TAUNTON'S
Fine Homebuilding
INDEX

TAUNTON'S

Fine Homebuilding®
INDEX

ISSUES 1-85
Compiled by Harriet Hodges

The Taunton Press

First printing: March 1994
Printed in the United States of America

A FINE HOMEBUILDING Book

FINE HOMEBUILDING® is a trademark of The Taunton Press, Inc., registered in the
U.S. Patent and Trademark Office.

The Taunton Press, 63 South Main Street, Box 5506,
Newtown, CT 06470-5506

In

Rea... hat subscribers to many other magazines don't.
For... back issues? And how do you easily find that
arti... know you read a few years ago but can't quite
put...

We... r back issues, but we can help with accessing
info... dex, which readers have been requesting for
som... We love hearing from our readers, but many of
you... n your own rather than calling us to find it. Even
for... asy way to find that missing piece of information
for...

And... e, or your back issues don't go back far enough?
We'... The index includes references to the reprint
boo... volumes. These books are in print and available
fro... es of contents of the reprint books on pp. 195-200.

It's... ough this index and see what's available and how
you... tool you can't live without. Let us know if it does
or...

How to use this index

16 August/ September 1983

- -

A Slice off the Cube Tim Snyder
Foundations on Hillsides Ronald J. Barr
Pier and Grade-Beam Foundations Michael Spexarth
Timber-Frame Layout Tedd Benson
Decorative Ironwork Rachel Carley
Reciprocating Saws Craig Stead
Underground Retreat Elizabeth Holland
Dry-Stack Block Rob Thallon
At the Top of the Mountain Paul Spring
Paul Schweikher, Architect
Stripping Trim Mark Alvarez
Building a Helical Stair Rick Barlow
Sculpted Stairway Jody Norskog

Barrett Co.: dry-stack block of, 16:57 (CBS)

Key to books:

(BK)   Building Baths and Kitchens
(CBS)   Building with Concrete, Brick and Stone
(CSH)   Craftsman-Style Houses
(DWS)   Building Doors, Windows and Skylights
(EEH)   Energy-Efficient Houses
(EF)   Exterior Finishing
(FC)   Finish Carpentry
(FRC)   Frame Carpentry
(FWS)   Building Floors, Walls and Stairs
(MFC)   More Frame Carpentry
(REM)   Remodeling
(SH)   Small Houses
(TB)   Tools for Building
(TFH)   Timber-Frame Houses

(CBS)
Builder's Library
Building with Concrete, Brick and Stone

Concrete
Small-Job Concrete
Gunite Retaining Wall
Building with Ferro-Cement
Stemwall Foundations
Rubble-Trench Foundations
Building a Concrete Bulkhead
Concrete and Masonry Fasteners
Building a Block Foundation
Insulating and Parging Foundations
Insulated Masonry Walls
Dry-Stack Block
Surface-Bonded Block
Site Layout
Stepped Foundations
Facing a Block Wall with Stone

This is primarily an index to technical information. As the above example shows, the basic format for each entry is the issue number followed by a colon and page numbers. A hyphen separating the page numbers within an issue indicates a continuous discussion of the topic, while a comma indicates intermittent discussion. Letters in parentheses following the page numbers indicate which *Builder's Library* or *Great Houses* book contains the same information (see the Key to Books on p. 6 and thereafter at frequent intervals throughout the Index). You can then refer to the Magazine tables of contents listings on pp. 181-194 or the Books tables of contents listings on pp. 195-200, or consult the index in a particular book to find the topic discussion.

A and I Bolt and Nut: screw gun supplies, 34:45 (TB)

A. O. Smith Water Products Co.: address for, 82:58

Abarbanel, Henry: home of, 3:68

Abatron, Inc.: address for, 62:41 (EF), 70:49, 72:41

ABC Coating Co., Inc.: epoxy-coated rebar, 33:32 (CBS)

Abee, Blair: on owner-building, 4:10

Abernathy, Ann:
on Oak Park, 56:82-87
Oak Park Home and Studio of Frank Lloyd Wright, The, cited, 56:82
on Wright's studio, 32:60-66
as joint author. *See* Kalec, Don.

Abitibi Building Products: address for, 83:44

Abledata computer program: using, 54:102

Ablobe: nature of, 21:20-21

Abrams, John:
light fixture by, 61:86
seating by, 66:88

Abrams, Lawrence and Kathleen:
Salvaging Old Barns and Houses, reviewed, 28:86

ABS: *See* Pipe: ABS.

Absolute Coatings, Inc.: address for, 67:54

Abundant Energy, Inc.: address for, 72:78 (FC)

Acadian style: house in, building, 73:36-41

Accessibility Book, The (Quarve-Peterson): reviewed, 63:106

Accessible Bathroom, The (Nickels): discussed, 35:45 (BK)

Accessible Entrance, An (Nickels): discussed, 35:45 (BK)

Accidents: *See* Injuries. Safety.

Accounting: books on, 36:94

Accurate Metal Weatherstrip Co., Inc.:
address for, 49:62 (SH), 81:6
drawer slides, 30:58, 59 (BK), 44:71 (BK)

Accu-Speed Glass Block Connectors: source for, 37:81

ACEC Research & Management Foundation: address for, 71:49

Acer saccharum: See Maple, sugar.

Acheson, Rus: designs tool, 35:56 (TB)

Ackerman, Johnson Fastening Systems: Polly-All, 41:54, 57 (CBS)

Acme Canvas Co.: address for, 55:67

Acme General Corp.: address for, 54:65 (FC)

Acme National Sales: address for, 52:104

Key to books:

(BK)   Building Baths and Kitchens
(CBS) Building with Concrete, Brick and Stone
(CSH) Craftsman-Style Houses
(DWS) Building Doors, Windows and Skylights
(EEH) Energy-Efficient Houses
(EF)   Exterior Finishing
(FC)   Finish Carpentry
(FRC) Frame Carpentry
(FWS) Building Floors, Walls and Stairs
(MFC) More Frame Carpentry
(REM) Remodeling
(SH)   Small Houses
(TB)   Tools for Building
(TFH) Timber-Frame Houses

Acorn Building Components: A-Therm Door, 6:60

Acorn Manufacturing: Colonial hardware, 20:12

Acorn Structures: sponsors conference, 19:22

Acoustic tiles: touch-up for, 41:14

Acoustical Manual: source for, 35:60, 63

Acrivue A: source for, 10:33 (DWS)

Acrylic:
cleaner for, 55:47, 49 (FC)
cutting, 55:47 (FC)
expansion rate of, 55:45-46 (FC)
gluing, 55:47, 48-49 (FC)
laminated roofing film of, 24:46
skylight, 55:45-49 (FC)
See also Finishes: acrylic. Glazing.

Acrylite: source for, 10:33 (DWS)

Acrylonitrile-butadiene-styrene pipe (ABS): *See* Pipe: ABS.

ACS Hoval: heat-recovery ventilators, 34:34 (DWS)

Action Leathercraft: tool bags, 42:64, 65 (TB)

Acton, Rad: built-in seating by, 66:91

ADA: *See* Drywall: airtight drywall approach.

Adam, Robert:
library by, 43:40, 41 (FWS)
plaster ornament by, 43:41 (FWS)

Adamo Building Corp.: house by, 38:24-29 (EEH)

Adams, Mary and Robert: restore Fountainhead, 12:27, 33

Adamson, Jim: mentioned, 29:28, 32, 38:8

Adaptable Housing: reviewed, 63:106

Adaptive Environments Center: discussed, 35:45 (BK)

Adaptive Equipment Center: address for, 54:102

Additions:
to adobe duplex, 22:40, 42
adobe-steel, 82:64-68
by amateur, 52:126
of bathroom, 75:66-67
bedroom, 46:38-41 (REM)
bow-ceiling, 5:22-24
built-up, 55:69 (REM), 57:43-47 (REM), 75:67
to Cape, 78:56-59
cantilevered, 22:65-66 (BK), 70:82-85 (REM)
corridor-attached, 59:74-77 (REM)
curved, sculptural, 2:56-59
design for, 3:52-53
double-envelope, 11:66-69
Edwardian, 59:48-51 (SH)
by enclosing exterior posts, 7:22 (BK)
framing for, 3:54, 55, 14:23-25
freestanding modular, 75:46-49 (REM)
gable-end strengthening for, 31:34 (DWS)
gable-roof solarium, 33:39 (EEH)
above garage, 60:43-45 (SH), 69:62-63 (REM)
under house, 81:68-71
by house raising, 59:74-77 (REM)
by jacking up roofs, 67:64-66 (REM)
of lean-to, 78:62-65 (REM)
long-range planning for, 75:66-67
with new floor, 81:53
to 1920s bungalow, 64:38-42 (CSH)
to north, lighting, 83:54-56
passive-solar stone, 43:58-61 (CBS)
of porch-sun decks, 51:50-53
to quonset hut, 67:20
of roof, 52:46, 48 (TFH)
screened-porch, 72:81-83 (REM)
second-story, 58:76-79 (MFC), 72:54-56 (REM)
design for, 9:28
shed-roof two-story solarium, 33:39 (EEH)
by "slice and stretch," 31:32-34 (DWS)
spa-room, 58:58-61 (CSH)
stair-tower, 56:68-72 (CSH)
against stone wall, flashing for, 83:56
sunroom, stone-glass, 77:74-75
third-story, 74:46 (EF, REM)
See also Renovation.

Adelman, Dennis: on radiant-floor heating, 22:68-71 (CBS)

Adhesive and Sealant Council: address for, 61:42, 65:45

Adhesive Engineering: concrete adhesive, 41:14

Adhesive Products Corp.: casting supplies from, 1:39 (FWS)

Adhesive Systems: address for, 65:44

Adhesives: *See* Glue. Thinset.

Adirondack style: illustrated, 40:38-42

Adjustable Clamp Co.: address for, 74:73 (FC)

Adjustable Scaffold Bracket Co.: pump jacks, 36:36 (TB)
ADO Products: address for, 65:96
Adobe:
  arches in, 30:39
  baseboards for, 30:41
  block,
      machines for, 28:80, 67:96
      wire reinforcement for, 34:86
  over block, 19:72-77
      solar design for, 58:80-85 (EEH)
  bond beams for, 5:49, 30:39
  books on, 27:84, 30:39
      reviewed, 43:102, 60:106
  bricks for, 5:49
  cannales in, 48:3
  casings in, 5:49
  ceramic fire-hardened, book on, 40:90
  clay for, 25:28
  course in, detailed, 67:96-98
  earthquake-proofing, 58:82 (EEH)
  finishes for, 30:41
  fireplace in, 43:76, 77
  foundation for, 5:46, 48-49
  greenhouse with, 5:48, 51
  house in style of, 43:75-79
  house of, 48:32-36
  information on, 23:49-50, 65:54
  institute of, 30:39
  insulation of, 5:49, 50, 22:43, 30:40, 41
  latillas with, 48:36
  laying, 30:39
  mass of, 26:12
  mortar for, 30:39
  nailers for, 30:39, 82:65-66
  old,
      heating system for, 22:43
      wiring in, 22:43
  plaster for, 5:47
  pumped, 21:20-21
  restoration of, 21:21
  roofs of, 5:46, 50-51
  R-values of, 5:46, 26:10-12
  screws for, 30:41
  sealer for, 30:41
  skim milk for, 25:28
  solar additions for, 17:63-67 (DWS)
  sprayed, 21:20-21
  stabilizing, 5:48, 58:82 (EEH)
      with asphalt-emulsion, 21:21, 30:39
  stucco for, 5:49-50, 82:68
  Tanzanian-round influenced, 30:37-42
  trim for, 5:47
  types of, 44:6, 82:65
  vigas for, 48:33, 58:85
  walls of, 5:46, 50-51
  windows in, 22:43, 30:40
  wiring in, 30:39
  See also Ablobe. Earth construction.
      Fechin house. Pottery House.
Adobe and Rammed Earth Buildings
  (McHenry): reviewed, 27:84

Adobe International: block machines, 28:80
Adobe (McHenry): cited, 27:84
Advanced Chemical Technologies Co.:
  SIL-ACT Silane concrete sealer, 33:32
  (CBS)
**Advanced Environmental Research
  Group:** address for, 76:104
Advanced Framing Systems: address for,
  76:92
Advanced Protective Products, Inc.:
  address for, 62:41 (EF)
Adwood Corp.: address for, 65:96, 74:73
  (FC)
Adzes: for finish work, 25:31
AEG Power Tool Corp.:
  address for, 63:73, 70:102
  caulking gun, electric cordless, 26:82
  circular saw, reviewed, 63:73, 76
  compound-miter saw, reviewed, 83:67-
  68
  cut-off saws, reviewed, 62:80-83
  drills, 35:38, 40-42 (TB), 82:36-41
  plunge routers, reviewed, 71:79, 80 (FC)
  power planes, reviewed, 54:78-79
  random-orbit sanders, reviewed, 77:68,
  69-70, 71, 72
  reciprocating saws, 35:90
AEG Telefunken: water heaters, 12:18
  (CSH)
Aero-Smith: *See* Danair Inc.
AFG-Solglass: sponsors conference, 19:22
AFM Enterprises: address for, 73:68
A-frame houses: building, 20:65-67
Against the Grain (McCormick): source
  for, 13:16
Aggraglaze: for sandstone floor, 9:45
A.G.L.: level-transits, 37:45 (TB)
Agress, Gene: cabinets by, 43:31 (CSH)
Ahlers, Thomas: on trial by drywall, 26:94
Ahlum, Dale: house by, 43:72-74 (SH)
Ahrens Chimney Technique: address for,
  70:79
AIN Plastics, Inc.: reviewed, 44:89
Air Changer Div.: heat-recovery
  ventilators, 9:59, 34:34 (DWS)
Air Chek, Inc.: address for, 67:51
Air cleaners:
  avoiding, 73:67
  electronic (EAC), described, 63:58-60
  source for, 85:87
  for toxic chemicals, source for, 73:70
Air compressors:
  carburetor cleaner for, 40:16
  cold-weather precautions for, 50:60
  hose repair for, 75:26
  portable, 49:84-89
  power drops in, 17:6
  safety seminars for, 49:102
  storage reel for, 69:32

tools for, suppliers of, 15:53 (TB)
See also separate tools.
Air conditioners: *See* Air cleaners.
  Cooling: electric units for. Energy
  consumption: excessive. Vents.
Air hat: homemade, 36:16
Air infiltration:
  blower doors and, 28:82
  dangers from, 77:65
  explained, 28:82, 77:64
  and heating bill, 77:65
  pamphlet on, 65:108
  preventing, system for, 77:64-67
  with radiant heat, 75:69
  See also Airtight-Wrap. Air-vapor
      barriers. Convection currents.
      Insulation.
Air Krete, Inc.:
  address for, 56:39, 73:69
  insulation,
      source for, 31:38 (CBS)
      using, 73:69
Air Nail Co.: address for, 56:54
Air quality:
  book on, reviewed, 75:110
  ensuring, 5:15, 22:16-18, 23:4, 29:72, 30:4
  indoor, plant cleaners for, 69:102
  low, dangers of, 1:10-12, 5:4
  in solar design, 84:88-89
  standards for, 5:15
Air structures: using, 51:42, 120
Air Vent, Inc.:
  address for, 57:46 (REM), 61:78 (EF)
  Principles of Attic Ventilation, cited, 56:41
  vent strips, 21:52 (DWS)
Air-change rates: for ADA, 37:65
Aircheck heat-recovery ventilator:
  source for, 34:34 (DWS)
AirCore Design Guidelines: source for,
  30:52 (CBS)
Airplane house: construction of, 6:54-57
Airsled, Inc.: address for, 72:90
Airtemp water heaters: mentioned, 5:65
Airtight-Wrap: source for, 39:90
Air-to-Air Heat Exchangers (Nisson):
  reviewed, 50:108
Air/vapor barriers:
  acoustical sealant for, 46:72
  with ADA, 40:4
  for balloon framing, 24:67, 68-69
  for crawl spaces, 56:14-16, 40
  debated, 9:56, 19:22, 63, 66, 68, 22:4,
      56:41, 74:98, 77:65
  defined, 19:67, 56:6
  degrade in,
      from heat, 22:18 (CSH)
      under slabs, 77:10
  and degree days, 19:66
  for door frames, 24:67
  double, in dry climates, 19:48
  drywall as, foil-backed, 81:43

for floors, 29:69-71
  dirt, 82:14
foil, source sheet for, 30:80
for foundations, 29:68-69
glossary for, 19:67
installation of, 19:68, 34:68 (SH)
and insulation placement, 15:59
integrity of, 18:7, 21:4
at joist-rafter intersection, 46:16
kraft paper as, 44:6
lack of, and insulation, 56:41
laminated, 15:59, 19:22, 68, 21:59, 22:18
  (CSH), 25:82 (EEH), 46:71-72
for maximum efficiency, 42:60-62
and moisture control, 50:100
paint as, 25:10, 73:69
patching, 50:4
placement of, 9:56, 13:4, 19:66, 21:8, 27:4,
  44:6, 56:62-63 (EEH), 66:46, 49
publication on, 32:90
puncture-resistant, 83:48
with radiant barriers, 80:57
against radon, 67:48
reinforced, 66:68 (EEH)
retrofitting, 20:35, 36, 37, 30:8, 31:8, 39:10
roofing membrane as, 64:47 (EF)
sealant for, 61:37
over sheathing, 82:14
source for, 68:83
test and repair of, 34:86
and thermal bridges, 31:8-10
trouble spots for, 12:66-67 (EEH)
and vinyl siding, 55:20
for walls, 29:70-72, 47:18
whole-house, 24:65, 67, 68-69, 43:73 (SH),
  63:82 (EEH)
for window frames, 24:67
See also Drywall: airtight (ADA). Heat-
  recovery ventilators. Polyethylene:
  sheeting. Relative humidity.
AirXChange Inc.: heat-recovery
  ventilators, 34:34, 37:4 (DWS)
Akmese, Kemal: spadome by, 67:116
Akzo Coatings Inc.: address for, 69:43
  (EEH), 83:87
Akzo Industrial Systems Co.:
  address for, 58:57
  mentioned, 73:68
Alabama: home conservation credits in,
  5:65
Alaska:
  building in, 14:82, 69
  Extension Service, address for, 50:61
  framing for, 40:6
  insulation for, 21:8
  solar tax credits in, 3:10
  solariums in, 19:71 (EEH)
  work precautions for, 50:60-63
Albany Woodworks, Inc.: reviewed, 56:92
Albaugh, E. Kurt:
  on floor trusses, 30:24-28 (FRC)
  on Poplar Forest, 42:74-79

Albert Berner GmbH & Co. KG: address
  for, 41:57 (CBS)
Albert Constantine & Son, Inc.: 800-
  number for, 55:4
Alclad roofing: described, 24:44
Alcoves: showcase, 52:64
Alden, Catherine: columns by, 69:88
Aldes Ventilation Corp.: address for,
  55:81
Alexander, Carl: sawblade by, 39:90
Alexander, Christopher, *et al.*:
  Pattern Language, A,
    cited, 13:16, 26:34, 33:36, 36:51-55,
      46:62, 85:91 (TFH, EEH)
    reviewed, 45:116
    using, 37:71, 72, 38:49-53, 52:62-67,
      80:51, 52, 62-67
  Timeless Way of Building, The, cited,
    13:16, 37:71
Alexander, Geoff:
  on conical roofs, 25:54-55 (FRC)
  on power miter saws, 19:42-45 (TB)
  on power planes, 14:42-45 (TB)
  turret by, 3:68
Alexander, John:
  on Architectural Woodwork Institute
    (AWI), 55:100
  on circular stair retrofit, 55:62-65
  window seat by, 66:89
Alexander, Rex:
  on kitchen, 69:50-54
  on refacing cabinets, 81:72-77
Alfano, Sal:
  on contracts, 28:54-57
  on estimating, 27:32-35
Alkco: address for, 52:98, 66:104, 73:75
Alkyd paint: *See* Paint: oil-base.
All Metal Inc.: glazing supplies, 14:12
All Savers Certificates: mentioned, 6:16
All Weather Inc.: quad-pane glass from,
  20:22
Allen, Dennis:
  bath remodel of, 22:65-67 (BK)
  on computer, 35:66 (TB)
  on concrete spiral stair, 20:50-53 (FWS)
Allen, Ed and Mary: brick work by,
  9:53-55 (CBS)
Allen, Edward:
  Fundamentals of Building Construction,
    cited, 37:4, 40:72 (FRC)
  How Buildings Work, reviewed, 45:116
  on nailed connections, 40:68-72 (FRC)
Allen, Edward, and Joseph Iano:
  Architects' Studio Companion, The,
    reviewed, 57:114-16
Allen, Gerald: as joint author. *See* Moore,
  Charles.
Allen, Kathryn: ceramics by, 59:91
Allen, Kathy: work by, 41:70-77 (FWS)
Allen, Roger:
  on capping foundations, 4:34-37 (FRC)
  on freeform fireplace, 28:100

Allen wrenches: for renovation, 12:51
  (TB)
Allen-Drerup-White, Ltd.:
  basement insulation study of, 19:4
  retrofit by, 15:58, 61, 62
  superinsulated house by, cheap, 17:4
Allergen-free products: *See* Healthy
  houses.
**Allergy and Environmental Health
  Association of Ontario:** address for,
  51:98
Allied Resin Corp.:
  address for, 49:44, 57:74 (FC), 70:49
  epoxy, 9:21-22, 16:10, 20, 21
Allmer, Karl: stone work by, 48:79-83
All-Weather Wood Foundation System:
  source for, 23:50
All-Weather Wood Foundation, The:
  quoted, 7:4
  source for, 5:40 (FRC)
Almaguer, Don Alfredo Avila: boveda
  by, 50:74-77
Alpen Inc.: high-performance windows
  of, discussed, 41:84-86, 55:78
Alpine Engineered Products, Inc.:
  address for, 50:42 (MFC)
Al-Said, Fahad: addresses conference,
  49:100-102
Alsco: address for, 83:45
Alt and Hyndman: *Roadside Geology,*
  cited, 50:86
Alternative Energy Engineering:
  address for, 52:100, 69:43 (EEH)
  catalogue, source for, 24:80
Alternative Energy Sourcebook: address
  for, 65:64 (SH)
Alternative Housing Arrangements:
  reviewed, 32:86
Alum-A-Pole Corp.: pump-jack poles,
  36:36 (TB)
Alumax: address for, 52:112
Alumco: soffit vents, 2:31 (EEH)
Aluminum:
  alloys of, salt-resistant, 65:6
  anodized, 24:44
  coated, 24:44
  corrosion of, 24:44, 46, 62:64, 66
    and cedar, 10:4
  countertop frame of, 84:80-81
  cutting, disc-grinder, 20:16
  foil, perm rating for, 19:67
  and galvanized steel, compatibility of,
    65:4-6
  glazing, for south walls, 8:42 (DWS)
  nobility of, 21:4
  paint, perm rating for, 19:67
  as roofing, 24:42, 44
  sheets, source for, 33:32 (CBS)
  simulating, 1:38 (FWS)
  welding, 84:80
  See also Siding: aluminum.

Alvarez, Mark:
on Florida house, 3:56-59 (EEH)
on garage remodel, 19:46-49
on heliodon, 13:18
Home Office, The, reviewed, 65:108
on Home Sweet Home conference,
20:22-26
on hydro-electric power, 15:66
on Japanese woodworker, 8:15-16
on paint stripping, 16:66-69 (DWS)
reviews Clark, 19:26
reviews Metz, 15:22
on Rodale building books, 7:60
on saltbox, 2:50-52 (SH)
Alvastra Community Land Trust (Mass.):
discussed, 17:20
Amana Tool Co.: address for, 46:12
Ambitech Industries Inc.: address for,
58:91
Ambrose, James: *Simplified Design of
Building Structures,* cited, 58:16
Amburgey, Terry:
on fungi, 72:64-66 (REM)
on pentachlorophenol, 15:21
on preservatives, 13:14
Amcraft Inc.: Craftseat, 41:86
American Aides Ventilation Corp.: heat-
recovery ventilators, 34:34 (DWS)
American Air Filter: heat pumps, 26:68
American Arbitration Association:
address for, 49:77
American Architecture since 1780
(Whiffen): reviewed, 2:62
**American Association for State and
Local History:** booklet by, 4:62
American Beauty: soldering iron of, 23:41
(DWS)
American Builder's Companion, The
(Benjamin): cited, 1:49, 5:25 (DWS), 53:88
American Bungalow, The (Lancaster):
reviewed, 31:80
American Chestnut Foundation: address
for, 84:108
American Clamping Corp.: address for,
74:73 (FC)
American Colloid Co.:
address for, 47:20, 56:83
Bentonite, 34:66 (BK)
Volclay clay panels, 2:37, 29:12
American Concrete Institute:
address for, 55:68, 65:52
books from, 23:49, 51:41
Guide to Shotcrete, 40:63 (CBS)
honeycomb standards of, 33:4
information from, 44:37 (CBS)
American ConForm Industries, Inc.:
address for, 78:6
**American Council for an Energy-
Efficient Economy (ACEEE):**
Most Energy Efficient Appliances, The,
discussed, 47:102
standards of, 47:102

*American Country Houses of the Gilded
Age* (Lewis): reviewed, 29:90
American Design and Engineering Inc.:
SawWalker, reviewed, 64:71
American Enka Co.: address for, 69:41
(EEH)
American Floor Products Co.: address
for, 46:52 (EEH)
American Forest and Paper Association:
address for, 85:120
Design Values for Wood Construction,
source for, 81:16
*National Design Specification for Wood
Construction,* source for, 81:16
**American Formulating &
Manufacturing:** address for, 67:92
American Gas Association: address for,
46:48
American Hardboard Association:
address for, 67:81, 83:45
American Homeowners Foundation:
publications from, 60:100
American House, The (Foley): cited, 2:62,
26:73 (SH)
American Houses (Langdon): reviewed,
44:94
American Hydrotech: waterproofing
supplies, 2:37
American Institute of Architects:
address for, 65:54
documents from, 28:54, 57:77
Environmental Resource Guide, 65:100-
102
ornament cards, 1:66
*Recommended Guide for Bidding
Procedures and Contract Awards,* 23:6
restoration corporation by, 72:98
See also Architects. Contracts.
American Institute of Building Design:
address for, 53:85, 77:108
**American Institute of Timber
Construction:**
address for, 65:53, 71:59 (MFC)
deflection standards of, 30:26 (FRC)
Glulam Beams, 23:49
Glulam Systems, 23:49
Timber Construction Manual, 6:6
Typical Construction Details, 23:49
American Ladder Institute:
address for, 84:53
Ladder Safety Resource, cited, 84:53
American Lamp Parts: address for, 27:63
American Levels: mentioned, 37:80
**American Life Foundation and Study
Institute:** plans from, 53:88
American Lighting Association:
address for, 71:106
"Lighting Your Life," cited, 54:52

American Marazzi Tile: address for, 55:86
American Micro-Tech, Inc.: address for,
72:100
American MorFlo Industries Inc.:
Nautilus water heater, 27:71 (CBS)
**American National Standards Institute
(ANSI):**
address for, 84:53, 85:16
ladder-safety standards from, 84:53
lockset standards of, 48:64 (FC, MFC)
and safety, 34:52 (TB)
American Olean Tile Co.: tiles, 1:62,
26:38, 39 (BK)
American Paint Scrapers: address for,
62:39 (EF)
American Plywood Association:
address for, 34:67 (SH), 51:82 (MFC),
58:75, 63:65 (MFC), 65:53, 67:81, 72:98,
76:16, 78:48, 83:45
on all-weather wood foundations, 23:49
booklet by, 4:62
Design-Construction Guide, 21:6
paint study by, 19:12
Permanent Wood Foundations, 68:66
Plywood Design Specification, 18:14
Publication Index, 23:49
sheathing information from, 37:69 (FRC)
stress-skin panel book from, 26:4
toolbox by, 29:40 (TB)
American Polysteel Forms:
address for, 76:39
insulation of, using, 76:41
American Saw & Manufacturing Co.:
address for, 68:81
BX cable cutter of, reviewed, 55:94-96
Lenox reciprocating sawblades, 11:14,
16:47 (TB)
American Small Business Computers:
address for, 82:92
**American Society for Surgery of the
Hand:** address for, 53:104
**American Society for Testing and
Materials:**
address for, 65:45
mentioned, 8:16
**American Society of Heating,
Refrigeration and Air-Conditioning
Engineers (ASHRAE):**
air standards of, 5:15
climate handbook of, 21:60
*Energy Conservation in New Building
Design,* 5:45
Handbook of Fundamentals, cited, 46:48,
60:51 (FC)
publications of, 23:51
**American Society of Plumbing
Engineers:** address for, 76:106
American Solar Energy Society:
address for, 65:52
China trip of, 1984, 26:82-83

conference of, 1984, 24:80

Passive Solar Design Handbook, 21:59, 30:52 (CBS, EEH)

American Solar Network: address for, 68:54

American Standard:
address for, 59:110
Perma-Door, 6:60
round soaking tub, 11:45 (SH)

American Tool Co., Inc.: address for, 74:73 (FC)

American Tower Co.: address for, 52:73

American Universal Corp.: address for, 62:76

American Vernacular (Kemp): reviewed, 49:114

American Wind Energy Association: publication of, 1:66

American Wood Preservers Bureau: address for, 63:65 (MFC)

American Wood Preservers Institute:
address for, 63:65 (MFC)
FHA Pole House Construction, 15:37, 23:49
Pole Building Design, 15:37

American Wood Systems: address for, 71:59 (MFC)

American Wood-Preservers' Association: address for, 63:65 (MFC)

America's Architectural Roots (Upton): reviewed, 53:108

America's Favorite Homes (Schweitzer and Davis): reviewed, 77:120

Ameropean Corp.: address for, 56:92

Amer-X6: galvanized roofing, described, 24:43

Ames, Dave: on remodeling loans, 76:70-71

Ames Taping Tool Systems: Crimper, 10:4

Ametek Microfoam Div.: address for, 55:67

Amoco Foam Products Co.: address for, 76:39

Amos, John: on balloon-truss framing, 24:65-69

Amperage: *See* Electricity.

Amputations: first-aid for, 53:102-104

Amsbary, Doug: on ridge vents, 21:51-52 (DWS)

AMTI Heating Products, Inc.: address for, 53:74

Amtrak house: construction of, 38:54-59

Amtrol, Inc.: address for, 56:16, 85:86

Anchor Staple & Nail: address for, 63:92

Anchors:
adhesive, 26:82
association for, 41:56 (CBS)
bolt,
drop-in, retrofit installation of, 29:34-36, 37, 38 (FRC)
drop-in, sources for, 29:34 (FRC)
reinforcing, with epoxy, 70:47
stud, source for, 29:34 (FRC)
for treated lumber, 63:65 (MFC)

bolts as, 29:34 (FRC)
for concrete, 3:6, 39:90, 78:30
adhesive, 26:82
driver for, 10:14
for drywall, 62:94
against earthquakes, 43:48, 49 (FRC)
epoxy, 70:49
floor, 43:46, 47 (FRC)
flush, described, 41:53 (CBS)
for foundations, 64:65 (MFC), 65:30, 70:47, 73:80, 77:80-81
for framing, 29:74-75, 62:59, 85:57
source for, 62:59
for gunite, 40:63 (CBS)
for hurricanes, 57:54
for ironwork, 16:44
lead, described, 41:53 (CBS)
for masonry, 26:82, 41:57
adhesive, 26:82
plastic, 41:56 (CBS)
post, 57:65-66, 69:47 (EF), 81:87
for rafters, 43:48 (FRC)
hurricane, 57:54
for shear-wall bracing, 85:57
for shotcrete, 40:63 (CBS)
sleeve, 41:53 (CBS)
sources for, 41:57 (CBS)
spacing of, 4:37 (FRC)
tie-back, earth-reinforcing, 40:63 (CBS)
for trusses, 39:90
types of, 9:30, 41:53-56 (CBS)
wedge-and-sleeve, 41:53-54 (CBS)
See also Metal connectors.

Ancient Carpenters' Tools (Mercer): cited, 6:29

Anderegg, Ray: house by, 44:64-68 (FRC)

Andersen Corp.:
address for, 53:68, 55:79, 65:62 (SH), 70:55 (EEH), 76:75 (FC)
Selection Guide of, 1:62
windows, 7:60
awning, 43:74 (SH)
custom , 36:74
production of, 60:46, 47-48 (FC)
systems, retrofit, 1:62
for ventilation, 17:63 (DWS)

Andersen, Tim:
on Arts-and-Crafts style beach house, 31:22-27 (CSH)

Anderson, Brent: *Underground Waterproofing,* cited, 29:12

Anderson, Bruce, ed.: *Fuel Savers, The,* reviewed, 70:120

Anderson (D. L.) Associates: wood preservatives, 1:6

Anderson, Kevin: on bricks, 53:51-53

Anderson, L. O.: *Woodframe Houses,* reviewed, 1:64

Anderson, Ralph: house by, 38:78-83 (CSH)

Anderson, Terry: stump house of, 23:92

Andrea Palladio: reviewed, 45:122

Andrews, Bruce: on table-saw molding, 2:48-49 (FWS)

Andrews, Steve:
on foam-core panels, 62:52-57 (TFH)
reports on EEBA conference, 33:84
reviews adobe book, 27:84
reviews Schwolsky-Williams, 18:78
reviews solar handbook, 16:14
on superinsulation conference, 22:16-18, 28:82

Angle iron: using, 8:30 (TFH)

Angle Square: evaluated, 10:61 (TB)

Angle ties: *See* Metal connectors.

Angles:
board "recorder" for, 77:58, 59
figuring, metric vs. imperial, 60:102
saw jigs for, 55:26, 28

Anglo American Enterprises Corp.: Vario Spade Bit Set from, reviewed, 50:95

Animal shelters: pictured, 67:86-87

Annebergshus: houses by, 40:51, 53

Anns, George: stair storage by, 85:95

ANSI: *See* American National Standards Institute.

Antes, John: house by, 48:79-83

Antifreeze: in-line injector for, 50:60

Anti-Hydro Corp.:
A-H Poly-Epoxy Bonding No. 100, 4:9
roofing membrane, 15:59

Antique Hardware Store: address for, 75:49 (REM)

Antiquing: described, 60:81-82

Antiquity Reprints: plans from, 53:88

Ants: *See* Insects.

Apache Board: over adobe, 5:49, 50

Apartments:
design for, 31:66, 68-69, 70, 77:87, 88-89
above garage, 69:62-63 (REM)

APC Corp.: address for, 62:48 (SH)

Apiaries: roof-top, 44:76

Apitong (Dipterocarpus grandiflorus): staircase of, 68:41

Apple Computer: for contractors, 35:65 (TB)

Apple Corps Guide to the Well-Built House, The (Locke): reviewed, 51:104-106

Apple, Inc.: address for, 49:46

Appliances:
alternative-energy, 52:100-102
ceramic cooktop, source for, 76:58
combination units, 52:102-106
custom coloring, 49:62 (SH)
dish/clothes washer (1940s), 22:28-30
dryers, nonvented, 83:6
earthquake-proofing, 64:60 (MFC)
efficiency of, 2:64, 47:102
listed, 33:84
floor drains for, 69:30
gas, backdraft problems with, 33:84

and heat-recovery ventilators, 24:69, 34:34 (DWS)
kitchen, 2:53-54 (BK)
microwave clothes dryer, reviewed, 72:100
moving, air beams for, 72:90
oven, side-opening, 76:58
painting, 62:48 (SH)
planning for, 2:53, 54, 55 (BK)
small,
    "garage" for, 58:38, 40 (REM)
    sources for, 60:45 (SH), 75:67
venting, need for, 28:82
washers, energy-efficient, 83:6
See also Dryers. Washing machines.
***Applications of Treated Poles and Posts
    for House Construction*** (SHC-BRC):
    source for, 29:92
Applied Hydroponics: address for, 72:63
Appropriate Technology (Darrow and
    Saxenian): reviewed, 64:112
Appropriate Technology Corp.: Window
    Quilt insulation, 39:51
Appropriate Technology Project:
    address for, 64:112
APR Industries, Ltd.: address for, 55:44
    (SH)
Aqua Star: water heater, 12:18 (CSH)
Aquabar B paper: advantages of, 22:67
    (BK)
Aquaculture: in-house, 73:70
Aquariums: salt-water, building, 72:62-63
Aquatek Lab: address for, 67:51
Araucaria angustifolia: See Parana pine.
Arbitration: process of, 57:76-77
Arbors:
    making, 49:44-45
    vaulted, 25:80
Arbortech Woodcarver: reviewed, 62:92
Arbutus menziesii: See Madrone.
Arch Technology Corp.: metal buildings,
    33:72
Arches:
    of A-frames, construction of, 20:65-67
    book on, 30:78
    brick,
        construction information for, 20:10
        laying, 9:53-55 (CBS)
    for casings, building, 69:82-84
    forces in, 32:30 (FRC)
    four-center, 69:82-83, 84
    layout for, 76:28
    log, 40:41
    mathematical history of, 25:4
    metal prefab, 33:72
    from sawn stock, 48:45, 46 (TFH)
    segmented plastered, 68:86, 87
    steel-framed, kits for, 76:92
    stuccoed, 45:38, 41
    trammel for, 35:14
    wooden, constructing, 6:25
See also Vaults.

Key to books:

(BK)	Building Baths and Kitchens
(CBS)	Building with Concrete, Brick and Stone
(CSH)	Craftsman-Style Houses
(DWS)	Building Doors, Windows and Skylights
(EEH)	Energy-Efficient Houses
(EF)	Exterior Finishing
(FC)	Finish Carpentry
(FRC)	Frame Carpentry
(FWS)	Building Floors, Walls and Stairs
(MFC)	More Frame Carpentry
(REM)	Remodeling
(SH)	Small Houses
(TB)	Tools for Building
(TFH)	Timber-Frame Houses

Architects:
    association for, 53:85
    becoming, 15:63
    and builders, 22:61-64, 24:4
    as builders, 15:63, 17:79 (SH) 37:74-7,
        38:8-10, 80:22-24
    building resources for, 45:106-10
    caretaker role of, 22:61
    and client relationships, 38:10-12
    communication imperatives for,
        45:94-106
    and computers, 25:83
    as construction managers, 76:57
    consultant service for, instant, 31:84,
        32:90
    as contractors, 15:63, 19:46
    discussion on, 12:38-39, 20:26
    and Document A-117, 23:6
    and Document A-201, 22:63, 64, 23:6, 8
    fees of, 12:39, 13:4, 14:4, 15:6
    finding, 12:39
    furniture suggestions by, 12:40
    information about, 22:4
    numbers of, 20:26
    query list for, 45:102
    and remodeling, 12:40
    responsibilities of, 31:42-43, 32:86
    revisions by, 12:39-41
    supply sources for, 41:35
    See also Contracts.
***Architect's Sketchbook of Underground
    Buildings, An*** (Wells): reviewed,
    65:106-108
***Architects' Small House Service Bureau
    (1929):*** *Authentic Small Houses of the
    Twenties,* cited, 53:88
Architects' Studio Companion, The
    (Allen and Iano): reviewed, 57:114
***Architectural and Building Trades
    Dictionary*** (Putnam and Carlson):
    reviewed, 47:112

Architectural Color (Porter): cited, 74:45
    (EF)
Architectural Energy Corp.: address for,
    71:47
Architectural Engineering Products Co.:
    copper coating, 24:46
Architectural Graphic Standards:
    cited, 58:41 (REM)
    old, compendium of, 65:108
    reviewed, 45:116
    source for, 51:18
Architectural Iron Co.: work of, 16:44
Architectural Masterworks: address for,
    47:95
Architectural Monographs: reviewed,
    43:102
Architectural Ornamentalism (Kemp):
    reviewed, 44:94
Architectural Precast Association:
    mentioned, 25:71
***Architectural Treasures of Early
    America*** (Early American Society):
    cited, 40:33, 34, 35 (FWS), 47:110-12
***Architectural Treasures of Early
    America, The*** (National Historical
    Society): reviewed, 47:110-12
Architectural Woodwork Institute:
    address for, 43:39 (FWS), 65:53
    services of, 55:100
    staircase information from, 36:61 (FWS)
Architecture:
    books on, 4:62, 33:88, 45:116-22
    children's classes in, 66:14-16, 68:8
    classical, book on, 45:120
    Colonial-style tract, 80:16-20
    community-generated, 33:88
    conference on, 47:100-102
    deconstructivist, 47:102, 80:16-20
    degree programs in, 63:100
    dictionary of, reviewed, 85:134
    guides to, reviewed, 2:62, 65:108
    history of, 31:82
    human-scale, books on, 13:16
    morality of, 3:60-61
    "organic," discussed, 63:100
    organization for, 63:100
    post-modern, 80:20-22
    Romanian school of, aiding, 62:4
    teaching, source book for, 68:8
    traditional, appeal of, 52:4
    vernacular,
        association for, 49:102
        conference on, 49:100-102
    See also Design. *various periods, schools.*
Architecture (Ching): reviewed, 45:116-20
Architecture in Education: source for,
    68:8
Architecture of Country Houses, The
    (Downing): cited, 46:82 (TFH)
Architecture of Historic Nantucket, The
    (Lancaster): cited, 77:89

Architecture Oregon Style (Meidell, ed.): reviewed, 33:88

Architecture Shop, The: houses by, 5:14

Architerra Austin: address for, 59:110

Architraves:
  defined, 20:60 (FWS)
  Greek Revival, 1:49
  types of, 20:61, 62, 63 (FWS)

ARCO Solar Inc.:
  photovoltaic cell, 44:63
  photovoltaic supplies, 4:55, 57, 8:46 (TFH)

Argue, Robert:
  Superinsulated Retrofit Book, The, 22:18 (CSH)
  on superinsulated retrofits, 22:18 (CSH)

Aristokraft, Inc.: cabinets of, discussed, 65:71, 72, 73

Arizona:
  home conservation credits in, 3:10, 5:65
  solar house in, 11:29-33 (EEH)

Arizona Polytech Corp.: foam forms, 40:86

Arkansas:
  home conservation credits in, 5:65
  solar tax credits in, 3:10

Armac Distributing Co.: address for, 69:54

Armco Steel: Refrasil board, 24:82

Armenia: post-earthquake aid for, 63:100-102

Armor-All Products Co.: address for, 48:57

Armour Products: Armour Etch kits, 39:8

Armstrong:
  Designer Solarian flooring, 22:47 (BK)
  flooring epoxy, 22:47 (BK)

Armstrong, Leslie:
  house by, 1:56-58
  Little House, The, 1:56, 57, 5:14
  on owner-built houses, 5:14

Arnold, Jamie: house by, 35:28-34

Aronie Concepts, Inc.: address for, 70:100

Arpin Products: Asbestite coating of, 24:83

Arrow Fastener Co., Inc.: address for, 57:86 (EF)

Arroyo Craftsman: address for, 47:4, 58:58 (CSH)

Art Deco: bathroom, 26:81 (BK)

Art Deco Style in Household Objects, Architecture, Sculpture, Graphics, and Jewelry (Menten): cited, 69:57

Art for Everyday (Conway): reviewed, 65:108

Art of the Painted Finish for Furniture, The (O'Neil): cited, 60:81

Arthur Brown Bros.: casting supplies from, 1:39 (FWS)

Artist-Blacksmiths' Association of North America: address for, 75:78

Artistic Brass: address for, 75:49 (REM)

Arts-and-Crafts style:
  Australian, 53:64, 65, 66
  bungalow in, 59:52-56 (CSH)
  casings after, 56:70, 72 (CSH)
  ceiling in, 69:40, 41 (EEH)
  cloud motif in, 59:85, 86 (CSH)
  color in, 73:64
  conference on, 54:100
  design service for, 54:100
  details from, 67:37, 80:40-45
  discussed, 73:54
  furniture in, source for, 54:100
  house plans for, 53:88
  houses in,
    Eastern, 82:82-87
    restoration of, 52:78-82
    small, 74:52-56
  kitchen in, remodel of, 67:72-76 (REM)
  lighting fixtures in, source for, 54:100
  newsletter for, 54:100
  Nova Scotian, 73:51
  outhouse in, 67:87
  restoring, 59:83-87 (CSH), 66:24-26
  studio in, 51:36-40 (CSH)
  tiles in, source for, 54:100
  See also Greene-and-Greene Brothers restoration.

Artwork: display clamps for, making, 65:32

Arus Imports: address for, 56:41

Arvin, Jeff:
  on earthquake-proofing timber frames, 40:43-45 (TFH)
  reviews forest book, 57:114
  on stress-skin panel wiring, 47:53-55 (TFH)
  on timber-frame enclosure, 24:54-59
  on timber-framing machines, 35:55, 56 (TB)

Arvin-Air: swamp coolers of, 17:45 (SH)

Asbestite: coating, source for, 24:83

Asbestos:
  danger from, 1:12
  dealing with, 20:6, 22:4-6, 24:83, 50:66-67
  information on, 22:4, 41:8-10, 42:4, 55:108, 70:18
  removing, 41:8-10, 42:4, 70:20
  repair tape for, 70:20
  respirators for, 22:4, 24:83
  substitutes for, 24:82, 31:34, 49 (DWS)
  testing for, 70:18-20
  ubiquity of, 24:82

Ash (*Fraxinus* spp.):
  black (*F. nigra*), as flooring, 43:29, 31 (CSH)
  white (*F. americana*), building with, 15:10

Ashland Chemical Co.: Isoset adhesive, 24:59

ASHRAE: *See* American Society of Heating, Refrigeration and Air-Conditioning Engineers.

ASHRAE Fundamentals Handbook: source for, 46:48

Askins: as joint author. *See* Mack, Robert C.

Asko, Inc.: address for, 83:6

Aslet, Clive, and Alan Powers: *National Trust Book of the English House, The,* reviewed, 32:86

Aspen (*Populus* spp.): brown stains in, 28:4

Aspenite: in superinsulated houses, 15:59

Asphalt:
  cements, discussed, 65:41, 44
  incompatibility of, with coal-tar, 9:4
  test for, 9:4, 12:4
  See also Bitumens. Membranes. Roofing.

Asphalt Roofing Manufacturers Association:
  address for, 57:89, 65:53 (EF)
  information from, 37:84
  publications of, 3:63, 23:50
  recycling programs of, 69:102
  Residential Asphalt Roofing Manual, 23:50

Associate Engineering Corp.: address for, 49:87

Associated General Contractors of America:
  contracts from, 57:77
  Recommended Guide for Bidding Procedures and Contract Awards, 23:6

Association for Preservation Technology, International: address for, 61:68, 65:45, 55, 70:49

Association for the Study of Traditional Environments: address for, 49:102

Association of Energy Engineers: address for, 65:52

Astaire, Lesley, and Roddy Martine: *At Home in Scotland,* reviewed, 54:106

Aston Industries, Inc.: heat-recovery ventilators, 34:34 (DWS)

Astro Chemical Co.: address for, 61:68

Astrolon: cost of, 8:30 (TFH)

At Home in Scotland (Astaire and Martine): reviewed, 54:106

A-Therm Door: source for, 6:60

Atkin, John: gate by, 52:89

Atlantic Boatworks: timber frames by, 36:49 (TFH)

Atlantic International, Inc.: address for, 59:63 (EEH)

Atlantic Trading Co., Ltd.: address for, 52:108

Atlantic Veneer Co.: address for, 55:96

Atlas Co., Inc.: address for, 67:54

Atlas Industries: stress-skin panels, 24:59

Atlas SCA: address for, 78:50

Atrium: Japanese, 4:53, 57 (TFH)

Atrium Door & Window Co.: address for, 76:75 (FC)
Atsko Inc.: address for, 50:63
Attics:
bathroom in, 13:41
design for, 13:39
floors of, reinforcing, 21:27
insulating, 27:10, 31:70
and convection losses, 79:110
loose-fill, 56:39-40
renovation of, 28:26-30
skylight in, 13:40, 41
staircase for, 13:40-41
and vapor-barrier concerns, 19:68, 29:70, 47:18
ventilation for, 7:52-53 (DWS)
Audel Carpenters and Builders Library
(Ball, ed. Leeke): reviewed, 76:118
Audel Mechanical Trades Pocket Manual (Nelson): reviewed, 64:112
Auerbach, Ezra:
on alternative energy, 62:68-71
reviews battery system, 51:92
Aug. G. Barkow Mfg. Co. Inc.: heat pumps, 26:68
Auro: distributor for, 67:90
Auro-Sinan Co.: address for, 73:68
Austin, C. K.: *Formwork to Concrete,* cited, 78:53
Austin, Henry: house by, 9:21-24
Australia: verandah houses of, 53:62-66
Authentic Small Houses of the Twenties
(ed. Jones):
cited, 53:88
reviewed, 44:94
Auto-body fillers: for wood, 35:14
Autodesk, Inc.: address for, 59:16, 82:92
Automated home systems: described, 53:72-76
Automotive vehicles: cold-proofing, 50:60-61
AutoSketch: reviewed, 81:114
Avanti Insulated Entry Door: source for, 6:60
Avila Mateo: brick vaults of, 23:26-31
Avonite, Inc.:
address for, 84:45
Avonite, reviewed, 32:82
See also Countertops: resin board.
Awls: for renovations, 12:51 (TB)
Awnings:
fabric for, 50:49
for south wall, 38:26, 27 (EEH)
AWWF: *See* Foundations: all-weather wood.
Axes:
broad-, using, 13:56, 57
rigging, described, 23:33-35 (TB)
technique with, 13:54-59
See also Handles.
Ayotte, Richard: on loft remodel, 70:80-81 (REM)

Azevedo, Jerry:
arched bridle joint by, 3:66
on Bai houses of southwestern China, 55:88-89
on bending form, 67:85 (FC)
on hot-tub, 42:118
on metal roofing, 24:42-46
on owner-builder code, 62:102
on radial-arm-saw cabinet, 69:71-72
on tile roofing, 60:36-41, 65:56-61 (EF)
Aztec International Ltd.: address for, 75:72

B

B and S Patent Developing Corp.:
chalklines, 25:69 (TB)
Babcock, Richard: mentioned, 27:84
Babitsky, Stephen: on worker's compensation, 18:16-17
Bacca floor finish: *See* Finishes: Swedish floor.
Back: *See* Injuries: cumulative.
Backer boards:
edge plane for, 42:20 (CSH)
gypsum-based, cutter for, 82:92-94
source for, 15:8, 37:8
for tilework, 85:16
using, 70:63-65 (EEH)
Backer rods: *See* Gaskets.
Backhoes:
marking for, 18:66 (CBS)
narrow bucket for, 18:66 (CBS)
Backstrom, Adam: on Scandinavian prefab houses, 23:84
Backyard Structures (Strombeck): cited, 53:89
Badanes, Steve:
on airplane house, 6:54-57
on architects, 38:8-10
on beach house, 63:36-41
on Jersey Devil Hill House, 29:28-33
on metal-skin house, 52:68-73
on troll bridge, 77:132
Baer, Morley, *et al.*: *Painted Ladies,* 35:72
Baer, Steve and Holly:
career of, 26:56
Dome Cookbook, The, 26:56
products of, 26:56
Zomehouse of, 26:52-57
Bahamas: building in, 67:59-63
Bahrman, Neal: on camper-shell toolbox, 57:71
Bailey Pottery Equipment: address for, 56:44
Bailey, Robert F.: *Pocket Size Carpenter's Helper, The,* reviewed, 46:104

Bailey's (mail-order tool catalog):
address for, 78:42
reviewed, 62:51
Bain, Delmar: mentioned, 32:73
Bainbridge Aquabatten Inc.: address for, 50:49
Bainbridge, David: on microclimates, 9:14-16
Baird, Bill: toolbox of, 74:86
Baird, Gary J.: reviews Generic CADD, 60:92-94
Baird, James E.: finds note, 48:104
Bake ovens:
books on, 64:20
building, 64:20-22
Baker, David: house by, 32:38-43
Baker, Jim: on English museum, 19:22-23
Baker, Larry: mentioned, 32:61
Baker, Stuart: on remodel, 65:76-79 (REM)
Baker, Victoria: on job well dug, 35:102
Balazs, Harold: downspout by, 9:75
Balconies:
chain-suspended, 32:63-64
column-supported, 73:48, 50
French, 75:49 (REM)
knotty-pine, 73:52, 55
roofed, 38:36, 37, 39 (CSH)
semicircular, 66:79 (SH)
Spanish Revival, 45:41
Swiss cutout, 70:74, 75
tiny cabin, 55:42, 43 (SH)
Baldcypress *(Taxodium distichum)*:
decay resistance of, 63:63 (MFC)
Baldwin Hardware Corp.:
address for, 50:73 (FC), 54:65 (FC), 68:44 (FC), 83:56
brass forging by, 48:64, 65 (FC, MFC)
Baldwin, John: on deck, 69:46-49 (EF)
Balin, Marty:
roof by, 26:6
room by, 25:92
Ball and Ball:
address for, 49:14
Colonial hardware, 20:12
strap hinge of, 12:20 (CSH)
Ball, John E. (ed. Leeke): *Audel Carpenters and Builders Library,* reviewed, 76:118
Ballantine, Tim: makes tenon, 12:1
Ballinger, Charles: on showerhouse, 46:74-75 (BK)
Ball-Paylor house: mentioned, 11:34-35
Bally Block: address for, 77:44
Balusters: *See* Staircases.
Band joists: *See* Joists: rim.
Bandsaws:
abrasive belt for, 35:72
circle-cutting jig for, 67:83 (FC)
dolly for, making, 77:94
makeshift, 50:30
metals on, 63:66, 67
portable, 35:57 (TB)

safety label for, 37:81
shingle jig for, 48:72, 73 (SH)
wheeled operation of, 17:14
See also Roller supports. Sawmills.
Bang and Olufsen: shelving system, 31:76
Bangkok Industries: teak, 39:74
Bangor Slate Co.: address for, 54:54
Banisters: *See* Staircases: balusters for.
Bannister, Phillip: house by, 10:48, 49 (SH)
Barbecue grill: gas, source for, 48:36
Barber, F. Drake: floor by, 79:91
Barclay Home Designs: address for, 53:89
Bard Mfg. Co.: heat pumps, 26:68
Barden, Albie:
on masonry stoves, 7:49 (CBS), 76:76-79
mentioned, 34:50
Bargagjy, Joan C.: as joint author. *See*
Diffrient, Niels.
Bargeboards: *See* Rafters: barge.
Barker, Ellen R.: on remodeling drama, 28:98
Barker, Vernon: house by, 31:72-73
Barking spud: described, 13:54-55
Barlow, Rick: on helical stair, 16:70-72 (FWS)
Barn Book, The (Corbett-Winder):
reviewed, 67:104
Barnacle Parp's New Chainsaw Guide
(Hall): cited, 78:43
Barnard, John:
Earth Sheltered Housing Design,
mentioned, 25:71
roof specifications of, 25:71
Barnes, Robert:
ablobe technique of, 21:20-21
mentioned, 10:16
Barnes, Roger:
on Fonthill, 6:29-35
on foundation disaster, 1:60
on redwood house, 1:52-55
reviews Wolfe, 9:68
Barnes, Susan: on ablobe, 21:20-21
Barnett Brass and Copper, Inc.: mail-
orders from, 44:4
Barns:
as building-material source, 11:51, 52, 22:14
connected, 10:26, 27
English conversions of, book on, 67:104
house from, 59:14
as houses, building, 59:42-47
plan sources for, 53:89
rebuilding, 44:72-75
Barr, Ronald J.: on pier-and-grade-beam
foundation, 16:31-33 (CBS)
Barr Specialty Tools: tools of, reviewed, 49:95
Barr, Tom: on passive cooling, 2:30-34 (EEH)
Barragan, Luis:
influence of, 70:64 (EEH)
staircase after, 48:33, 35

Key to books:

(BK)   Building Baths and Kitchens
(CBS)   Building with Concrete, Brick and Stone
(CSH)   Craftsman-Style Houses
(DWS)   Building Doors, Windows and Skylights
(EEH)   Energy-Efficient Houses
(EF)   Exterior Finishing
(FC)   Finish Carpentry
(FRC)   Frame Carpentry
(FWS)   Building Floors, Walls and Stairs
(MFC)   More Frame Carpentry
(REM)   Remodeling
(SH)   Small Houses
(TB)   Tools for Building
(TFH)   Timber-Frame Houses

Barrett, Alfred: makes boring mistake, 80:114
Barrett Co.: dry-stack block of, 16:57 (CBS)
Barrett, David:
passively cooled house by, plans for, 51:8
plans duplex rehab, 26:33-37
Barrett Manufacturing Co.: address for, 41:57 (CBS)
Barrett, Nancy: on Skidompha house, 17:79 (SH)
Barrett, Niall: goat shed by, 67:86
Barricade: vs. Tyvek, 39:90
Barron, Errol: on Louisiana Country
House, 59:57-61
Barrows, John E.: on Earl Covey, 40:38-42
Bars:
built-in compartment for, 15:78, 79 (CSH)
nosing for, curved painted, 62:60
Barth, Aileen L.: on Nantucket house, 77:86-89
Basalt: building with, 8:24 (CBS)
Base hooks: using, 77:58, 59
Baseboards:
caulking, 14:14, 61:26
cherry and walnut, 68:87
coping, 34:40-41, 36:6 (FWS)
curved, cold-molded, 38:45
cutlist form for, 76:53 (FC)
described, 34:40 (FWS)
fitting, to tile, 14:14
installing, 34:40-41 (FWS), 76:51-53 (FC), 77:58
lamello slot-joined, 49:28
mahogany coved, 67:73 (REM)
measuring blocks for, 34:40-41 (FWS), 77:58
at odd angles, 37:8-10
plate-joined, 70:53 (FC)
and radiused corners, 43:78-79

shims for, adjustable, 62:28
spline joint for, 25:16
and stair skirtboard, 68:60-61
wiring chases in, 47:54 (TFH), 48:52
See also Miters.
Baseclad:
for foundation insulation, 8:6
mentioned, 29:12
Basements:
adding, 32:62-63
baseboards for, 23:14
building, 10:34
cooling room in, retrofitting, 48:58-60
damp, dealing with, 19:8, 26:12
deckboard floor for, 32:58
digging, under house, 12:46-47, 39:38, 81:68-71
insulating, 19:4, 26:12
temperatures of, 13:8
as temporary shelter, 10:34
vapor barriers for, 19:68, 21:58 (EEH), 41:10, 81:71
ventilation for, 79:24
wall nailers for, embedded, 69:30
waterproofing, 81:70
See also Crawl spaces. Foundations.
Radon.
Basic Building Code: discussed, 5:44, 45
Basic Carpentry (Capotosto): reviewed, 35:70 (TB)
Basic Coatings: address for, 85:63
*Basic Construction and Materials
Takeoff* (Jones):
mentioned, 23:49
reviewed, 29:92
Basic Design Measurements for Sitting:
source for, 53:14
Basketball:
backboards, integrating, 28:74, 75
courts, by garages, 44:76
Basswood *(Tilia americana)*: for trim, 19:52-53, 42:55 (DWS, FWS)
BATA Shoe Co.: address for, 50:62
Bathroom Design (Snow): reviewed, 47:112
Bathroom Machineries: address for, 80:70
Bathroom Planning Standards: source for, 29:92
Bathrooms:
adding, 28:28-29, 30
angled, 52:16
Arts-and-Crafts style, 26:81 (BK)
association for, 72:98, 82:104
attic, 21:29
bins for, 45:52 (CSH)
black-and-white checkered, 82:87
blocking for, 82:50
book on, 47:112
built-ins for, 13:60-63 (BK)
for children, 45:52 (CSH), 47:89
concrete, 37:27, 28 (BK)

corrugated glass in, 21:40, 42
design for, 30:63, 52:20 (CSH)
    booklet on, 29:92
    courses on, 72:98
divided-sector, for privacy, 74:60-61
dividers for, wood-slab, 80:91
duckboard for, vinyl, 37:28 (BK)
energy-efficient, 66:4, 80:70
faucets for, 25:49 (BK)
    lever-handled, 76:57, 58
    water-saving, 84:82-84
fireplace in, 75:85
fixtures for, handmade, 36:68-69 (BK)
floors in, wood, 22:67 (BK)
formal, 80:91
gallery of, 80:88-91
glass for, specialty, 76:66-69 (REM)
glass-roofed, 48:79, 81, 82, 83
with greenhouse, 59:66 (EEH)
for handicapped, 6:51, 53:69, 70, 71, 65:77,
    79 (REM), 76:56
    books on, 35:45 (BK)
handrails for, 25:47-48 (BK), 53:70
hardware for, 75:49 (REM)
Japanese-influenced, 32:42-43
marbleized, 60:78
medicine cabinets for, flush-mounted,
    75:49 (REM)
modular, 52:26-28
murals in, 45:52 (CSH)
1950s' future, 34:74
odors from, diagnosing, 62:18 (CSH),
    65:8
open, 41:47-48
planters for, orchid, 59:90
plant-filled, 38:48 (SH)
plywood, 46:36
remodeled, for loft, 70:81 (REM)
sinks for,
    circular pedestal, 12:62 (DWS)
    Craftsman bracket for, 69:56
    for handicapped, 76:58
skylights in, 73:73, 75
soap holder for, magnetic, 49:59 (SH)
stone, 25:47-49 (BK), 80:91
supply source for, 69:63 (REM)
of terra-cotta blocks, 21:40, 42
tiled,
    with bench, 80:89
    columned, 80:89
    with geometrical designs, 80:90
    handmade, 59:90
    marble, 69:56-57, 80:77, 90
    mosaic-, 34:76
    organic, 66:53
    process of, 22:65-67 (BK)
    with seconds, 76:68-69 (REM)
tiny, 11:43, 45, 13:65, 66 (SH, SH), 75:66-67
towel bars for, hot, 59:86, 87 (CSH)

vanities for,
    integral, 22:65-67, 25:48-49 (BK)
    painted under glass, 84:80-81
venting, 64:20
as whole-room showers, 21:40-41, 42,
    25:47 (BK)
windows for,
    bay, 22:66, 67 (BK)
    diamond, 68:86
    stained-glass, 73:88, 91
See also Bathtubs. Drain lines. Hot tubs.
    Showers. Toilets.

Bathtubs:
acrylic, mortar base for, 73:87
alcove-enclosed, 80:58
attic gable installation of, 21:29
blocking for, 22:35-36 (FRC)
cast-concrete, 37:28 (BK)
certification program for, NAHB, 76:108
cold-molded fiberglassed, 38:45
deep round, 11:45, 71 (SH)
drain placement for, 29:52 (BK)
drop-in wide-rimmed, source for, 73:62
enameled metal and composite, 59:110
ferro-cement, 13:52, 53 (CBS)
fiberglass, filling voids beneath, 68:30
furred-out plumbing box for, 22:66, 67
    (BK)
with grab bars, built-in, 69:63 (REM)
insulating, 10:52 (SH)
Japanese-style, 19:40-41 (BK), 61:61 (SH)
layout for, 21:72, 76, 77 (FRC)
lightweight, mortar bed for, 26:16
moving, 64:130
old, source for, 42:30 (CSH)
placement of,
    and framing, 49:51-52 (MFC)
    reverse, 7:10
round deep, 11:45 (SH)
shelf around, tiled, 45:52 (CSH)
/showers, integral cast, 4:31, 33
tiled, Arts-and-Crafts style, 26:80 (BK)
urethane foam, 65:96
whirlpool, address for, 76:68 (REM)
See also Hot tubs. Plumbing. Porcelain:
    refinishing.

Batterboards:
reusable system for, reviewed, 62:94
setting up, 11:27, 28:16 (CBS)
See also Site layout.

Batteries:
cold-weather precautions for, 50:60
rechargeable, care of, 35:39 (TB)
Bau-Biology: information on, 65:54
Bauer Corp.: address for, 84:55
Bauer, Jerry: mentioned, 34:8
Bauhaus:
book on, reviewed, 9:68
and Mies van der Rohe, 46:35
Bauman, M. Garrett: on nature's
    reclamation, 59:118

Baxter (J. H.) and Co.:
poles, 15:27
treated shingles, 11:8
Bayliss Autovents: mentioned, 32:37, 34:4
B&D Window and Sash Co.: address for,
    76:67 (REM)
BDC Electronics, Inc.: dangerous-fume
    detectors, 39:92
BeA America Corp.:
nailer, discussed, 47:74 (FC)
pneumatic tools, 15:53 (TB)
Beach, John: on Sowden house, 14:66-73
Beach houses: in Mexico, building,
    63:36-41
Beadboard: *See* Polystyrene, expanded.
Beadex Manufacturing Co., Inc.:
address for, 46:90, 66:67 (EEH)
Beading: tool for, 21:18
Beads: vertical attached, 71:44, 45 (REM)
Beadwall: source for, 26:56
Beals, Joseph:
on building window frames, 84:76-79
on classical columns, 64:54-57
on Greek Revival addition, 54:68-71
    (REM)
on interior doors, 72:50-53 (FC)
reviews Foad, 69:108-10
reviews Gray, 64:110
reviews Kitchen, 70:120-22
reviews National Park Service booklets,
    72:108
Beams:
boom lift for, 6:8
box,
    building, 71:76-77 (MFC)
    built-up insulated, 55:42-44 (SH)
    built-up shear, 79:82, 83, 84
    cherry, 68:84, 87
    for continuous lift, 9:6
    curved, 2:56-59
    for curved construction, 25:39-41
        (EEH)
    framing system for, 72:98
    plywood, 18:14, 52:69-73
built-up, 31:34 (DWS), 64:20, 68:85, 69:6,
    77:20
    calculations for, 49:6-8
    for coffered ceilings, 84:69-71
    curved, 68:58-59
    glue for, 77:77 (REM)
    with insulation layers, 79:32
    stepped, 45:57, 59
of butt-joined timbers, 7:36, 37 (DWS)
cantilevered, 20:33
    Cor-Ten steel, 75:59
    exterior, with corbels, 72:39-40
    gusset, 57:53, 54-55
    shaped, 45:41
carved, 7:23 (BK)
    wire-brushed, 24:30 (CSH)
cased, 29:56, 58-61 (CSH)

ceiling, veneering, 56:77
chamfered, 28:59, 60-61 (TFH)
   exterior, 70:74
     fire protection from, 33:42 (FWS)
     Japanese treatment of, 24:63 (TFH)
checks in, 14:10
composite, 2:27, 29, 49:73 (EEH)
   built-in-place, 13:6
concrete,
   bond, pouring, 82:66-67
   precast double tee, 66:84-85
   reinforced, method for, 74:50-51
corbeled Swiss, 70:74
cord, 22:54, 56, 57, 58 (CSH)
coved, 28:59, 61 (TFH)
curves in, 14:14
   bandsaw cutting of, 17:14
   makeshift bandsaw for, 50:30
damaged, connector plates for, 32:57
for definition, 45:64 (SH)
dividing by three, 74:114
dovetailed, pictured, 28:58 (TFH)
dressing, with floor sander, 69:30
exterior,
   detailing of, 51:60
   flashing of, 9:48-49 (erratum, 10:6, EF)
ferro-cement, circular, 25:60
girder,
   adding, 79:87
   bracing, 77:85
   on metal plates, 51:38-39 (CSH)
   placing, 77:83-84, 79:82
   posts for, 77:83-85
   preservative for, 79:24
   repairing, 79:22-24, 86-87
   spans for, 77:85
   splicing, 77:85
   steel, knee braces for, 79:81
glulam, 1:63, 47:84, 86, 62:85 (MFC), 68:71
   (EF)
   associations for, 71:59 (MFC)
   books on, 71:59 (MFC)
   care of, 71:59 (MFC)
   curved, making, 20:8
   custom, 77:52, 53
   cutting, caveats for, 71:58 (MFC)
   described, 71:55 (MFC)
   finished sizes of, 71:56 (MFC)
   grades of, 71:56 (MFC)
   metal connectors and, 71:58-59 (MFC)
   site-built, 73:43, 45 (EEH)
   strength of, 71:55-56 (MFC)
   "top" designation on, 31:8
   and wood shrinkage, 81:55
gunstock, joined, 28:59 (TFH)
hewing, 39:59 (CBS)
honeycomb-paper, 81:106
I-, hardboard for, 67:81
jacking, cautions for, 48:4
jacks for, improvised A-brace, 53:28-30
Japanese temple dimensions for, 24:63,
   64 (TFH)

Japanese wedged drying of, 19:38-39
   (BK)
lamb's tongues on, 28:59, 60-61 (TFH)
laminated,
   camber of, 33:4
   exposed, 37:34-35
   information on, 65:53
   limitations of, 60:43 (SH)
   publications on, 23:49
laminated-veneer I-, 50:42-43 (MFC)
lateral supporting, rules for, 70:14
logs as, 40:40, 41
metal I-, raising jig for, 62:87 (MFC)
metal strapping for, hand-wrought,
   51:36-37, 39 (CSH)
moving, 8:31-33, 9:43, 14:48, 50 (TFH),
   34:14, 62:30, 65:51 (TFH), 70:32
notched, for rafters, 65:49-50 (TFH)
for plank floors, 33:42 (FWS)
quirk-beaded, 28:59 (TFH)
repairing, 70:49
replacing, 72:39-40
sandblasting, 22:43, 53:46, 49 (SH)
scarf joints in, 38:83 (CSH), 70:47
sizing, 4:46, 47, 42:10 (FRC)
steambending, 48:46-47 (TFH)
steel, 4:44, 6:49-50, 16:51, 52, 53 (FRC)
   cantilevered, 11:55-56, 57
   for deck, 30:33, 35-36
   I-, as floor joists, 67:66 (REM)
   I-, insulating, 68:86
   I-, source for, 79:82
   paint for, 73:73
   placing, 70:84 (REM)
   rectangular-tube, 73:73, 76, 78-81
   source for, 73:79
summer,
   carved, 28:58, 61 (TFH)
   defined, 6:42-43 (TFH)
support for, temporary, 7:22 (BK)
Swedish insulated concrete, 40:54
types of, compared, 71:56-58 (MFC)
used mortised, supporting, 6:38 (FRC)
wood I-, 52:55, 56:58, 60 (EEH)
   connectors for, 51:82 (MFC)
   for vaults, 51:82-85 (MFC)
See also Plates. Raising. Ridge beams.
   Sills.
Bean (L. L.), Inc.: address for, 50:62
Bear Creek Lumber: address for, 75:84
Bear Wear, Inc.: tool bags, 36:89, 42:65 (TB)
Beard, Bill: reviews Grabow, 33:88
Beard, Don: roof by, 57:91
Beattie, Drew: columns by, 69:89
Beatty, Herb:
   on energy publications, 56:110
   house by, origin of, 51:8
   on passive cooling, 49:72-75 (EEH)
   on radiant barriers, 58:96-98
Beatty, Paul: foundation design by, 40:44,
   45 (TFH)

Beauties of Modern Architecture, The
   (Lafever): mentioned, 29:63
Beaver, Byron: on builder's day, 68:118
Beaver Blade chainsaw blade: reviewed,
   43:96
Bechhoefer, William: on temperate-
   climate design, 19:61-65 (EEH)
Beck, Jim: owner-contracting by, 6:27
Beck, Michael: on free-form building,
   66:55
Beckedorf, Lloyd: mentioned, 34:49
Beckman, Richard M.:
   on building house, 81:83-87
   on Seattle house, 64:75-79
Bedrooms:
   adobe-imitative, 43:78
   bed recess in, arched, 32:42
   built-ins for, 37:38
   design for, 30:63
   engawa nook as, 43:28, 29 (CSH)
   over garage, 80:87
   1950s' future, 34:74, 75
   lavatory for, 37:38
   modular, 52:26-28
   tables for, flip-up bed, 46:39 (REM)
   with terrace door, 80:48
   two-tier efficiency, 62:49 (SH)
   ventilating panels for, 73:64, 65
   See also Sleeping lofts.
Beds:
   art-deco red gum, 14:68-69
   built-in, 12:31, 38:43, 44, 45, 49:60 (SH),
     66:38, 39 (SH)
     for kneewall space, 76:42-45 (REM)
     plywood, 46:38-40 (REM)
   cantilevered, 66:86
   foldaway,
     hardware for, 73:100
     Murphy, choices in, 73:100
     sources for, 75:4
   by Frank Lloyd Wright, 56:87
   headboards for,
     built-in, 73:57, 80:80
     cast-concrete, 29:33
     console, 46:38-39 (REM)
   leather/steel, 46:36
   platform, 23:75, 77
   slide-out, 66:89
Beech *(Fagus grandifolia)*:
   for floors, 37:8
   hardness group of, 40:69 (FRC)
   radial splits in, 13:8
   red stain for, 36:26 (CSH)
Bees: *See* Insects.
Beetles: *See* Insects.
Behavior of Flooring: source for, 53:14
Behr Process Corp.: address for, 48:73
   (SH)
Belair, Dick: on stone stairway, 76:60-62
Belcher, Clay: on fluorescent lighting,
   54:49-53

Bellcomb Technologies: address for, 81:106

Bellock, Bob: on gas nail gun, 33:82 (TB)

Bellows, Roy: iron work by, 48:84

Bellows Free Academy (VT): rehabilitation classes at, 29:88-89

Belt sanders: *See* Sanders.

Belts: *See* Tool belts.

Belvederes:
active, 8:63-65 (EEH)
for coastal house, 29:74-77
concrete, 30:65-69 (CBS)
over tetrahedron, 6:49, 50
for tropics, 3:56-59 (EEH)
truss system for, 43:69-70 (TB)
See also Gazebos.

Bench stones:
concrete truing of, 13:12
diamond, 13:12
dressing of, 18:61 (TB)
oil,
vs. water, 18:59, 61 (TB)
water saturation of, 13:12

Benches:
as balustrade, 66:89
and bed, built-in, 38:43, 45
built-in, 2:60, 3:58, 59, 12:31, 21:41, 35:32, 33, 42:38 (EEH), 51:52
body-contoured, 53:14
deck, 39:54, 55 (CSH)
exterior, 25:81, 45:69
heated, 44:79
slabwood, 33:77
upholstered, 45:63 (SH)
cantilevered,
exterior-interior, 66:36, 37 (SH)
laminated strips, 66:90
deck, 46:69 (EF), 80:45
comfortable, 82:52-53
integral, 29:45, 46 (FRC), 69:46-49 (EF)
equipment-hiding, 58:59 (CSH)
fireplace-flanking, 59:37 (SH)
for hall window bay, 59:39-40 (SH)
Inglenook Greene-and-Greene, 17:33 (CSH)
kitchen, 58:40, 41 (REM)
limestone carved, 54:73
nails for, 85:47
plaster-over-block, 48:34, 35
revising, for comfort, 12:41
rustic cedar, 13:76
for sauna, 51:44, 45
in staircases, 6:66
stone kitchen, 42:69 (CBS)
See also Countertops. Drawers.
Tambours. Window seats.
Workbenches.

Benchmark Insulated Entry Door:
source for, 6:60

Benchstones:
alumina ceramic, reviewed, 77:94-96
diamond,
reviewed, 48:91
source for, 76:84 (FC)
Japanese water, source for, 76:84 (FC)

Bend Industries: insulated block, 31:39 (CBS)

Bend Millworks Systems: address for, 65:80 (MFC)

Benda Industries: address for, 46:90

Bender, Richard: on architects, 20:26

Bender, Tom:
on house burning, 27:94
on overhead glass, 16:21 (CSH)
reviews preservation book, 4:58
on storage stair, 15:70-71 (FWS)

Bendheim (S. A.): address for, 59:104, 67:75 (REM)

Bending: *See* Kerf-bending. Lamination. Steam bending.

Bending strength:
defined, 7:25, 27-28, 32:30-31 (FRC, TFH)
figuring, 4:46 (FRC)

Benite sealant: for flooring, 27:12

Benjamin, Asher:
American Builder's Companion, The, cited, 53:88
Country Builder's Assistant, The, influence of, 20:62 (FWS)
mentioned, 29:63
Practical House Carpenter, The, mentioned, 1:49

Benjamin, John: reviews film, 1:66

Benjamin Moore & Co.:
address for, 67:54, 68:85, 70:112
Benwood one-hour varnish, 7:6
exterior alkyd primer, 6:23

Benjamin Obdyke, Inc.: Cedar Breather shingle underlayment, reviewed, 79:100

Benson, Arthur: begins Montauk Association, 37:52

Benson, Tedd:
Building the Timber-Frame House, cited, 5:10, 8:15, 11:18
builds frame, 38:74-75, 76-77 (TFH)
and Habitat for Humanity, 49:98
reviews Phleps, 17:80
on timber framing, 12:22-26, 16:38-41 (CSH, TFH, TFH)
timber-framing course of, 11:16-18
on timber-framing machines, 35:55, 56 (TB)

Bent Hill Settlement: restored house in, 1:48-51

Bentonite:
gel, 2:36, 37
as leak sealer, 2:36, 37, 34:66 (BK)
sheets, using, 29:12
sources for, 2:37, 56:83
spray-on, 2:36, 37
using, 26:73 (SH)

Bents:
fiberglass V-shaped, 34:71
footings for, separate, 18:28, 29
plywood asymmetrical box, 18:26-27, 29
steel, 23:76, 77
See also Post-and-beam. Timber framing.

Benzene: live plants removing, 69:102

Berg, Bob:
glass by, 42:80-81 (DWS)
on stained glass, 42:32-35 (DWS)

Berg, Bruce R.: on metal connectors, 43:44-49 (FRC)

Berg, Donald J., ed.: *Modern American Dwellings,* reviewed, 4:58

Berger Instruments: level-transits, 37:45 (TB)

Berglund, Magnus:
on Earth Systems Conference, 28:80-81
on mobile mills, 17:18-20
on rammed earth, 11:20-25, 34:35-39
on Rex Roberts house, 28:68-72
on soil-cement tile floors, 27:56-59
on stone house, 18:44-49
Stone, Log and Earth Houses, 34:39

Bergman Tool Mfg. Co.: Bluebird snips, 39:63

Berkeley Bar Bender: using, 26:64-65 (CBS)

Berkey, Brian: house-building saga of, 14:36-40

Berkus, Barry: NEST house by, 26:82

Bernard Maybeck (Woodbridge): reviewed, 83:120-22

Berndt, Lawrence: windows by, 38:75 (TFH)

Berner International Corp.: heat-recovery ventilators, 34:34 (DWS)

Berol USA: drafting tools, 26:58 (TB)

Berridge Manufacturing Co.: copper coating, 24:46

Berry, Kevin: mentioned, 25:42, 44, 45 (TFH)

Berry, Mark:
deck by, 39:52-55 (CSH)
mentioned, 29:57 (CSH)

Berry, Wendell: *Unsettling of America, The,* cited, 45:24

Berwick, Arnold: on sawed-off finger, 55:100

Beryllium copper: machining of, danger in, 42:4

Besco: period plumbing, 42:30 (CSH)

Besinger, Curtis:
on essential design question, 38:100-102
reviews *Japanese Folkhouses,* 32:86

Best Way Tools: screwdrivers, take-apart, 36:88

Bethlehem Steel:
address for, 52:73
Galvalume roofing, 24:43-44

Better Heating-Cooling Council:
    address for, 46:48
    heat-pump information from, 26:68
Better Use of Your...Electricity
    (Hackleman): reviewed, 24:80
Bevan, David: toolbox of, 74:87
Bevel boards: making, 77:58, 59
Bevel gauges:
    choosing, 4:21 (TFH)
    combination, source for, 67:90
    discussed, 57:94
    locking levers of, aligning, 79:6
    for renovations, 12:50 (TB)
    using, 77:58
Bevels:
    with planer, jig for, 17:37 (DWS)
    on posts, jig for, 62:44
BGP Systems: boilers, 27:71 (CBS)
BHMA: *See* Builder's Hardware
    Manufacturer's Association, Inc.
BIA: *See* Brick Institute of America.
Bianco, Jeffrey Dale: on Catskill retreat
    house, 66:78-81 (SH)
Bibbins, Bill: mentioned, 34:8
Bicknell Manufacturing Co.:
    address for, 55:8, 58:46
    stone masonry tools, 15:4, 35:36 (CBS)
Bickner, Jeff: tiles by, 6:20, 21 (CSH)
Bierman-Lytle, Paul: on healthy houses,
    73:67
Biesemeyer Manufacturing Co., Inc.:
    address for, 53:58, 74:76
    T-Square miter-saw stop system of,
    19:44 (TB)
Big Fin: source for, 26:56
Bill, David: *Practical Home Energy
    Savings,* reviewed, 76:118
Bilsom International, Inc.: safety
    products, 34:55 (TB)
BiltBest Windows: address for, 55:79
B-I-N primer-sealer: source for, 39:10
Binks Manufacturing Co.:
    address for, 48:74
    respirators, 42:55 (DWS)
    sprayer Model 7, 42:56 (DWS)
Binney and Smith: Liquitex latex paint,
    9:24
Bins: for artwork, 64:86, 87 (REM)
Bio-Energy Systems: SolaRoll, 6:56, 57
Biofa Naturprodukte: distributor for,
    67:90
Biofire, Inc.: address for, 73:102
Birch (*Alnus* spp.): hardness group of,
    40:69 (FRC)
Birch (*Betula* spp.):
    color matching, 48:78
    for paint, 42:55 (DWS)
    yellow (*B. lutea),* red stain for, 36:26
    (CSH)
Birchard, John:
    on barn-house, 59:42-47
    on board-and-batten, 75:52-56 (EF)

Doormaking Patterns and Ideas,
    cited, 83:61
    reviewed, 68:106
light fixture by, 45:52 (CSH)
*Make Your Own Handcrafted Doors and
    Windows,* cited, 83:61
on site-built door, 83:57-61
on wooden light fixtures, 27:60-63 (BK)
Bird Roofing Products, Inc.: address for,
    65:79 (REM)
Bird's mouths:
    described, 10:63, 66, 68 (FRC)
    gang-cutting saw for, 35:54, 55 (TB)
Birkerts, Gunnar: mirror-windows by,
    44:78-79
Birren, Faber: *Color Psychology and Color
    Therapy,* cited, 74:45 (EF)
Bischoff, Jim: mentioned, 27:31
Biscuit joinery: *See* Joinery: plate.
Bisson Tread Bevel: reviewed, 48:90
Bits:
    for acrylic, 55:47 (FC)
    auger,
        sharpening, 4:25 (TFH)
        shell, 13:26-27 (TFH)
        for timber framing, 4:23 (TFH)
    back-out flat for, 34:14
    Bullet, reviewed, 55:92, 63:4
    carbide panel, source for, 56:4
    clogged, cleaning, 49:28
    with countersinks, 62:43
    finger-pull, source for, 83:72
    for hammer drills, 41:52-53 (CBS)
    Hole Hawg, cautions for, 39:37 (BK)
    for holes in insulation, 56:28
    hole-saw,
        clearing, 75:28
        for locksets, 79:41, 100
        plug clearance for, 48:24
        plug-ejecting, 79:100
    for laminate trimming, 75:61-62, 63
    nail-pouch carrier for, 42:22 (CSH)
    from nails, 10:12, 31:8
    planetor,
        for extremely hard woods, 57:69
        (TFH)
        source for, 28:40 (FWS)
    router,
        adjustable slot, 64:92
        face-frame, 55:36, 41 (FC)
        for jointing, 83:58
        storage for, 56:26
    screwdriver,
        extended, making, 83:28
        sharpening, 42:16
    shank of, shortening, 54:26
    shaper, cope-and-pattern cutters, 58:38
        (REM)
    small, making, 20:16
    spade,
        chainsaw-file sharpening for, 42:18
        (CSH)

    interchangeable-cutter kits of,
        reviewed, 50:95
    refiling, 8:10-12
    scribers from, 79:30
    split-point, recommended, 63:4
    stair-rail boring, reviewed, 63:90
    tapered-countersink-stop, 49:67
    waxing, 62:28
Bitumens:
    applying, 2:35-36
    below-ground use of, 2:35-36, 37
    sources for, 2:37
    against termites, 6:63
    type test for, 12:4
    See also Asphalt. Membranes.
Bituthene:
    and ice damming, 71:14
    See also Membranes.
Bix Process Systems, Inc.: paint removal
    by, 16:66-69 (DWS)
Black & Decker, Inc.:
    accuses Japanese, 82:104
    address for, 63:74, 70:49, 53 (FC)
    Bullet bit, reviewed, 55:92, 63:4
    buys Elu, 43:92
    circular saw, reviewed, 63:73-74, 76
    compound-miter saws
        model 9425, reviewed, 29:86
        model 1707, reviewed, 43:92
    cut-off saw, reviewed, 62:80-83
    drills,
        cordless, 35:40-42 (TB)
        VSR, reviewed, 82:36-41
    hinge butt mortising template, 31:29,
        30-31 (TB)
    jigsaw blades, 33:60 (TB)
    jigsaws,
        cordless, 33:62 (TB)
        model 3159-10, 33:61, 62 (TB)
        scrolling-head, 33:61-62 (TB)
    miter saws,
        model 39, 19:42, 20:4 (TB)
        model 3091, 19:42 (TB)
    Piranha blade, reviewed, 50:95, 56:92
    plunge routers, reviewed, 71:79, 81, 82
        (FC)
    power planes, reviewed, 54:78-79
    radial-arm saw #1712,
        portable, 36:88
        reviewed, 57:60, 61, 62
    reciprocating saw, 16:45, 46, 48, 49, 18:18
        (TB)
    router #3310, for mortising, 31:29 (TB)
    Sawcat, 24:38, 41 (TB)
    saws, worm-drive,
        clips for, 24:10
        model 3051, 24:37, 40, 41 (TB)
        6½ in., 24:40 (TB)
    screw gun, Versa Clutch, 34:43 (TB)
    staple gun, reviewed, 85:102

tables,
    Workmate, 12:50 (TB)
    Workmate, as miter-saw stand, 20:4-6
    See also DeWalt.
Blackhawk Industries, Inc.: heat-
recovery ventilators, 34:22, 34
Blacksmithing:
    courses in, 8:14-15
    See also Ironwork.
Blaine Window Hardware, Inc.:
    address for, 64:49 (FC)
    tape balances of, 20:8
    window parts, 44:89
Blanco America, Inc.: address for, 66:106
Blazeck, Jerome: house by, 36:70-75
Bliss, Robert: on architects, 20:26
Block:
    adobe simulation with, 19:72-79
    with aircrete, 64:102
    associations for, 64:102, 70:110
    Bahamian, 67:61
    bond beam for, 9:65, 66
    cement/polystyrene, 83:108
    coating for, source for, 66:38 (SH)
    cold-weather, 51:41-42
    concrete funnel for, 64:32
    concrete "stones" for, 47:94
    cooling,
        publications on, 30:80
        retrofits for, information on, 30:80
    cores of, concrete pumping to, 30:37-38
    cracks in, repairing, 4:8
    curved, rebar locating for, 30:37, 39
    cylindrical, 44:59
    demonstration house of, 70:110
    for double-envelope heat storage, 11:66, 67
    Dow units for, 10:22, 23
    dry-stack, 16:55-57 (CBS)
        McIBS, features of, 17:4
    exterior-wall, repairing, 61:24
    fiber for,
        type-E, 27:12
        type-K alkali-resistant, 27:12
    for fireplaces, 4-in., 20:54, 55 (CBS)
    glass, 37:46-51 (DWS)
        corner, source for, 60:92
        laminated colored, 67:62-63
        in passive-solar systems, 10:48, 49, 52 (SH)
        plastic preset, reviewed, 85:108
        plastic, reviewed, 62:92
        for tall circular window, 45:60-61, 62, 64 (SH)
    hand-cast textile, 16:4
    hurricane-proofing, 78:86
    insulated, 9:6, 31:38-41, 36:73-74, 46:71 (CBS)
        costs of, 31:41 (CBS)
        hollow-core, 23:82-84
        lightweight, 40:53-54

Key to books:

(BK)   Building Baths and Kitchens
(CBS)   Building with Concrete, Brick and Stone
(CSH)   Craftsman-Style Houses
(DWS)   Building Doors, Windows and Skylights
(EEH)   Energy-Efficient Houses
(EF)   Exterior Finishing
(FC)   Finish Carpentry
(FRC)   Frame Carpentry
(FWS)   Building Floors, Walls and Stairs
(MFC)   More Frame Carpentry
(REM)   Remodeling
(SH)   Small Houses
(TB)   Tools for Building
(TFH)   Timber-Frame Houses

    source for, 71:52
    two-piece stacking, 70:110
    waterproofed, 66:38 (SH)
    insulation of,
        exterior, 31:41 (CBS)
    and joist floor, 70:110
    leca,
        block, foundations of, 40:53-54
        block, walls of, 40:53-54
    lining up, devices for, 25:66 (TB)
    lintels in, site-cast, 74:50-51
    moldings with, fastening, 47:28
    mortar for, 71:16
    by oneself, design for, 55:57, 59
    for partitions, 70:110
    perm rating for, 19:67
    plastering, 15:74 (FWS)
    as plenum, 1:43-44, 23:44 (EEH)
    of precast interlocking units, 70:110
    pumice, 58:82 (EEH)
        for fireplace arch, 48:36
    and radon, sealing against, 67:49
    reinforcing, 66:38 (SH), 83:14
    rock connection for, 19:76
    sandblasted, 27:48, 66:38 (SH)
    sand-filled, for heat storage, 19:63 (EEH)
    with service raceways, 70:110
    Sparfil, 23:82-84, 31:38, 39 (CBS)
        insulation for, 31:39, 41 (CBS)
    speed, 81:69, 71
        16-in., 69:41 (EEH)
    split-faced, as stone, 52:86
    strength of, 83:14
        vs. stone masonry, 9:6
    stuccoed, 40:12
        with premixed cement, 54:86 (TFH)
    surface-bonded, 12:34-37 (CBS), 46:62, 65, 71 (TFH), 69:41 (EEH)
        home mix for, 16:6
        mortar for, 69:41 (EEH)
    terra-cotta, for bathroom, 21:40, 42

    textile, hand-cast, 14:67, 70-73
    thermal breaks in, 25:12
    truss anchors for, 39:90
    vacation tower-house of, 67:59-63
    veneered,
        with brick, 24:10
        with plaster, 15:74 (FWS)
        with stone, 11:52, 36:73-74, 43:58-61 (CBS), 54:83-87 (TFH), 58:46-48, 84:56-59
        with tile, 69:57
    vents in, 44:60
    walls of,
        cavity, 31:40 (CBS)
        composite, 31:40-41 (CBS)
        double, 54:84, 85-86 (TFH)
        filled, 25:71
        fluid, 19:72-77
        freestanding, 36:12
    waterproofing, 55:57
    See also Chimneys. Efflorescence.
Fireplaces. Foundations. Masonry:
repointing. Metal connectors.
Pavers. Trombe walls.
Block and tackle: for timber raising, 1:19-21 (TFH)
Blocking:
    adhesive for, 19:56 (FRC)
    in bathrooms, 82:50, 84:6
    in ceilings, 84:6
    for closets, 82:51
    for crown molding, 82:51
    cutting, 3:33, 34 (TB)
    defined, 3:33, 34 (TB)
    discussed, 13:40, 82:48-51
    for door openings, 84:6
    for drywall backing, 82:50
    fire-stop, 20:4, 35, 21:71 (FRC), 82:48
        for balloon frames, 62:62 (MFC)
        foam-sealant, cautions for, 49:4-6
        and soffit vents, 23:12
    for green-wood construction, 7:42
    with headers, 82:49
    inefficiency of, 19:56 (FRC)
    for joists, 82:49
        end, 19:57, 59 (FRC)
    for kitchens, 84:6
    let-in, for drywall stop, 33:52 (SH)
    metal, 19:56 (FRC)
    requirements for, 19:56 (FRC)
    for siding, 82:49
    for staircases, 82:51
    for stucco, 22:35 (FRC)
    for subfloor, 82:49
    vented, 8:29 (TFH)
Blomberg: address for, 73:81
Blomberg, Nancy J.: *Navajo Textiles,* cited, 67:58
Bloodgood Plan Service: plans from, 53:87, 89

Bloomer, Kent, and Charles Moore: *Body, Memory, Architecture,* reviewed, 45:116

Bloomfield, Neal: on adobe house, 30:37-41

Blower doors:
and air-vapor barrier repair, 34:86
described, 33:56

Blow-In-Blanket System: address for, 59:53 (CSH)

Bluebird aviation snips: source for, 39:63

Blueboard: *See* Drywall: plastering. Plaster.

Blueprints:
frame for, 21:16
horizontal basket for, 31:14

Blumenson, John: *Identifying American Architecture,* described, 4:62

Blunk, J. B.: trusses by, 27:28

BNZ Materials, Inc.: address for, 59:82

Board foot: defined, 23:59 (FWS)

Board-and-batten: *See* Siding.

Boat house: described, 9:76

Bob Vila's This Old House (Vila): reviewed, 5:60

BOCA: *See* Building Officials and Code Administrators.

Body, Memory, Architecture (Bloomer and Moore): reviewed, 45:116

Bogie, Charles: sunbursts by, 29:78

Boiardi Products Corp.: mentioned, 68:68

Boice-Crane: radial-arm saw, 36:49 (TFH)

Boilers:
controls for,
computerized, 22:69-70 (CBS)
low-tech, 22:70 (CBS)
low-temperature problems with, 22:70 (CBS)
and radiant-floor heating, 22:69-70 (CBS)

Bokum, Nori: mentioned, 45:46 (TFH)

Boldrick, Charlie: on double-envelope addition, 11:66-69

Bollinger, Don:
on floor inlays, 63:78-80
on floor sanding, 14:58-59 (FWS)
on flooring, 13:42-47 (FWS), 49:63-67
on Swedish floor finishes, 36:42-45 (FWS)

Bollman house: concrete blocks in, 16:4-6

Bolton house:
restoration of, 17:29-34, 19:4 (CSH)
See also Greene and Greene Brothers.

Bolts:
lag, installation of, 64:65 (MFC)
toggle, described, 41:55-56 (CBS)
See also Anchors. Metal connectors.

Bomanite Corp.: patterning tools of, 7:6

Bon Tool Co.: address for, 63:50, 68:96

BonaKemi USA, Inc.:
address for, 67:54, 85:63
floor-finishing courses of, 69:100

Bondo auto-body putty: concrete patching with, 20:51, 52 (FWS)

Bon-Don thinset mortar: source for, 37:8

Bonsal (W. R.) Co.:
address for, 46:62, 71 (TFH), 69:41 (EEH), 85:16
surface-bonded mix, 12:37 (CBS)

Book of Masonry Stoves, The (Lyle):
cited, 15:21
quoted, 36:30 (CBS)
reviewed, 37:88

Bookcases:
on balcony, 73:48
in bed alcove, 76:43, 44, 45 (REM)
built-in,
fireplace-wall, 59:37 (SH)
pivoting, 38:43, 45
cherry glass-doored, 61:72-73
concrete, 6:34
corner recessed, 74:54
display shelves in, 26:42
fluted-stile cherry, 77:79 (REM)
formal, 40:37 (FWS)
gallery of, 58:86-87
Greene and Greene, 17:33, 24:30 (CSH)
high, 27:76, 77
integral, 37:35
ladders for, rolling, 55:86
in library renovation, 61:120
low, with planter tops, 75:47, 49 (REM)
as revolving door, 85:94
sculpted Mackintosh, 54:39
stock, modified, 26:42
tall-wall, 55:85, 86

Bookkeeping: need for, 25:12

Books: house of, 53:124

Boorstein, James:
on early pocket doors, 54:67 (FC)
on restoration, 29:63-67

Booth, Don: *Double-Shell Solar House, The,* reviewed, 1:66

Booth, Don, Jonathan Booth, and Peg Boyles: *Sun-Earth Buffering and Superinsulation,* reviewed, 28:86

Booth, Jonathan: as joint author. *See* Booth, Don.

Boots:
cold-weather, 50:62-63
dressings for, 50:63
hiking, for work, 56:4
steel-toed felted, 50:63

Borax: as wood preservative, 63:65 (MFC)

Borden Inc.:
address for, 65:41
Elmer's Concrete Bonder, 43:10
plastic resin glue, 16:75 (FWS)

Borers: *See* Insects.

Boring machine: for timber framing, 4:23 (TFH)

Bornhurst, Rick: trim by, 41:68-69 (CSH)

Bosch (Robert) Power Tool Corp.:
address for, 63:74, 68:45 (FC), 73:104, 76:65 (MFC), 81:61
circular saws, reviewed, 63:74, 76
cut-off saws, reviewed, 62:80-83
door bucks, 31:30 (TB)
drills,
cordless, 35:41 (TB)
cordless #1920-VSRK, 35:40-42 (TB)
VSR, reviewed, 82:36-41
hammers, #11304 Brute demolition, 18:18
hinge butt mortising templates, 31:29, 30-31, 49 (TB)
jigsaw blades, 33:60 (TB)
lubricator for, 33:61 (TB)
jigsaws,
model 1581, 18:17-18, 33:61, 62 (TB)
model 1578 electronic, 18:17-18
plunge routers, reviewed, 71:79, 83-84 (FC)
power planes, reviewed, 54:77, 78-79
random-orbit sanders, 64:96
reviewed, 77:69, 70, 71, 72
router bits, two-flute carbide, 13:12
router #1601, for mortising, 31:29, 49 (TB)
vacuum attachment by, 54:77

Boschen, Dick: columns by, 69:89

BossAire: heat-recovery ventilators, 34:34 (DWS)

Bostik Construction Products:
address for, 82:87
2000 caulk, source for, 32:48 (BK)

Bostitch:
framing nailers, reviewed, 56:52, 53, 54-55, 57
nail guns, 15:51 (TB), 47:74-75 (FC)
pneumatic tools, 15:53 (TB)
powder-actuated tools, 21:34 (TB)

Boston Design Corp.: address for, 80:104

Boston Shutter and Door, Inc.: products of, reviewed, 43:92-94

Bottomley, Bill:
on environmental concerns, 52:12
reviews Arbortect Woodcarver, 62:92

Bouknight, Joanne Kellar:
on conference, 47:100-102
on Florida study, 55:100-102
on HABS, 52:8-12
on Harwell Hamilton Harris, 55:70-74
on land trusts, 59:24
on new products, 52:98-108, 75:92
reviews architecture books, 45:116-22
reviews bathtub, 59:110
reviews bending lauan, 55:96
reviews building school, 51:98
reviews design book, 57:114
reviews drafting gear, 56:92-94
reviews *Encyclopedia,* 50:108
reviews glass, 59:102-104
reviews glass block, 59:110

reviews Kemp, 49:114
reviews London, 49:114
reviews Metposts, 56:92
reviews remote-control unit, 59:106
reviews slate, 57:96
reviews Snow, 47:112
reviews stair, 59:104-106, 74:90
reviews tile modules, 59:106-10
on steamboat house, 52:41-45
on stock house plans, 53:85-89
on wood windows, 60:46-51 (FC)
Boulder house:
building, 19:72-77
Gerry Jones collaboration on, 21:6
Bouton (H. L.) Co.: safety products, 34:55
(TB)
Bovedas:
building, 23:27-29, 50:74-77
mathematics of, 24:4
Bowen Jiffy:
Futura floor finish, applying, 36:42-45
(FWS)
Swedish finish, 36:12
Bower, John: *Healthy House, The,*
reviewed, 64:112
Bowerman, Tom R.: house by, 37:62-65,
38:14, 100
Bowlin Equipment Co.: address for, 54:81
(EF)
Bowman, Robert: on angle indicator,
27:82
Bow-roof houses: construction of, 33:45-
47 (TFH)
Bowyer, Jack: *Handbook of Building Crafts
in Conservation,* reviewed, 24:86
Box, Jim: on caulk, 8:16
Box joints: *See* Joinery.
Boyd, Bruce: on Snyder house, 9:42-45
Boyles, Peg: as joint author. *See* Booth,
Don.
BPCO, Inc.: address for, 72:88
BPI Systems: computer program, 35:66
(TB)
Braces:
arched steambent, 48:45-46 (TFH)
gunstock, designing, 54:16
See also Corbels.
Bracing: *See* Framing: bracing.
Brackets:
carved, 7:23 (BK)
custom metal, 62:89
patterns for, 35:72
plaster, 28:52 (FWS)
sawblade for, 35:72
staircase, 36:57 (FWS)
Victorian, copying, 35:72-73
wall, using, 36:38 (TB)
See also Scaffolding: brackets for.
Brackett, Len:
Japanese house by, 4:52-57 (TFH)
on Japanese-American house, 43:28-33
(CSH)

Brackman, Barbara: on Dinsmoor
preserve, 68:120
Bracy, Ron: builds bowstring-truss house,
33:44-47 (TFH)
Bradford White Corp.: address for, 82:58
**Bradley (E. H.) Building Products
Limited of Swindon:** stone slats of,
49:71
Brady, Mark:
Growing a Housebuilder, reviewed,
64:112
on hired help, 43:114
Branch, Quentin:
house by, 39:49-51
mentioned, 34:37
Branch, Toby: pictured, 34:36
Branch River Foam Plastics, Inc.:
address for, 61:78 (EF), 76:39
circulators, 33:12
recyling, 69:102
stress-skin panels, 24:59
vented roof panels, 26:4
Branch Woodworking: deck by, 42:36-39
Branham, Fechin Eya: mentioned, 25:26,
28, 31
Brass:
association for, 63:4
care for, 33:10
coating for, 34:6
corrosion of, 62:66, 67
hardware from, making, 63:66-68
nobility of, 21:4
polishing, in electric case polisher,
76:28-30
tung-oil heat treatment for, 33:10
Brass-Craft: polybutylene fittings, 39:90
Braun, Lee: on header, 62:87 (MFC)
Brazing: process of, 63:67
Brennan, Terry:
*Food and Heat Producing Solar
Greenhouse, The,* 10:17
reviews solar collector book, 15:22
on solar greenhouses, 10:16
Brennen, Alexander:
on second-story addition, 58:76-79
(MFC)
on site-built stairs, 62:42-45
Brewer, George: on Bahamas cabin,
67:59-63
Breyer, Donald E.: *Design of Wood
Structures,* cited, 58:16
Brian's Tool Sales: custom cutters, 28:61
(TFH)
Brick:
from Alberta (Can.), 66:42, 43, 45
arches in, 9:52, 53, 54-55, 11:4
below-grade, waterproofing, 82:20
(CSH)
bonds in, 9:53-54, 14:33 (CBS)
books on, 23:49, 32:10, 58:48

bottles as, 36:104
carrying, 67:6
cement for, 43:50 (CBS)
cleaning, 4:39, 14:35, 37:8, 43:55 (CBS)
clinker, source for, 53:53, 55:10
curved battered, 56:83
cutters for, 20:14, 64:82-83
pneumatic, 43:92
reviewed, 61:92
cutting, 3:43, 55, 33:70-71 (CBS)
drilling, vacuum for, 28:16
finish for, 14:35, 22:43 (CBS)
fire-, 26:4, 36:31-32 (CBS)
source for, 71:52
flashing saw-kerf in, 4:64
grout-lock wall, 25:51
information on, 65:53
faxed, 70:112
joint-reinforcing product for, 37:38
joints of, 43:53 (CBS)
roped, 11:4
laying, 9:53, 55, 14:34-35, 43:51-55 (CBS)
in cold weather, 51:41-42
exchange program for, 32:82
layout for, 14:33, 34, 43:50, 51 (CBS)
lightweight vault, 23:27
lintel widening in, 12:8
mortar for, 43:50 (CBS)
mosaics in, making, 64:80-83
old,
book on, 49:114
cleaning, 52:51 (TFH)
matching, 32:65, 63:70-71
paint on, removing, 8:6
paths of, arched screed for, 20:16
perm rating for, 19:67, 68
pickling, 62:22 (CSH)
plaster on, removing, 22:10
powder-actuated tools with, 21:30-33
(TB)
production of, 53:51
as quoins, 64:39, 40 (CSH)
raked, shims for, 20:78
repairing, 17:12, 20:44-46, 29:10, 69:68-69
(REM)
restoring, book on, 24:86
salvaged, 2:46, 66:75-76
sand for, 43:50 (CBS)
sandblasting, 8:6
sanding, 22:43
saws for, 36:64-65 (BK)
sealants for, 2:45-47, 14:35, 29:10 (CBS)
sewage aggregate for, 22:18 (CSH)
smoothing, 22:43, 37:8
source for, 33:68 (CBS), 64:80
strength of, tensile, 26:10
tests for, 64:24

tooling, 9:53, 55, 14:35 (CBS)
tools for, 14:33, 34, 43:52-53 (CBS)
trompe l'oeil detail for, 39:38, 41
truss anchors for, 39:90
types of, 53:53
varnish for, pre-grout, 23:12
veneer,
    flashing of, 32:10
    hurricane damage to, 57:104-106
walls of,
    cavity, 31:40 (CBS)
    duct work in, 25:51
    sculpted, 15:84
waterproofing, 64:81
weep holes in, screening, 6:4
See also Efflorescence. Floors: brick.
    Masonry: repointing. Metal
    connectors. Mortar.
Brick Institute of America:
address for, 65:53
Colorless Coatings for Brick Masonry,
    23:49
fireplace information from, 22:6
masonry heater information from, 22:6
Moisture Control in Brick and Tile Walls,
    23:49
publications from, 32:10
Salvaged Brick, 23:49
on sleeve anchors, 41:53 (CBS)
vaulted ceiling information from, 20:10
Brickner, Lou: mentioned, 34:55 (TB)
Brickwood, Casey: on blueing hardwood,
    17:14
Bridge City Tool Works, Inc.: reviewed,
    62:51
Bridges:
cantilevered, 66:84-85
draw-, 6:60
entryway steel, 79:80, 82-83
laminated cypress, source for, 56:92
small arched, glued stringers for, 42:8-10
suspended interior, 85:73
Tassajara, of laminated girders, 68:70-72
    (EF)
troll under, 77:132
Bridges and Cupolas (Strombeck): cited,
    53:89
Bridges, Pam: ceramics by, 59:91
Bridle joints: *See* Joinery.
Brierly, Cornelia: leads tour, 38:100
Briggs, Alba: mentioned, 32:34
Briggs, Don: mentioned, 30:39
Briggs Industries, Inc.: address for, 63:94
Bright, David: on bench, 82:52-53
Brill, Harry: mentioned, 32:74
Brill, Lesley and Megan: remodel of,
    19:46-49
Brill, Michael: quoted, 45:28
Brinkman (L. D.) Co.: linoleum of, 22:45
    (BK)
Bristol Design (Tools) Ltd.: address for,
    65:8

Key to books:

(BK)   Building Baths and Kitchens
(CBS)   Building with Concrete, Brick and Stone
(CSH)   Craftsman-Style Houses
(DWS) Building Doors, Windows and Skylights
(EEH)   Energy-Efficient Houses
(EF)   Exterior Finishing
(FC)   Finish Carpentry
(FRC)   Frame Carpentry
(FWS)   Building Floors, Walls and Stairs
(MFC)   More Frame Carpentry
(REM)   Remodeling
(SH)   Small Houses
(TB)   Tools for Building
(TFH)   Timber-Frame Houses

Britslate North American, Inc.: address
    for, 57:96
BRK Electronics: smoke-detector recall,
    72:100
Broadaxes: *See* Axes.
Broadstreet, Jim: *Building with Junk and
    Other Good Stuff,* reviewed, 67:104
Brock, Peter S.: on Woodstock house,
    38:72-77 (TFH)
Brockschmidt, Art: on cabin building,
    63:118
Brockway-Smith Co.: address for, 59:40
    (SH), 73:50
Brody, J. J.: *Mimbres Painted Pottery,*
    cited, 67:58
Bronze:
coating for, 34:4
faucet handles of, 26:80 (BK)
nobility of, 21:4
simulating, 1:38 (FWS)
Brooks, F. A.: *Introduction to Physical
    Micro-Meterology, An,* 9:16
Brooks, H. Allen: *Frank Lloyd Wright and
    the Prairie School,* cited, 69:57
Brooks, John: builds economically,
    73:56-59
Brooks, Walter: house by, 23:72-77
Brosco: wooden awning windows, 15:43
Brown, Arthur:
career of, 11:34
designs of, 11:29-35 (EEH)
house by, performance of, 11:31 (EEH)
Brown, Azby: *Small Spaces,* reviewed,
    85:132
Brown Book, The (Maddex): reviewed,
    31:80
Brown, Chris: columns by, 69:88
Brown, Delores: sink by, 7:67 (BK)
Brown, Ellie: house by, 19:69 (EEH)
Brown, G. Z.: *Sun, Wind, and Light,*
    reviewed, 37:88, 45:116

Brown, S. Azby: *Genius of Japanese
    Carpentry, The,* reviewed, 58:106
Brown, Sanborn G.: *Count Rumford,* 3:40
    (CBS)
Brownback, Jeanne: at conference, 28:82
Browne, Dan: *House Building Book, The,*
    reviewed, 1:64
Brownell, Bruce: sand system by, 28:81
Brownstone:
house, restoring, 5:36-39, 20:10-12
porches, repairing, 9:21-24
sealer for, 20:12
suppliers of, 5:36, 39
Broyles, Gary: furniture by, 35:29, 33, 34
BRS computer service: described, 46:60
Brubaker, Michael: on fated digging,
    79:130
Bruce & Dana, Inc.: address for, 76:58
Bruce Hardwood Floors: address for,
    57:67
Bruck, Robert: addresses conference,
    49:98
Bruder (M. A.) & Sons, Inc.: address for,
    75:49 (REM)
Bruder, Will:
bathroom by, 80:88
house remodeling by, 27:48-53
on remodeling design, 27:53
Brungraber, Ben: mentioned, 29:86
Bruno, Robert: house by, 4:68
Brunskill, R. W.: *Timber Building in
    Britain,*
cited, 42:44 (TFH)
source for, 44:4
Brushes:
bristle, 42:59 (DWS)
care of, 67:71
carrier for, 21:16
for latex paint, care of, 67:69, 70
for paint, 14:14, 42:59 (DWS)
for varnish, 48:78
varnish keeper can for, 62:30
water storage for, 62:30
wiper for, bent-wire, 82:26
Bryan, Gordon: ceramics by, 59:91
Bryant Laboratores: address for, 75:78
Bryant Steel Works: stove parts from,
    21:63 (CBS)
BSG Software: address for, 71:48
Bubblestone:
defined, 2:23 (CSH)
walls of, 2:20, 23-25 (CSH)
Bubel, Mike and Nancy: *Root Cellaring,*
    cited, 72:14
Buckingham Virginia Slate Corp.:
address for, 20:39 (EF)
Buechel Stone Corp.: address for, 68:85
Buege, David: on gingerbread house,
    12:76
Buehner Block Co.: dry-stack block of,
    16:57 (CBS)

Buffalo Sand Blasting Sands Co., Inc.:
address for, 81:47

Buffelen Woodworking Co.: Thermal Door, 6:60

Buffing: *See* Sharpening.

Buhler, Steve: house by, 11:42-45 (SH)

Build a House (Cary): cited, 7:4

Build It Underground (Carter): reviewed, 16:14-16

Build Your Own Energy-Saver Home (Wilson): cited, 1:66

Builder: New American Home by, 28:73-77

Builders:
allowances for, 52:44
apprentice programs for, high-school, 79:112
arbitration for, 49:77, 57:76-77
associations for, 47:68-71, 55:100, 77:108
audits for, quality-control, 77:108
bank aid to, 59:14
books for, 62:79, 71:69
books on, reviewed, 51:104-106
business structuring for, 62:78-79
card container for, 77:30
and change orders, 71:69, 74:6
client meetings with, 69:80-81
competition for, English, 61:98-100
computer approach for, 59:14
construction-management contract for, 76:57
consultation service for, instant, 31:84, 32:90
contracts for,
sample, 60:100
source for, 57:77
as designers, location hotline for, 77:108
dictionaries for, reviewed, 47:112-14, 50:108
donated work by, 62:106
emotional toll on, 49:126
employee management for, 47:69-71, 76:6
employee-owned corporations for, 74:53
energy-efficiency certification program for, 68:100-102
environmental responsibility of, 53:4
and fairness issues, 51:4
freeze alarm for, 39:14
good-neighbor stance for, 49:26-28
and hazardous materials, booklet on, 62:114
and homeless, programs for, 61:100-102
and hurricane-damage culpability, 78:87
incorporated, 62:78-79
information sources for, 23:48-51, 37:29 (BK)
job-closeout scheduling for, 69:79-81, 71:6
learning time of, 47:104-106
legal liability of, 49:76-77

magazine for, 20:80-81
math book for, reviewed, 85:132
multi-skilled, working as, 45:20-28
OSHA penalties for, 69:100
in partnership, 62:78
project notebook for, reviewed, 77:122
in proprietorship, 62:78
radios for, designing, 62:102-104
and subcontractors, 6:26-27
advice for, 69:81, 73:58
contracts with, 6:26-28
tape recorder for, 48:4
worker's compensation insurance for, 18:16-17
See also Carpenters. Cold weather. Construction. Contracts.

Builders Book Source: source for, 23:51

Builders for Social Responsibility: wins design competition, 75:102

Builder's Foundation Handbook (Carmody, Christian, and Labs): reviewed, 74:98

Builder's Guide to Accounting (Thomsett): source for, 36:94

Builder's Guide to Solar Construction, The (Schwolsky and Williams): reviewed, 18:78

Builder's Hardware Manufacturer's Association, Inc. (BHMA):
Directory of Certified Locks and Latches, 48:65 (FC, MFC)
lockset standards of, 48:64 (FC, MFC)

Builder's paper:
aluminum-laminated, 49:75 (EEH)
asphalt-emulsion sandwich, 22:67 (BK)
foil-backed, perm rating for, 19:67
moisture problems with, 56:42
perm rating of, 19:67
resin,
as sheathing, 19:68
for standing-seam roofs, 39:62
for roof, wire hold-down for, 85:32
under shingles, 25:63
under stucco, mesh vapor-barrier, 31:27 (CSH)
for superinsulated houses, 11:4-6, 13:4
using, 19:68
as vapor barrier, 44:6

Buildex:
address for, 41:57 (CBS), 61:74, 62:94, 65:86
screw gun, reviewed, 85:70, 71

Building codes:
on accessible housing, book on, 63:106
all-state, book on, 46:104
"alternative-owner," formulating, 62:102
associations of, 50:58
books on, 3:10
reviewed, 57:114
on ceiling heights, 60:43 (SH)
changes in, 3:10
on chimneys, 75:44

computer compliance programs for, 71:48, 49
costs of, 3:10
discussed, 5:44-45
and earthquakes, 67:4
electrical, 2:42, 5:45, 6:39, 7:44
energy-efficient, savings of, 65:102
enforcement of, 50:58-59
equivalency provisions in, 3:10
fire prevention, 5:44, 37:4
on fireplaces,
chimneys, 69:76-78
Rumford, 71:104
on flues, 85:8
on foundations, frost-protected shallow, 74:104
on handrails, 30:4
house built to, 69:38-43 (EEH)
and increased building costs, 67:36
information on, 23:48, 65:54, 55
lumber-grading requirements of, 81:16
models of, 50:58
and oriented strand board, 85:118-20
performance, 5:33
on plumbing, 5:45, 7:44, 29:51, 39:37 (BK)
regional models of, 24:44
requirements of, 7:44
for residential structures, 5:44
on roof venting, 21:51 (DWS)
on staircases, 42:49 (FWS), 65:66-67
Southern, 74:92
and story addition, 1:40-42 (FRC)
in Vermont, 50:65
violations of, and Andrew damage, 78:86, 87
and wind resistance, 60:4
working with, 64:75-79
See also Basic Building Code. National Building Code. National Electrical Code. National Fire Prevention Code. National Plumbing Code. One-and-Two Family Dwelling Code. Standard Building Code. U. S. Department of Housing and Urban Development (HUD). *under state names.* Uniform Building Code. Uniform Plumbing Code. Zoning ordinances.

Building Community: Puerto Rican work of, 62:106

Building Construction Illustrated (Ching): reviewed, 1:64, 3:4, 45:116, 78:110

Building inspectors:
associations for, 50:58
job of, 50:58-59

Building Officials and Code Administrators (BOCA): 1993 code, discussed, 83:110-12
rack resistance standards of, 40:6
on skylight glass, 49:14

Building permits:
dealing with, 7:44-45
Building Regulations (Vitale): source for, 3:10, 5:43
Building Systems Product File and Directory: source for, 32:6
Building Technology Publications 1982: source for, 23:48
Building the Timber-Frame House (Benson): cited, 5:10, 8:15, 11:18
Building Value into Housing Awards: source for, 23:48
Building with Frank Lloyd Wright (Jacobs): source for, 3:27
Building with Junk and Other Good Stuff (Broadstreet): reviewed, 67:104
Building with Logs (Mackie): cited, 8:70, 27:84
Building without Barriers for the Disabled (Harness and Groom): source for, 6:51
Building Your Own House (Roskind): cited, 53:47, 50 (SH)
Bulkheads:
aluminum, 33:32 (CBS)
concrete, building, 33:32-35 (CBS)
steel, 33:32 (CBS)
wooden, 33:31-32 (CBS)
Bulwinkle, Mark: steel garden of, 10:76
Bungalows:
with arched trusses, 39:66-69 (TFH)
book on, 31:80-82
details from, for large house, 80:40-45
See also Greene and Greene Brothers.
Bunker, B.: *Cruck Buildings,* cited, 42:41 (TFH)
Burch, Monte: *Tile Indoors and Out,* cited, 69:57
Burden, Ernest: *Living Barns,* 28:86
Burdett, Kent: on Rumford fireplaces, 3:40-43 (CBS)
Burdick, William E.: on working alone, 55:56-61
Bureaus: built-in, 45:64 (SH), 49:60 (SH), 74:56
Burgel, James A.: trailer model by, 83:130, 132
Burger, Alewyn: as joint author. *See* Konya, Allan.
Burgess & Associates: toilets, reviewed, 78:94
Burinsky, Joseph: on double envelope, 23:42-47 (EEH)
Burke Co.:
address for, 78:50
coil nuts, 14:6
concrete accessories, 26:65, 29:30, 31 (CBS)
Burlin, Brenda: newel post by, 71:89
Burnham, Franklin: columns by, 69:88
Burnham Corp.: address for, 75:94, 85:86
Burns, Jack: house by, 39:48-51 (FWS)

Burr, Duncan: pours glue down sink, 12:74
Burritt, Carroll: on Eastfield Village, 8:14-15
Burther, Darwin: mentioned, 30:33, 34
Burton, Robin: on aircrete, 64:102
Bus stop: simple, 55:73
Bush, Rick: develops cellular concrete, 30:76
Bush, Sam: on entryway, 3:15-18 (DWS)
Business: *See* Construction.
Butcher Co.: address for, 67:76 (REM)
Butcher, Solomon D.: *Pioneer History of Custer County, A,* 31:54
Butcher's Bowling Alley paste wax: tinted, 42:30 (CSH)
Butt gauges:
discussed, 57:94
homemade, 8:10
Butt joints: *See* Joinery.
Butternut *(Juglans cinerea):*
for cabinets, 12:61, 62 (DWS)
kitchen in, 69:50-54
radial splits in, 13:8
source for, 69:52
Button, Stephen D.: houses by, 14:60-61
Butyl:
with acrylic, 10:33 (DWS)
compatibility of, 17:65 (DWS)
sources for, 2:37
See also Membranes.
Butz, Sam and Marion: newel post by, 71:88
Byrne, Michael:
on glass block, 37:46-49 (DWS)
on laying tile, 17:70-75 (BK)
on mortar-bed showers, 32:46-52 (BK)
reviews Craftseat, 41:86
Setting Ceramic Tile, 37:49 (DWS) cited, 56:7, 69:57
on tiled countertops, 25:32-37 (BK)
Bystrom, Elizabeth Ogden: house design after, 31:66-71

C

C. P. D. Services: address for, 48:69
Cabarga, Leslie: bathroom by, 80:89, 90
Cabinetmaking: courses in, 8:14-15
Cabinets:
appliance "garages" in, 58:38, 40 (REM), 67:75, 76 (REM)
arced, 48:53
Arts-and-Crafts style, 22:60 (CSH)
bar in, 15:78, 79 (CSH)
base-rail system for, 30:59, 60 (BK)
beaded, 71:44, 45 (REM)
built-in, 36:29 (CSH), 85:64-67

carousels for, making, 69:53-54
carved, 62:75, 76
carving, 47:64-67
cases for, 9:35 (BK)
cherry, 45:51 (CSH), 80:52, 53
cherry veneer plywood, 59:45-47
Colonial corner, source for, 63:49
crown molding with, 59:50-51 (SH)
curved, 58:36-41 (REM)
custom, 66:66, 67 (EEH)
source for, 73:50
design of, 13:61-62 (BK)
dish storage for, vertical, 15:78 (CSH)
dish-drying, 44:52, 53 (SH)
drawings for, 9:32, 33 (BK), 13:61 (BK)
dumbwaiter with, 15:77 (CSH)
European-style,
high-tech, 62:60-61
installing, 85:53
face frames for, 9:32, 33-35, 13:61, 62 (BK)
finish for, 9:38, 17:69 (BK), 47:67, 58:41 (REM), 59:56 (CSH), 66:45, 71:45 (REM), 72:62, 73:69, 70, 74:76-77
finishing, 37:29 (BK), 48:75-78
fir, 53:49 (SH)
quartersawn, 59:56 (CSH)
Formica-edged, 66:50
garbage-can compartments in, 15:78, 79 (CSH)
glass sided and bottomed, 59:77 (REM)
glue for, 30:60 (BK)
grained, 60:82
Greene and Greene style, 17:30-31 (CSH)
handholes in, cut-out, 21:43
for handicapped, 53:70, 71
wheeled boxes as, 76:58-59
hanging,
cleats for, 3:6
system for, 58:39, 41 (REM)
hardwood-plywood-glass, 69:50-54
installing, 9:38 (BK), 39:14, 85:48-52
island, 45:51 (CSH), 59:66 (EEH), 71:42-45 (REM)
jacks for, 15:18, 27:16, 69:32
reviewed, 52:98, 78:92
scissors, 9:10
Japanese-style maple/bubinga, 43:31 (CSH)
kitchen, white, with cherry, 80:52
with KorTron, 62:76, 77
lacquering, in place, 81:76
laminated, 37:29 (BK)
curved, 15:77-79 (CSH)
lazy Susans in, 15:77 (CSH)
with leaded glass, 67:72, 73, 75 (REM)
levelers for, 74:74, 76, 81:26
library undercounter, 61:74-75
makers of, 9:41 (BK)

manufactured,
  accessories for, 65:74
  association for, 65:74
  discussed, 65:71-74
  particleboard in, coatings for, 65:61
    (EF)
  stock vs. custom, 65:71, 74
materials list for, 9:33 (BK)
molding for, 69:51, 54
nail guns for, 15:49 (TB)
nontoxic recycled, 81:106
oak,
  quartersawn, 58:36-41 (REM), 66:45
  white-stained, 64:40, 42 (CSH)
oak/cherry paneled, 75:80, 83, 84
old-wood, source for, 56:92
open-shelved over base, 63:55, 57
    (REM), 69:8
panels for, frame-and-panel, 69:52
particleboard, 8:65-66, 67 (EEH)
peninsula, installing, 85:52
plate-joined, 70:52-53 (FC)
plywood, avoiding, 73:67
redwood, 79:73, 74
reveneering, 81:72-77
scribing, integral spline for, 9:10
shelves in,
  supports for, 9:38 (BK), 69:53
  swing-up, 67:75, 76 (REM)
shutter panels for, 8:65 (EEH)
site-built, 79:76-79
slides for, 30:58 (BK)
in solid wood, 73:69, 70
  cautions for, 69:54
  unstable, 37:28-29 (BK)
with Southwestern motifs, 67:57
spacing for, 85:48
Spanish Revival, 45:42, 43
stapling, 13:61, 62 (BK), 30:60 (BK)
stock for, 30:59-60 (BK)
substrate for, attaching, 78:28, 79:8
supply sources for, 81:72, 76
tenons for, routed slip, 27:40-42 (TB)
32mm, 74:74-78, 85:53
tiled-edge, radiused, 62:76
tiles let into, 51:74, 75 (EEH)
toe-space for, 58:38, 39 (REM)
tools for, 9:33 (BK)
trays for, sliding, 45:68, 69
veneering, with plastic-laminate, 30:60-
    61 (BK)
with vertical aluminum strips, 66:45
Victorian, new, 71:71, 73
wall-divider, 62:75, 76
wood-edged laminate, 52:60 (CSH)
See also Countertops. Doors. Drawers.
    Hardware. Hinges. Pulls.
Cabins:
  building, 54:83-87 (TFH)
  cantilevered, over river, 73:71-75
  delapidating, for movie, 56:48-51
  designing, 44:38-39 (SH)

energy-efficient, building, 55:42-44 (SH)
  insulation for, 44:39 (SH)
  Japanese-influenced, 52:36-40 (TFH)
  Kansas-style, 52:57-61 (CSH)
  large Arts-and-Crafts style, 80:40-45
  Lindbergh-box, 74:116
  Minnesota-lake Norwegian-style, 80:59-
    61
  post-and-beam, 46:80-83 (TFH)
  roof system for, 44:40-41 (SH)
  stone-glass, 48:79-83
  water supply for, 44:39-40 (SH)
  See also Log building.
Cables: sleeve-forming tool for, 42:39
Cab-O-Sil: described, source for, 1:37, 39
    (FWS)
Cabot Stains: address for, 66:38 (SH)
Cabrera, Manuel Serrano: restores
    mudejar ceiling, 26:44-45
CAD-CAM for the Macintosh
    Professional: source for, 49:50
CADD: See Computers.
Cadet: address for, 59:72 (SH)
Cadley, William R.: on carved timber
    frame, 28:58-62 (TFH)
Cadmium: toxicity of, 10:10
Cahill, Okie: mentioned, 26:56
Cahoon, Geof: on "fat" glass, 41:84-86
Caine, Robert: on eyebrow roof, 44:64-68
    (FRC)
Cal Western Supply:
  address for, 46:55 (BK)
  Flexwrap form inserts, 39:34 (BK)
Calandruccio, Peter: on Daniel house,
    33:24-30
Calculated Industries, Inc.:
  address for, 51:92, 57:78, 69:92, 76:48
    (CSH, MFC)
  ultrasonic tape, reviewed, 78:54-55
Calculators:
  conversions on, 36:62 (FRC)
  framing, reviewed, 51:92
  roof problems on, 10:61 (TB)
  for roofs, 57:70, 78 (TFH)
  scientific, for framing, 36:62-63 (FRC)
  See also Computers.
Caldwell Manufacturing Co.: address for,
    84:79
Caliche: information on, 23:49-50
California:
  architectural coating standards of,
    49:14
  building code changes in, 3:10
  computer land searches in, 46:59
  dry-stack block in, 16:57 (CBS)
  energy loans in, 4:14
  energy standards of, 19:10
  handrail requirements, coded, 30:4
  home conservation credits in, 5:65
  solar tax credits in, 3:10
  water-heater rebates of, 1:9

California Design 1910: cited, 49:79
California Drywall-Lathing
    Apprenticeship and Training Trust:
    address for, 51:84 (MFC)
California Energy Commission: address
    for, 78:104
California Heat Pump: heat pumps, 26:68
California Redwood Association:
  address for, 65:53, 83:45
  assistance from, 33:90
  information from, 23:50
  publications from, 33:90
Calipers:
  discussed, 57:94
  from squares, 40:16
Calisch, Doug: sculpture by, 69:124
Callister, Charles Warren: house by,
    27:26-31
Cal-White marble sand: source for, 20:52
    (FWS)
Cameo California Metal Enameling Co.:
  countertops by, 44:53 (SH)
Cameras: Polaroid indestructible, 68:96
Campbell, Barry: builds house, 34:58-61
    (FRC)
Campbell, Guy: on cement mixer, 25:90
Campbell, Roy: shingles by, 65:88-89
Campers: See Gypsy wagon.
Can Ray Inc.: heat-recovery ventilators,
    34:34 (DWS)
Canada:
  energy demonstration in, 47:104-106
  R-2000 program of, 34:86
Canada Mortgage and Housing Corp.:
  Construction and the Environment, cited,
    83:110
Canadian Home Builder's Association:
  address for, 34:86, 51:96, 71:47
Canadian Housing Information Centre:
  address for, 75:100
Canadian Log Builders Association,
    Int'l.: address for, 47:100, 68:8
Cantherm Heating Ltd.: heat pumps,
    26:68
Cantieni, Piero: reviews sawblades,
    85:102
Cantilevers:
  construction, retrofitted, 70:82-84
    (REM)
  defined, 32:31-32 (FRC)
  design with, 32:38-43, 66:70-72
  and vapor barriers, 29:70-71
  vertical, 32:32, 33 (FRC)
Cape May (Thomas and Doebley): cited,
    14:61
Capen, Judith M.:
  on architect-client relations, 38:10-12
  on Capitol Hill townhouse, 39:38-42
  on remodel, 31:32-34 (DWS)

Capital

Capital: defined, 20:60 (FWS)
Capotosto, John: *Basic Carpentry,* reviewed, 35:70 (TB)
Capp and Bush: *Glass Etching,* 39:8
Caradco: address for, 76:75 (FC)
Carbide Tooling and Design: address for, 83:58
Carbon monoxide:
  danger from, 1:12, 5:15
  detector for, 39:92
Care Covers: reviewed, 48:91
CAREIRS: *See* Conservation and Renewable Energy Inquiry and Referral Service.
Carhartt Mfg. Co.: address for, 50:62
Caribbean: house for, 50:53-57
Caring for Your Old House (Kitchen): reviewed, 70:120-22
Carl Heinrich Co.: level-transits, 37:45 (TB)
Carl Zeiss Inc.: levels, 37:45 (TB)
Carley, Rachel: on decorative ironwork, 16:42-44
Carlin, Earl P.: on Amtrak house, 38:54-59
Carlisle Corp.:
  lead-caulked copper roofing, 32:65
  rubber roofing, 32:65
Carlisle SynTec Systems:
  address for, 51:53
  elastomeric membranes, 44:80
Carlisle Tire and Rubber Co.: membrane sheeting, 2:37, 7:37, 9:4, 16:52, 29:12 (DWS)
Carlsen, Gregg:
  on plunge routers, 71:78-84 (FC)
  tars roof, 36:102
Carlson, Peter: on exterior newel posts, 84:60-63
Carmody, John, Jeffrey Christian, and Kenneth Labs: *Builder's Foundation Handbook,* reviewed, 74:98
Carmody, John, and Raymond Sterling: *Earth Sheltered Housing Design* (2nd ed.), reviewed, 31:82
Carne, John and Linda: library of, 26:40-42
Carothers, John: builds trusses, 38:82 (CSH)
Carpal tunnel syndrome: preventing, 64:68
Carpenter, Scott M.: on curved corners, 83:62-63
Carpenter, Timothy: on Sea Ranch chapel, 64:50-53
Carpenter Gothic: *See* Gothic.
Carpenter Handy Square: evaluated, 10:61 (TB)
Carpenters:
  calculator for, reviewed, 51:92
  concerns of, polled, 70:110
  Florida study of, 55:100-102

four-day work week for, 47:71
  Japanese, book on, 58:106
  risk rating of, 34:51 (TB)
  school for, reviewed, 51:98
  SEP-IRA accounts for, 47:71
  tests for, 63:20, 64:24, 65:4
  tool writeoff for, 47:71
  See also Builders. Cold weather.
Carpenter's Dream (Heilman): reviewed, 62:112
Carpentier, Don: courses of, 8:14-15
Carpentry and Building Construction (Feirer and Hutchings): metric edition of, 35:71 (TB)
Carpentry and Building magazine: reprints from, 4:58
Carpentry and Construction (Miller and Baker): reviewed, 71:112
Carpentry (Koel): reviewed, 35:68-69 (TB)
Carpentry (Lewis): reviewed, 56:110
Carpentry (Syvanen): reviewed, 3:60
Carpets:
  adhesive padding for, reviewed, 54:92-94
  avoiding, 73:67, 70
  fusion-bonded, 38:59
  gases from, 54:16
  mastic for, avoiding, 73:67
  natural-fiber, 73:70
  protectors for, in remodeling, 75:94
  underlayment for,
    nontoxic, 54:6, 14-16
    from old tires, 81:106
Carports: *See* Garages.
Carrier Corp.: heat pumps, 26:68
Carroll, John:
  argues metric, 60:100-102
  on continuity, 57:126
  on old houses, 52:4
  reviews brick cutter, 61:92
  reviews laser level, 84:94
  reviews masonry book, 62:112
  on tools, 57:94-96
Carroll Cable Co.: address for, 50:60
Cars:
  courtyard for, 80:85
  See also Garages.
Carse, David: on spec house, 80:50-53
Carson, George: table saw of, 1:22 (TB)
Carter, Brian: on relining chimneys, 70:76-79
Carter, David: *Build It Underground,* reviewed, 16:14-16
Carter, Geoffrey: on Montgomery Place, 61:67-71
Carter, Neal: wins competition, 75:102 (addenda, 78:8)
Cartrette, Katherine: house by, 34:46-50
Carver, Norman F., Jr.:
  on architecture, 39:74
  career of, 39:70

Form and Space of Japanese Architecture, 39:70
Iberian Villages, 39:74
Italian Hilltowns, 39:74
Japanese Folkhouses,
  cited, 39:70
  reviewed, 32:86
Carving:
  of cabinets, process of, 47:64-67
  custom, source for, 66:104-106
  layout for, 67:56-58
  machine for,
    reviewed, 62:92
    source for, 64:96
  painting, preparation for, 67:58
  for pediment, 75:59
  of sunburst, for mantel, 54:56-57
  See also Cabinets: carving.
Cary, Harold: *Build a Home,* 7:4
Cary, Jane Randolph: *How to Create Interiors for the Disabled,* 6:51, 35:45 (BK)
Casa Adobe, La (Lumpkins): reviewed, 43:102
Cascade Holistic Economic Consultants, Inc.: address for, 67:100
Cascade Pacific Industries: address for, 77:16
Casein glue: *See* Glue.
Casings:
  arched, 56:67, 69:82-86 (FC)
    swan-neck laminated, 29:56-58 (CSH)
  Arts-and-Crafts style, 22:59-60 (CSH), 52:80, 56:70, 72 (CSH)
  ceramic, 41:76, 77
  corner-block, 30:56, 57 (DWS)
  curved, 27:10, 44:68 (FRC), 55:52
  door,
    fitting to walls, 32:4
    surfacing of, 32:4
  drywall abutting, 46:51 (EEH)
  and drywall, considerations for, 30:55 (DWS)
  edges of, easing, 30:57 (DWS)
  for entryways, jamb for, 3:16 (DWS)
  jambs of, 26:26-29, 30:55 (DWS)
    arched, 69:84-86
    repairing, 75:28
    steel-reinforced, 81:82
    thermal-break, 37:26, 27 (BK)
  limestone, 37:60
  mating of, to walls, 30:57 (DWS)
  mitered, 4:6, 30:56, 57 (DWS)
  molded, in cob wall, 83:89
  mortised, 85:66, 67
  nail holes in, filling, 30:57 (DWS)
  nailing, 30:56 (DWS)
  plate-joined, 70:50, 52, 53 (FC)
  for pocket doors, jamb repair for, 63:28
  publication on, 30:55 (DWS)
  relieving, 30:55 (DWS)
  removing, 30:57 (DWS)

reveals in, 47:83 (SH)
  jig for, 23:14
for skylights, pre-routed jambs for,
  70:106
spray-painting, 42:58-59 (DWS)
square-cut, 30:56, 57 (DWS)
staining, 30:57 (DWS)
steel, 46:34, 35-36
stock for, 30:55 (DWS)
tools for, 30:55 (DWS)
of tree trunks, 83:89
window,
  double-hung, 35:4
  jambless, 83:86, 87
  jambs for, extension, 33:53-54 (DWS),
    67:83 (FC)
  jambs for, thermal-break, 37:26, 27
    (BK)
  jambs for, vinyl, 84:76, 79
wiring around, 47:54 (TFH)
See also Doors. Trim. Windows.
Cassella, Steve: on fantail deck stairs,
  83:74-76
Casting:
  jig for, 1:38-39 (FWS)
  materials for, 1:36-39 (FWS), 5:10, 39,
    29:66, 70:48, 49
  process of, 1:38-39, 29:65-66 (FWS)
  of stone elements, 5:38, 39
Cast-in-Place Walls: cited, 78:53
cast-iron:
  for plumbing, 29:52 (BK)
  See also Ironwork.
Castlegate Thermal Entry Door: source
  for, 6:60
Castlelog: reviewed, 64:112
Catalytic elements: deficiencies of, 39:4
Cathedral of St. John the Divine:
  workshops at, 54:100-102
Cathers, Donald M.: *Furniture of the
  American Arts and Crafts Movement,*
  36:29 (CSH)
Catnic Components Ltd.: lintels, 43:59-60
  (CBS)
Cat's paws: for nail pulling, 32:53, 54, 55
  (TB)
Cauldwell, Rex:
  on polybutylene pipe, 78:74-78
  reviews water heater, 69:92-94
  on submersible pumps, 67:96
  on water heaters, 82:54-58
  on watertight receptacles, 77:96
Caulk:
  for acrylic, 10:33 (DWS)
  acrylic,
    copolymer, 82:14
    latex colored, 64:96
  adhesive, 15:40 (EF)
    waterproof, 2:23 (CSH), 6:23, 68:45
      (FC)
  air-infiltration-preventing, 77:67
  aluminum tape for, 42:22 (CSH)

Key to books:

(BK)   **Building Baths and Kitchens**
(CBS)   **Building with Concrete, Brick and Stone**
(CSH)   **Craftsman-Style Houses**
(DWS)   **Building Doors, Windows and Skylights**
(EEH)   **Energy-Efficient Houses**
(EF)   **Exterior Finishing**
(FC)   **Finish Carpentry**
(FRC)   **Frame Carpentry**
(FWS)   **Building Floors, Walls and Stairs**
(MFC)   **More Frame Carpentry**
(REM)   **Remodeling**
(SH)   **Small Houses**
(TB)   **Tools for Building**
(TFH)   **Timber-Frame Houses**

applying,
  drip-free, 51:24
  exterior, 62:41 (EF)
avoiding, 46:70-73
backer rod for, 62:41 (EF)
butyl, for shower pans, 32:48 (BK)
for casings, 32:4
for cold weather, 51:42, 81:96
compatibilities of, 8:16, 42, 43, 10:4
as countertop glue, 84:81
for Exolite, 17:65 (DWS)
exterior, source for, 62:41 (EF)
for fiberglass panels, 1:32
Geocel, 14:14
guns for,
  care of, 25:16
  electric cordless, 26:82
  extension, 12:12
  improvised, 77:30
  long-handled, 64:94
  power, 70:100-104
  reviewed, 42:90
oil-based, 8:16, 48:68
for paint, 42:58-59 (DWS)
paintable, 42:58-59 (DWS), 71:72
  interior/exterior, reviewed, 42:88-90
polyurethane, 12:4, 58:14
priming for, 8:43 (DWS)
against radon, 67:48
ratings for, derivation of, 11:4
for skylights, 3:48, 11:64 (DWS)
smoothing,
  with ice cube, 65:30-32
  with potato, 35:14
for soundproofing, 35:63
tape for, expanding bitumened foam,
  58:14
for tilework, 85:16
for tiny cracks, 32:4
toolable, 37:26 (BK)
trimmer for, 28:16

tubes of,
  caps for, 29:16, 48:24, 53:26, 81:28
  clear, reviewed, 42:88-90
  declogging, 60:28
  extending, 34:14
urethane,
  black, 37:26, 29 (BK)
  marine-grade, 55:4
  source for, 73:81
warming, with car motor, 60:28
See also Sealants.
Caves: fabricated, 64:132
Cawley, Frank: on arched A-frame,
  20:64-67
CB and S Stone Co.: business of, 37:56-61
CBC Environmental Services: reviewed,
  70:20
CCA: *See* Wood preservatives: copper
  arsenate.
Ceco Corp.: Entergy Entry Door, 6:60
Cedar, Eastern red *(Juniperus
  virginiana):*
  qualities of, 8:25 (CBS)
  radial splits in, 13:8
Cedar Shake and Shingle Bureau:
  address for, 65:53, 67:104, 83:45
Cedar *(Thuja* spp.):
  acids of, and zinc, 24:44
  and copper, corrosion with, 77:51
  decay resistance of, 69:16-18
  Northern white *(T. occidentalis),*
    for clapboards, 31:37
    hardness group of, 40:69 (FRC)
    radial splits in, 13:8
    shingles of, 18:8, 28:66
  for timber framing, 26:10, 30:6
  trim-grade, source for, 75:84
  Western red *(T. plicata),* color
    matching, 48:78
Cedar Valley Shingle Systems: address
  for, 54:44 (EF), 83:41
CeeFlow Skylights:
  address for, 48:90, 61:78 (EF)
  reviewed, 48:90
*Ceiling-Floor Partition Separation
  Studies* (Jones): source for, 29:92
Ceilings:
  adjustable, insulated, 2:31, 32 (EEH)
  air infiltration through, preventing,
    77:66-67
  air/vapor barriers for, 24:82, 31:8-10
  arches in, framing, 71:14
  Arts-and-Crafts style, 58:59 (CSH), 69:40,
    41 (EEH)
  barn-roof natural, 66:62 (REM)
  beaded, pictured, 51:37, 40, 51, 80, 81
    (CSH), 59:60
  beamed, 5:34-35
    Arts-and-Crafts style, 24:30, 32 (CSH)
    composite, 2:27, 29

concrete, 6:30, 31
Japanese-style, 54:37, 38
joint for, 5:12
bevel-siding, cedar, 58:51, 52-53
boards in, scribing, 77:60-62
bow, building, 5:22-24
brackets for, casting, 1:38-39 (FWS)
burlap for, 52:78, 79, 82
cast, 6:34-35
stone, 41:39-40
catalogue for, 51:90
cathedral, 43:78, 79
bow-roof, 33:47 (TFH)
circulators for, 33:12
double, 66:71, 72
exposed-rafter, 57:66
framing, 21:71 (FRC), 77:16-20
for hot climates, 70:16-18
with I-beam, 45:37
insulated truss for, 19:22
insulating, 33:12, 56:37, 38, 66:66 (EEH)
multifaceted paneled, 75:49 (REM)
thermal bridging in, 31:10
ventilating, 21:51-53 (DWS), 57:46
(REM), 61:78 (EF)
cedar, 41:47
chimney penetrations of, fire codes on,
69:78
clapboarded, 78:62, 65 (REM)
code height for, 21:27
coffered, 31:48 (FWS), 68:84, 85, 75:36, 37
(MFC), 80:75-76, 84:69-71
applied, 75:47, 48, 49 (REM)
framing for, 75:36-40 (MFC)
compound-curved Plexiglas, 52:72, 73
coved,
corner braces for, 8:51 (FWS)
drywall, 18:14 (addendum, 20:4)
flat-, 20:74, 75
plaster, 15:10
radiused, 8:51 (FWS)
and vaulted, 56:72 (CSH)
curved,
battened, 52:71, 72, 73
gussets for, 35:76
designing, 10:26, 28
domed,
elliptical, constructing, 71:14
plotting, 34:59 (FRC)
dropping,
with drywall, 39:40
over garage, 64:85 (REM)
drops for, turning, 56:77
fir, tongue-and-grooved, 38:82-83 (CSH)
flat, superinsulated, 66:66 (EEH)
floating, above trusses, 71:74, 75 (MFC)
and floor junctions, booklet on, 29:92
furring out, for drywall, 81:38-39
Greek Revival, 1:50, 51
gridded, 15:30, 31
as heating plenum, 22:28, 29

heights for,
minimum, 60:43 (SH)
varying, 52:65, 66, 66:37, 38 (SH)
illuminated dropped, 49:61 (SH)
insulating, 28:12, 61:76-77 (EF)
board for, 48:58, 59
with pulled batts, 79:20
Japanese-style,
boarded, 43:31 (CSH)
and insulation, 43:29-31 (CSH)
joists for,
in hip roof, 69:44-45 (MFC)
sandblasted, 22:43
lapped redwood, 9:64, 65
leveling, with transit, 68:22
as light fixtures, 80:76
lighting, 62:48 (SH)
lighting grill in, 3:21
mahogany,
pegged, 24:76, 77
plywood, 18:30
metal-framed, 32:71 (FRC)
mixed-wood, color evening for, 58:16-18
mudejar, reconstructing, 26:43-45
painted,
depth-foiling, 59:55 (CSH)
Scandinavian-style, 77:91
with painted skylight, 60:82
paneled,
building, 56:74-77
fiberboard, 18:28
random-fitted, 17:68-69 (BK)
reversed, 55:85
sliding, 17:42, 43 (SH)
stress-skin, 24:58
of Tectum, 55:73
plaster,
finishing, 34:61 (FRC)
repair of, 4:9
rosette, 1:36 (FWS)
trimmed hole in, 18:14
plywood, 55:73
porch, beadboard for, 66:49
pyramidal, 80:54-55
radiant heat for, 10:52 (SH), 76:8
raising, 62:46 (SH), 77:77-78 (REM)
redwood,
exposed, 45:38, 42, 43, 50
split, 45:50 (CSH)
roof as, 3:58, 59 (EEH), 20:30, 31, 32, 55:60
sagging,
correcting, 62:85-86 (MFC)
drywall nailing channel for, 18:42
scale of, 52:20 (CSH)
shiplap, cedar, 6:18, 19 (CSH)
skip sheathing, exposed, 73:64, 65
sliding-panel system for, 29:60-61 (CSH)
slotted metal, 52:71, 72, 73
soundproof, 28:10, 31:48, 35:63 (FWS)
stovepipes for, 46:14
of strand board and T-111, 39:71
strapping for, 29:33, 46:71

texturing, 67:67-68
tile,
adhesives for, 58:75
replacing, 69:30
timber-frame, 65:48-51 (TFH)
simulated, 69:62 (REM)
tongue-and-groove, 27:30, 31, 40:77
(EEH), 53:49 (SH), 56:71 (CSH), 59:37
(SH), 59:54, 56 (CSH), 61:52, 53 (SH)
transitions with, 80:52
truncated-cone, 56:87
of 2x4s, rounded, 68:38
vaulted, 80:54, 58
with applied coffers, 75:40-42 (MFC)
barrel-, 56:86-87
vaulted kitchen, 48:53
ventilating, 28:12, 61:76-77 (EF)
V-grooved, 66:86, 87, 67:36
wood, diagonal, 36:72
See also Vaults.
Cellars: See Basements.
Cellon-processed wood: described, 15:21
Celotex Corp.:
address for, 48:58, 54:62, 56:79
insulation board of, 18:47
Thermax sheathing, 29:69, 31:70
Celtite, Inc.: address for, 41:57 (CBS)
Cement:
asphalt, discussed, 65:41, 44
association for, 71:16
casting with, 5:10
Finnish, 21:65 (CBS)
house of, frame for, 66:53, 55
hydraulic, using, 83:14-16
Keenes, and drywall, 50:4
refractory, source for, 69:76, 71:52
and sawdust, flooring from, 32:66
siding of, reviewed, 77:96
spalling with, 32:4
stains from, removing, 49:26
waterproof, as additive, 37:46 (DWS)
for wood models, source for, 22:51
(FRC)
See also Backer boards. Concrete. Soil
cement.
Cement Mason's Guide (PCA):
cited, 55:68
source for, 44:14
Cement mixers:
travails with, 25:90
wheeled carrier for, 48:24
Cemesto panels: described, 39:72, 74
Cem-Fil Corp.:
alkali-resistant glass fibers, 23:12
type-K fiber, 27:12
Center for Accessible Housing: address
for, 79:112
Center for Building Technology:
Building Technology Publications 1982,
23:48
information from, 23:48

Center for Environmental Design Research: address for, 65:54

Center for Maximum Potential Building Systems:
address for, 65:54, 83:88
cob (mud/straw) house after, 83:88-89
sawdust bricks of, 15:10
work of, 23:49-50, 28:81

Center for Renewable Resources:
booklet by, 4:62

Center for Resourceful Building Technology:
address for, 69:100, 71:112, 81:106, 85:124
Guide to Resource Efficient Building Elements, cited, 81:106, 85:124

Center for Understanding the Built Environment: curricula from, 66:14

Centrum Vinduer: visited, 31:76, 77

Ceramic Houses (Khalili): reviewed, 40:90

Ceramic Tile Institute:
address for, 65:54
Prevention of Cracked Ceramic Tile Thinset over Concrete Slabs, 23:50
publications from, 23:50

Ceramic Tile Manual, The: source for, 17:74 (BK)

Ceramic tiles: *See* Tile.

Ceramicboard: source for, 39:90

Ceramics:
custom-made, 41:70-75 (FWS)
See also Light fixtures. Sinks.

Cerritor: address for, 52:104

CertainTeed Corp.:
address for, 66:66 (EEH), 80:49, 83:45
Form-A-Drain pipe, reviewed, 84:98
Insul-Safe II, 37:26 (BK)

Certifoam: source for, 18:33 (CBS)

CES, Inc.: address for, 67:51

Chainsaw Lumbermaking (Malloff): source for, 42:41 (TFH)

Chainsaw Savvy (Soderstrom): cited, 78:43

Chainsaws:
accessories for, 7:31
books on, 7:31, 78:43
care of, 61:85, 78:42-43
choosing, 78:42-43
in circular-saw format, 60:84, 85 (MFC)
electric, for log joinery, 34:48, 49
for log building, 2:38, 13:56, 59
lumber dressing with, 1:54
miter guide for, 31:76
parts for, 7:29, 30, 61:84-85
plunge-cutting, German, 35:57 (TB)
rafter cuts with, 28:37 (FRC)
safety features of, 61:82
sizes of, 61:82-84
supply sources for, 7:31, 61:84
using, 61:82-83, 118, 78:38-43, 79:6-8
worm-drive, accuracy of, 75:83
See also Sawmills: chainsaw.

Chainsaws (Oulette): cited, 78:43

Chair rail: *See* Molding.

Chairs:
Australian deck, retractable-armrest, 53:64, 65
half-cylinder laminated, 14:68-70
hammer-handle, 21:41, 42
hexagonal, 12:31
lounge, sculpted, 12:43, 44, 45 (REM)
Mackintosh, 54:37, 39, 40
Maloof rocking, 68:37
Mies van der Rohe, 46:36
with storage, 12:41
two-board, 25:29
Wright-style, 20:77
See also Benches. Dining rooms: built-in seating for. Window seats.

Chalklines:
anchor-helper for, 44:24
automatic, reviewed, 43:94-96
colors for, 21:72 (FRC), 68:96
double, using, 3:6
erasing, 18:12
for framing layout, 21:72-74 (FRC)
in log building, 13:56-59
on masking tape, 85:30
for moist conditions, 21:72 (FRC)
one-man, tool for, 21:20
protecting, 55:110
refined, 39:14
for renovations, 12:50 (TB)
for shingles, 57:88 (EF), 60:8
for site layout, 26:16
string for, 25:64, 69 (TB)
uses of, 4:22, 25:69 (TB, TFH)
varnishing, 44:24
on wet concrete, 47:32

Challis Stairways, Inc.: address for, 63:90

Chamberlain, Samuel: *New England Doorways,* cited, 54:68 (REM)

Chamberlain, Samuel and Narcissa:
Southern Interiors of Charleston, South Carolina, 40:33 (FWS)

Chamberlin, John: shingling by, 27:80-81

Chambers, Robert W.: on log house, 34:46-50

Chambers, S. Allen, Jr.:
reviews McLaughlin, 53:110-12
reviews Schweitzer and Davis, 77:120

Chamfers: on beams, 28:60-61 (TFH)

Champion International: address for, 69:96

Chandeliers: *See* Light fixtures.

Channel markers:
homemade, 21:77 (FRC)
source for, 21:20

Chapels:
Adirondack stone, 40:42
Sea Ranch, building, 64:50-53

Chappell, Steve: mentioned, 29:86

Charger Corp.: address for, 55:87

Charles Friedheim Co.: dry-stack block of, 16:57 (CBS)

Charles G. G. Schmidt & Co.: address for, 61:68

Charles Hubbard Associates, Inc.: Sparfil concrete blocks, 23:84

Charles Roccaforte Associates: address for, 53:89

Charleston (SC):
hurricane damage to, 57:104-106
porches of, 2:14-17

Charrette:
address for, 56:94
architect supplies, 41:35

Chase Panels: stress-skin panels, 24:59

Chase, Sara:
on rehabilitation books, 5:60
reviews restoration book, 24:86

Chassis punch: source for, 54:48

Chattem Consumer Products: address for, 46:90

Chauvin, Tim: on barn raising, 34:98

Chemical anchors: described, 41:54-55 (CBS)

Chemical sensitivity:
design around, 46:70-73
sources of, book on, 46:104
See also Healthy houses.

Chemonite: defined, 15:27

ChemRex, Inc.: address for, 62:43, 66:38, 77:67 (SH)

Chem-Tech, Inc.: address for, 70:49

Chem-Trete masonry sealer: source for, 20:12

Chemtron Metaseal: qualities of, 9:56

Cheney, Tod: on radially sawn clapboards, 31:35-37

Cheney Co.: address for, 53:68

Chernega, John and Joan: bedroom of, 46:38-31 (REM)

Chesavage, Jay: on fixed-glass windows, 51:76-78 (FC)

Chestnut (*Castanea dentata*):
ammonia darkening of, 36:26 (CSH)
association for, 84:108
virus for, protective, 84:108

Chestnut, Jim:
on crown molding, 68:81
reviews compound-miter saws, 83:64-69
reviews nailer, 68:92-94
workshop trailer by, 70:132

Chests: *See* Bureaus.

Chicago:
historic preservation in, 3:10
home finance hotline in, 3:63
restoration book for, 4:62

Chicago Faucet: address for, 76:58

Chicago Historical and Architectural Landmarks: booklet by, 4:62

Chicken houses: Texan, 55:124

Chida, Ted: roof tiling by, 45:74-75 (CSH)

Childers Products Co.: address for, 77:8-10

Children:
architecture classes for, 66:14-16, 68:8
architecture source book for, 68:8
clubhouse for, 84:136
house designed around, 45:49-53 (CSH)
renovation classes for, 29:88-89
rooms for, design of, 38:51, 53

Childress, William: reviews pattern roller, 71:94

Chilson, Chip: fireplaces by, 35:32

Chimneys:
and air-vapor barriers, 9:59, 29:72
block, with liners, 5:6
bookcase recesses in, 38:28 (EEH)
building, 14:38
"buttressed," 82:83, 84
camera scanners for, 70:78
canted, 13:39
caps for, 2:23, 4:41, 21:50, 76:18 (CBS, CSH)
    copper, 4:65
    curved, 5:22, 24, 28, 29
    English-style, 38:72-73 (TFH)
    poured-concrete, 46:26-28
    sculpted metal, 9:75
cast one-piece, 70:79
central massive, 38:28, 32-33, 34 (EEH)
cleanout doors for, 4:38 (CBS)
cobblestone, 42:26-27 (CSH)
codes on, 21:46-47 (CBS), 69:76-78, 75:44
cover for, copper, 27:75, 76
crickets for, 9:48, 49, 21:48 (CBS, EF), 47:61-63 (EF)
    glazed, 73:72, 74
    nails in, 49:4
dampers for, 46:14, 51:6
    automatic balancing, 4:50, 51
    fire-resistant heat-sensitive flaps for, 23:44 (EEH)
    low-leakage, 4:50, 51
    roof-top, 57:4
decorative-pot, source for, 74:49 (REM)
draft difficulties with, 14:65
ductwork in, 48:36
in earthquakes, 64:61 (MFC)
embellished, 32:76-77
enlarging above roof, 21:47 (CBS)
European-profile, 59:36, 41 (SH)
exterior,
    clapboarded, 45:47 (TFH)
    insulating, 54:87 (TFH)
    stuccoed, 38:66, 67, 68
fiber for, fireproof, 31:34 (DWS)
fiberglass gasket for, 51:44
flashing for, 4:64, 9:48, 49, 11:4, 21:46, 48-50 (CBS, EF), 65:60 (EF)
    retrofitted, 50:16-18
    seacoast, 74:56
    through-pan, 12:4, 14:6, 21:48-49 (CBS)
    and wood shrinkage, 81:55

Key to books:

(BK)   Building Baths and Kitchens
(CBS)   Building with Concrete, Brick and Stone
(CSH)   Craftsman-Style Houses
(DWS)   Building Doors, Windows and Skylights
(EEH)   Energy-Efficient Houses
(EF)   Exterior Finishing
(FC)   Finish Carpentry
(FRC)   Frame Carpentry
(FWS)   Building Floors, Walls and Stairs
(MFC)   More Frame Carpentry
(REM)   Remodeling
(SH)   Small Houses
(TB)   Tools for Building
(TFH)   Timber-Frame Houses

flue liners for, 75:44-45
    assembly clamp for, 74:24-26
    ceramic, 21:46 (CBS)
    installing, 4:39-40 (CBS), 83:16-18
    large, source for, 85:8
    in seismic areas, reinforcing, 85:8
    webbed, 13:65 (SH)
flues in, 21:47 (CBS), 22:6
    sizing, 10:4
flue-tile enclosed metal, 55:60-61
foundations for, 6:42 (TFH)
gas lines in, 48:36
glass let into, 33:30
hearth of, replacing, 4:40 (CBS)
history of, 13:23 (TFH)
hot-water coils in, 38:34
leaks in, 27:12
limestone, 36:72, 74
liners for,
    Heatilator, 36:74
    removing, 70:76, 77
    square vs. round, 4:38 (CBS)
for log buildings, flashing, 17:8
masonry, sealing, 76:18 (CSH)
metal,
    cantilevered support for, 73:82, 87
    chases for, 37:38
    clearances for, 37:4
    coal-acid resistant, 12:8
    disadvantages of, 5:6
    downdrafts with, 49:18
    flashing for, 56:80
    flues for, welded, 41:29
    galvanized, 83:85
    insulation for, 56:37
    standards for, 46:14
    suspended, 18:70, 71
    ties for, 21:47 (CBS)
mortar for, 4:39 (CBS)
mosaic cobblestone, 41:36, 37, 39
openings in, filling, 70:78-79
outside air for, book on, 49:18

outside, difficulties with, 13:65, 49:18 (SH)
pipe as, with windows behind, 80:54
placement of, 44:41 (SH)
as plenum, 24:76
rain hoods for, 59:71, 73 (SH)
refractory cement for, 75:45
reinforcing, 4:38, 39 (CBS)
relining, 4:38-41 (CBS)
    continuous, 9:16, 70:76-79
repairing, 50:65-66
    floor protection for, 4:38 (CBS)
restoration of, 29:64, 65
roof platform for, 21:47-48 (CBS)
and roof sheathing, 21:46, 47 (CBS)
safety information on, 46:14
sculpted, 22:72
sealants for, 27:12
as service conduits, 4:39, 76 (CBS)
settling of, dealing with, 16:8-10
skylights surrounding, 48:36
spiraled, 74:49 (REM), 75:43-45
with stairs attached, 38:33
stone, 45:76, 78 (EEH)
    with block core, 6:44-47 (TFH)
    building, 30:86
    cylinder, 8:23-24, 25 (CBS)
    single-form, 14:65
stuccoed, 64:39, 40 (CSH)
supply sources for, 70:77, 78, 79
tops of,
    enlarging, 35:71 (TB)
    remaking, 27:83
Tudor-style, 52:48 (TFH)
over urethane core, 24:76
vent-incorporating, 59:63 (EEH)
wet, diagnosing, 76:18-20 (CSH)
See also Fireplaces. Wood stoves.

China:
architecture of, book on, 45:116
Feng-shui in, 26:83
masonry in, 26:83
solar technology in, 26:82-83

Ching, Francis D. K.:
Architecture, reviewed, 45:116-20
Building Construction Illustrated, reviewed, 1:64, 3:4, 45:116, 78:110
Interior Design Illustrated, reviewed, 51:104

Chisels:
bricklaying, 43:53 (CBS)
carrier for, nail-pouch, 42:22 (CSH)
corner, 4:22 (TFH)
    retractable, 79:44
for framing, 4:22, 12:23 (CSH, TFH)
hand-forged, 49:95
honing, glass bed for, 53:26-28
millwright's, described, 4:22 (TFH)
for renovations, 12:51 (TB)
sharpening, 12:23, 18:56-61 (TB)
truing, 4:24 (TFH)
See also Slicks.

Chloraloy 240 vinyl:
source for, 32:47, 36:69 (BK)
uses of, 20:12
Chlordane:
danger from, 1:12
nature of, 5:12
against termites, 22:12
using, 6:52
Chlorinated hydrocarbons:
against termites, 6:52
substitute for, 28:10
toxicity of, 28:10
See also Chlordane. Polyethylene.
Chlorofluorocarbons: avoiding, 73:67
Christoffersen, John: builds tower, 37:50 (DWS)
Christoph, Ann: on landscaping, 44:50-53 (SH)
Christopher Alexander (Grabow): reviewed, 33:88
Chromated copper arsenate: *See* Copper arsenate.
Chronomite Laboratories, Inc.: water heater, 12:18 (CSH)
Church, Frederic: house by, 78:79-81
Church, Gary: cabinets by, 45:51, 53 (CSH)
Church:
conversion, process of, 13:67-69
reconstruction of, 66:118-117
Cinder block: *See* Block.
Cinva-Ram: source for, 26:77 (SH)
Circles:
arcs of, with slat, 47:65, 66
drawing, 32:16
with framing square, 54:24
See also Curves.
Circular saws:
anti-splinter flange for, 58:8, 76:65 (MFC)
with bar and chain, 60:84, 85 (MFC)
base tape for, 57:28
bearings for, unsealing, 50:60
bevels with, 62:44
bracing with, let-in, 3:34, 22:36, 37 (FRC, TB)
bushings for, copper, 31:14
chainsaw blade for, 43:96
chainsaw/bandsaw blade for, 39:90
choosing, 3:33, 24:41 (TB, TB)
books on, 7:60
crosscut guide for, 48:42
cut-off fixture for, 8:12, 12:12
cuts with,
bevel, 3:35 (TB)
clean, 9:12
double, 19:14
framing side, 16:8
pocket, 3:34 (TB), 24:40 (TB)
square, 9:12, 16:12, 77:84
dado kit for, 60:84-85 (MFC)
door-trimming jig for, 10:14
with dust bag, 44:88
gauge block for, 48:41

guards of, and accidents, 34:53-54 (TB)
guides for, clamp, 76:63-65 (MFC)
horsepower of, 63:73
kickback with, preventing, 85:30-32
for left-handed, 65:8
lightweight, reviewed, 44:88
lube for, low-viscosity gear, 50:60
maintaining, 27:6, 63:76-77
notching with, 3:35 (TB), 85:55
plastic-laminate cutting with, 9:39 (BK)
plywood cutting with, 1:22, 23, 24:37-38 (TB)
professional-grade, reviewed, 63:72-77
protectors for, contact-paper, 27:16
protractor guide for, shop-built, 55:26
for rafter cutting, 60:84-85 (MFC)
ripping with, 3:35 (TB)
finger-fence for, 10:12
stair-gauge fixture for, 10:14
roofing with, sawblade set for, 12:12
safety with, 3:35, 4:4 (TB), 55:56
sawhorse bracket for, 71:26
shoe for,
laminate, 53:41-42 (FC)
reviewed, 67:90
shooting boards for, making, 76:64-65 (MFC)
sidewinder vs. worm-drive, 27:6
siding with, base-strip guide for, 67:28
with 60° capacity, 68:96
speed control on, 18:18
stack cutting with, 3:33 (TB)
tables for, 1:22-23, 60:84 (MFC, TB)
for timber framing, 4:23, 35:54, 55 (TB, TFH)
trim,
compared, by brand, 48:40-43
crosscut guide for, 48:42
/framing, reviewed, 79:102-104
gauge block for, 48:41
25-in. three-phase, 35:54, 55 (TB)
worm-drive,
discussed, 24:36-41 (TB)
end cuts with, 25:4
flush-cut, source for, 53:38 (FC)
framing with, 24:36 (TB)
handles for, 27:6
hangers for, 24:10, 55:92
light, 25:4
maintaining, 24:38-40 (TB), 27:6, 70:66-67
safety with, 24:38 (TB), 27:6
See also Arbortech Woodcarver. Cut-off saws. Miter saws, power. Sawblades.
Circulation space: minimizing, 52:14-16
Cisterns:
book on, 10:55 (BK)
constructing, 10:54-55 (BK), 50:55
Citation Homes: address for, 68:62
Cladium mariscus: See Sedge.
Clair International Development Corp. Ltd.: Wasco shingles, 28:66

Clairson, International, Inc.: address for, 53:44 (SH), 66:67 (EEH)
Clamps:
band, improvising, 74:72-73 (FC)
bar, site-built, 55:26
from bolts, 74:24, 26
cam-action, source for, 53:61
continuous-threaded coil rod for, 14:6
cutting-guide, for plywood, 76:63, 65 (MFC)
discussed, 74:70-73 (FC)
as drywall lift, 74:26
flue-pipe assembly, 74:24-26
as framing positioner, modifying, 76:28
handscrew, improvised, 74:72, 73 (FC)
as hold-downs, 65:30
irregular-angle, 74:73 (FC)
locking C-, holster for, 74:26
from masking tape, 85:30
pipe,
extenders for, reviewed, 85:106-108
extending, 19:14
for rope lift, modifying, 76:28
sources for, 74:73 (FC)
spring,
coil, 54:92
miter, 84:63
reviewed, 54:92
Clapboards: *See* Siding.
Clapp House: restoration of, 32:56-59
Claris Corp.: address for, 49:50
Clark, Brent: on timber-framing, 36:46-50 (TFH)
Clark, Martha Fuller: on dating buildings, 27:82
Clark, Nancy: on remodeling, 27:48-53
Clark, Roger, and Michael Pause:
Precedents in Architecture, reviewed, 45:120
Clark, Sam:
on business of building, 22:61-64
on design for handicapped, 53:71
Designing and Building Your Own House Your Own Way, cited, 1:23, 13:16 (TB), 83:77
on kitchens, 14:54-57 (BK), 35:43-45 (BK)
Motion-Minded Kitchen, The, reviewed, 19:26
on on-site shop, 1:22-23 (TB)
reviews accessible housing books, 63:106
reviews Beck, 58:106
reviews kitchen book, 41:94-96
reviews solar design book, 28:86
on ticksticking, 20:49 (FWS)
Clark, Timothy: on AOB house, 69:38-43 (EEH)
Clarke, Duane: mentioned, 32:53, 54 (TB)
Classic Engineering: address for, 79:42
Classical Language of Architecture, The (Summerson): reviewed, 45:120

Clay-Burn Sales Inc. USA: Ceramicboard, 39:90

Clayton, David:
house by, 6:67 (FRC)
redwood house by, 1:52-55

Cleary, Barbara: quoted, 6:14

Clerestories:
alcove, 18:28, 29
band of, 20:75, 76
circular, 25:58, 59, 60-61
for cooling, 40:74 (EEH)
doors for, sliding glass, 15:31
raised double-sided, 34:65-66 (BK)
in rustic shelter, 21:66, 67, 68
under shed roof, 39:49, 51
as solar chimney, 17:41 (SH)
south-facing, 8:37, 38, 41 (EEH)
timber-framed, 25:10
trim for, 20:75
vents for, automatic, 34:4

Cleveland Steel Specialty Co.: metal connectors, 43:49 (FRC)

Clevenger, Jerry: radial-arm-saw cabinet by, 69:71-72

Climate:
books on, 9:16, 60
design parameters for, 21:60-61
micro-, factors affecting, 9:14-16

Climatic Atlas of the U. S.: source for, 9:16

Climatic Design (Labs and Watson): source for, 37:90

Climatic Information for Building Design in Canada: source for, 9:16

Climatology of the U. S.: source for, 9:16

Clipson, Colin: addresses conference, 47:100

Cloroben Chemical Corp.: address for, 62:18 (CSH)

Clorox Co.: Olympic acrylic latex stain, 28:72

Closets:
blocking for, 82:51
broom, retractable, 44:52 (SH)
circular, 12:61 (DWS)
design for, 30:63
fixtures in, requirements for, 20:12
for handicapped, 53:68
behind headboard, freestanding, 83:84
mold in, dealing with, 74:98
with plywood carcases, 83:70-73
plywood sheathing for, as shelf-support backing, 81:28
"secure," building, 57:26-28
wardrobe for, making, 78:44-47

Clothing:
cold-weather, 50:61-63
See also Boots. Cold weather.

Clubhouses: children's shingled, 84:136

CMS Industries, Inc.: address for, 69:76, 75:45

Coal: chimney corrosion problems with, 12:8

Coaldrake, William:
on Japanese carpentry, 48:102-104
reviews Japanese show, 51:96

Coal-tar pitch:
incompatibility of, with asphalt, 9:4
test for, 9:4, 12:4
See also Bitumens.

Coat hooks: carved, 21:35

Coatings:
fiberglass-reinforced, 73:74
nontoxic,
discussed, 69:8
reviewed, 67:90-92
stirrer for, drill-powered, 67:26

Cob construction: *See* Earth construction.

Cobb (T. M.): address for, 71:71

Cobblestone cottage: building, 54:83-87 (TFH)

Cobos, Richard: on green-wood woes, 8:49

Cockroaches: chemical for, 6:53

Codes: *See* Building codes. *individual building category. individual code names.*

Coefficient of performance: explained, 14:16

COFI-ROOF panels: reviewed, 53:98

Cold Spring Granite Co.:
address for, 75:84
video from, 71:106

Cold weather:
Arctic, working in, 68:100
gloves for, 56:4
work precautions for, 50:60-63
working in, 51:41-42, 56:4

Cold Weather Concreting (ACI): cited, 55:68

Cole, John: as joint author. *See* Wing, Charles.

Cole, Katherine H., and H. Ward Jandl: *Houses by Mail,* source for, 28:45

Cole, Roy F.: on restoring a porch, 2:14-17

Collar ties: *See* Rafters.

Collyer, Grahame: on solar addition, 43:58-61 (CBS)

Colonial Brick Corp.: address for, 55:10

Colonial Saw Co., Inc.: address for, 46:41 (REM), 70:53 (FC)

Colonial Stair & Woodwork Co.: staircases, 36:60-61 (FWS)

Colonial style:
books on, 63:45
details of, adapting, 63:45-49
sources for, 63:45-46
See also Plans.

Colonnade:
defined, 29:48
interior dividing, 68:85

Color:
absorptance and, 2:6
adding, to stains, 83:86-87

books on, 74:45 (EF)
consulting firm in, 74:45 (EF)
discussed, 74:41-45 (EF)
for house parts, choosing, 74:42 (EF)
from nature, 52:85-87, 83:83-84, 86
schemes for, 74:44 (EF)
test method for, 74:42 (EF)
wheel of, 74:43 (EF)

Color Clad roofing: conical installation of, 30:40-41

Color Psychology and Color Therapy (Birren): cited, 74:45 (EF)

Color Putty Co.:
address for, 69:4
filler, mixing shades of, 20:14
source for, 30:57 (DWS)

Colorado:
Boulder,
PUD code, 10:42, 19:46-47, 26:36
rehab loans, 26:34
zoning in, 34:57 (FRC)
dry-stack block in, 16:57 (CBS)
modular house for, 9:63
solar tax credits in, 3:10

ColorCaulk, Inc.: address for, 85:16

Colorcore: used, 43:79

Colorless Coatings for Brick Masonry: source for, 23:49

Columbia Paint and Coatings: address for, 78:69

Columns:
bases of, 2:16, 17
beam-supporting, retrofitting, 81:70
bedding compound for, 61:70
books on, cited, 61:69, 64:54
built-up, 52:59, 60 (CSH)
center steel-support, 55:59
classical,
making, 64:54-57
mock, 75:59
concrete, 6:34, 35, 30:67 (CBS), 58:49-50
cast, 45:50 (CSH)
for foundations, 8:65 (EEH)
poured, 27:26-27, 29, 77:51, 52
concrete-block, tying to adobe, 82:65, 66
constructing, 6:23-24, 25
corbels for, 48:35
cow's-head bracketed, pictured, 53:64, 65
doors between, fitting method of, 30:69 (CBS)
exterior, ventilating, 68:14
fiberglass, 2:16
fluting, 9:22-23, 11:37 (DWS)
of 4x4s, sheathed, 71:62, 63 (REM)
in French-American tradition, 26:72, 73
gallery of, 69:88-89
galvanized-steel tubing, 52:73
glulam,
carved, 59:53-55, 56 (CSH)
tapered, 51:80-82 (MFC)
Greene-and-Greene strapped, 72:39

hollow, screening, 75:4
I-beam, 46:33
indented square, 37:26 (BK)
Ionic, 50:67
Lally,
  boxing, 78:30
  camouflaging, 72:26-28
  column reinforcement for, 9:22, 23
  defined, 19:55 (FRC)
load-bearing, post anchors for, 81:87
mahogany houseboat, 12:71
making, 61:69-71, 63:46, 47, 66:49
maple, turned, 33:75
metal, saddle for, 52:71
octagonal, 48:37-39, 68:85
plinths for, 2:16, 17
  aluminum, 68:14
porch, repairing, 75:74
replacing, 2:15-17
of 6x6s, doubled, 80:44, 45
with Sonotubes, 30:67 (CBS), 50:56, 57
  "Mermaidic," 45:86
for spiral stair, 70:87, 89
square,
  fieldstone, 45:57
  interior, 64:41 (CSH)
steel-pipe adjustable, 68:85
stone-simulating, 9:20, 22-24
support, retrofitting, 81:53
templates for, 6:23
ventilation for, 75:74
weatherproofing, 68:14
wood for, 6:23
wooden, commercial, 1:63
Comfortable House, The (Gowans):
  reviewed, 37:90
Command-Aire Corp.: heat pumps, 26:68
Common difference (rafters): defined,
  10:63 (FRC)
Common-Sense Stairbuilding and
  Handrailing (Hodgson): cited, 43:37
  (FWS)
Communities:
  house designs for, 73:82-87
  land trusts for, 17:20, 59:24
  Usonian, 66:26-28
Compact House Book, The (ed. Metz):
  reviewed, 20:80
Compactors: tethered self-running, 76:30
Comparative Climatic Data for the
  United States: source for, 21:60
Compasses:
  impromptu, 32:16
  large layout, making, 63:10
  for renovations, 12:51 (TB)
  scribing with, 77:58-60
  See also Trammels.
Complete Book of Kitchen Designs
  (Rand and Perchuck): cited, 77:45
Complete Foundation and Floor
  Framing Book, The (Ramsey):
  reviewed, 46:104

Complete Heat Exchanger Book, The:
  source for, 34:33 (DWS)
Complete Home Restoration Manual,
  The (Jackson and Day): reviewed,
  82:112
Complexity and Contradiction in
  Architecture (Venturi):
  cited, 45:116
  reviewed, 45:120
Composite materials:
  association for, 85:122
  wood-plastic, 85:122
Composition board:
  cart for, reviewed, 81:92
  discussed, 67:77
  and fungi damage, 72:64 (REM)
  high-density insulating, 68:86
  See also Fiberboard. Hardboard.
    Oriented strand board.
    Particleboard.
Compotite Corp.: Composeal 40, 32:47
  (BK)
CompServCo: address for, 49:50
Compu-Arch: address for, 49:50
Computer Shoppe: address for, 49:50
Computerizing Your Construction
  Business (Coulter): reviewed, 33:88
Computers:
  books on, 33:88, 36:94
  CADD programs for,
    AutoSketch, 81:114
    libraries for, window, 60:49 (FC)
    Macintosh, 49:46-50
    MiniCad, 49:48, 50
    timber-frame, reviewed, 60:92-94
  comments on, 36:4-6
  for contractors, 35:66 (TB)
  costs of, 35:67 (TB)
  costs-estimator program for, 67:104
  data storage for, 35:67 (TB)
  design system for, buying, 49:50
  design with, 25:83
    mentioned, 26:58 (TB)
    program evaluations of, 82:104
    programs for, 82:92
  Dreams program for, 49:50
  energy programs for, 34:86, 51:96, 56:36,
    64:106
    reviewed, 61:106, 71:46-49
  estimating program for, reviewed,
    62:112
  handicapped source-list program for,
    54:102
  hardware choices, 35:66 (TB)
  job-scheduling program for, 69:80
  libraries for, template, 49:49-50
  MacDraft program for, 49:48-49, 50
  MacDraw program for, 49:48-49, 50
  Macintosh, newsletter for, 68:108
  MacPaint program for, 49:46-48, 50
  models generated by, 59:14-18
  newsletter about, 83:122

possibilities in, 35:64-65 (TB)
Power-Draw program for, 49:48, 50
printers for, 35:67 (TB)
  architectural, 49:49
programs for,
  Compuserve, using, 46:59-60
  HOTCAN II, 34:68, 86 (SH)
publications on, 49:50
research with, 46:58-60
software for, 35:64-66, 67 (TB)
  book on, 75:110
  on remodeling, 83:122
solar-design program for, 79:120
Thunderscan program for, 49:49-50
uses of, 59:14
See also Automated home systems.
  Calculators.
Computers (Thomsett): reviewed, 36:94
Comstock, William T.: *Victorian Domestic*
  Architectural Plans and Details,
  cited, 66:47
  reviewed, 44:94
Concept Builders Supply:
  Sawklip, 24:10
Concepts in Wood: address for, 81:76
Concresive concrete adhesive: source
  for, 41:14
Concrete:
  adhesives for, 41:56 (CBS)
    source for, 66:55
  admixtures for, 13:31, 34 (CBS), 51:41
    antifreeze, 77:110
    bonding-agent, 85:82
    drying-retardant, 13:22 (TFH), 33:33
      (CBS), 58:49, 50, 66:45
    latex, 32:47, 51-52 (BK)
    plasticizer, 30:67 (CBS), 48:67, 58:59-61
      (CSH)
    water-reducing, 13:31, 16:37 (CBS),
      44:34 (CBS)
    water-reducing, high-range, 33:33
      (CBS)
  aggregate for, 13:28, 30-31, 33, 35, 15:8
    (CBS)
    exposed, 66:38, 39 (SH), 66:42, 43, 45
    exposed, house of, 58:49-53
    faulty, 21:10
    lightweight, 26:74 (SH)
    sewage, 22:18 (CSH)
  air-entrained, 2:23, 13:31, 33, 34 (CBS,
    CSH), 31:76-77
    agents for, 48:67, 58:61 (CSH)
  arch blocks of, casting, 69:82-83
  associations for, 23:50, 25:71, 30:52
    (CBS), 48:69, 50:49, 55:66, 68, 74:50,
    77:104
  auger-cast pile, 59:81
  backfilling to, 44:37 (CBS)
  beams of, cast, 6:34-35, 66:84-85
  blankets for, 55:67
  bonding, with epoxy, 70:46-47, 49

books on, 19:8, 44:12, 37 (CBS), 51:41, 55:66, 68, 78:53
 cited, 58:48, 68:14
 reviewed, 47:110
boots for, 13:31 (CBS)
bricks of, homemade, 64:22-24
bulkheads of, 33:32-35 (CBS)
calcium chloride for, 13:31 (CBS), 48:67
castable, 36:32 (CBS)
casting, 5:38, 39, 20:33-34
cellular, qualities of, 30:76
cement types for, 13:28-30, 34 (CBS)
/ceramic hybrid, 28:82
channels in, 10:48, 51 (SH)
 pipe, 27:16
characteristics of, 32:33 (FRC)
chipped, repairing, 70:48
chute for, making, 20:16
coatings for, 40:12
 below-ground, 2:35
cold joints in, epoxy binder for, 16:37 (CBS)
coloring, 7:6, 8:6-8, 11:47, 48, 49, 20:34, 21:72, 26:74, 76, 28:69, 66:59 (CBS, FRC, SH)
 for mottled look, 33:12
 pigment for, source for, 66:59 (SH)
 stains for, choosing, 40:10-12
 stains for, and incompatible finishes, 40:10-12
compactors for, tethered self-running, 76:30
compressive-strength tables for, 55:66, 67
from contaminated soil, 81:106
countertops, making, 77:42
cracked, replacing, 68:14-16
cracks in,
 initiators for, 48:68
 patches for, source for, 66:55
 preventing, 48:67
 repairing, 65:14, 68:14-16
 sealing, 8:27 (CBS)
in crawl space, through register opening, 71:24-26
curing, 11:48-49, 13:31, 33:33-34 (CBS), 48:67, 55:66-68, 60:55
 cold-weather, 13:31, 35 (CBS), 51:41-42
 colored, 55:67
 compounds for, 13:31 (CBS), 44:37 (CBS)
 compounds for, and finish bonding, 55:67
 wax compound for, 26:74 (SH)
curved, Masonite lap siding for, 30:37, 39
cutting, 83:16
delivery of, for tight space, 58:59-60 (CSH)
deterioration of, 4:9, 21:10
 arresting, 15:12-14

over dirt forms, 6:35, 68
dowel connectors in, epoxying, 41:14
drilling, 46:67, 51:28 (EF)
drills for, 41:52-53 (CBS)
elevation stakes for, copper pipe, 82:26-28
epoxy-coated rebar for, custom service of, 33:33 (CBS)
estimating, 79:67, 69
 inch-to-yard conversion for, 17:14
 metric vs. imperial, 60:100-102
expansion, using, 3:6
"farmer," 80:48, 49
fasteners for, 55:65
faults in, 13:30 (CBS)
finishes for, 4:27, 10:8
 liquid acrylic, 66:86
 problems with, 10:8
 wax, 66:86
finishing, sand-, 73:62
floating, 32:52 (BK), 83:49-51
 with power trowel, 83:52-53
fly ash in, 44:34 (CBS)
over foam-form, 69:64-66
for foundations, 48:67
funnel for, 64:32
grids in, angled, 12:28, 29
grout for, bonding, 11:47 (CBS)
hand-mixing, 13:35 (CBS)
 planning for, 55:57
headers of, casting, 18:46
hollow-core planks of, 1:43, 44, 45, 46 (EEH), 8:4, 14:38, 25:71
honeycombed, 33:4
 repair of, 37:74
house of, 50:53-57, 77:104
for humidity control, 7:35 (DWS)
information on, 23:49-50, 65:52-53
insulating, 20:10
as interior finish, 7:38, 39, 11:46 (CBS, DWS)
jitterbugging, 13:29, 31 (CBS)
joints in,
 control, 48:67-68
 control, caulk for, 48:68
 decorative expansion, 11:48, 49 (CBS)
kneeboards for, 83:49, 50
lightweight, 13:29-30, 20:10, 52 (CBS)
 insulated Danish, 31:76-77
 source for, 66:102
lintels of, site-cast, 74:50-51
"log" cabin of, 5:68
metal connectors for, 43:44-45 (FRC)
mix designs for, 13:30-31, 35 (CBS)
mixers for,
 machine, 13:35 (CBS)
 vintage heavy-duty, 27:6
 wheeled carrier for, 48:24
moldings with, fastening, 47:28
for monolithic pour, 68:57
nails for, 15:51 (TB), 32:55 (TB)
nature of, 13:28 (CBS)

new, over old, 4:9
ordering, 13:30, 31, 32, 33 (CBS), 44:34, 37 (CBS), 83:47
 for foundations, 4:37 (FRC)
paint for, epoxy, 70:49
painted, 11:47, 49 (CBS)
panels of, sawdust-cement, 48:48-53
parging for, source for, 60:55
patching of, Bondo, 20:51, 52 (FWS)
patterning, tools for, 7:6, 27:56, 58, 71:94
perm rating for, 19:67
piers, 19:69, 70 (EEH)
pipes in, plastic, 27:16
pitted, leveling, 11:10
plastering, 15:74 (FWS)
post bases for, galvanized, 39:53 (CSH)
post-tensioned, 2:33-34, 7:14 (EEH)
pouring, 33:33 (CBS)
 around ducts, 55:83
 and temperature calculations for, 78:52
 two-stage, 11:47, 48 (CBS)
powder-actuated fasteners for, 21:30-34 (TB)
pozzolan in, 13:29 (CBS)
precast cellular, installation of, 30:76
pressure of, calculating, 78:52
psi of, 34:4, 44:34, 37 (CBS)
pumice, 77:55-57
pumping, 4:31, 37, 30:37-38 (FRC)
recesses in, 4:27, 37:27 (BK)
refractory, 64:20
reinforcing for, 6:34, 29:30
 fibers for, 48:67
 mesh, 15:4, 48:90, 63:82 (EEH)
removing, 81:70
repairing, 34:64 (BK)
resurfacing, 15:14
 book on, 15:14
as roofs, 63:36, 37, 39-40
 cast, 6:35
R-value chart for, and density, 20:10
in salt water, protection for, 33:32 (CBS)
salt-residue in, moisture wicking by, 19:8
sand for, 13:28, 34-35 (CBS)
sanding, 52:40 (TFH)
screeding, 32:51 (BK), 83:46, 48-49
 body strategies for, 85:80
 to set tile, 11:48, 49 (CBS)
sculpture, exterior, 78:88
sealers for, 2:36, 6:34-35, 55, 11:10, 30:69, 33:32, 68:49 (CBS)
 cementitious membrane, 11:10
 cure-retardant, 51:42
 nontoxic, source for, 67:92
 source for, 66:59 (SH)
segregation problems with, avoiding, 69:61
self-leveling, 48:12

shingles of, 22:18 (CSH)
siding, 83:45
sills of, casting, 18:46
slag in, 13:29 (CBS)
small-job, 13:34-35 (CBS)
small-section system for, 65:36
solar absorption of, 9:14
spalling of, 32:4
  carbon-dioxide, 51:42
  repairing, 71:14-16
spandrels of, precast, 25:71
for stairs, 44:14-16, 49:28
on stone, 38:41
  contour gauge for, 31:14
"stone" blocks of, 47:94
"stone" from, cast, 59:48-49 (SH)
strength of, 13:30, 31, 35 (CBS)
  vs. stone masonry, 9:6
supply source for, 65:92
surface-evaporation table for, 55:68
and temperature, 83:51
testing,
  by cylinder, 33:33 (CBS), 55:66-67
  slump, 13:30 (CBS), 44:34-35, 37 (CBS)
in trenches, unstable, 75:58
types of, 55:66
vibrating, cautions with, 4:37, 13:30
  (CBS, FRC)
vibrator with, using, 74:51
walls,
  high curved, 30:66 (CBS)
  with insulation, integral, 58:50-51
  openings in, cutting, 41:10
  panels of, precast, 85:82-83
  tilt-slab, 4:27-28
water in, 13:30, 34 (CBS)
  cautions for, 30:67 (CBS)
  and strength, 77:6-8
  wicking of, 19:8
as waterproofing, for foundations, 69:16
waterproofing, 30:69 (CBS)
waterproofing, wet, 65:16
wet, chalk lines on, 47:32
whitewashing, 20:53 (FWS)
windows of, precast, 48:82
wiring in, 48:53
over wood framing, 11:47-49, 14:4-6
  (CBS)
and wood, gluing, 55:65
wood texturing for, 10:48, 51 (SH)
working, 13:31 (CBS)
See also Anchors. Block. Cement.
  Columns. Earth construction. Floors.
  Forms. Foundations. Gunite. Metal
  connectors. Mortar. Rebar. Roofing:
  concrete tile. Sealants. Showers. Soil
  cement. Staircases: concrete. Walks.
Concrete block: See Block.
Concrete Formwork (Koel): reviewed,
  63:106
Concrete Masonry and Brickwork: cited,
  58:48

Key to books:

(BK)   Building Baths and Kitchens
(CBS) Building with Concrete, Brick and Stone
(CSH) Craftsman-Style Houses
(DWS) Building Doors, Windows and Skylights
(EEH) Energy-Efficient Houses
(EF)   Exterior Finishing
(FC)   Finish Carpentry
(FRC) Frame Carpentry
(FWS) Building Floors, Walls and Stairs
(MFC) More Frame Carpentry
(REM) Remodeling
(SH)   Small Houses
(TB)   Tools for Building
(TFH) Timber-Frame Houses

*Concrete Masonry Handbook for
  Architects, Engineers, Builders:* cited,
  78:53
Concrete Masonry Paving Block: source
  for, 23:50
Concrete Restoration Services: address
  for, 48:68
Condensation:
  air-vapor barriers against, 46:16
  controlling,
    book on, 74:98
    through design, 63:82 (EEH)
  discussed, 39:10, 63:18
  and fungi, 72:66 (REM)
  and glazing, 55:81
  and insulation, 46:16, 56:41-42
  prevention of, 72:66 (REM)
  publication on, 22:4
  in wall, 22:4
*Condensation and Related Problems in
  the Home:* cited, 56:14-16
Condominiums: Manhattan-style, 62:58-61
Conduit bender: making, 21:16
Conerly, Tom: on moment framing, 74:58
  (MFC)
Cones: constructing, formula for, 4:6
Conley, Kate: reviews architecture books,
  2:62
Connecticut:
  pension-fund mortgages in, 4:14
  solar tax credits in, 3:12
Connecticut Stone Supplies: address for,
  77:44
Conproco Corp.:
  address for, 73:74
  source for, 12:37 (CBS)
Conquer-Dust Floor conditioner:
  recommended, 33:70 (CBS)
Conrad, Bernie: on porch disaster, 76:126
Conran's Habitat: address for, 66:67
  (EEH), 73:50

**Conservation and Renewable Energy
  Inquiry and Referral Service
  (CAREIRS):**
  address for, 65:52
  landscaping brochure from, 82:106
  reviewed, 33:90
  services of, 23:51
Conservation Energy Systems: heat-
  recovery ventilators, 34:34 (DWS)
Conservation in Buildings: source for,
  32:90
Conservation Materials Ltd.: Incralac,
  34:6
Conservation Services: address for, 70:49
Consoweld Corp.: address for, 9:41 (BK)
Constant, Caroline: *Palladio Guide, The,*
  reviewed, 32:86
Construction:
  with appropriate technology,
    associations for, 64:110-12
  and architect partnership, 24:4
  associations for, 44:46-49 (TB), 47:106,
    72:100, 77:104
  bibliography on, annotated, 46:104
  bids in, 22:61-62, 28:28-29
  billing procedures in, 22:61
  bookkeeping in, 25:12
  books on, 1:64-66, 36:94, 46:104, 53:47
    (SH), 55:58, 56:110, 71:112, 83:77
    in appropriate technology, 64:110-12
    exercise, 30:78
    metric, 35:71 (TB)
    out-of-print, 5:12
    reviewed, 35:68-71 (TB), 55:108-10,
      56:110, 64:112, 69:108-10, 74:98,
      78:110, 83:120
  budgeting for, 2:27-28
  Colonial, book on, 79:120
  competition in, 72:100
  costs of, 8:4, 83:110
    checklist for, 27:33
    owner equity and estimating, 4:42-43
    and profit, 27:35
    reducing, 2:26-28
  courses in, 13:14-16
  custom, cost of, 83:87
  energy-assessment laboratory for,
    71:104
  energy-efficient,
    information on, 66:4
    programs for, 64:104-106
    southern, information on, 66:22-24
    stratagems for, 66:4
  estimating for,
    book and disk on, 67:104
    books on, 27:35, 55:100
    chart for, 4:42-43
    computer program for, reviewed,
      62:112
    methods for, 27:32-35
    present-worth formula for, 74:4-6

films on, 1:66
flow chart for, 44:47-48 (TB)
glossary of, 3:33 (TB)
help with, association for, 56:104
history of, reviewed, 82:112
information on, 65:52-55
metric, guide for, 72:100
in multiple, 73:82-87
and OSHA, 34:52-53 (TB)
and owned land, 6:26
by owner, 4:10-13, 10:48-49, 52, 12:66
   (EEH, SH)
   aid firm for, 4:12
   costs of, 82:81
   guides for, 55:55-61
   perils of, 4:12, 14:36-40
   savings in, 4:10, 6:27, 26:77 (SH)
and permits, 6:26
recycling strategies for, 83:108-10
rules for, general, 4:6-7
scheduling for, 6:26, 28
   book on, 46:104
tax considerations for, 7:43
by women, books on, 13:16
See also Contracts. Financing.
   Instruction. Materials.
Construction Accessories Co.: address
for, 81:94
Construction adhesive: *See* Glue.
Construction and the Environment
   (Canada Mortgage and Housing Corp.):
   cited, 83:110
Construction Dictionary: reviewed,
   47:112
*Construction Estimating Reference
   Data:* mentioned, 27:35
Construction Geometry (Walmsley):
   reviewed, 30:78
Construction Index: reviewed, 46:104
Construction Industry Standards
   (OHSA): source for, 36:34, 37 (TB)
*Construction Manual for Concrete and
   Formwork:* source for, 29:30
Construction Master calculator:
   reviewed, 51:92
Construction Materials (Hornbostel):
   reviewed, 67:104
Construction Materials and Processes
   (Watson): reviewed, 3:61
Construction Sealants and Adhesives
   (Panek and Cook): cited, 65:45
Consumer Information Catalog:
   reviewed, 69:110
Consumer Information Center:
   Consumer's Resource Handbook, 23:49
Consumer Products Safety Commission:
   asbestos information from, 41:10
   800-number for, 41:10
   phone number, 24:83
Consumer's Resource Handbook:
   source for, 23:49
Contact cement: *See* Glue.

Contact Lumber Co.: address for, 48:91
Container Home Supply: address for,
   61:61 (SH)
ConTech PL 200 adhesive: source for,
   34:59 (FRC)
Conti, Vinnie: fireplace by, 40:31
Continental Chemical: 3C Brand 202
   construction adhesive, for floors, 18:7
Contracting: *See* Construction.
Contractor (Gerstel): cited, 47:71
Contractors: *See* Builders.
*Contractors Handbook on Indiana
   Limestone, The:* source for, 37:59
Contracts:
   for additions, 31:33 (DWS)
   AIA, 31:33 (DWS)
      A-111, 28:54, 57
      A-117, 23:6
      A-201, 22:63, 64, 23:6
   checklist for, 28:56-57
   and cost plus, 22:62-63
   and cost plus estimate, 22:63-64, 23:6-8,
      28:54-55
   and cost plus fixed fee, 28:54
   and cost plus with guaranteed
      minimum, 28:55-57
   handshake, 45:24
   importance of, 28:54, 55
   time-and-materials, disadvantages of,
      38:77 (TFH)
Controlled Energy Corp.: address for,
   80:70
Convection currents:
   heating with, 10:45
   tracing of, 1:5
   trouble spots for, 12:66-67 (EEH)
Conway, Patricia: *Art for Everyday,*
   reviewed, 65:108
Cook, Jeffrey:
   speaks at conference, 18:16
   on Zomehouse, 26:52-57
Cooke, Gary: on shingle thatch, 23:52-56
Cooks Supply of New York: refrigerators,
   custom, 38:59
Cooledge, Harold N., Jr.: mentioned,
   11:70
Cooley, Richard:
   on brotherly love, 54:118
   on long division, 74:114
Cooling:
   AirCore floors for, 30:51 (CBS)
   belvedere for, 3:56-59, 8:63-65 (EEH)
   center researching, 30:80
   by convection, 80:70
      with fans, 59:66, 67 (EEH)
   Cracker-style energy-efficient, plans for,
      68:102
   cupola for, 60:59 (EEH)
   Danish system for, 31:77
   design aid for, reviewed, 79:120

design for, 2:30-33, 15:14 (EEH), 49:72-75
   (EEH), 51:8, 52:68-73
   in tropics, 85:74-75
dogtrot adaptation for, 37:72-73
electric units for,
   chases for, in cathedral ceiling, 66:72
   computer-run, 73:70
   condensation with, 12:10, 15:14
   downsizing, 80:58
   ductless, source for, 75:94
   and heat-pump water-heater, 2:64
   high-velocity systems for, 61:12
   information on, 46:48
   in restorations, 29:65
   SEER rating for, 61:12
and habitation stratum, 54:61
from heat pumps, 26:66, 78:70
with house mass, 48:33
hydronic floor, discouraged, 69:18
leaky pipes in, repairs for, 67:98
masonry wind catcher (*malqaf*) for,
   47:110
with metal floor-plenums, 60:59 (EEH)
passive system for, 8:63-65 (EEH)
publications on, 30:80
radiant barriers for, 56:39
with rammed earth, 42:10
rock beds for, 16:29
roofs for, 36:71
site selection for, 3:19
for subtropics, passive, 15:14
swamp coolers for, 17:45 (SH)
systems for,
   below-grade, 58:80-83 (EEH)
   hybrid, 85:86-87
   integrated, 33:84, 63:85 (EEH)
   passive, 11:31, 32-33 (EEH), 26:56, 41:4,
      40:73-77 (EEH)
   sizing, 48:4
towers for,
   evaporative-cooling, 47:110, 58:82
      (EEH), 71:106
   windowed, 55:42, 44 (SH)
with trellises, 60:56, 58 (EEH)
tunnel for, 15:75 (CSH)
underground tubes for, 11:9, 69:39-41
   (EEH)
venetian blinds for, 59:65, 66 (EEH)
with wall air space, 54:62
and wall mass, 63:18-20
water-to-air coil for, 69:18
whole-house ventilation for, 46:64, 65
   (TFH)
See also Insulation.
Coombs, Peter: penthouse design by,
   31:63-65
Cooper Group, The: Weiss sheet-metal
   shears, 32:68 (FRC)
Cooper Tools:
   ultrasonic tape, reviewed, 78:54-55
   reviewed, 64:96
Coopering: *See* Columns.

COP (coefficient of performance):
explained, 26:66
Cope, William S.: on design, 1:24-27, 3:44-45
Coped joints: *See* Joinery. Molding.
Copeland, Gerry:
on barrel vaults, 51:79-82 (MFC)
on budget bungalow, 59:52-56 (CSH)
on energy-efficient house, 42:60-63
Copper:
and acid rain, 27:83
association for, 63:4
bathroom in, 26:80 (BK)
brass no-solder fittings for, 65:96
and cedar, 77:51
chimney tops of, 20:29, 34
coating for, 34:6
corrosion of, 62:64-65, 66
and cedar, 10:4, 12:57
for countertops, disadvantages of, 16:4
for fire-sprinkler systems, 47:6
flue sleeves of, 20:34
hardware from, making, 63:66-68
kitchen uses of, 14:4
and lead, door panels of, 23:31
lead-coated, about, 61:49
nobility of, 21:4
for plumbing, 29:52 (BK)
as roofing, 3:16, 17, 24:42 (DWS)
for sinks, 21:42
tubing,
types of, 3:48, 50, 10:40 (BK)
working with, 10:40-41 (BK)
See also Wood preservatives.
Copper Development Association:
address for, 63:4
Copper Green: mentioned, 29:37 (FRC)
Copperfield, David: *Electrical Independence Booklets,* 24:80
Cor-A-Vent:
address for, 61:80 (EF)
corrugated vent strips, 26:82
source for, 33:12
Corbels:
carved, 5:8, 25:29, 34:76
source for, 66:104-106
Greene-and-Greene, 72:39, 41
interior plastered, 38:70
shaped, 22:56, 57, 58 (CSH)
strapped, 83:88
triangular
exterior, 25:30
interior, 9:67, 25:29
Corbett-Winder, Kate: *Barn Book, The,* reviewed, 67:104
Corbo, Robert: on remodeling, 69:24
Cordwood Masonry Houses (Roy): cited, 2:68
Core Builders: mentioned, 20:48
Corian:
address for, 84:45
See also Countertops: resin board.

Cork *(Quercus suber):* for floors, 52:106-108
Corley Plan Service and Plansamerica:
plans from, 53:85, 87, 89
Corlis, Michael: builds living area, 75:80-85
Cornell Corp.: address for, 61:78 (EF)
Corner boards: Greek Revival, 1:49
Cornerite: source for, 23:12
Cornerstones: women's building course of, 13:16-18
Cornices:
for barn renovation, 66:61 (REM)
of built-up stock, 32:43
cantilevered, decorated, 24:14
captioned, 35:70 (TB)
concrete textile-block, 14:72
coved, framing, 74:48, 49 (REM)
crown and dentil, 63:46, 48, 49
defined, 20:60 (FWS)
over entrances, 3:14, 17 (DWS)
Federal, 1:59
formal, for dormers, 41:64-65 (FRC)
Greek Revival, 1:49, 29:67
interior, 20:75, 78
modillions with, 24:14
ornaments for, custom-cast, 53:57
returns of, 24:14
building, 15:39, 40-41 (EF), 77:46-49 (EF)
rebuilding, 14:25-26
sheet-metal, information on, 17:12
types of, 15:38, 39, 20:60 (EF, FWS)
Victorian ornate, rebuilding of, 53:54-57
water table for, 15:41 (EF)
with windows, interior, 38:88-89
Corning Glass Works: etching information from, 39:8
Corrie, James: solarium by, 85:148
Corrin, Rich:
brick wall by, 15:84
garden sculpture by, 35:104
Cor-Ten weathering steel:
defined, 19:6
non-availability of, 27:4-6
as roofing, 24:42, 43
Corylus cornuta: See Hazel.
Cotswolds, The (Whiteman): reviewed, 49:114
Cottages: *See* Cabins. Small houses.
Cotterman Co.: ladders of, 19:47-48
Cottonwood *(Populus* spp.*):* hardness group of, 40:69 (FRC)
Couches: *See* Sofas.
Coulter, Carelton III: *Computerizing Your Construction Business,* 33:88
Council of American Building Officials:
address for, 65:54
on skylight glass, 49:14
Council of Forest Industries of British Columbia: address for, 53:98

Countertops:
attaching, 79:79
backsplashes for, 77:45
butcher-block, source for, 77:44
cantilevered, for handicapped, 76:58-59
cart for, reviewed, 81:92
certification program for, NAHB, 76:108
concrete, making, 77:42
contact-cement bucket for, 55:28
copper, 14:4
cutting, support for, 82:28
drop-leaf, 44:52, 53 (SH)
edging, clamps for, 74:72, 73 (FC)
enameled, 44:53 (SH)
with epoxy overlay, 70:48
finish for, 2:6, 9
Fireslate for, cement-based, 71:45 (REM)
granite, 51:62, 52:72, 67:72, 74, 75-76 (REM)
sheets for, 44:88
tiles for, 75:83, 84
half-round, constructing, 58:37-38, 40 (REM)
for handicapped, 53:70, 71
hardwood edgings for, 78:66-67
ifilele, 45:51, 53 (CSH)
maple, 66:66, 67 (EEH)
marble, 82:70, 71
materials for, compared, 77:40-45
nosing for, 58:40-41 (REM)
nosing inlay for, 58:41 (REM)
into out-of-square space, 68:28-30
oversized, 78:64-65 (REM)
painted, under glass, 84:80-81
plastic laminate, 43:79, 77:40-42
applying, both-sides, 47:28
backsplashes in, 75:65
bending plywood for, 55:96
over curves, 62:61
designer nonglossy, 30:60 (BK)
edgings for, hardwood, 69:51, 54, 78:66-67
estimating for, 75:60
filing, 75:64, 65
filling, 78:67
forms of, 75:60
gluing, 30:61 (BK), 62:61, 75:64-65
gluing, spacers for, 29:16, 61:24
gluing, spray adhesive for, 75:62, 64
inlaid, 49:62 (SH)
moldings of, 77:42
qualities of, discussed, 77:40-42
samples of, express-mail, 69:102
sawblades for, 30:60 (BK), 72:47 (MFC)
seams in, 41:8, 75:61, 63-64
sink clips with, 75:65
striped, source for, 62:61
substrate for, 75:61, 63
substrate for, acclimation of, 75:62-63
substrate for, attaching, 78:28, 79:8

tools for, 75:60-61
ungluing, 75:65, 77:8
white, 34:63 (BK)
working with, 75:60-65
resin board, 77:42, 84:40-45
  color matching, 28:6
  colors of, 37:81
  cutting, 84:41, 42
  discussed, 77:41, 42
  gridded, 64:42 (CSH)
  installing, 27:44-47, 34:66, 84:44-45
    (BK)
  literature on, 27:47 (BK)
  mentioned, 37:81
  possibilities of, 84:90-91
  sources for, 34:64 (BK), 84:45
  templates for, 84:41
split reglued boards for, 61:73-74
stainless-steel, 45:51, 52 (CSH), 77:44, 45
stone, 77:44, 45
  making, 51:63
substrate for, attaching, 78:28, 79:8
synthetic, sawblades for, 72:47 (MFC)
tile, considered, 77:42-43
wood, 77:43-44
and wood shrinkage, 81:56, 59
See also Tile.
Country Designs: plans from, 53:85, 86, 87, 89
Country Floors: address for, 54:54
Countryside Chimney Sweep Supply:
  address for, 70:77
Courtaulds Coatings, Inc.: address for, 70:48
Courterco: address for, 69:53
Courtyards:
  Japanese, 45:70-71, 72 (CSH)
  Spanish Revival, 45:38-43
Coveralls: insulated, 50:62
Covert & Associates: house by, 80:78-81
Cox, William T., Jr.: reviews knife
  sharpener, 84:94-96
CPVC: *See* Polyvinyl chloride.
Cracker style: house in, 57:63-67
Craftsman Book Co.: address for, 57:78
  (CSH, MFC)
Craftsman Heritage Collection, The:
  address for, 54:100
Craftsman Homeowner Club newsletter:
  source for, 54:100
Craftsman style: *See* Arts-and-Crafts
  style.
Cranes:
  pivoting, for hot-tub cover, 69:64-65, 66
  shop-built, 55:59, 60
  waterlift, making, 62:30
CRATerre:
  address for, 28:81
  focus of, 30:74
  institute plans of, 30:76
Crawford, Bruce: bench by, 66:90
Crawford (J. A.) Co.: address for, 48:68

Key to books:

(BK)   Building Baths and Kitchens
(CBS) Building with Concrete, Brick and Stone
(CSH) Craftsman-Style Houses
(DWS) Building Doors, Windows and Skylights
(EEH) Energy-Efficient Houses
(EF)   Exterior Finishing
(FC)   Finish Carpentry
(FRC) Frame Carpentry
(FWS) Building Floors, Walls and Stairs
(MFC) More Frame Carpentry
(REM) Remodeling
(SH)   Small Houses
(TB)   Tools for Building
(TFH) Timber-Frame Houses

Crawford Products Co.: address for, 62:41
  (EF), 71:72
Crawl spaces:
  book on, 56:14-16
  condensation in, treating, 48:14, 64:22
  foundation with, 44:32-37 (CBS)
  inaccessible, wiring snare for, 44:26
  moisture control for, 56:14-16
  as plenum, 78:71
  pressurizing, 50:100
  vents for, 51:71
Creative Structures, Inc.: glazing by, 46:52 (EEH)
Creative Wood Design: bookcase by, 58:87
Credo Co.: hole saw, reviewed, 79:100
Creek beds: creating, 80:66
Creosote:
  cautions for, 62:18-20 (CSH)
  discussed, 63:63, 65 (MFC)
  levels of, 63:64 (MFC)
  masking, impossibility of, 62:20 (CSH)
Crestline: address for, 76:75 (FC)
Crick Tool Inc.: address for, 58:45
Crimpers: single-blade hand, source for, 67:43 (EF)
Criterium Engineers: address for, 77:108
Croghan Island Mill: address for, 73:75
Crosbie, Michael J.: on adding story, 74:46-49 (EF, REM)
Cross (A. T.) Co.: address for, 77:58
Crosscutter compound-miter saw:
  reviewed, 43:92
Crossfields Products Corp.: address for, 59:82
Crystal Cabinetworks, Inc.: address for, 66:66 (EEH)
Cuadra Directory of Online Databases:
  described, 46:60
Cubic Industries, Inc.: address for, 76:39

Cupolas:
  adding, 74:46, 47 (EF, REM)
  for barn renovation, 66:60, 61 (REM)
  frame, 50:78, 80, 81 (SH)
  glazed, framing, 83:55, 56
  rectangular skylighted, 45:44-47 (TFH)
  stuccoed brick, 50:74, 77
  for ventilation, 57:63, 65
Cuprinol Group: address for, 79:24
Curtain Wall Co.: address for, 76:96
Curtain-rod holders: blocking for, 82:51
Curtains: Mylar insulating, 58:83 (EEH)
Curves:
  adjustable template for, reviewed, 68:94
  shaper jigs for, 60:74-77
Curwick, Rick: stone masonry by, 80:55, 57
Custom Building Products: address for, 50:77, 62:60
Custom Woodworker's 1993 Buying Guide: source for, 81:76
Custom Woodworking Business: address for, 81:76
Customer Technology Applications Center: number for, 72:100
Cut-off saws:
  cutting wheels for, 62:84
  for masonry, 50:18
  reviewed, by brand, 62:80-84
  safety with, 50:18, 62:80
  uses of, 62:80
Cypress, bald *(Taxodium distichum)*:
  decay resistance of, 50:72 (FC)
  old, source for, 56:92
  for siding, 45:58
  for trim, 45:58, 59

D. & J. Wood Press: address for, 72:62
D. C. Precision Tools, Inc.: address for, 70:106
da Vignola, Giacomo Barozzi:
  Comparison of Orders, cited, 64:54
Dadd, Debra Lynn: *Nontoxic Home, The,* reviewed, 46:104
Daggett house: restoring, 49:38-43 (REM)
Dahlke, Tom: on spiral staircase, 18:50-52 (FWS)
Dakin, Robert:
  construction by, 29:73-77
  on foam, 46:96
Dallaire, Gene: reviews Shurcliff, 6:58
Daly's Wood Finishing Products:
  address for, 59:56 (CSH), 70:91 (errata, 72:6)
Dampers: *See* Chimneys.
Dampness in Buildings (Gratwick): cited, 47:20

Danair Inc.: framing nailers, reviewed, 56:54-55, 56, 57

Danex, Inc.: address for, 59:102

D'Angelo, Robert: on marbleizing, 60:80-81

Daniel house: restored, 33:24-30

Daniels, Farrington: *Direct Use of the Sun's Energy,* 26:56

Danish Building Export Council: address for, 31:77

Dankoff, Mark (Windy): catalog from, 24:80-82

Danville Plywood Corp.: address for, 55:96, 83:63

DAP, Inc.: address for, 65:42

Darkrooms:
designing, 10:50 (SH)
solar heat for, 10:49-51 (SH)

Darrah, Dennis:
on drywall detailing, 63:50-53
on purpleheart framing, 57:68-70 (TFH)

Darrow, Ken, and Mike Saxenian: *Appropriate Technology,* reviewed, 64:112

Darworth Co.: address for, 30:49, 53:79 (REM), 84:81

Dasco: levels, 37:80

DashWood Industries, Ltd.: address for, 76:75 (FC)

Data Pro: described, 46:60

Database of Databases: described, 46:60

Daughters of Painted Ladies (Larsen and Pomada): cited, 66:47, 74:45 (EF)

Dave Pate and Sons: replace foundation, 32:62-63

David Barrett and Associates: address for, 53:89

David White:
level AL8-22, 37:45 (TB)
level transit 8830, 37:45 (TB)
level transit LT8-300, 37:45 (TB)

Davidson, Dale: mentioned, 32:58

Davidson, Jane: as joint author. *See* Vila, Bob.

Davidson, Joel: *New Solar Electric Home, The,* cited, 62:71

Davidson, Joel, and Richard Komp: *Solar Electric Home, The,* reviewed, 24:80

Davidson Ladders, Inc.: address for, 84:55

Davidson, Leslie Barry: Acadian house by, 73:36, 41

Davis, A. J.: on hillside house, 38:24-29 (EEH)

Davis, D. R.: heat-loss studies of, 2:31 (EEH)

Davis, Jack: reviews Allen, 36:94

Davis, Kelly: on small house, 66:36-39 (SH)

Davis, Wink: on Montana solar house, 8:37-41 (EEH)

Davis Kitchens: address for, 52:106

Davits: *See* Cranes.

Day, Ron: mentioned, 29:33

Dayton Speed Air: compressors, 15:52 (TB)

Dayton Superior Corp.: address for, 78:50

De Boer, Bill: mentioned, 32:73, 75

De Cristoforo, David: on miter saws, 57:58-62

De Cristoforo, R. J.: reviews SmartLevel, 53:94

De Marre: as joint author. *See* Lehr.

Deadbolts: *See* Locksets.

Deadman: constructing, 33:34-35 (CBS)

Dean, William: *Terms of the Trade,* reviewed, 47:112

DeAngelo, Raymond: on architects and computers, 25:83

DeBlois, Christopher: on sizing beams, 71:56-57 (MFC)

Debris chute: from concrete-forming tube, 58:24

Dec International, Inc.: address for, 46:72

Deca Dome:
building, 46:42-43
structural attributes of, 49:6

DeCew, Tom: gates by, 52:91

Dechar, Peter: cabinets and countertops by, 2:54 (BK)

Decking: *See* Decks. Floors: plank-and-beam. Floors: sub.

Dec-Klips:
metal connectors, 43:49 (FRC)
source for, 35:90

Decks:
all-surrounding, 80:65, 67
anchors for, post cam-lock, 69:47 (EF)
balusters for,
router-edged, 39:54 (CSH)
Victorian, 48:70, 73 (SH)
benches for, 29:45, 46 (FRC)
board spacer for, reviewed, 65:92
boards for, spacing, 82:26
bracing, 84:28-30
brighteners for, 50:18-20
built-in, 38:43, 45
butt ends in, caulking, 82:26
cantilevered, 21:8-10, 32:40, 41-42, 73:71, 82:80, 81
with steel, 79:81, 82, 83, 84
stuccoed, 51:60
for tower, 67:62
cap, 9:48, 49 (EF)
columns for,
concrete, 30:35
heavy-duty, 68:72-73 (EF)
corbel support for, 29:29, 31
costs of, 29:42 (FRC)
no-object, wood for, 61:12-14
designing, 29:42 (FRC)
fascia for, laminated, 39:53 (CSH)
fastening for, invisible, 56:28

finish for, 27:55, 29:43, 39:54-55 (CSH, FRC), 50:18-20
fiberglass coating, 47:87
firepit for, 39:55 (CSH)
flashing, 9:48, 21:8-10 (EF)
for mounting blocks, 45:87
footings for, calculating, 81:6
foundations for, 6:22-23, 69:46-47 (EF), 79:64-69
grates for, over basement windows, 69:48 (EF)
Greene-and-Greene, restoring, 72:39-41
Greene-and-Greene style, 39:52-55 (CSH)
ground-level subtle, 52:86
for handicapped, at-grade, 73:60
I-beams with, 30:36
installation for, 29:44-46 (FRC)
joinery in, gutter-spike reinforcements for, 75:26
joists for,
double, 5:7
log, 24:63 (TFH)
water kerf in, 78:41
ledgers for, 29:44 (FRC), 46:67, 68 (EF), 47:8
offset, 30:35
PVC pipe, as spacers for, 49:4
low simple, 74:55
lumber for, 29:42-43 (FRC)
cutting tips for, 69:48 (EF)
membrane-covered, 79:82
metal connectors for, 43:45-46, 49 (FRC)
mildewcide for, 61:14
nails for, 29:43 (FRC), 85:47
aluminum, avoiding, 85:120-22
finish, 39:53 (CSH)
pattern for, 82:26
observation, 59:78, 79
for ocean-side cabin, 54:61, 62
panels for, tapered, 68:86
pedestal octagonal, 45:47 (TFH)
persuaders for, 57:26, 62:30, 85:30
reviewed, 84:96-98
piers for, 29:43 (FRC)
planter for, integral, 69:47, 48 (EF)
platform, 27:72, 73
pocket second-story, 68:86, 87
for pool surrounds, 18:7
over porch, waterproofing, 51:52-53
posts for,
caps for, making, 56:73
cut-off jig for, 40:16
power-washing, 84:134
premade, on grade, 50:16
pressure-treated, finish for, 77:104-108
railings for, 29:46 (FRC)
curved laminated, 39:54 (CSH)
installation gauge for, 49:28
removable, 48:24
steel, 66:86, 87
supports for, 46:66 (EF)
redwood radiused, 39:52-55 (CSH)

removable, 56:69 (CSH)
as roofs, 44:76, 80-81, 80:70, 77
    of concrete pavers, 80:77
    low-cost, 84:12
    modified-bitumen, 70:71 (EF)
    system for, 55:84
rooftop, 7:8, 9:4
    flashing for, 12:59, 60
    gutters for, 12:60
    roofing under, 12:58-60
round brick, 45:34
sawblades for, Teflon-coated, reviewed, 56:92
screw gun for, remote-drive, 85:71
screwed-from-below, 45:75 (CSH)
seat brackets for, 72:90
for spa, building, 69:46-49 (EF)
span tables for, source of, 23:50
stairs for, 29:46 (FRC)
    on quadrant, 83:74-76
    spiral, 54:80-82 (EF)
    stringer methods for, 76:16
steel, 30:18, 21
steel clips for, 35:90
steel-framed, 78:20
sunshade for, 75:67
tables for, built-in, 30:35
through-pan, 9:48 (EF)
tiling, 16:8
tongue-and-groove, weatherproofing, 81:46
as transitional spaces, 80:52
trellis for, 51:50-53
    overhanging, 39:55 (CSH)
unstable, bracing, 82:16
Victorian tiny, 48:70, 73 (SH)
over water, 80:62
waterproofing, 52:39 (TFH), 61:14, 69:42 (EEH)
weatherproofing, 6:23, 20:12
weather-worthy, building, 46:66-69 (EF)
"Wolmanized," and finishes, 55:18-20
wood for, 6:23
wood preservative for, 69:48 (EF)
and wood shrinkage, 81:56-57
of wood/concrete planks, 47:87
wood/plastic lumber for, 85:122
wrap-around, 42:36-39
Decorating: books on, 36:94
Decorating with Paint (Innes): cited, 60:81
Decorators Supply Corp.: address for, 47:6
Decra-Led, Ltd.: address for, 74:78
Dectron, Inc.: Dry-o-tron dehumidifier, 45:80 (EEH)
DeDominicis, Al: on bell tower, 30:42-45
Deflection:
    calculating, 7:24-27 (TFH)
    defined, 7:25, 32:31 (FRC, TFH)
DeForest House: pictured, 37:55

Deft Inc.: address for, 48:75
Degenkolb, Henry: evaluates site, 15:27-28
DeGrange, Connie: on asbestos, 24:82-83
Dehumidification:
    by air tube, 11:8
    heat pump for, 2:33 (EEH)
    for interior swimming pools, 45:80 (EEH)
Del Monte, Gerard: on financing, 59:14
Delaware: solar tax credits in, 3:12
Dellett, Jack: mentioned, 28:77
Delphi computer service: described, 46:60
Delta Industries: stress-skin panels of, 25:44 (TFH)
Delta International Machinery Corp.:
    address for, 70:53 (FC)
    compound-miter saws,
        model 36-040, discussed, 57:59, 94
        reviewed, 83:64, 65-66, 67
    Getting the Most Out of Your Shaper,
        cited, 50:72 (FC)
    miter saw, mentioned, 82:92
    portable table saw, reviewed, 64:71-73, 68:4
    radial-arm-saw safety retrofits from, 43:96
    safety design at, 34:55 (TB)
    safety labels for, 37:81
    Sawbuck, reviewed, 57:58-59, 62
    sawmill, portable, 35:90
Delta-Flo Manufacturing Co.: address for, 66:66 (EEH)
DeMasi, Victor:
    on graining, 60:78-82
    reviews Ripolin, 61:90-92
    reviews Shivers, 77:120-22
Demers, Steve: house by, 38:40-45
Demetras, Jeff: mentioned, 25:53
Demolition:
    process of, 53:122
    reasons for, 10:44
    saw for, 10:44
Dempsey, Jim: mentioned, 29:28-29
Denarco Sales Co.: address for, 68:64, 77:67
Denison, Chris: on etched glass, 24:52-53 (DWS)
Denmark:
    concrete of, lightweight, 31:76, 77
    door manufacture in, 31:76, 77
    electric heating system in, 31:77
    export office of, 31:77
    influence of, 35:28-34
    shelving system from, 31:76
    window manufacture in, 31:76, 77
    See also Prefabricated houses: Scandinavian.
Denmark, Marvin: reviews Walmsley, 30:78

Dennis, Mark: on owner-building, 4:10-12
Denny, Nelson: on addition, 5:22-24
Denny Products: address for, 61:12
Dentils: two-by-four, 15:26-28
Denver Flux: flux, 42:35 (DWS)
Department of Energy National Solar Data Network: glazing tests of, 20:22
Department of Veterans Affairs: address for, 65:54
Department of Veterans Benefits:
    Handbook for Design, 23:48
    information from, 23:48
Derbigum HPS roofing: source for, 37:26 (BK)
Derricks:
    A-frame, 34:10
    pivot-beam, 34:10
Des Champs Laboratories, Inc.:
    address for, 66:66 (EEH)
    heat-recovery ventilators, 34:34 (DWS)
Design:
    ad hoc, 17:76-79, 18:4, 25:56-61 (SH)
    for affordable housing, bill for, 62:106
    for air quality, book on, 75:110
    approach to, with clients, 74:52
    for arches, 69:83
    for Arctic Circle, 68:100
    bilateral symmetry in, 38:38-39 (CSH)
    books on, 33:88, 35:94, 45:116-22, 46:66 (EF), 52:36 (TFH), 77:51
        cited, 69:86, 87
        reviewed, 18:78, 62:114
    by builders, hotline for, 77:108
    with cantilevered bays, 32:41, 43
    for carved projections, 69:87
    for coastal areas, 29:73-74
    Colonial, book on, 47:110-12
    with Colonial motifs, 63:45-49
    with color, 55:70, 71, 74, 56:70-71 (CSH), 73:60-65, 74:40-45
        books on, 73:64
        video planner for, 70:112
    for community houses, 73:82-87
    competitions for, 72:100, 75:102
    computer program for, reviewed, 81:114
    computer-aided, 25:83, 49:46-50
    conferences on, 47:100, 72:100
    consultant in, 29:57 (CSH)
    contemporary, book on, 44:89
    contest book of, 20:80
    continuity in, 52:4
    contrast in, 66:16-22, 80:51-52
    around courtyard, 80:82-87
    for demolition, 26:34, 35
    difficulties with, 14:36-37
    digital measuring wheel for, reviewed, 69:92
    ecological conscience in, 52:12
    economy in, 52:12-24

energy-efficient, 59:72 (SH), 63:81-85
(EEH), 65:62-65 (SH), 66:4, 68:82-83,
72:70-75 (EEH), 78:68-71, 81:104-106,
82:102, 85:4
average insolation and, 21:60
blueprints for, 36:92
books on, 71:47, 72:108
centers for, 69:100, 83:88
certification program for, 68:100-102
and climate, 21:60-61, 44:76-81
and climate, book on, 54:61
and condensation index, 21:61
for cooling, 80:54-58, 85:74-75
for cooling, passive, 41:4
degree-day zones for, 21:60-61, 56:36,
40
for desert, 66:82-87
and earth-sheltering effectiveness,
21:61
and evaporative cooling
effectiveness, 21:61
and heating degree-days, 21:60
insulation guidelines for, 56:36
environmentally responsible, 76:4
by family compromise, 52:36-40 (TFH)
for farm structures, information on,
65:54
"farmhouse," 83:82-87
by framing views, 33:49-50 (SH)
with gables, inverted, 55:74
geometry in, 38:86-87
around golden section, 34:56-58 (FRC)
Gothic Revival,
books on, 61:45 (SH)
discussed, 61:45 (SH)
for handicapped, 53:67-71
plans for, 52:100
sources for, 35:45 (BK)
for health, 46:70-73, 55:104, 73:66-70
aids for, 53:108
books on, 49:6
and composition board, 67:80, 81
finishes for, 67:90-92
information on, 65:54
organization for, 62:104-106, 66:4
project on, 51:98
for hillside, 66:69-73, 69:38-43 (EEH)
historic,
reviewed, book on, 53:108
source for, 52:8-12
for hot climate, 79:70-74
for humid climate, 8:63-67, 28:73-77
(EEH)
for hurricane resistance, 54:58-62, 59:78-
82, 60:4, 85:72-75
program for, 57:106
improving, 12:39, 40-41
information on, 65:52-53, 54
interior, books on, 30:78, 51:104
around intersecting squares, 47:84-87

in-the-field, drafting boards for, 56:92-94
of kitchens and baths, courses on, 72:98
around landscape, 52:83-87
for light and energy efficiency, 81:83-87
with light, natural, 80:78
and lighting, 55:57
vs. making, 38:102
for materials efficiency, 84:46-49
math book for, reviewed, 85:132
by milk crate, 45:84
minimum size, 10:44
Modernist, 55:74
modular, 55:73-74, 66:59 (SH)
Alden Dow's, 10:21-24
building blocks for, 10:22, 23
from centerline, 71:37-38, 41 (EEH)
drafting of, 11:4
by exterior grid, 43:72-74 (SH)
in fiberglass, 34:70-75
hexagonal, 9:62, 64, 65, 11:4
as house core, 52:26-28
hybrid, 52:24-28 (CSH)
Japanese, 4:52-53 (TFH), 19:41 (BK),
43:31 (CSH)
metal prefabrication for, 33:72-73
NEST, 26:82
with notepads, 56:26-28
parallelogram, 12:28, 29
for pole building, 15:32
Quonset ribs in, 33:26, 73
in units of 2 ft., 73:58
in units of 3x3, 48:48
in units of 3 ft. 6 in., 79:50-52
in units of 4 ft., 39:71, 74, 66:38 (SH)
in units of 4-ft./8-ft. alternates, 52:58-
59 (CSH)
in units of 5 ft., 38:87-88
in units of 6 ft. 8 in., 73:73
in units of 10 ft., 71:37-38 (EEH)
vertical, 30:23
windows for, 16:30, 43:74 (SH)
motifs in, cut-out, 73:63, 64, 65
and motive, 38:102
multi-level, 12:42-44 (REM)
around nautical imagery, 52:41-45
by NCAT, 32:90
19th-century, book on, 61:69
for ocean-side locations, 54:58-62
organic,
curved, 8:25 (CBS)
defined, 66:41-42, 52-53
overcare in, 12:62 (DWS)
for Pacific Northwest, 8:25 (CBS)
paint-choosing service for, 62:104
parallelogram, for steep, narrow site,
38:30-34
Pattern Language method of, 52:62-67
by pattern relationships, 36:51-55
"Persian," 78:79-81
of portable houses, 19:29
for privacy, 38:58

process of, 66:41, 66:83
defined, 45:16-20, 102-106
reality consideration for, 30:63
for retrofits, 1984 conference on, 25:82-
83
risk/certainty dichotomy in, 52:57-61
(CSH)
of round forms, 44:78-80
scale in, 52:20 (CSH)
altering, 73:53
Scandinavian, collection of, 77:90-91
sequence for, 80:83-87
Shaker, 79:87-88
for sheet-metal, book on, 61:49
around sight lines, 42:50-52 (SH)
sketching for, 1:24-27
of small space, 19:49, 31:22-27, 32:38-43,
33:48-52 (CSH, SH)
source book for, reviewed, 57:114
spiral, 35:74-77
standardizing in, 52:20 (CSH)
for steep sites, 38:24-24, 60-65, 41:44-48
(EEH), 51:58-63, 79:80-84
for strict-permit area, 64:75-79
for structural strength, 79:80-84
and style, 12:4
for subdivisions, cluster, 59:68-73 (SH)
subtractive, 44:78, 79
for subtropics, 15:14
with sun's orbit, 59:57-58, 60
for sunspace, analysis of, 16:14
sun-tempered, 16:14
by synthesis, 1:24-27
for temperate climate, 19:61-65 (EEH)
thermal mass in, 72:70 (EEH)
brick as, 44:78, 81
cement plaster as, 29:32
and concrete density, 20:10
concrete slab as, 51:72 (EEH), 54:14
designing, 33:40 (EEH)
drywall as, 34:29 (DWS)
energy-efficient, 72:70 (EEH)
for erratic climate, 29:28
floor and chimney as, 38:26 (EEH)
floors as, 34:29 (DWS)
plaster as, 31:58-61 (FWS), 51:61
rock beds as, 12:65-66 (EEH), 15:62,
16:29
rock beds as, mildew in, 15:10
sand as, 7:37-39 (DWS), 28:81
sizing, 84:86-87
for tilework, 69:56-57
book on, 62:112-14
tilted axis, 13:68, 69-70
timber-frame, plans for, 47:44, 53:85-89
(TFH)
and traffic patterns, 10:48, 49, 51-52 (SH)
around transitions, 52:40 (TFH), 80:52
trees in, 17:4-6
for tropics, 38:78-83 (CSH)
for updated Cape, 56:58-63 (EEH)
variables in, 3:44-45

and ventilation effectiveness, 21:61
for vibration resistance, 54:61
and village metaphor, 28:77
water in, 38:66, 68-70
for west-facing site, 34:8-10
for wetlands, 57:63-67
by women, 84:108-10
around wood shrinkage, 81:54-59
with wood, specification books for, 81:16
See also Architects. Computers. *different building types.* Drafting. Energy. Plans.

Design and Application Manual for Exterior and Interior Walls (Red Cedar Shake and Shingle Bureau): cited, 54:42-44 (EF)

Design and Construction Handbook for Energy-Saving Houses, A (Wade): reviewed, 7:60

Design and Construction Manual for Residential Buildings in Coastal High Hazard Areas: source for, 29:74

Design and Control of Concrete Mixtures (PCA): cited, 55:68

Design and Fabrication of Stressed Skin Panels: mentioned, 26:4

Design Basics: address for, 53:89

Design for Affordable Housing (HUD): cited, 53:89

Design for Glued Trusses: source for, 23:50

Design for Independent Living (Lifchez and Winslow): discussed, 35:45 (BK)

Design of Glued and Nailed Plywood Web Beams: source for, 72:98

Design Values for Wood Construction (American Forest and Paper Association): source for, 81:16

Design with Climate (Olgyay): cited, 54:61
source for, 9:16

Design-Construction Guide: source for, 21:6

Designing and Building Your Own House Your Own Way (Clark): cited, 7:42, 13:16

Designing for the Disabled (Goldsmith): source for, 6:51

Designing Houses (Walker and Milstein): reviewed, 18:78

Designing Staircases (Mannes): cited, 70:90

DesigniT Corp.: drywall saw, reviewed, 79:100

Designs for Low-Cost Wood Homes: described, 4:62

Designs of Inigo Jones, The (Jones): cited, 42:74

Desks:
built-in, with recessed drawers, 47:88
cantilevered, 46:38, 40, 41 (REM), 61:73
in library renovation, 61:120

DeSmidt, Gene:
addition by, 25:92
on soundproofing, 35:60-63
on Tassajara, 68:70-73 (EF)

Desmond, Dan:
on energy myths, 33:56-57
on framing defects, 6:36-38 (FRC)
on vapor barriers, 19:66-68

De-Sta-Co: address for, 74:73 (FC)

Detailing for Acoustics (Lord and Templeton): source for, 35:63

Details and Engineering Analysis of the Illinois Lo-Cal House: source for, 4:8

Detergents: for house washing, 62:38 (EF)

Dethier, Jean:
organizes earth-building exhibit, 30:74
plans earth college, 30:76

Devcon Corp.: address for, 70:49

DeVido, Alfredo: earth-sheltered house by, 71:36-41 (EEH)

Devoe and Raynolds Co.: address for, 48:75

Dew point:
defined, 19:67
explained, 63:18

DeWalt Industrial Tool Co.:
compound miter saws, Crosscutter #1707, reviewed, 43:92, 57:59-60, 62
reviewed, 83:67, 68-69
plate joiner, mentioned, 82:92
power miter saw #3090, 19:42, 20:4 (TB)
radial-arm saw, 24-in., 36:49 (TFH)
rotary hammer of, mentioned, 82:92
service policy of, 82:92
VSR drill, reviewed, 82:36-41

Dexter Lock Co.:
brass doorknob manufacture of, 48:65 (FC, MFC)
Dexlock, 48:62 (FC, MFC)

DF Windows: address for, 76:75 (FC)

Dial indicators: source for, 53:58

Dialog computer service: described, 46:60

Diamond Co.: wide flooring, 32:75

Diamond Machining Technology, Inc.:
address for, 48:91
whetstones of, 13:12, 18:61 (TB)

Diamond veneer plaster: source for, 28:10

Diaz, Ana: on metal corrosion, 62:64-67

Dickinson, Duo:
on design, 45:94-106
on hillside house, 66:69-73
Small House, The, reviewed, 40:90

Dictionary of Architecture and Construction, The (Harris): reviewed, 47:112

Dictionary of Tools (Salaman): reviewed, 47:112

Die grinders: pneumatic, 47:67

Diedrich Chemical: address for, 84:72

Dieldrin: against termites, 22:12

Diem, Andrew H.: on arbitration, 57:76-77

Diesel oil: stain of, removing, 13:6-8, 15:14

Dietz, Albert G. H.: designs Monsanto house, 34:70, 72, 75

Dietz (R. E.) Co.: address for, 74:90

Dietzgen Corp.: drafting tools, 26:58 (TB)

Diffrient, Niels, Alvin R. Tiller, and Joan C. Bardagjy: *Humanscale 1-2-3,* discussed, 35:45 (BK)

DiGaetano, Louis S., and Kathleen Haugh: on fire-damage restoration, 4:16-20

Digitool Corp.: ultrasonic tape, reviewed, 78:54-55

Dillon, Pat: entryway by, 3:14-18 (DWS)

Dimar Canada Ltd: Quadriset, reviewed, 64:92

Dimension Lumber: address for, 53:55

Dimmers: *See* Lighting.

Dining rooms:
alcove for, 45:63 (SH)
built-in seating for, 66:88
enlarging, 71:60-63 (REM)
incorporating, with kitchen, 63:54-57 (REM)
space requirements of, 52:20 (CSH)
two-story windowed, 79:53, 54

Dinsmoor, Samuel P.: house by, 68:120

Direct Safety Co.:
first-aid kits, 36:4
safety products, 34:55 (TB)

Direct Supply Co.: address for, 81:72

Direct Use of the Sun's Energy (Daniels): source for, 26:56

Directory of Audio-Visuals, Publications, and Promotion Material: source for, 23:50

Directory of Special Libraries and Information Centers: coverage of, 23:51

Directory of State Building Codes and Regulations (McIntyre): reviewed, 46:104

Disabled: *See* Handicapped.

Disc grinders: cutting with, 20:16

Discovering Timber-Framed Buildings (Harris): cited, 42:44 (TFH), 47:45 (TFH)

Dishracks: doweled, 12:12

Dishwashers:
cord length for, 58:4
installation of, 39:42, 54:46-48, 58:6
pans for, 54:48
placement of, 10:45

selecting, 2:54 (BK)

water-saving, 73:104

Display niches:

caps for, molded, 39:92

glass shelves for, 68:37

in kitchen, 67:72, 73, 75 (REM)

tokonoma, 82:84, 85

Disston Co.:

address for, 69:73, 81:40

Deck Blade, reviewed, 50:95

handsaws,

dating, 27:4

discussed, 20:69 (TB)

Tiger Force blade, reviewed, 50:95

Diversified Fastening Systems, Inc.:

address for, 41:57 (CBS), 70:79

toggle bolts, 41:56 (CBS)

Dividers:

discussed, 57:94

with levels, source for, 34:49

for log building, 34:49

pen for, 34:49

DLS Aquatics: address for, 72:63

DMA Radtech, Inc.: address for, 67:51

DML, Inc.:

address for, 84:42

dado blade, 40:87

Dobsevage, Ruth:

on energy conference, 25:82-83

reviews children's book, 15:22

reviews Kangas, 10:70

reviews Walker, 44:94

Docker, James: on eyebrow windows, 65:80-84 (MFC)

Dodge, John: stoves of, 7:49 (CBS)

Dodge Cork Co., Inc.: address for, 52:108

Dodge Reports: computer access to, 46:59

Doebley, C.: as joint author. *See* Thomas, G.

Doghouses:

architectural, 67:87

for tropics, 49:128

Dog-trot: defined, 29:48

Doidge, Dave: gate by, 52:89

Dome Cookbook, The (Baer): mentioned, 26:56

Domer, Dennis: addresses conference, 47:102

Domes:

of arcuate segments, tapered, 67:116

book on, reviewed, 65:108

concrete, 50:56

concrete-roof, 30:67-68 (CBS)

forces in, 32:30 (FRC)

leaded glass, 31:50 (FWS)

of molded foam, 39:92

See also Bovedas. Deca Dome.

Domestic Water Conditioning (Lehr, Gass, Pettyjohn, De Marre): cited, 10:55 (BK)

Donahoe, Richard: house by, 55:82-87

Key to books:

(BK)   Building Baths and Kitchens

(CBS)   Building with Concrete, Brick and Stone

(CSH)   Craftsman-Style Houses

(DWS)   Building Doors, Windows and Skylights

(EEH)   Energy-Efficient Houses

(EF)   Exterior Finishing

(FC)   Finish Carpentry

(FRC)   Frame Carpentry

(FWS)   Building Floors, Walls and Stairs

(MFC)   More Frame Carpentry

(REM)   Remodeling

(SH)   Small Houses

(TB)   Tools for Building

(TFH)   Timber-Frame Houses

Donahue, Bob: timber framing by, 36:49 (TFH)

Donnell, Bill and Mayra: clapboard mill of, 31:36-37

Door and Hardware Institute: *Buyer's Guide* (5th ed.), cited, 48:65 (FC, MFC)

Doormaking Patterns and Ideas (Birchard):

cited, 83:61

reviewed, 68:106

Doors:

air-vapor barriers with, 9:57, 58, 29:70, 72

aluminum, black anodized, 37:26 (BK)

arched, 64:77, 78

eight-panel, 36:77 (DWS)

interior, 33:51 (SH)

lintel, 1:55

transoms for, 13:71

Arts-and-Crafts style, 22:59-60 (CSH), 69:42, 43 (EEH)

associations for, 6:60, 40:86, 60:50 (FC)

backing for, improving, 70:32

of barn siding, 66:74

batten,

distressed, 31:73

iron-hinged, 36:77 (DWS)

making, 7:32-33 (DWS)

with sliding-dovetails, 25:31

beadboard for, 10:46 (DWS)

bevels for, 8:35 (DWS), 53:42 (FC)

bifold,

bumpers for, 7:12

pivot, over carpet, 70:34

biscuit joinery for, discouraged, 85:6

books on, 36:41 (DWS), 68:106, 72:50 (FC)

bottoms of, cutting, 35:69 (TB)

bowing of, correcting, 10:8

bucks for,

in block work, 84:57

carpenter's vise for, 35:91

clamps as, 3:6, 9:12, 28:16, 74:72 (FC)

folding, on portable workbench, 69:74

plywood wedged, 8:35 (DWS)

quick, 54:24, 56:26

simple slotted, 9:4

site-made, 33:16

bumpers for, cork, 85:32

cabinet,

breadboard-end, 49:41, 43 (REM)

catches for, 9:37-38 (BK)

commercial, source for, 72:62

curved, 12:62, 63 (DWS)

custom, 65:72-73, 68:96

hanging, jigs for, 1:15 (FWS)

hutch-style caned, 44:52, 53 (SH)

making, 85:67

mounting, 47:67

overlay, 13:63 (BK)

panel, 2:54 (BK), 9:37-38 (BK), 58:38-39 (REM)

panel, with glass, 69:50-51, 53

panel, random-pieced, 17:68-69 (BK)

repairing, 81:76

canopy for,

collector, 6:57

fiberglass, 63:54, 56 (REM)

carrying, 55:26-28

cart for, reviewed, 81:92

carved, 21:35, 29, 31, 34:77

and adzed, 25:30-31

custom, 37:76-77 (DWS)

center-pivot, 10:12-14, 18:31, 32

chapel teak and glass, 64:53

classical interior, building, 72:50-53 (FC)

clearances for, 53:41, 42 (FC)

club brace for, reviewed, 85:102-104

collage, 13:53 (CBS)

crosscutting, methods for, 53:41-42 (FC)

curved, laminated, 38:45

custom, 51:90

vs. commercial, 38:53

sources for, 63:40, 67:58, 73:75

cut-down, matching, 60:45 (SH)

designing, 15:12, 83:61

dowel joinery for, 83:58-60

edge-trimming jig for, 10:14

ends of, finish for, 10:8

estimates for, 27:34

fanciful, 40:78

fasteners for, 7:32, 33 (DWS)

figuring, metric vs. imperial, 60:102

finish for, 3:16, 8:36, 10:46, 15:12 (DWS), 48:75-78, 83:61

fireproof formal, 31:49 (FWS)

fitting, 3:17, 8:35 (DWS)

flashing, 8:60-65, 9:47 (EF)

foldaway, reviewed, 73:100

folding, 2:20, 24, 25 (CSH)

glass-mahogany, 63:40, 41

noise-insulated, 65:77 (REM)

steel and glass, 19:31

for 4-ft. module, 39:72
frame-and-panel, 72:50-53 (FC)
  mock, 28:52, 53 (FWS)
  for 32mm cabinets, 74:77
  and wood shrinkage, 81:54, 58-59
framing for, 8:34-35 (DWS), 21:71,
  22:34-35, 27:76 (FRC), 82:43, 84:48
  failures with, 6:38 (FRC)
  hurricane-proofing, 78:86-87
French, 45:40, 42
  canopy for, 72:88
  custom, 83:56
  framing for, 21:71 (FRC)
  nonwarping, 82:96
  painting, 13:70-71
  retrofitting, 68:42-46 (FC)
gang of, installing, 26:32 (DWS)
garage,
  exposed counterweights for, 16:63-64
   (TFH)
  hurricane-proofing, 78:86
  installing, 74:57-59 (MFC), 76:6-8
  replacing panels of, 53:28
  roll-up, glazed, 41:48
  roll-up, source for, 52:69
gasketing, for noise control, 58:57
gauge blocks for, 30:55-56 (DWS)
glass inset for, 15:78 (CSH)
glue for, 83:59
gluing up, 10:46, 47 (DWS)
  process for, 85:6-8
graining, process of, 85:18-20
gridded, 15:31
grills in, 25:29-31
half-circle nail-studded, 6:30
hand of, 8:35 (DWS), 26:26-27 (DWS)
for handicapped, 6:51, 53:68, 69, 71, 65:77
  (REM), 76:55
hanging, 10:6, 21:16, 26:26-32, 28:4, 29:4
  (DWS), 68:46 (FC)
  butt marker for, 49:95
  hinge-mortise plane for, 49:95
  jig for, 65:32
  into out-of-true opening, 81:26-28
  with plumb bob, 74:64-65 (FC)
  production, 53:38-42 (FC), 58:8
  roller for, 49:26
  scribing anchor for, 53:41 (FC)
  for security, 31:14
  worm-drive flush-cut saw for, 53:38
   (FC)
hatch, 38:45, 46:53 (EEH)
height of, standard, 21:70, 71 (FRC)
in hung walls, 8:30 (TFH)
insulated,
  commercial, 6:60-62
  for cooling room, 48:58-60
  curtain as, 70:56 (EEH)
  making, 10:46-47 (DWS)
Japanese-style, 45:74 (CSH)

laminated, 29:61 (CSH)
  curved, making, 15:79 (CSH)
lead, shaped, 23:31
leaded glass inserts for, 54:40-41
level-holding trick for, 39:14
louvered, 38:80 (CSH)
  custom, 68:96
making, 3:15-16 (DWS), 10:8, 46-47
  (DWS), 62:73-74, 76
  book on, 50:69 (FC)
  on-site, 83:57-61
map on, routed, 7:66 (DWS)
metal-skinned, boring, 83:28
modular, 27:73, 75, 66:59 (SH)
molding for, 3:16 (DWS)
  drip, raked, 61:43, 44 (SH)
mortised, wedging, 74:24
old,
  source for, 56:92
  stripping, 59:50 (SH)
one-over-one, 77:89
ornate, gallery of, 56:88-89
out-of-plumb, fixing, 15:18, 69:14, 71:16
oval, 17:77 (SH)
overlapping, 18:32
painting of, spray, 42:55-56 (DWS)
paneled, 3:16 (DWS)
  circular, making, 12:62-63 (DWS)
  with copper and lead, 23:31
  etched-and-stained, 36:77, 73:90, 91
   (DWS)
  playhouse, quick, 61:44-45 (SH)
  profiles of, 20:61, 62, 63 (FWS)
  of random pieces, 17:68-69 (BK)
  with rice-paper, 69:42, 43 (EEH)
  rounded, 15:78 (CSH)
  with rounded glass, 72:52-53 (FC)
  stick-, 23:29
papering, 6:8
particleboard in, 15:12
pediments for, 75:59
  with urn, 72:53 (FC)
placement of, 77:88
plates of, chainsaw cutting, 78:41
pocket, 7:23 (BK)
  circular, 12:61 (DWS)
  constructing, 54:65, 66 (FC)
  early, repairing, 54:67 (FC)
  frame kits for, 54:63-66 (FC)
  glass, 49:73, 75 (EEH)
  Greek Revival, 29:63, 67
  installing, 6:10, 24:22
  manufacturers of, 54:65 (FC)
polystyrene core for, 17:42, 43 (SH)
prehung, installing, 58:26, 74:62-65 (FC)
projecting, 83:56
quad-pane glazed, source for, 20:22
rabbeted stops on, 5:33-34

from recycled material, 81:106
redwood/catalpa, 35:51, 52 (BK)
restoring, 1:49
reveals for, 3:55, 30:55 (DWS)
  jig for, 23:14
roofing panels as, 36:16
rustic, metal-clad, 83:89
sandblasted, 53:46, 50 (SH)
sculpted, 46:84-85
  from built-up strips, 68:39-40
sheathed-over, chainsaw cutting, 78:40
shoji, 29:56-57 (CSH)
shopmade, 50:81 (SH)
shower, steam-tight, 52:112
sidelights for, 54:69, 70, 71 (REM)
sliding, 38:80, 82 (CSH)
  canvas, 4:27, 29, 31
  closer for, automatic, 82:96
  curved, tracks for, 15:78, 79 (CSH)
  Danish, 31:76, 77
  French, 68:43 (FC)
  glass, 4:55 (TFH)
  handicap-sill insert for, 53:68
  insulated, 17:42-43 (SH)
  Japanese, 4:54-55 (TFH)
  size problems with, 37:29 (BK)
  steel, 22:28
  stop for, 74:52
soundproof, 31:49, 35:63 (FWS)
source for, 51:90, 61:59 (SH)
of Southern long-leaf yellow pine, 39:76
with Southwestern motifs, 67:56-58
stained-glass, 1:55, 42:33 (DWS)
stainless-steel clad, 27:52-53
steel foam-core, drilling, 53:26, 58:24-26
stone-faced, 40:100
storage, compound-curved, 29:33
storm, making, 57:75 (FC)
and storm doors, damage from, 53:14-16
in stress-skin panels, 24:55, 57, 58
styrene and plastic-laminate, 38:48 (SH)
tenons for, loose, 83:60-61
threaded-rod adjustment in, 68:39, 40
thresholdless, 76:56
thresholds for,
  for handicapped, 53:68, 71
  in situ replacement of, 19:34-36 (DWS)
  installing, 23:14-16
  stone, 24:30 (CSH)
of tongue-and-groove stock, 28:70, 71
tops for, angled, 74:53
tracks for, 4:31
transoms for, 77:88
trimming, 8:35 (DWS)
unprimed, commercial, 10:51 (SH)
vandal-proof system for, 30:69 (CBS)
vertical board, 3:24
widening, in masonry wall, 12:8
window grid for, 73:59
windows in, half-round, 80:67
wood for, 50:16

workbenches for, 53:40, 41 (FC), 81:64, 66, 82:6
See also Butt gauges. Carving. Casings. Entryways. Glazing. Handles. Hardware. Hinges. Latches. Locksets. Mortises. Pulls. Screens. Templates. Trim. Weatherstripping.

Doran, William: on tall forms, 78:48-53

Dormers:
arched,
     framing for, 23:66, 67
     plaster for, 23:66
backing for, 41:63-64 (criticized, 36:6, FRC)
curved, 52:43, 44
described, 41:60 (FRC)
diamond-windowed, 68:86
eyebrow, 20:29, 30-31, 52:56
     building, 65:80-84 (MFC), 84:28
     framing, 65:81-84 (MFC), 76:74, 75 (FC)
     mitered-glass, 59:65, 67 (EEH)
flashing for, 70:42
flush-wall, 38:72, 73 (TFH)
framing, 35:71 (criticized, 36:6, TB)
gable, 59:36, 38-39 (SH)
     adding, 40:10
     mid-ridge, 52:48 (TFH)
     shingled, 59:75 (REM)
     steep, 83:89
hipped, 52:53, 54, 55, 60:43 (SH)
     Arts-and-Crafts style, 76:66, 67, 68 (REM)
inverted, flashing, 80:87
large, 46:62, 63 (TFH)
with light well, 78:57, 58
methods for, 41:60, 62-63, 64 (FRC)
moldings for, crown, 41:64-65 (FRC)
pedimented, 41:64-65 (FRC)
as plant space, converting to, 70:42-43
ridge, 5:30
shed, 35:50 (FRC), 59:42, 45
     adding, 15:12, 24:47-51, 28:26-30, 35:46 (FRC)
     distinctive, 35:80-81 (FRC)
     pocket, 54:86 (TFH)
     small, 80:59
shoring up around, 49:39-40 (REM)
ventilating, 61:78 (EF)
Victorian modern, 31:67, 68, 70

Dost, William: *Procedure for Classification of Stains Which Develop on Wood in Service,* 47:16

Double Shell House, The (Booth): reviewed, 1:66

Double Star, Inc.: address for, 78:6

Double-envelope houses:
books on, 1:66, 6:58, 15:22
building, 11:66-69, 23:43-46 (EEH)
church conversion to, 13:69-71
fire precautions for, 23:44 (EEH), 34:4-6

problems with, 23:43 (EEH)
sprinkler system for, 25:6
See also Superinsulated houses.

Douglas fir *(Pseudotsuga menziesii)*:
decay resistance of, 61:12, 63:63 (MFC)
drying, 29:4
for framing, 4:54 (TFH)
furniture of, 35:33, 34
green, 8:14
hardness group of, 40:69 (FRC)
vs. hem-fir, 19:4
managed forests of, 47:43
for paint, 42:55 (DWS)
for pole building, 15:32
price rise of, 82:104
sawdust of, as concrete additive, 48:51
span capability of, 33:43 (FWS)
stairway of, 28:40-41 (FWS)
timber framing with, 28:10-12, 40:45 (TFH)
for trim, 49:91

Douglas Products: ventilation units from, reviewed, 50:94

Dover Publications, Inc.: house plans from, 53:88

Dover Resources Co.: address for, 53:61

Dovetails: *See* Joinery.

Dow, Alden:
career of, 10:20-25
style of, 12:4

Dow Chemical Co. USA: address for, 46:71, 96, 48:58, 56:38, 76:37, 39, 82:94
caulk 795, Exolite compatibility of, 17:65 (DWS)
Dursban, 28:10
and fully halogenated chlorofluorocarbons, 49:102
polystyrene blueboard, 18:8, 31:70
polystyrene extruded, 18:33 (CBS)
processed wood from, described, 15:21
silicone rubber from, 1:39 (FWS)

Dow Corning Corp.: address for, 58:57

Dowels:
drilling for, 83:58
joinery with, 69:51, 53
making, for doors, 83:58
spring-loaded, 11:14
See also Joinery.

Dowman Products, Inc.:
cement and mortar colors, 21:72 (FRC)
Fixall patching compound of, 22:44 (BK)

Downen, Steve: on solar farmhouse, 37:70-75

Downing, Andrew Jackson:
Architecture of Country Houses, The, cited, 46:82 (TFH)
discussed, 53:88
house plans after, source for, 53:86

Downing, Antoinette: mentioned, 25:83

Downspouts:
gargoyle, 55:84, 87, 56:70, 72 (CSH)
sculpted copper, 9:75
as visual element, 17:28, 29 (CSH)

Dowrick, D. J.: *Earthquake Resistant Design,* cited, 29:38 (FRC)

Drafting:
detail requirements for, 46:4
leads for, 30:4
module system of, 5:30, 31
paper sizes for, 46:4
pens for, cheap cleaning of, 30:4
portable boards for, source for, 56:94
process of, 43:63-67 (SH, TB)
reproduction of, 26:62 (TB)
supplies for, 26:58-62 (TB), 28:4, 30:4, 43:63 (SH, TB), 56:94

Drafting (Syvanen): source for, 43:67 (TB)

Drafts: *See* Air infiltration.

Drainage systems:
board for, using, 55:57-58, 59
books on, 50:86
cleanouts for, 50:85, 86, 54:4
code on, source for, 39:37 (BK)
discharge systems for, 50:86
ensuring, around house, 71:16
filter fabric for, 2:37, 18:4, 40:63 (CBS), 50:85
floor drains for, air-tight, source for, 67:48
foundation forms for, 39:34 (BK)
foundation retrofit for, 48:12
French drains for, 21:66, 22:43, 45:69
frozen, thawing, 84:30
for fungi protection, 72:66 (REM)
gravel for, 50:85
inspection of, 39:36 (BK)
installing, 39:33-37 (BK)
labels on, 39:35 (BK)
locating, dowser for, 75:26-28
pipes for, 50:82-84
     preformed PVC, reviewed, 84:98
problems with, solving, 69:24
retrofitting, 50:84-86
for site, 11:10
surface-drainage matting for, 69:41 (EEH)
tile, filter fabric for, 2:37, 18:4, 40:63 (CBS)
tools for, 39:37 (BK)
vents in, 39:35, 36, 37 (BK)
See also Gutters. Plumbing.

Dranjer Corp.: address for, 67:48

Drawers:
bin, 15:79 (CSH)
with biscuit joiner, 78:46, 47
bumpers for, cork, 85:32
for cabinets, 9:36, 15:77, 78 , 30:58-59, 62 (BK, CSH)
     designing, 65:74
     making, 79:78, 79
     manufactured, 65:72

carving, 47:64-67
constructing, 9:36-37 (BK)
curved laminated, 15:77, 78, 79 (CSH)
faces for,
adjusters for, 58:39 (REM), 74:77
beaded, 71:44, 45 (REM)
custom, 68:96
laminated, 30:59, 62 (BK)
shaping, 83:72-73
file, horizontal, 37:35, 37
guides for, wooded, 76:42 (REM)
joints for, 37:29 (BK)
finger, 30:62 (BK)
rabbet, on table-saw, 77:30
kitchen-cabinet,
"compost," 14:57 (BK)
custom, 40:66-67 (BK)
kneewall recessed, 47:88
knife, 15:78, 79 (CSH)
maple, dovetailed, 69:53, 54
overlay, making, 13:60, 62-63 (BK)
pan-shaped, 17:68 (BK)
pivoting/sliding, 74:75, 78
repairing, 81:76
slides for, 9:37, 13:62 (BK), 58:39-40
(REM)
ball-bearing, 30:58, 59 (BK)
discussed, 44:71 (BK)
mounting jig for, 13:61 (BK)
self-closing, 69:53
source for, 53:45 (SH)
with story poles, 83:72
wooden, 71:44 (REM), 83:73
spice, 67:76 (REM)
steam-table inserts for, 27:44, 45, 46
(BK)
32mm system for, 74:77
types of, 9:35 (BK)
under-bed alcove, 76:42-45 (REM)
under-counter, 61:75
custom, 2:54 (BK)
under-stairs, 15:70-71 (FWS)
vertical board, 2:54 (BK)
vertical pullout, 2:54 (BK)
See also Pulls.
*Drawing House Plans with Bob
Syvanen* (Syvanen): source for, 43:67
(TB)
Drawing tables: dust covers for, from
shades, 49:26
Drawings:
of Japanese house, 47:128
protecting, with clear Contact, 75:28
Drawknives:
French, for shingles, 30:49
hand-forged, 49:95
in timber framing, 4:22 (TFH)
Dremel Co.: modelmaking tools of, 22:51
(FRC)
Drerup, Oliver: on steel-panel roofing,
15:62

Key to books:

(BK) Building Baths and Kitchens
(CBS) Building with Concrete, Brick and Stone
(CSH) Craftsman-Style Houses
(DWS) Building Doors, Windows and Skylights
(EEH) Energy-Efficient Houses
(EF) Exterior Finishing
(FC) Finish Carpentry
(FRC) Frame Carpentry
(FWS) Building Floors, Walls and Stairs
(MFC) More Frame Carpentry
(REM) Remodeling
(SH) Small Houses
(TB) Tools for Building
(TFH) Timber-Frame Houses

Dresser Industries, Inc.: address for,
47:67
Dressing rooms: design for, 46:40, 41
(REM)
Drill presses:
cup-hinge jig for, 74:77
doweling jig for, 72:51 (FC)
metal drilling with, 63:66, 67
mortising with, long-stock jig for, 50:71,
72 (FC)
peg-hole jig for, 58:36 (REM)
registration jig for, 15:16
rosette corner-block maker for, 48:90-91
safety labels for, 37:81
sheet metal on, safely, 82:28
for timber framing, 4:23 (TFH)
Drilling:
body strategies for, 85:81
in concrete, method for, 51:28
with jig, 83:58
for lag bolts, 51:48 (EF)
for lockset mortises, bit for, 82:6
of long holes, 28:40 (FWS)
of metal-skinned doors, 83:28
of round stock, with V-block and
alignment rod, 81:26
of stone, 9:42, 43
stop block for, 61:6
32mm, jigs for, 74:76
from two sides, 15:16
vacuum device for, 28:16
Drills, hand:
bit holder for, 3:7
caulking gun for, 70:100-102
chucks for,
keyed, 82:37-38
keyless, 43:96, 82:38-40
on retracting key ring, 67:26
cordless,
brands of, compared, 35:38-42 (TB)
choosing, 35:41-42 (TB)
reviewed, 62:94-96

countersinks for, 81:40
depth gauge for, 18:12
grounding for, 82:41
as hacksaw, improvised, 54:26
hammer, for concrete, 41:52-53 (CBS)
hole-saw nail-remover for, 81:26, 84:28
mixing with, 33:16
plaster, 15:73 (FWS)
stirring rod for, 67:26
nail spinner for, 49:94
overhead use of, lever aid for, 67:26
plumb-bob aid for, 62:28
for rafter-pin joinery, 35:57 (TB)
as routers, 71:26
for timber framing, 4:23 (TFH)
variable-speed reversible (VSR),
reviewed, 82:36-41
See also Bits. Screw guns.
Dring, Bill: mentioned, 32:61
Drip edges: with router, 39:14
Driveways:
automated snow melting from, 53:76
epoxy repair for, 70:48
Driwood Moulding Co.: address for, 63:46
Droplights: TuffSkin bulbs for, 29:35 (FRC)
Drum walls:
in greenhouse, 32:100
See also Zomehouse.
Dryers:
and backdrafting, solutions for, 81:16-18
and heat-recovery ventilators, 23:82,
81:16-18
microwave, discussed, 72:100
venting, 64:20
Dryline: *See* String.
Dry-rot: chemicals against, 29:37 (FRC)
Dryvit Systems, Inc.:
address for, 82:82
See also Insulation.
Drywall:
acoustic qualities of, 11:50 (CBS)
adhesives for, 10:4, 58:75, 81:40
adobe-style, 43:78-79
airtight (ADA),
disadvantages of, 77:65
expounded, 50:100
gaskets for, 37:62, 40:4
process of, 37:62-65
over rigid insulation, 42:8
and air/vapor barriers, ceiling, 31:8-10
anchors for, reusable, 62:94
to angled spaces, 11:12
appearance of, vs. plaster, 38:28 (EEH)
askew, problems with, 13:60-61 (BK)
associations for, 58:75, 81:56
backing for, 82:50
banjo for, 23:60, 61 (FWS)
battens for, 35:14
bazookas for, 23:60 (FWS)

beads for,
  archway, 63:52
  corner, 23:61 (FWS), 43:78-79, 63:51, 52,
    66:66-67 (EEH), 81:40, 43
  corner, bullnose, source for, 60:44-45
    (SH)
  corner, radiused, 46:90
  corner, rigid, 63:50-51
  corner, rust bleed-through with,
    39:10, 67:71
  J-, 63:51, 52
  L-, 63:51, 52
  large-radius aluminum, 37:81
  U-, 63:52
bending, 9:12, 44:24, 83:62
  by form, 7:56
  over trusses, 11:69
books on, 51:83 (MFC), 58:75, 81:43
  reviewed, 70:120
butt joints with, 81:40, 43
carrying,
  cart for, 81:92, 83:30
  by folding for transport, 24:22
  hook for, 7:12
ceilings in, 8:52-53, 54 (FWS)
  coved, 18:14
channel for,
  RC-15, 18:42
  resilient, 35:63 (erratum, 36:6)
  U-, bending, 51:84 (MFC)
clips for, using, 84:48
corners for, 8:55, 57 (FWS)
  rounded, 63:52
  taping, 10:4
crimper with, 10:4, 63:50-51
curved, 5:24, 31:71
  achieving, 44:68 (FRC)
  mantel of, 39:39
cutouts in, 8:53, 55 (FWS), 81:40, 41
  cutter for, 23:61 (FWS)
  locating, 25:16
  marking, 10:12
  template for, light-fixture, 49:28
  wiring outlet jig for, 57:28
cutter for, battery-operated, 43:96
cutting, 8:54-55 (FWS), 81:42, 44
delivery of, 8:52, 32:69 (FRC, FWS)
dented, repairing, 79:30-32
dropcloths for, heavy, 24:6
economizing with, 66:66-67 (EEH)
exterior, source for, 66:38 (SH)
fasteners for, 83:4
fillers for, 23:61, 63-65 (FWS)
film strips on, 51:84 (MFC)
finish for, 8:56-57, 23:65 (FWS)
  dustless, 10:4, 6
  supplies for, 50:95
  textured, 77:78 (REM)
  textured, matching, 71:26
fire resistance of, 83:4

fire-resistant, source for, 76:96
fire-retardant, 55:44 (SH)
glazing of, 45:48 (TFH)
gluing,
  to concrete block, 19:63 (EEH)
  recommendations for, 81:56
hanging, 23:61 (FWS), 81:38-43
interior vs. exterior, 70:14
Keenes cement for, disadvised, 50:4
kicker for, homemade, 61:24
layout for, 81:40-42
leveling for, 23:61 (FWS)
lifts for, 5:6, 7:10, 8:4, 81:40
  commercial, 50:52
  making, 50:50-52
  pipe-clamp, 74:26
  for solo hanging, 57:26, 72:26
metal-framed, 30:6
moisture-resistant, 83:4
  around windows, 63:52
nailing, 6:64, 8:54-55, 15:49 (FWS, TB)
  errors with, covering, 40:16
  pops in, fixing, 48:24
and noise control, 35:60-63 (erratum,
  36:6), 58:54-55, 57, 62:18, 60, 61 (CSH)
as noncombustible surface, 13:10
  (erratum, 15:8)
paint for, 67:70
patches for, 18:14, 22:14, 54:26
patterns for, foam-sheet, 47:28
perm rating of, 19:67
planning of, 8:53 (FWS)
plaster for, water-resistant, 45:80 (EEH)
plastering, 15:72-74 (FWS), 45:84-86
  problems with, 26:94
raised-panel, 44:89
removing, 19:14, 47:30
return for, backing, 68:30
risks from, 34:51 (TB)
sanders for, 10:4
sanding, 63:52-53, 82:77
screw guns for, 34:42-45 (TB)
screws for, 6:8, 10:4, 12:51 (TB), 81:38-40
  spacing of, 83:4
screws in, magnetized, finding, 33:16
scribing, 81:41, 42, 43
seams in, 10:4, 23:61, 62-63 (FWS)
  kitchen, 41:14
Sears, Roebuck early, 28:44
sequence for, 81:39-40, 43
sizes of, 8:52 (FWS)
  odd, source for, 32:69 (FRC), 82:94
skim-coat technique for, 31:27 (CSH)
spackling, 8:56-57 (FWS)
over steel, 31:63, 65, 32:71 (FRC)
stilts for, 23:63 (FWS)
  from joint-compound buckets, 49:26
as structural component, 25:51
substitute for, discussed, 64:92-94
supply source for, 63:50

tapes for, 8:55, 9:4, 23:61, 26:41 (FWS)
  compared, 82:73
  fiberglass vs. paper, 84:6
temperature limits of, 15:8
tool bags for, 42:66, 67 (TB)
tools for, 8:54-55, 57, 12:51, 32:69 (FRC,
  FWS, TB), 82:72-73
training in, CA, 51:84 (MFC)
trim in, 63:50-53
trimmer for, edge, making, 62:28
trowels for, 8:55, 23:62, 63 (FWS)
  crown, 23:62 (FWS)
  rubber, 31:4
types of, 81:43
uncased, 8:66 (EEH)
on vault, 51:85 (MFC)
water absorptance of, 54:61
waterproof, 31:63
over wood lath, 32:58, 59
and wood shrinkage, 81:55-56
See also Casings. Joint compound.
  Screws.
Drywall (Harris): reviewed, 70:120
Duca, Tom:
  bookcase by, 58:86
  roof by, 57:91
Duckboards: vinyl, source for, 37:28 (BK)
Ductwork:
  in attic, and ice dams, 75:16
  condensation problems with,
    correcting, 15:14
  flex, avoiding, 46:70-73
  hiding, 26:41-42
  insulation for, 1:62
  pressure drops in, 34:33 (DWS)
  sheet-metal, 73:70
Duffy, Gerald J.: on housebuilding, 9:72
Duffy, Thomas: on curved doors, 12:61-63
  (DWS)
Dufort, Robert: on repainting, 62:36-41
  (EF)
Dulaney, Daniel: house by, 43:75-79
Dumbeck, Lawson: on theft, 55:122
Dumbwaiters:
  choices among, discussed, 73:102-104
  source for, 55:86
  triangular, 55:84, 86
  for wood, reviewed, 64:92
Dumond Chemicals, Inc.: address for,
  76:4, 84:72
Dumont Industries: address for, 55:60,
  70:79
Dunbar, Jean:
  on Church house, 78:79-81
  on raising finished walls, 58:62-66
Dunham, Rodger: ceramics by, 59:90
Dunham-Bush Inc.: heat pumps, 26:68
Dunkley, Don:
  on coffered ceilings, 75:36-40 (MFC)
  on floor framing, 19:54-60 (FRC)
  on hip and gable roofs, 10:65-69 (FRC)
  on hip roofs, 57:78-83 (CSH, MFC)

on plumb and line, 23:68-71 (FRC)
reviews Gross, 60:106
reviews layout tool, 21:20
on soffits, 63:69 (MFC)
Dunlap, Wayne A.: as joint author. *See* Wolfskill, Lyle A.
Dunleavy, Steve: on built-up cedar roofing, 58:67-71 (EF)
Dunn, Chris: on body strategies, 85:76-81
Dunning, Scott: on orchestrating disaster, 69:122
Duo-Fast Corp.:
address for, 75:72
framing nailers, reviewed, 56:52, 53, 54-55, 56, 57
nail gun, 25:47:74-75 (BK)
pneumatic tools, 15:53 (TB)
safety seminars by, 49:102
screw gun, reviewed, 85:70, 71
stapler, Model E electric, 2:52 (SH)
Duo-Therm: water-heating heat pump, 5:65
DuPont (E. I.) de Nemours & Co., Inc.:
address for, 19:12, 69:63 (REM)
Corian publications from, 27:47 (BK)
800-number for, 37:81
Freon hot-water system, 29:86-88
heat-resistant materials from, 24:82
Lucite, 10:33 (DWS)
Tedlar film of, 16:30
DuPont, Peter, and John Morrill:
Residential Indoor Air Quality and Energy Efficency, reviewed, 75:110
DuPree, Russell: on noise control, 58:54-57
Duprey, Kenneth: *Old Houses on Nantucket,* cited, 77:89
Durabond drywall filler 90: using, 23:61, 26:41 (FWS)
Duraco: power planes of, reviewed, 54:78-79
Duracote Corp.: Foylon, 8:30 (TFH)
Dura-Finish: for floors, 22:12
Dural International Corp.:
address for, 48:68
No-clamp contact cement, 36:69 (BK)
Duramem: source for, 40:32
DuraSeal floor finish: cited, 22:12, 33:12
Dura-Stilt Corp.: stilts from, 23:63 (FWS)
Durastone Corp.:
Durastone, 44:88
sheets, source for, 44:88
Duratherm Window Corp.:
Castlegate Thermal Entry Door, 6:60
teak windows, 35:34
Durbahn, Walter E., and Sundberg:
Fundamentals of Carpentry (2 vols.), 3:4
Duro Dyne Corp.: address for, 67:40 (EF)
Duro-Last: address for, 80:70

DUR-O-WAL, Inc.:
address for, 66:38 (SH)
joint-reinforcing product, 37:38
wall ties, source for, 41:39
Dursban: source for, 28:10
Dust:
OSHA standards on, booklet on, 58:90
plastic-bag collection of, 85:32
Dust masks:
as filters, 40:16
See also Respirators.
Dust-collection systems:
central house-cleaning, installing, 60:60-62
debris scoop for, 55:28
filter-fan, 48:24
in floor slab, 43:69 (TB)
for power planer, 71:24
for power tools, 54:77
for shop,
liner for, 60:26
small, 60:63
simple worksite, 83:28
See also Vacuums.
Dutch barn-house: mentioned, 10:26, 27
Dutch Thatched Roofing Co.: thatch, 39:90
Dutcher, William:
on Mullgardt house, 52:78-82
pot rack by, 81:88
remodels barrier-free house, 73:60-65
Dutt, Gautam: on gas furnaces, 22:18 (CSH)
Dwellings, Settlements, and Tradition: discussed, 49:102
Dwyer: address for, 52:106
Dyer, Sam: cabinet by, three-sided, 8:65, 11:34 (EEH)
Dyes: aniline, for color matches, 5:12
See also Stains.
Dykstra, Gerritt: house by, 80:40-45
Dynamit Nobel of America: Chem-Trete masonry sealer of, 20:12
Dyson, Arthur: house by, 57:52-57, 73:42-45 (EEH)
DYWIDAG Systems International USA, Inc.: rebar, threaded, 33:34 (CBS)

E

E & E Special Products: address for, 62:92
E. I. Syndrome, The (Rogers): mentioned, 49:6
EAC: *See* Air cleaners, electronic.
Eagle Industries, Inc.: address for, 65:96
Eagle Window and Door, Inc.:
address for, 55:79, 82:68
windows of, 60:48, 50 (FC)

Ear board: defined, 15:39-40 (EF)
Early American Society: *Architectural Treasures of Early America,* mentioned, 47:110-12
Early Domestic Architecture of Connecticut (Kelly):
cited, 40:33 (FWS), 49:43 (REM)
source for, 28:58 (TFH)
Early Nantucket and Its Whale House (Forman): cited, 77:89
Earth: temperatures of, 13:8
Earth and Sun Development Co.: mentioned, 34:37
Earth construction:
block, machines for, 28:80
cob, house of, 83:88-89
conferences on, 10:16-17, 28:80-81
in the East, 28:81
in France, 30:74-76
information on, 23:49-50
rammed-,
vs. adobe, 39:49
in Australia, 58:96
block machines for, 28:80
bond beams with, concrete, 11:24
books on, 27:84, 34:39, 67:96
books on, reviewed, 60:106
and cooling, design for, 63:18-20
course in, detailed, 67:96-98
design with, 10:16, 11:25, 39:48-51, 42:10 (FWS)
durability of, 10:16, 13:4, 6
finish for, 10:16, 11:23
framing of, 15:6-8
in France, 30:74-76
history of, 10:16, 11:21
information on, 23:49-50, 65:54
insulating, 34:37-38
partitions for, interior, 19:10
performances of, 34:37, 38, 39:51
process of, 10:16-17, 11:21-25, 15:10-12, 34:36-39
rot invulnerability of, 13:4, 15:6-8
and solar, 39:48-51 (FWS)
stuccoed, 30:74-76, 54:86 (TFH)
with tires, 60:120
walls with, plastered interior, 39:51
sheltered,
bermed, 45:56, 76-81, 88, 89, 77:50-54
books on, 3:60-61, 15:22, 16:14-16, 31:82, 65:106-108, 69:110
cautions for, 7:39 (DWS)
costs of, 16:53
design aid for, 40:29
for erratic climate, 29:28-33
on expansive clay, 6:55
ferro-cement, 44:112
Flexicore roof in, 25:71-72
foundations for, 7:36 (DWS), 29:28-31, 48:50-51
with fully integrated systems, 72:70-75 (EEH)

heat storage for, 7:37-38 (DWS), 29:28, 32, 33
information on, 65:55
insulating, 2:32-33 (EEH), 25:72, 29:28, 30, 32, 33
liability insurance for, 2:37
Mendocino-style, 52:74-77 (SH)
mortgages and, 2:12-13
on native materials, 71:36-41 (EEH)
need for, urgent, 73:4, 77:6
performance of, 7:38-39 (DWS), 16:53, 29:33
plenum floors in, 7:36 (DWS)
political correctness of, argued, 77:4-6
process of, 2:30-37 (EEH)
roofs for, 7:36-37 (DWS), 16:52, 29:29, 30, 31-32
sites for, 2:35, 7:35 (DWS)
skylights for, 7:37 (DWS), 40:30-31
Usonian, 3:20-27
ventilation for, 7:36 (DWS)
walls for, curved, 73:45 (EEH)
waterproofing for, 2:35-37, 16:52, 25:72, 29:12, 40:32
wiring for, hidden, 40:32
sprayed-earth system for, discussed, 71:104
straw-clay method of, 30:74
See also Adobe. Membranes.
Earth Manual, The (Margolin): cited, 50:85
Earth Ponds (Matson): cited, 7:43
Earth Press block machines: discussed, 28:80
Earth-sheltered houses: *See* Earth construction.
Earth Sheltered Housing Design (Barnard): mentioned, 25:71
Earth Sheltered Housing Design (Carmody and Sterling): reviewed, 26:14-16
Earth-Sheltered Residential Design Manual (Sterling, Fanan, and Carmody): reviewed, 16:14-16
Earth Systems Development Institute: address for, 30:39
exposition by, 28:30-81
Earth tubes: designing, 11:8
Earthbuilder: address for, 30:39
Earthbuilders' Encyclopedia, The (Tibbets):
cited, 67:96
reviewed, 60:106
Earthen Building Materials: 1982 conference, 10:16-17
Earthquake Hazards and Wood Frame Houses: source for, 29:38 (FRC)
Earthquake Research Center: on adobe brick, 34:86
Earthquake Resistant Design (Dowrick): source for, 29:38 (FRC)

Earthquakes:
and adobe block, reinforced, 34:86
books on, 29:38 (FRC)
bracing for, shear-wall, 85:57
building for, 63:102, 64:60-65 (MFC)
damage from, 29:34 (FRC)
danger from, areas of, 47:106
design for, information on, 65:52, 54
discussed, 40:45 (TFH)
forces in, analyzed, 64:61-63 (MFC)
foundations for, 73:79-80
concrete-pile, 82:78-80
retrofitted, 40:12
framing for,
steel, 74:58 (MFC)
timber, 40:43-45 (TFH)
joist blocking for, 29:37-38 (FRC)
map of, 64:100
nails for, 85:47
post-to-pier connections against, 31:4, 40:44 (TFH)
reinforcing against, 29:30-31
Research Center on, 34:86
retrofitting against, 29:34-38 (FRC)
roof sheathing for, 85:47
safety council on, 47:106
seismic anchors against, 43:48, 49 (FRC)
stucco in, 64:61 (MFC)
Earthship (Reynolds): reviewed, 69:110
Eastern Chem-Lac Corp.: address for, 67:75 (REM)
Eastfield Village: courses of, 8:14-15
Easton, David:
on French earthbuilding, 30:74-76
mentioned, 28:81
mobile sawmill of, 17:18
Rammed Earth Experience, The, 34:39
rammed-earth houses of, 11:21-25 19:10, 34:38, 39
on rammed-earth construction, 58:96
on sod roofs, 56:78-81
soil/cement floors by, 27:56-59
Easy Access Housing: address for, 77:110
Easyheat, Inc.: address for, 75:72
Easylink: using, 46:59-60
Eaton, Larry: solar houses by, 33:84
Eaves:
Arts-and-Crafts style, 80:66
defined, 10:63 (FRC)
glazed, 80:44, 58
latticed, 43:69 (TB)
venting, 52:50, 51 (TFH)
wide light-shielding, 80:79
EBCO: Pentron Work Lights of, reviewed, 50:94
Ebony: logs, source for, 29:58 (CSH)
Eck, Jeremiah:
on architectural reality, 80:24-26
on cottage building, 59:36-41 (SH)

Eckerman, Michael: stone masonry by, 82:88-89
Ecology:
book on, reviewed, 60:106
interior,
book on, 61:106
organization for, 60:102
See also Energy. Solar design.
Economic and Social History of New England 1620-1789 (Weeden): cited, 47:48 (EF)
Ecotope: address for, 71:48
Ecrates plywood: described, 36:89
Edelstein, Monte: mentioned, 29:33
Edging: for resin board, 84:40, 43
Edinger, J.: *Watching for the Wind,* 9:16
Edrington, David: on *A Pattern Language,* 36:51-55
Edwil Co.: address for, 56:39
Edwin Lutyens (Architectural Monographs): reviewed, 45:122
EEBA: *See* Energy Efficient Building Association.
Eemax Inc.: address for, 70:56 (EEH)
Effective Building Products:
Bentonize spray montmorillonite clay, 2:37
Waterstop-Plus gel montmorillonite clay, 2:36-37
Efflorescence:
danger of, 26:4, 32:4
preventing, 25:10
treating, 25:10, 32:4
Effron, Edward: *Planning and Designing Lighting,* reviewed, 54:106
Egee, Paul: bathroom by, 80:91
Eggert, Sebastian:
on cedar/basalt house, 8:22-27 (CBS)
on installing manufactured stairs, 39:44-48 (FWS)
Egypt: architecture of, book on, 47:110
Ehlers, Jake:
on houseboat, 12:68-71
on pattern shingling, 18:53-54
Ehrenhaft, George: on addition, 52:126
Eich, Bill: on permanent wood foundations, 68:62-66
Eicher, R. F.: on scrounging, 29:98
Eifler, John:
on Jacobs house, 81:78-82
on Usonian house, 80:46-49
Eighteenth-Century Houses of Williamsburg, The (Whiffen): reviewed, 43:102
Eklind: Allen wrenches, 12:51 (TB)
Ekstrom Carlson: plunge bits, 27:38 (TB)
Ekus, Lou: storage unit by, 85:94
Elco Industries, Inc.: address for, 41:57 (CBS)
Eldenwood Enterprises: address for, 62:94

Electric heating:
baseboard,
Danish, 31:77
vapor-barrier degrade behind, 22:18 (CSH)
costs of, 10:52 (SH)
heat film for, 34:68-69 (SH)
off-peak storage, 1:44, 45 (EEH)
radiant-panel, automated, 53:76
with solar design, 10:52 (SH)
in superinsulated houses, 22:18 (CSH)
Electrical Independence booklets (Copperfield): source for, 24:80
Electrical Independence Guidebook and Catalogue, The: source for, 24:80
Electricity:
amperage of,
figuring need for, 2:42, 43
and motor quality, 24:41 (TB)
bucket power station for, 83:28
centralizing, 52:14
codes for, 5:45
importance of, 2:42
cords for,
cold-resistant, 50:60
Velcro binders for, 81:28
demand for, figuring, 62:70-71
generators for, selecting, 74:16
grounding of, 83:6
line trenches for, 17:10
outlets for, painting around, 67:68
photovoltaic,
appliances for, 8:46-47, 24:80
catalogs of, 24:80-82
cells for, manufacture of, 72:75 (EEH)
center researching, 30:80
computer program for, 8:48
costs of, 8:48, 80 (FWS)
hydro, 69:43 (EEH)
information on, 65:52
inverters for, 24:80, 72:72-73 (EEH)
mounting, 72:73-74 (EEH)
publications on, 8:47, 12:72, 24:80-82
systems for, 8:46-47, 55-56, 72:72-74 (EEH)
systems for, and propane generator, 26:64 (CBS)
test house for, 72:70-75 (EEH)
unit for, 44:63, 49:72 (EEH)
vs. utility, 70:112
savings in, huge, 66:4
solar, catalog for, 52:100
switch for, transmitter-controlled, 80:98
systems for,
alternative, 69:43 (EEH)
emergency, 78:85
home, 68:106-108
hydroelectric home, 15:66-69
solar-battery, reviewed, 51:92
underground lines for, locating, 75:26-28
voltage of, defined, 2:43

water-power, units for, 64:12
wattage of, defined, 2:43
See also Energy. Extension Cords. National Electrical Code. Solar design. Wiring.
Electro Damp-Proofing, Ltd.: address for, 47:20
Electromagnetic fields: danger from, 82:20 (CSH)
Electro-osmosis waterproofing: book on, 47:20
Electroplating: *See* Coatings, solar.
Elements of Color, The (Itten): cited, 74:45 (EF)
Elephants: house in shape of, 71:128
Elevators:
exquisite handmade, 8:76
residential, 38:56
Elgar Products, Inc.: address for, 57:75 (FC)
Eli Townsend & Son, Inc.: address for, 53:89
Eljer Industries: address for, 70:56 (EEH)
Elkay Manufacturing Co.: address for, 80:100
Elke, Louaine Collier: on space efficiency, 53:43-45 (SH)
Elking, Bert: on sewage aggregate, 22:18 (CSH)
Elkins, Henry: block machines by, 28:80
Elkins, Stephen: on playhouse, 61:43-45 (SH)
Ellerman-Kreun house: picture of, 5:68
Elliott, Cecil D.: *Technics and Architecture,* reviewed, 82:112
Ellipses:
for cones, building, 8:50-51 (FWS)
drawing, 5:25 (DWS), 8:50-51 (FWS), 34:58 (FRC), 35:14, 54:57
See also Circles.
Ellis, George:
Modern Practical Joinery, cited, 54:71 (REM)
Modern Practical Stairbuilding and Handrailing, reviewed, 64:110
Ellis, Harvey: work of, 36:28-29 (CSH)
Ellis, Jeffrey: on shingled solar house, 12:64-67 (EEH)
Ellison, David: ceramics by, 59:88-89
Elmer's Concrete Bonder: source for, 43:10
Elmer's Midget Helper brick cutter: reviewed, 61:92
Elmroth, Arne: on Swedish superinsulation, 22:18 (CSH)
Elon, Inc.: address for, 79:22
Elu: bought by Black and Decker, 43:92
Emary, A. B.: *Handbook of Carpentry and Joinery,* cited, 50:69 (FC)
Emerson, Ron: mentioned, 29:53

Emerson and Cuming, Inc.:
address for, 70:49
casting resins of, 1:39 (FWS)
Emerson Electric Co.: address for, 57:86 (EF)
Emery, Jared: on hanging doors, 8:34-36 (DWS)
Emglow Products Corp.:
address for, 49:87
compressors, 15:51 (TB)
Emhart Corp.:
Bostik 2000, 32:48 (BK)
Para-bolt anchor bolts, 29:34 (FRC)
Empire Comfort Systems: address for, 65:64 (SH)
Empire Level Manufacturing Corp.: address for, 58:45
Empire Molding Co., Inc.: address for, 68:79 (FC)
Empire Stove Co.: gas heater 235, 34:69 (SH)
Empro Manufacturing Co.: shunt resistor, 8:47
Emrie, Paul: newel cap by, 55:65
Emulsa-Bond Stir-in Bonding Primer: for stucco, 16:8, 18:8
Encyclopedia of Architecture (Wilkes): reviewed, 50:108
Encyclopedia of Associations: coverage of, 23:48, 51
Encyclopedia of Wood, The: reviewed, 64:112
End grain: sealant for, 72:41
EnerComp. Inc.: address for, 71:48, 76:39
Enercon Inductries Ltd.: heat-recovery ventilators, 9:59
Energ-G Block Corp.: address for, 76:39
Energy:
alternative,
books on, 62:71
source catalogs for, 52:100-102
source for, 69:43 (EEH)
appropriate technology for, books on, 64:110-12
books on, 23:51, 33:56, 37:88, 60:51 (FC), 61:106, 64:112, 72:108
centers for, 61:77 (EF), 69:100, 74:104, 106
"customer technology," 72:100
codes on, 56:36, 65:102
classes in, 5:45
conference on, 56:110
course in, 1981, 2:64
demand for, figuring, 62:70-71
efficiency,
analyzing, 33:56, 57
associations for, 47:102, 60:51 (FC), 64:100, 102
batteries for, 62:68, 69-71
books on, 67:104, 70:120, 76:118, 81:114
building details for, 29:68-72
Canadian demonstration of, 47:104-106

Canadian program and, 34:86
centers for, 53:108-10, 61:77 (EF), 71:112, 81:104, 106, 83:88
computer programs for, 34:68, 86 (SH), 37:88
design for, 42:60-63, 66:4, 81:104-106
design for, competition in, 72:100
Florida programs in, 66:22-24
investments in, formula for, 74:4-6
landscaping for, brochure on, 82:106
Middle Eastern tactics for, 47:110
myths concerning, 33:56-57
newsletter on, 84:124
product list of, 71:112
recycling strategies for, 83:108-10
retrofits for, 25:82-83, 65:18
of solar house, 84:88
tax credits for, 2:12
technical aid on, free, 56:42
utility programs in, 64:104-106, 70:112
Washington standards of, 42:60-63
through water-saving devices, 84:82-84
window labels for, 78:104
generators for, 62:69
heat-loss areas for, 65:18
light-bulb saving, 65:102, 74:104
recycling, programs for, 69:102
renewable, information on, 65:52, 55
resource addresses on, 30:80
savers, award-winning, 71:106
and stack effect, 33:56
waste of, through air handlers, 67:98
water-power, 62:68-69, 71
    information on, 65:52
    units for, 64:12
wind, 62:69
    information on, 65:52
    inquiry and referral service for, 33:90
    publications on, 1:66
See also Appliances. Ecology. Electricity. Insulation. Solar design.
Energy Business Association: 1987 conference of, 46:96
Energy Conservation Features Inherent in Older Homes: source for, 23:48
Energy Conservation in New Building Design (ASHRAE): coverage of, 5:45
Energy Crafted Homes: energy-efficiency certification program of, 68:100-102
Energy Development Inc.: Vent-Aire EC20 heating-cooling-ventilation system, 33:84
Energy-Efficient Building: source for, 32:90
Energy Efficient Building Association (EEBA):
    address for, 65:52
    conference, 1986, 33:82-84 (TB)
    confers award, 33:84
    described, 28:82
    retrofit contest, 1987, 33:84

Key to books:

(BK)   Building Baths and Kitchens
(CBS)   Building with Concrete, Brick and Stone
(CSH)   Craftsman-Style Houses
(DWS)   Building Doors, Windows and Skylights
(EEH)   Energy-Efficient Houses
(EF)   Exterior Finishing
(FC)   Finish Carpentry
(FRC)   Frame Carpentry
(FWS)   Building Floors, Walls and Stairs
(MFC)   More Frame Carpentry
(REM)   Remodeling
(SH)   Small Houses
(TB)   Tools for Building
(TFH)   Timber-Frame Houses

Energy-Efficient Florida Home Building: reviewed, 56:110
Energy-Efficient Home Construction: source for, 32:90
Energy-Efficient Windows Program: publications of, 1:66
Energy-Guard Door: source for, 6:60
Energy Information Directory: source for, 23:51
Energy, Mines and Resources Canada: R-2000 program of, 34:86
Energy Savings Solutions Inc.: address for, 79:110
Energy Systems and Design: address for, 64:12
Energy Technology Laboratories: address for, 84:84
Energy-Wise Home Buyer: described, 4:62
Enerjee: address for, 59:102
Enermatrix, Inc.: heat-recovery ventilators, 34:34 (DWS)
Ener-Quip Inc.: heat-recovery ventilators, 34:34 (DWS)
Enertex Systems, Inc.: stress-skin panels, 24:59
Engel, Heino: *Measure and Construction of the Japanese House,* reviewed, 34:92
Engineered Components, Inc.: Amer-X6 roofing, 24:43
Engineering Development, Inc.: address for, 63:85 (EEH), 73:70 heat-recovery ventilators, 34:34 (DWS)
Engineering sites: records of, 52:8-12
England, John: on job-site foot injuries, 79:56-57
Engleke, Jim: designs remodel, 18:41
English architecture: book on, 45:122
English Cottages (Evans and Green): reviewed, 29:90
English Historic Carpentry (Hewett): cited, 15:4

Enner-Corp Management Ltd.: Ennerex heat exchanger, 25:53
Ennerex heat exchanger: mentioned, 25:53
Entablatures:
    constructing, 6:24-25, 11:39-40 (DWS)
    defined, 20:60 (FWS)
    Greek Revival, 1:49
    stone-simulating, 9:22-24
    See also separate elements.
Entergy Entry Door: source for, 6:60
Enterprise Companies, The: vapor-barrier paints, 9:8, 19:68
Entry Door System: source for, 6:60
Entryways:
    airlock, knock-down, 70:56 (EEH)
    arched,
        angular, 69:83
        chamfered stone, 57:73 (FC)
        laminated, 29:56-57 (CSH)
        plaster, 45:42, 43
        roof over, 7:50-51, 28:73, 74, 75
        stone, 52:48-49 (TFH)
    Arts-and-Crafts style, 59:83, 84 (CSH), 80:42
    barrel-vaulted, 53:63
    books on, 1:49, 54:68 (REM)
    bridges for, 52:72, 73, 79:80
    canopy for, 72:88
    casing for, 3:17 (DWS)
    for chapel, 64:53
    Colonial, 63:45, 46
    color for, 74:42 (EF)
    corner, 38:25-26, 27 (EEH)
    corner posts for, heavy, 80:59
    cornices for, 1:59, 3:16, 17 (DWS)
    designing, 3:14, 15 (DWS), 11:36 (DWS)
    diagram of, 11:38 (DWS)
    doors for, 3:14, 15-17 (DWS)
        double-, history of, 11:36, 38 (DWS)
    Edwardian, concrete and plinth, 59:51 (SH)
    entablature for, 11:39-40 (DWS)
    flat-roofed building-supported, 63:41
    formal, details of, 3:14 (DWS)
    framing for, exposed, 83:84
    gabled,
        with cornice return, 77:49 (EF)
        French-doored, 44:74-75
        Japanese, 68:72 (EF)
        multi-, 64:79
    gate for, in chain-link hedge, 19:33
    Greek Revival, 1:48, 50, 54:68-71 (REM)
    for handicapped, 53:71, 73:62
    headers for, fretwork, 68:38, 40
    hip-roofed, overlapping, 48:49
    Japanese simple, 45:74 (CSH)
    latticed quarter-circle, 45:32, 33, 34, 35
    moldings for, 11:37 (DWS)
    mosaic for, 59:88
    needs for, 52:63
    overhang, shingled, 57:53, 54

pedestals for, 11:37 (DWS)
pediments for, 11:40-41 (DWS)
    carved, 75:59
    with columns and pilasters, 77:86, 87
pilasters for, 3:16-17 (DWS), 11:37 (DWS)
recessed, 45:61 (SH), 51:14, 55:20
skylight for, pyramidal acrylic, 73:59
for small house, 74:55
supports for, peeled-post, 43:77, 79
Victorian restored, 4:20
walls for,
    curved, 27:49
    extended, 38:25-26, 27, 108 (EEH)
Warm Door, 6:60
over water, 80:62
wing for, new, 30:32-39
wood for, 3:15 (DWS)
Envelope houses: See Double-envelope
houses.
Environment Air Ltd.: heat-recovery
ventilators, 34:34 (DWS)
Environmental Action Resource Service:
services of, 23:51
Environmental Builder: source for,
62:106
Environmental Building News:
reviewed, 84:124
*Environmental Hazards in Residential
Construction:* source for, 55:108
Environmental Noise Control (Magreb):
source for, 35:63
Environmental Outfitters: address for,
73:67
Environmental Protection Agency (EPA):
air-change studies of, 1:12
architectural coating standards of,
    49:14
on asbestos, 24:83
on chlordane, 5:12
and fully halogenated
    chlorofluorocarbons, 49:102
radon directives of, 70:8
woodstove rulings of, 49:98
Environmental Research Associates:
Thorn water heater, 12:18 (CSH)
Environmental Resource Guide (AIA):
discussed, 65:100-102
EPDM:
acrylic glazing with, 10:32, 33 (DWS)
gaskets of, 10:32, 33 (DWS)
sources for, 2:37
See also Membranes.
Epoca Co.: Epoc 5 epoxy paint, 27:12
*Epoxies for Wood Repairs in Historic
Buildings* (Phillips and Selwyn):
cited, 62:41 (EF)
source for, 16:21 (CSH)
Epoxy:
capsules, for foundations, 73:73
casting with, 1:39 (FWS)

cold-molding, 70:48
for concrete, 41:14
for concrete bonding, 4:9, 15:12-14
and concrete coatings, compatibility
    with, 40:12
construction, described, 70:45-49
grout, 77:42, 43
wood-consolidant, 16:20-21 (CSH)
    described, 70:45-49
    for porch work, 81:46
    as restoration material, 61:68
    for rot repair, 48:68-69, 72:41
    source for, 81:51
See also Fillers. Glue.
Epoxy Repairs for Exterior Wood
(Leeke): source for, 70:49
E&R Manufacturing Co.: brick cutter,
reviewed, 61:92
Ergenics: Maxorb black foil, 10:51 (SH)
Erling Anderson: baseboard heating,
31:77
Ernest, Ethan: corrugated plywood by,
36:89
Ernest Co.: Ecrates plywood, 36:89
Ernst, Scott: on brick mosaics, 64:80-83
Esherick, Wharton:
furniture by, 21:38-40, 41
house by, 21:35-43
staircase by, 34:8
Essenco Inc.: insulated E-block, 31:39-40,
41 (CBS)
Estoban Corp.: address for, 70:78
Estwing:
framing hammers, 23:32, 33 (TB)
rock picks, as slater's hammers, 27:16
ESWA heat film: installing, 34:68-69 (SH)
Etcon: ground-fault circuit-interrupter
testers, 9:4
ETEC:
distance-estimating device, 39:92
ultrasonic tape, reviewed, 78:54-55
E-Tech: water heater, 5:65
Ethylene propylene diene monomer:
See EPDM.
Euclid Chemical Co.: address for, 58:59
(CSH)
Eugene Toy and Hobby: mail-order
materials from, 22:51 (FRC)
Eurocal: address for, 80:67
Euroglass Corp: glass block, French, 37:49
(DWS)
Evan Pollitt Architect: address for, 53:89
Evans, Tony, and Candida Lycett Green:
English Cottages, reviewed, 29:90
Evans Rule Co.: chalklines, 25:69 (TB)
Evaporative cooler: *See* Swamp cooler.
Evelyn Nesbit and Stanford White
(Mooney): source for, 37:53
Everseal Manufacturing Co., Inc.:
address for, 47:87
Ever-Straight Door: source for, 6:60

Ewald, Richard: on Arctic building, 68:100
Ewen, Ted: on porch addition, 6:22-25
Ewenstein, Neal: as joint author. *See*
Wade, Alex.
Exact Level and Tool Co.: address for,
58:45
Excalibur Hand Tools Ltd.: address for,
58:45
Excalibur Machine and Tool Co.:
address for, 74:76
Excavations:
hose water-power for, 2:5
under house, Bobcat for, 12:46-47
Exolite:
butyl tape for, 10:32 (DWS)
glazing for, 17:63, 65 (DWS), 34:4
heat-forming, 10:30-33 (DWS)
long lengths of, 31:33 (DWS)
for octagonal greenhouse, 32:35
skylights, 2:31 (EEH)
source for, 10:33 (DWS)
for water walls, 26:57
See also Caulk. EPDM. Glazing: acrylic.
Expanko Cork Co., Inc.: address for,
52:108
Experience Book (Wilkins): source for,
24:82
Experiencing Architecture (Rasmussen):
reviewed, 45:116
Export Hamel International: address for,
53:94
Exposed Cedar (Western Wood Products
Association): cited, 47:16
Extension cords:
bucket power station for, 83:28
carry-case for, 34:14
for groud-fault protection systems, 8:4
heavy-duty, making, 76:30
length of, proper, 85:120
plug locks for, 42:88
plugs with, right-angle, 83:30
recall of, 71:106
storing, 76:92-94
straps for, making, 82:28
winders for, 57:14
Extension offices: county, services of,
23:51
Exterior Finishing: source for, 23:50
**Exterior Insulation Manufacturing
Association:** information from, 31:41
(CBS)
Exterior Wood in the South (from
Southern Forest Products Association):
cited, 84:4
Exterior Wood in the South (from U. S.
Forest Products Laboratory): cited,
83:45
Eyedroppers: uses for, 3:7
Eyes:
sunglasses for, for cold-weather work,
50:62
See also Safety.

Faber-Castell Corp.: drafting tools, 26:58 (TB)
Fabric:
Arts-and-Crafts style, source for, 54:100
dacron translucent, 50:49
Scottish, source for, 54:106
Facades: improving lines of, 12:38-39, 40
Fafnir: router guide bearing, 13:12
Fagus grandifolia: See Beech.
Failsafe Systems: plumbing fittings, 27:71 (CBS)
Fairbanks house: construction of, 13:23-27 (TFH)
Fairey, Philip: on air-handler losses, 67:98
Fairmont Foundry Co., Inc.: work of, 16:44
Falk gaslights: source for, 14:31
Fallingwater (Kaufmann): reviewed, 45:122
Family rooms: New American, 26:75-77 (SH)
Fanan, William: as joint author. *See* Sterling, Ray.
Fancy Cut Shingles: address for, 46:75 (BK)
Fanlights: book on, reviewed, 64:110
Fanlights (Gray and Sambrook): reviewed, 64:110
Fans:
destratification, 21:58 (EEH)
mount for, quieting, 44:24
over-coil, source for, 63:85 (EEH)
whole-house, use of, 5:15
Farah, Tony: newel post by, 71:89
Farallones Institute:
Integral Urban Houses, The, reviewed, 6:58
provides design aid, 40:29
Farm buildings:
as house potential, 15:64-65
information on, 23:50
Farmer (W. D.): plans from, 53:87, 89
Farmer's Home Administration (FmHA):
construction information from, 23:49
financing by, 4:14, 5:14, 10:48, 52 (SH)
Information for Contractors, 10:52 (SH)
Farmhouses:
classical, 38:84-89
remodeling of, 12:46-49
Farmline Thermoply: mentioned, 2:52 (SH)
Farmstead Planning Handbook: source for, 23:50
Farrell and Thurrell Joiners: house by, 47:44-47 (TFH)

Farrow, H. William, Jr.: on radios, 62:102-104
Farrow, John: workshop of, 8:75
Fasca Inc.: Insul-Flue, 34:8
Fascia:
beveling, 63:69 (MFC)
boards for, angled, 66:57, 59 (SH)
color for, 74:42 (EF)
compound-curved, laminating, 44:68 (FRC), 73:43, 45 (EEH)
cuts for, double matching, 19:14
decorative projections for, 81:50-51
defined, 10:63 (FRC), 20:60 (FWS)
described, 10:63 (FRC)
freestanding, for screened porch, 72:82, 83 (REM)
grooving, for soffits, 63:69 (MFC)
hanging, jig for, 53:26
stepped, 45:58
sub-,
beveled, 68:76 (MFC)
loadbearing, 75:83, 84
vented, double-board, 45:85, 87
Fas'N'Go: reviewed, 57:94
Fast, Victor: stain by, 32:27 (CSH)
Fast Products: sling by, reviewed, 56:92
Fast Track Estimating for Remodelers (Northwest Construction Software): reviewed, 83:122
Faswal: address for, 76:39
Fathy, Hassan: *Natural Energy and Vernacular Architecture,* 47:110
Faucets:
aerating, 1:62
ceramic temperature-sensing, 75:92-94
custom-cast bronze, 26:80 (BK)
single-control, double-swivel, 1:62
wall-mount, with sprayer, 27:45, 47 (BK)
water-saving, 61:66, 84:82-84
Faulkner, Howard:
on superinsulated houses, 19:22
on superinsulated saltbox, 34:67-69 (SH)
at superinsulation conference, 22:18 (CSH)
Favour, Jock: gate by, 52:90
Faxon, Tom: trim by, 49:91
Fay Jones (Ivy): reviewed, 78:110
F-Chart Software:
address for, 71:49
hot-water system sizing, information on, 29:88
Fearn, Richard: on backyard Edwardian, 59:48-51 (SH)
Fechin, Nicolai: house by, 25:26-31
Fechin Institute: mentioned, 25:31
Federal architecture:
books on, 1:49
cornices on, 1:59
defined, 1:49
details of, 20:59, 61-62 (FWS)
moldings in, 31:46, 47 (FWS)

Federal Home Loan Bank Board: mentioned, 2:8, 10
Federal Home Loan Mortgage Corp. (Freddie Mac): mentioned, 2:13
Federal Housing Administration (FHA):
FHA Pole House Construction, source for, 15:37, 23:49
programs of, 4:14
rack-resistance standards of, 40:6
Federal National Mortgage Association (Fannie Mae): rehabilitation mortgages of, 4:14
Feet: injuries to, treating, 79:56-57
Feierabend, Peter: louver jig by, 37:28-29 (BK)
Fein Power Tools, Inc.:
cordless drills, 35:41 (TB)
random-orbit sanders, 64:96, 77:69, 70, 71
screw guns, 34:43, 44-45 (TB)
VSR drill, reviewed, 82:36-41
Feirer, John L., and Gilbert Hutchings: *Carpentry and Building Construction,* reviewed, 35:71 (TB)
Feirer, Mark:
on Avonite, 32:82
on beads for, corner, 46:90
on chateau, 65:120
on columns, 69:88-89
on doors, 46:84-85
on Florida Solar Energy Center, 30:80
on glass-block spacers, 37:81
on heat-recovery ventilators, 23:80-82
on Idea farm, 62:106
on information sources, 23:48-51
on insulating foundation forms, 76:36-41
on job-site safety, 34:51-55 (TB)
on laminated-veneer lumber, 50:40-45 (MFC)
on literacy program, 65:102
on making models, 22:50-53 (FRC)
on NAHB convention, 39:90-92
on new products, 36:89, 44:88-89, 52:108-10, 66:102, 106, 67:90
on NFPA, 64:106
on Norman Carver, 39:70-74
on redwood association, 33:90
reviews books, 33:88, 44:94
reviews cable cutter, 55:94-96
reviews CAREIRS, 33:90
reviews code book, 46:104
reviews concrete-block book, 46:104
reviews *Construction Index,* 46:104
reviews dictionaries, 47:112
reviews drywall book, 70:120
reviews *Habitat News,* 36:94
reviews Hoosier book, 43:102
reviews HUD book, 32:86
reviews HUD USER, 36:92
reviews Lander, 34:92
reviews Le Corbusier book, 43:102
reviews Lewis, 34:92

reviews Lumpkins, 43:102
reviews NCAT, 32:90
reviews *Old-House* book, 31:82
reviews *Palladio Guide, The,* 32:86
reviews plastic block, 62:92
reviews pocket guide, 43:102
reviews Polycutter, 43:92
reviews *Right-to-Know,* 62:114
reviews *Shelter,* 62:114
reviews trim book, 31:82
reviews Victorian paint book, 43:102
reviews *Whole Earth Review,* 30:78
reviews *WoodHeat,* 30:78
on SHC-BRC publications, 29:92
on steel-framing supplies, 32:69 (FRC)
on stone working, 37:56-61
on sunblock, 46:90
on teahouses, 44:82-83
on U.S. FPL, 37:84
on Victorian modern, 31:66-71
on WWPA, 31:84
Feist, William:
on exterior finishes, 27:54-55
on siding, 83:44-45
Fejes, Mark: house by, 19:69-71 (EEH)
Feldman, Pattie: reviews computer
software, 83:122
Feldman, Russell: on Canadian
bargeboards, 76:86-87
Felker Operations: address for, 70:59
Felt, builder's: *See* Builder's paper.
Feltner family: stone company of, 37:56-61
Fences:
balustrade for, 25:75
of boards, horizontal mitered, 66:2
cement-bonded particleboard, 70:63-65
(EEH)
finish for, 25:76
gallery of, 51:86-87
installing, 25:76, 77
moldings for, 24:74-75
paint illusions with, 46:26
posts for,
caps for, 56:73
hollow, 25:73-74
rotted, splinting, 10:14
slatted, 24:80
urns for, 25:76
Victorian-style wood, 28:49, 53 (FWS)
Fences (machine):
for housed rabbets, 77:30
router, adjustable infeed, 55:40-41 (FC)
Fenestra Insulated Door: source for, 6:60
Feng-shui (Rossbach): reviewed, 45:116
Ferguson, Robin: on double-helix stair,
42:45-49 (FWS)
Ferrell, Douglass:
on building windows, 41:41-43 (DWS)
on lumberyards, 31:51-53
on tool bags, 42:64-67 (TB)

Key to books:

(BK)	Building Baths and Kitchens
(CBS)	Building with Concrete, Brick and Stone
(CSH)	Craftsman-Style Houses
(DWS)	Building Doors, Windows and Skylights
(EEH)	Energy-Efficient Houses
(EF)	Exterior Finishing
(FC)	Finish Carpentry
(FRC)	Frame Carpentry
(FWS)	Building Floors, Walls and Stairs
(MFC)	More Frame Carpentry
(REM)	Remodeling
(SH)	Small Houses
(TB)	Tools for Building
(TFH)	Timber-Frame Houses

Ferro-cement:
armatures for, 13:50, 52, 53 (CBS), 50:47-
48
association for, 50:49
beam of, circlar, 25:60
finish for, 50:49
house of, 44:112
mentioned, 20:10
mix for, 13:50-52 (CBS), 50:48-49
publications on, 50:49
R-value of, 20:10
urethane foam with, 50:49
See also Concrete.
Ferrocement Materials and
Applications: cited, 50:49
Fetchko, Joe: on site-cast lintels, 74:50-51
FHA: *See* Federal Housing Administration.
Financing.
FHA Pole House Construction: source
for, 15:37, 23:49
FHP Manufacturing Division: heat
pumps, 26:68
Fiber optics: for lighting, Japanese, 51:96
Fiberboard:
asphalt-impregnated, 19:68, 48:69
association for, 67:81
cart for, reviewed, 81:92
dust from, 67:80-81
edge treatment for, 71:72
formaldehyde-free, 73:70
source for, 67:81
gypsum, discussed, 64:92-94
medium-density, formaldehyde in, 22:16
for paneling, 71:72
for shelving, 71:72
uses of, 67:80
Fiberboard Surface Bonding Cement:
source for, 12:37 (CBS)
Fiberglas Canada Inc.: address for, 8:6,
46:72, 48:68

Fiberglass:
avoiding, 46:70-73, 73:67
casting of, 5:39
fabrication of, 34:72-73
HVAC unit, 33:84
jigsaw blades for, 33:60 (TB)
1950s design in, 34:71-75
panels of,
flexible, 27:63
source for, 63:54 (REM), 70:56 (EEH)
rewettable cloth, 22:4
rice-paper, simulated, 39:74
shingles of, textured, 24:50 (FRC)
as shower pan, disadvantages of, 32:46
(BK)
troubles with, 42:110
See also Insulation.
Fibermesh, Inc.: address for, 48:67, 63:82
(EEH)
FibreCem Corp.: address for, 82:14
Ficam pesticide: using, 6:52-53
Fiebiger P. A., Inc.: work by, 16:44
Field (G. L.) Manufacturing Co.:
Dec-Klips, 35:90
Field Guide to American Architecture, A
(Rifkind): reviewed, 2:62
Field Guide to American Houses, A
(McAlester): reviewed, 31:82, 45:120-22
Fields Corp.: address for, 65:58 (EF)
Fieroh, Len: on Oak Park, 56:82-87
Fierro, Bernard: mentioned, 32:34
Files:
for plastic-laminate, 75:64
for renovation, 12:51 (TB)
saw, 20:71 (TB)
Fillers:
applying, 42:56 (DWS)
auto-body, 35:14
avoiding, 73:67
colorants for, 48:77
colored, making, 20:14, 21:14, 48:77
crazy glue,
and baking soda, 65:43
and sawdust, 65:43-44
epoxy, 55:87, 70:47, 49
for end gaps, 55:87
for floors, 14:12
recommended, 30:57 (DWS)
spackling compound for, 30:57 (DWS),
71:72
See also Putty.
Fillion, Deborah: on fierce-faced door,
40:100
Fillmore Design Group: address for,
53:89
Filon Products: address for, 63:54 (REM)
Filter fabric:
fiberglass, draining, 29:12
for foundations, 53:49 (SH)

nylon, 73:68
qualities of, 50:85
for underground drainage, 2:37, 18:4, 40:63 (CBS)
Filters: for air quality, 5:15
Financing:
adjustable (AML), 5:16
All-Savers Certificates and, 6:16
Chicago hotline on, 3:63
construction estimation cost for, 4:42-43
of contract sale, 2:10
deeds of trust for,
first, 2:10
second, 2:10
wraparound, 2:10
earth-sheltered houses and, 2:13
for energy-efficient houses, 2:13, 4:14
FHA-insured loans for, 2:13, 10:48 (SH), 26:34
first-home incentives for, 4:14
FmHA loans for, 4:14
HUD-insured loans for, 2:13
land-lease, 2:10
lease-purchase, 2:10
loans for, 203(K), 76:70-71
mortgage revenue bonds for, 4:13-14
for owner-building, 59:14
for owner-contracting, 4:10-13
from pension funds, 4:14
Sears, Roebuck 1920s, 28:45
See also Mortgages.
Fine Homebuilding: design competition of, 75:102
Fine Paints of France: Ripolin paint, reviewed, 61:90-92
Finger joints: *See* Joinery.
Fingernails: smashed, treating, 79:57
Finials: exterior, metal, 43:80-81
Finish work:
contracting, 10:49 (SH)
nail guns for, 15:49, 50, 52, 53 (TB)
See also Trim.
Finishes:
alkyd, alcohol-resistant, 56:86
bleaching, 52:67
brightening, 50:18-20
clear, 59:56 (CSH)
sanding, 48:77
for decks, 72:41
drip-catching cuffs for, 41:14
for end grain, 36:12
exterior, 1:6, 3:8, 6:23, 27:75, 76, 50:88 (CSH), 51:49 (EF), 81:46, 47
book on, 50:20
choosing, 27:54-55
clear, 48:73 (SH), 73:75
clear, problems with, 51:53, 69:43 (EEH)
composite, 54:14
oil, 51:40 (CSH), 52:66, 68:72 (EF)
publication on, 23:50

floor,
paint for, thinned, 49:62 (SH)
polyurethane, problems with, 14:12
fuel oil as, 50:18
glazed, 60:78-79
interior,
clear types of, 48:75
oil, 51:45
sunlight-resistant, 85:75
water-resistant, 47:22
for ironwork, 75:78
Japanese-style, 43:31-32, 33 (CSH)
for kitchens, 9:38 (BK), 47:67, 67:73, 75 (REM)
lacquer, 9:38 (BK)
catalytic sprayed, 77:79 (REM)
dye and, 59:50-51 (SH)
for interiors, discussed, 48:75
nontoxic, sources for, 67:90-92
repair for, 45:53 (CSH)
sanding, 48:77
spraying, 48:77-78
water-based, using, 81:76
latex, watered-down, 33:52 (SH)
life of, 27:55
linseed-oil mixture, 34:50
for log houses, 14:53
exterior, 66:77
interior, 66:77
nontoxic, 44:41 (SH)
information on, 67:90, 92
sources for, 67:90-92
oil, on rags, house burning from, 27:94
oil, tinted, 69:40, 43 (EEH)
oil/varnish, 68:39
on oily woods, 22:12
penetrating-oil, 2:6, 9, 62:76
applying, 27:55
choosing, 27:54, 55
coloring, 67:58
and lacquer, 58:41 (REM)
maintenance of, 67:58
rosewood-oil, 37:29 (BK)
for teak, 22:12
restoration of, restraint with, 19:4
scrubbable, 42:30 (CSH)
sealer-over-glaze, 59:50-51 (SH)
shellac,
lightening, 56:86
nontoxic, sources for, 67:90-92
ship-quality, 38:45
stilt aids for, 32:16
for stone, 55:87
teak oil, using, 22:12
toxicity of, 10:10
for treated lumber, 55:18-20, 63:64 (MFC), 77:104-108
tung oil, 17:64 (DWS), 22:12, 33:12, 73:68, 70
applying, 73:70
white tint for, 31:27 (CSH)

turpentine-alcohol, over old paint, 29:89
urethane, 69:54
nonyellowing, 75:49 (REM)
and tung oil, 70:91
varnish, 7:6, 14:53, 38:45
acrylic, 44:41 (SH)
alkyd, sanding, 48:77
alkyd, spraying, 48:75, 77-78
alkyd-resin, mentioned, 8:6
avoiding, 73:67
brushing, 48:78
design without, 46:70-73
over epoxy, 70:48
linseed-modified alkyd, 56:86
marine, exterior, 50:88 (CSH)
marine, over teak, 22:12
nontoxic, sources for, 67:90-92
polyurethane, 9:38, 14:35 (BK)
polyurethane, marine two-part, 19:35 (DWS)
polyurethane, and sanding sealer, 8:6
polyurethane satin, 47:67
polyurethane, over softwood, 14:12
polyurethane, spraying, 48:75, 78
polyurethane, over teak, 22:12
polyurethane, for tile, 1:55
polyurethane, tinting, 42:30 (CSH)
respirator for, 48:74
sequence for, 48:74
spar, source for, 72:62
spraying, 48:75-78
stilt aids for, 32:16
storage life of, extending, 71:26
two-part boat, 19:35 (DWS)
water-based,
applying, 85:62-63
interior, 69:54, 75:84
water-repellent, 50:18-20, 63:64 (MFC)
wax,
for concrete, 66:86
and oil, applying, 67:58
source for, 66:45
for tile, 67:76 (REM)
wax/turpentine/oil, 20:78
wood-floor, 3:58, 4:20, 7:6 (EEH), 13:47 (FWS), 14:12, 22:12, 33:12, 35:77, 48:73 (SH), 61:54 (SH), 77:88, 79:87
color-stability tests for, 67:52-53
courses in, 69:100
Craftsman, 36:26-27 (CSH)
for fir, heavy-duty, 65:16-18
penetrating-oil, 67:55, 77:88
polyurethane, disadvised, 33:12
refinishing, 56:86
safety with, 72:4-6
Swedish, 14:12, 22:12, 36:42-45 (FWS), 67:55
Swedish, over end-grain blocks, 36:12
Swedish, on oily woods, 22:12
for teak, 22:10-12

tung oil, 33:12, 73:68, 70
urethane as, moisture-cured, 67:53-54
urethane as, oil-modified, 67:54
urethane as, water-based, 67:54-55
urethane-tung oil, 70:91
varnish, 7:6
water-based, 83:87, 85:61-63
water-based vs. solvent-, 49:14
See also Paint. Sanding sealer.
Sandpaper. Sealants. Sealers.
Sprayers. Stains. Wood
preservatives.
Finishes on Metals: source for, 32:6
Finishing Touch, The: source for, 37:59
Finishing Wood Interiors: source for,
37:84
Finnish masonry heaters: *See* Masonry
stoves.
Fir *(Abies* spp.):
color matching, 48:78
decay resistance of, 63:63 (MFC)
managed forests of, 47:43
nature of, 17:8, 40:69 (FRC)
span capability of, 33:43 (FWS)
for timber framing, 26:10, 30:6
Fir and Hemlock Door Association: tests
of, 6:62
Fire:
board impervious to, 70:63 (EEH)
damage from,
on oily rags, 27:94
professionals in, 4:18
restoration after, 4:16-20
electrician-caused, punishment for,
69:100
extinguishers, types of, discussed, 58:91
house impervious to, 66:52
prevention of,
association for, 62:104, 64:106
books on, 31:71, 62:104
codes for, 5:44, 37:4, 69:76-78
for double-envelopes, 25:6
drywall for, 81:43
and faulty smoke detectors, recall of,
72:100
floor planks for, 47:87
for job site, 60:4
Oakland (CA), information on, 72:100
for old inn, 50:65
planning for, 75:4
for shingles, treatments for, 77:16
wood resistant to, 33:90
See also Blocking: fire. Building codes.
Ladders. Lightning. National Fire
Prevention Code. National Fire
Protection Association. Smoke
detectors. Sprinkler systems.
Fire Drum Corp.: fireplace of, 3:59 (EEH)
Fire stops: *See* Blocking: fire.

Firepits:
building, 9:45
suspended chimney for, 18:70, 71
Fireplaces:
adobe, 5:47, 25:26-29
air ducts to,
danger in, 69:76
need of, 28:82
angled stepped, 31:24, 25, 27 (CSH)
arched,
fashioning, 48:36
with flanking cabinet, 80:64
stone, 15:76, 77 (CSH)
Arts-and-Crafts style, 52:78, 80, 82:85, 86
attic installation of, 21:28
block, 20:54, 55, 56 (CBS)
sandblasted, 27:52, 66:38 (SH)
books on, 46:65 (TFH), 47:8, 51:18
cited, 57:4, 63:48
boxes for, brick-lined, 77:78 (REM)
brick, 20:56-57 (CBS), 22:6
freeform, 28:100
cantilevered, 66:85
side, 52:49 (TFH)
central, 77:89
fitted stone, 59:63, 64 (EEH)
freestanding, 46:83 (TFH)
cleaner for, 37:8
closed-combustion, 72:72 (EEH)
coastal, code on, 43:4
cobblestone, 40:40, 42, 54:87 (TFH)
hearth for, 12:42-44 (REM)
codes on, 69:76-78
in Colonial style, 63:47, 48
concrete,
cast, 20:32-34, 45:50 (CSH)
double-stepped, 52:37, 40 (TFH)
"farmer," 80:49
geometric, 4:27
half-round copper-hooded, 58:51
raised, 83:87
sewer-pipe, 3:52
and cookstove, 21:62-65 (CBS)
corner,
dual, framing for, 82:16-20
projecting, 80:61
tiny, 47:80 (MFC, SH)
Craftsman, 36:26, 27 (CSH), 39:56, 61
(CBS)
cricket, glazed chimney, 73:72, 74
damper exfiltration allowance for, 69:76
dampers for, 21:57 (EEH), 22:6, 43:14,
51:18
air-tight, 54:14
chimney-top, 57:4
dating, 27:83
draft in, 43:12-14
with duct system, 34:26, 27 (DWS)
efficiency of, 15:20
Federal, 31:47 (FWS)
fieldstone, 35:74, 77, 45:57
fire rating for, upgrading, 30:6

fireboxes in, 22:6, 26:4
airspace for, 22:6
insulation for, 24:4
joints for, 24:4
flues for,
hidden, 3:27
insulating, 24:4
footing for, 20:54, 55 (CBS)
formal simple, 68:84
framing for, 20:54, 55 (CBS)
freestanding,
dual-purpose, 48:33, 34, 35
firebrick, 3:59 (EEH)
rock, 3:53
gas grill in, 48:35, 36
gas-log, adding, 77:78-79 (REM)
granite, 30:19-20, 21, 31:73, 40:41, 42
Greene-and-Greene,
brick, 72:38
tiled, 17:32, 33 (CSH)
hearth of,
replacing, 4:40 (CBS)
slab for, 20:54, 55 (CBS)
slate, source for, 54:54
Heatilator, 2:33 (EEH), 20:34
hoods for,
copper, 5:35
of welded tie-plates, 15:30, 31
infill for, 24:4
island adobe, 43:75-76, 77, 78
keystone for, carved, 54:73
in kitchens, stucco, 21:43
large, flue sizing for, 43:12
leaky, repairing, 27:12
limestone-faced, 57:65, 67
lintel for, 20:57 (CBS)
as low room dividers, 66:49
in masonry stoves, 42:68-73 (CBS)
metal, life of, 43:4
metal box in, 65:38
mortar for, 22:6
with ovens, 40:31, 79:89
paired, masonry-stove and open, 66:58,
59 (SH)
patio, 4:26, 33
plain, 11:33 (EEH)
plastered recessed, 38:70, 71, 108
prefabricated, efficient, 10:44
Preway, 1:45 (EEH)
raised,
adobe-concrete block, 19:74, 75
concrete, 45:67
stone, 79:55, 80:60, 83:88
river-rock, 46:63 (TFH)
Rumford, 45:45 (TFH), 59:37, 39 (SH)
code approval of, 71:104
as renovation, 3:40-43 (CBS)
sandstone, 75:85
ashlar, 35:32, 33
massive, 35:37 (CBS)
see-through, 75:85
flue for, 10:4

shallow, 2:23 (CSH)
simple, 73:85, 87
smell from, treating, 54:14
smoke chamber for, 20:58 (CBS)
stainless-steel, welded, 9:74
steel-tube, 16:60-61, 63 (TFH)
stone, 3:21, 25, 45:78, 79 (EEH)
   massive, 32:28 (CSH)
   wishbone, 37:73
stoned corner, 33:66
surrounds for,
   carved, 54:73
   carved pilastered, 69:82, 86-87
   cherry, 77:79 (REM)
   concealed-door, 77:88
   concrete, 66:42
   copper, 38:43
   custom ceramic, 41:70-75, 76, 77 (FWS)
   drywall, 64:41, 42 (CSH)
   granite, 51:62
   limestone, 73:85, 87
   paneled, 73:41
   simulated masonry, 57:47 (REM)
   source for, 63:49
   tile, 56:47
Thermal Energy Storage Systems
   (TESS), precast-block fireplace of,
   15:20-21
three-sided, 8:65 (EEH), 11:34, 80:80
tiled, 6:21 (CSH)
tiles for,
   architectural, 59:106-10
   handmade, 59:88-91
tiling, 37:8
tools for, custom, 80:61
as transition markers, 80:52
two-sided, 39:51, 52:80
wood lift for, reviewed, 64:92
Wright-designed, 41:30
See also Bake ovens. Chimneys.
   Firewood storage. Flues. Inglenooks.
   Mantels. Masonry stoves.
Fireplaces (Magers and Kern): cited, 46:65
   (TFH)
Fireslate 2, Inc.: address for, 71:45 (REM)
Firestone Building Products Co.:
   address for, 64:45 (EF)
Firestone Tire and Rubber Co.: EPDM,
   2:37
Firestops: *See* Blocking.
Firewood storage:
   cast-concrete bin for, 61:54 (SH)
   formal, 4:16
   hidden, 21:26, 28, 29
   kitchen, 42:52, 69 (SH)
   under stair landing, 39:60 (CBS)
   wooden box for, 21:28, 29
First-aid kits:
   comprehensive, reviewed, 58:90-91
   loupe for, 68:28
   source for, 36:4

Fischer, Marvin J.: *Pocket Guide to the
   National Electric Code,* reviewed, 44:94
Fisette, Paul:
   on airtight house, 63:81-85 (EEH)
   on glazing, 55:78-81
Fisher, E. Lee: on economical framing,
   84:46-49
Fisher Hill Products: address for, 48:60
Fi-Shock, Inc.: address for, 85:60
Fisk, Pliny:
   center headed by, 83:88
   at conference, 28:81
Fiske Bros. Refining Co.: address for,
   50:60
Fittings, Inc.: Runtal radiators, 38:28
   (EEH)
Fitzgibbon, James W.:
   career of, 33:25-26, 29
   house by, 33:24-30
   See also Daniel house.
Five Star Manufacturing: address for,
   50:60-61
Fixall patching compound: mentioned,
   22:44 (BK)
Flagg, Ernest:
   architecture of, 5:28-35, 7:4
   Small Houses, 5:28
Flagpoles: retractable, 45:82, 87
Flagstone:
   defined, 40:46 (CBS)
   walks of, laying, 40:46-49 (CBS)
Flaharty, David: on plaster restoration,
   57:38-42
Flair Homes, Ltd.:
   Energy Demo (Manitoba), report of,
     47:104-106
   superinsulated tract houses of, 24:82
Flake board: *See* Oriented strand board.
Flakt, Inc.: heat-recovery ventilators,
   34:34 (DWS)
Flametest fireproofing: source for, 31:49
   (FWS)
Flashing:
   for adjoining roofs, 8:8
   aluminum corner, corrugated, 76:96
   over asphalt-polyethylene, 58:67-68 (EF)
   base, 11:64 (DWS)
   for beams, 9:48 (EF)
   bending,
     brake for, quick, 57:28
     jig for, 9:10
   with board-and-batten, 75:54 (EF)
   cant strip for, 9:48, 12:57 (EF)
   for cantilevered construction, 66:72
   cap, 9:48, 49 (EF)
   caulking of, 12:4
   for chimneys, 9:48, 49, 14:6, 21:46, 48-50
     (CBS, EF), 65:60 (EF), 81:55
     stone-ender, 6:44, 46, 47 (TFH)
   with clapboards, 47:48-51 (EF)

   clips for, 9:50 (EF)
   of columns, 68:14
   concrete as, insufficiency of, 54:41
   for concrete stoop, 57:28
   copper,
     and cedar problems, 49:4, 77:51
     lead-coated, 21:68
   counter-, 9:49, 11:65 (DWS, EF)
     retrofitting, 50:16-18
   for crickets, 47:61-63 (EF)
   for curbs, 15:8, 58:14
   curved,
     copper, 4:64
     making, 56:66-67 (FC)
   cutting, with disc-grinder, 21:16
   dams with, 9:50 (EF)
   for decks, 21:8-10, 29:44-45 (FRC), 51:53,
     72:39, 40
   dispensers for, 65:32
     making, 77:32
   of doors, 8:60-61, 9:47 (EF)
   of dormers, shed, 35:50 (FRC)
   eave,
     shield membrane for, 57:86 (EF)
     for slate roofs, 22:4
   EPDM, 51:53
   folded water-tight, 49:83
   for foundation foam, 8:38, 39, 41 (EEH)
   and galvanic action, 9:50, 12:57 (EF),
     50:6
     preventing, 72:80 (FC)
   with galvanized coil, prepainted, 82:14
   for gutters, 9:47, 15:41, 67:39, 42 (EF)
   for half-timbers, curved, 68:59
   head, 11:65 (DWS)
   hurricane-proofing, 78:85, 86
   of insulation, exterior perimeter, 18:8
   for joists, exterior, tabbed, 61:24-26
   lead for, 53:78, 79 (REM)
   litho plates for, 21:18
   making, 9:46, 47, 48 (EF)
   materials for, 9:46, 50 (EF)
   with membranes, 64:46-47, 52-53 (EF)
   with metal lath, 47:59, 49:4
   modified bitumen for, 37:26 (BK), 70:71
     (EF)
   nails with, 58:14
   neoprene, for ABS pipe, 39:37 (BK)
   for newel post, exterior, 70:69, 70, 71 (EF)
   of pipes, roof-penetrating, 79:83, 84
   for porch roofs, 75:73
   for rafter ends, 77:51, 52
   retrofitting, 50:65-66
   for roof abutments, 8:8
   for roof valleys, 57:87-89 (EF), 60:6, 8
   for roofs, 9:48-50, 12:56, 57 (EF), 34:50
     sidewall-juncture, 11:4, 12:4, 19:8
     standing-seam, 9:8, 39:65
   screws for, 9:49, 11:64 (DWS, EF)
   for shingles, 58:70-71 (EF), 60:6, 8
     composition, 57:88-89 (EF)

for skylights, 3:48, 49, 11:60-61, 62, 63, 64, 65, 18:36-39 (DWS), 55:48 (FC), 65:59, 60 (EF)
  vertical, 70:42
for sloped glazing, 72:80 (FC)
for solar panels, 69:18
soldered, 9:48, 49 (EF)
step, 9:48, 49, 11:59, 61, 64-65 (DWS, EF), 57:89 (EF)
of stone wall, into addition, 83:56
of stone-to-wood junctions, 8:27 (CBS)
strip, 11:59, 61, 64 (DWS)
tape for, flexible, 65:58, 60 (EF)
tarred vs. soldered, 21:48 (CBS)
terne-coated stainless-steel, 73:75
for tiles, 60:38, 65:56, 57, 59, 60 (EF)
of valleys, 11:4
  for shingles, 1:5, 2:4
for vents, 56:80, 65:60-61 (EF)
for vertical-wall abutment, 19:8, 20:12
for walls, 8:60-62, 9:48 (EF)
for walls on slab, 58:14
for windows, 8:60-61, 9:47, 10:6 (EF)
  eyebrow, 76:74, 75 (FC)
See also Metals: galvanic corrosion of.
Flashlights: eyeglasses-style, 50:94
Flash-Rite Co.: address for, 76:96
Flecto Co. Inc.:
  address for, 48:75
  Varathane Plastic Oil, 45:53 (CSH)
Fleming, Edward S., Jr.:
  on Georgetown renovation, 47:79-83 (MFC, SH)
  on hybrid building, 52:24-28 (CSH)
Fletcher, Banister: *History of Architecture, A,* reviewed, 45:120
Flexible Materials, Inc.: address for, 66:102
Flexicore concrete planks:
  for floors, 8:4
  hauling, 14:38
  installing, 25:71-72
  roof of, 25:70-72
  second floor from, 1:43, 44, 45, 46 (EEH)
Flexi-Therm block: pictured, 31:39 (CBS)
Flex-Trim Moldings, Inc.: address for, 47:95
Flexwatt Corp.: address for, 75:72, 77:88
Flexwrap form insert: source for, 39:34 (BK)
Flies, cluster: *See* Insects.
Floetrol paint additive: source for, 17:32 (CSH)
Flood, Jon:
  shelter by, 21:66-68
Flood Co.:
  address for, 50:88, 51:49, 62:41, 69:48, 83:86 (CSH, EF)
  Emulsa-bond Stir-in Bonding Primer, for stucco, 16:8, 18:8
  paint additives of, 17:32 (CSH)

Flood plains: house design for, 17:40-45 (SH)
Floor sanding: *See* Sanding.
Flooring:
  apitong as, 73:81
  ash, black, 43:29, 31 (CSH)
  Australian cypress, source for, 71:94-96
  books on, 53:14, 63:80
  cherry, 38:74, 75, 77 (TFH)
  composition, removing, 41:8
  cork, discussed, 52:106-108
  fir/padauk, 27:48, 51-52
  glass-block, reviewed, 59:110
  for handicapped, 76:59
  and humidity, 53:14
  ifilele, 45:51, 53 (CSH)
  ledgers for, metal, 43:71 (TB)
  linoleum,
    history of, 22:45 (BK)
    removing, 41:8-10, 42:4, 44:4, 84:28
    source for, 22:45 (BK)
  Magnesite, composition of, 32:66
  maple, tung-finished, 73:68
  marble tile, 80:74, 77
  mastic asphalt, 43:61 (CBS, SH)
  mesquite, source for, 59:106
  nails for, 85:47
  oak,
    association for, 67:78
    bleached varnished, 45:45, 48 (TFH)
    and oriented strand board underlayment, 67:78-79
  old-wood, source for, 56:92
  particleboard as, 67:79-80
  pine,
    Norwegian, 73:50
    old, 73:37-38
    wide, source for, 32:75
  plank, 55:59
    cherry, 61:52, 54 (SH)
    cupping of, 53:14
    custom-milled, 23:58, 59 (FWS)
    installing, 39:14, 53:6, 54:4-6, 63:48
    laminated, source for, 39:92
    oak, source for, 57:67
    Swiss wedge board for, 70:75
    varieties of, 53:4-6
    wood/concrete/urethane, 47:87
  plate-joined, 70:52, 53 (FC)
  plywood panels for, 80:71
  resilient, laying, 22:44-49 (BK)
  sawdust-cement poured, 32:66
  slate, 75:47, 49 (REM)
    over slab, 81:71
  softwood, polyurethane problems with, 14:12
  sub-, nails for, 85:46
  teak, 39:74
  tiles for, rubber, 46:52 (EEH)
  vinyl,
    duckboard, 37:28 (BK)
    no-wax, 64:87 (REM)

and oriented strand board, 67:78
  source for, 56:63 (EEH)
wood,
  acoustic qualities of, 11:50 (CBS)
  aging, 6:47 (TFH)
  air-dried vs. kiln-dried, 33:10-12
  association for, 81:102, 104
  baselines for, 13:44-45, 46 (FWS)
  board width for, 19:8, 23:59 (FWS), 81:59
  cracks in, repairing, 1:6, 14:12
  curved, laying, 46:12
  drying, 37:8
  of end-grain blocks, 36:10-12
  fasteners for, 81:104
  grades of, 23:59 (FWS)
  in humid locales, 54:61
  information on, 65:54
  inlaid, process of, 63:78-80
  installing, 5:10, 29:12, 27:12
  jack for, reviewed, 64:92
  laminated, making, 5:10
  layout of, 13:44, 45, 46 (FWS)
  over linoleum, 16:10
  manufacturers of, 23:50
  matching, to addition, 70:84, 85 (REM)
  measurement of, 23:59 (FWS)
  milling, 23:59 (FWS), 37:8
  moisture level for, 13:43-44, 19:8, 23:58, 59 (FWS)
  mosaic, 21:40, 41
  nailer for, power, 13:45 (FWS)
  nailing, 13:45-46 (FWS)
  nails for, 13:4, 42-44, 29:12, 63:48
  nailset for, rectangular, 11:12
  persuaders for, 4:7, 61:12, 62:30, 64:4, 84:96-98, 85:30
  pine, wide, 78:58-59
  plainsawn vs. quartersawn, 23:58-59 (FWS)
  prefinished, 59:49-50, 73 (SH)
  preparation for, 13:42-43 (FWS)
  publications on, 23:50
  quartersawn, 29:12
  removal of, tool for, 32:54, 55 (TB)
  screw-hole plugs for, 24:12
  screwing down, 33:10-12
  screws for, 7:8, 19:8-10, 24:12
  sealant for, 27:12
  shiplap joints in, 23:58, 59 (FWS)
  shrinkage of, 24:64, 29:12 (TFH), 43:8
  species for, 23:57 (FWS), 37:8
  splines for, 19:8
  stairwell nosing with, 13:47 (FWS)
  storing, 31:10
  strip, patching, 64:30-32
  strip, types of, 13:42 (FWS)
  supplies of, finding, 23:57 (FWS)
  thickness for, 27:12
  tongue-and-groove, matching, 7:23 (BK)
  tongue-and-groove, removing, 11:12

Vermont Federal, 1:49-51
wedges for, 74:73 (FC)
with wide gaps, filling, 79:88
Floors:
adding, 81:53
to raised-roof addition, 67:66 (REM)
in renovation, 64:85 (REM)
air infiltration through, preventing,
77:65-66
AirCore, 38:65 (CSH)
construction of, 30:50-54 (CBS)
and termites, 35:10
air/vapor barrier for, 42:60-61
Alaskan slab, 18:68 (CBS)
anchors for, metal, 43:46, 47 (FRC)
appliance drains for, 69:30
beams for,
built-up, 43:73, 74 (SH)
composite, 2:27, 29
block,
air channels in, 17:45 (SH)
system for, 70:110
blocking for, 19:59 (FRC)
reinforcing, 43:47 (FRC)
bluestone, 3:53
brick, 66:45
advantages of, 34:6
broom grouting of, 23:12, 38:41-42
care of, 33:70 (CBS), 66:45
dry slab for, 66:45
finish for, 33:70 (CBS)
gap filling in, 23:12
on gravel, 38:41-42
laying, 5:50, 51, 9:27, 14:32-35, 23:12,
33:70 (CBS)
layout for, 33:68 (CBS)
mortarless, 33:68-71 (CBS)
paraffined, 23:12
patterns for, 33:69-70 (CBS)
pavers for, 38:82 (CSH)
-paving, 38:82, 83 (CSH)
radiant heating with, 37:10
in sand, 5:50, 51, 22:43, 33:68-69 (CBS)
screeding, 33:69 (CBS)
sealer for, 33:70 (CBS)
tongs for, 33:69 (CBS)
wheelbarrow for, 33:69 (CBS)
bridging for, 19:56 (FRC)
metal, 43:47-48 (FRC)
for cabin, 7:30, 31, 14:48, 32:75
ceiling as, 5:34-35
cherry, 68:85, 87
concrete, 4:27, 20:74
air-radiant, 33:40 (EEH)
brown, 11:31, 32 (EEH)
collector, 51:72, 73 (EEH)
colored, 66:59 (SH)
colored, mottled, 33:12
direct-gain, 33:40 (EEH)
expansion strips in, 19:77, 30:19, 21, 23
exposed-aggregate, 66:38, 39, 42, 43,
45 (SH)

Key to books:

(BK)   Building Baths and Kitchens
(CBS)   Building with Concrete, Brick and Stone
(CSH)   Craftsman-Style Houses
(DWS)   Building Doors, Windows and Skylights
(EEH)   Energy-Efficient Houses
(EF)   Exterior Finishing
(FC)   Finish Carpentry
(FRC)   Frame Carpentry
(FWS)   Building Floors, Walls and Stairs
(MFC)   More Frame Carpentry
(REM)   Remodeling
(SH)   Small Houses
(TB)   Tools for Building
(TFH)   Timber-Frame Houses

finish for, 7:38 (DWS), 66:86
over gravel, 3:21, 19:77
gridded, 7:6, 12:28, 28, 29, 30, 31, 32
hollow-plank, 1:43, 44, 45, 46 (EEH),
8:4, 14:38, 25:70-72
level pour for, 20:74
pebbled, 17:42, 45 (SH)
pebble-finish, 27:30, 31
pigmented, 6:55, 11:47-50, 18:31 (CBS)
as plenum, 7:36, 38 (DWS)
post-tensioned, 2:34 (EEH)
pour of, timing, 17:45 (SH)
over rock bed, 12:66, 67 (EEH)
scored, 66:59, 84, 85, 86 (SH)
slab, 4:27
slab, insulating, 44:4
slab, waterproofing, 65:16, 71:16
small-section system for, 65:36
vapor-barrier retrofit for, 41:10
over wood, 11:47-50, 14:4-6, 26:73, 74
(CBS, SH), 75:70
construction protection for, 8:6
costs of, by type, 11:50 (CBS)
crib walls for, 19:55 (FRC), 69:68 (REM)
decking for, 19:55 (FRC), 43:20
dropping, for headroom, 32:59
ductwork in, 19:59 (FRC)
earthen, vapor barrier for, 79:24
earthquake-proofing, 64:64 (MFC)
epoxy for, source for, 70:49
evaluating, 10:43
exterior stone, drainage pans for, 46:35,
37
flagstone, 33:64, 66
framing, for bow window, 44:65 (FRC)
girders for, 19:55 (FRC)
glass, 38:62, 63
glued system for,
book on, 76:16
nonvibrating, 76:16-18
hardboard, 12:44 (REM)
heat-storing, 7:37-38 (DWS)

from honeycomb-paper panels, 81:106
importance of, 19:55 (FRC)
information on, 65:53, 55
instruction in, 75:100, 76:16
as insulated sealed unit, 5:57 (FRC)
insulating, 7:12, 19:59 (FRC), 29:69, 33:41
(FWS), 37:63, 51:70, 71, 55:43 (SH),
73:74, 77:78 (REM)
Japanese, 4:56-57 (TFH)
joists for, 19:54, 55, 56-59, 22:8 (FRC)
laying for, 21:4
strengthening, 13:40
for kitchens, wood, 15:10, 78:65 (REM)
kraft paper/fiberglass, 34:73
laying, cutout block for, 36:4
ledgers for, Micro-Lam, retrofitting,
81:53
leveling, 75:66
with light vents, perimeter, 47:82, 83
(SH)
loads on, 33:43 (FWS)
masonry, support for, 84:86
nail guns for, 15:49, 52, 53 (TB)
nailing,
double-, 11:53
face-, nails for, 77:88
nails for, 85:47
nonslip, for handicapped, 53:69, 70
nonwax conditioner for, 33:70 (CBS)
oak/slate, curved, 8:27 (CBS)
oil stain on, removing, 13:6-8
oriented strand board for, 67:78
panel-framing method for, 35:8
panels for, paper, 81:104, 106
parquet, gallery of, 79:90-91
particleboard/marble, 39:39
perimeter-insulated raised, 46:96
plank,
drilling template for, 49:67
fir, 71:72-73
grades of, 49:64
layout and installation for, 49:64, 65,
66-67
moisture barrier for, 49:64-66
movement in, calculating, 49:66
nailer for, 49:65, 66
plugs in, tapered bit for, 49:67
screws for, 49:67
subflooring for, 49:64
plank-and-beam,
cutout block for, 36:4
disadvantages of, 33:41, 36:4 (FWS)
as plenums, 2:23, 25, 12:67 (CSH, EEH)
data source for, 23:49
plumbing in, 19:59 (FRC)
plywood, adhesive for, 18:7
polybutylene piping for, 21:12
porch,
renovating, 75:73
slope for, 75:73
porphyry stone, 70:65 (EEH)
posts in, scribing to, 77:62-63

poured, self-leveling, 48:12
prefab Scandinavian, 40:53
protecting, 64:30, 67:55, 75:94
    paper for, 55:76 (MFC), 71:96
publications on, 23:49, 50
    cited, 75:100
reinforcing, 10:8-10, 43
on sand, 8:38, 39 (EEH)
sandstone, 9:44, 45
savings in, 84:47
screens for, removable, 77:30-32
screwed, 55:59
second-story, and vapor barrier, 29:70-71
second-story tiled collector, 1:43, 44, 45, 46, 47 (EEH)
sheathing bump-stick for, 37:66 (FRC)
sill placement for, 19:55-56 (FRC)
slab,
    cracks in, 68:14-16
    gravel base for, 66:68 (EEH)
    insulation for, 66:66 (EEH)
    radon exhaust system for, 66:68 (EEH)
    topping, 19:47
slate for, 21:8
solar-gain masonry, tile mortar for, 46:14-16
soundproofing, 28:10, 31:48 (FWS), 35:60-61, 46:64 (TFH)
space under, furred-out, 55:59
splined single-layer, 6:47 (TFH)
Squeakenders for, reviewed, 62:92
squeaking, dealing with, 7:8, 28:10
stone, 33:77
    Aggraglaze for, 9:45
    installing, 68:47-49
strengthening, 60:43-44 (SH), 74:14
stress-skin panel, 24:58, 40:12
for structural strength, 79:82
sub-, 13:42-43, 29:12 (FWS), 19:59-60 (FRC)
    adhesives for, 58:74-75
    constructing of uneven boards, 18:7
    cutting in place, 3:34 (TB)
    dropping, 67:73 (REM)
    eliminating squeaks from, 28:10, 42:18 (CSH)
    estimates for, 27:34
    gluing, 84:47
    leveling, 18:7
    OSB, water-resistant, 75:94
    remote-drive screw gun for, 85:71
    supplies of, finding, 23:57 (FWS)
    support systems for, 19:55 (FRC)
    test report on, 81:102-104
    tongue-and-groove plywood for, 37:66-67 (FRC)
system for, nonvibrating, 75:100

tile, 1:55, 8:38, 41, 31:68, 69 (EEH), 45:42, 66:53, 54
    baseboard fitting to, 14:14
    considerations for, 52:61 (CSH)
    and deflection, 85:16
    over ferro-cement, 13:51, 52 (CBS)
    layout for, 17:70-71 (BK)
    making, 18:48
    mastic for, 17:70, 72, 18:4 (BK)
    radiant heat for, 85:87
    in solar design, 10:49, 50, 51 (SH)
    source for, 55:86
    supports for, 38:28 (EEH)
    as thermal mass, 34:29 (erratum, 36:6, DWS)
    underlayment for, 67:78
timber-framed, soundproofing, 62:18 (CSH)
transitions in, flush, 31:34 (DWS), 76:56
trusses for, 19:55, 24:67, 68, 69, 25:16, 30:25-27, 43:75-76 (FRC)
underlayment for,
    allergen-free, 54:14-1
    5/16-in. cement-board, source for, 64:96
    need for, 19:60 (FRC)
    self-leveling, 48:12
vapor barrier for, 29:69
and wall ratio, for materials efficiency, 84:46-47
wax for, nonyellowing, 33:70 (CBS)
wood,
    framing for, 23:61 (FWS)
    headers for, 13:46, 47 (FWS)
    self-leveling underlayment for, 48:12
and wood shrinkage, 81:55, 56, 58-59
See also Flooring. Radiant-floor heating.
Floresca, José L.: on fantail deck stairs, 83:74-76
Florida:
    carpenter shortage in, 55:100-102
    conservation credits in, 3:12, 5:65
    early house in, 3:56-59 (EEH)
    passively cooled houses for, 49:72-75 (EEH), 51:8
    south, building codes for, 6:50
Florida Power and Light: house by, 40:73-77 (EEH)
Florida Solar Energy Center:
    activities of, 30:80
    address for, 65:52, 74:106
    on air-handler inefficiencies, 67:98
    energy-efficient Cracker house by, plans for, 68:102
    mentioned, 40:73 (EEH)
    programs of, jeopardized, 66:22-24
    prototype houses by, 30:80
    publications of, 30:80
    on radiant barriers, 52:68
    services of, 23:51, 30:80, 49:72 (EEH)
    solar-rating program of, 68:55
Flues: *See* Chimneys.
Fluorescent lighting: *See* Lighting.

Flutes (grooves): making, 54:55-56, 71, 61:69-70 (REM)
Flux: *See* Soldering.
FM transceiver headsets: source for, 34:50
FmHA: *See* Farmers Home Administration. Financing.
Foad, E. V.: *Purpose-made Joinery,* reviewed, 69:108-10 (CSH)
Foam: *See* Caulk. Insulation.
Foam Laminates of Vermont: stress-skin panels by, 24:58, 59, 29:74, 76, 77
Foam Plastics of New England, Inc.:
    address for, 56:63 (EEH)
    stress-skin panels, 24:59
Foam Products Corp.: address for, 24:59
Foam Tech, Inc.: address for, 85:18
Foamglas: for slab insulation, 26:10
Foamular: source for, 18:33 (CBS)
Focal Point:
    address for, 56:63 (EEH)
    foam-core moldings, 39:92
Foley, Joseph H.: on ground-fault protection, 6:39-41
Foley, Mary Mix: *American House, The,* cited, 26:73 (SH)
    reviewed, 2:62
Foley-Belsaw: molder-planers, reviewed, 55:50-55
Foliage for Clean Air Council: address for, 69:102
Follansbee Steel Corp.:
    address for, 73:75
    terne roofing of, 24:44, 39:62, 41:4
Fomo Products, Inc.:
    address for, 47:54 (TFH), 77:67
    Fomofill sealant, 24:56
Fontaine, André: on Arts-and-Crafts style, 82:82-87
Fonthill: construction of, 6:31-35, 68
Food and Heat Producing Solar Greenhouse: source for, 10:17
Food storage: tunnel for, 15:75, 77 (CSH)
Foote, Steven: sleeping loft by, 39:104
Footings:
    block,
        precast interlocking, 70:110
        two-piece insulating, 70:110
    concrete, and rock, 51:68
    for concrete piers, 79:64-65, 67
    for decks, calculating, 79:67, 81:6
    drainage tiles for, preformed PVC, 84:98
    for erodable desert sites, 66:84
    for exterior spiral stair, 54:80, 81 (EF)
    forming, 44:33-35 (CBS), 61:55-56
    gravel-bed, for AWW foundations, 68:63-64
    hand-dug, 55:56, 57
    independent, 18:28
    insulating, 63:82, 83 (EEH)
    lack of, disaster with, 3:64
    levels for, laser, 84:94

for porches, 81:46
pouring, 12:35, 15:44-45 (CBS)
precast, 40:86-87
raising house for, 28:12
reinforcing, 35:8
retrofitting, 52:49-50 (TFH), 58:77 (MFC)
for sand, 63:38
slab-integral, insulating, 29:68-69
See also Foundations.
Forbo North America, Inc.: address for,
56:63 (EEH)
Ford, David K.: on log building, 7:29-31
Ford, Len: on wall disaster, 33:94
Ford, Lynn:
career of, 23:30
doors of, 23:31
Ford, O'Neil: boveda house by, 23:26-31
Ford, Robert M.: on Mississippi house,
8:63-67 (EEH)
Ford Glass Div.: high-performance glass
of, discussed, 41:84-86
*Foreign Building and Construction
Literature in English:* source for,
55:108
Forest City Tool: address for, 55:63
Forest Products Journal: source for,
23:50
Forest Products Laboratory: *See* U. S.
Department of Agriculture Forest
Products Laboratory.
Forest Products Research Society:
address for, 65:45, 65:53
Forest Products Journal, 23:50
services of, 23:50
Forests:
acid rain and, 49:98
association for, 65:102
hurricane damage to, 57:104
managed,
coppicing in, 19:23
Western, 47:38-39, 42-43
old-growth,
book review on, 57:114
importance of, 49:98-100
publication on, 67:100
responsibility to, 59:4, 60:4, 61:4-6, 63:4-6,
64:4-6, 65:102, 69:42 (EEH), 71:6, 73:67,
75:4-6
Russian slant on, 67:100
saving, book on, 75:110
2-4-D spraying of, 47:43
in U. S. life, book on, 54:106
*Forgotten Art of Building a Good
Fireplace, The* (Orton): cited, 47:8, 51:18
Forklift: job-site, reviewed, 61:90
*Form and Space of Japanese
Architecture* (Carver): mentioned,
39:70
Formaldehyde:
in composition board, 67:80, 81
danger from, 1:12, 5:15

from kitchen cabinets, 22:16
levels of, reducing, 66:67-68 (EEH)
limits for, 67:81
plants removing, 69:102
publications on, 55:108
sealants for, 46:73
Forman, Henry Chandlee: *Early
Nantucket and Its Whale House,* cited,
77:89
Formbloc Inc.: insulated block, 31:39
(CBS)
Formica Corp.:
address for, 9:41 (BK), 62:61
See also Countertops: plastic-laminate.
Forms:
aluminum, 6:55
custom, 34:39
backing for, polycarbonate, 49:45
bending, 58:50, 67:83, 84, 85 (FC)
blockouts for, 44:37 (CBS)
books on, 63:106, 78:53
boxes for,
cardboard, 75:26
drywall, 13:12
bracing, 41:14, 78:53
brackets for, 78:50
building, 61:55-57
circular, 30:66-67 (CBS), 58:50
for windows, 29:30, 31
for concrete, 7:54, 55, 32:16, 37:27 (BK),
44:32-37 (CBS)
contour gauge for, giant, 65:32
curved, 30:37, 67:81
for walls, 29:30, 31, 30:66-67 (CBS)
design for, 47:6
dirt as, 6:35, 68
foam, 40:86, 69:64-66
insulating, 76:36-41
and pests, 76:37-38, 78:6-8
sources for, 76:39, 78:6
for laminating molding, 74:79 (FC)
for lintels, simple, 74:51
modular metal, 2:20, 22, 23-25 (CSH)
nailers for, 82:92
nailing, 24:22-24
for pier and grade-beam foundations,
16:36-37, 28:16 (CBS)
pipe-cavity, 46:55 (BK)
plastic-laminate, 20:50, 51 (FWS)
plyform for, 78:48
plywood for, bending, 55:96
plywood-sheathed metal, 73:73
for pours on rock, 30:33-34, 35, 74:67
for pumice-crete, 77:55, 56
PVC, 28:16
for rammed earth, 11:22, 23, 24, 34:36-37,
38-39
release for, 26:65, 37:27 (BK, CBS), 30:67
(CBS), 44:35, 37 (CBS), 47:4, 6, 78:48-50
coated plywood for, 69:96
reusing, 26:73 (SH), 47:4, 6

round fiberboard, using, 79:67, 68, 69
slip, 51:69-71
smooth, 46:4
Sonotube, 27:27, 30:35, 50:56
for columns, 27:27, 30:67 (CBS)
for deck supports, 29:43 (FRC)
step, 49:28
stops for, 24:22
stud-and-waler, designing, 78:48-53
void self-destructing, for expansive
soils, 70:63 (EEH)
walkways for, 78:52
for wall panels, precast, 85:82-83
wire sealing, 63:26
See also Lamination. Metal connectors.
Forms and Surfaces:
address for, 66:50, 102, 73:59
glass block, Japanese, 37:49 (DWS)
pulls, 30:59 (BK)
Forms Plus:
address for, 76:39
insulation of, using, 76:41
Formwork to Concrete (Austin): cited,
78:53
Forti-Fiber:
Aquabar B paper, 22:67 (BK)
polyethylene from, 36:12
Foss, Merl: mobile sawmill of, 17:18-20
Foster, Bill: mentioned, 36:61 (FWS)
Foster, Hugh:
on power planes, 54:76-79
reviews Pearson, 61:106
reviews Wells, 65:106-108
Foulkes, Robert: on small houses, 67:34-
37
Foundation for Architecture:
address for, 68:8
Architecture in Education, source for,
68:8
Foundations:
adobe, repairing, 22:40-41, 43
all-weather wood,
advantages of, 68:62
backfill for, 7:4
constructing, 5:40-42, 7:4 (FRC), 68:62-
66
designing, 5:40-41 (FRC)
footings for, 68:63
nails for, 6:4
performance of, 3:9, 72:4
plywood for, 7:4
prefabricated, source for, 68:62
publications on, 5:40, 23:49, 34:67
(FRC, SH)
short-wall, 34:67-68, 69 (SH)
for unstable ground, 15:58-59
wood treatment for, toxicity of, 28:10
anchor bolts in, 64:65 (MFC)
accuracy with, 65:30, 73:80, 77:80-81
retrofitted epoxied, 70:47
Arts-and-Crafts style modern, 82:82

asphalt-impregnated fiberboard for, 48:69
backfilling to, 7:4, 15:48, 26:73 (CBS, SH), 48:68
    protection for, 24:68
of bedrock, 24:29 (CSH)
block,
    backfilling to, 15:44-48 (CBS)
    with block bond beam, 59:60
    coating, 12:37 (CBS)
    corner poles for, 15:46, 25:66-77 (CBS, TB)
    cracks in, repairing, 81:16, 83:14
    failure of, avoiding, 81:16
    insulated, 54:84-86 (TFH)
    pilasters with, 12:37 (CBS)
    repairing, 61:24
    rock-faced, 11:51, 52
    scored-stucco, 66:79, 80 (SH)
    surface-bonded, 69:41 (EEH)
    waterproofing, 15:46-48 (CBS)
bolts in, vs. drive pins, 21:32 (TB)
books on, 29:12
    reviewed, 74:98
brick,
    raised, 38:72, 73 (TFH)
    repairing, 17:12
brick-veneered, flush-to-siding, 66:46, 48, 49
buttresses for, 7:36, 39, 26:73, 75 (DWS, SH)
butylated-asphalt membrane for, 15:59
cantilevered, with I-beams, 66:70-72
capping,
    blocks for, 6:4
    brick for, 4:34 (FRC)
    concrete, 4:34, 35 (FRC)
    forms for, 4:36-37 (FRC)
    pour for, 4:37 (FRC)
    process of, 4:34-36 (FRC)
circular, 7:54, 55
coatings for,
    fiberglass-reinforced, 73:74
    nontoxic, 73:68
code requirements for, 50:59
color for, 74:42 (EF)
columns as, earth-filled steel, 11:55, 58
concrete,
    beveled, 56:69, 70 (CSH)
    disadvantages of, 12:34 (CBS)
    and drilled-rock, 9:43
    pad, 55:42-43 (SH)
    pier, 7:30, 19:69, 70 (EEH), 73:71, 73
    pile, 69:58
    pile, auger-cast, 59:81
    pile, earthquake-resistant, 82:78-80
    repairing, 4:9
    sill keyway for, 19:39 (BK)
    stemwall, methods for, 47:4
contracting for, dual, 43:20
cracks in, repairing, 48:68-69

Key to books:

(BK)   Building Baths and Kitchens
(CBS) Building with Concrete, Brick and Stone
(CSH) Craftsman-Style Houses
(DWS) Building Doors, Windows and Skylights
(EEH) Energy-Efficient Houses
(EF)   Exterior Finishing
(FC)   Finish Carpentry
(FRC) Frame Carpentry
(FWS) Building Floors, Walls and Stairs
(MFC) More Frame Carpentry
(REM) Remodeling
(SH)   Small Houses
(TB)   Tools for Building
(TFH) Timber-Frame Houses

crawl-space, 44:32-37 (CBS)
    framing, 77:80-85
cut-and-fill, 80:55
for decks, 69:46-47 (EF)
and drain lines, 39:33-34 (BK)
drain retrofit for, 48:12
drainage for, 8:6, 15:48, 17:4, 18:4, 20:4 (CBS), 48:68
    drywell, 3:21, 48
    and filter fabric, 2:37, 18:4, 40:63 (CBS)
    placing, 62:6
    tile, preformed PVC, 84:98
dressing, against the cold, 81:122
earth-bermed, 38:34
    insulating, 46:62-63 (TFH)
for earth-bermed walls, 48:50-51
earthquake-resistant, 40:44 (TFH), 63:102, 64:64-65 (MFC)
and earthquakes, 29:34-38 (FRC)
for earth-sheltered houses, 7:36 (DWS)
enlarging, 1:42 (FRC)
    for veneer, 24:10
estimates for, 27:34
evaluating, 10:42-43
under existing houses, 7:22-23 (BK), 9:29, 31, 28:12, 39:38-39, 42:26 (CSH), 49:39 (REM)
    jacking for, 77:16
expansion joints in, 6:55
in expansive clay, 34:58-59 (FRC)
failure of, 14:40, 29:34, 35 (FRC)
filter fabric for, 53:49 (SH), 73:68
floating, 52:49-51 (TFH)
"flying buttress" repair rig for, 49:39, 40 (REM)
form clips for, reviewed, 65:92
freeze-protection for, 36:12
frost-line levels for, 79:66, 68
and fungi protection, 72:66 (REM)
grade beam over graveled trench, 67:96
on granite outcrops, 74:66-67

on gravel pads, for wetlands, 57:64-65, 66
hurricane-proofing, 52:69, 57:64-66, 59:79, 81, 78:82
    pilings for, 49:73 (EEH)
insulating, 8:6, 15:48, 17:8, 18:8, 33-34, 38:41, 43:20, 73, 56:38, 60:53, 54, 55, 63:82, 83, 65:62, 66:66 (CBS, EEH, SH)
    with OSB, 48:68
    polystyrene for, parged, 18:33-35 (CBS)
    and termites, 20:6
insulation-drain board for, 56:38
for Japanese houses, 4:53, 54 (TFH)
loads on,
    analyzed, 32:29 (FRC)
    lateral, 17:4
for log buildings, 7:30, 14:52
nails for, 85:46
Norwegian corner-post, 72:84-85
old,
    underpinning, 47:81 (MFC, SH)
    waterproofing, 56:83
one-step form and insulation for, reviewed, 53:96-98
parging for, source for, 60:55
"perching" of, 48:67
pier and grade-beam, 16:31-37, 34:58-59, 42:50-53, 52:75-76, 69:58-61 (CBS, FRC, SH)
    booklet on, 29:92
    for coastal areas, 29:73-76
    concrete tie beams in, 27:29
    for decks, 29:43-45 (FRC), 79:64-69
    drilling for, 51:59-60
    against earthquakes, 31:4
    over expansive soils, 70:61-63 (EEH)
    hammer leads for, 32:4-6
    for log studio, 48:71, 73 (SH)
    pier reinforcing for, 40:44, 61 (addendum, 41:4, TFH)
    post cut-off jig for, 40:16
    prefab Scandinavian, 40:54
    on rock, 74:66-67
    on rocks, form contour-gauge for, 31:14
    for soft clay, 73:40-41
    steel, 46:34, 37
pier and post, 82:102
pier-block, drywall forms for, 13:12
piers for, retrofitted, 60:43 (SH)
plans for, care in, 43:65-66 (TB)
plastic wrap for, 18:45, 47
for playhouse, 61:43, 44 (SH)
pole and concrete, 46:49-50 (EEH)
for porches, 75:74
post, 4:44, 45, 5:54-55, 56 (FRC)
post-and-glulam, creep-resistant, 53:47-49 (SH)
pouring, disasters with, 1:60
powder-actuated fasteners for, 21:30-34 (TB)

rebar for, 4:37 (FRC)
repair of, 4:9, 6:12, 10:10, 43, 21:10, 79:86
 with epoxy, 70:48, 49
 experts in, finding, 48:69
 exterior extensive, 48:69
replacing, 32:62-63
retaining wall, gravity-type, tie-in with,
 14:12
on rock, 38:41, 73:48
 epoxy-bonded rebar for, 73:73
rubble-trench, 9:25
 constructing, 18:66-68 (CBS)
 and earthquakes, 20:6, 22:4-6
 for park shelter, 21:66
 reinforcing, 19:4
 with Scandinavian prefab houses,
  40:54
 for stone masonry, 14:63
 trenches for, 3:22, 24, 9:25, 18:66, 67
  (CBS)
 under whole house, 24:66, 67, 69
for rugged site, 47:86
sealer for, 63:82 (EEH) 77:57
settled, dealing with, 85:20-22
shallow, 5:30
 frost-protected, new codes on, 74:104
 remedies for, 17:8-10
for shelter, 21:66
shifting, dealing with, 51:16-18
shoring up, 14:10-12
sills in,
 attaching, 77:81
 moisture-barrier for, 18:4
 placement on, 56:83
site considerations for, 47:4-6
slab, 4:27
 adding, 15:64
 Alaskan, 18:68 (CBS)
 colored, 28:68-69, 71
 cracks in, 68:14-16
 cutting, 83:16
 existing, wall building on, 83:14-16
 failure of, 81:80, 82
 fill for, 25:67 (TB)
 gravel base for, 66:68 (EEH)
 insulating, 17:8, 22:69, 26:10, 29:68-69,
  31:70, 44:4, 81:18 (CBS)
 insulation for, 66:66 (EEH)
 on-grade, 31:70
 pouring, 83:46-51
 pouring, under house, 81:70-71
 radiant-heated, 19:69, 70 (EEH), 24:10,
  58:59-61 (CSH), 60:55
 radon exhaust system for, 66:68
  (EEH)
 raised, pouring, 30:39
 repairing, 32:10
 savings with, 84:47
 suspended, 58:59, 60-61 (CSH)
 thermal breaks in, 54:14
 for tropics, 85:75

tunneling under, water-hose method
 for, 2:5
vapor barriers for, 77:10
vapor barriers for, puncture-
 resistant, 83:48
vapor barriers for, seamless, 46:71-72
waterproofing, 65:16, 71:16
slab-on-grade, 55:82-83
 over gravel, 60:51-55 (FC), 62:4-6
 repairs of, 32:10
slab-on-pier, 73:56, 59
slab-piling, 46:75 (BK)
on soft soils, 73:40-41
soil for, evaluating, 43:8
and soil moisture, 48:67
spot, joining, 17:8-10
squareness of, checking, 77:80
stake grease for, improvised, 51:24-26
star-shaped, 25:56-59
and steel bents, 23:76, 77
steel column connections with, 6:50
for steep sites, 16:31-33, 34-37, 38:31-34
 (CBS), 26:63-65 (CBS)
 plate leveling for, 19:56 (FRC)
stemwall, 44:32-37 (CBS), 51:4
stone, 83:88, 89
 -faced, 19:38, 39 (BK)
 -faced block, 32:73, 74
 insulating, 18:6
 pier-block, 51:36-38, 39 (CSH)
 repairing, 69:68-69 (REM)
 -veneered block, 77:74-75
 waterproofing, 69:14-16
on stone formations, below-grade, 36:6
for stone masonry, 8:23-24, 26 (CBS),
 41:68 (CSH), 51:68, 70
strengths of, compared, 9:6
stucco for, 7:36, 18:8, 33-35 (DWS)
 synthetic, 43:77
and substrates, 48:66 (MFC)
for superinsulated houses, 15:58-59
super-strength, 14:27, 28
and surface rock, 43:8
termite-proofing, 6:53
as thermal link, 20:10
as thermal mass, 70:54-55 (EEH)
threaded rod for, 4:37 (FRC)
trenches for, root-sawing in, 15:16
for tropics, 61:60 (SH)
for turret, 68:57
undersizing of, for floor-plate fit, 39:10
on unstable ground, 6:55, 15:58, 16:31-33,
 34-37 (CBS)
in unstable trenches, 75:58
vapor barriers for, 19:68
walls of, forming, 61:57
water pressure in, relieving, 17:4
waterproofing, 2:37, 55, 26:73, 29:12 (SH),
 55:57-58, 59, 70:54 (EEH)
 book on, 47:20
 electro-osmosis, 47:20

retrofitting, 47:18-20
wood pile, driven, 69:58-60
See also Basements. Drainage systems.
 Filter fabric. Footings. Forms.
 Membranes. Radon.
Foundries: list of, 16:44
Fountainhead:
 address for, 84:45
 construction of, 12:27-32
 furniture for, 12:28
 restoration of, 12:32-33
Fountains: interior, poured-concrete,
 77:54
Four Books of Architecture (Palladio):
 cited, 42:74
Four Seasons Greenhouses: skylight
 insulation, 35:8
Four-square houses: discussed, 71:63
 (REM)
*Fourteenth National Passive Solar
 Conference Proceedings, The:*
 reviewed, 56:110
Fox, Jim: house by, 47:84-87
Fox Industries Inc.: latex cement bonding
 agent of, 19:47
Foylon: cost of, 8:30 (TFH)
*Framed Houses of Massachusetts Bay,
 1625-1725, The* (Cummings):
 mentioned, 13:26, 15:4, 16:6 (TFH)
Framing:
 askew, problems with, 13:60-61 (BK)
 balloon, 13:40,
  19th-century, 18:41
  for strength, 79:82
 balloon-and-post, 22:56 (CSH)
 balloon-truss, 24:65-69
 beams in,
  box, headers for, 19:10
  box, insulated, 55:43 (SH)
  cantilevered, 20:33
 books on, 23:48, 49, 50, 35:70-71 (TB),
  46:104, 47:43, 110, 71:112, 72:57
 for Boston ridge, 63:43-44
 bracing, 22:36-37 (FRC)
  gable, 78:85-86
  let-in, 22:36-37 (FRC), 85:54-55
  let-in, vs. sheathing in, 37:6
  metal-angle, 85:55-56, 75
  need for, 22:36-37 (FRC)
  of raised walls, 22:39 (FRC)
  retro-, 55:16-18, 57:16
  shear-wall, 85:57
  sheathing as, 85:56
  teepee, 22:39 (FRC)
  types of, 22:36 (FRC)
 broken-plate tension-ring, 76:67 (REM)
 for ceiling height, additional, 59:37 (SH)
 chainsaws for, 78:38-41, 79:6-8
 checking, with transit, 73:80
 for chimneys, 82:16-20
  fire codes on, 69:77-78
 clips for, 14:24

code requirements for, 50:59
communal, 59:74-77 (REM)
composite, 3:57, 58 (EEH)
    lightweight, 3:24, 25, 26
for concrete over, 11:47, 48 (CBS)
of corners, 47:30, 50:30, 82:45
    in California, 29:69
    with clips, 82:102
    details for, 72:60-61
    OVE method for, 84:48-49
of curves, 29:31, 31:70
for curvilinear upper story, 57:53-54
cutting of, 3:33-35 (TB)
defects in, 7:22 (BK)
dimensions for, choosing, 72:57
for doors, 22:34 (FRC)
    French-, retrofit, 68:42, 44, 46 (FC)
for double-envelope house, 23:44, 45, 46
    (EEH)
for double-wall construction, 42:61,
    66:66, 68 (EEH)
for drywall, 81:38
earthquake-proofing, 64:60-65 (MFC)
Eastern vs. Western, 35:8-10
of eaves, "falling," 74:82-85 (MFC)
energy-efficient, 61:106
evolution of, 79:50
of fascia, freestanding, 72:82, 83 (REM)
firestops in, 25:12
of forms, round, 44:79
of gable overhangs, 38:38 (CSH)
of gable-end, 22:35 (FRC)
    glassed, 66:43-44
for gazebo, 55:83
girts in, trussed, 6:36, 37 (FRC)
for glass, fixed heavy, 73:49
hanger notches for, 27:16
headers for,
    built-up retrofitted, 68:46 (FC)
    details for, 72:57-60
    flush, 56:65 (FC)
    insulated, 82:102
    intersecting, 51:78 (FC)
    long-span, 55:75-77 (MFC)
    raising jig for, 74:59 (MFC)
    reinforcing, 67:66 (REM)
    retrofitting, 46:26
hurricane-proofing, 59:79, 81, 74:69,
    78:82, 83, 86-87
    steel vs. wood, 78:87
information on, 47:43, 65:53
and insulation concerns, 29:68-72
intersections in, 21:71 (FRC)
    filler blocking for, 22:14
    45°, studs for, 26:16
    square, 47:84-87
of jambs,
    extension, scribing trick for, 58:26
    production, 53:38-42 (FC), 58:8
jigs for, 4:7

with joists,
    prebored, 55:59
    rim, steel-post supported, 82:79, 80
for kneewalls, retrofitted, 74:14
layout for,
    chalklines for, 21:72-74 (FRC)
    detailing of, 21:75-77 (FRC)
    flat, 21:75-77 (FRC)
    marking plans for, 21:69-72 (FRC)
    on-edge, 22:32, 33 (FRC)
    principles of, 21:69 (FRC)
    stick for, 21:77 (FRC)
    tool for, 21:20
learning, hard lessons in, 71:126
low-cost, 73:59
for materials efficiency, 84:46-49
modular,
    exposed, 55:72
    Japanese, 43:31 (CSH)
moment, for steel, 74:58 (MFC)
nail guns for, 15:49, 50, 53 (TB)
nail hinges for, 7:10, 49:26
nailing, 82:45-47
    no-nail wiring zone for, 21:18
nails for, 22:32-33 (FRC), 85:46
19th-century, defects in, 6:36-38, 39:42
    (FRC), 49:39 (REM)
number system for, 22:31 (FRC)
of octagons, 9:2
    bay, 26:12 (erratum, 27:6)
    corner posts in, 32:36
    prefab, 32:34-36
old, allowable deviation in, 14:23
openings in,
    bracing, 6:38 (FRC), 7:22 (BK)
    rake-wall, 62:62 (MFC)
Optimum Value Engineering (OVE),
    23:48, 84:46-49, 85:4
    books on, cited, 84:49
    criticized, 85:4
of oval domed room, 71:14
under peaks, 7:12
pencil-and-crayon holder for, 78:30
persuaders for, 32:16, 76:28, 77:32, 78:92
sans plans, 17:76-77 (SH)
plates in,
    failures of, 6:36, 37 (FRC)
    precut, 20:16
    with strap ties, 78:86
    triple 2x6s, 66:44-45
platform, 13:40
    origins of, 46:78-79
for playhouse, 61:43, 44 (SH)
with plumbing layout, 29:52 (BK), 49:51-
    53 (MFC)
    protective plates with, 39:36, 37 (BK)
for porches, 81:44-47
preparation for, 22:31-32 (FRC)
rack resistance of, 37:6, 40:4-6
rafter-beam joint for, 8:27 (CBS)
with rebar, 66:55
Rex Roberts method of, 28:69-70

ring-support system in, 20:30
of rooftop-addition, 57:43-44, 45-46
    (REM)
of saltbox, open-plan, 4:44-47 (FRC)
with saplings, 30:29-30
Scandinavian-style, 43:73-74 (SH)
screwed, 55:59
for shack, take-down, 56:49-50
shims for, metal, 77:78 (REM)
sizing of, aids for, 13:8
of soffits, 73:58
    fascia-supported, 63:69 (MFC)
span computer for, 13:8
square cuts in, importance of, 9:51
    (FRC)
steel, 78:20
    advantages of, 32:67, 71, 35:4 (FRC),
        76:92
    books on, 30:6, 35:4, 85:118
    estimating, 35:4
    with I-beams, 31:64
    kits of, 76:92
    plumbing, 35:4
    popularity of, 85:118
    process of, 2:56-57, 58, 23:76, 77, 32:68-
        71 (FRC)
    Stud-Lok tool for, 40:87
    with tubes, 73:78
step motif in, 15:75, 76 (CSH)
straightedge for, stair-gauge, 27:16
strapping in, for strength, 28:69-70
string aids for, 25:67 (TB)
for stucco, 2x12s, 45:38
studs in,
    backing, 21:71 (FRC)
    bowed, correcting, 81:38
    bowed, straightening, 60:28, 65:32
    defined, 21:71 (FRC)
    finger-jointed, 82:94
    foam-filled, 40:51
    height of, finding, 21:71 (FRC)
    king, 21:71 (FRC)
    layout of, 21:77 (FRC)
    lengthening, in foundation repair,
        4:34-37 (FRC)
    locating, 36:16, 53:30, 82:44-45
    magnetized screws in, finding, 33:16
    metal, 30:6
    separating, 4:6
    solid vs. staggered, 8:8
    straightener for, 64:30
    trimmer, 21:71 (FRC), 22:34-35 (FRC)
style of, choosing, 72:57
for superinsulation, 38:52-53, 56:62
    (EEH)
    modified, 37:25-26 (BK)
for tetrahedron, 6:48-50
and thermal bridges, eliminating, 63:82-
    84 (EEH)
tie rods with, 25:51-52
for tight envelope, 78:68-69
for toilets, 84:6

with truss frames,
    advantages of, 7:4
    process of, 5:55-57 (FRC)
of turret, 68:56-58
on 2-ft. centers, 19:10, 84:47-48
2x-and-gusset hybrid, 40:50, 52, 53
with 2x4s, double, 78:68-69
with 2x6s,
    changes caused by, 19:10, 21:6
    34:68 (SH), 51:60, 53:49 (SH)
of walls, 22:33-34, 35 (FRC)
    chalklines for, 82:42
    circular, 25:60
    layout for, 82:42-44
    plates for, 82:42-44
    prefab, 58:62-66
    pre-fab load-bearing, 62:72-77
    preframed, positioning trick for, 34:16
    rake, balloon, 62:62-63 (MFC)
    rake, methods for, 72:67-69 (MFC)
    round, 7:56
    shear, interior, 79:82
weak, girder reinforcement for, 14:23-25
for windows, 22:34, 24:6 (FRC)
and wood shrinkage, 81:54-59
Z-splice in, 59:86 (CSH)
See also Anchors. Metal connectors.
    Plumb and line. Post-and-beam.
    Roofs. *separate joints.* Timber
    framing. Trusses. *various building
    parts. various tools.*
France: property regulations in, 33:67
Francis, Kenneth: mentioned, 32:34
Francis turbines: described, 15:66
Frandon Lead Alert Kit: address for,
    84:75
Frane, David: on lap-joint windows, 76:72-
    75 (FC)
*Frank Lloyd Wright and the Prairie
School* (Brooks): cited, 69:57
**Frank Lloyd Wright Home and Studio
Foundation:** address for, 32:66
**Frank Lloyd Wright Memorial
Foundation:** Wright house plans from,
    41:26-31
Frank Lloyd Wright to 1910 (Manson):
    cited, 69:57
Franklin International: address for, 47:65,
    48:55, 65:41, 69:83, 71:96, 81:96
    glue information from, 30:60 (BK)
Frederick, Linden:
    on tool-barrow, 69:75
Frederick Shohet, Inc.: address for, 67:75
    (REM)
Frederickson, Steven R.: on building
    inspectors, 50:58-59
Fredriksson, Don: *Plumbing for Dummies,*
    19:82
Freeborn Tool Co.: address for, 58:38
    (REM)

Free-form: *See* Design: organic.
Freeze alarm: telephonic, homemade,
    39:14
Freezers: undercounter, 44:52, 53 (SH)
French, Roger:
    mentioned, 9:14, 15:67
    phase-change systems of, 10:18
French-American architecture: solar
    house in, 26:72-77
Freon:
    hot-water system, homemade, 29:86-88
    in phase-change systems, 10:18
Frerking, Michael: houses by, 34:37-38
Freshwater and Marine Aquarium:
    cited, 72:63
Freud, Inc.:
    address for, 46:12, 64:70, 70:53 (FC),
        72:52 (FC)
    plunge routers, reviewed, 71:79, 84 (FC)
    power planes, reviewed, 54:78-79
    Teflon sawblade, for laminates, 30:60
        (BK)
Friedlander, Matthew: designs radiant
    floor, 38:77 (TFH)
Friedman, Keith: mentioned, 26:41
Friedman, Renee: as joint author. *See*
    Goodall, Harrison.
Friedman, Rodney: mentioned, 28:77
**Friedrich Air Conditioning &
    Regrigeration Co.:** heat pumps, 26:68
Friends of Kebyar: address for, 63:100
Frieze blocks:
    defined, 10:63, 68 (FRC)
    installing, 10:68 (FRC)
    windows as, 85:73, 75
    See also Blocking.
Friezes:
    Arts-and-Crafts style, 52:79, 81-82
    defined, 15:39, 40, 60 (EF)
    doorway, 11:38, 39 (DWS)
    furring out, for shingles, 28:64
    Greek Revival, 1:49
    of joined wood, 6:24
    tile, 59:88-89
Froelich, Chris: greenhouse by, 4:48
Froes: using, 30:48
Frog Tool Co.: chisels of, 12:23 (CSH, TFH)
From Bauhaus to Our House (Wolfe):
    reviewed, 9:68
From the Ground Up (Wing and Cole):
    cited, 7:42
From the Walls In (Wing): quoted, 5:4
Frost, Thomas, Jr.: newel post by, 71:89
Frost heave: explained, 17:8-10
Frost point: defined, 19:67
Frothane insulation: source for, 31:38
    (CBS)
FTR Insulated Shutter Systems: address
    for, 53:14
Fuel Savers, The (Anderson, ed.):
    reviewed, 70:120

Fuge, Paul:
    on buying green lumber, 7:40
    on flooring, 23:57-59 (FWS)
Fuktskyddsmatta **membrane:** described,
    40:54
Fulgham, Darnell:
    house by, 9:25, 26, 27
    roofing detail by, 11:6
Full Length Roof Framer, The
    (Riechers): cited, 10:60 (TB)
Fuller, Buckminster: mentioned, 33:29
Fuller, Millard: discussed, 53:104
Fuller (H. B.) Co.:
    address for, 62:85 (MFC)
    insulation adhesive, 34:49
Fuller O'Brien Paints: address for, 77:79
    (REM)
Fuller Tool Co.:
    address for, 49:67
    tapered bits, 34:45 (TB)
Fuller (W. L.), Inc.: address for, 62:43
Fuller's earth: mentioned, 13:6
Fulper Glazes, Inc.: address for, 54:100
Fulper, Rada, Julia and Anne: ceramics
    by, 59:88
Functional Aids for the Handicapped
    (Robinault): mentioned, 6:51
Fundamentals of Building Construction
    (Allen):
    professional edition of, 37:4
    reviewed, 36:94, 71:112
    source for, 40:72 (FRC)
Fungi:
    conditions for, 72:64-65 (REM)
    preventing, 72:65-66 (REM)
Fungicides: toxic, 1:6
Furman, Jim: on stained glass, 21:54-55
    (DWS)
Furman Lumber, Inc.: address for, 64:94
Furnima: address for, 62:74
Furnishings: book on, reviewed, 65:108
Furniture:
    Arts-and-Crafts style, source for, 54:100
    built-in, 9:63, 64, 65, 66, 36:24, 26, 27-28,
        29, 38:43, 44 (CSH)
        bay-window seating, 12:41
        benches, suggestions for, 12:41
        circular tables, 23:74-75
        concrete, 6:33
        hutch, 85:64-67
        triangular, 12:28, 31
        wooden, 24:76
    concrete bureau, 6:33
    custom, source for, 67:58
    design of, integrated, 10:22, 24-25
    glides for, Teflon homemade, 31:14
    old-wood, source for, 56:92
    for parallelogram house, 12:28, 31, 32
    plastic 1950s, 34:74-75
*Furniture of the American Arts and
    Crafts Movement* (Cathers): source
    for, 36:29 (CSH)

Furring strips: metal, 32:68-71 (FRC)
Fuse box: *See* Wiring: service panel for.
Futagawa, Yukio: *Wooden Houses,* 12:72
Futura floor finish: source for, 36:12, 44 (FWS)
Future Energy Products Ltd.: heat-recovery ventilators, 34:33, 34 (DWS)
Future Enterprises: address for, 63:94

- -

G. D. E. Products: address for, 68:94
Gableboards: See Rafters: barge.
Gables:
carving for, 83:79
Chinese painted, 55:88
gallery of, 50:90-91
metal ornaments for, 43:80-81
overhangs for, 52:52, 53
trim for, inexpensive, 59:71-73 (SH)
truncated, 52:52
See also Walls.
Gabriner, Vicki: on women's building course, 13:18
Gacioch, Marti: on house for handicapped, 32:82
Gaebel Enterprises: address for, 56:94
GAF Corp.: fiberglass shingles, 29:76, 38:38 (CSH)
Gaggenau:
address for, 76:58
stoves, mentioned, 40:67 (BK)
Gallaway, Bob M.: as joint author. *See* Wolfskill, Lyle A.
Gallery: defined, 29:48
Galvagrip primer: recommended, 33:75
Galvalume roofing: described, 24:43-44
Galvanizing: *See* Metal: galvanic corrosion of. *specific metals or substance.*
Galveston (TX):
history of, 39:77-79
restoration projects at, 39:76-77
Gammelin, Jeff: on stonework, 26:69-71 (CBS)
Garages:
attached formal, 38:86, 87
AWW foundations for, 68:66
bracing for,
retro-, 55:16-18, 57:16
wall, 85:56
carport,
gabled, 59:70 (SH)
as main entry, 12:29, 32
roof failure of, 81:81-82
rustic, 35:30
behind columns, 73:40
concrete floors in, hollow-core precast, 38:34

converting, into library, 77:76-79 (REM)
design of, 30:63
doors of, replacing panels of, 53:28
floors over, framing for, 74:58 (MFC)
handicapped-accessible, 53:67, 68, 69
with hyperbolic/paraboloid roof, 21:38
overhead-door safety cable for, 26:16
plan sources for, 53:89
remodelings of, 12:42-45, 19:46-49 (REM)
siding for, on doors, 74:59 (MFC)
Garcia, Javier Sanchez: restoration efforts of, 22:84
Garden Pools, Fountains, and Waterfalls: cited, 13:6
Gardens:
as drywells, 3:21, 22
enclosed, 55:72, 73, 79:70, 72, 74
integral, 4:26, 31
sunken, 4:26, 28-29
water, creating, 80:66, 67
See also Landscaping.
Gargoyles: for downspouts, 56:70, 72 (CSH)
Garland Commercial Industries, Inc.: address for, 71:43 (REM), 75:67
Garland-White and Co.:
address for, 51:63
latex grout waterproofing, 22:12
thinset mortar, 25:35, 36, 37:8 (BK)
Garrett, Jim: iron work by, 51:36-40 (CSH)
Garrett Wade Co.:
address for, 46:90
chisels of, 12:23 (CSH, TFH)
reviewed, 62:51
Garvey, Helen: *I Built Myself A House,* cited, 83:77
Garvin, James:
on framing, 27:83
mentioned, 27:82, 83
Gas:
barbecue grill, source for, 48:36
code on, 49:18
earthquake protection with, 29:38 (FRC)
furnaces, 2:65, 5:4
in superinsulated houses, 22:18 (CSH)
heaters, propane quick-delivery, 34:69 (SH)
helicopter delivery of, 15:66-67
induced-draft fans for, 49:18
lighting with, 14:30-31, 16:6
lines for,
chases for, in slab-on-grade, 60:53-54
in chimney, 48:36
and door retrofits, 68:43 (FC)
earthquake-proofing, 64:62 (MFC)
locating, dowser for, 75:26-28
in trenches, 17:10
venting requirements for, 49:18
Gas Appliance Manufacturer's Association: address for, 46:48

Gas Research Institute: HVAC unit, 33:84
Gaskets:
with ADA, 37:62-65
air-infiltration-preventing, 77:67
extruded EPDM sill, 83:16
split backer rod, commercial source for, 40:4
split, using, 37:62-63
from surgical tubing, 48:55, 56
urethane, source for, 68:64
Gasoline:
care with, 13:8
cleaning with, danger of, 15:14
respirator for, 15:14
safety cans for, 44:88
Gass: as joint author. *See* Lehr.
Gately, David K.:
mentioned, 27:31
on skylights, 55:45-49 (FC)
Gates:
in adobe wall, 5:9
Arts-and-Crafts style, 59:83, 84 (CSH)
Australian incised, 53:65
entrance, 40:79
forged, 75:75, 78, 79
gallery of, 52:88-91
garden, building, 60:28
iron, 48:84
iron and copper, 14:67, 68
latch for, 49:45
making, 49:44-45
metal custom, 62:89
metal-wood sculpted, 63:86-87
posts for,
fiberglass, 48:84
Galveston, 39:79
slatted, 25:80
Spanish Revival, 45:40, 41
Gates, John Humboldt: on windows, 36:76 (DWS)
Gates and Sons, Inc.: address for, 78:50
Gates Engineering Co.:
butyl sheeting, 29:12
elastomeric-membrane roofing, 9:4
EPDM, 2:37
Gazebos:
contemporary, 55:82-87
defined, 29:48
gallery of, 75:86-87
pondside, 75:57-59
Gazebos and Other Garden Structures (Strombeck): cited, 53:89
Geiger, R.: *Climate Near the Ground, The,* 9:16
Geller, Howard: addresses conference, 33:84
General Conditions of the Contract for Construction: explained, 22:64
General Electric:
address for, 54:51, 57:56
fixtures, 15:57 (BK)
Silglaze 1200 caulking, 1:32, 8:16

General Elevator: residential elevators, 38:56

General Fire Extinguisher Corp.: address for, 58:91

General Hardware Mfg.: plumb bobs, 25:69 (TB)

General Products Co.: Benchmark Insulated Entry Door, 6:60

Generators:
belt-driven, 15:68
with DC system, 8:47
gas-powered, 67:62
See also Energy.

Generic CADD: reviewed, 60:92-94

GEnie: using, 46:59-60

Genie Industries: Superlift, reviewed, 61:90

Genius of Japanese Carpentry, The (Brown): reviewed, 58:106

Gentle Architecture (Wells): reviewed, 3:60

Gentrex Corp.: address for, 53:96

Geocel Corp.:
address for, 53:79 (REM), 82:14
caulk,
adhesive, 43:74 (SH)
mentioned, 14:14

Geodesics, Inc.: mentioned, 33:29

GeoHeat Co.: heat pumps, 26:68

George, David: mentioned, 33:26

George, Doug: wins award, 33:84

George, Eugene: on Texas house, 38:66-71

George, Gene and Mary Carolyn: on Ford boveda house, 23:26-31

George Cook House: bell-tower restoration of, 30:42-45

George Enterprises, Inc.: address for, 63:90

George Jackson and Sons: plasterwork by, 43:41-43 (FWS)

Georgia:
architecture, details in, 20:59 (FWS)
coastal house for, 29:73, 77
home conservation credits in, 5:65
solar tax credits in, 3:12

Georgian Period (Ware, ed.): mentioned, 47:112

Georgia-Pacific Corp.:
address for, 66:80 (SH), 82:94
Metal Products Catalog, 32:69 (FRC)

Geotech Systems Corp.: address for, 55:57

Germer, Jerry:
reviews Jackson and Day, 82:112
reviews Konzo and MacDonald, 81:114
reviews Lechner, 72:108
on screened-porch addition, 72:81-83 (REM)

Gerow, Daniel: mentioned, 30:35

Gerstein, Rosalyn: on small houses, 10:48-52 (SH)

Key to books:

(BK)   Building Baths and Kitchens
(CBS)   Building with Concrete, Brick and Stone
(CSH)   Craftsman-Style Houses
(DWS)   Building Doors, Windows and Skylights
(EEH)   Energy-Efficient Houses
(EF)   Exterior Finishing
(FC)   Finish Carpentry
(FRC)   Frame Carpentry
(FWS)   Building Floors, Walls and Stairs
(MFC)   More Frame Carpentry
(REM)   Remodeling
(SH)   Small Houses
(TB)   Tools for Building
(TFH)   Timber-Frame Houses

Gerstel, David:
on building library, 26:40-42
on change orders, 71:69
Contractor, 47:71
on orderliness, 44:46-49 (TB)
on organization, 47:68-71

Gerster, Anton: shelter by, 21:66

GFCI: *See* Wiring: ground-fault protection, circuit interrupters for.

Ghost Ranch (NM) solar conferences: mentioned, 26:56

Gibralter:
address for, 84:45
See also Countertops: resin board.

Gibson, Scott:
on cob house, 83:88-89
on insulation convection loss, 79:112
reviews catalog, 81:114-16
reviews *EBN,* 84:124
reviews energy-efficient practices, 83:108-10
reviews Hamilton, 85:132
reviews Kindersley, 85:134
reviews Rybczynski, 84:124
on siding, 83:40-45

Giddings, Jean: bedspread by, 46:38, 39, 41 (REM)

Giedion, Sigfried: *Space, Time and Architecture,* quoted, 46:79

Gilbreth, Frank and Lillian: efficiency studies of, 19:26, 22:63

Gilder, Cornelia Brooke: on stone masonry, 5:37, 39

Gilding:
described, 60:82
of letters, 72:48
paint remover and, 4:8-9
process of, 3:8

Gill, Brendan: *Many Masks,* reviewed, 50:108

Gill, Irving: concrete use of, 11:46, 14:70 (CBS)

Gillespie Corp.: address for, 73:104

Gillette, Joseph: on misplaced septic tank, 47:126

Gil-Lift: cabinet lift, reviewed, 78:92

Gilligan, Sean: uses computer, 35:66 (TB)

Gin poles: using, 8:31, 32, 33, 34:10 (TFH)

Gingerbread house: described, 12:76

Girders: *See* Beams.

Girouard, Mark: *Life in the English Country House,* reviewed, 45:122

Girts: *See* Beams.

Givoni, Baruch: *Man, Climate and Architecture,* 2:33 (EEH)

Givoni air tubes: mentioned, 2:31, 33 (EEH)

Gladding McBean: roofing tiles, 24:31 (CSH)

Glas-Kraft, Inc.: address for, 71:96

Glass:
art, types of, 23:37 (DWS)
cast-in-concrete, 12:28, 31
and caulk compatibility, 8:16
cleaner for, 55:47, 49 (FC)
coating for, metallic oxide, 20:22
corners in, 51:78 (FC), 66:42
mitered, 12:30-31
corrugated factory, 21:40, 42
cutting, 23:37-38 (DWS)
early production of, 24:52 (DWS)
energy-efficient, 81:102
etched,
acid technique for, 24:52, 53 (DWS), 39:8, 42:34 (DWS)
sandblasting, 24:53 (DWS), 39:8, 42:34 (DWS)
and stained, gallery of, 73:88-91
as exterior unit, unframed, 33:26
"fat" high-performance, discussed, 41:84-86
film with, and radiant heat, 82:102
heat mirror, 72:70 (EEH)
insulated,
association for, 51:78 (FC)
booklet on, 11:64 (DWS)
and caulk, 8:16
double-seal, 8:42 (DWS)
making, 14:12
setting, 51:78 (FC)
single-seal, 8:42 (DWS)
templates for, 51:78 (FC)
tests of, 11:4
window-making for, 50:70-73 (FC)
as interior wall, unframed, 33:30
laminated, 18:36 (DWS)
advantages of, 16:21, 18:4 (CSH)
large panels of, framing for, 16:62-63 (TFH)
leaded, windows of, making, 23:36-41 (DWS)
low-e, source for, 38:26 (EEH)
nature of, 24:52, 26:4-6 (DWS)

overhead, safety considerations with, 16:21, 18:4 (CSH)
plate, blown, 59:102-104
publications on, 39:8
quad-pane system for, 20:22
as roof, 13:66 (SH)
school of, 39:8
shading coefficients for, 78:69-70
for skylights, 18:36 (DWS)
specialty, discussed, 76:67 (REM)
stained,
    came for, custom, 42:34 (DWS)
    construction of, 21:54-55 (DWS)
    copperfoiling, 42:33, 34, 35 (DWS)
    examples of, 42:80-81 (DWS)
    panels of, 64:41-42 (CSH)
    polyester overlay, 47:95
    in skylights, 49:6
as structural member, 60:74, 77
tempered, 16:21, 18:4, 36 (CSH), 49:14-16
window, hand-blown, source for, 67:75 (REM)
wire, 18:36 (DWS)
See also Caulk. Glazing. Skylights.
Glass Art Magazine: source for, 39:8
Glass Certification Council: *Certified Product Directory,* cited, 11:64 (DWS)
Glass Etching (Capp and Bush): source for, 39:8
Glass Glazed Site-Built Solar Collector: reviewed, 15:22
Glass Studio Magazine: source for, 39:8
Glasshaus, Inc.: glass block, German, 37:49 (DWS)
Glaverbel: high-performance glass of, discussed, 41:84-86
Glazing:
acrylic, 57:55, 56-57
    butyl-tape problems with, 34:4
    caulk for, 10:33, 17:65, 32:37, 34:4 (DWS)
    curved, installing, 17:65-66 (DWS)
    disadvantages of, 10:30, 31, 32, 38:70 (DWS)
    example of, early, 17:77-79 (SH)
    expansion formula for, 10:32 (erratum, 12:4, DWS)
    house of, 23:72-77
    overhead seamless, 31:33-34 (DWS)
    perm rating of, 19:67
    process of, 10:32-33 (DWS), 32:37
    for roofs, 38:66, 70
    in solar collectors, 3:48
    for water walls, 26:57
aluminum-neoprene, 34:66 (BK)
argon in, 55:80
for bathroom, specialty glass for, 76:66-69 (REM)
choosing, 33:37 (EEH)
commercial, types of, 60:49 (FC)

compared, by brand, 55:79
compounds for, nontoxic, 46:71
and condensation, 55:81
custom, 73:74, 75:6
double-pane,
    divided-light, sources for, 40:86, 67:14
    fiberglass, source for, 6:54
dry, 8:16
efficient, source for, 80:71
EPDM, for greenhouses, 65:62 (SH)
evacuated, 55:81
of fiberglass, 1:32
for glass panels, problems with, 12:48-49
for glass wall, floating, 66:60-62 (REM)
heat-resistant, 53:16
of insulated windows,
    dessicant for, 14:12
    edge sealant for, 14:12
lead, imitation, 74:78
with low-e coatings, 55:78-80
    argued, 84:86
    gas-filled, 73:45 (EEH)
    placement for, 57:14-16
    triple Heat Mirror, 80:70-71
manufacturers of, analyzed, 55:79
neoprene gasket system for, 48:36
orientation of, 33:37 (EEH)
process of, 45:48 (TFH)
putty for, softening, 60:26-28
quad-pane, 20:14, 22, 33:37 (EEH), 34:68 (SH)
research on, 33:37 (EEH)
R-values of, 55:79, 80
sealants for, 61:42
single,
    and low-e coatings, 64:22, 64:22 (addenda, 65:4)
    and storm windows, 64:22
sloped,
    caps for, aluminum, 75:6
    process of, 72:76-80 (FC)
specialty glass for, 76:66-69 (REM)
switchable, 55:81
tapes for, 7:37, 11:62, 63, 25:12 (DWS)
for 32mm cabinets, 74:77
for three-level sunspace, 46:52 (EEH)
tilt of, 33:37 (EEH)
tri-pane, source for, 34:68 (SH)
triple vs. double, 16:14
types of, defined, 55:78-80
UV-filtering, 53:16
ventilated, 59:65, 66 (EEH)
and window R-values, 57:6
See also Glass.
Glazing Recommendations: source for, 11:4
Gleason, Robert: on cantilevered kitchen, 70:82-85 (REM)

Glendenin Bros., Inc.: copper nails of, 20:42 (EF)
Glen-Gery Corp.: address for, 64:80
Glessner Corp.: address for, 68:49
Glick, Ruth: on family architecture, 39:31
Glidden Co.:
Glid-Wall, 43:10-12
Insul-Aid vapor barrier paint, 9:8, 19:68
vapor-barrier paint, 37:65
XIM Sealer, 33:30
Glid-Wall: source for, 43:10
Glitsa American Inc.:
address for, 49:14
floor finish, application of, 36:42-45 (FWS)
varnish, 14:12, 35:77
Globe Building Materials, Inc.: address for, 63:4, 82:6
Glossebenner, Alfred: *How to Look It Up Online,* cited, 46:60
Gloucester Co.: Phenoseal adhesive caulking, 6:23, 15:40 (EF)
Gloucester (MA) Development Team: house renovations of, 6:14-16
Gloves:
for cold-weather work, 50:63
recommendations for, 56:4
Glue:
for acrylic, 55:47, 49 (FC)
air-infiltration-preventing, 77:67
anaerobic, 65:41, 44
authority on, 50:42 (MFC)
booklets on, 58:75
bottles for, 3:7
for carved panels, 47:65
casein, 65:41, 44
caulk as, 84:81
choosing, chart for, 65:41
for cold weather, 51:42
in composition board, 67:77
for concrete, 4:9, 41:14, 56
for concrete-wood joinery, 55:65
construction,
    avoiding, 73:67
    caulk as, 43:74 (SH), 73:81
    in noise control, 58:56
    for staircase parts, 39:48 (FWS)
contact-cement, 65:41, 42-43
    application-storage bucket for, 55:28
    down garbage disposal, 12:74
    no-clamp, for vinyl sheeting, 36:69 (BK)
    for plastic laminate, 41:8
    removing, 61:26
    spacers for, 61:24
    spray, recommended, 75:62, 64
    water-based, 81:76
cornstarch, 4:55 (TFH)
cyanoacrylate, 65:41, 43-44
design without, 46:70-73
discussed, by type, 65:40-45, 86
for dissimilar materials, 53:79 (REM)

epoxy,
adherence of, 70:47
aerosol, source for, 65:86, 70:49
books on, 62:41 (EF), 67:4
curing, 70:46
discussed, 65:43
for exterior use, 9:21-22, 36:14, 57:72-74 (FC)
for flooring, 22:47 (BK)
forms of, 70:46, 47
heat resistance of, 13:10
house repairs with, 62:6, 37, 40-41
for lamination, 42:48-49 (FWS), 44:68 (FRC)
light sensitivity of, 50:68
mixing of, with electric drill, 33:16
qualities of, 16:20-21 (CSH)
sources for, 16:10, 21, 42:10, 39, 48:55, 81:51
spray, source for, 65:86
for tile, 17:70 (BK)
using, 65:41, 43, 70:47-49
waterproof, 49:44
exterior, 3:16 (DWS), 42:10, 39, 54:14, 62:6, 70:69 (EF), 83:59
for finished wood, 55:65
for flexible construction, 35:8
on floors, loosening, 44:4
for headers, 62:85 (MFC)
hide, 65:41, 44-45
for restorations, 29:66-67
hot-melt, 65:41, 44, 79:49 (EF)
for mockups
information on, 23:50, 65:45
for insulation board, 34:59 (FRC)
Isoset, for stress-skin panels, 24:59
for lamination, 65:86, 70:90, 74:81 (FC), 77:77 (REM)
quick-setting, 65:86
liquid, roller bottle for, 65:42
marine sealant, 33:46 (TFH)
for model making, 22:51, 79:49 (EF, FRC)
for oily wood, 29:57-58 (CSH)
organic, heat-resistance of, 13:10
phenol-formaldehyde, described, 50:42 (MFC)
plastic resin, 65:41, 44
setting time for, 16:75 (FWS)
for plastic laminate, 62:61
for plywood floors, 18:7
for polyethylene, 32:48 (BK)
polyvinyl acetate (PVA),
discussed, 65:40-43
white vs. yellow, 65:41-42
properties of, 58:72-75
for resin board, 37:81, 84:42-43
resorcinol, 65:41, 42
clamping pressure for, 42:46 (FWS)
for exterior use, 42:10
for exterior use, cautions for, 36:14
for restoration, 29:66-67
severing wood from, 51:24

special, 58:75
for stress-skin panels, 24:59
for subfloors, 7:8, 19:60 (FRC), 62:43
tapes as, 65:45
tiles, 62:76
for tiles, 78:84
roof-, source for, 65:58 (EF)
for treated lumber, 63:65 (MFC)
urea-formaldehyde, 50:42 (MFC), 65:41, 42
mixing, 74:81 (FC)
wallpaper, removing, 64:30
waterproof, one-part, 71:96
yellow, source for, 48:55
See also Cement: hydraulic. Epoxy: wood consolidant. Loctite.
Glued Laminated Timbers for Residential and Light Commercial Construction: cited, 71:59 (MFC)
Glues and Glued Products: source for, 23:50
Gluing and Clamping (Spielman): cited, 65:45
Glulam Beams: source for, 23:49
Glulam beams: *See* Beams.
Glulam Systems: source for, 23:49
Gluts: making, 30:48
Godine, David R.: *Great Camps of the Adirondacks,* 40:42
Goerzen, Les: reviews Whiffen, 43:102
Goettsch, Kenny: cabinets by, 38:62-63, 65 (CSH)
Goff, Bruce:
design elements by, 33:25-26
house by, 78:124
Goggles: defogging, 27:16
GoJo hand cleaner: cited, 42:59 (DWS)
Gold Bond Building Products Co.:
address for, 66:55, 68:87
Gypsolite, 23:61 (erratum, 24:6, FWS)
Gold, Jeff:
on house on mined site, 80:62-67
on Snyder house, 9:42-45
Gold leaf: *See* Gilding.
Goldbeck, David: *Smart Kitchen, The,* reviewed, 58:106
Goldberg, Alan: on house rebuilding, 3:51-55
Goldblatt Tool Co.:
address for, 43:52 (CBS), 50:52, 58:45, 70:79
pattern roller, reviewed, 71:94
reviewed, 62:51
stamping tools, 27:58
trowels, 31:61 (FWS)
Golden section: house design around, 34:56-58 (FRC)
Goldfish Pools, Water-lilies, and Tropical Fishes (Thomas): cited, 13:6
Goldman, Elizabeth: on children's architecture, 66:14-16

Goldman, Mark S.:
columns by, 69:88
on earthbuilding class, 67:96-98
on train-station renovation, 81:50-53
Goldner, Steven: ceramics by, 59:88
Goldsmith, Selwyn: *Designing for the Disabled,* 6:51
Goldstein, Eliot Warren:
on alpine house, 44:76-81
on cantilevered house, 79:80-84
on trusses, 71:74-77 (MFC)
on Usonian community, 66:26-28
Gomito Distributors, Inc.: layout tool of, 21:20
Good House, The (Jacobson, Silverstein and Winslow): excerpted, 66:16-22
Good Housekeeping: New American home by, 28:73-77
Good Times Stove Co.: stove parts from, 21:63 (CBS)
Goodale, Douglas: on arch-top windows, 56:64-67 (FC)
Goodall, Harrison, and Renee Friedman: Log Structures, 16:21 (CSH)
Goodfellow, Bob: on newels, 82:63
Goodin, Mark: on redwood, 70:106
Goodrich (B. F.):
butyl, 2:37
EPDM, 2:37
Goody, Marvin: designs Monsanto house, 34:70, 71
Goodyear Tire & Rubber Co.: address for, 64:45 (EF)
Googie (Hess): source for, 27:31, 30:23
Gopher Glove: address for, 56:4
Gordon, Bob:
addition by, 30:50-54 (CBS)
dormer by, 23:66-67
Gordon, Bruce:
on batten doors, 7:32-33 (DWS)
on small house, 13:64-66 (SH)
Gordon, J. E.: *Structures, or Why Things Don't Fall Down,*
reviewed, 45:116
source for, 7:28 (TFH)
Gore, Robert H.:
on Florida house, 57:63-67
Gorsuch Foundry: work of, 16:44
Gossage Tool Co.: address for, 81:96
Gothic:
Carpenter, example of, 39:78-79
over Federal style, 76:128
for playhouse, 61:43-45 (SH)
Revival,
books on, 61:45 (SH)
building in, 59:36-41 (SH)
Gott, Peter: log-building techniques of, 13:54-59
Gougeon Brothers, Inc.: address for, 48:55, 50:68, 61:68, 65:43, 70:49, 81:46, 51

Gouges

Gouges: hand-forged, 49:95
Gould, Peter: on stone chimney, 30:86
Gowans, Alan: *Comfortable House, The,* reviewed, 37:90
Grabow, Stephen: *Christopher Alexander,* reviewed, 33:88
Grace (W. R.) and Co.:
 address for, 51:45, 52:56, 55:57, 57:86, 58:67, 59:39, 63:42, 70:81, 71:14, 77:57 (EF, SH, REM)
 Bituthene sheet, 25:72
 butyl sheets, 29:12
 modified bitumins, 2:37
 Polycel One, 15:59
 Zonolite, 31:38 (CBS)
Grainger (W. W.) Co.: address for, 49:87
Graining:
 described, 60:80, 81
 mentioned, 5:10-12
 process of, 60:81, 85:18-20
 See also Finishes: glazing.
Gran Quartz Trading Co.: address for, 55:8
Granado, Jesus: on plastic laminate, 9:39-41 (BK)
Granberg Industries: chainsaw mills, 7:31
Grandmothers: houses by, 45:70 (CSH)
Granite:
 for countertops, 77:44, 45
 psi of, 32:33 (FRC)
 sheets of, 44:88
 tiles, source for, 75:84
Granite City Tool Co.: address for, 48:12, 55:8
Granke, Dennis: mentioned, 38:38 (CSH)
Grant Hardware Co.:
 address for, 51:51, 53:45 (SH), 54:65 (FC)
 drawer slides, 9:37 (BK), 44:71 (BK)
Graphic Guide to Frame Construction
 (Thallon): cited, 71:112, 72:57
Graphsoft, Inc.: address for, 49:50
Grashow, Jim: model buildings by, 21:84
Grass America Inc.:
 address for, 30:58, 61-62 (BK), 69:53
 concealed hinges, 13:63 (BK)
 cup hinges of, 44:70-71 (BK)
 hardware, 35:34
 hinges, jig for, 15:6
Gratwick, R. T.: *Dampness in Buildings,* 47:20
Gray, Alexander Stuart, and John Sambrook: *Fanlights,* reviewed, 64:110
Gray, John: mentioned, 36:61 (FWS)
Gray, Ralph Gareth: on earthquake resistance, 64:60-65 (MFC)
Gray, William Whitie:
 on handsaw sharpening, 48:122
 on shoring up, 69:67-69 (REM)
Graystone Block Co., Inc.: address for, 71:52

Key to books:

(BK) Building Baths and Kitchens
(CBS) Building with Concrete, Brick and Stone
(CSH) Craftsman-Style Houses
(DWS) Building Doors, Windows and Skylights
(EEH) Energy-Efficient Houses
(EF) Exterior Finishing
(FC) Finish Carpentry
(FRC) Frame Carpentry
(FWS) Building Floors, Walls and Stairs
(MFC) More Frame Carpentry
(REM) Remodeling
(SH) Small Houses
(TB) Tools for Building
(TFH) Timber-Frame Houses

Great American Marketing, Inc.:
 caulking gun by, reviewed, 42:90
Great Camps of the Adirondacks
 (Godine): cited, 40:42
GREBE: reviewed, 71:112
Greek Revival:
 details of, 1:49, 20:59, 62-63 (FWS)
 entryway in, 54:68-71 (REM)
 porch in, 6:22-25
 restoration of, 1:48-51, 29:62-67
Green, Candida Lycett: as joint author. *See* Evans, Tony.
Green, Patrick: toolshed of, 27:96
Green (A. P.) Refractories Co.: Sairset mortar, 36:32, 42:71 (CBS)
Green Bull, Inc.: address for, 84:55
Greene, Charles:
 furniture plans by, 24:32 (CSH)
 James house by, 24:27-32 (CSH)
 later career of, 24:27, 32 (CSH)
 publications on, 24:32 (CSH)
 See also Greene and Greene Brothers.
Greene, Herb: on refining owner-builder designs, 12:38-41
Greene and Greene (Makinson):
 cited, 27:62 (BK)
 source for, 29:57 (CSH)
Greene and Greene Brothers:
 Bolton house by, 17:28-34 (CSH)
 books on, 45:122
  cited, 72:41
 career of, 24:27, 32 (CSH)
 construction by, 22:56-58 (CSH)
 deck in style of, 39:52-55 (CSH)
 furnishings by, 17:29 (CSH)
 Gamble house by, 59:87 (CSH)
 mentioned, 32:26 (CSH)
 porches of, 29:50
 Pratt house, restoration of, 72:36-41
 sprayed concrete of, 14:70
Greenheart Durawoods, Inc.: address for, 73:68

Greenhouses:
 air isolation for, 46:73
 aquaculture unit for, 73:70
 bathroom as, 38:48 (SH)
 benches for, 32:37
 book on, 7:60
 braces for, corner, 13:4
 cantilevered, 56:58-59 (EEH)
 ceilings for, slat, 13:68, 70, 71
 colors for, 4:49
 condensation in, 10:17
  preventing, 16:10
 crops in, 10:17
 desert, 41:36-40
 design for, prefab, 32:34-36
 doors for, Thermopane, 5:51
 energy calculations for, 10:17
 example of, 33:39 (EEH)
 floors for, 32:34
  deck, 13:68, 70, 71
 glazing,
  acrylic, 10:32, 33 (DWS)
  difficulties with, 14:64
  end-wall, 10:17
  EPDM, 65:62 (SH)
  roof, 10:17
 heat for, 4:48-49, 51, 10:17, 16:10
  forced-air, 4:49-51
  radiant system, 4:48-49
  storage for, water, 37:72
 hot tubs in, 8:41 (EEH)
 for house heat, 4:48, 58:80-85 (EEH), 65:62-64 (SH)
 hydroponics in, 73:70
 insulation for, 10:17
  reverse, 41:39
 integrating, 35:4, 38:26-27 (EEH)
 masonry, 14:63, 64
 octagonal, 32:34-36
 passive-solar, 32:100
 pit, with Trombe walls, 46:63, 65 (TFH)
 plans for, 10:17
 posts for, corner, 32:36
 as room connector, 11:66, 67
 shades for, 4:51, 5:51
 shallow, 1:54, 55
 skylights for, 4:48, 49, 51
 sunken, 40:28, 30, 31
 ventilation in, 10:17
 vents for,
  automatic, 32:100, 34:4
  heat-recovery ventilator pump controls for, 4:51
  temperature-sensitive window, 32:35, 37
  turbine, 5:51
 against wall, bermed, 59:62-65, 66 (EEH)
 walls in, drum, 32:100
 See also Glazing. Solariums.
Greenlaw, Bruce:
 on Abledata program, 54:102
 on ACEEE, 47:102

70

on air structure, 51:120
on cathedral workshops, 54:100-102
on CFC, 49:102
on circular saws, 48:40-43
on Colonial detail, 63:45-49
on cut-off saw blades, 62:84
discusses low-flush toilets, 48:102
on drywall lifts, 50:52
on EPA woodstove standards, 49:98
on frost-protected shallow foundations, 74:104
on healthy houses, 51:98
on history, 48:104
on HUD books, 55:108
on hurricane, 57:104-106, 128
on ladders, 84:50-55
on molder-planers, 55:50-55
on NSFC, 64:102
offers excerpts, 67:100
on PIRF floors, 46:96
on pneumatic tool seminars, 49:102
on portable table saws, 64:70-74
reviews books, 65:108
reviews Building Community, 62:106
reviews Crosscutter miter saw, 43:92
reviews Dadd, 46:104
reviews energy resource, 71:112
reviews fire prevention book, 62:104
reviews Garbage, 60:106
reviews hand-tools book, 51:104
reviews HOME, 56:104
reviews Langdon, 44:89
reviews LeGwin, 77:122
reviews lighting book, 54:106
reviews Nabokov and Easton, 69:110
reviews NAHB show, 82:92-94
reviews NAHB software book, 75:110
reviews Naversen, 46:104
reviews new books, 64:112, 67:104, 68:108
reviews Nisson, 70:122
reviews pocket guide, 46:104
reviews radon book, 53:110
reviews Ramsey, 46:104
reviews Saw Boss, 44:88
reviews Tibbets, 60:106
reviews Whiteman, 49:114
on roof safety, 61:102
on sealants, 61:36-42
on siding painting, 60:100
on timely events, 65:100-102
on tool shed, 44:63
on wood, 69:54
Greenlee Tool Co.:
address for, 54:48
horizontal mortiser, 36:49 (TFH)
Greenman, Ronald R.:
on bullet bits, 55:92
on fire extinguishers, 58:91
on mail-order, 62:50-51
reviews blind nailer, 54:92
reviews door-hanging tools, 49:95
reviews Pocket Caddy, 63:92-94

reviews saw shoe, 67:90
on smoke detectors, 46:96-98
Greenwood House, The (Hackenberg):
cited, 7:42
reviewed, 4:58
Grefco, Inc.: Permalite, 36:73
Gridley, Roy and Marilyn: belvedere of, 30:64-69 (CBS)
Griendling, Rich:
on concrete and glulams, 77:50-54
on curtainless shower, 79:62-63
Griesbach, C. B.: *Historic Ornament,* cited, 69:87
Griffen, Walter Burley: Knitlock system of, 16:6
Griffith, David: house designed by, 25:50-53
Griffoul, Michelle: ceramics by, 59:90
Grillworks, The: registers of, reviewed, 60:96
Grinders:
abrasive belt,
choosing, 18:59 (TB)
types of, 18:59 (TB)
mini-,
random-orbit sanding heads for, 77:70
speed control for, source for, 77:70
portable, for brick mortar removal, 2:46
power wheel,
dressing, 18:59 (TB)
grit for, choosing, 18:58 (TB)
safety labels for, 37:81
tool rests for, 18:58 (TB)
using, 18:58-59 (TB)
using, free-hand, 18:58-59 (TB)
safety with, 50:4, 18
Griskivich, Stan: reviews Shapiro, 29:90
Griskivich, Stan and Toni:
greenhouse shutters by, 13:48-49 (DWS)
house by, 2:50-52 (SH)
Groff, Richard D.: on heating system, 85:84-87
Grohe America, Inc.: plumbing fixture, 35:34
Groom, James N.: as joint author. *See* Harkness, Sarah P.
Groove-V-Guide: source for, 37:81
Gross, Marshall:
Roof Framing,
cited, 57:78 (CSH, MFC)
reviewed, 60:106
videos by, reviewed, 60:106
Ground hydrants: *See* Pumps: pitcher.
Grout:
additives for, 25:34, 35 (BK)
for heat resistance, 71:54
for block, 16:57 (CBS)
for brick, 25:51
broom application of, 23:12, 38:41-42
colored, source for, 82:87
for concrete, bonding, 11:47 (CBS)
epoxy, 77:42, 43

epoxy impervious, 77:42, 43
and gravel, for stone masonry, 23:14
gun for, 5:6
placing, 68:69
soil-matched, 61:60 (SH)
for tiles, 17:75, 25:37, 32:52, 36:66 (BK)
siliconing, 78:28
using, faxed advice on, 70:112
waterproof, 22:12
See also Mortar. Tiles.
Grovco Sales Co.: window springs, 20:8
Grove, Scott: on decks, 29:42-46 (FRC)
Grove Park Inn: described, 54:100
Grover, Christopher:
on deck, 39:52-55 (CSH)
reviews Ching, 51:104
reviews Riggs, 30:78
Grow, Lawrence, comp.: *Seventh Old House Catalog, The,* reviewed, 70:122
Growing A Business (Hawken):
reviewed, 67:104
Growing a Housebuilder (Brady):
reviewed, 64:112
Growing Food in Solar Greenhouses (Yanda, Wolfe): cited, 10:17
Grumman: solar panels, 42:53 (SH)
Grundfos Pumps Corp.:
address for, 59:87 (CSH), 72:14
ceramic-bearing pump, 27:71 (CBS)
Grunewald, John: staircase by, 35:75, 78-79
G-U Hardware: address for, 54:65 (FC)
Guaranteed Energy Efficient Systems, Inc.: address for, 84:88
Guardian Industries: high-performance glass of, discussed, 41:84-86
Guazzoni, Alan: on pondside gazebo, 75:57-59
Guerra, Glenn: on cherry ceiling, 56:74-77
Guest houses: *See* Cabins.
Gugler, Kent: work by, 52:90
Guide to Affordable Houses (Wade):
cited, 46:80 (TFH)
mentioned, 25:46 (TFH)
Guide to Hand Tools (Hand Tools Institute): reviewed, 51:104
Guide to Resource Efficient Building Elements (Center for Resourceful Building):
cited, 81:106
source for, 85:124
Guide to Shotcrete: source for, 40:63 (CBS)
Guide to Southern Pine Shakes (Southern Forest Products Association): cited, 84:4
Guild, The: reviewed, 44:94
Gullfiber AB: trusses by, 40:53
Gulliford, Andrew:
on cave dwellers, 63:120
Los Angeles talk by, 20:22
on sod houses, 31:54-57
Gun blueing: suppliers of, 17:14

Gunebo Corp.: powder-actuated tools from, 21:34 (TB)

Gunite:
architectural use of, 14:70
as fill, 19:73, 75
for foundations,
    retaining wall, 53:48-49 (SH)
    waterproofing, 69:14
retaining wall of, 40:60-63 (CBS)
See also Earth construction. Shotcrete.

Gunite and Shotcrete Contractors Association: address for, 40:63 (CBS)

Gurney, Susie: reviews Thomsen, 68:106-108

Gusdorf, Edmund B.: boathouse by, 9:76

Gustav Stickley (Smith): sources for, 36:29 (CSH)

Gutters:
alternative to, tiled-ditch, 77:54
aluminum, installing, 67:38-41 (EF)
avoiding, 27:75
book on, source for, 58:14
box,
    problems with, 27:10-12
    repairing, 27:12, 61:68-69
chain and catch-basin substitute for, 66:42
for cisterns, 10:53 (BK)
for colonial additions, 5:22
concealed, 77:46 (EF)
copper,
    built-in, 53:55-56, 57
    integral, for snow country, 38:72, 73, 75 (TFH)
and cornices, 15:39-41 (EF), 77:46-49 (EF)
downspouts for,
    gargoyle, 55:84, 87, 56:70, 72 (CSH)
    sizing, 67:38, 41, 42 (EF)
    wooden, 80:61
for eaves, 66:46, 47
flashing for, 9:47 (EF), 67:39, 42 (EF)
galvanized, installing, 67:38, 41, 42-43 (EF)
hangers for, 67:38-39 (EF)
inlaid, installing, 61:46-49, 63:4
necessity of, 48:67, 67:38 (EF)
pans as, integral, 75:83-84
profiles of, 67:38 (EF)
screens for, discussed, 69:4
for sod roofs, 56:79
sound-deadening, 70:32-34
Swiss, 70:75
tiles for, barrel, 24:29, 30 (CSH)
for turret, 68:59
wood,
    curved, 31:71
    with deep cornices, 24:14
    installing, 6:66, 22:12
    replacing, 14:25
Yankee, 27:75
See also Downspouts.

Gutterson, Henry: on roofs, 10:26 (erratum, 24:6)

Gwinnup, Roger: on header problems, 62:85-87 (MFC)

Gym lockers: black, 37:28, 29 (BK)

Gypboard: *See* Drywall.

Gypcrete: mentioned, 27:69 (CBS)

Gypcrete Corp.: address for, 82:68

Gypsolite:
source for, 23:61 (FWS)
using, 26:41

Gypsum Association: address for, 58:75, 81:56

Gypsum board: *See* Drywall.

Gypsum Construction Handbook (USG):
cited, 51:83 (MFC)
source for, 35:4, 81:43

Gypsum plaster: as adhesive, 65:41, 45

Gypsy wagon: building, 50:87-89 (CSH)

H

H and H Industries: visited, 31:76

Haas Wood and Ivory: millwork, 44:67, 68 (FRC)

Haase, Ronald W.:
on glass block, 37:47 (DWS)
on glass-block tower, 37:50-51 (DWS)

Haberfeld, Louise: on aquarium, 72:62-63

Habiger, Robert: gazebo by, 75:86

Habitat for Humanity:
builds timber-frame, 56:104
discussed, 53:104

Habitat News: reviewed, 36:94

HABS: *See* Historic American Building Survey.

Hackenberg, Larry: *Greenwood House, The,* reviewed, 4:58

Hackett, Clifford: on concrete-plane roof, 25:72

Hackleman, Michael: *Better Use of Your...Electricity,* reviewed, 24:80

Hacksaws:
power, improvised, 54:26
for renovation, 12:51 (TB)

Haddon Tool: Lumber-Maker chainsaw mill, 7:29, 31

Haegler, Jeff: on log house, 32:72-75

Haegler, Steve: mentioned, 32:73

HAER: *See* Historic American Engineering Record.

Haertling, Charles: house by, 58:49-53

Häfele America Co.: address for, 52:102, 54:65 (FC), 62:61, 65:86, 73:100, 74:73, 77 (FC)
hardware, 35:34

Hagerty, Bob:
house by, 43:75-79

Hagstrom, Carl:
on concrete, 83:46-51
drills, 78:122
reviews solar-design book, 79:120
on twisted chimney, 75:43-45

Hairston, Gale: house by, 45:54-59, 88

Haivala Concrete Tools: patterning tools of, 7:6

Hale, Jonathan: on Wright house, 65:100

Hall, Christopher: on stone-glass addition, 77:74-75

Hall, David: house by, 80:40-45

Hall, Doug: mentioned, 29:30

Hall, Walter: *Barnacle Parp's New Chainsaw Guide,* cited, 78:43

Hall, Wayne: on epoxy wood consolidation, 16:20-21 (CSH)

Halls:
bridge as, 13:70
for handicapped, 6:51, 76:55
minimizing, 52:14-16
plumbing of, 23:71 (FRC)

Halo Lighting:
address for, 62:48 (SH)
fixtures, 15:56, 57 (BK)

Halstead Enterprises, Inc.: framing nailers, reviewed, 56:52, 53-55

Hamilton, Douglas:
about, 45:130
house by, 45:70-75, 89 (CSH)

Hamilton, Johnny E., and Margaret S.: *Math to Build On,* reviewed, 85:132

Hamilton, Richard: designs Monsanto house, 34:70

Hammer, Martin: on header, 62:87 (MFC)

Hammers:
body strategies with, 85:81
bricklaying, 43:52 (CBS)
choosing, 12:51 (TB)
cold-proofing, 50:60
copper, 40:87
copper/beryllium, 40:87
deadblow urethane, source for, 39:63
demolition,
    electric, 18:18
    sling for, 19:14
drop, 29:74-75
drywall, 8:54 (FWS)
framing, 23:32-35, 30:10 (TB)
gauged roofing, discussed, 57:94-96
handles for,
    choosing, 84:30
    fiberglass-reinforced, 30:10
    securing, 84:30
for metal, 32:53, 55 (TB)
as nail pullers, 32:54-55 (TB)
for roofing, 57:94-96
rotary, 82:92
    bits in, unsticking, 34:14
    safety with, 29:38 (FRC)
    using, 29:35-36 (FRC)

safety with, 62:4
Side-Strike, reviewed, 81:96
slater's, 27:16
sledge,
    handle protector for, 79:32
    using, 34:16
slide, 46:90
steel, deadening of, 25:4
tinner's, for standing-seam roofing,
    sources for, 39:63
See also Axes: rigging. Handles.
Hammond, Jon: straw-bale studio of,
    24:70-72
Hand cleaners: salad oil as, 55:28
Hand Tool Safety Guide (Hand Tools
    Institute): cited, 84:6
Hand Tools Institute:
    Guide to Hand Tools, reviewed, 51:104
    Hand Tool Safety Guide, cited, 84:6
Handbook for Building Homes of Earth
    (Wolfskill, Dunlap and Gallaway):
    source for, 34:39
Handbook for Ceramic Tile Installation:
    cited, 23:50
Handbook for Design:
    cited, 23:48
    source for, 53:67
Handbook of Building Crafts in
    Conservation (Bowyer): reviewed,
    24:86
Handbook of Carpentry and Joinery
    (Emary): cited, 50:69 (FC)
Handbook of Doormaking,
    Windowmaking, and Staircasing:
    cited, 72:50 (FC)
Handbook of Toxic and Hazardous
    Chemicals and Carcinogens: source
    for, 73:67
Handcrafted Doors and Windows
    (Rowland): source for, 36:41 (DWS)
Handicapped:
    advocacy group for, 35:45 (BK)
    bathroom design for, 23:16
    bathtub for, cushioned, 65:96
    building checklist for, 77:108-10
    building information for, 6:51, 23:48,
        32:86, 35:45 (BK) 53:67, 55:8-10, 108,
        63:106, 65:54
        computerized, 54:102
    call system for, 65:77, 79 (REM)
    design for, 6:51
    handles for, door, 48:65 (FC, MFC)
    houses for, 39:48-51 (FWS), 50:102, 53:67-
        71, 76:54-59
        development, 32:82
        plans for, 52:100, 53:89
    housing center for, 79:112
    kitchen for, 35:43-45 (BK)
    remodel for, 73:60-65
    room for, 6:51
    suite for, 65:76-79 (REM)
    suppy sources for, 35:45 (BK)

in wheelchairs, offset hinge doors for,
    19:10
Handles:
    door,
        ebony, 29:56 (CSH)
        nylon, 46:53 (EEH)
    flip-up casement window, reviewed,
        76:94
    for handicapped, 48:65 (FC, MFC), 76:57,
        58
    radiused stainless-steel, 48:53
    replacement, epoxying, 15:16
    steel, deadening of, 25:4
    See also Latches.
Handmade Hot Water Systems
    (Sussman): cited, 46:65 (TFH)
Handrails: *See* Railing.
Hands: injury to, 83:80-81
    treating, 79:57
Handsaws:
    blades for, replaceable, reviewed,
        85:102
    case for, 49:28
    choosing, 20:69 (TB)
    coping, for crown molding, 51:64-65
        (FC)
    crosscut, 20:58 (CBS)
    for drywall, reviewed, 79:100
    files for, 20:71 (TB)
    Japanese folding, reviewed, 72:88-90
    Japanese pruning, for rough cuts, 48:55
    jointing, 20:71 (TB)
    keyhole, for drywall, 8:54 (FWS)
    for miter boxes, wooden, 65:75 (FC)
    nibs on, 56:14, 60:4, 62:6
    old, buying, 54:94-96, 120
    pit, using, 13:26, 27 (TFH)
    profile of, 27:4
    for renovation, 12:51 (TB)
    rip, 20:68 (TB)
    set of, 20:68-69, 70, 71 (TB)
    sharpening, 30:70, 71-72, 48:122
    "shortcut," reviewed, 69:92
    sizes of, 20:68 (TB)
    tendon danger from, avoiding, 81:6
    for timber framing, 4:23 (TFH)
    tool-box bracket for, 58:26
    using, 20:72 (TB), 78:60-61
    vises for, 20:71 (TB)
Hangers: *See* Metal connectors.
Hanisch, Ric: on saunas, 35:51-53 (BK)
Hanke, Paul:
    on caretaker house, 47:84-87
    discusses Habitat for Humanity, 53:104
    on green wood, 7:40-42
    on Hanna studio, 2:56-59
    mentioned, 20:81
    on plank floors, 33:42-43 (FWS)
    reviews Abrams, 38:86
    reviews earth-shelter books, 16:14-16,
        32:82
    reviews Gill, 50:108

    reviews Japanese book, 19:26
    reviews Syvanen, 3:60
    reviews Woodbridge, 83:120-22
    on Sparfil blocks, 23:82-84
    on surface-bonded block, 12:34-37 (CBS)
Hann, Marlys: on Catskill house, 48:79-83
Hanover Wire Cloth, Inc.: address for,
    57:75 (FC)
Hansbrough, Jim: reviews *Brown Book,*
    The, 31:80
Hansen, Daryl E.: on addition, 51:50-53
Hansen, David: on heat-recovery
    ventilators, 23:80-82
Hansen, Gunnar: on seaside home, 38:40-
    45
Hanson, David: remodel by, 44:51-53 (SH)
Hanson, Keith: addresses conference,
    33:84
Hanson, Sven:
    reviews hole saw, 79:100
    on solid-surface countertops, 84:40-45
Hanson, Tim: on drywall lift, 50:50-52
Harboe, Thomas: on Frank Lloyd Wright,
    20:73-79
Har-Car Aluminum Products: address
    for, 49:73 (EEH)
Hardboard:
    association for, 67:81, 83:45
    for cabinets, 30:59 (BK)
    cart for, reviewed, 81:92
    for floors, 12:44 (REM)
    nails for, 67:81
    siding from, 83:42-43, 44
    uses of, 67:80, 81
Hardcast Inc.:
    address for, 65:58 (EF)
    aluminum stripping, 42:22 (CSH)
Hardman Saunders Co.: columns of, 9:22
Hardware:
    Austrian nylon, 35:34
    authentic, sources for, 31:82, 81:114-16
    backsplash-attachment clips, 75:65
    bolts, cremorne, 5:33
    cabinet, 35:34
        sources for, 52:98, 102
    cabinet, kitchen
        European, 44:69-71 (BK)
        installing, 85:52
    catches, bullet, 69:54
    connector plates, 30:26 (FRC)
    Corian, sculpting, 66:55
    Craftsman, 36:28 (CSH)
    deck clips, 35:90
    door, 57:75 (FC)
        commercial, 3:55
        foreign/American hybrids, 39:92
        French, 68:43-44 (FC)
        for handicapped, 53:68, 71
        installing, 8:36 (DWS)
        slide-and-hinge hybrid, 49:62 (SH)
        sliding, closer for, 82:96
        sliding-screen, 51:51

door-knocker,
    hand-forged, 66:77
    iron, 48:84
eccentric, catalog of, 64:112
faucet, cross-handle, source for, 75:49
    (REM)
gun blueing for, 17:14
hand-forged, source for, 67:58
for handicapped, 76:57, 58
icebox, 18:32
importance of, 80:53
internalized, German, 35:57 (TB)
lazy-Susan, source for, 69:54
leg bracket, folding, 56:94
making, 63:66-68
marine-grade, 67:61
national show of, 36:88
neoprene, source for, 66:50, 102
nylon colored, source for, 73:59
old, matching, 75:100
pocket-door, 54:64, 66 (FC), 56:6
pull-out, source for, 52:102
in restoration, 1:49
for seacoast, 59:81
security, source for, 85:102-104
source for, 63:41
storage containers for, bucket,
    reviewed, 69:96
window, bronze, 51:8
wooden threaded, 35:31
See also Bolts. Hinges. Latches. Metal
    connectors. Pulls.
*Hardwood Flooring Finishing/
Refinishing Manual:* cited, 23:50
*Hardwood Flooring Installation
Manual:* cited, 23:50
Hare, Robert: on converting old store,
    20:44-48
**Harkness, Sarah P., and James N.
Groom:** *Building without Barriers for the
Disabled,* source for, 5:51
Harlen Metal Products: metal
    connectors, 43:49 (FRC)
Harlow house: pocket shutters of, 8:74
Harmon, Frank: on beach house, 59:78-82
Harmonson Stairs: stairbuilding by, 43:38-
    39 (FWS)
Harnden, Cherie: ceramics by, 59:90
Harper, Douglas: *Working Knowledge,*
    reviewed, 55:108
Harper, Rick: on curved wall, 7:16-20
    (FRC)
Harreluk, Bob: shingles by, 65:88
Harrington Tools: drywall knives, 23:63
    (FWS)
Harris, Cyril, ed.: *Dictionary of
Architecture and Construction, The,*
    reviewed, 47:112

Harris, Harwell Hamilton:
    architecture of, 55:70-74
    book on, 55:74
Harris, Richard: *Discovering Timber-
Framed Buildings,* 47:45 (TFH)
Harris, W. Robert: *Drywall,* reviewed,
    70:120
Harris Hydroelectric: address for, 64:12
Harris (J. W.) Co.:
    Stay-Brite silver-bearing solder, 29:88
    Stay Clean liquid flux, 39:65
Harris Packaging Corp.: address for,
    70:63 (EEH)
Harrison, Gregory: on safe stairs, 65:66-
    68
Hart Tool Co.: Tweaker, reviewed, 50:94,
    78:92
Hartelius, Dennis:
    brick wall of, 15:84
    garden of, 35:104
Harter Concrete Products Co.: dry-stack
    block of, 16:57 (CBS)
Hartford House: exhibit of, 50:102
Hartsell, Thomas L.: as joint author. *See*
    Van Den Branden, F.
Hartzler, Neil: on garage conversion,
    77:76-79 (REM)
Hasluck, Paul N.: *Manual of Traditional
Woodworking,* cited, 69:87
Hassinger, Herman:
    about, 45:130
    house by, 45:82-87, 89
Hasson, Will: on kitchen cabinets, 9:32-38
    (BK)
Hastings, Diane: on chicken house, 55:124
Hastings Tile & Il Bagno Collection:
    address for, 68:96
Hat channels: source for, 13:10
Hatchets:
    broad, source for, 30:49
    framing, 30:10
    shingling, described, 12:52, 53
    See also Axes: rigging.
Hats:
    burnoose, reviewed, 72:88
    for cold-weather work, 50:62
Haubold of America, Inc.: framing
    nailers, reviewed, 56:52, 53, 54-55
Haugh, Kathleen: as joint author. *See*
    DiGaetano, Louis S.
Haun, Larry:
    on blocking, 82:48-51
    on cutting plywood, 76:63-65 (MFC)
    on door hanging, 53:38-42 (FC)
    on fast-framing roofs, 60:83-87 (MFC)
    on framing crawl-space foundation,
        77:80-85
    on hip roof, 69:44-45 (MFC)
    on rake walls, 72:67-69 (MFC)
    on staircases, 67:44-46
    on valley framing, 79:58-61

Very Efficient Carpenter, The,
    cited, 77:85, 79:61, 82:48, 84:16, 85:56
    videos by, 85:56
    on wall bracing, 85:54-57
Haust, David: on drywall bending, 7:54, 56
Hawaii:
    exterior finishes for, 24:12
    house for, 61:58-61 (SH)
    solar tax credits in, 3:12
Hawken, Paul: *Growing A Business,*
    reviewed, 67:104
Hawks:
    for drywall, 8:54 (FWS)
    for plaster, 15:3, 74
Haws, Irving: house by, 44:64-68 (FRC)
Hay, Harold: mentioned, 26:56
Hayes, Roy: mentioned, 32:34
Haynes, Charles: solar houses by, 5:14
Hayton, Richard:
    on design, 8:25 (CBS)
    house by, 8:22-27 (CBS)
Hayward, Charles: *Woodwork Joints,* 42:42
    (TFH)
Hayward, Judy: mentioned, 27:83
Hazel *(Corylus cornuta):* in thatching,
    22:73, 74, 75, 76, 77
Hazzard, Ed: house by, 6:18-21 (CSH)
Header joist: *See* Joists: rim.
Headers:
    adding,
        in attics, 62:85, 86 (MFC)
        to balloon frame, 62:85, 86 (MFC)
        to joist end, 62:87 (MFC)
        to save drywall, 62:86 (MFC)
        schemes for, 64:6-8
        to truss ends, 62:85 (MFC)
    built-up box beam, 19:10
    built-up, with insulation layers, 79:32
    concrete, casting, 18:46
    continuous, 31:24, 25, 27 (CSH), 42:29-30
        (CSH)
        interior, 17:33 (CSH)
    corbeled, 63:55 (REM)
    defined, 10:63 (FRC), 21:71 (FRC)
    dropped, blended in, 28:52 (FWS)
    "falling," framing, 74:82-85 (MFC)
    flitch-plate, 55:75, 76, 77 (MFC)
        installing, 56:83-84
        shear plates for, 58:6-8
    flush hidden, adding, 64:6-8
    and foundation considerations, 62:87
        (MFC)
    4x12s for, 21:71 (FRC), 22:33 (FRC)
    jack, 21:71 (FRC)
    jamb, 21:71 (FRC)
    laminated,
        commercial, 1:63
        pre-engineered, 62:85 (MFC)
        -veneer lumber, 50:44-45 (MFC)
    long-span, no-rack techniques for, 62:87
        (MFC)
    plywood, 84:47, 48

retrofitting, 46:26, 53:26

screws for, vs. nails, 64:8-10

steel I-beam, solo handling of, 62:87 (MFC)

Health and Safety Hazard Identification Program (UBC): source for, 34:55 (TB)

Health codes: ubiquity of, 5:45

Healthy House, The (Bower): reviewed, 64:112

Healthy houses:

book on, reviewed, 64:112

building, 73:66-70

design consultant for, 73:67

product source for, 73:67

sealant for, 61:37

See also Safety.

Heard, Brooks: on Australian verandah, 53:62-66

Hearing: *See* Safety.

Heart Interface inverter: source for, 24:80

Hearth Warmers: address for, 70:56 (EEH)

Heartland Products: address for, 77:22

Heartwood Owner-Builder School:

courses of, 13:14-16

program of, reviewed, 51:98

Heat: nature of, 33:56

Heat Controller, Inc.: heat pumps, 26:68

Heat exchangers: *See* Heat-recovery ventilators.

Heat Exchangers Inc.: heat pumps, 26:68

Heat guns:

disadvantages of, 1:33 (FWS)

source for, 62:38-39 (EF)

use of, 3:4

Heat loss: finding, 46:47-48

Heat Mirror:

glazing, in divided-light casements, 38:65 (CSH)

high-performance glass of, discussed, 41:84-86

using, 34:65-66 (BK)

Heat plates: source for, 62:38 (EF)

Heat pumps:

air-source, 26:66

air-to-water,

filters for, 46:72

Swedish, 46:72

as coolers, 26:66

geothermal, discussed, 72:72 (EEH)

ground-source, 26:66-68

hybrid, 26:66

inefficiency of, 26:68, 48:4, 78:70, 85:84

Swedish triple-function, 22:18 (CSH)

water-source, 14:16

Heat Pumps: source for, 26:68

Heat Recovery Ventilation for Housing: source for, 22:18 (CSH), 32:90

Heath Zenith: address for, 80:98

Key to books:

(BK)   Building Baths and Kitchens

(CBS) Building with Concrete, Brick and Stone

(CSH) Craftsman-Style Houses

(DWS) Building Doors, Windows and Skylights

(EEH) Energy-Efficient Houses

(EF)   Exterior Finishing

(FC)   Finish Carpentry

(FRC) Frame Carpentry

(FWS) Building Floors, Walls and Stairs

(MFC) More Frame Carpentry

(REM) Remodeling

(SH)   Small Houses

(TB)   Tools for Building

(TFH) Timber-Frame Houses

Heather Power Tool, Ltd.: dividers, 34:49

Heatilator, Inc.:

chimney liners, 36:64 (BK)

copy of, in masonry stove, 42:69 (CBS)

Heating, Cooling, Lighting (Lechner): reviewed, 72:108

Heating, Refrigeration and Air Conditioning Institute (Canada): heat-recovery courses by, 34:34 (DWS)

Heating systems:

adding, 78:58

air cleaners for, electrostatic, 67:92

air infiltration through, preventing, 77:67

boilers for, 85:86

automated hydronic, 53:74, 75, 76

care of, 46:45

ceiling radiant, source for, 76:8

centralizing, 52:14

considering, 35:4

COP of, 26:66

design aid for, reviewed, 79:120

design temperature for, 46:48

efficient, 10:44-45

electric,

back-up, 66:59 (SH)

baseboard, concealed, 80:70, 71

ceramic-storage, 43:74 (SH), 75:49 (REM), 82:102

fan-assisted, 60:44 (SH)

German, thermal storage units for, 70:112

in-line duct, 66:66, 68 (EEH)

kickspace, 48:80, 83

zoned fan-forced, 59:72 (SH)

electric radiant,

advantages of, 75:69

ceiling, source for, 77:88

suppliers of, 75:72

fan-coil unit for, source for, 56:61 (EEH)

filters for, 46:45, 47, 72

forced-air,

continuous-cycle, 66:45

distribution for, 46:46-47

hot-water hybrid, 85:84-87

solar integrated, 59:67 (EEH)

furnaces for, designing, 46:44-48

gas, 46:46

efficient, 65:78 (REM)

high-efficiency, 31:69

water-heater and HRV forced-air, 56:59-61 (EEH)

greenhouse as, window-wall, 69:40, 43 (EEH)

heat pumps, 78:70

geothermal, 69:18, 72:72 (EEH)

hot-water,

book on, 46:65 (TFH)

centralizing, 52:14

circulating pump for, 33:12, 42:53 (SH)

electric boiler for, 42:53 (SH)

electric instaneous, 80:70

energy-efficient, 80:70

fireplace-integrated, 46:63, 65 (TFH)

flat-plate collector, 49:72, 75 (EEH)

Freon-charged, testing, 29:86-88 (erratum, 30:4)

gas, flues for, 49:18

hot-air hybrid, 79:52

Skylids in, 26:56-57

solar-assisted, 42:53 (SH)

thermosiphon, 29:88

thermosiphon, air-panel, described, 5:4

thermosiphon, collector for, 3:48-50

thermosiphon, mentioned, 1:47 (EEH)

underground extensions of, 65:18

woodstove heat exchanger for, 33:12

hydronic coils for, in-duct, 74:14-16

information on, 46:48

integrated, 63:85 (EEH)

with integrated cooling, ventilation, 33:84

kerosene through-the-wall, 40:59

leaky, repairs for, 67:98

metal positive-pressure flues for, 55:60

multi-fuel trash-burning, reviewed, 65:94-96

new, savings from, 33:57

oil-to-gas conversion of, 2:65, 5:4

outside air for, need of, 28:82, 46:46

plenums for,

crawl-space, 37:27 (BK)

metal, in concrete, 60:58-59 (EEH)

propane backup unit for, 65:64 (SH)

registers for, reviewed, 60:94-96

sensors for, 53:76

sizing, 26:68, 46:47-48

for solar houses, 84:88

solar panels for, 71:106

solar-tempered, 73:45 (EEH)

swimming pool as, 45:80 (EEH)
and time constants, 65:65 (SH)
types of, 46:45-46
vent dampers for, advisability of, 33:57
wood,
    cautions for, 70:79
    efficiency of, 36:33 (CBS)
    furnace for, 70:79
    restrictions on, 36:33 (CBS)
    water stove, 45:68
wood/oil,
    high-fire forced-draft, 55:60
    hot-water, 38:28 (EEH)
wood/propane/electric, 55:85
wood/solar, 65:62-65 (SH)
See also Air cleaners. Ductwork.
    Fireplaces. Masonry stoves. Radiant-
    floor heating. Radiators. Solar
    design. Thermal mass. Thermostats.
    Trombe walls. Wood stoves.

Heat-recovery ventilators:
and air quality, 1:12, 3:4, 5:4, 15
airtight installation of, 42:62-63
and appliances, 23:82
books on, 32:90, 50:108
brands of, 9:59
centrifugal fan, 34:33 (DWS)
choosing, 22:16-18
and clothes dryers, 23:82, 81:16-18
for cold areas, 19:71 (EEH)
and combustion air, 23:82
computer-run, 73:70
condensation with, 23:82
considerations with, 30:4, 37:65
costs of, 23:82, 28:81
courses on, Canadian, 34:34 (DWS)
defrosting, 34:32 (DWS)
drawbacks of, 23:4, 24:82, 46:72
duct work with, 23:82
efficiency of, 37:10
explained, 9:59, 11:6
for healthy houses, 73:70
heat pump as, Swedish air-to-water,
    22:18 (CSH)
humidistat controlled, 24:53 (DWS)
information on, 65:52
integrated-system, 33:84
large, 66:66 (EEH)
maintenance of, 23:82
need for, 19:68, 28:81-82
operating, 65:65 (SH)
placement of, 23:82
problems with, 28:82, 34:30-31, 32 (DWS),
    37:10
purposes of, 34:31-31 (DWS)
against radon, 67:50-51
and range hoods, 23:82
redundant, 70:56 (EEH)
size of, 23:82
for small spaces, 34:69 (SH)
source for, 3:4
system for, 34:33-34 (DWS), 78:70-71

through-the-wall, 23:82
two-speed, 24:69
types of, 34:32-33 (DWS), 37:4
and vent stacks, 23:82
whole-house, 23:80-82
workshop on, 23:80-82
See also Heat pumps: air-to-water.
Heatway: address for, 77:54
Hebert: molder-planer of, 19:52 (FWS)
Hechter, Doug: on leaded glass, 23:36-51
    (DWS)
Heckmann Building Products Inc.: metal
    connectors, 43:49 (FRC)
Heilman, Dan: *Carpenter's Dream,*
    reviewed, 62:112
Heim, David: on slate roofs, 20:38-43 (EF)
Heineken, Alfred: bottle house by, 36:104
Heinlein, Terrence: addresses
    conference, 47:102
Heinz, Thomas A.: on Jacobs II house,
    3:20-27
Helfant, David Benaroya:
    on foundation drainage, 50:82-86
    on seismic retrofits, 29:34-38 (FRC)
Heliodons: Sun Light, 13:18
Heller, Robert: as joint author. *See*
    Salvadori, Mario.
Helliwell, Boh: on spiral house, 35:74-77
Hem-fir: explained, 17:8, 19:4
Hemlock (*Tsuga* spp.):
    durability of, 11:4
    nature of, 17:8, 19:4, 40:69 (FRC)
    span capability of, 33:43 (FWS)
    for timber framing, 7:6, 26:10
Hemp, Peter:
    on framing for plumbing, 49:51-53 (MFC)
    on installing dishwasher, 54:46-48
    reviews Ratch-Cut, 53:94-96
    Straight Poop, The, cited, 49:53 (MFC)
Hempe Manufacturing Co.: miter boxes,
    36:88-89
Henderson, Lamar: on barrel vaults,
    51:82-85 (MFC)
Hennin, Pat: on hung walls, 8:28-30 (TFH)
Hennin, Pat and Patsy:
    film by, 1:66
    on framing saltbox, 4:44-47 (FRC)
Henry A. Landes house: pictured, 39:78
Henry Dreyfuss Co.: modular bathroom,
    34:74
Henry (W. W.) Co.: address for, 66:55,
    77:67
Herbert Malarkey Roofing Co.: address
    for, 64:92
Herbertson, Ross:
    on adhesives, 65:40-45
    on epoxies, 70:45-49
    reviews gypsum fiberboard, 64:94
Heritage Custom Kitchens: address for,
    65:73

Herman, Alfred and Helen: entryway of,
    3:12
Hermannsson, John: stair storage by,
    85:95
**Hertzberg, Ruth, Beatrice Vaughan, and
    Janet Greene:** *Putting Food By,* cited,
    72:14
Hess, Alan:
    Googie, mentioned, 27:31, 30:23
    on Hillmer house, 30:18-23
    on Mauer House, 18:26-32
    on 1950s future house, 34:70-75
    on Onslow-Ford house, 27:26-31
Hewi, Inc.:
    address for, 46:53 (EEH), 73:59
    hardware, 35:34
    nylon-coated door hardware by, 48:65
    (FC, MFC)
Hexicon: soldering iron of, 23:41 (DWS)
Hibben, Thomas: earth construction by,
    28:81
Hickey, Neil: owner-building advice from,
    4:12-13
Hickman, Barry: mentioned, 26:56
Hickman, David: custom bath by, 36:68-69
    (BK)
Hickman (W. P.) Co.: zinc roofing of, 24:44
Hickory (*Carya* spp.):
    hardness group of, 40:69 (FRC)
    pignut, for flooring, 37:8
Hicks Starter Vent: address for, 61:80 (EF)
Hida Tool and Hardware Co., Inc.:
    address for, 76:82 (FC), 83:92
Hide glue: *See* Glue.
**_High-Efficiency Showerheads and
    Faucets_** (Rocky Mountain Institute):
    cited, 84:83
High-Pressure Decorative Laminates:
    cited, 9:41 (BK)
Hi-Lift Jack Co.: address for, 72:90
Hill, Daniel Milton:
    on cottage cluster, 59:68-73 (SH)
    on energy detailing, 29:68-72
Hill, Jeffrey O.: *Professional Dome Plans,*
    reviewed, 65:108
Hillbrand, Deane: mentioned, 35:50 (FRC)
Hillen, Robert: library shelves by, 65:85-
    87
Hilley, John:
    on chimneys, 21:46-50 (CBS)
    fireplaces by, 20:54-58 (CBS)
    mentioned, 14:33, 35 (CBS)
    stuccoes foundations, 18:35 (CBS)
Hillmer, Jack:
    career of, 30:22
    house by, 30:18-23
    mentioned, 27:31
Hilti Fastening Systems, Inc.:
    address for, 77:67
    adhesive anchoring devices, 26:82
    foam-sealant applicator CB2000, 39:92

framing nailers, reviewed, 56:52, 53, 54-55

masonry anchors, 41:57

nailer, discussed, 47:74-75 (FC)

pneumatic tools, 15:53 (TB)

powder-actuated fasteners,
    model DX350, 23:69 (FRC)
    model DX36M, 39:90-92

powder-actuated tools, 21:36

Quik Bolts, 29:34 (FRC)

Hines, Thomas S.:

on Richard Neutra, 19:28-33

Richard Neutra and the Search for Modern Architecture, mentioned, 19:33

Hinges:

antique, sources for, 20:12

for batten doors, 7:32 (DWS)

bearings for, thrust, 14:14

bifold/pivot,
    over carpet, 70:34

cabinet, 65:73-74
    adjustable, source for, 58:41 (REM)
    installing, 30:58 (BK)
    source for, 69:53

cup, 30:58, 59 (BK), 44:69-71 (BK)
    concealed, 44:69-71 (BK)
    installing, 26:29-31 (DWS)
    specialty, 44:70-71 (BK)
    for 32mm cabinets, 74:77

decorative, stamped-brass, source for, 39:92

drill-press attachment for, 74:77

fiche slot, Flagg use of, 5:33, 34

frictionless, 14:14

Grass,
    concealed, 13:63 (BK)
    jig for, 15:6

hook-and-eye, 5:33, 34

installing, 8:35-36 (DWS), 9:37-38 (BK), 53:42 (FC), 55:4-6, 78:28

maker of, 10:46 (DWS)

making, 63:66-68

marker for, 49:95

massive wrought, 36:77 (DWS)

MED offset, 19:10

offset, 19:10

oil reservoir for, 18:14

for overhead bifold shutters, 13:49 (DWS)

painting, 67:58

piano, 12:32

pin, brass integral, 50:73 (FC)

pivot, 47:67

plane for, 49:95

rising butt,
    cheaper, 55:4
    discussed, 49:14

router bits for, 53:40, 41 (FC)

router jigs for, 16:12, 28:4-6

router templates for, 31:28-31, 53:40, 41, 55:37-38, 68:45 (FC, TB)
    reviewed, 70:104-106

screws for, long, 21:16

for security, 31:14

shimming, 10:6

springing, 53:42 (FC)

strap, with jamb lead, 20:12

for thick doors, 10:46 (DWS)

Hinges and Handles: address for, 71:72

Hinton, Kem Gardner:

about, 45:130

house by, 45:32-37, 88

Hintz, Berny N.: on hybrid building, 52:24-28 (CSH)

Historic America (USGPO): described, 52:10-12

Historic American Building Survey (HABS):

plans after, 53:86, 88, 89

plans from, 47:44 (TFH)

resources of, using, 52:8-12

Historic American Engineering Record (HAER): resources of, 52:8-12

Historic Architecture of Maine: source for, 47:44 (TFH)

Historic Ornament (Griesbach): cited, 69:87

Historic preservation:

assessment forms for, 61:67

books on, reviewed, 68:106, 108, 70:120-22, 72:108, 77:120-22

Chicago, 3:10

consultants on, 70:49

epoxy for, books on, 67:4, 70:49

information on, 65:55, 67:4

national, 3:10

of store-stable, grant for, 20:44-48

See also National Trust for Historic Preservation. Restoration.

Historical Replications:

address for, 71:71

plans from, 53:86, 88, 89

History of Architecture (Kostof): reviewed, 45:120

History of Architecture, A (Fletcher): reviewed, 45:120

History of Cornwall, Connecticut, A (Starr): cited, 49:38 (REM)

History of the English House, A (Lloyd): cited, 69:86

Hitachi Power Tools USA Ltd.:

address for, 63:74

bandsaw #600A, praised, 29:57 (CSH)

C-8FB saw, reviewed, 57:60, 61-62

chain mortiser, 21:10, 22:16

circular saws, reviewed, 63:74, 76

compound-miter saw, reviewed, 83:66-67

cut-off saw, reviewed, 62:81-83

drills,
    cordless, 35:41 (TB)
    VSR, reviewed, 82:36-41

framing nailers, reviewed, 56:52, 54-55

import duties on, 84:108-10

jointer-planer F-1500, for timbers, 36:58 (FWS)

knife cutter CK12D, cordless, reviewed, 43:96

miter saws, 19:42-43 (TB)

nailer, discussed, 47:74-75 (FC)

plunge routers, reviewed, 71:79, 81, 82, 84 (FC)

pneumatic tools, 15:53 (TB)

power planes, 14:42-43 (TB)
    reviewed, 54:77, 78-79

trade practices of, 82:104

Hitchcock, Henry-Russell:

In the Nature of Materials, reviewed, 45:122

on Rudolph Schindler, 4:30

Ho, Morris: owner-contracting by, 6:27

Hoadley, R. Bruce: *Understanding Wood,* mentioned, 13:8, 81:59

Hock Handmade Knives: address for, 76:82 (FC)

Hockman, John: in R-2000 program, 34:86

Hoddick, Fritz: deck by, 39:52-55 (CSH)

Hodgen, William: house plan by, 53:62

Hodges, Harriet: reviews Lyle, 37:88-90

Hodges, Julian:

gate by, 52:91

stair by, 25:81

Hodgson, Fred:

Common-Sense Stairbuilding and Handrailing, 43:37 (FWS)

Modern Carpentry, cited, 54:71 (REM)

Hoechst Celanese Corp.: address for, 50:85

Hoffman, Eric: on stone house, 41:66-69 (CSH)

Hoists: gas-powered, source for, 57:86 (EF)

Hoitsma:

address for, 58:62

pump jack, 36:36 (TB)

walking jacks, operation of, 22:38 (FRC)

Hold-downs:

for bar clamp, 74:71 (FC)

cam-action clamps for, 74:72 (FC)

foundation,
    custom-made, 9:30
    Simpson, 9:30

frame-sill, self-regulating, 44:6

pipe-clamp, 65:30

shear panels as, 53:48, 49-50 (SH)

Holden, Barry: book house by, 53:124

Hold-N-Lock: cord coupler, reviewed, 79:100-102

Hole Hawg bit: cautions with, 39:37 (BK)

Holes:
filler for,
  auto-body, 35:14
  colored, 30:57 (DWS)
  making colored, 20:14
filling, 48:77
  for painting, 42:56 (DWS)
location of, transferring, 31:16
pigmented wax for, 20:78
plugs for, 49:45
spackle for, 30:57 (DWS)
Holladay, Martin: on aid to Armenia, 63:100-102
Holland, Elizabeth:
  on acrylic glazing, 10:30-33 (DWS)
  on brick arches, 9:53-55 (CBS)
  on building course, 13:14-16
  on greenhouse conference, 10:17-18
  on land trusts, 17:20
  on penthouse, 31:63-65
  on tankless water heaters, 12:16-18
  on underground house, 16:50-53
Holliday, J. Michael: dog houses by, 49:128
Hollingsworth, Fred Thornton: on Malmgren house, 66:40-45
Holloway, Paul: on stone floors, 68:47-49
Holly Hydra woodstove water heater: source for, 26:64 (CBS)
Hollyhock House: mentioned, 16:4
Hollywood Disappearing Attic Stair Co.: long-rise stairs from, 43:71 (TB)
Holmboe Manufacturing Co.: address for, 65:92-94
Holmes, Dwight: house by, 3:56-59 (EEH)
Holmstrom, Matt:
  on ADA approach, 50:100
  on bearing-wall strategies, 55:75-77 (MFC)
  on standing-seam roofs, 39:61-65
Holt, Georgina: ceramics by, 59:88
Holz-Her: framing nailers, reviewed, 56:54-55
Homasote Co.:
  address for, 54:16, 58:61 (CSH), 66:102, 83:79
  as allergen-free underlayment, 54:16
  foam-panel laminate, 28:12
  from recycled paper, 66:102
  stress-skin panels, 24:59
Home Accessibility Information Series: discussed, 35:45 (BK)
Home Building and Woodworking in Colonial American (Wilbur): reviewed, 79:120
Home Building Cost Cuts (HUD): reviewed, 36:92
Home Design Alternatives, Inc.: address for, 53:89
Home Energy Cost Estimator: source for, 33:56

Key to books:

(BK)	Building Baths and Kitchens
(CBS)	Building with Concrete, Brick and Stone
(CSH)	Craftsman-Style Houses
(DWS)	Building Doors, Windows and Skylights
(EEH)	Energy-Efficient Houses
(EF)	Exterior Finishing
(FC)	Finish Carpentry
(FRC)	Frame Carpentry
(FWS)	Building Floors, Walls and Stairs
(MFC)	More Frame Carpentry
(REM)	Remodeling
(SH)	Small Houses
(TB)	Tools for Building
(TFH)	Timber-Frame Houses

Home Office, The (Alvarez): reviewed, 65:108
Home Ownership Made Easy (HOME): services of, 56:104
Home owning: costs of, 65:102
Home Planners, Inc.: address for, 53:89
Home Sweet Home 1983 (Los Angeles) conference:
  report on, 20:22-26
  catalog of, 20:26
Homeless: shelter for,
  book on, 61:100
  groups providing, 61:100-102
  raffled, 64:102-104
Homeowner's Complete Handbook for Add-On Solar Greenhouses and Sunspaces, The (Shapiro): reviewed, 29:90
Homeowner's Guide to Building with Concrete, Brick and Stone, The (Portland Cement Association): reviewed, 62:112
Homer, Vince: furniture by, 37:35, 37
Homes for Creative Living (Jones): cited, 77:51
Homestead Design:
  address for, 53:89
  plans from, 53:85, 87, 89
Homestyles Plan Service: address for, 53:89
Hondo Lead Co.: custom came, 42:35 (DWS)
Honeywell, Inc.:
  address for, 67:51, 85:87
  generator, 8:47
  thermostats, 44:89
  Tradeline low-leakage damper, 4:50, 51
Honing: *See* Sharpening.
Honor-Bilt houses: *See* Sears, Roebuck.
Honychurch, Douglas: on making molding, 40:33-37 (FWS)

Hood, Sallie: on small house, 38:35-39 (CSH)
Hood, Vic:
  cabin restorations by, 14:46-51
  mortar formulas of, 26:51
Hoopengardner, Jack: carpet padding by, 54:92-94
Hoosier Landmarks: reviewed, 43:102
Hoover Universal: treated shingles, 11:8
Hope's Landmark Products, Inc.: address for, 51:8
Hopkins, Lynn: on timber frame, shingle-style, 79:50-55
Horn, Spencer: houseboat by, 12:68-71
Horn (A. C.): address for, 51:42
Hornbostel, Caleb: *Construction Materials,* reviewed, 67:104
Horrobin, Peter J.: as joint author. *See* Simpson, John W.
Horsepower: *See* Motors.
Horsley, David: on insulation nightmare, 39:102
Horst, Jack: on heat pumps, 26:66-68
Hot tubs:
  ad lib building of, 42:110
  chemical-storage tub for, 35:58 (TB)
  concrete, making, 37:27, 28 (BK), 69:64-66
  under etched-glass window, 73:88
  foundation for, 69:47 (EF)
  integrated water heating for, 56:16
  Japanese pressure-treated, 51:96
  lids for, fiberglass, 69:64, 66
  plywood plastic-lined, 66:38, 39 (SH)
  silo-contained, 38:57, 58
  source for, 69:46 (EF)
  See also Spas.
Hot Weather Concreting (ACI): cited, 55:68
HotCan: *See* Computers: energy programs for.
Hot-melt glue: *See* Glue.
Hotte, Eleanor B.: as joint author. *See* May, Elizabeth E.
Hot-water heaters:
  anode maintenance for, 60:16
  automated, 53:74-76
  Big-Fin solar, 58:83-84 (EEH)
  breadbox, 28:72
  choosing, 82:54-57
  comparative costs of, 5:64
  connectors for, flexible, 17:53 (BK)
  corrosion in, discussed, 65:6
  deposits in, vacuuming, 84:30
  desuperheaters for, 72:72 (EEH)
  electric in-line, 70:56 (EEH)
  extending, outside underground, 65:18
  flueless high-efficiency, 68:53
  Freon-charged, homemade, 29:86-88 (erratum, 30:4)

gas,
    defective, 2:64
    high-efficiency, 60:55
    sealed-combustion, 63:85 (EEH)
gas-solar-wood, 69:43 (EEH)
heat pump, 2:64, 5:64-65, 26:66
heat-exchanger panel, disadvantages
    of, 10:18
high-volume, 85:84, 86
installing, 82:57-58
insulation for, 1:62
integrated, 63:85 (EEH)
    adding, 56:16
lifetime warranted, reviewed, 69:92-94
maintenance of, 82:59
noise from, diagnosing, 84:12-14
phase-change systems, explained, 10:18
point-of-use, 72:14
pumps for,
    circulating, 59:87 (CSH)
    small, 72:14
relief valve for, 17:53 (BK)
remote, quicker service from, 72:14,
    76:20 (CSH)
sizing information for, 29:8
in slab-on-grade, 60:54
solar, 38:65 (CSH), 52:73, 68:50-51
    -and-wood, 65:62-65 (SH)
    -assisted, 42:53 (SH)
    batch heater, 68:53, 55, 70:56 (EEH)
    bleed, 68:52
    for cabin, 8:47
    center researching, 30:80
    costs of, 5:65
    demonstrations of, 30:80
    drainback, 68:52, 53
    flush-set, 59:65-67 (EEH)
    glycol closed-loop, 68:51-52, 53
    hybrid, 68:54-55
    integrated, 72:72 (EEH)
    pre-heating for, 6:57, 60:59 (EEH)
    publications on, 1:66, 4:62, 30:80
    rating agencies for, 68:55
    sizing, 68:50
    sources for, 60:16
    thermosiphon, 29:88, 50:55, 68:51,
      52-55
    /woodstove/propane system for,
      24:64 (TFH)
supply sources for, 82:58
switches for, magnetic float, 29:88
tankless, 12:16-18
    electric, 34:69 (SH)
    pressure requirements of, 14:6
    problems with, 14:6
    pumps for, 14:6
troubleshooting, 82:59
utility support of, 1:9
water vapor from, 22:10
woodstove unit for, 24:64 (TFH)
See also Energy. Metals: galvanic
    corrosion of.

Hou, Jiyao: mentioned, 28:81
Houben, Hugo: mentioned, 28:81, 30:76
House, Cathi and Steven: on central-
    corridor house, 80:78-81
House, Lloyd: sauna by, 13:76
House (Kidder): reviewed, 32:86
House and Building Mover, The: source
    for, 5:19
House and House: house by, 83:82-87
House Building Basics: described, 4:62
House Building Book, The (Browne):
    reviewed, 1:64
House moving:
    by air, 40:4
    of church, 66:118-17
    costs of, 5:19
    disaster when, 2:66
    dismantling for, process of, 11:51-52
    lifting for, 28:12
    publications on, 5:19
    sequence of, 5:19-21, 32:58
House of the Future (1950): MIT design
    of, 34:70-71
House raising: *See* Raising.
House Restorer's Guide, The (Lander):
    reviewed, 34:92
House Style Book, The (ed. Sudjic):
    reviewed, 36:94
Houseboats:
    engineering of, 12:70-71
    Seattle, history of, 12:69
    shoe-style, 43:116
Household Conservation Catalog:
    source for, 1:63
Household Paint Selector, The: source
    for, 23:50
Householder, Jerry: *Scheduling for
    Builders,* reviewed, 46:104
Houses and Gardens by E. L. Lutyens
    (Weaver): reviewed, 45:122
Houses by Mail (Cole and Jandl): source
    for, 28:45
Housing Affordability Act: discussed,
    62:106
Housing codes: *See* Building codes.
    individual trade codes.
*Housing Construction Process Flow
    Manual* (HUD): source for, 36:92
Housing developments: architecture of,
    80:16-20
*Housing Interiors for the Disabled and
    Elderly* (Raschko): discussed, 35:45
    (BK)
Housing Special Populations: source for,
    55:108
Houston's #3 preservative: for exterior
    doors, 3:16 (DWS)
How Buildings Work (Allen): reviewed,
    45:116
How to Build a House Simply (Zink):
    source for, 28:68

*How to Build Storm-Resistant
    Structures:* source for, 23:50
How to Buy Construction Lumber
    (Oviatt): mentioned, 8:14
*How to Create Interiors for the
    Disabled* (Cary): mentioned, 6:51, 35:45
    (BK)
How to Create Your Own Painted Lady
    (Larsen and Pomada): cited, 74:45 (EF)
How to Look It Up Online
    (Glossebenner): cited, 46:60
*How to Select and Renovate an Older
    House* (Sherwood): mentioned, 28:86
Howard, Bion D.: on insulated block,
    31:38-41 (CBS)
Howard, John: mentioned, 32:57, 58
Howard, Robin: roof by, 57:90
Howard Manufacturing Co.: address for,
    84:55
Howlett Enterprises: guard rails, 41:41
    (DWS)
Hoyt Heater Co.: 110v., 20-gal. water
    heater, 11:45 (SH)
HRV: *See* Heat-recovery ventilators.
HTC Products: feed tables, 34:55 (TB)
Hubbell, James T.:
    chapel by, 64:50-53
    door by, 1:55
    on free-form house, 66:51-54
Huber, Barry:
    on shingle thatching, 23:52-56
    as joint author. *See* Cooke, Gary.
HUD: *See* U. S. Department of Housing
    and Urban Development.
Huddleston, Charley: on self-contracting,
    6:26-28
Hugh Products: HC6478 laminating glue,
    24:59
Hughes, John R.:
    on allergen-free house, 46:70-73
    on heat-recovery ventilators, 34:30-34
      (DWS)
    on retrofit superinsulation, 20:35-37
    reviews DuPont and Morrill, 75:110
    reviews Nisson, 50:108
    on superinsulated houses, 9:56
Hughes, Ken: on gunite, 40:60-63 (CBS)
Human Ecology Action League:
    described, 60:102
Humanscale 1-2-3 (Diffrient, Tiller and
    Bardagjy): discussed, 35:45 (BK)
Humidifiers: heat-pump water-heater,
    2:64
Humidity: automated control of, 53:76
Humphrey Co.: gaslights, 14:31
Hunt, Rob:
    on bathroom built-ins, 13:60-63 (BK)
    on shutters, 17:35-39 (DWS)
Hunter, Lake: on Barker house, 31:72-73
Hunter, Linda Mason: on four-square
    remodel, 71:60-63 (REM)
Hura, Terry: fireplace by, 35:74, 77

Hurd, M. K.: *Concrete Craftsman Series-2,* cited, 78:53

Hurd Millwork Co., Inc.:
address for, 55:79, 65:77 (REM), 76:75 (FC)
wooden awning windows, 15:43

Hurr, Doug and Jeff: mentioned, 29:33

Hurricane ties: *See* Metal connectors.

Hurricanes:
damage from, 57:104-106, 128
design for, 59:78-82, 60:4, 67:59-63, 85:72-75
lessons from, 78:82-87
and oriented strand board, 85:118-20
projectile-proof room for, 78:87
and wood buildings, report on, 85:120
See also Design. Foundations.

Husqvarna Power Products: address for, 53:83

Huston, Don and Stan: houses by, 34:38

Hutches: *See* Cabinets.

Hutchings, Gilbert: as joint author. *See* Feirer, John L.

Hutton, Ted: on passive cooling, 40:73-77 (EEH)

Hyde, Cassie: staircase by, 30:88

Hyde, Christopher: on timber frame, 47:44-47 (TFH)

Hyde Manufacturing Co.:
address for, 43:52, 56:42 (CBS)
model 45600 Pry Bar, 19:34 (DWS)

Hydro-Ban 500: mentioned, 11:10

Hydrocal: source for, 1:37, 39, 29:66 (FWS)

Hydrocide: mentioned, 15:48 (CBS)

Hydrocote Co., Inc.: address for, 69:54, 74:77, 75:84, 81:76

Hydrolevel: address for, 85:60

Hydronics Institute: address for, 65:102

Hydroponics: in-house unit for, 73:70

Hydrostone:
casting with, 5:10
source for, 1:37, 39 (FWS)

Hydrotherm, Inc.: address for, 61:12

Hydrozo Water Repellent #7N: source for, 14:35 (CBS)

Hy-Lite Acrylic Blocks: address for, 85:108

Hymes, Sidney:
on business structure, 62:78-79
reviews turntable saw, 51:90-91
reviews workstation, 71:94

I Built Myself A House (Garvey): cited, 83:77

Iberian Villages (Carver): cited, 39:74

Ice machines: avoiding, 73:67

ICONDA computer service: described, 46:60

Idaho:
home conservation credits of, 5:65
solar tax credits in, 3:12

Idea Development Inc.: address for, 46:52-53 (EEH)

Ideal Roofing Co., Ltd.: address for, 75:59, 82:14

Identifying American Architecture: described, 4:62

Ifilele: floor of, 45:51, 53 (CSH)

IFL, Inc.: address for, 82:96

Ifö Sanitär: plumbing fixtures, 35:34

Igloo Products Corp.: address for, 81:92

Igloos: building, 1:68

Illinois: dry-stack block in, 3:12, 16:57 (CBS)

Illinois Lo-Cal House, The: safety tests of, 4:8

Illinois Tool Works Co.: address for, 76:96

Illuminating Engineering Society: *Lighting Handbook,* cited, 54:52

Imadan Enterprises: address for, 83:98

Imai, Makoto: tea room by, 32:39, 40

Imperial Gypsum Veneer system:
described, 4:19-20
plaster, source for, 28:10

Impex-Allied Fastening Systems: powder-actuated tools from, 21:34 (TB)

Impingement: preventing, 64:69

Impregnations: nontoxic, sources for, 67:90-92

Impson, Loren:
on ferro-cement house, 44:112
mentioned, 28:80

In the Bank...or Up the Chimney?: described, 4:62

In the Nature of Materials (Hitchcock): reviewed, 45:122

Inca: radial-table saw #810, reviewed, 46:90

Inclinator Co. of America: address for, 55:86, 73:104

Incralac metal lacquer: source for, 34:6

Independent Living for the Handicapped and the Elderly (May, Waggoner and Hotte): discussed, 35:45 (BK)

Independent Protection Co., Inc.: address for, 84:68

Index Manufacturing Co.: workstation of, reviewed, 71:94

Indian Blankets and Their Makers (James): cited, 69:57

Indian Sand Treewax: recommended, 33:70 (CBS)

Indian shutters: *See* Shutters: sliding panel.

Indiana:
dry-stack block in, 16:57 (CBS)
historic buildings of, book on, 43:102
solar tax credits in, 3:12

Industrial Abrasives Co.:
address for, 48:77
silicon paper, 42:58 (DWS)

Industrial Millwork Corp.: address for, 68:87

Industrial Plastics Supply: silicone rubber from, 1:39 (FWS)

Industrial Products Co.: safety products, 34:55 (TB)

Industrial Thermo Polymers Ltd.: address for, 85:16

Infiltration Control: source for, 32:90

Infloor Heating Systems: address for, 75:72

Information on Demand: services of, 46:60

Information Resources in Housing and Urban Development (HUD): source for, 36:92

Information sources:
contracting, 23:48
design, 23:48-49
energy, 23:51
finish, 23:50
general, 23:51
government, 23:49
structural, 23:49-50
trade, 23:48-49
See also *separate agency, association or building category.*

Infrared imaging:
described, 33:57-57
findings of, 58:4

Infraspection Institute: address for, 56:41

Ingersoll-Rand:
address for, 49:87
random-orbit sanders, reviewed, 77:73
tamper #341, 34:39

Inglenooks:
baronial, building, 69:82-87
early English, 60:71, 72
with folding doors, 2:20, 22 (CSH)
pictured, 38:75 (TFH)
ventilation for, 37:34

Initiative for Environmental Sensitivity in Construction, The (TIES): reviewed, 62:104-106

Injuries:
amputations, first-aid for, 53:102-104
cumulative,
to back, preventive strategies for, 85:76-81
nature of, 64:66-67
preventing, 64:67-69, 67:4-6
preventing, through yoga, 65:8
See also First-aid kits. *individual process or machine.* Safety.

Inlay: face, router bit for, 58:41 (REM)

Innamorato, Dan: reviews extension-cord holder, 76:94-94
Innes, Jocasta: *Decorating with Paint,* cited, 60:81
Innovative Data Design, Inc.:
address for, 49:50
MacDraft program, 35:66 (TB)
Innovative Design (Raleigh, N. C.):
AirCore systems by, 30:50 (CBS)
Inogon Level and Angle Indicator:
evaluated, 27:82
Insect repellents: nontoxic, sources for, 67:90-92
Insects:
bees, removal of, 55:4
beetles,
anobiid, discussed, 60:69 (REM)
damage from, assessing, 40:10
discussed, 64:6
ivory-marked wood-boring, 58:18
and old lumber, 2:6
powderpost, discussed, 58:18, 60:67-69 (REM)
carpenter ants,
dealing with, 43:14-16, 44:4, 56:14
discussed, 60:66-67 (REM), 64:6
and foam-core panels, 62:57 (TFH)
carpenter bees,
dealing with, 29:10
wood preferences of, 29:10
cluster flies, dealing with, 53:14, 84:12
termites,
and air-core floors, 35:10
borate preservatives against, 85:22, 75
chemicals for, 6:52-53, 22:12, 29:37 (FRC)
controlling, 5:12, 6:53
discussed, 60:64-66 (REM), 64:6
and foundation insulation, 7:12, 53:96-98
foundation shields against, 4:36-37, 6:53, 20:6 (FRC)
nature of, 6:52-53
roof shields against, earth-bermed, 22:12
safer insecticide for, 28:10
wood resistant to, 33:90
Insolation: explained, 5:52 (DWS)
Insta-Foam Products, Inc.:
address for, 65:44
Frothpak insulation of, 20:31
Installation Guidelines for Solar DHW Systems: cited, 1:66
Instant Flow Water Heaters: source for, 12:18 (CSH)
Insteel Construction Systems, Inc.:
address for, 78:100
Institute for Community Economics:
address for, 59:24

Instruction:
in architecture, 63:100
association for, 56:104
in building, 45:106-10
in floor-laying, 75:100
for high-school students, 79:112
in masonry, workshop for, 74:106
in preservation, sourcebook of, 74:106
Romanian, aiding, 62:4
on roofing, 60:100
site-specific, workbook for, 56:110
in stairbuilding, 43:38-39 (FWS)
testing of, 63:20
Insul Block Corp.: insulated blocks, 31:39 (CBS)
Insul-Aid: vapor barrier paint, 6:55, 19:68, 37:65
Insulated Door: source for, 6:60
Insulated Steel Door Systems Institute:
standards of, 6:62
Insulation:
adding, 30:8, 39:10, 56:40-42, 65:18
reason for, 35:4
adhesive for, 34:49, 59 (FRC)
for adobe exteriors, 22:43
for A-frame houses, 20:67
asphalt-treated board, 83:79
assistance with, 56:42
with automatic curtains, 34:24, 26, 28-29 (DWS)
backer rod for, 47:22
baffles for, 56:39
batts of,
furring for, 18:41-42
pull placement of, 79:20
below-grade,
spray foam for, 8:38, 39, 40 (EEH)
in wet and dry soils, 8:6
in block, double-wall, 54:84, 85-86 (TFH)
blown-in,
adhesively bound, 59:53 (CSH)
drama with, 13:74
fiberglass vs. rock wool, 25:10
hole mistake for, 70:130
moisture control with, 25:10
problems with, 32:59
vapor barrier for, 9:8
book on, reviewed, 61:106
for cabins, seasonal, 29:10
for Canadian winters, 73:55
ceiling, R-factors for, 46:16
cellulose, 8:40 (EEH)
defined, 56:37-38
disadvantages of, 19:67-68, 73:69
vs. other, 58:4, 59:53 (CSH)
perm rating for, 19:67
sulfated, caveats against, 72:108
wet-spray, defined, 56:38
cementitious foam,
advantages of, 73:69
defined, 56:39
certification program for, NAHB, 76:108

CFC, ozone depletion and, 49:102
chicken-wire support for, 7:12
choosing, 33:56
code requirements for, 50:59
for cold climate, 21:58-59 (EEH), 44:81
compressed, 35:63
compressible draining, 8:6
for concrete floors, 44:4
convection losses with, 79:110
cost-effectiveness considerations with, 33:56-57
cutting, 19:14
design aid for, reviewed, 79:120
doubled, vapor barrier in, 21:8
for double-envelope walls, 4:8
of drain lines, 39:36 (BK)
drain-board, 56:38
exfiltration check of, 33:56
exterior, 1:43, 3:8 (EEH)
Dryvit system, as above-grade, 8:38, 39 (EEH)
Dryvit system, described, 3:8
Dryvit system, mentioned, 19:63 (EEH)
Dryvit system, Outsulation of, 63:83, 84 (EEH)
Dryvit system, on penthouse, 31:63
Dryvit system, whole-house use of, 1:43 (EEH)
fiberglass, 12:10
foil-faced, problems with, 12:10
fiberglass, 29:12
alkali-resistant loose fibers of, 27:12
batts, cutting of, 16:12, 20:6
blown-in, source for, 66:66 (EEH)
and cancer, 56:42
compression of, 28:6, 29:4, 30:4, 56:37
cutter guides for, 37:81
defined, 56:37
disadvantages of, 34:49, 58:4, 59:53 (CSH), 73:67, 68
high-density, 64:4
installing, 56:36-37
nonsettling, 37:26 (BK)
perm rating for, 19:67
sack-enclosed, 79:110
sealing off, 46:71
for slabs, 26:10
slivers of, removing, 1:5
toxicity of, 85:124
vs. urethane, for roofs, 24:6
waterproof, 29:12
for floors, 5:56, 57, 51:70, 71 (FRC)
foam,
air-infiltration-preventing, 77:67
bit for, 56:28
vs. blown, 24:12
cleaner for, 56:26
expanding, source for, 77:67
and freon, 56:42
gaskets for, 34:49

and insect damage, 78:6-8
magnesium, 24:12-14
vs. other, 58:4
ozone-friendly, 79:104
packing as, 11:14
packing as, caution for, 13:4
reading labels of, 46:96
sealing off, 46:71
trimming, 56:26
foam-board,
  fire protection for, 29:6
  laminates, 28:12
  over plaster, 33:4
  recesses in, 55:58
  steel channel for, 32:68, 71 (FRC)
foam-core panels,
  for Arctic Circle, 68:100
  associations for, 62:56, 57 (TFH), 64:10
  book on, cited, 62:57 (TFH)
  and carpenter ants, 62:57 (TFH)
  dome of, 46:42-43
  exterior camouflaging of, 67:37
  and fire hazard, 62:53, 56 (TFH)
  installing, 62:54-55 (TFH)
  manufacturers of, 62:57 (TFH)
  and ozone layer, 62:57 (TFH)
  pricing, 62:54 (TFH)
  recycling, 69:102
  structural, in small house, 67:35
  types of, 62:52-54, 55 (TFH)
  and wood siding, 64:10-12
foil, 56:39
  single-sided, 22:4
foil-faced, polyethylene over, 29:10
formaldehyde, danger of, 2:64-65
for foundations, 2:36, 37, 55:57-58, 59
  shallow, frost-protected, 74:104
framing for, 82:45
frauds in, 56:42
gas-filled, discussed, 71:104
holders for, under-floor, 33:41 (FWS)
information on, 33:90, 65:52
infrared findings on, 58:4
installing, arm protectors for, 51:26
isocyanurate,
  danger from, 70:112
  defined, 56:38-39
  for foundations, 43:20
  installing, 20:10, 29:69-70
  ozone depletion and, 49:102
  over plaster, 33:4
  in shutters, 13:48, 49 (DWS)
  source for, 29:69, 31:70
  stress-skin panels, 4:8
  underground, 2:31 (EEH)
kinds of, compared, 56:36-42
labeling of, 1:10
liquid system for, two-part pressurized,
  20:31
for log houses, 53:84
of masonry cavity walls, 43:59-60 (CBS)

mass and, 31:38 (CBS)
for maximum heat retention, 72:70
  (EEH)
for metal buildings, 33:75
and moisture, 4:8, 41:4 (addendum,
  42:4)
  book on, 74:98
Mylar curtain for, 58:83 (EEH)
vs. new furnace, 33:57
night, 16:14
non-ozone-damaging, 85:16-18
for old houses, booklet on, 72:108
one-third-two-thirds rule for, 61:106
optimal, 66:4
ostrich feathers for, 36:6
pests in, dealing with, 7:12, 56:42
phenolic foam, 35:8, 50:79-81 (SH), 56:39
placement of, 50:100
plastic foam, avoiding, 73:69
polystyrene,
  and asphalt, 18:33 (CBS)
  expanded, defined, 56:38
  extruded, defined, 56:38
  extruded, panels of, 82:94
  parged, 18:33-35 (CBS)
  source for, 48:58
  tapered, 75:83
publications on, 56:36, 42
in renovations, 1:9, 10:44, 24:12-14
Rex Roberts method of, 28:69-70
risks with, 34:51 (TB)
rock wool, defined, 56:37
rodent-proof pipe, 77:8-10
for roofs, 8:40, 25:45 (EEH, TFH), 51:70,
  71, 54:62
R-values of, discussed, 33:57
sawdust as, 48:49
sheathing, 31:70
under siding, rough, 4:8
for skylights, 35:8
for sod roofs, 56:79
for solar design, 60:58 (EEH), 84:87-88
for soundproofing, 35:60-63, 58:57, 62:60,
  61
sound-suppression blankets as, 55:59
sprayed, 66:55
for stairs, fold-down, source for, 67:92
vs. stud cavities, 13:14
studies of, 13:14
styrofoam, flammability cautions with,
  4:8
subsurface, 26:10
thermal mapping of, 56:41
for timber-frame remodel, 79:86
for tropics, 61:60 (SH), 85:74
in truss frames, 5:56, 57, 19:69-71 (EEH,
  FRC)
with trusses, advantage of, 59:53, 55
  (CSH)
urea-formaldehyde,
  danger of, 1:12, 2:64-65, 72:108
  perm rating for, 19:67

urethane,
  board, for retrofits, 39:10
  defined, 56:38-39
  foam, 40:58-59, 50:49
  foam, improved, 68:6-8
  foamed-in-place, 63:83, 84 (EEH)
  foamed-in-place, problems with,
    65:62 (SH)
  R-value of, 56:79
  spray, 34:66 (BK), 43:4
  UV-resistant coating for, source for,
    66:55
vacuum, 56:42
vent protectors for, 56:39
vermiculite for, 46:62 (TFH)
video on, reviewed, 61:106
for windows, 8:30 (TFH)
and wind-washing, 47:18
zones for, by degree-days, 56:36, 40
See also Air infiltration. Air-vapor
  barriers. Computers: energy
  programs for. Curtains. Radiant
  barriers. Shutters. Simple Caulk and
  Seal method.
Insulblock Forming System: foam forms,
  40:86
Insul-Flue: source for, 34:8
Insulite: Schindler use of, 4:31
Insul-Mold: galvanized metal insulation
  darts, 33:41 (FWS)
Insul-safe II: source for, 37:26 (BK)
Insul-Tray:
  address for, 56:39
  insulation trays, 33:41 (FWS)
Insurance:
  and risks, 34:51 (TB)
  See also Safety.
Integral Urban House, The: reviewed,
  6:58
Integrated systems: urban, book on, 6:58
Intercoms: telephone-operated, 70:106
Interior Design Illustrated (Ching):
  reviewed, 51:104
Interior Finish (Syvanen): cited, 8:52
  (FWS)
**Intermediate Technology Development
  Group of North America:** address for,
  64:112
International Air Filter: address for,
  70:20
**International Association of Lighting
  Designers:** address for, 54:52
**International Association of Plumbing
  and Mechanical Officials:** Uniform
  Plumbing Code, 39:37 (BK)
**International Association of Stone
  Restoration and Conservation:**
  address for, 71:104
**International Conference of Building
  Officials:**
  on powder-driven pins, 21:32 (TB)
  on skylight glass, 49:14

International Cushioned Products: address for, 65:96

International Design Systems: patterning tools of, 7:6

International Ferrocement Information Center: address for, 50:49

International Foundation for Earth Construction: mentioned, 28:81

International Handbook of Finnish Sauna, The (Konya and Burger): mentioned, 39:4

International Institute for Bau-Biologie and Ecology: address for, 65:54

International Masonry Institute: *Directory of Audio-Visuals, Publications, and Promotion Materials,* 23:50

International Paint Co.: address for, 61:70
Interlux Polythane Super Gloss boat varnish of, 19:35 (DWS)

International Solar, Inc.: phase-change systems, 10:18

International Staple and Machine Co.: nailer, discussed, 47:74-75 (FC)
pneumatic tools, 15:53 (TB)

International Style: beginnings of, 19:29
house in, 34:24-29 (DWS)

International Symposium on Traditional Dwellings and Settlements: conference by, 49:100-102

International Technology Sales Corp: AEG Telefunken water heater, 12:18 (CSH)

International Tile and Supply Corp.: Japanese roofing tiles, 45:74 (CSH)

Interpane Coatings Inc.: high-performance glass of, discussed, 41:84-86

Introducing Supplemental Combustion Air (USDOE): cited, 46:46

Introduction to Early American Masonry (McKee): cited, 5:39

Introduction to Physical Micrometeorology, An (Brooks): cited, 9:16

Iowa: solar tax credits in, 3:12

IPS: address for, 55:47 (FC)

Ireland, David: corrugated house by, 7:68

Ireland, Geoff: on moving mud, 77:130

Ireton, Kevin:
on attic studio, 64:84-87 (REM)
on barrel vaults, 51:79 (MFC)
on becoming a carpenter, 20:90
on compound-miter saw, 57:94
on Daggett house, 49:38-43 (REM)
on door hardware, 48:61-65 (FC)
on foam forms, 40:86
on hand injury, 83:80-81
on healthy house, 73:66-70
on kitchen cabinets, 65:69-74
on mail-order tool concern, 57:94

Key to books:

(BK)   **Building Baths and Kitchens**
(CBS) **Building with Concrete, Brick and Stone**
(CSH) **Craftsman-Style Houses**
(DWS) **Building Doors, Windows and Skylights**
(EEH) **Energy-Efficient Houses**
(EF)   **Exterior Finishing**
(FC)   **Finish Carpentry**
(FRC) **Frame Carpentry**
(FWS) **Building Floors, Walls and Stairs**
(MFC) **More Frame Carpentry**
(REM) **Remodeling**
(SH)   **Small Houses**
(TB)   **Tools for Building**
(TFH) **Timber-Frame Houses**

on masonry fasteners, 41:52-57 (CBS)
on Meadowcreek Project, 37:75
on new products, 44:88-89, 55:92, 62:92-94, 66:102, 104-106, 70:106, 72:88, 76:92-96
on Norway building, 46:76-79
on OSHA, 36:37 (TB)
on plastic laminate, 77:40-45
on plate joinery, 70:50-53 (FC)
on plunge router, 57:96
on pocket doors, 54:63-66 (FC)
reviews Boston Shutter and Door, Inc., 43:92-94
reviews care cover, 48:91
reviews caulk equipment, 42:88-90
reviews Craftseat, 41:86
reviews dumbwaiter, 64:92
reviews Goo Stick, 64:94
reviews Harper, 55:108
reviews Magneto, 74:90
reviews miter-saw stand, 49:94
reviews new tools, 43:94-96
reviews Owen, 83:120
reviews Pinecrest, 51:90
reviews plastic mesh, 48:90
reviews Quadriset, 64:92
reviews Quarton tools, 49:95
reviews rail-boring jigs, 63:90
reviews rosette maker, 48:90-91
reviews sanders, 64:96
reviews seminars, 56:104
reviews sinks, 68:94-96
reviews stair-tread template, 48:90
reviews tools, 64:96
reviews 2-By Turner tool, 78:92
reviews vapor cube, 49:94
reviews veneered moldings, 48:91
reviews workpants, 70:100
on roof venting, 61:76-80 (EF)
on screw guns, 46:90
on stairbuilders, 43:34-39 (FWS), 53:104
on stock staircases, 36:56-61 (FWS)

on synthetic materials, 47:94
on timber-framing conference, 49:98-100

Irland, Richard: on panelized frame, 62:72-77
reviews Birchard, 68:106

Iron: cast, corrosion of, 62:66
corrosion of, 62:64, 65

Ironing boards: fold-out, source for, 53:45 (SH)

Ironwork:
aging, by patinating, 75:78
anchoring, 16:44
association for, 75:78
cast vs. wrought, 16:42
defined, 17:47, 19:4-6, 75:76-77
designing, 17:47-49
examples of, 16:43, 17:90
fabrication of, 16:42-44, 17:48
fences of, installing, 17:50-51
finishes for, 17:50, 51, 75:78
grills of, 25:29, 30
joinery in, 75:77-78
nobility of, 21:4
painting, 16:44
rust on, removing, 16:44
sources for, 16:44
in Spanish colonial style, 75:75-79
in stone, problems with, 5:37
strength of, 32:33 (FRC)
uses of, 17:47
wrought, defined, 40:6

Irwin Co.: chalklines, 25:69 (TB)

Is Solar Water Heating Right for You?: source for, 1:66

Isaacs, John: masonry walls by, 35:30, 34

Isabel O'Neil Studio Workshop: address for, 60:81

Isadore Haumont House: about, 31:55, 57

Ise shrine (Kyoto): mentioned, 32:26-27 (CSH)

Iseo Locks Inc.: address for, 54:65 (FC)

Ishakawa, Masahiko: mentioned, 38:74 (TFH)
woodworking of, 8:15-16

Isham, Norman: house by, 4:17

Island City Woodworks: history of, 39:75

Islands: building on, 54:58-62

Isobutylene isoprene: *See* Butyl.

Isotech Consultants, Inc.: Quadrex screws, 34:45 (TB)

Italian Hilltowns (Carver): cited, 39:74

Itten, Johannes: *Elements of Color, The,* cited, 74:45 (EF)

Itzkowitz, Howard Frank: on particleboard floors, 39:43 (FWS)

Ives (H. B.) Co.: address for, 50:69 (FC), 54:66 (FC), 56:6

Ivy, Robert Adams, Jr.: *Fay Jones,* reviewed, 78:110

J and R Enterprises, Inc.: address for, 74:76

J. C. Trading Co.: rice paper, 27:63

Jaakola, Lasse:
on architect as builder, 15:63
houseboat by, 12:68-71

Jacklin, Robert: window seat by, 66:90

Jack-Post Corp.: address for, 68:85

Jacks:
A-brace, improvised, 53:28-30
for house raising, 28:12
hydraulic, for roof lifting, 9:6
load-rating caution for, 48:4
post and wedge as, 2:15
post, for roof lifting, 9:6
pump,
aluminum poles for, 36:36 (TB)
source for, 36:36 (TB)
using, 36:36-37 (TB)
safety with, 51:6-8
scissor, drill arbor for, 9:10
screw, for roof lifting, 9:6
for settled walls, 85:20-22
stresses on, discussed, 51:6-8
walking, 2:5, 22:38 (FRC)
wall, 29:16, 58:62, 65
shop-built, 47:46 (TFH)
See also Columns: steel-pipe adjustable.
Shoring.

Jackson, Albert, and David Day:
Complete Home Restoration Manual,
The, reviewed, 82:112

Jackson, Neil: addresses conference,
47:100-102

Jackson Mfg.: defective water heaters,
2:64

Jacobs, Herbert and Katherine:
Building with Frank Lloyd Wright, 3:27
Wright houses of, 3:20

Jacobs II house (Wright):
costs of, 3:21
design of, 3:20-27
1980 heating costs, 5:4

Jacobsen, Arne: plumbing components
by, 1:62

Jacobson, Max:
A Pattern Language, mentioned, 20:10
on peaking a flat roof, 1:40-42 (FRC)
roofs by, 10:26-29
on steep-slope design, 41:44-48
on thin-mass house, 11:46-50 (CBS)

Jacobson, Max, Murray Silverstein and
Barbara Winslow: *Good House, The,*
excerpted, 66:16-22

Jac-Tac Inc.: address for, 54:94

Jaffe, Rubin: addition by, 30:32, 33

Jalowy, Leroy: cuts stone, 37:57, 58

Jambs: *See* Casings.

James, Fred: film by, 1:66

James, George Wharton: *Indian Blankets*
and Their Makers, cited, 69:57

James, Peter: on remodel, 68:22, 74:60-61

James Hardie Building Products, Inc.:
address for, 77:96, 83:45
fiber/cement shingles, 39:90
Hardieplank, discussed, 85:8

Jamestown Distributors: address for,
67:63

Jandl, H. Ward: as joint author. *See* Cole,
Katherine H.

Jantzen, Steven: on upward addition,
67:64-66 (REM)

Japan: Good Living Show, reviewed, 51:96

Japan Trading Co.: address for, 69:43
(EEH)

Japan Woodworker, The: address for,
76:83 (FC)

Japanese, The (Reischauer): praised,
34:92

Japanese Folkhouses (Carver):
mentioned, 39:70
reviewed, 32:86

Japanese Homes and Their
Surroundings (Morse):
on baths, 19:38 (BK)
reviewed, 45:122

Japanese Joinery (Nakahara): cited, 46:4

Japanese style:
architecture, book on, 45:122
bath house, constructing, 19:37-41 (BK)
carpentry,
museum of, 62:128
traditional vs. machine, 48:102-104
houses,
American, 32:38-43, 43:28-33 (CSH)
books on, 19:26, 32:86, 34:92, 39:70
construction of, 4:53-57 (TFH)
developments in, 28:82
disadvantages of, 24:60, 61 (TFH)
firepits in, 4:53 (TFH)
houses after, 39:70-74, 45:71-75, 89
(CSH)
hybrid, 24:61-64 (TFH)
as influence, 9:42-45, 16:58-65, 29:56-61,
30:18-23, 39:74 (CSH, TFH)
joinery in, 46:4
modular nature of, 4:52-53, 19:41 (BK,
TFH)
proportions in, 43:28 (CSH)
raising of, 24:63 (TFH)
roofs for, 4:54 (TFH), 19:38, 40 (BK)
and shingle style, 12:64 (EEH)
stress-skin panels for, 43:28-31 (CSH)
temple proportions for, 24:63, 64
(TFH)
timber grades for, 4:52 (TFH)
timbers for, care of, 24:63 (TFH)
tokonohmah in, 4:57 (TFH)

Japanese Touch for Your Home, A
(Yagi): reviewed, 19:26

Jaraslow, Abby:
on rustic shelter, 21:66-68
as joint author. *See* Robinson, David.

Jarvis, Glen:
on attic remodeling, 21:26-29
kitchen vent by, 7:67 (BK)

Jarvis, Mike: develops Truslock, 37:80

Jasco Speedmatic stripper: for old
houses, 1:33 (FWS)

Jatoba (Hymenaea courbaril):
availability of, 40:6
pictured, 37:24-25, 27 (BK)
qualities of, 37:29 (BK)
trim of, 49:91

J-Deck, Inc.:
mentioned, 24:59
stress-skin panels of, 25:44, 39:73 (TFH)

Jefferson, Thomas:
book on, reviewed, 53:110-12
Poplar Forest by, 42:74-79
skylight by, 42:79

Jefferson and Monticello (McLaughlin):
reviewed, 53:110-12

Jellum, Keith:
chimney cap by, 9:75
weather vane by, 9:75

Jencks, Charles: *Towards a Symbolic*
Architecture, reviewed, 35:94

Jenks (W. S.) & Son: address for, 70:53
(FC)

Jenn-Air stove: on inside wall, 34:66 (BK)

Jensen, Jim: built-in sofa by, 66:89

Jenson, Roy K.: on header, 62:87 (MFC)

Jersey Devil:
formation of, 38:8-10
Hill House, construction of, 29:28, 33
house by, 52:68-73

Jersey Devil Design-Build Book
(Crosbie): source for, 29:33

Jetton, Bill: work by, 81:89

Jevning, Steve: on paint choosing, 62:104

Jigs: medium density overlay (MDO) for,
28:39 (FWS)

Jigsaws:
bases for, 33:59-60 (TB)
custom, 43:20
battery-operated, reviewed, 43:96
blade guard for, 54:24
blades for, 33:60 (TB)
no-splinter, 76:65 (MFC)
brands of, compared, 33:61 (TB)
cordless, 33:62 (TB)
disadvantages of, 77:94
top-handle electronic, 18:17-18
types of, 33:58-62 (TB)
using, 33:60-61 (TB)

Jilson Corp.: Stud-Lok, 40:87

Jim Walter Corp.: Insulated Steel Entry
System, 6:60

JJJ Specialty Co.: address for, 76:75 (FC)
Job sites:
  air-dome enclosed, 51:120
  bench for, quick, 81:28
  lamp for, portable, 67:28
  literacy program for, 65:102
  machinery stands for, wheeled, 69:70-72
  magnet pickup for, 77:32
  nonelectrified, tools for, 67:62
  power center for, wheeled, 69:71-72
  storage reels for, 69:32
  tables for, quick, 79:32
  towelettes for, 72:90
  waste from,
    debris plow for, 65:30
    recycling, 76:104
  work tree for, 51:24
  workbenches for, 69:32
    wheeled, 69:73-75
  workbench-storage box for, 65:46-47
    (FC)
  See also *various articles of clothing.*
Joe Frogger: using, 77:62-63
Johansen, John M.: house by, 3:51
John B. McCreary house: mentioned, 14:60, 61
John L. Darragh house: pictured, 39:79
John Starer house: concrete blocks in, 16:4
John Sterling Corp.: address for, 54:65 (FC)
John Stortz and Son, Inc.:
  address for, 71:68
  slater's tools, 20:40 (EF)
John Wagner Associates, Inc.: screw
  gun, reviewed, 85:69-70
John Winnie house: restored, 40:55-59
Johnson, Charles F.:
  boulder house by, 19:72-77 (erratum, 21:6)
  house by, criticized, 11:4
  on Rocky Mountain house, 9:62-67
Johnson, Philip: house by, 80:16
Johnson, Thomas: on three-way switches, 81:48-49
Johnson, Timothy:
  reviews stairbuilding books, 41:94, 64:110
  stairbuilding by, 43:36-38 (FWS)
Johnson, Warren: on pole building, 64:58-59
Johnson Controls Inc.: Penn aquastat of, 18:6
Johnson (G. A.) and Son: repair Wright studio, 32:61
Johnson (L. E.) Products, Inc.: address
  for, 54:65 (FC), 63:41
Johnson Level and Tool Manufacturing Co.:
  address for, 58:45
  Angle Square, 10:61 (TB)
Johnson Metal Products: Rigi-Door, 6:60

Johnson Products: pocket-door frames
  of, 54:65 (FC)
Johnston, David: on ranch remodel, 70:26
Johnston, Randy: mentioned, 34:50
Joinery:
  angle iron for, 8:30 (TFH)
  with bolts, double-ended handrail, 60:77
  with box beams, 72:98
  bridle,
    arched, 3:66
    jig for, 69:52
    in long, twisted stock, 48:71-72 (SH)
  butt,
    clamps for, 74:70, 71 (FC)
    dowel-anchored, 30:10
    half-lap spiked, 65:51 (TFH)
    metal connectors for, 43:48, 49 (FRC)
    modified V-groove for, 9:12
    plate-joined, 70:51, 52 (FC)
    vs. scarf joints, 51:67 (FC)
  concealing, 6:12
  coped, 31:49 (FWS)
    angled jig for, 71:24
    in crown molding, 54:4
    making, 51:64-67 (FC)
  double-bladed, 28:59, 60 (TFH)
  dovetail,
    half-lap, 65:50 (TFH)
    plate-locking, 43:32 (CSH)
    with router, indexed, 55:41 (FC)
    and shrinkage, 7:6
    with tenoned post, 65:50 (TFH)
  dowel,
    for doors, 83:58-60
    for doors, on drill press, 72:51
  for drawers, 30:62 (BK)
  edge, clamps for, 74:71, 72, 73
  exposed, 38:62-63 (CSH)
  finger,
    Arts-and-Crafts style, 22:58, 59 (CSH)
    pegged and chamfered, 17:34 (CSH)
    on table saw, 30:62 (BK), 53:60
  four-way timber, 18:7-8, 20:4
  glue-joint, 85:65
  gutter-spike reinforcements for, 75:26
  Japanese, 4:55, 8:15-16, 24:62-63 (TFH), 43:29, 31, 32 (CSH)
    post-to-top-plate, 19:39 (BK)
  lap,
    half-, V-shaped, 41:68-69 (CSH)
    for window sash, 76:72-74 (FC)
  miter,
    arrowhead, 82:85, 87
    bamboo pins for, 26:16
    by chainsaw, guide for, 31:76
    clamping, 54:92, 74:71, 72, 79:49 (EF), 84:63
    for countertop edgings, 78:67
    on crown molding, 51:65-66 (FC)
    in curved molding, 63:10-12

  double-angle, production cutting of, 15:18
  handsaw adjustment of, 44:68 (FRC)
  ledger-cap, jig for, 84:71
  lock, with router, 55:64
  measuring from, 85:30
  opened, from wood shrinkage, 81:57, 58
  plate-joined, 70:50, 52 (FC)
  radial-arm-saw jig for, 17:16
  shooting board for, making, 76:82 (FC)
  mortise and tenon,
    bolts with, 19:8
    drawboring of, 7:6
    by hand, speed of, 11:17
    multiple intersecting, 15:4, 17:7-8
    and non-uniform stock, allowances for, 16:38-41 (TFH)
    with router, 27:40-42 (TB)
    shouldered, making, 12:22-26 (CSH, TFH)
    shrinkage allowance in, 7:6
    wedging tight, 74:24
  mortises,
    chain mortiser for, 22:16, 63:90-92
    for door latches, 28:4
    for door latches, chiseling, 79:43
    drill-press jig for, 50:71, 72 (FC)
    in heavy timbers, with router template, 10:38-39
    for hinges, 27:40, 41, 42 (TB)
    for hinges, chiseling, 8:36 (DWS), 78:28
    for hinges, templates for, 31:28-31 (TB)
    jig for, 83:60
    for locksets, routing, 79:44
    machine for, reviewed, 62:92
    with router, 27:37, 40-42 (TB), 35:79 (FWS), 79:44
    staircase, router jig for, 55:38-39 (FC)
  plate,
    advantages of, 70:50 (FC)
    for doors, discouraged, 85:6
    epoxy with, 70:53 (FC)
    machines for, new, 82:92
    for narrow stock, 70:53 (FC)
    supply sources for, 70:53 (FC)
    using, 70:50-53 (FC)
    wardrobe with, 78:44-47
  in plywood, 30:60 (BK)
  pocket-screw, 85:66, 67
    machine for, reviewed, 83:92-96
  restoration of, book on, 24:86
  scarf,
    assembly jig for, 53:61
    biscuit joinery for, 76:28
    for board-and-batten, 75:56 (EF)
    vs. butt joints, 51:67 (FC)
    clamping, 76:28
    for clapboards, 51:28

double-keyed, 17:34 (CSH)
epoxied, design for, 70:47
swallowtail, 43:32 (CSH), 46:4
table-saw jig for, 53:61
V-groove for, 9:12
"segmented," 52:61 (CSH)
spline-and-groove, 85:65, 66-67
steel brackets in, hidden, 17:14
Swiss-chalet, 70:73, 75
tenons,
    loose, for doors, 83:58-61
    on rough stock, sizing, 48:73 (SH)
    round, on table saw, 55:26
    rounding of, with plug cutter, 17:37 (DWS)
    with router, 18:74-76 (DWS)
    table-saw jig for, 19:51, 36:41 (DWS, FWS), 50:71, 72 (FC)
tongue-and-groove, curved, routing, 46:12
See also Timber framing.

Joint compound:
applying, 82:76-77
avoiding, 73:67, 69
over block, interior, 40:12
care of, 82:75-76
dust from,
    disaster with, 4:66
    vacuuming, 8:4
mentioned, 23:61 (FWS)
mixing of, electric, 33:16
nontoxic, 67:90-92, 73:69
pan for, large, 48:24
over plaster, 28:10
quick-dry, 26:41, 62:60
recommended, 30:57 (DWS)
setting-type, recommended, 84:6
types of, 82:73-75

Jointer/planers:
German massive, 35:58-59 (TB)
for timber framing, 35:58-59, 36:48 (TB, TFH)

Jointers:
baluster shaping on, 6:21 (CSH)
bricklaying, 43:53, 55 (CBS)
glue joints with, 85:65
mammoth, 36:49 (TFH)
power planes as, 14:45 (TB)
routers as, 1:23, 83:58 (TB)
safety labels for, 37:81
See also Roller supports.

Joists:
adding, for addition, 24:49 (FRC)
angle ties for, 29:37, 38, 44 (FRC)
association for, 82:67
band, sizing, 84:47
blocking for, against earthquakes, 29:37, 38 (FRC)
butted, nailed, 6:6
cantilevered, 27:72, 67:62
composite, 2:27

cutting to fit, 3:33 (TB)
decay problems with, 68:6-8
for decks, 29:44 (FRC)
doubled exterior, leak prevention for, 61:26
dovetailed, 28:59 (TFH)
doweled, 6:6
dry vs. green, 19:57 (FRC)
for exposed ceilings, 65:48-51 (TFH)
extending, through wall, 70:42
failure in, correcting, 10:10
hanger nails for, 50:59, 63:42, 75:16, 85:43, 46
hangers for, 6:6, 19:69-70, 21:27-28 (EEH), 43:45, 46-47 (FRC), 72:28
    installing, 75:14-16, 76:8
housed, 5:12, 6:6
hurricane ties for, 29:74-75
laminated, 50:41, 45 (MFC), 81:53
    commercial, 1:63
lapped, 19:56 (FRC)
    failures with, 6:38 (FRC)
layout of, 19:56 (FRC)
ledger strips for, 6:6
nailing, 19:57-59 (FRC)
nails for, 85:46
placement of, for plumbing, 49:51-53 (MFC)
plumbing holes in, 39:37 (BK)
post connection for, 4:46, 64 (FRC)
prebored, for wiring, 55:59
premarking, 82:44
quirk-beaded, 28:59, 61 (TFH)
repairing, with epoxy, 70:49
replacing, 28:50, 37:8 (FWS)
retrofitting, corner trimming for, 50:30
rim, 19:57 (FRC)
for round houses, central support for, 44:60
stacking, 82:44-45
steel web, using, 82:67

strength of, 74:14
strengthening, 50:67-68, 56:83-84, 64:30, 68:16, 74:14
    with cable, 47:57, 58
    plywood for, 62:28
    sisters for, 65:30 (addenda, 72:6)
    sisters for, split prevention for, 72:6
    with steel I-beam, 68:22
strongback for, 24:50 (FRC)
structural calculations for, 6:6, 23:50, 27:4
support for, in foundation repair, 4:35 (FRC)
for third-floor addition, 74:47-48 (REM)
timber-framed, repairs to, 1:51
"tweaker" for, 50:94
of 2x4s, built-up, failure of, 81:80-81
of 2x12s, paired, 55:59
wood I-beams for, 56:58, 60 (EEH)
See also Metal connectors.

Jokes: for builders, 79:112
JOMY Safety Ladder: address for, 46:90
Jones, E. Fay:
book about, reviewed, 78:110
on Wright, 38:106
Jones, Faye C.: color studies of, 2:6
Jones, Gerry: Boulder house by, 21:6
Jones, Inigo: *Designs of Inigo Jones, The,* cited, 42:74 (FC, TFH)
Jones, Jeremy: *Homes for Creative Living,* cited, 77:51
Jones, M. Dean: on steep-site house, 38:60-65 (CSH)
Jones, Paul: mentioned, 28:81
Jones, Robert T., ed.: *Authentic Small Houses of the Twenties,* reviewed, 44:94
Jones, Rudard A.: *Basic Construction and Materials Takeoff,* reviewed, 29:92
Jonsereds chainsaw: for log building, 2:38
Jordan, Roger: on owner-building, 4:10
Jordan International: ebony logs, 29:58 (CSH)
Joseph, Stanley: on Finnish sauna, 51:42-45
Joshi, Kirti: mentioned, 29:74
Josiah Durkee house: mentioned, 1:48-51
Jotul USA, Inc.: Nor-Metal table saw, 26:82
Journeyman Products, Ltd.: address for, 69:96
Joyce, Tom: ironwork by, 75:75-79
JPS Elastomerics Corp.: address for, 64:45 (EF)
Judge, Dr. James: on Pueblo burials, 18:65
Juglans cinerea: *See* Butternut.
Julius Blum, Inc.:
address for, 46:41, 58:41, 69:53, 74:76 (REM)
cup hinges of, 44:70-71 (BK)
work of, 16:44

Juniperus virginiana: See Cedar, Eastern red.
Junkers water heater: source for, 12:18 (CSH)
Juno Lighting: fixtures, 15:57 (BK)
Jurgens, Kenneth E.: on pressure-treated poles, 15:37
Justrite Manufacturing Co.: gas cans, 44:88

K & B Associates:
   address for, 76:39 (errata, 77:10)
   insulation of, using, 76:41
Kaddies, Inc.: Tool Kaddie from, reviewed, 50:94-95
Kaercher, Bruce C., Jr.: on electric radiant floors, 75:68-72
Kahn, Lloyd, ed.: *Shelter,* reviewed, 62:114
Kahrs Floors: address for, 59:49 (SH)
Kalcoat: *See* Plaster: veneer.
Kalec, Don: on Wright's studio, 32:60-66
Kalwall Corp.:
   address for, 58:83 (EEH), 69:42 (EEH)
   fiberglass, 6:54, 56, 57
   solar components catalog, 1:63
   Sun-Lite Premium II glazing panels, 1:32
   Sun-Lite tubes, 19:63-65, 21:56-58 (EEH)
   tubes, for hydroponic-aquaculture pond, 73:70
   in windows, 16:30
Kampel Enterprises, Inc.: address for, 64:96, 78:67
Kanalflakt, Inc.: address for, 66:68 (EEH)
Kangas, Robert: *Old-House Rescue Book, The,* reviewed, 10:70
K'angs: *See* Masonry stoves.
Kansas:
   solar house for, 26:72-77
   solar tax credits in, 3:12
Kaplan, Matthew: on kitchen design, 2:53-55 (BK)
Kapland, Helain S., and Blair Prentice: *Rehab Right,* reviewed, 2:62
Karnak Chemical Corp.:
   mastic 920, source for, 18:34 (CBS)
   One-Kote roofing, 34:28 (DWS)
Karp, Ben: *Ornamental Carpentry of 19th-century American Architecture,* 18:53
Karpilow, Miles:
   mantel by, 6:20, 21 (CSH)
   on staircase, 49:78-82
Kasko K1-10 insulation: source for, 31:38 (CBS)
Katz, Gary M.: on lockset installation, 79:40-45, 81:60-63
Katz, Howard:
   on freestanding addition, 75:46-49 (REM)

on kitchen remodel, 26:38-39 (BK)
   on playful house, 43:72-74 (SH)
Kaufman, Alice, and Christopher Selser: *Navajo Weaving Tradition, The,* cited, 67:58
Kaufman, David: reviews Rocky Mountain Institute publications, 53:108-10
Kaufmann, Edgar, Jr.: *Fallingwater,* reviewed, 45:122
Kaufmann Footwear: address for, 50:62
Kavanaugh, Karla: on silo house, 7:54-57
Kawecki, Joseph: on Tyvek, 25:82
Kayner, Alex: house by, 38:40-45
Kearns, Steve:
   on cold roofs, 63:42-44
   on prehung doors, 74:62-64 (FC)
   on Sun Valley Manhattan, 62:58-61
Keel: *See* Lumber crayon.
Keene's plaster: using, 34:64 (BK)
Keeping room: 17th-century replica of, 6:47 (TFH)
Keldman, Eric: interviewed, 31:77
Keller, Tom: mentioned, 29:32
Keller Industries: address for, 84:55
Kelly, David: *Secrets of the Old Growth Forest,* reviewed, 57:114
Kelly, Ed: roof by, 11:44, 45 (SH)
Kelly, J. Frederick: *Early Domestic Architecture of Connecticut,* cited, 28:58, 40:33 (FWS, TFH), 49:43 (REM)
Kemlite Co.: address for, 72:62
Kemmer, Jeff: mentioned, 34:50
Kemp, Jim:
   American Vernacular, reviewed, 49:114
   Architectural Ornamentalism, reviewed, 44:94
Kempster, David: curved flashing by, 4:64
Kenco Safety Products: address, 34:55 (TB)
Kencraft Co.: Router Master pad of, reviewed, 55:92-94
Kenlan, Joseph:
   on flagstone walks, 40:46-49 (CBS)
   stone masonry workshop, 74:106
   on stone walls, 49:54-57
Kennedy, Clyde R.: on salvaged house, 66:74-77
Kennedy, Stephen:
   Practical Stonemasonry Made Easy, mentioned, 44:57
   on stone masonry, 27:65-67, 44:54-57 (CBS)
Kennelly, Robert: housing, moving of, 5:19-21
Kenneth Lynch and Sons: work of, 16:44
Kenny, Kathleen: on housebuilding, 82:78-81
Kentucky Wood Floors: jatoba, 40:6
Kenwood House (England): plaster in, 43:40-41 (FWS)

Kerf-bending:
   for bullnose step, 82:61-62
   for molding, 31:71, 82:62
   of plywood, 68:58
Keriakin, Joseph: develops cellular concrete, 30:76
Kern, Barbara and Ken: *Owner-Built Pole Frame House, The,* reviewed, 8:70
Kern, Hansel: stonework by, 41:66-67 (CSH)
Kern, Ken:
   death of, 34:55 (TB)
   Owner-Built Home, The, mentioned, 3:29, 7:42 (CBS), 28:68, 72
Kern, Ken, and Steve Magars: *Owner-Builder's Guide to Fireplaces, The,* 22:6
Kern, Ken, Steve Magers, and Lou Penfield: *Owner-Builder's Guide to Stone Masonry, The,* 3:30 (CBS)
Kern-Tac Inc.: Pleko Therm System cement-stucco coating, 18:8
Kerosene: as paint-thinner substitute, 15:18
Kerr, John: on Roundhouse, 44:58-62
Kerr house (Grand Rapids, Ohio): pictured, 32:77
Keson Industries, Inc.: chalklines, 25:69 (TB), 43:94-96
Kessler, Helen J.:
   on Arthur Brown, 11:29-33 (EEH)
   mentioned, 10:17
Kett Tool Co.: power shears #K-200, 39:63
Keuffel and Esser: drafting tools, 26:58 (TB)
Kevin Roche, John Dinkeloo Associates: Wright house work of, 20:73, 74
Kevlar fire-resistant material: source for, 24:82
Key Technology, Inc.: address for, 67:51
Keys: off-center hole in, for differentiation, 76:30
Keystone Retaining Wall Systems: address for, 47:94
Khalili, Nader: *Ceramic Houses,* reviewed, 40:90
Kickers: defined, 10:68 (FRC)
Kidder, Tracy: *House,* reviewed, 32:86
Kielman, Rolf: house by, 52:41-45
Kiley, Martin D., and Moselle, William M.: *1991 National Construction Estimator,* reviewed, 67:104
Kiln-drying: *See* Wood: drying.
Kilpela, Don: reviews AutoSketch, 81:114
Kilroy, Hugh: folding roof by, 85:148
Kilz primer:
   mentioned, 42:57 (DWS)
   source for, 39:10
Kimball, Herrick:
   on plastic-laminate countertops, 75:60-65
   on pressure-sensitive veneer, 81:76-77
   reviews flooring persuader, 84:96-98

on ⅜-in. VSR drills, 82:36-41
on water levels, 85:58-60
Kindersley, Doris: *Visual Dictionary of Buildings,* reviewed, 85:134
Kindt-Collins Co.: casting metals of, 1:39 (FWS)
King, Peter:
on architectural ceramics, 41:70-75 (FWS)
on handmade tiles, 56:43-47
King, Scott: on chop-saw workstation, 65:46-47 (FC)
King-Post Nailed-Glued Roof Trusses Using 2x4 Members (SHC-BRC): source for, 29:92
King Refrigerator Co.: address for, 52:106
Kinney Brick Co.: mentioned, 33:68 (CBS)
Kirk, Ross: on solo timber-raising, 1:19-21 (TFH)
Kirkhuff, Pat: gate by, 52:91
Kit houses: *See* Prefabricated houses.
Kitchel, Joseph:
on chimney renovation, 4:38-41 (CBS)
on staircase renovation, 1:14-18 (FWS)
Kitchen, Judith L.: *Caring for Your Old House,* reviewed, 70:120-122
Kitchen Cabinet Manufacturers Association: certification program of, 65:74
Kitchen Design Center: address for, 65:74
Kitchen Planning Principles, Equipment, Appliances (SHC-BRC): source for, 29:92
Kitchen Planning Standards: source for, 23:49
Kitchen ranges: *See* Ranges.
Kitchen Systems Division: address for, 75:94
Kitchens:
additions to,
cantilevered, 70:82-85 (REM)
lean-to, 78:62-65 (REM)
angular, small, 12:31, 32
Arts-and-Crafts style, 67:72-76, 69:6-8 (REM)
black-and-white, 82:84, 87
1930s, 44:52, 53 (SH)
association for, 72:98, 82:104
backsplashes for,
ceramic, 59:90, 91
recessed, 49:62 (SH)
behind bifold doors, 85:94
black-and-white, 45:35
black-trimmed, 37:24 (BK)
blocking for, 82:51
books on, 19:26, 23:49, 42:53 (SH), 58:106, 77:45
breezeway-extended, 63:38

centers in,
cleanup, 14:54-55 (BK)
cooking, 14:54-55 (BK)
mix, 14:54-55 (BK)
chair in, drafting, 35:43, 44 (BK)
children's alcove in, 45:51 (CSH)
compact units for, 52:102-106
corridor, 16:60, 27:29, 30 (TFH), 59:77 (REM)
design of, 2:53, 55, 14:56-57, 30:23 (BK)
courses on, 72:98
display niches in, 67:72, 73, 75 (REM)
double-Pullman, 61:51, 54 (SH)
drywall in, seam position of, 41:14
enlarging, 7:21-23 (BK), 63:54-57 (REM)
visually, 39:41-41
farmhouse, 36:54-55, 38:50-51
fir, pickled, black accented, 83:86
galley, 36:72, 45:68, 52:44, 64:78
granite, plaster and wood, 53:49 (SH)
with greenhouse, integral, 59:62-65, 66 (EEH)
for handicapped, 6:51, 35:43-45 (BK), 53:70, 71, 73:62, 63, 65
herb-garden access from, 30:23
industrial-look, 33:75
information on, 65:55
intercom system for, 6-volt, 67:73, 75 (REM)
islands for,
central, 80:65
double-wide, 73:53
mobile work, 26:38-39 (BK)
Japanese-style, 43:31 (CSH)
low-maintenance, 70:65 (EEH)
marble tile for, 80:76
modular, 52:26-28
New American, 28:76-77
1950s future, 34:74, 75
1950s-style remodel, 26:38-39 (BK)
octagonal, 24:76, 77
one-roomed from many, 68:22
outlets for,
retractable extension cords for, 26:39 (BK)
strip, 39:41, 40:67 (BK)
pass-throughs in, 11:45, 38:38-39, 74 (CSH, SH)
racks for,
drain/storage, 27:45, 35:43, 44 (BK)
pot, 81:87, 88-89
pull-out, 47:89
remodeling, 34:62-66 (BK)
for two cooks, 73:16-20
renovating, 2:53-55 (BK)
for light, 62:46-48 (SH)
ridge dormers in, 5:34
round, 7:57
sculptural, 21:43
shelves for, dish-drainer, 52:40 (TFH)
silo-centered, 38:58-59
sites for, 14:54, 55 (BK)

small, 11:43-44, 13:65, 66, 33:50-51, 38:48, 41:94-96 (SH)
steel and wood, 46:36
storage in, 14:54, 57 (BK)
dual-purpose, 85:94
industrial bins for, 26:38, 39 (BK)
summer, acrylic-roofed, 38:66, 70
sunny tile-floored, 85:92
table in, small built-in, 67:75 (REM)
timber-framed,
open, 45:48 (TFH)
simple, 79:54
tiny, 75:67
triangular compact, 45:63 (SH)
U-shaped, open, 65:78 (REM)
vacation-house, 67:63
sans wall cabinets, 78:62-65 (REM)
windows for, stained glass, 73:88
wiring for,
exposed, 46:51 (EEH)
raceway, 71:43 (REM)
Wright-inspired, 65:39
See also Appliances. Cabinets. Countertops. Drawers. Faucets. Lighting. Ranges. Refrigerators. Sinks. Ventilation.
Kitkitdizze: building of, 9:42-45
Klahn, Jim: window seat by, 66:89
K-Lath: source for, 31:27 (CSH)
Klein, Gary: builds rondavels, 30:30-31
Klein Tools, Inc.:
address for, 58:45
Proper Use and Care of Hand Tools, 34:55 (TB)
safety-insulated tools from, 84:98
Klenk Industries, Inc.: address for, 75:61
Kleyman, Jim: mentioned, 21:59 (EEH)
Knape & Vogt Manufacturing Co.:
address for, 58:39 (REM), 69:53
drawer slides, 13:62 (BK)
Knapke, Paul: discusses staircases, 36:60-61 (FWS)
Knauss, Bill: houses by, 34:37
Knepper, David: rural houses by, 5:14
Knight, Robert W.: interviewed, 31:42-43
Knives:
caulk-trimmer, 28:16
drawer for, 15:78 (CSH)
edge-trimming, source for, 81:74
for marking, 4:22 (TFH)
race, 4:22 (TFH)
razor, 22:51 (FRC)
for renovation, 12:51 (TB)
sharpener for, reviewed, 84:94-96
in ship joinery, 38:41, 43
for thatching, 22:75
utility,
for blueboard, 15:73 (FWS)
for drywall, 8:54 (FWS)
for plaster, 11:10
swivel-lock, 76:92

Knots:
trucker's, 8:33 (TFH)
tying, 25:64-65 (TB)
Knowlton, Everett: village by, 20:92
Koehn, Stan: on solar farmhouse, 37:70-75
Koel, Leonard:
Carpentry, reviewed, 35:68-69 (TB)
Concrete Formwork, reviewed, 63:106
Koenig, Harry:
builds house, 25:50-53
house by, 37:34-38
Koh-I-Noor Rapidograph Inc.: drafting
tools, 26:58 (TB)
Kohler Co.: address for, 69:63, 73:62, 76:58,
68, 82:96 (REM)
Kolbe & Kolbe Millwork Co., Inc.:
address for, 55:79, 76:75 (FC)
windows of, 60:49, 50 (FC)
Kolle, Jefferson: on new products, 79:100-
104, 81:92-96, 83:92, 98, 84:98, 85:102-106
Kollman, Michael S.: on Caribbean
house, 50:53-57
Kolva, Dennis: replaces window, 44:110
Komac Paint Co.: Plastique Exterior Tung
Oil, 17:64 (DWS)
Komp, Richard J.:
Practical Photovoltaics, cited, 62:71
as joint author. *See* Davidson, Joel.
Konya, Allan, and Alewyn Burger:
*International Handbook of Finnish
Sauna, The,* cited, 39:4
Konzo, Seichi, and Marylee MacDonald:
Quiet Indoor Revolution, The, reviewed,
81:114, 83:6
Kooistra, Jan Dirk:
quoted, 46:79
Koontz, Thomas:
on building basics, 32:29-33 (FRC)
at conference, 28:81
Koppers Co., Inc.:
address for, 50:20, 79-81 (SH)
foam-panel laminate, 28:12
KMM roll roofing, 9:4
modified bitumens, 2:37
phenolic foam, 35:8
treated shingles, 11:8
Korad acrylic film:
described, 24:46
difficulties with, 28:6
Koral, Bill: uses air structure, 51:120
Koralewsky, Frank: lockset by, 48:124
Korfil Inc.: insulated block, 31:38, 39, 41
(CBS)
Kornegay, Burt: on moving church,
66:118-17
Korpan, Dean: masonry repairs by, 5:36,
37, 38, 39
Koster, John: reviews *House,* 32:86
Kostof, Spiro: *History of Architecture, A,*
reviewed, 45:120

Kramer, Tim: mentioned, 32:73
Krayenhoff, Meror: shoeboat by, 43:116
KRC Research Corp.: epoxy sealant, 11:10
Kreh, Richard T.:
on block foundations, 15:44-48 (CBS)
on bricklaying, 43:50-55 (CBS)
on repointing, 2:45
Krimmel, Max: on bees, 50:126
Kristensen, Paul: house by, 38:72-77 (TFH)
Kroin Inc.: address for, 1:62, 49:60 (SH)
Krommenie Co.: linoleum of, 22:45 (BK)
KSD Industries: address for, 52:112
Kupferer, Kate, ed.:
Residential and Commercial Sunspaces,
reviewed, 68:108
Timber Frame Homes, reviewed, 68:108
Kupfermuehle: jointer/planer, 35:59 (TB)
Kuranar: fluorocarbon resin paint,
discussed, 24:46
Kurlander, Ira: on garage remodeling,
12:42-45 (REM)
Kurtz, Bill: on owner-building, 4:10
Kushner, Ira: on attic conversion, 13:39-41
Kutz, Dr. Joseph E.: gives amputation
advice, 53:102-104
Kwikset Corp.: address for, 53:68
Kynar 500: fluorocarbon resin paint,
discussed, 24:46

La France Equipment Corp.: first-aid kits,
36:4
La Miniatura: textile blocks in, 16:4-6
La Torre, John, Jr.: on curved crown
molding, 74:79-81 (FC)
Lab Safety Supply: address for, 61:68
Labadie, John: on belt-sander longevity,
72:118
Labels: removing, 54:28
Labor: estimates for, 27:34-35
Labs, Kenneth:
heat-loss studies of, 2:31 (EEH)
on *Sunhouse,* 37:88
Labs, Kenneth, and Donald Watson:
Climatic Design, 37:90
Lacquer: *See* Finishes.
LaCrosse Footwear: address for, 50:63
Ladder hooks: for roofing jobs, 39:63
Ladder Inspection and Repair Guide
(Ladder Man, Inc.): address for, 84:55
Ladder jacks: using, 36:37 (TB)
Ladder Man, Inc.: *Ladder Inspection and
Repair Guide,* cited, 84:55
Ladders:
accessories for, 84:54
angle for, quick guide to, 61:26
association for, 84:53

to balcony, 74:53
baskets for, 61:26
bootees for, 79:30
cold-proofing, 50:60
duty ratings of, 84:50
escape, folding, reviewed, 46:90
extension, 84:51, 52-53
library, making, 65:86-87
loading-dock, steel, 19:47-48, 49
loft, 18:49
materials for, 84:50-51
ridge-hung, T-device for, 34:14
rolling, 13:65-66 (SH), 55:86, 61:120
reviewed, 52:98
safety with, 57:85 (EF), 84:53
scaffolds with, 57:85 (EF)
ship, for cupola access, 74:49 (REM)
sources for, 19:48, 55:86, 60:94, 84:54
specialty, 84:52, 53-54
stand-off and shelf for, 42:16-18
step-, 17:62 (FWS), 84:51, 52
three-legged, reviewed, 60:94
tool pouch for, 42:22 (CSH)
various, source for, 52:98
wheels for, 65:86, 87
Lafever, Minard:
Beauties of Modern Architecture, The,
29:63
Modern Builders Guide of 1833, 29:63
Laffin, Peter: mentioned, 25:39, 40 (EEH)
LaFrance, Allan: reviews miter saw,
85:104-106
Lagerquist, Gordon:
on island house, 61:50-54 (SH)
studio by, 51:36-40 (CSH)
Lamarra, John: on owner-building, 4:10
Lamb, Jane: on Maine studio, 50:78-81
(SH)
Lamberti, Vic: designs pole system, 39:28
Lambie, Alec: on corrugated house, 7:68
Lamb's tongues: on beams, 28:60-61 (TFH)
Lameyer, Ted:
reviews Brown, 85:132
reviews Ivy, 78:110
Lamin-Art: address for, 9:41 (BK)
Laminate slitters: discussed, 75:60, 61
Laminate trimmers: radiused grooves
with, 62:30
Laminated beams: *See* Beams: glulam.
Laminates:
aluminum polychromed, 39:90
metal dust, 39:90
plastic, solid-colored, 39:90
wood, reconstituted, 39:90
wood/phenolic/melamine, 39:90
See also Plastic laminate.
Lamination:
banding machine for, 42:47 (FWS)
for casings,
arched, 29:57-58 (CSH), 69:83-84
curved, 67:82-85 (FC)

clamping techniques for, 42:46-47, 48-49 (FWS)
clamps for, site-built, 74:24, 26
contact-cement bucket for, 55:28
creep with, dowels for, 62:30
with epoxy, 70:48, 49
  cold-cure, 44:68 (FRC)
glue for, 42:46, 47, 48 (FWS), 44:75, 55:63, 65:86, 69:83, 74:81 (FC)
of molding, crown, curved, 74:79-81 (FC)
of oily wood, 29:57-58 (CSH)
for paneling, 56:75
for rail, 70:88, 89-90
  exterior, 54:82 (EF)
See also Forms. Staircases. Steam bending.
LaMonica, Dennis: outhouse by, 67:87
LaMontagne, Armand: stone-ender by, 6:42-47 (TFH)
Lamps: *See* Light fixtures.
Lancaster, Clay:
  American Bungalow, The, reviewed, 31:80
  Architecture of Historic Nantucket, The, cited, 77:89
Lance, Mary: on Lynn Ford, 23:30
Lance, Steve: on deconstruction, 53:122
Land: computer searches for, 46:59
Land trusts: *See* Communities.
Lander, Hugh: *House Restorer's Guide, The,* reviewed, 34:92
Landmark Designs, Inc.:
  address for, 30:63
  plans from, 53:88, 89
Landmark Yellow Pages: reviewed, 68:106
Landscape architects: working with, 52:83-84
Landscape Architecture (Simonds): reviewed, 45:116
Landscape Lighting Book, The (Moyer): reviewed, 85:132-34
Landscaping:
  Craftsman-California style, 44:50-53 (SH)
  edible, 44:51 (SH)
  energy-efficient, 3:19
  integral, 4:26-27, 28-29, 31-33
  irrigation system for, 44:51 (SH)
  and microclimate, 9:16
  for radiation moderation, 34:10
  vertical, with vines, 15:26-27, 30, 31
  Victorian, book treating, 11:70
  See also Sites.
Landscaping for Energy Efficient Homes (CAREIRS): source for, 82:106
Lane, Charles A.:
  on design and climate, 21:60-61
  on waterproofing houses, 2:35-37
Lanford, Marilyn: reviews Sudjic, 36:94
Lang, Christoper: reviews sander, 64:94-96

Lang, Paul: on Russian fireplaces, 7:46-49 (CBS)
Langdon, Philip: *American Houses,* reviewed, 44:94
Lange: woodstoves, 1:45, 47 (EEH), 4:38 (CBS)
Langford, Berry: on ferro-cement office, 50:46-49
Langsner, Drew:
  on ax techniques, 13:54-59
  Logbuilder's Handbook, A, 13:59
  reviews Suzuki, 12:72
  on shingles, 30:46-49
  on Swiss chalets, 70:72-75
Lanterns: exterior forged, with mica, 75:77
Lap joints: *See* Joinery.
Laparade, Claude: mentioned, 33:67
Larch (*Larix* spp.):
  decay resistance of, 63:63 (MFC)
  span capability of, 33:43 (FWS)
Larry W. Garnett & Assoc., Inc.:
  address for, 53:89
  plans from, 53:85, 89
Larsen, Michael, and Elizabeth Pomada:
  Daughters of Painted Ladies, cited, 74:45 (EF)
  How to Create Your Own Painted Lady, cited, 74:45 (EF)
Larsen Products Corp.: Plaster-Weld, 23:10, 28:10, 43:10
Larsen trusses: *See* Trusses: Larsen.
Larson, John and Sandra: house by, 38:30-34
Larson, Merwin: on S. D. energy standards, 33:84
Larson, Steve:
  on powder-actuated tools, 21:30-34 (TB)
  on remodel plumbing, 17:52-55 (BK)
  on Victorian addition, 14:22-26
Lasar, Stephen:
  about, 45:130
  on Chinese solar technology, 26:82-83
  house by, 45:76-81, 89 (EEH)
  on making skylights, 11:62-64 (DWS)
  on solar design, 1:43-47 (EEH)
  on thermosiphons, 3:48-50
  on timber-frame remodel, 79:85-89
Laschever, Jon: reviews construction books, 1:64-66
Laschever, Sara: reviews Sloan, 11:70
Laser Alignment: levels, 37:45 (TB)
Laser Tools, Inc.: level of, reviewed, 84:94
Lassiter, Leonard: scorps by, 34:49
Lasso, Robert: light fixtures by, 27:60, 63 (BK)
Latapoxy 210: for tile floors, 17:70, 72 (BK)
Latch bolts: *See* Locksets.
Latches:
  Bean, 1:49
  carved ebony, 21:35
  forged, 67:57, 75:77
  magnetic adjustable, source for, 80:102

Norfolk, 1:49
for pocket doors, 54:66 (FC), 56:6
sculpted handmade, 68:39, 40, 88-89
Suffolk, 1:49
wooden, 10:75
See also Hardware.
Latex paint: *See* Paint.
Latham, Sarah: on restoring brownstones, 5:36-39
Lathes:
  column jig for, 64:55-57
  fluting columns on, jig for, 64:55-56
  post-turning, 39:76
  safety labels for, 37:81
Lathing hatchet: *See* Hatchets: shingling.
Lathrop Tool Works: reviewed, 48:91
Laticrete International, Inc.:
  additives, 37:46 (DWS)
    latex, 17:75 (BK)
  address for, 71:54
  admix #3701, source for, 32:47 (BK)
  800-number for, 70:112
  #8510, source for, 37:46 (DWS)
  Latapoxy #210 thinset epoxy, 17:70, 72 (BK)
  latex grout waterproofing, 22:12
  mortar-grout admix, 25:34, 35 (BK)
  #9235, 20:12
  roofing membrane, 16:8
  #301-335, uses of, 20:12
Latta, Jay: on marble, 69:55-57
Lattice work: back-lit gable-end, 29:58, 59-61 (CSH)
Lauan: *See* Mahogany, Philippine.
Laundries:
  accessories for, 53:44, 45 (SH)
  chutes for, 14:26, 43:79
  concealed, 28:52, 53 (FWS)
  drain lines for, 39:36, 37 (BK)
  hampers for, in-wall, 60:45 (SH)
  and office combination, 44:52-53 (SH)
  and sauna combination, 33:52 (SH)
  space for, 53:43-45 (SH)
  upstairs, 59:70, 72 (SH)
Laurence, Vincent:
  on earthquakes, 64:100
  on information resources, 65:52-55
  on nontoxic coatings, 67:90-92
  reviews books, 70:120, 122
  reviews curve template, 68:94
  reviews preservation book, 68:106
  reviews Reynolds, 69:110
  on stainless fasteners, 63:92
  on tubular incandescents, 66:102-104
  on WARP, 65:102
  on workshop trailer, 70:132
Laurence (C. R.) Co., Inc.:
  address for, 65:44
  glazing products, 10:4
Lauritzen, Peter: on log studio, 48:70-73 (SH)

Lautner, John:
career of, 18:29, 32
and Frank Lloyd Wright, 18:26, 29
See also Mauer house.

Lauziere, Stephen: reviews pocket cutter, 83:92-96

Law, Tom:
on cabinet installation, 85:48-52
on carpentry texts, 35:68-71 (TB)
on circular stair, 9:60-61
on crown molding, 51:64-67 (FC)
on handsaws, 20:68-72 (TB), 54:94-96, 118, 78:60-61
on hanging doors, 26:26-32 (DWS)
on miter boxes, 65:75 (FC)
reviews hinge-mortise template, 70:104-106
reviews Lewis, 56:110
reviews sharpening stones, 77:94-96
reviews short-cut handsaw, 69:92
reviews Walmsley, 69:108
on sawhorses, 43:56-57 (TB)
on scribing, 77:61
on sharpening sawblades, 24:33-35 (TB)
on shingles, 25:62-63
on simplified roof framing, 10:62 (FRC)
on site layout, 11:26-28 (CBS)
on toolboxes, 29:39-41 (TB)
video by, 85:52
on workbenches, 81:64-66

Lawler Machine and Foundry Co.: work of, 16:44

Lawrence, Greg: on coffered ceilings, 75:37 (MFC)

Lawrence, Lena: on house design, 30:63

Lawrence Berkeley Laboratory:
address for, 71:104
air-change studies of, 1:12

Lawrence Brothers, Inc.: address for, 54:65 (FC)

Layout: *See* Site layout.

Layout sticks: *See* Story poles.

Layout tees: *See* Roofs: framing.

Lazy Susans: making, 69:53-54

Lazzaro, Victor: on house and studio, 27:72-77.

Le Corbusier:
books on, 43:102
quoted, on human scale, 23:29

Le Messurier International Timbers, Inc.: address for, 71:96

Leach, Thomas:
bookcase by, 58:87 (addendum, 60:8)
on hot-climate house, 79:70-74
on learning carpentry, 80:22-24

Lead:
corrosion of, 62:64, 65
detector kit for, 71:96
melting, 46:56 (BK)
nobility of, 21:4
in paint, danger from, 76:4
panels of, 23:31

Key to books:

(BK)	Building Baths and Kitchens
(CBS)	Building with Concrete, Brick and Stone
(CSH)	Craftsman-Style Houses
(DWS)	Building Doors, Windows and Skylights
(EEH)	Energy-Efficient Houses
(EF)	Exterior Finishing
(FC)	Finish Carpentry
(FRC)	Frame Carpentry
(FWS)	Building Floors, Walls and Stairs
(MFC)	More Frame Carpentry
(REM)	Remodeling
(SH)	Small Houses
(TB)	Tools for Building
(TFH)	Timber-Frame Houses

protection against, 61:68
publications on, 55:108
as roofing, 25:59, 60-61
strips, for fake glazing, 74:78
for window cames, 23:36, 38 (DWS)
See also Flashing. Windows: leaded.

Lead Industries Association: mentioned, 25:61

Lead shields: described, 41:53 (CBS)

LeadCheck Swabs: address for, 84:75

Leaded glass: *See* Windows: leaded.

Leahy (R. J.) & Co.: address for, 68:73 (EF)

Leather:
alcohol-forming, 46:26
forming, for sheath, 51:26-28

Leather punch: for screw-hole plugs, 84:28

Leca: *See* Block.

Lechner, Norbert: *Heating, Cooling, Lighting,* reviewed, 72:108

Lee, John:
belvedere by, 30:64-69 (CBS)
solar house by, 26:72-77

Lee Valley Tools Ltd.:
chisels of, 12:23 (CSH, TFH)
screen-door hardware, 36:39 (DWS)

Lee-Carmichael house:
building of, 11:46-47 (CBS)
performance of, 11:49-50 (CBS)

Leek, Stephen: career of, 18:43

Leeke, John:
Epoxy Repairs for Exterior Wood, source for, 70:49
on window sash, 18:72-77 (DWS)

Leger house: described, 6:58

Lego, William: on miter-saw stand, 69:70-71

LeGwin, J. Hardy: *Project Notebook,* reviewed, 77:122

Lehigh Safety Shoe Co.: address for, 69:96, 81:4

Lehman Hardware: reviewed, 52:100-102

Lehn, Ted. P.: on lightweight-concrete wall house, 48:48-53

Lehr, Gass, Pettyjohn, and De Marre: *Domestic Water Conditioning,* cited, 10:55 (BK)

Leitch & Co.: address for, 51:63

Lelen, Kenneth: on rebuilding, 3:51-55

Lemire, Ed: house by, 38:40-45

Lemle, Brad: on bottle house, 36:104

Lennox Industries, Inc.:
address for, 61:12
heat pump, as dehumidifier, 2:33 (EEH)

Lenox:
Hackmaster bimetal blades, manufacture of, 16:47 (TB)
reciprocating-saw blades, source for, 11:14

Leonite International Inc.: patterning tools of, 7:6

Lepre, Vincent:
on restoration, 29:63-67
on Wright restoration, 20:73-79

Leslie Iron Works: circular staircase, 10:50, 51 (SH)

Lesser, Stan:
on Atlantic Boatworks, 36:49 (TFH)
house by, 33:76-77

Lettering:
painted, gilded, 72:48-49
pounce table for, 72:48

Levelers: for legs, 74:74, 76

Leveling rods:
commercial, 37:41 (TB)
making, 37:14

Levels:
with angle-finding capacity, 27:82
brands of, discussed, 37:45 (TB)
bricklaying, 43:52 (CBS)
choosing, 37:80
combination, source for, 67:90
described, 37:39-40 (TB)
digital, 58:44
read-out, reviewed, 53:94, 58:6
with electronic sound, 44:89
electronic, source for, 71:96
extensions for, 23:69, 80 (FRC)
for framing, 58:43
laser, 37:45 (TB)
reviewed, 84:94
lighted-vial, 65:96
line, 25:66, 67 (TB)
magnetic, 34:6
90°, finding, 84:94
pocket, optical, 29:43 (FRC)
for renovations, 12:50 (TB)
sighting with, 27:67 (CBS)
6½-ft., wedging for door jambs, 39:14
sources for, 58:45
specialty, 58:44
string, 29:43 (FRC)

testing, 47:18, 49:8
tuning, 81:28
types of, 58:42-44
using, 37:41-44 (TB)
versatility of, discussed, 57:96
vials in, 58:43, 44-45
  replacing, 47:18
water,
  advantages of, 77:22, 85:58
  commercial, 42:86-88, 85:60
  making, 70:32, 85:58-60
  source for, 74:78
  using, 6:8, 8:4, 11:27, 29:43 (CBS, FRC), 85:48, 59-60
water drops as, 8:24 (CBS)
Leventhal, Michael: house by, 45:49-53, 88 (CSH)
Levin, Edward M.:
  about, 45:130
  on Fairbanks house, 13:22-27 (TFH)
  on frame design, 45:46 (TFH)
  house by, 45:44-48, 88 (TFH)
  on laminated timber, 48:44-47 (TFH)
  mentioned, 29:86
  on timber-framing, 4:21-25, 7:24-28 (TFH, TFH)
Levin, Per: Swedish housing report by, 28:82
Levine, Betsy:
  on Grashow models, 21:84
  on house in boulders, 19:72-77
  on octagon house, 11:6
  on porches, 14:60-61
Levine, Jeffrey: on slate quarrying, 71:65-68
Levine, Paul:
  on cabinets, 30:58-62 (BK)
  on European hardware, 44:69-71 (BK)
  on laminate edgings, 78:66-67
  Making Kitchen Cabinets, cited, 78:67
Levine, Richard: solar house by, 16:26-30
Leviton Mfg. Co. Inc.: address for, 46:39 (REM), 53:74
Levolor Lorentzen Inc.: sloped-surface shades, 31:34 (DWS)
Levy, Daniel A.: on Ernest Flagg, 5:28-35
Lewis, Arnold: American Country Houses of the Gilded Age, reviewed, 29:90
Lewis, Gaspar J.: Carpentry, reviewed, 56:110
Lewis, Jack R.: Support Systems for Buildings, reviewed, 34:92
Lexel caulk: reviewed, 42:88-90
LexFoam Mfg. Inc.: address for, 75:83
Lexson, Steve: on Pueblo construction, 18:63, 65
Libbey-Owens-Ford Co.: address for, 80:26
Liberty Fasteners, Inc.: address for, 46:90

Libraries:
  formal, 31:49, 50 (FWS)
  from garages, 84:69-71
  ladders for, rolling, 84:55
  renovated, 61:120
  Spanish-Revival style, 26:40-42
Liczwinko, John: on concrete wall panels, 85:82-83
Liddle, Alan: seating by, 66:90
Lido Inc.: tool box from, reviewed, 49:95
Lienemann, Mike:
  on shingle thatching, 23:52-56
  as joint author. See Cooke, Gary.
Lie-Nielsen, Susan: wins competition, 75:102 (addenda, 78:8)
Lie-Nielsen Toolworks, Inc.: address for, 76:83 (FC)
Lietz-Sokkisha: transit level #20, 37:45 (TB)
Lifchez, Raymond, and Barbara Winslow: Design for Independent Living, cited, 6:51, 35:45 (BK)
Life in the English Country House (Girouard): reviewed, 45:122
Life-Support Technics conferences: mentioned, 26:56
Lifting:
  aids for, 85:81
  body strategies for, 85:80, 81
Light: ultraviolet, blocking, 55:8
Light fixtures:
  for alcove, 76:43, 44, 45 (REM)
  for aquariums, 72:63
  Art Nouveau, 54:40
  Arts-and-Crafts style, 42:29, 30 (CSH), 52:78, 81, 54:100, 59:85-87 (CSH)
    source for, 58:58 (CSH)
  bathroom, Arts-and-Crafts style, 45:52 (CSH)
  built-in, 54:50, 53
    wooden, making, 27:60-62 (BK)
  catalog for, 51:90
  ceramic semicircular, 73:50
  chandeliers,
    Art Nouveau, 54:37
    branding-iron, 48:85
    forged, with mica cups, 75:78, 79
    glass, 73:89
  cheap, 52:40 (TFH)
  compact-fluorescent, efficiency aids for, 74:104
  cord bracket for, wooden, 27:63
  cove box, source for, 51:52
  custom, source for, 67:58
  decorative, 15:56 (BK)
  drywall-formed, 63:53
  energy-saving, 66:4
  exterior,
    aluminum, 52:72, 73
    benches, 51:52
    boxed, 79:70-71, 73
    copper, 45:38

  Craftsman, 74:55
  ridge-flag, 52:70
  shingled, 10:75
  source for, 69:49 (EF)
  tower for, 52:72, 73
  wood-framed, 52:36, 40 (TFH)
fluorescent, 54:49, 76:45 (REM)
  dimmers for, 75:6
  high-output, source for, 72:63
  vs. incandescent, 75:6
  indirect, 54:53
  shadowless-cove, 75:6
  slimline, reviewed, 52:98-100
glass-veneered, source for, 43:31, 33 (CSH)
glass-and-steel sculpted, 66:52, 54
Greene-and-Greene style, 17:28, 31, 33, 34, 38:65, 72:41 (CSH)
halide, source for, 72:63
hanging,
  slatted, 21:40
  wooden, making, 27:63
industrial, 52:44, 45
insulation for, 56:37
iron round, 25:28-29
job-site,
  flashlight, 67:28
  portable, 60:26
  tripod, 47:28
kitchen oak/Plexiglas, 80:76
laminated curved, 15:77, 78 (CSH)
lantern,
  forged, with mica, 75:77
  shoji-like, 39:70, 74
linear incandescent, in soffits, 73:73
mahogany tusk, 24:76, 77
mica for, 75:78, 79
neon entry, 33:75
parts sources for, 27:63
plaster, 31:62 (FWS)
plaster molded, 53:46, 50 (SH)
Plexiglas, 55:73, 74
portable, 15:56 (BK)
prairie-style, 45:59
punched-copper sheet, 80:58
recessed, 15:56 (BK)
  compact low-voltage, source for, 60:44 (SH)
  heat loss with, 18:7
  insulatable, 61:78 (EF)
  in newel post, 2:20-22, 25 (CSH)
  source for, 62:48 (SH)
  stairwell, 45:57
room-length wood/glass, 43:28, 29, 33 (CSH)
safety rules for, 27:60-61 (BK)
salvaged, 66:76
Scandinavian, 35:34
scribing for, 77:30
shades for, board, 3:26, 27
shopmade, gallery of, 61:86-87
Skywalker, 31:47, 50 (FWS)

sources for, 66:67 (EEH)
stairwell, 66:43, 45
Stickley, 36:24, 27 (CSH)
switch for, transmitter-controlled, 80:98
theatrical, 38:48 (SH)
30-volt, early, 66:77
track,
    indirect, 62:48 (SH)
    miniature, 52:100
    source for, 62:48 (SH), 71:43 (REM)
in trusses, indirect, 75:81, 84
tubular incandescent, source for,
    66:102-104
wall,
    corner, 74:52, 56
    sconce, ceramic, 30:70-71
    sconce, forged, 75:79
    semicircular, 74:53, 56
    wooden, making, 27:60 (BK)
Wright-style, 21:76, 77 (FRC)
wrought-iron, 51:36-37, 40 (CSH)
See also Lighting.
Lighthouse house: pictured, 33:96
Lighting:
accent, 15:57 (BK)
acrylic diffusers for, 15:60
by adjustable lamps, 48:81, 83
for alcoves, 70:44
alternative, catalogs for, 52:100-102
associations for, 54:52
by back-lit Nerf balls, 29:33
book on, reviewed, 54:106
built-in, 66:38-39 (SH)
    between collar ties, 67:37
    indirect, 44:41 (SH)
ceiling panels for, 10:24, 25
colors of, 54:50-51
from compact fluorescents, 70:112
cove, 51:51, 52, 53
with cupola and transoms, 83:54-56
Danish, 35:29, 33, 34
degree program in, 69:100
diffusers for, pine-and-linen, 49:61, 62
    (SH)
dimmers for, 15:56 (BK)
    autotransformer, 17:6
    quieting, 39:14
    solid-state, 17:6
drop, on tracks, 38:59
drywall template for, 49:28
fiber-optics, Japanese, 51:96
fluorescent,
    advances in, 2:64
    bulbs for, compact, 67:92
    constant illuminance system for,
        54:53
    dimmers for, 54:53
    guide to, 54:49-53
    solar-powered, 8:47
    switches for, 54:53
    types of, 15:55, 56 (BK)

by gas, 14:31
headlamp for, 4:6
for house numbers, 56:71-72 (CSH)
incandescent,
    argument for, 24:82
    types of, 15:54 (BK)
indirect, 15:57 (BK)
information on, 6:4
    hotline for, 71:106
for kitchens, 2:54-55, 40:64-65 (BK),
    43:78, 79
    ceiling task, 80:76
    recessed, 67:72, 73, 74 (REM)
landscape, book on, 85:132-34
light well for, countertop, 18:32
low-voltage, 15:55, 18:30 (BK)
lumens of, 15:54 (BK)
peanut, 3-watt, 8:47
publications on, 54:52
recessed,
    for kitchen, 67:72, 73, 74 (REM)
    mini-, source for, 60:44 (SH)
rheostats for, 15:56 (BK)
ridge-suspended, 60:42, 44 (SH)
skylights for, venting, 62:48 (SH)
soffit,
    exterior, 19:32, 33
    low-voltage, 69:46, 47 (EF)
sources for, 15:57 (BK)
staircase, with encased fluorescence,
    56:71 (CSH)
switches for, oak-leaf, 31:72
system for, 75:84
task, 15:56-57 (BK)
track, in kitchen, 78:65 (REM)
valances for,
    in closets, 83:70, 72
    full, 46:38, 41 (REM)
    torsion-box, 62:59
See also Light fixtures.
Lighting Handbook (Illuminating
    Engineering Society): cited, 54:52
Lighting Your Life: cited, 54:52
Lightning:
association on, 47:20-22
book on, 47:22
danger from, assessing, 47:20-22
protection against, 47:20-22
rods,
    information on, 84:68
    installing, 84:68
*Lightning Protection for Home, Family
    and Property:* cited, 47:22
Lightolier, Inc.: address for, 52:100, 61:78
    (EF), 62:48 (SH), 71:43 (REM)
    fixtures, 15:56, 57 (BK)
Lightstat:
    address for, 83:92
Lightweight Processing Co.: aggregate,
    20:52 (FWS), 21:52 (DWS)

Lil Otto Hydroworks: address for, 64:12
Lilypons Water Gardens: catalog from,
    13:6
Lime: as adhesive, 65:41, 45
Limestone: *See* Stone.
Limestone Institute of America:
    information from, 37:59
Lincoln, Ray: on pickup tool storage,
    41:58-59 (TB)
Lincoln Electric Co.: address for, 84:80
Lincoln Wood Products, Inc.: address
    for, 76:75 (FC)
Linde, Tom: on tankless water heater,
    12:16, 18
Lindemann, William N.: on Viking castle,
    77:90
Lindsay Finishes, Inc.: address for, 70:49
Lindsey, Larry: acrylic use of, 10:30, 31, 33
    (DWS)
Linear Link VCS-12 chainsaw: accuracy
    of, 75:83
Line-Design portable drafting board:
    reviewed, 56:94
Linen Re-Creations: address for, 54:100
Linfoot, Lance: roof by, 57:90
Linseed oil:
    in high humidity, 29:77
    house burning from, 27:94
    for log buildings, 14:53
Lintels:
    built-up, 27:76, 77
    concrete,
        preformed, 83:14
        site-cast, method for, 74:50-51
        and wood, 14:73
    recessed frameless, 27:76, 77
    steel prefabricated (English), 43:59-60
        (CBS)
Lipfel, Arthur: mentioned, 1:8
Lipnosky, Andrew: dacha of, 26:96
Lipson, Eric: on Deca Dome, 46:42-43
Lipstick: uses of, 25:16
Liquid Nails: for staircase parts, 39:48
    (FWS)
Liquitex: latex paint, 9:24
Liriodendron tulipifera: See Yellow
    poplar.
*List of Publications of Interest to
    Architects, Builders, Engineers and
    Retail Lumbermen:* source for, 23:50
Litchfield, Michael W.:
    Renovation, reviewed, 14:76, 65:106
    on venting, 1:34-35 (BK)
Lite-Form, Inc.:
    address for, 76:39
    insulation of, using, 76:41
Literacy training: programs for, 65:102
Lithocarpus densiflorus: See Tan oak.
Lithochrome Chemical Stain: source for,
    11:10, 28:69

Little House, The:
building, 1:56-57
criticisms of, 1:57-58
See also Small houses.
Little House, The (Armstrong): variations on, 1:56, 57
Littleton Millwork: address for, 56:61 (EEH)
Lively, John:
on butt-hinge mortising, 8:36 (DWS)
on Craftsman houses, 36:24-29 (CSH)
on Fechin house, 25:26-31
on gas nail gun, 33:82 (TB)
on Greene-and-Greene revival, 22:54-60 (CSH)
on Island City Woodworks, 39:75-77
on Mexican stone masonry, 22:84
on NAHB conference, 21:20, 26:82
on sharpening, 18:56-61 (TB)
on timber-frame power tools, 35:54-59 (TB)
Living Barns (Burden): mentioned, 28:86
Living Systems: mentioned, 34:37
Living the Good Life (Nearing): source for, 14:63
Livos Plant Chemistry:
address for, 67:90
distributor for, 73:69
Liz's Antique Hardware: address for, 75:100
Lloyd, John: on fireplace-chimney codes, 69:76-78
Lloyd, Nathaniel: *History of the English House, A,* cited, 69:86
Load: defined, 7:25 (TFH)
Lo-Cal house: discussed, 9:56
Locke, Jim: *Apple Corps Guide to the Well-Built House, The,* reviewed, 51:104-106
Lockhart, Brian: on rammed-earth house, 39:49-51
Lockman, Heather: on restoring house, 66:24-26
Locks: *See* Doors: club brace for. Locksets.
Locksets:
backset, narrow, 83:56
Baldwin Lexington pattern, 3:16 (DWS)
bored, installing, 79:40-45
boring jigs for, 79:42
brass, 48:65 (FC)
cylindrical, 48:62-63, 64 (FC)
deadbolt, 48:62-64 (FC)
keyless, 48:65 (FC)
French door, 5:33
hand of, 26:26-27 (DWS), 81:60
for handicapped, 48:65 (FC)
levered, 53:68, 71
installing, 8:36, 10:46 (DWS), 81:61-63, 82:6
interior, 48:64 (FC)
jig for, 53:40 (FC)
kinds of, 48:61 (FC)

Key to books:

(BK)	Building Baths and Kitchens
(CBS)	Building with Concrete, Brick and Stone
(CSH)	Craftsman-Style Houses
(DWS)	Building Doors, Windows and Skylights
(EEH)	Energy-Efficient Houses
(EF)	Exterior Finishing
(FC)	Finish Carpentry
(FRC)	Frame Carpentry
(FWS)	Building Floors, Walls and Stairs
(MFC)	More Frame Carpentry
(REM)	Remodeling
(SH)	Small Houses
(TB)	Tools for Building
(TFH)	Timber-Frame Houses

latch for, locating, 55:28
lever-handled, 48:65 (FC)
mortise, 76:57, 58
locating, 48:65 (FC)
mortise, 48:61-62 (FC)
mortiser for, 48:62 (FC), 81:61
pin-tumbler cylinder, 48:63 (FC)
precious-metal inlaid sculpted, 48:124
quality of, 8:36 (DWS), 48:64-65 (FC)
retrofit jig for, 21:18
tubular, 48:62-63, 64 (FC)
Weiserbolt, 48:64 (FC)
Loctite: for router bearings, 41:69 (CSH)
Loctite Corp.: address for, 65:44, 70:49
Loewen Windows: address for, 76:75 (FC)
Loferski, Joseph R.: on nails, 85:42-47
Lofts:
adding, 38:47-48 (SH)
ladders for, 13:65-66, 18:49 (SH)
octagonal, 24:76, 77
post-and-picket rail for, 18:49
railing for, tubular-steel, 19:47
sleeping, 48:81, 83
See also Mezzanines.
Loftus, John: Colonial motif work of, 63:45-49
Log Builders Association of New Zealand: address for, 47:100
Log building:
addition to, timber-framed, 34:50
Adirondack-style, 40:38-42
associations for, international, 47:100
barking in, 13:55
books on, 8:70, 16:21, 23:12, 27:84, 34:49, 50, 92 (CSH)
butt joints in, 7:29, 30
cantilevered, 66:76, 77
for Central Park shelter, 21:67
chainsaw cuts for, 61:82-83
chainsaw milling for, 7:29-31
chainsaws for, 2:38, 39-41, 13:56, 59, 53:83-84

chimneys for, 17:8
chinking,
about, 14:50-51, 53, 28:6, 32:74
barbed-wire reinforcement for, 26:48
delayed, 12:10
gaps for, 26:49
metal lath for, 26:48-49
mortar for, 12:10, 26:50-51
plastered insulating, 66:77
technique for, 26:50, 51:44-45
traditional, problems with, 26:48
construction of, 14:46-47
cracks in, sealing, 9:6, 12:10
disadvantages of, 44:39 (SH)
dismantling, 14:47-48
dovetails for, sawn, 48:70-71 (SH)
electrical chases for, 32:75
European, book on, 12:72, 17:80
finish for, 1:6, 7:31, 14:51, 53, 34:50, 48:73 (SH)
exterior, 66:77
interior, 47:22, 66:77
foundations for, 7:30, 14:48, 49, 52
gable ends in, 7:30-31
gaps in, spacing, 26:49
Greek Revival, 18:84
gun ports in, 66:77
hewing for, 13:56, 57, 34:46
and humidity controls, 14:52, 53
information source for, 68:8
insulating, 2:41, 7:30, 31, 26:48, 32:74-75, 34:49
insulation value of, 13:14
jacks with, 34:50
Japanese use of, 24:63 (TFH)
kerfing in, 34:48, 49-50
kits for, choosing, 18:6-7
lag screws in, 34:49
logs for,
concrete, 5:68
cutting, 44:10
jointing, 24:63, 34:46 (TFH)
limestone, 68:120
quarter-round, 7:29-31
used, 66:75-77
maintenance for, 14:53
mid-wall stabilizing cleat for, 34:49
mortar for,
cement/sawdust, 51:6
flexible, 47:22
New Zealand conference on, 47:100
Norwegian,
antecedents of, 46:76-78
scribe method of, 6:6, 34:48-49
notches for,
dovetailed, 34:46-49
half-dovetail, 13:57-59, 14:52, 51:43-44
octagonal, 23:12
round, 2:38-41, 13:57, 14:52
V-, 13:57

openings in, 7:30, 31
overhangs for, 14:52-53
"palace" of, 41:108
penta-treated, sealant for, 15:21
pins for, 32:73, 74
plans for, 8:70, 53:89
plumbing in, 14:48
preservatives for, 13:14, 34:46
by reconstruction, 32:72-75
restoration of, 14:46-51, 16:21 (CSH)
roofs for, 14:50, 51, 32:74, 53:6
rot in, repair of, 16:20-21 (CSH), 70:48-49
sanding, interior, 4:9
school for, 8:70, 34:49
sealers for, 8:8, 13:14, 61:37, 40
seasoning of, 26:49
shrinkage in, 34:49
sites for, 14:52
squaring up in, 13:55
stackwood method for, 51:6
Swedish chinkless, 53:80-84
Swiss-chalet, described, 70:72-75
trimming out, 14:51
types of, 14:47
V-grooving for, 6:6
for Victorian studio, 48:70-73 (SH)
and water vapor, 47:22
windows for, commercial, 32:73
wiring, 14:48
wood splitting in, minimizing, 13:8
woods for, 13:55, 14:52
See also Dividers. Scribers.
Log House Plans (Mackie):
cited, 27:84, 53:89
reviewed, 8:70
Log Structures (Goodall and Friedman):
cited, 16:21 (CSH)
Logbuilder's Handbook, A (Langsner):
source for, 13:59
Loggia:
defined, 29:48
See also Porches.
Loken, Steve:
builds recycled house, 81:104-106
resource recycling center of, 69:100
Londino, Bill: cast concrete by, 5:38, 39
London, Mark: *Masonry,* reviewed, 49:114
Long, John F.: houses by, 34:36, 38
Long Island Lighting Co.: heat-pump water-heater policy of, 5:65
Longo, Matthew Adams: on kitchen addition, 78:62-65 (REM)
Looking Around (Rybczynski): reviewed, 84:124
Loomis, Harwood: on single-ply roofing, 64:43-47 (EF)
Loos, Adolf:
influence of, on Neutra, 19:29
mentioned, 9:68
Lopez, Rich: on rehabilitating duplex, 26:33-37

Lord, Al: inlay by, 45:80 (EEH)
Lord, Peter, and Duncan Templeton: *Detailing for Acoustics,* 35:63
Los Angeles Shoji and Decorative Products, Inc.: address for, 61:59 (SH)
Lotus 1-2-3: for contractors, 35:66 (TB)
Lotz, William: on vapor barriers, 19:22, 20:81
Louda, Frank: shingled fixture by, 10:75
Louis Mian, Inc.: address for, 67:75-76 (REM)
Louis Poulsen and Co.: light fixtures, 35:34
Louisiana:
building code changes in, 3:10
historic preservation in, 7:14
solar tax credit in, 3:12
Louisiana-Pacific Corp.: address for, 64:94, 71:72, 75:94, 80:49, 82:94, 83:43
800-number for, 83:44
Inner-Seal waferboard, 37:80
Louisville Ladder Corp.:
address for, 84:55
Louvers: insulated, source for, 43:92-94
Loveday, Evelyn: as joint author. *See* Wolfe, Ralph.
Low-Cost Green Lumber Construction (Seddon): mentioned, 7:42
Low-Cost Pole Building Construction (Wolfe, Merrilees and Loveday): reviewed, 8:70
Lowell, Daniel: mentioned, 34:50
Loy, Trey:
on concrete, 13:28-32 (CBS)
on moving heavy timbers, 8:31-32 (TFH)
on string tools, 25:64-69 (TB)
Lstiburek, Joseph:
on airtight drywall approach, 37:62-65, 50:100
Moisture Control Handbook, reviewed, 74:98
on sealing houses, 28:82
Lubricants: dry, source for, 79:75
Lucas (George) House: design of, 31:44-47 (FWS)
Lucchesi, Peter III: on spiral stair, 48:37-39
Lucite: source for, 10:33 (DWS)
Luckey, Tom: staircases by, 53:90-91
Ludwig, Jerry:
reviews Bill, 76:118
reviews Ching, 78:110
Lumber:
associations for, 63:63, 65 (MFC), 77:110
buying, guide to, 85:124
cold-weather handling of, 51:42
creosote-treated, 63:63 (MFC)
crooked, straightening, 70:32
Danish care of, 31:76, 77
delivery of, planning for, 23:16
design values of, seminars on, 70:110

dry, for staircases, 84:16
flag for, easy-tie, 34:16
for framing,
kiln-dried vs. green, 8:14
price rise of, 82:104
grades of, western, 47:40, 42-43
grading, agencies for, 81:16
handling, 85:81
harvesting, process of, 81:16
"in-grade,"
testing of, 56:104-106
values for, pamphlet on, 71:104
for Japanese temples, mill providing, 83:112
laminated-veneer,
described, 50:40-43 (MFC)
working with, 50:43-45 (MFC)
pressure-treated,
finish for, 77:104-108
handling, 77:83
hazards of, 83:6
types of, 63:62 (MFC)
warpage in, 81:56, 57
rack for, on-site, 67:26
strength of, books on, 81:16
stress-rated, 47:40
supply of, in crises, 78:100-102
threats to, 63:61-62 (MFC)
tongue-and-groove laminated, custom, source for, 55:60
treated,
fastening, 63:64-65 (MFC)
finish for, 63:63 (MFC)
as green wood, 63:64 (MFC)
information sheet on, 63:65 (MFC)
labels of, 63:62-63 (MFC)
orientation of, 63:64 (MFC)
for playgrounds, 63:65 (MFC)
recommended, 68:6
retouching, 63:65 (MFC)
toxicity of, 56:14
water repellents for, 63:64 (MFC)
for tropics, 61:61 (SH)
U. S. use of, book on, 54:106
western, booklets on, 71:104
"Wolmanized," and finishes, 55:18-20
wood/plastic, source for, 85:122
See also Wood preservatives.
Lumber and Plywood Saving Manual (NAHB): cited, 84:49
Lumpkins, William: *Casa Adobe, La,* reviewed, 43:102
Lundberg Studios: lantern from, 45:38
Lundie, Edwin:
cabins by, 80:59-61
kitchen by, 85:94
Lunstead Metals: address for, 82:86
Lush, Mary: on tin houses, 59:20-24
Lusk, Tommy: on movie shack, 56:48-51
Lustron houses: construction of, 22:26-30

Lutyens, Edwin: book on, 45:122
Lyemance International: address for, 57:4
Lyndon, Donlyn: as joint author. *See* Moore, Charles.
Lynn Ladder and Scaffolding Co., Inc.: address for, 84:55

MacCluer, C. R.: on Freon-charged system, 29:86-88
MacCluer-Mitchell Engineering: hot-water system sizing, information on, 29:88
MacDonald, John S.: on Maine house, 74:66-69
Macdonald, William G.: crawl-space drama of, 17:90
MacDraft program: discussed, 35:66 (TB)
Mace, Ronald L.: *System, The,* discussed, 35:45 (BK)
MacGregor, Malcolm: on early building, 27:82-83
Machanic, Mindy:
  reviews construction books, 3:61
  reviews design book, 18:78
  reviews Farralones book, 6:58
Machinery:
  cold-weather precautions for, 50:60
  cords for,
    cold-resistant, 50:60
    coupler for, 79:100-102
  lubricant for,
    dry, 79:75
    low-viscosity gear, 50:60
  mounts for, epoxy-mix, 70:48
  old, restoring, 39:75-77
  outfeed rollers for, from shades, 49:26
  pads for, sheet-rubber, 35:60
  pneumatic, cold-weather precautions for, 50:60
  See also *specific tool or machine.* Tools.
Macintosh Apple Users Group (MAUG): described, 46:60
Macintosh Construction Forum (Savage): reviewed, 68:108
Macintosh Plus: for contractors, 35:66 (TB)
Mack, Robert C.:
  Cleaning and Waterproof Coating of Masonry Buildings, The, cited, 5:39
  Preservation Briefs No. 1, 4:4
Mack, Robert C., and Askins: *Repointing of Historic Masonry Buildings, The,* mentioned, 4:4

Mackall, Louis:
  on Adelman barn, 66:60-63 (REM)
  light fixture by, 61:86
  staircase by, 1:59
MacKay, Richard:
  on ceiling disaster, 22:82
  on poodle malevolence, 15:82
Mackie, B. Allan:
  Building with Logs,
    cited, 23:12, 27:84
    reviewed, 8:70
  Log House Plans,
    cited, 27:84, 53:89
    reviewed, 8:70
  Notches of All Kinds, cited, 23:12, 27:84
  Picture Book of Log Homes, reviewed, 27:84
Mackie School of Log Building: mentioned, 34:49
Mackinac Island: cabin on, 46:80-83 (TFH)
Mackintosh, Charles Rennie: Hill House by, 54:36-41
Macklanburg-Duncan Co.: address for, 43:52 (CBS), 50:73 (FC), 58:45, 77:67
  Carpenter Handy Square, 10:61 (TB)
Maclay, William: builds roll-top house, 25:38-41 (EEH)
MacMath, Richard:
  on stone walls, 3:28-32 (CBS)
  on sunspaces, 33:36-40 (EEH)
MacMillan Bloedel Building Materials Ltd.: address for, 50:42 (MFC), 66:49
MacMillan Small Business Handbook, The (Stevens): cited, 62:79
MacWrite program: for contractors, 35:66 (TB)
Maddex, Diane: *Brown Book, The,* reviewed, 31:80
Madigan, Chris: reviews timber-framing book, 27:84
Madrone *(Arbutus menziesii):* floors of, 24:64 (TFH)
Mafell-Maschinenfabrik:
  bandsaw Z3, guard for, 37:4
  chain mortisers, 21:10, 35:56 (TB)
    unavailability of, 22:16
  circular saws, 35:54, 55 (TB)
  drilling machine, 35:57 (TB)
  organizes trip, 35:55 (TB)
  portable bandsaws, 35:57-58 (TB)
  power plane ZH 280, 35:56 (TB)
  Schnieder tenoner, 35:58 (TB)
  slot mortiser, 35:57 (TB)
  tools, 35:54-59 (TB)
Magarian, Rick: stair by, 6:20 (CSH)
Magazine wrappers:
  of biodegradable plastic, 53:4
  composition of, 54:6
Magee, Vishu: on pumice-crete, 77:55-57
Magers, Steve: as joint author. *See* Kern, Ken.

Magers, Steve, and Ken Kern: *Owner-Builder's Guide to Fireplaces, The,* mentioned, 46:65 (TFH)
Magic Seal Corp.: address for, 77:67
Magid Glove and Safety Manufacturing Co.: safety clothing, 34:55 (TB)
Magnesite: floor of, 32:66
Magnesium: nobility of, 21:4
Magnetic variation: charts of, 5:53 (DWS)
Magnets: uses of, 15:18
Magnolia Sash Cord: address for, 64:49 (FC)
Magrab, Edward B.: *Environmental Noise Control,* 35:63
Mahogany, Honduras *(Swietenia* spp.):
  aged finish for, 17:34 (CSH)
  bending, 16:74 (FWS)
  respiratory ailments from, 12:71
Mahogany, Philippine *(Shorea* spp.):
  for bending, 17:64 (DWS)
    reviewed, 55:96
Mahoney, Kevin M.: on porches, 81:44-47
Mahony, John: on Humboldt house, 25:56-61
Mail chutes: installing, 3:18 (DWS)
Mailboxes: gallery of, 54:88-89
Mail-order companies:
  houses from, book on, 77:120
  legal requirements for, 62:50-51
  reviewed, 62:50-51
Maine:
  architecture in, 31:42-43
  brownstone damage in, 9:21
  house in style of, 73:46-50
  solar tax credits in, 3:12
Maine Wood Heat Co., Inc.:
  address for, 66:59 (SH), 79:73
  Finnish heaters of, 7:49 (CBS)
  masonry cookstove parts from, 21:62 (CBS)
Maintaining Your Old House in Cambridge (Sullivan, Woodford, *et al.*): reviewed, 68:108
Maize, Dave: doors by, 37:76-77 (DWS)
Majestic Co.: address for, 77:78-79 (REM)
Major Energy Conservation Retrofits: source for, 32:90
Make Your Own Handcrafted Doors and Windows (Birchard): cited, 83:61
Making Kitchen Cabinets (Levine): cited, 78:67
Makinson, Randell L.:
  Greene and Greene,
    cited, 24:32, 27:62, 29:57, 72:41 (BK, CSH)
    reviewed, 45:122
  as joint author. *See* McCoy, Esther.
Makita USA, Inc.:
  address for, 63:75
  chain mortisers, 21:10, 22:16
    model 7104, for timber framing, 36:50 (TFH)

chainsaws, electric, 34:48, 49
circular saws, 18:18
    reviewed, 63:74-75, 76-77
    for timber framing, 35:55 (TB)
compound-miter saws, reviewed, 83:67
cut-off saws, reviewed, 62:80-84
drills, cordless, 35:41 (TB)
    model 6012-HDW, 35:38, 40-42 (TB)
    VSR, reviewed, 82:36-41
jigsaw blades, 33:60, 61 (TB)
    model 4301 BV, 33:61, 62 (TB)
miter saws,
    accurate cuts with, 20:6
    model LS1400, 19:42, 43 (TB)
    safety with, 22:6
    sawdust guard for, 32:16
    model 2400B, 19:42, 43 (TB)
planer-blade sharpener, #9820-2, 18:18
plunge routers, reviewed, 71:79, 81, 84
    (FC)
portable table saws, reviewed, 64:70-73,
    68:4
power planes, 35:56 (TB)
    model 1805B, 4:22 (TFH)
    model 1900B, 14:42, 45 (TB)
    reviewed, 54:77, 78-79
    for timber frames, 28:59 (TFH)
random-orbit sanders, reviewed, 77:69,
    72, 73
reciprocating saws, discussed, 16:45, 46
    (TB)
screw guns, 34:42 (TB)
trade practices of, 82:104
trim saws, reviewed, 48:40-43
Malakoff, Peter:
    deck by, 39:52-55 (CSH)
    on remodeling, 29:56-61 (CSH)
Malco Products, Inc.:
    address for, 67:43 (EF)
    roofing tools, 39:63
Malek, Stan: on renovation, 62:46-49 (SH)
Malicoat, Conrad:
    fireplace by, 28:100
    freeform brick fireplaces of, 28:100
Mallets: for timber framing, 4:23-24 (TFH)
Malley, Pat: mentioned, 6:19 (CSH)
Malloff, Will:
    Chainsaw Lumbermaking, 10:35, 41:51,
        42:41 (TB, TFH)
    homemade chainsaw mill of, 10:35-37
        (TB)
Malone, Robert: on studio apartment,
    60:43-45 (SH)
Maloney, Jim:
    on ADA, 37:65
    on conference, 46:96
    on controlling air leakage, 77:64-67
Maloof, Sam:
    career of, 68:40
    latches by, 68:39, 40, 88-89
Mameco International Corp.: address
    for, 48:68, 67:42 (EF)

Man, Climate and Architecture (Givoni):
    mentioned, 2:33 (EEH)
Mandan Indian earth lodge: influence of,
    9:42-43
Mann, Dale, and Richard Skinulis:
    Complete Log House Book, The, 23:12
Mannarino, Frank: on chainsaw mishap,
    61:118
Mannes, Willibald:
    Designing Staircases, cited, 70:90
    Techniques of Staircase Construction,
        reviewed, 41:94
Mannington Resilient Flooring: address
    for, 64:87 (REM)
Mansfield Plumbing Products: address
    for, 67:63
Manson, Grant Carpenter: *Frank Lloyd
    Wright to 1910,* cited, 69:57
Mantels:
    Arts-and-Crafts style, 29:56, 61 (CSH)
    assembled ornate, 27:76, 77
    carved, 6:21 (CSH)
        source for, 66:104-106
    cast-concrete tinted, 54:87 (TFH)
    Colonial, making, 40:33, 34, 35 (FWS)
    in Colonial style, 63:47, 48-49
    for corner fireplace, projecting, 80:61
    curved, 52:44, 45
        of drywall, 39:39
    Federal-style, building, 54:54-57
    fire codes on, 69:78
    of foam, molded, 39:92
    Greek Revival, 1:50, 51
    marbleized, 60:79
    showcase niche over, 29:56, 61 (CSH)
    table-saw-made, 49:41, 43 (REM)
    tiles for, 54:54, 57
Mantistique Saw and Planing Mill:
    address for, 67:36
Manual of Traditional Woodworking
    (Hasluck): cited, 69:87
Manville Corp.: address for, 64:45 (EF),
    68:86
Many Masks (Gill): reviewed, 50:108
Mapei Corp.: address for, 62:76
Maple, red *(Acer rubrum):* for flooring,
    37:8
Maple, sugar *(Acer saccharum)*:
    for flooring, 37:8
    hardness group of, 40:69 (FRC)
    radial splits in, 13:8
Maps: topographical, site-specific, 73:71-72
Marble:
    for countertops, 77:44
    for floors, inset squares of, 39:39, 40, 42
    hardness of, 69:55
    installation advice for, faxed, 70:112
    matching, height control for, 11:14
    psi of, 32:33 (FRC)
    simulating, 1:38, 60:79-81 (FWS)
    tiling with, 69:55-57

Marble Institute of America: soapstone
    information from, 39:42
Marbleizing: described, 1:38, 60:79-81
    (FWS)
Marchat, Tim: quoted, 29:89
Marcheske, Jan and Mike: mentioned,
    32:73-75
Marcus, Jim: Victorian models by, 29:100
Marcus, Karl:
    on masonry stove, 42:68-73 (CBS)
    masonry stove by, 36:30-33 (CBS)
Marden, Lori:
    reviews *Wood,* 54:106
    reviews Zuckerman, 75:110
Mardon Industries: address for, 48:90
Margolin, Malcolm: *Earth Manual, The,*
    cited, 50:85
Margolis, Angelo: on nail guns, 15:49-53
    (TB)
Maria Soccorro Industries, Inc.: address
    for, 84:55
Marietta Millworks: address for, 55:16
Marina Sheet Metal: address for, 82:81
Mark II Sharpening System: source for,
    18:59 (TB)
Markertek Video Supply: address for,
    57:4
Marking:
    knife for, 4:22 (TFH)
    masking tape for, 85:30
    panel gauge for, 4:22, 24:22 (TFH)
    See also Measuring.
Marking gauges:
    discussed, 57:94
    dual, making, 24:22
    for risers and treads, 35:14
Marks, Alan:
    on Canadian video, 61:106
    reviews Airstream Helmet, 58:90
    reviews Japanese book, 58:106
    reviews steam showers, 52:110-12
Marks, Ted: on Maine house, 73:46-50
Marnicki, Richard: mentioned, 30:35, 36
Marquart Block Co. (Waterloo, IA): dry-
    stack block of, 16:57 (CBS)
Marsh, Katherine: Briarcombe art colony
    of, 20:28-34
Marshall, David: on skylight flashing,
    49:83
Marshall, John: renovates duplex, 26:33-
    37
Marshall, Tom: mentioned, 26:34
Marshall Brass: address for, 27:71 (CBS)
Marshalltown Trowel Co.:
    address for, 31:61, 43:52, 58:45 (CBS,
        FWS)
    taping banjo, 23:61 (FWS)
Marshco Products:
    random-orbit sanding heads, 77:70
Marti, Felix:
    on clamps, 74:70-73 (FC)
    light fixture by, 61:87

reviews caulking guns, 70:100-104
reviews digital plan measure, 69:92
reviews featherboard, 69:94-96
reviews System 150, 53:96-98
on screw guns, 34:42, 45 (TB), 85:68-71
on table-saw tools, 53:58-61

Martin, Elizabeth:
builds Victorian modern, 31:66-71
on wrap-around deck, 42:36-39

Martin, Paul: mentioned, 27:84

Martin Fireproofing Georgia, Inc.:
address for, 47:87

Martinez, Ray: makes flue forms, 41:29, 30

Martin-Senour Co.: address for, 71:72

Marts, Sam: on small houses, 67:37

Martz, Elsa: on superinsulated house,
70:54-56 (EEH)

Marvair Co.: heat pumps, 26:68

Marvel, Jonathan: on superinsulated
house, 66:64-68 (EEH)

Marvel Industries: address for, 52:106

Marvin Windows and Doors:
address for, 47:59, 50:81, 54:87, 55:79,
59:61, 65:78, 67:14, 76:75, 94, 82:96,
83:56 (FC, REM, SH, TFH)
curved windows, reviewed, 55:92
custom windows, 36:74
double-hung windows, 32:73
insulated windows, 18:42
small-light double-pane windows, 40:86
window production of, 60:47, 48, 49, 51
(FC)

Marx, Robert L.: on addition, 83:54-56

Maryland: solar tax credits in, 3:12

Masking tape:
applying, 67:68
gentling, 46:26
for painting, brand of, 42:56 (DWS)
plywood marking with, 76:65 (MFC)
professional quality, 48:75
reliability of, 67:68
removing, 67:71
trimming, 48:75
uses of, 85:30

Masks:
dust, high-quality, 48:74
See also Respirators.

Mason Industries: address for, 62:18
(CSH)

Masonite Corp.:
address for, 71:72, 83:42
Flametest fire-resistant material, 31:49
(FWS)
trusses by, 40:53

Masonry:
and air/vapor barrier, 21:4
book on, reviewed, 47:110
cavity walls with, 31:40 (CBS)
cleaning, 56:83
cold-weather, 51:41-42

with cordwood, 2:68
crack patchers for, source for, 66:55
cutting, 50:18
drilling, accurate method for, 51:28
epoxy coatings for, 70:48, 49
historic, research aid on, 65:55
instruction in, 8:14-15
mortar of, repointing
repointing, 4:4
grout bag for, 30:10
mortar for, 2:45, 46, 47
process of, 2:45-47
restoration, books on, 4:4
rising damp in, 32:4
sandblasting, danger of, 4:4
silicone treatment of, 4:4
wall-insulation product for, 1:62-63
See also Anchors. Block. Brick.
Chimneys. Concrete. Efflorescence.
Metal connectors. Rebar. Stone
masonry.

Masonry (London): reviewed, 49:114

**Masonry Heater Association of North
America:** address for, 71:54

Masonry heaters:
advantages of, 76:77
air source for, 70:56 (EEH)
association for, 71:54
books on, 15:21, 37:88-90, 71:50, 51
bread-warming shelf in, 42:69, 71 (CBS)
bricks for, 42:71 (CBS)
builders of, 38:74 (TFH), 66:59 (SH)
building, 7:47-49, 42:68-73, 76:76-79 (CBS)
vs. cast-iron, 40:4
cookstoves in, 12:62-65, 39:60 (CBS,
DWS)
dampers for, 36:32, 42:71 (CBS)
described, 7:46, 49, 36:33 (CBS)
designing, 7:47, 42:68 (CBS)
with fireplaces, 42:69, 71, 46:63, 64, 65,
66:58-59 (CBS, SH, TFH)
building, 42:68-73 (CBS)
of granite, 34:50
hardware sources for, 71:52, 79:73
heat exchange in, 46:4-6
as heating systems, 66:58-59, 70:56,
79:73-74 (EEH, SH)
k'ang,
construction of, 36:31-33 (CBS)
efficiency of, 36:30-31 (CBS)
kits for, custom, 73:100-102
mortar for, refractory, 42:71 (CBS)
options with, 76:78
performance tests of, 71:54
precast system for, 15:20-21
soapstone, performance of, 70:56 (EEH)
tiled, building, 71:50-54
variations in, 21:63 (CBS)

Masonry Institute of America: address
for, 57:4

Masonry Specialty Co.:
address for, 43:52 (CBS)
Quic-kut outlet cutter, 23:61 (FWS)

Masonry Stove Guild Newsletter:
mentioned, 7:49 (CBS)

Masons: risk rating of, 34:51 (TB)

Mason's Blend fireclay: mentioned, 36:32
(CBS)

Mass: *See* Thermal mass.

Massachusetts:
building code in, 9:4
for fireplaces, 20:54 (CBS)
for underground piping, 17:12
pension-fund mortgages in, 4:14
solar tax credits in, 3:12

**Massachusetts Dept. of Labor and
Industries:** asbestos bulletin, 22:4

Master Appliance: address for, 62:38 (EF)

Master Builders, Inc.: address for, 51:41,
66:59 (SH)

Master Level: address for, 58:45

Masterchem Industries, Inc.:
address for, 67:71, 68:45 (FC)
Kilz primer, 39:10, 42:57 (DWS)

Mastin, Bill:
on enlarging kitchen, 63:54-57 (REM)
work by, 81:89

Materials:
by barge, 54:59-60
book on, reviewed, 67:106
certification program for, NAHB, 76:108
characteristics of, analyzed, 32:32-33
(FRC)
computer-ordered, 69:102
dimension estimating for, ultrasonic
device for, 39:92
energy-efficient, source for, 69:100
estimating checklists for, 23:49, 29:92
lumberyard estimating of, 31:51-52
organization for, 44:46-49 (TB)
performance of, book on, 26:4
salvaged, 52:74-77 (SH)

*Materials and Components of Interior
Design* (Riggs): reviewed, 30:78

Mateson Chemical: Cover-Up asbestos
coating, 24:83

Math to Build On (Hamilton): reviewed,
85:132

Matson, Tim:
cabin cellar of, 10:34
Country Planet, A, 32:44 (DWS)
Earth Ponds, 7:43
on gaslight, 14:30-31
on mud rooms, 32:44-45 (DWS)
on tax shelters, 7:43

Matteson, Thor: on winding stair, 51:46-49
(EF)

Mattesons Mill: shingles, 30:4

Mattewood: chair of, 39:92

Mauer house: construction of, 18:26-31

Mautz Paint Co.: address for, 70:49

Max Katz Bag Co.: address for, 66:68 (EEH)

Max-Bond adhesive: for staircase parts, 39:48 (FWS)

Maxi-Flow water heaters: source for, 12:18 (CSH)

Maxorb black foil: mentioned, 10:51 (SH)

May, Cliff: Los Angeles 1983 talk by, 20:22, 26

May, Elizabeth E., Nora R. Waggoner and Eleanor B. Hotte: *Independent Living for the Handicapped and the Elderly,* 35:45 (BK)

Maybank, Bruce: superinsulated houses of, 24:82

Maybeck, Bernard:
arch form by, 10:28
book on, reviewed, 83:120-22
career of, 2:24 (CSH)
Kennedy house by, 10:29
staircase bench by, 6:60
trellis by, 1:59
Wallen II house by, 2:18-25 (CSH)

Maycock, Paul D., and Edward N. Stirewalt: *Photovoltaics,*
cited, 8:47
reviewed, 12:72

Mayes Bros. Tool Mfg. Co.:
address for, 58:45
Squangle, 10:60 (TB)

Mayline, The: source for, 26:62 (TB)

Maze (W. H.) Nail Co.: address for, 46:51 (EEH), 54:61, 58:14, 64:8, 77:49 (EF)

Mazria, Edward: *Passive Solar Energy Book, The,*
cited, 5:53, 19:63, 65, 21:56, 37:71 (DWS, EEH)
reviewed, 45:116

McAlester, Virginia and Lee: *Field Guide to American Houses, A,* reviewed, 31:82

McArthur, Scott: house by, 46:49-53 (EEH)

McAvoy, Randy: bookcase by, 58:87

McBride, Fay: work by, 34:76-77

McBride, Scott:
builds Victorian house, 31:66-71
on casement windows, 50:69-73 (FC)
on chimney crickets, 47:61-63 (EF)
on cornice returns, 77:46-49 (EF)
on cross gables, 76:46-50 (MFC)
on dormers, 35:46-50, 41:60-65 (FRC)
on exterior woodwork, 70:68-71 (EF)
on framing, 82:42-47
on glass/maple staircase, 60:74-77
on job-site chainsaws, 78:38-43
on Octagon restoration, 53:54-57
on reciprocating saw, 41:84
reviews calculator, 51:92
reviews cord coupler, 79:100-102
reviews Litchfield, 65:106
reviews textbooks, 71:112
reviews weatherstripping, 78:92-94

Key to books:

(BK)   Building Baths and Kitchens
(CBS) Building with Concrete, Brick and Stone
(CSH) Craftsman-Style Houses
(DWS) Building Doors, Windows and Skylights
(EEH) Energy-Efficient Houses
(EF)   Exterior Finishing
(FC)   Finish Carpentry
(FRC) Frame Carpentry
(FWS) Building Floors, Walls and Stairs
(MFC) More Frame Carpentry
(REM) Remodeling
(SH)   Small Houses
(TB)   Tools for Building
(TFH) Timber-Frame Houses

reviews Wing, 74:98
on roof framing, 28:31-37 (FRC), 74:82-85 (MFC)
on scaffolding, 36:34-38 (TB)
on traveling bandsaw, 77:94

McClean, Mike: dacha by, 26:96

McCloskey Corp.:
address for, 64:49 (FC)
Glaze Coat, 45:48 (TFH)

McCollum, Roy: on cisterns, 10:53-55 (BK)

McCormick, Dale L.:
Against the Grain, 13:16
on caulk compatibility, 8:16
course by, 13:16-18
on fixed-glass windows, 8:42-43 (DWS)

McCoy, Esther: on Schindler house, 4:26, 30, 32

McCoy, Esther, and Randell L. Makinson: *Five California Architects,* 4:30

McDaniel, Malcolm:
on curved wall, 7:16-20 (FRC)
mentioned, 28:39 (FWS)

McDermid, H. R.: reviews plywood jointed panels, 53:98

McDonald, Bill: on limestone, 37:59

McDonald, Clark: quoted, 1:12

McDonald house: pictured, 39:79

McDonald, Margot Kally: measurement system of, 73:20-22

McDonald (A. Y.) Mfg. Co.: DC pumps of, 24:82

McDowell, Doug: on adobe house, 5:48-51

McFeely Hardwoods and Lumber: address for, 53:18, 67:79

McGahey, Robert: on solar house, 46:61-65 (TFH)

McGrath, Ed:
on superinsulated curved house, 19:69-71 (EEH)
Superinsulated House, The, 19:69 (EEH)

McGrath, Richard: on models, 59:14-18

McGrew, Dave: on insulation, 13:14

McGuire-Nicholas: tool bags, 42:64, 65 (TB)

McHenry, Paul Graham, Jr.:
Adobe and Rammed Earth Buildings, reviewed, 27:84
on adobe restoration, 22:40-43
at exposition, 28:80

McIBS Co.:
dry-stack block of, 16:57, 17:4 (CBS)

McIntyre, Maria, ed.: *Directory of State Building Codes and Regulations,* reviewed, 46:104

McIntyre Tile, Inc.: address for, 71:54, 76:68 (REM)

McKee, Bob: columns by, 69:88

McKee, Harley: *Introduction to Early American Masonry,* 5:39

McKie Wing Roth, Jr.: plans from, 53:85, 86, 87, 89

McKim, Charles: buildings by, 37:53

McKim, Mead and White: history of, 37:53

McLaughlin, Jack: *Jefferson and Monticello,* reviewed, 53:110-12

McLean, Bruce: stained glass by, 6:18, 20, 21 (CSH)

McLellan-Sweat house: fence of, 25:73-77

McLeod, John A., III: on nails, 85:42-47

McMahon, Brian: on roof remodel, 72:54-56 (REM)

McMillan Development Inc.: houses of, for handicapped, 32:82

McMullen, Ernie: house by, 38:40-45

McNeice, Donald: on large house, 2:26-29

McNichols Co.: address for, 54:4

McPherson, Inc.: toilets, reviewed, 78:16

McRaven, Charles: on chinking, 26:48-50

McReynold, Sandy: turret by, 3:68

McRose Leather: tool bags, 42:65 (TB)

MDO: *See* Medium-density overlay.

Mead, Ro: ceramics by, 59:91

Mead, Stephen:
on fire sprinklers, 44:42-45 (BK)
on job closeouts, 69:79-81
on paint removal, 84:72-75
on steel framing, 32:67-71 (FRC)

Mead, William: buildings by, 37:53

Meader, Lon: constructs penthouse, 31:63-65

Meadowcreek Project: programs at, 37:75

Meadows (W. R.), Inc.: address for, 66:86

Mean radiant temperature (MRT): defined, 22:68 (CBS)

Meaning in Western Architecture (Norberg-Schulz): reviewed, 45:120

Means, Graeme:
about, 45:130
bathroom by, 80:89
on Eurostyle house, 35:28
house by, 45:60-64, 89 (SH)

Means Illustrated Construction Dictionary: reviewed, 47:112

Measure and Construction of the Japanese House (Engel): reviewed, 34:92

Measurement Limited: ultrasonic tape, reviewed, 78:54-55

Measuring:
digital wheel for, reviewed, 69:92
inside, precise, 13:12
metric,
    argued, 60:100-102, 62:6-10, 78:8
    vs. British, 33:4
    council on, 76:6
    mandated, 76:6
    mandated, booklet on, 72:100
from miter points, 85:30
pencil-and-crayon holder for, 78:30
plus/minus system for, 78:28-30
scribed, for recessed fixtures, 77:30
sequence for, 63:26, 64:32
system for, 73:20-22
tapes for,
    choosing, 4:21-22 (TFH)
    intervals with, marking, 82:44
    for renovations, 12:50 (TB)
    slip stick for, 22:14
    ultrasonic, evaluated, 78:54-55
tickstick method for, 20:49 (FWS)
transfer method for, 32:16
ultrasonic tools for, evaluated, 78:54-55
See also Story poles.

Mechanical Plastics Corp.: address for, 41:57 (CBS)

Mechanical Properties of Visually Graded Lumber: source for, 56:106

Mechanics liens: releases of, 6:28

Medallions: of molded foam, 39:92

Medford Corp.: particleboard, 40:36 (FWS)

Medicine cabinets: layout for, 21:72, 76, 77 (FRC)

Medinger, Larry: on movable insulation, 28:46-48 (DWS)

Medite Corp.:
address for, 73:70
source for, 40:36 (FWS)

Medium-density overlay: for concrete forms, 46:4

Meehan, Christopher: on radon, 67:47-51

Meehan, Tom: on tile backsplash, 68:67-69

Meem, John Gaw: carved corbel by, 5:8

Meguire's Inc.: address for, 55:47 (FC)

Meidell, Pamela S., ed.: *Architecture Oregon Style,* reviewed, 33:88

Meier, Hans W.: quoted, 22:64

Melamite: defined, 39:41

Melin, Charles: house by, 38:60-65 (CSH)

Melody, Ingrid:
on Florida Solar Energy Center, 66:22-24
reviews FSEC plans, 68:102

Membership: source for, 23:48

Membranes:
acrylic laminated, 24:46
acrylic/latex elastomeric, 50:49
air-infiltration-preventing, 77:67
air-permeable plastic, Swedish, 40:54
applying, 64:47 (EF)
asphalt flame-bonded, 35:77
asphalt/polyethylene, under shingles, 58:67-68 (EF)
associations for, 64:45 (EF)
below-ground use of, 2:35, 29:12
bitumen,
    for roofs, 52:56
    self-adhering, 51:45
bitumen/plastic/aluminum, 9:4
bituthene, sheeting, 25:72, 29:12
book on, 64:45 (EF)
butyl, 2:37, 29:12
    below-ground use of, 2:35, 29:12
butylated asphalt 50-mil, 15:59
cement system, mentioned, 11:10
chemical resistances of, 67:6
copolymer alloy/nylon, 80:70
discussed, 2:35-36, 37
eave-shield, source for, 57:86 (EF)
elastomeric, 9:4, 12:58, 59, 60, 34:28, 29 (DWS)
    mentioned, 2:35, 36, 37
    for roof deck, 44:80-81
EPDM, 2:35, 37, 7:37, 16:52 (DWS)
    below-ground use of, 2:35, 7:37 (DWS)
    roofing, 51:53
    roofing, single-ply, 43:16
fiberglass, coating, 47:87
flame-bonded, 50:49
for flat roof, choosing, 72:16
floor-protecting adhesive, source for, 75:94
for foundation waterproofing, 55:57-58, 59, 77:57
installing, 47:20
neoprene walk-on, 59:82
nylon/asphalt, source for, 66:55
nylon filtering, 73:68
plastic corrugated, 40:54
for pocket deck, 68:86
polyethylene,
    /asphalt, 25:72, 29:12
    cross-laminated, 19:22, 34:68 (SH), 36:12
    40-mil, source for, 22:12, 32:46-47, 32:46 (BK)
    20-mil chlorinated, 56:79-80, 81
polyvinyl chloride,
    below-ground use of, 2:35
    40-mil, 36:69 (BK)
for roofs, 15:59, 16:52, 59:39 (SH), 63:42, 81:81
rubber, 32:65
    for roofs, 32:65
under shingles, 64:53

for shower pans, 70:81 (REM)
shrinkage of, 56:80
single-ply,
    vs. built-up, 64:43-44 (EF)
    vs. multi-ply, 67:6
snake-protection racket for, 47:28
sources for, 64:45 (EF)
sprayable, 40:32
thermoplastic, reinforced, source for, 65:79 (REM)
for tilework, 61:12, 85:16
torch-down, source for, 66:50
types of, 64:44-47 (EF)
underlayment for, composition-panel, 68:86
urethane, coal-tar, 40:32
See also Air/vapor barriers. Filter fabric.

Memphremagog Heat Exchangers:
address for, 65:65 (SH)
business of, 23:80

Mendelsohn, Erich: and Richard Neutra, 19:29

Mendoza, George: *Need A House? Call Ms. Mouse,* reviewed, 15:22

Menefee, Dave: cottage by, 54:83-87 (TFH)

Menicucci, David F.: on electronic air cleaners, 63:58-60

Menten, Theodore: *Art Deco Style in Household Objects, Architecture, Sculpture, Graphics, and Jewelry,* cited, 69:57

Mepla, Inc.:
address for, 58:39 (REM)
cup hinges of, 44:70-71 (BK)

Mercer, Henry Chapman:
Ancient Carpenters' Tools, 6:29
career of, 6:29-31
Museum, 6:29
tiles after, 56:43-47
See also Fonthill.

Mercier, Mickey: mentioned, 30:42

Meree & Spindler: address for, 53:89

Merillat Industries: address for, 73:50

Merit Metal Products Corp.: address for, 54:65 (FC)

Meroni: push-button doorknob by, 48:65 (FC, MFC)

Merrilees, Doug: as joint author. *See* Wolfe, Ralph.

Mesirow, Kip:
on Japanese-style bath house, 19:37-41 (BK)
reviews McAlester, 31:82

Mesquite *(Prosopis* spp.): bricks from sawdust of, 15:10

Metabo Corp.:
address for, 63:75
circular saw, discussed, 63:75, 77
cut-off saw, reviewed, 62:80-84
drills,
    cordless, 35:41 (TB)
    VSR, reviewed, 82:36-41

plunge routers, reviewed, 71:79, 81-82 (FC)

power planes, reviewed, 54:77, 78-79

random-orbit sanders, reviewed, 77:71, 72

Metal:

bandsawing, 63:66, 67

casting, low-melt, 1:38, 39 (FWS)

compatibilities of, 10:4

drilling, 63:66, 67

for floor inlay, 63:78-80

galvanic corrosion of, 10:4, 21:4, 22:6-8, 24:46, 62:65-67

of aluminum and steel, 53:16, 65:4-6

of aluminum, seaside, 65:6

anodes in, distance effect of, 65:6

defined, 24:46

in water heaters, 65:6

from wood acids, 24:46

galvanic series for, 62:64

galvanized, primer for, 33:75

grinding, 63:67-68

holes in, large-diameter, tool for, 54:48

jigsaw blades for, 33:60 (TB)

nobility of, 21:4

polishing, 63:68

rusty, epoxy paint for, 70:49

sealers for, nontoxic, source for, 67:92

sheet,

association for, 61:49

books on, 61:49

brake for, improvised, 74:73 (FC)

drilling, safely, 82:28

working, book on, 63:66

See also *specific metal or product.*

Metal Blueing Products, Inc.: gun blueing of, 17:14

Metal brakes:

site-built, 57:28

for standing-seam roofs, 39:63

Metal connectors:

angle-tie, 29:37, 38, 44 (FRC), 43:48 (FRC)

beam-hanger, custom, 79:83

for beams, in lifting operation, 72:55-56 (REM)

bracing, 43:47 (FRC)

bracket,

for pole building, 39:28

post-to-beam, 17:14

calculations source for, 55:58

cap, 43:48 (FRC)

clip, 43:48-49 (FRC)

drywall, 84:48

framing, 63:42

for concrete, 43:44-45 (FRC)

and masonry, 41:52-57 (CBS)

custom, 43:49 (FRC)

ornamental, 62:89

in earthquake proofing, 64:60, 64, 65 (MFC)

exterior, as ornament, 43:80-81

for foundations, 43:44-45 (FRC), 74:59 (MFC)

for framing, 56:50

bracing, 85:55, 57

marine-grade, 67:61

shim, 77:78 (REM)

with glulams, 71:58-59 (MFC)

hanger, 43:46-47 (FRC)

with headers, 62:85 (MFC)

hold-down, 29:38 (FRC), 81:87

in hurricane proofing, 78:86

hurricane-tie, 29:38 (FRC), 43:48, 49 (FRC)

job-site lessons on, 47:4

joist-hanger, 6:6, 19:69-70, 21:27-28 (EEH), 43:45, 46-47 (FRC)

installing, 75:14-16, 76:8

kerfs for, 27:16

large, source for, 46:68 (EF)

source for, 82:18 (CSH)

substitute for, 5:12

ladder-tie, 54:84-85 (TFH)

L-strap, 29:38 (FRC)

nailing, care with, 44:6

pier-to-beam, 52:69, 71

plate-to-rafter, tested, 74:36-39 (MFC)

for pole buildings, 15:33-34, 36, 83:78-79

post cam-lock, 69:47 (EF)

post-anchor, 81:87

post-to-pier, 79:69

powder-actuated, 21:30-34 (TB)

ring, 43:48 (FRC)

for roofs, recommended, 85:47

shear-plate, 43:48 (FRC)

snap-tie, 30:66 (CBS), 44:33, 35, 36, 37, 47:4, 6 (CBS), 78:50-52

sources for, 43:49 (FRC), 51:82 (MFC), 56:50

spike-grid, 43:48 (FRC)

split-ring, making, 8:30 (TFH)

stainless,

custom, source for, 68:73 (EF)

source for, 63:92

strap, 43:46 (FRC), 85:57

T-, 29:38 (FRC)

for timbers, 51:36-40 (CSH)

utility, in coils, 67:92

structural calculations with, books on, 58:16

for timbers, 43:48 (FRC)

tinnerman nut, 69:30

for treated lumber, 63:64 (MFC)

for trusses, 43:48-49, 69-70 (FRC)

retrofitting, 55:69 (REM)

slotted, source for, 74:14

two-layer, 73:72, 74-75

of various metals, source for, 63:92

for wood shrinkage, 81:55, 56, 59

wood-to-concrete, 43:44-45, 49 (FRC)

See also Anchors. Bolts. Nails. Rebar. Screws. Staples.

Metal Construction News: source for, 32:6

Metal Home Digest: cited, 85:118

Metal snips: source for, 32:68 (FRC)

Metalbestos:

address for, 55:60

pipe, air space for, 34:8

Metalwork: ornamental Ukrainian, 72:120

Metcalf, Charles: on glass vanity, 84:80-81

Methane: detector for, 39:92

Metposts: reviewed, 56:92

Metric Guide for Federal Construction: source for, 72:100

Metropolitan Home: remodeled house of, 26:82

Metz, Don:

ed., *Compact House Book, The,* reviewed, 20:80

house by, 16:50-53

Superhouse, reviewed, 15:22

Metzler, Joseph G.: on diagonal floor plan, 68:82-87

Mexico:

building in, 63:36-41

Vallecillo, stone masonry in, 22:84

Meyer Equity, Inc.: Accu-Speed Glass Block Connectors, 37:81

Mezzanines:

circular, 3:24-25

concrete, 6:34

hangers for, 3:24, 26

See also Balconies.

Mica: using, 57:96

Michaud, Jacqueline M.: interviews Knight, 31:42-43

Michigan: solar tax credits in, 3:12

Microbes: danger from, 1:12

MicroCAD News: source for, 49:50

Microclimate: See Climate.

Microclimate (Rosenburg): mentioned, 9:16

Micropump: geared sealed magnetic pumps 200-655, 29:88

Microsoft: Multiplan program, 35:66 (TB)

Microzinc Products: described, 24:44

Mid-State Power Tools: address for, 51:90

Mid-Valley Distributors: address for, 51:48 (EF)

Midwest Plan Service:

address for, 65:54

Designs for Glued Trusses, 23:50

Farmstead Planning Handbook, 23:50

Mildew:

assault by, dealing with, 53:104-106

controlling, 6:12, 29:10

book on, 74:98

Mies van der Rohe, Ludwig:

exhibit on, 38:100-102

Farnsworth House of, 46:32-37

Mileaf, Harry: on architects and computers, 25:83

Millar, William: *Plastering Plain and Decorative,* mentioned, 47:8

Miller, Charles:
on acrylic pyramid, 23:72-77
on Art Nouveau bungalow, 31:92
on backyard shop, 43:68-71 (TB)
on Benny Soto, 35:35-37 (CBS)
on brick wall, 15:84
on California dacha, 26:96
on California pole house, 15:26-31
on Casa Paloma, 48:32-36
on cedar sauna, 13:76
on Charles Greene house, 24:27-32
(CSH)
on computers, 35:66 (TB)
on Craftsman studio, 51:36-40 (CSH)
on dry-stack block, 16:57 (CBS)
on earthquake research, 34:86
on earth-sheltered house, 52:74-77 (SH)
on fabricated cave, 64:132
on Fay McBride, 34:76-77
on fire ladders, 46:90
on Greek Revival cabin, 18:84
on Greene and Greene restoration,
72:36-41
on Hawaiian retreat, 38:78-83 (CSH)
on Home Sweet Home program, 20:22-26
on house/shop, 73:76-81
on hurricane lessons, 78:82-87
on insulation, 56:36-42
on ironwork, 75:76
on Japanese house, 32:38-43
on Japanese-style house, 4:52-57 (TFH)
on lumbering, 47:38-43
on Mackintosh Hill House, 54:36-41
on Maloof house, 68:36-41
on Mendocino house, 45:49-53 (CSH)
on NAHB convention, 26:82, 32:82
on new Victorians, 71:70-73
on passive-solar conference, 18:16
on pocket sliding screens, 8:74
pot rack by, 81:89
on Pottery House, 41:26-31
on powder-actuated tools, 21:30-34 (TB)
on pyramidal room, 25:92
reviews renovation book, 2:62
reviews skylight, 48:90
on sconces, 30:70-71
on shingled Whale House, 19:84
on Sierra Nevada farmhouse, 83:82-87
on Sowden House, 14:84
on steel garden, 10:76
on stump house, 23:92
on tile, 17:74 (BK)
trim by, 49:91
on Turman-Buhler house, 11:42-45 (SH)
on Wharton Esherick house, 21:35-43
on Wright exhibit, 47:102-104
on Wright seminars, 38:102-106
on Wright-like house, 73:42-45 (EEH)
Miller, Doug: on slip-form walls, 51:68-71
Miller, Rex, and Glenn E. Baker:
Carpentry and Construction, reviewed,
71:112

Key to books:

(BK)	Building Baths and Kitchens
(CBS)	Building with Concrete, Brick and Stone
(CSH)	Craftsman-Style Houses
(DWS)	Building Doors, Windows and Skylights
(EEH)	Energy-Efficient Houses
(EF)	Exterior Finishing
(FC)	Finish Carpentry
(FRC)	Frame Carpentry
(FWS)	Building Floors, Walls and Stairs
(MFC)	More Frame Carpentry
(REM)	Remodeling
(SH)	Small Houses
(TB)	Tools for Building
(TFH)	Timber-Frame Houses

Miller, Tony: layout tool by, 21:20
Miller Manufacturing, Inc.: address for,
73:104
Miller Material Co.: insulated block, 31:39
(CBS)
Miller Paint Co.: address for, 67:92, 73:69
Milliken Carpet: fusion-bonded tiles,
38:59
Millwork:
custom, 44:67 (FRC)
Japanese-style, 43:31-32 (CSH)
See also Trim.
Milner, Ron: on hot tub, 69:64-66
Milstein, Jeff: as joint author. *See* Walker,
Les.
Milwaukee Electric Tool Co.:
address for, 63:75, 65:92
cord recall by, 71:106
drills,
cordless, 35:41 (TB)
with keyless chucks, 43:96
VSR, reviewed, 82:36-41
hacksaws, 12:51 (TB)
hinge butt mortising template, 31:29, 30-
31 (TB)
jigsaws,
model 6287, 33:59-60 (TB)
model 6255, 33:61, 62 (TB)
offset blade adaptor for, 2:5
plumber's tool kit, 39:37 (BK)
sanders, random-orbit, reviewed, 77:70,
71
sanding heads, random-orbit, 77:70
sawblade plant of, 18:18
saws,
circular, reviewed, 63:75, 77
contractor's, 7:60
model 6065, 27:6
worm-drive 6377, 24:37 (TB)
Sawzall,
accessories for, 16:46 (TB)
as concrete vibrator, 4:37 (FRC)
curves with, 14:14
discussed, 16:45-46 (TB)
reviewed, 41:84
siding removal with, 2:5
tools of, book on, 7:60
Milwaukee Valve Co.: quick-acting
valves, 27:71 (CBS)
Mimbres motifs: book on, 67:58
Mimbres Painted Pottery (Brody): cited,
67:58
Mine Safety Corp.: Comfo II respirator,
10:10
Mineral spirits: cheap, 42:59 (DWS)
Mineral wool: perm rating for, 19:67
Minimum Cost Housing Studies:
mentioned, 5:12
Minnesota:
dry-stack block in, 16:57 (CBS)
first-home incentive in, 4:14
solar tax credits in, 3:12
vernacular house of, 38:50
Vietnam veteran loans in, 4:14
Minnesota Diversified Products:
Certifoam extruded polystyrene, 18:33
(CBS)
Minwax Co. Inc.:
address for, 67:58, 69:54
Dura-Seal, for teak, 22:12
floor finish, 33:12, 36:44 (FWS)
POR-ROK concrete, 34:64 (BK)
Miracle Adhesives Corp.: address for,
77:67
Mirafi Inc.:
address for, 50:85, 53:49 (SH)
140N filter fabric, source for, 40:63 (CBS)
Mirror of Sweden Inc.: TASSO wallpaper,
35:34
Mirrors:
bottom-lighted, 76:44, 45 (REM)
specialty-glass backing for, 76:67 (REM)
Missell, R. W.:
on building deck, 46:66-69 (EF)
on ridge vent, 61:80 (EF)
Mission style: molding in, 31:46, 47 (FWS)
Mississippi:
clay of, difficulties with, 12:27, 28, 32-33
house in, 8:63-67 (EEH)
solar tax credits in, 3:12
Mississippi Power and Light: heat-pump
water-heater policy of, 5:65
Mitchell, Chuck: on passive cooling, 2:30-
34 (EEH)
Mitchell, James: *Short Log & Timber
Building Book, The,* reviewed, 34:92
Mitchell, Pete: cabinetry by, 40:32
Mitek Wood Products: address for, 50:42
(MFC)
Miter boxes:
awkward shapes in, 39:45 (FWS)
compound-angle, 36:88-89
skid-proofing, 67:28
wooden, making, 65:75 (FC)

Miter joints: *See* Joinery.
Miter Right: chainsaw guide, reviewed, 31:76
Miter saws, power:
angles on, 55:28
cold-weather precautions for, 50:60
compound,
blades for, 19:44 (TB)
blades for, carbide, 21:4
blades for, carbide, caution for, 4:6
brakes on, 19:42-43 (TB)
case for, bed-extension, 34:14
choosing, 19:42-43 (TB)
cuts with, accurate, 20:6
described, 19:42 (TB)
guards for, 19:45, 20:4, 21:4 (TB)
large stock with, 5:7
laser-sight, reviewed, 85:104-106
limits of, extending, 19:45 (TB)
miter corrections on, 4:6
outrigger support and stop gauge for, 19:44 (TB)
radial, 20:4-6
reviewed, 29:86, 43:92, 57:58-62, 94, 83:64-69
safety considerations with, 21:4, 22:6, 23:4
sawdust guard for, 32:16
setting up, 19:43-44 (TB)
sliding, 84:108-10
steel-cutting wheel for, 32:68 (FRC)
tables for, 5:6-7, 19:43, 44, 20:4 (TB)
tables for, extension-wing, 23:16
using, 19:42, 44-45 (TB)
workstation for, 65:46-47 (FC)
for crown molding, station for, 71:85-86 (FC)
cuts on, radial, clamp for, 60:77
safety labels for, 37:81
stands for,
portable, 49:94
wheeled expanding, 69:70-71
workbench for, making, 76:30
workstation for, reviewed, 71:94
Miters: *See* Joinery.
Mitsubishi Electric Sales America:
heat exchangers, 3:4
ventilators, deficiencies of, 23:4
Mjurbeck Hus: houses by, 40:51
MK Diamond Products, Inc.: address for, 70:59
MLCS: address for, 77:70
Mobil Chemical Co.: address for, 85:122
Mobile Dimension Mill:
capacities of, 17:18
performance of, 17:18-20
Mockbee, Samuel: house by, 80:16, 20
Models:
cardboard, 21:84
for chapel, 64:50
in clay, 66:52, 53
computer-generated, 59:14-18

corners for, 43:4, 44:6
cutting for,
hints for, 43:4
jig for, 22:52-53 (FRC)
for framing, difficult, 2:59
making, 22:51-53, 41:34-35 (FRC)
materials for, 22:51, 52, 41:33-34, 35, 42:49 (FRC, FWS)
people and trees for, 43:4
quick, rough, 17:76 (SH)
for remodeling, 27:49
Victorian, 29:100
Modern American Dwellings (ed. Berg): reviewed, 4:58
Modern Builders Guide of 1823 (Lafever): mentioned, 29:63
Modern Carpentry (Hodgson): cited, 54:71 (REM)
Modern Carpentry (Wagner): reviewed, 35:70-71 (TB)
Modern Movement: Mies van der Rohe beginnings of, 46:32-37
Modern Practical Joinery (Ellis): cited, 54:71 (REM)
Modern Practical Stairbuilding and Handrailing (Ellis): reviewed, 64:110
Modest Mansions (Prowler): reviewed, 40:90
Modillions: defined, 24:14
Mod-Lok urethane foam sheets: source for, 24:76
MoDoHus: houses by, 40:53
Modric, Inc.: lever handles by, 48:65 (FC, MFC)
Modulars, Inc.: Wonderboard, 15:8
Modulus of elasticity: defined, 7:25 (TFH)
Moisan, Rick: on Cape remodel, 78:56-59
Moist-Stop: source for, 36:12
Moisture:
condensation of,
book on, cited, 56:16
and space heaters, 51:42
controlling, books on, 70:122, 74:98
generation of, 24:6
house movement of, 50:100
interior, publication on, 32:90
from new houses, 24:6
from spas, controlling, 79:24
in wood,
consultants for, 81:59
and humidity level, 81:56
See also Air-vapor barriers. Mildew. Relative humidity.
Moisture and Home Energy Conservation: source for, 23:50, 32:90
Moisture Condensation: mentioned, 4:8
Moisture Control for Homes (Nisson): reviewed, 70:122
Moisture Control Handbook (Lstiburek): reviewed, 74:98

Moisture Control in Brick and Tile Walls: mentioned, 23:49
Mold:
controlling, book on, 74:98
See also Stains (blemishes).
Molded Fiber Glass Tray Co.: address for, 75:49 (REM)
Molder/planers:
beveled molding on, 19:52 (FWS)
defined, 55:50-51
grain orientation for, 19:53 (FWS)
knives for,
custom, 55:55
making, 19:52 (FWS)
reviewed, 55:50-55
sander capacity on, 55:54, 55
for whole-house job, 40:34 (FWS)
Molding:
applied, for mantel, 54:57
Arts-and-Crafts style, 31:46, 47 (FWS)
attachment for, crossed-nail, 81:26
backing blocks for, 71:86, 87 (FC)
band, Greek Revival, 1:49
bed, defined, 15:39, 40, 20:60 (EF, FWS)
beveled continuous, walnut, 68:84, 87
bolection,
defined, 21:60
example of, 20:61 (FWS)
books on, 54:71 (REM), 57:51
butt joints in, filling, 49:28
cap, Greek Revival, 1:49
carved, source for, 66:104-106
cast polyurethane, 47:95
ceramic, reviewed, 59:106-10
chair rail, 20:60-63, 40:36-37 (FWS)
choosing, 57:48
clamps for, 74:72, 73 (FC)
finger, 54:92
closet, as source for, 53:26
coping, 67:26-28
cornice, copying, 61:68
cove,
custom veneered, 56:75-77
kerf-bending, 82:62
rubber, mitering, 70:34
crown, 31:44, 47 (FWS), 40:35, 36, 37 (FWS)
blocking for, 82:51
built-up, 67:12
with coffered ceilings, 75:40 (MFC)
coping, 12:12, 54:4, 67:26-28
curved, installing, 55:16
curved, laminated, 74:79-81 (FC)
custom, source for, 53:55
cutting, 10:12, 53:57
described, 15:39, 40-41 (EF)
for dormers, 41:64-65 (FRC)
installing, 51:64-67 (FC)
miter box for, 12:12
other-end-holding, 64:32
two-piece, installing, 71:85-87 (FC)

wide, compound-miter calculations
for, 68:79-80 (FC), 70:4 (errata, 72:6)
wide, coping, 68:81
wide, jigsaws for, 68:81
wide, source for, 68:79 (FC)
curved, 69:82-84, 85
custom, source for, 55:16
jig for, 76:73, 74-75 (FC)
kerf-bent, 31:71
making, 27:10
mitering, 63:10-12
on molder/planer, 55:52
custom, 62:60
eave crown to raked crown, mitering,
54:68, 69-71 (REM)
for entrances, 3:14, 16 (DWS)
estimating, 57:50-51
Federal, 31:46, 47 (FWS)
for fence posts, making, 25:74-75
flexible,
polyester, 47:95
source for, 55:16
foam,
resilient, source for, 56:63 (EEH)
urethane, 39:92
veneered, 39:92
gaps with, caulking, 2:6, 4:9
glossary of, 11:38 (DWS), 20:60-63 (FWS)
Greek Revival, defined, 1:49
Greek-key fretwork, 40:35 (FWS)
head, 54:37
history of, 20:59-63 (FWS)
information on, 65:53
installing, to untrue surfaces, 2:6
making, 40:33-37 (FWS), 54:71 (REM)
savings with, 28:50 (FWS)
with table saw and shaper, 85:67
Mission-style, 31:46, 47 (FWS)
with multiplane, 11:37 (DWS)
neo-Victorian, 31:44-47 (FWS)
old-wood, source for, 56:92
painting, 63:49
plaster, 28:50-51 (FWS)
plastic-laminate, 77:41
preserving, book on, 77:120-22
PVC pipe as, 80:71
radiused, 28:50 (FWS)
rake,
Carpenter Gothic, 61:43, 44, 45 (SH)
defined, 15:41 (EF)
Greek Revival, 1:49
reproduction, supplier of, 27:82, 83
rope, source for, 63:45, 46, 70:4
with router, 18:74-76 (DWS)
on site, 51:24
saws for, reviewed, 57:58-62
on shaper, 72:52-53 (FC)
for staircase, router-made, 55:62, 63
stone-simulating, 9:22
"stretching," 53:61
on table saw, 2:48-49, 74:80-81 (FC, FWS)

trimmer for, framer's, 30:61 (BK)
veneered, 48:91
See also Casting. Molder/planers.
Plaster.
Molding machine: mammoth, 39:75
Moller, Lee: on stuccoed house, 43:75-79
Moment of inertia: defined, 7:25, 26 (TFH)
Monahan, Kevin: on island building, 31:90
Monel: nobility of, 21:4
Monier Roof Tile Inc.: concrete tiles,
43:77
Monitor Products Inc.: furnaces, 40:59
Monitron electric boiler: source for,
42:53 (SH)
Monkton, James: *National Stair Builder,*
43:38 (FWS)
Mono sealant:
properties of, 34:4
source for, 32:37
Monrad, Eric and Philip: telephone bin
by, 10:75
Monrad, Philip: gate by, 25:80
Monsanto, Juan: drawings by, Los
Angeles exhibit of, 20:22
Monsanto Chemical Co.:
address for, 71:106
House of the Future, 34:70-75
Montana:
heat-pump water-heater policy in, 5:65
solar construction in, 8:37-41 (EEH)
solar tax credits in, 3:12
Montmorillonite clay: *See* Bentonite.
Montooth, Charles: pot rack by, 81:89
Monzini compounds: casting with, 1:37-
38, 39 (FWS)
Mooney, Michael M.: *Evelyn Nesbit and
Stanford White,* 37:53
Moore, Charles:
addresses conference, 47:100
Los Angeles 1983 exhibit by, 20:22
as joint author. *See* Bloomer, Kent.
**Moore, Charles, Gerald Allen and
Donlyn Lyndon:** *Place of Houses, The,*
cited, 45:102
reviewed, 45:116
Moore, Peter: mentioned, 38:74 (TFH)
Moore, Thomas B.: on pole house, 15:32-
36
Moore Products: address for, 56:37
Moose Creek Restorations Ltd.:
moldings of, 2:48-49 (FWS)
Mor-Ad adhesive:
source for, 40:12
for stress-skin panels, 24:59
Morales, Everett: stonework by, 36:70-75
Morash, Russ, prod.: *This Old House,*
reviewed, 5:60
Moravian Pottery and Tile Works:
history of, 6:31

More Power to You! (Thomsen):
reviewed, 68:106-108
Morehouse, Don: shingles by, 65:89
Mor-Flo Industries, Inc.: address for,
56:61 (EEH), 63:85 (EEH), 68:53, 82:58
Morgan (C. E.): Wedgewood Entrance
System, 6:60
Morgan Products, Ltd.:
address for, 55:63
staircase production by, 36:56, 58-60, 61
(FWS)
Morgenrath, Jali: cord lock by, reviewed,
42:88
Morrell, C. Leigh: hardware by, 10:46
(DWS)
Morrill, John: on energy standards,
47:102
Morris, Duncan: chainsaw mill by, 41:49-
51 (TB)
Morse, Edward S.: *Japanese Homes and
Their Surroundings,*
cited, 19:38, 34:92 (BK)
reviewed, 45:122
Morse, Jeff:
on bathroom remodel, 76:66-69 (REM)
on Briarcombe, 20:28-34
Morse-Libby mansion: porch repair of,
9:20-24
Mortar:
additives for, 32:47 (BK), 37:46 (DWS)
for heat resistance, 71:54
latex, 65:45
adhesive, for roof tile, source for, 65:58
(EF)
backer boards with, 37:8
for bedding, 44:54-55, 56
for block wall, freestanding, 36:12
bond strength of, 26:10
for bovedas, 50:74
for brickwork, patching, 17:12, 29:10
cement/sawdust, 51:6
colorants for, 62:20 (CSH)
coloring,
to age, 73:75
to match, 52:51 (TFH)
for countertops, 25:34, 35 (BK)
curing time for, 44:57
for deck stone, 55:84
fortifier for, 37:46 (DWS)
for glass block, 37:46 (DWS)
handling, 44:56-57
historic, research aid on, 65:55
sans lime, strength of, 71:16
for masonry stoves, 21:65 (CBS)
Mexican-vault type, 23:27
nature of, discussed, 65:45
for pointing, 44:54-55, 56, 57
pump for, 70:79
refractory, 36:32, 42:71 (CBS)
source for, 71:52

of slurried stone, 70:63 (EEH)
as spalling corrective, 32:4
for stone masonry, 8:24, 13:37, 14:63, 26:70, 39:4, 57 (CBS)
for stonework, 39:4, 57, 51:69, 84:58-59 (CBS)
surface-bonding, for stone masonry, 12:37 (CBS)
temperature for, 44:55
for tile, 70:14
  floor, 85:16
  roof, source for, 65:58 (EF)
  source for, 71:54
  vertical, 37:8
with vermiculite, 46:63 (TFH)
for waterproofing, 69:14
See also Cement. Grout. Log building: chinking. Thinset.
Mortensen, Irv: on renovation, 59:18-20
Mortgages:
assumption of, 2:10
bonds for, 4:13-14
earth-sheltered houses and, 2:12-13
kinds of, 2:8-10
See also Construction. Financing.
Mortisers:
chain, 21:10-12, 35:56, 57, 36:50 (TB, TFH)
  manufacturers of, 21:10
  reviewed, 22:16
horizontal, 36:48 (TFH)
Mortises: *See* Joinery.
Morton Chemical Co.: Mor-Ad adhesive, 24:59
Mosaics:
in brick, 64:80-83
tile, 59:88-91
Moser, Cliff: on porch remodel, 42:112
Mosher, Dale F.: on crown molding, 71:85-87 (FC)
Moslemi, Al: on sawdust/cement, 48:51
Moss: removing, 48:12
Moss, Roger, and Gail Caskey Winkler:
Victorian Exterior Decoration,
cited, 74:45 (EF)
reviewed, 43:102
Most Energy Efficient Appliances, The: cited, 47:102
Motion-Minded Kitchen, The (Clark): reviewed, 19:26
Motors:
brake for, reviewed, 58:91
comparing, 24:41 (TB)
DC, source for, 24:82
horsepower of,
  developed, 24:41 (TB)
  electrical, 24:41 (TB)
  full-load, 24:41 (TB)
  rated, 24:41 (TB)
speed control for, source for, 77:70

Moulage: described, 1:36, 39 (FWS)
Mountain Energy and Resources, Inc.:
heat-recovery ventilators, 34:34 (DWS)
Moving: *See* House moving.
Moving Historic Buildings: source for, 5:19
Mowat, William and Alexander: *Treatise on Stairbuilding and Handrailing, A,*
cited, 43:35 (FWS)
reviewed, 41:94
Moyer, Janet Lennox: *Landscape Lighting Book, The,* reviewed, 85:132-34
Moyler, Alan: on barn house, 11:51-53
Mr. Steam: address for, 52:112
MRT: *See* Mean radiant temperature.
Mudrooms:
ample, 52:16-20
design of, 30:63, 32:44 (DWS)
examples of, 32:44-45 (DWS)
positioning, 80:83
Mudsills: *See* Sills.
Mulcahy, Michael: on remodeling, 62:126
Mulder, David: stairbuilding by, 43:34-36 (FWS)
Mulfinger, Dale:
on house design, 85:88-93
on Lundie's cabins, 80:59-61
on *Pattern Language* house, 38:49-53
Mullen, Peter: on Caribbean house, 85:72-75
Muller, Gayle M.: on mildew, 53:104
Mullgardt, Louis Christian:
house by, 52:78-82
staircase after, 49:78-82
Mullineaux, Peter: quoted, 41:86
Multiplan program: for contractors, 35:66 (TB)
Munroe, Tony: bookcase by, 58:86
Munsell Color Products: address for, 74:45 (EF)
Murals: restoration of, 56:85-86, 87
Murco Wall Products, Inc.: address for, 67:92, 73:69
Muriatic acid: in mortar cleanup, cautions with, 14:35 (CBS)
Muro North America, Inc.: screw gun, reviewed, 85:69, 70
Murphy Bed Co., Inc.: address for, 73:100
Murphy, Tim: on tub disaster, 65:118
Murray, Craig W.: on pueblo modern, 67:56-58
Murrell, Robin: *Small Kitchens,* reviewed, 41:94-96
Muscardini, Michael: mentioned, 32:43
Museum of Modern Art (New York City):
Mies van der Rohe exhibit, 1968, 38:100-102
Music rooms:
of wood, 38:44-45
wood and drywall, 38:52

Muskegon Power Tool Corp.: address for, 75:83
Muti Inc.: address for, 55:92
Mutual Hardware Corp.: reviewed, 62:51
Mutual Materials: brick pavers, 38:82 (CSH)
Mylar:
cost of, 8:30 (TFH)
curtains of, insulating, 34:24, 26, 28-29 (DWS)
against glare, 34:66 (BK)
Mylen Industries: address for, 75:49 (REM)
Myofascial pain: preventing, 64:69
Myson: Super III Fan Convector, 33:12

Nabokov, Peter, and Robert Easton:
Native American Architecture, reviewed, 69:110 (addenda, 71:4)
Nacul Architectural Center: address for, 53:89
NAHB: *See* National Association of Home Builders.
NAHB Bookstore: source for, 23:48
Nail guns:
about, 13:45, 15:49-53 (FWS, TB)
accidents with, 34:53, 54 (TB)
air-powered,
  coil-fed, 56:53, 56, 57
  maintenance for, 56:57
  reviewed, by brand, 56:52-57
  for roof shingles, 57:85 (EF)
butane-powered, reviewed, 56:55
case for, making, 76:28
cordless
  finish, reviewed, 68:92-94
  for formwork, 82:92
flooring, source for, 49:66
internal-combustion, 32:82
nails for, 56:56, 85:44, 46, 47
  hot-dipped galvanized, 25:4
propane, 33:82 (TB)
roof skid-proofing, 64:30
and shear-wall bracing, 85:57
source for, 13:45 (FWS)
Nail pullers:
choosing, 32:53-55 (TB)
sliding handle, pictured, 32:53 (TB)
Nailed Plywood Beams: source for, 72:98
Nailers, blind: reviewed, 54:92
Nailers, Inc.: tool bags, 36:89, 42:65 (TB)
Nailers, power. *See* Nail guns.

Nailite International, Inc.: address for, 78:104, 83:45

Nails:
aluminum, avoiding for decks, 85:120-22
bags for,
lining, 65:30
from old jeans, 42:22 (CSH)
organizing, 63:28
reviewed, 62:94
barn-spike, 20:10, 85:45
bent, breaking, 10:12
box, 22:33, 85:45 (FRC)
casing, 85:45
and cedar, corrosion with, 10:4
cement-coated, hammer for, 23:35 (TB)
clamp-driven, 68:28
clips for, 63:42
coated, 22:32-33 (FRC)
common, 22:32, 85:45 (FRC)
copper, 20:40-42, 85:45 (EF)
cut,
authentic, 49:64
source for, 63:48
for decking, 29:43, 85:47 (FRC)
depths for, 75:56 (EF), 85:44
dimensions of, 40:70 (FRC)
as drills, 31:8
driver for, homemade, 8:10
in earthquake proofing, 64:61, 64-65 (MFC)
on edges, 22:32, 33 (FRC)
extension method for, 23:16
in feet, problems from, 79:56-57
for flooring, 13:42, 44 (FWS), 81:104, 85:46, 47
for foundations, 85:46
for framing, 85:46-47
galvanized,
double hot-dipped, 68:64
electroplated, bleeding with, 51:77 (FC)
for green wood, 7:41-42
hammerless driving of, 63:26
hammers for, slide, 46:90
for hardboard, 67:81
for headers, vs. screws, 64:8-10
heating, for cold-weather work, 11:14, 50:63
hidden use of, 23:14, 30:22
holders for, 29:16
holes from, filling, 48:77
injury from, 34:51 (TB)
jigsaw blade for, 33:60 (TB)
joints with,
clinched, 40:71 (FRC)
codes on, 40:68 (FRC)
designing, 40:70-72 (FRC)
joist-hanger, 50:59, 63:42, 75:16, 85:43, 46
magnet holder for, 15:18
magnet pickup for, 77:32
for nail guns, 15:51, 85:44, 47 (TB)
hot-dipped galvanized, 25:4

needlepoint, 3:17 (DWS)
oiling, 9:12
one-handed start for, 5:6, 6:4
in oriented strand board, 67:78-79
overdriven, danger in, 64:64-65 (MFC)
pails for, sectioned, 46:26
painted, 47:73 (FC)
pattern for, 66:72, 67:64 (REM)
in high-wind areas, 85:120
in hurricane areas, 79:4
in plywood, 54:61
penetration of, for siding, 81:56
pennyweight of, explained, 85:44
pilot holes for, 85:44
plastic, 30:76
plugs for, tapered, 85:108
in plumbing zone, caveats against, 49:53 (MFC)
predrilling with, 10:12, 20:78
for rafters, inadequacy of, 74:36-39 (MFC)
recyled, 81:106
removing, 50:30, 55:26
from fragile boards, 34:4
with hole saw, 81:26, 84:28
tool for, 19:34 (DWS), 33:6
tool for, reviewed, 78:92
with Vise-grips, 36:4
weather conditions for, 71:24
ring-shank,
galvanized, source for, 46:51 (EEH)
for movement resistance, 81:55, 56
vs. screw, 85:44-45
silicon bronze, source for, 68:73 (EF)
stainless, 58:61 (CSH)
roofing, square-head, caveats for, 76:8
rosehead, source for, 43:73 (SH), 78:58
safety with, 62:4
setting, 47:52 (EF)
shanks of, discussed, 85:44-45
for shear-wall bracing, 85:57
shim strips with, removable, 24:22-24
shingle holder for, 17:14
for shingling, 8:52, 55, 62
small, holding, 70:34
spinner for, 49:94
spiral, heat-treated, source for, 20:67
split prevention with, 9:12, 10:14, 11:12
splitless, 77:49 (EF)
stainless,
efficacy of, 49:4
source for, 63:92
stains from, removing, 49:26
for staircases, 1:17 (FWS)
strength of, 9:51 (FRC)
technique for, 22:33-34 (FRC)
in tight spots, 22:14, 48:24
for treated lumber, 63:64 (MFC)
types of, 32:53, 85:42-47 (TB)
of various metals, source for, 58:14
and wood shrinkage, 81:55-56, 57

wrought,
flooring with, 11:53
source for, 77:88
See also Nail guns. Putty.
Nailsets:
from car spring, 11:12 (erratum, 13:4)
clip for, 14:14
grip for, 34:16
from powder-actuated fasteners, 47:28
for renovation, 12:51 (TB)
Nakahara, Yasuo: *Japanese Joinery,* 46:4
Nana Windows and Doors: address for, 73:100
Nantucket:
architecture of, books on, 77:89
house in style of, 77:86-89
Nantucket Doorways (Stackpole and Summerfield): cited, 77:89
Nash, George:
on barn rebuilding, 44:72-75
on gravel foundations, 60:52-55
quick turnaround of, 85:146
on renovating porches, 75:72-74
reviews Audel, 76:118
reviews Elliott, 82:112
reviews Locke, 51:104-106
reviews Wilbur, 79:120
reviews window-repair book, 84:124
on rotted sills, 53:77-79 (REM)
on timber-framed ceilings, 65:48-51 (TFH)
on valley framing, 68:74-78 (MFC)
Nasscor, Inc.: address for, 52:112
NATAS: *See* National Center for Appropriate Technology: assistance service.
National Association of Architectural Metal Manufacturers: on acrylic film, 28:6
National Association of Home Builders (NAHB):
Acoustical Manual, 35:63
address for, 55:68, 65:54, 84:49
blockwork house by, 70:110
builders' show of, reviewed, 82:92-96
concrete book from, 68:14
conventions of, 21:20, 26:82, 32:82
Cost Buster House of, 21:6
Lumber and Plywood Saving Manual, cited, 84:49
Membership, 23:48
NAHB Bookstore, 23:48
National Housing Center Library of, 23:48
New American Home for 1985, 28:73-77
Optimum Value Engineering (OVE) of, 21:6, 22:31 (FRC), 84:46-49
Plenwood system of, 23:49
product certification program of, 76:108

Reducing Home Building Costs with OVE Design and Construction, cited, 23:48, 84:49
Research Center,
  information from, 21:6, 20, 23:48
  address for, 65:54, 76:108, 77:104
Residential Concrete from, 44:37 (CBS)
scheduling book from, reviewed, 46:104
Software Catalogue for Home Builders, 33:88
Software Directory for Builders, reviewed, 75:110
window-testing program of, 60:51 (FC)
National Building Code:
history of, 5:44
See also Building codes.
National Building Code (Canada): on foundation concrete, 48:67
National Cancer Institute: phone number, 24:83
National Casein Co.: address for, 65:86, 77:77 (REM)
National Center for Appropriate Technology:
address for, 29:90, 56:42, 61:77, 65:52 (EF)
assistance service, 800 number for, 22:18, 32:90, 65:52 (CSH)
award program of, 71:106
Heat Recovery Ventilation for Housing, 22:18 (CSH)
Moisture and Home Energy Conservation, 23:51
publications of, 23:51, 32:90
scope of, 23:51, 32:90
National Climatic Center, The:
address for, 21:60
Climatic Atlas of the U. S., source for, 9:16
Climatic Information for Building Design in Canada, source for, 9:16
Climatology of the U. S., source for, 9:16
National Concrete Masonry Association:
address for, 65:53, 70:110, 74:50, 77:104
AirCore Design Guidelines, 30:52 (CBS)
AirCore floor system of, 30:50-54 (CBS)
Catalog of Publications, 23:50
Concrete Masonry Paving Block, 23:50
exterior insulation pamphlet, 31:41 (CBS)
insulation studies, 31:38-41 (CBS)
precast footer blocks by, 40:86-87
Precast Lintels for Concrete Masonry Construction, cited, 74:50
Removal of Stains from Concrete and Masonry Walls, 23:50
Second Generation Passive Solar Systems, 30:52 (CBS)
Sunspaces, 23:50

Key to books:

(BK)	Building Baths and Kitchens
(CBS)	Building with Concrete, Brick and Stone
(CSH)	Craftsman-Style Houses
(DWS)	Building Doors, Windows and Skylights
(EEH)	Energy-Efficient Houses
(EF)	Exterior Finishing
(FC)	Finish Carpentry
(FRC)	Frame Carpentry
(FWS)	Building Floors, Walls and Stairs
(MFC)	More Frame Carpentry
(REM)	Remodeling
(SH)	Small Houses
(TB)	Tools for Building
(TFH)	Timber-Frame Houses

National Conference of States on Building Codes and Standards Inc.:
address for, 65:55
National Council of the Housing Industry: New American Home by, 28:73-77
National Design Specification for Wood Construction: source for, 7:28, 40:68 (FRC, TFH)
National Earth Shelter Builders Association: address for, 31:82
National Electrical Code:
copies of, 8:44
on exposed conduit, 48:4
on ground-fault protection, 6:39
importance of, 2:42, 5:45
source for, 5:45
National Electrical Manufacturers Association: *High-Pressure Decorative Laminates,* cited, 9:41 (BK)
National Endowment for the Arts: handmade house grant, 15:76 (CSH)
National Endowment for the Humanities: Home Sweet Home (1983) conference of, 20:22-26
National Fenestration Rating Council: mentioned, 81:102
National Fire Prevention Association: address for, 69:76
National Fire Prevention Code: source for, 5:45
National Fire Protection Association:
Black Tiger Fire Case Study, reviewed, 62:104
double-envelope sprinkler system design from, 25:6
on fire-sprinkler systems, 44:42 (BK), 47:6
information from, 44:45 (BK)
lightning-rod information from, 84:68
prefab-chimney regulation of, 34:8
publications from, 31:71, 75:44

smoke-detector standards from, 46:98
woodstove rules of, 11:10
National Forest Products Association:
address for, 63:65 (MFC), 65:53
All-Weather Wood Foundation System, 23:50
National Design Specification for Wood Construction, 23:50, 40:68 (FRC)
plank-and-beam framing manual, 33:43 (FWS)
Span Tables for Joists and Rafters, 23:50
wood foundations report, 34:67 (SH)
Wood Framing Details, 21:6
National GeoThermal: heat pumps, 26:68
National Gypsum:
Gypsolite, 23:61, 6, 26:41, 31:58 (FWS)
Two-Way Hardwall plaster, 31:58 (FWS)
National Hardware Show:
1986, reviewed, 36:88-89
1987, reviewed, 43:94-96
National Historic Preservation Act: and owner signature, 3:10
National Historical Society: *Architectural Treasures of Early America, The,* reviewed, 47:110-12
National Information Center for Children and Youth with Handicaps: services of, 55:8-10
National Institute for Occupational Safety and Health (NIOSH):
number for, 72:6
roof-safety booklet from, 61:102
on scaffolding safety, 72:100
services from, 34:52, 55 (TB)
National Institute of Building Sciences:
address for, 63:65 (MFC), 65:55, 72:100, 76:6
Building Seismic Safety Council (BSSC), 47:106
toll-free number, 47:106
National Kitchen and Bath Association:
address for, 72:98
evaluates computer programs, 82:104
National Manufacturing Co.: address for, 54:65 (FC)
National Oak Flooring Manufacturers' Association:
address for, 53:14, 65:54, 67:78, 81:104
Hardwood Flooring Finishing-Refinishing Manual, 23:50
publications of, 23:50
National Paint and Coatings Association:
address for, 70:14
Household Paint Selector, The, 23:50
publications of, 23:50
National Park Service:
Cleaning and Waterproof Coating of Masonry Buildings, The (Mack), 5:39
Historic American Building Survey of, 52:8-12

Preservation Assistance Division, 82:102

Preservation Briefs, reviewed, 72:108

National Particleboard Association: address for, 65:54, 72, 67:81

publications from, 23:50

National Plumbing Code: source for, 5:45

National Precast Concrete Association: mentioned, 25:71

National Referral Center: services of, 23:51

National Register of Historic Places: *See* National Trust for Historic Preservation.

National Research Council of Canada: books from, 51:41

National Roofing Contractors Association: address for, 64:45 (EF), 65:54

information from, 37:84

NRCA Roofing & Waterproofing Manual, 37:84

NRCA Steep Roofing Manual, 37:84

National Safety Council: *Accident Prevention Manual for Industrial Operations,* 64:74

described, 34:52 (TB)

National Sash and Door Jobbers Association: staircase information from, 36:61 (FWS)

National Small Flows Clearinghouse: address for, 64:102

National Solar Data Network: *See* U.S. Department of Energy.

National Solar Heating and Cooling Information Center: publications of, 1:66

National Stair Builder (Monkton): cited, 43:38 (FWS)

National Starch & Chemical Corp.: address for, 65:45

National Supaflu Systems, Inc.: address for, 70:79

mentioned, 9:16

National Technical Information Service: address for, 65:55

Design and Construction Manual for Residential Buildings in Coastal High Hazard Areas, 29:74

Energy Conservation through Building Design, 23:51

Federal Energy Technology Catalog, 23:51

Passive Solar Design Handbook (vol. II), 3:46

Passive Space Heating and Cooling, 23:51

services of, 23:51

National Telephone Supply Co.: sleeve-forming tool, 42:39

National Tile Roofing Manufacturers Association: address for, 60:41, 65:61 (EF)

National Trade and Professional Associations of the U. S.: coverage of, 23:51

National Trust Book of the English House, The (Aslet and Powers): reviewed, 32:86

National Trust for Historic Preservation: guide book on, 31:80

National Register of, book on, 31:80

1982 meeting of, 7:14

Preservation and Conservation, 4:58, 5:39

National Water Well Association: heat-pump information from, 26:68

National Wood Flooring Association: address for, 75:100

National Wood Window and Door Association: insulated divided-light window information from, 40:86

Native American Architecture (Nabokov and Easton): reviewed, 69:110

Natural Energy and Vernacular Architecture (Fathy): reviewed, 47:110

Natural House, The (Wright): mentioned, 16:4, 18:66 (CBS)

Natural House Book, The (Pearson): reviewed, 61:106-108

Naturalite-EPI: address for, 73:59

Nature and Art of Workmanship, The (Pye): cited, 52:58 (CSH)

Nature Co.: address for, 47:28

Navajo motifs: book on, 67:58

Navajo Textiles (Blomberg): cited, 67:58

Navajo Weaving Tradition, The (Kaufman and Selser): cited, 67:58

Naversen, Kenneth: *West Coast Victorians,* reviewed, 46:104

Nayso, Inc.: address for, 83:92

NCAT: *See* National Center for Appropriate Technology.

Nearing, Scott and Helen: *Living the Good Life,* 14:63

Nebraska: solar tax credits in, 3:12

NED Corp.: address for, 64:83

Need A House? Call Ms. Mouse (Mendoza): reviewed, 15:22

Neeley, W. Scott:

on new Victorian, 66:46-50

on Texas in-fill house, 70:61-65 (EEH)

Neighborhood Reinvestment Corp.: rehab financing of, 6:14

Neilsen-Winter Corp.: stress-skin panels of, 25:44, 58, 59 (TFH)

Nelson, Carl A.: *Audel Mechanical Trades Pocket Manual,* reviewed, 64:112

Nelson, Dale: on stairway, 37:30-33 (FWS)

Nelson, Glenn: mentioned, 29:28

Neoprene: with acrylic, 10:33, 12:4 (DWS)

Nerf balls: back-lit, 29:33

Neri, Ernest: quonset-hut addition by, 67:20

Nesbit, Evelyn: career of, 37:53

NEST: *See* New Expanding Shelter Technology.

Net Free Ventilation Area (NFVA): defined, 19:68

mentioned, 7:53, 21:51 (DWS)

Neufeld, Larry:

houses by, 1:43, 45 (EEH), 45:76-81, 89 (EEH)

stone-faced block walls of, 13:36-38 (CBS)

Neufeld-Lasar Design Build Co.: house by, 1:45 (EEH)

Neutra, Richard:

book on, 19:33

building by, 19:29-33

concrete use of, 14:70

Nevada:

building code changes of, 3:10

home conservation credits in, 5:65

solar tax credits in, 3:12

Nevamar Corp.: address for, 9:41 (BK)

Nevins, Richard: gate by, 52:89

New Alberene Stone Co. Inc.: soapstone, 39:42

New American Home:

discussed, 28:73-77

1986 version of, 32:82

New Craftsman Furnishings: address for, 54:100

New Elements of Hand Railing, The (Riddell): cited, 43:38 (FWS)

New England: Northeast Utilities solar plans for, 33:84

New England Builder:

fire of, 22:6

mentioned, 25:54 (FRC)

reviewed, 20:80-81

New England Doorways (Chamberlain): cited, 54:68 (REM)

New England Solar Energy Association: conferences of, 9:14, 19:22, 25:82-83

New Expanding Shelter Technology (NEST): exhibition of, 26:82

New Hampshire: solar tax credits in, 3:12

New House Planning and Idea Book: reviewed, 20:80

New Jersey: solar tax credits in, 3:12

New Life for Old Dwellings: described, 4:62

New Mexican Furniture (Taylor and Bokides): cited, 67:58

New Mexico:

earth-building codes of, 34:36

Housing Rehabilitation Section, 5:16

solar conferences in, 26:56

Solar I housing development in, 34:36, 38

solar tax credits in, 3:12

New Morning Windows, Inc.: address for, 76:75 (FC)

New Practical Builder and Workman's Companion, The (Nicholson): update of, 24:86

New Solar Electric Home, The (Davidson): cited, 62:71

New York:
  Energy Research and Development Authority catalog, 3:63
  historic preservation grants of, 20:44
  home conservation credits in, 5:65
  Preservation League of, 5:39
  solar tax credits in, 3:12

New York City:
  Consumer Farmer Foundation, 6:16
  cooperative reclamation in, 6:16
  Department of Housing Preservation and Development, 6:16
  Facade Improvement Program of, 5:39
  penthouse construction in, 31:63-65
  restoration grants of, 5:39
  Urban Homesteaders Assistance Board, 6:16

New York Landmarks Conservancy:
  Repairing Old and Historic Windows, reviewed, 84:124
  sandstone restoration booklet of, 5:39

New York State Energy Research and Development Authority:
  solar greenhouse plans, 10:17

New York Wire Co.: address for, 57:75 (FC)

NewAire: heat-recovery ventilators, 34:34 (DWS)

Newman, Morton: *Standard Structural Details for Building Construction,* reviewed, 47:110

News, The: source for, 46:48

Newsnet computer service: described, 46:60

Newspaper: recycled, into panels, 66:102

Newtech Hardware: address for, 56:94

Newtex Industries: Zetex fireproof board of, 24:82

Newtron Products Co.: address for, 67:92

Nextel solar coating: mentioned, 1:30

Neymark, Shel: ceramics by, 59:90

NFPA 13 Installation of Sprinkler Systems: source for, 44:45 (BK)

NFPA 13D-1984 Sprinkler Systems: source for, 44:45 (BK)

NFVA: *See* Net Free Ventilation Area.

Nichols, Edward: on house additions, 15:64-65

Nicholson, Peter: *New Practical Builder and Workman's Companion, The* (1823), update of, 24:86

Nickels, Karen: *Accessible Bathroom, The,* discussed, 35:45 (BK)

Nicklas, Mike: AirCore systems by, 30:50 (CBS)

Nicolai Co.: Energy-Guard Door, 6:60

Nicopress: source for, 42:39

Nicro Fico pulleys: source for, 13:49 (DWS)

Nikolich, Mike: mentioned, 33:82 (TB)

1991 Consumer Guide to Home Energy Saving (Wilson): reviewed, 67:104

1991 National Construction Estimator (Kiley and Moselle): reviewed, 67:104

1993 Old-House Journal Catalog: reviewed, 81:114-16

1993-94 Buyer's Manual: source for, 85:124

NIOSH: *See* National Institute for Occupational Safety and Health.

NIOSH Alert: source for, 72:100

NIOSH Recommended Standards for Occupational Exposure to Methylene Chloride (GPO): mentioned, 1:33 (FWS)

Nisson, J. D. Ned:
  addresses conference, 33:84
  Air-to-Air Exchangers, reviewed, 50:108
  Moisture Control for Homes, reviewed, 70:122
  quoted, 28:82

Nitrogen dioxide: danger from, 1:12

Nitterhouse Concrete Products, Inc.: mentioned, 25:71

Nitto Kohki USA, Inc.: pneumatic cutter, 43:92

Niu, Stanley H.: tests plate-to-rafter connections, 74:36-39 (MFC)

No Problem!: address for, 47:100

Noble Co.:
  address for, 56:80, 61:12, 85:16
  Chloraloy 240, 20:12, 32:47, 36:69 (BK)
  Noblebond, 32:48 (BK)
  Nobleseal membrane, 44:14
  Nobleweld, 32:48 (BK)
  Vaporseal roofing membrane, 16:8, 20:12, 29:12, 37:47 (DWS)

No-Clamp contact-cement: source for, 36:69 (BK)

Noise:
  acoustical sealants against, 61:40-41, 62:60, 61
  blankets against, sound-suppression, 55:59
  books on, 29:92, 58:57
  with concrete surfaces, 11:50 (CBS)
  consultant in, 82:6
  dampening, strategies for, 58:54-57, 62:18 (CSH), 62:60, 61
  decibels of, 35:63
  design mitigating, 11:50, 31:48, 69, 35:60 (CBS, FWS)
  with drywall, 11:50 (CBS)
  earplug storage for, 37:14
  eliminating, room for, 35:60-63
  of fans, control of, 30:51 (CBS)
  with frame floor, 11:50 (CBS)

  insulation against,
    fiberglass, 32:67 (FRC)
    between separate stud walls, 54:61
  in open plans, 1:45 (EEH)
  pads against, rubber waffle, source for, 62:18 (CSH)
  panels cutting, cement-bonded particleboard, 70:63 (EEH)
  from plumbing, correcting, 79:20, 82:6
  resilient channel against, 56:62 (EEH), 58:56-57
  sealing out, in remodels, 65:76-77 (REM)
  with stucco, 11:50 (CBS)
  terminology of, 58:54
  types of, 35:63

Noise Control: source for, 29:92

Nomex fire-resistant material: source for, 24:82

Nontoxic Home, The (Dadd): reviewed, 46:104

Nooker, Clyde and Charlotte: sell Wright studio, 32:61

Norberg-Schulz, Christian:
  Meaning in Western Architecture, reviewed, 45:120
  on Norwegian architecture, 46:77-78
  Wood Houses, 12:72

Norco Windows, Inc.: address for, 55:79, 76:75 (FC)

Nord (E. A.) Co.:
  columns of, 1:63
  Entry Door System of, 6:60

Nordic floor finish: applying, 36:44 (FWS)

Norfield Corp.: Norcore honeycomb panels, reviewed, 36:89

Norfield Tools and Supplies: address for, 58:41 (REM)

Norgard, Richard: on spiral stair, 54:80-82 (EF)

Norgren: address for, 50:60

Normbau, Inc.:
  address for, 73:59
  nylon-coated door hardware by, 48:65 (FC, MFC)

Nor-Metal: table saw, 26:82

Norsaw: 805-X saw, reviewed, 57:60, 61, 62

Norskog, Jody: on sculpted staircase, 16:73-77 (FWS)

North American Log Builders Association: 1982 meeting of, 13:14

North American Plywood: address for, 83:63

North American Refractories Co.:
  address for, 71:52
  Refracrete castable refractory concrete, 36:32 (CBS)

North Carolina:
  pension-fund mortgages in, 4:14
  solar tax credits in, 3:12

North Dakota: solar energy tax credits in, 3:12

Northeast Sustainable Energy Association:
address for, 72:100
design competition of, 75:102

Northeast Utilities:
plans from, 53:87, 89
Solar Home Planbook, 33:84

Northeastern Lumber Manufacturers' Association:
address for, 65:53
grading rules from, 33:43 (FWS)
services of, 23:50

Northeastern Lumbermen's Association:
funds Fairbanks house, 13:27 (TFH)

Northeastern Scale Models, Inc.: mail-order materials from, 22:51 (FRC)

Northland Corp.: address for, 75:67

Northland Glass: quad-pane from, 20:22

Northrop, Lowell: on stripping paint, 1:33 (FWS)

Northrup Inc.:
heat pumps, 26:68
Solarflair water heater, 5:65

Northwest Aluminum: address for, 59:72 (SH)

Northwest Construction Software: *Fast Track Estimating for Remodelers,* reviewed, 83:122

Norton Construction Products: on diamond cut-off blades, 62:84

Norton Sealants Operation: gaskets, 40:4

Norway:
building in, 46:76-79
See also Prefabricated houses: Scandinavian.

Norwegian Homes, Ltd.: address for, 23:84

Nose auger: *See* Bits: shell auger.

Notches of All Kinds (Mackie): cited, 23:12, 27:84

Notter, George, Jr.: on architects, 20:26

NOVI Development Corp.:
cellular concrete of, 30:76
plastic nails from, 30:76
polymer-based stucco of, 30:76

Noyes, Eliot: house by, 16:50

NRCA Roofing and Waterproofing Manual: reviewed, 37:84

NRCA Steep Roofing Manual: reviewed, 37:84

NRG Barriers, Inc.: stress-skin panels, 24:59

Nuding, Stephen: on crown molding, 68:79-80 (FC)

Nudor Corp.: Wood Insulated Door, 6:60

Nuess, Mike: on continuous ventilation, 78:68-71

Nuheat Manufacturing Industries:
address for, 75:72

Numbers: house, gallery of, 64:88-89

Nunan Mansion (Jacksonville, OR):
pictured, 32:76

Key to books:

(BK)   Building Baths and Kitchens
(CBS)   Building with Concrete, Brick and Stone
(CSH)   Craftsman-Style Houses
(DWS)   Building Doors, Windows and Skylights
(EEH)   Energy-Efficient Houses
(EF)   Exterior Finishing
(FC)   Finish Carpentry
(FRC)   Frame Carpentry
(FWS)   Building Floors, Walls and Stairs
(MFC)   More Frame Carpentry
(REM)   Remodeling
(SH)   Small Houses
(TB)   Tools for Building
(TFH)   Timber-Frame Houses

Nursery: dormered, 80:75

Nutech Energy Systems, Inc.: heat-recovery ventilators, 34:34 (DWS)

Nutone Inc. Scovill:
heat-recovery ventilator AE-2000, 34:69 (SH)
heat-recovery ventilators, 34:34, 37:4 (DWS)

Oak Park Home and Studio of Frank Lloyd Wright, The (Abernathy): cited, 56:82

Oak Park Studio (Wright): restoration of, 32:62-66

Oak (*Quercus* spp.):
acids of, and zinc, 24:44
ammonia darkening of, 36:26, 67:75 (CSH, REM)
bleached finish for, 45:48 (TFH)
color matching, 48:78
hardness group of, 40:69 (FRC)
quartersawn, 58:36, 41 (REM)
flooring difficulties with, 29:12
red (*Q. rubra*), for timber framing, 7:6, 30:6
white (*Q. alba*),
for timber framing, 30:6
decay resistance of, 63:63 (MFC)

Oak, tan: *See* Tan oak (*Lithocarpus densiflorus*).

Oakland Carbide Engineering Co.:
address for, 70:90
spiral cutters, 27:38-39 (TB)
trimming bit TA 170 flush-cut, 10:38

Oak-Over veneered moldings: reviewed, 48:91

Oatey Co.:
address for, 65:44
neoprene flashing, 39:37 (BK)

Oberschulte, William: on computers, 35:64-67 (TB)

Ober-Stenerson Sales Corp.: laminate-veneer finish materials, 39:90

Occidental Leather:
address for, 63:94
tool bags, 42:65 (TB)

Occupational Safety and Health Administration (OSHA):
address for, 84:53
and house construction, 36:37 (TB)
and injury rate, 34:53 (TB)
OSHA Safety and Health Standards Digest, 34:52 (TB)
publications from, 34:55 (TB)
Safety Standards for Stairways and Ladders, cited, 84:53
scaffolding regulations, 36:34, 37 (TB)

Occupational Safety and Health Review Commission (OSHRC): described, 34:52 (TB)

Ocean sites: maintenance for, 68:16-18

Octagonal structures:
building, 9:25-27, 24:76, 26:12 (erratum, 27:6), 30:42-45, 32:34, 35, 36, 37, 63-64, 34:56-61 (FRC)
center for, locating, 24:76
drawings for, 11:6
golden rectangle with, 34:56-58 (FRC)
log, 23:12

Oda, Noritsugu: drawings by, 47:128

Odate, Toshio: reviews Engel, 34:92

Odell, Robert: mentioned, 24:92

Odors:
diagnosing, 78:16-20
smoke, removing, 4:18

Office of Scientific and Technical Information: address for, 65:52

Offices:
accounting process for, 45:94
architectural showcase as, 80:72-77
in balconies, 73:55
book on, reviewed, 65:108
design for, 44:51-53 (SH)
ferro-cement, building, 50:46-49
fourth-floor, 45:66
in-home, building, 45:28, 94
semi-enclosed, 73:62, 63
over shop, 73:77, 79, 80, 81
space for, creating, 53:43-45 (SH)
See also Studies. Studios.

Ohaks, Uldis: on ornamental metalwork, 72:120

Ohannesian, Paul B.:
on bungalow makeover, 56:68-72 (CSH)
light fixture by, 61:87

O'Hare, Michael: on Corian, 27:44-47 (BK)

Ohio:
microclimate studies in, 9:14-16
solar credits in, 3:12
Ohio Sealants: address for, 78:84
O'Keefe's, Inc.: address for, 76:56
Oklahoma:
dry-stack block in, 16:57 (CBS)
solar tax credits in, 3:12
Okon, Inc.: address for, 82:68
Olana: building of, 78:79-81
Old House Journal: product bulletin of, 1:63
Old House Journal Catalog, The:
cited, 48:65 (FC, MFC)
reviewed, 31:82, 70:120
source for, 43:39 (FWS), 64:49 (FC)
Old House Rescue Book, The (Kangas):
reviewed, 10:70
Old Houses on Nantucket (Duprey):
cited, 77:89
Oldham Saw Co.: abrasive cutting
wheels, 32:68 (FRC)
Olean Tile Co.: address for, 75:49 (REM)
Olenik, Sandra: heliodon by, 13:18
Olgyay, Victor: *Design with Climate,* cited,
9:16, 54:61
Olin: Solar-Bond absorber plates, 1:32
Olive Knot Products: address for, 76:65
(MFC)
Olschner, Joey: on Hardieplank, 77:96
Olson, Ken: solar-design course of, 69:100
Olympic:
acrylic latex stain, source for, 28:72
exterior stains, 45:41
use of, 22:57 (CSH)
Wood Preservative, for redwood, 3:8
Olympic Foundry: Hi-jacks, 22:38 (FRC)
Omnia: address for, 76:58
Omni-Tech Energy Products, Inc.:
Thermal-Krete, 24:12-14, 31:38 (CBS)
Onduline roofing:
disadvantages of, 46:51 (EEH)
installing, 6:56-57
mentioned, 20:10
nature of, 26:72, 73, 74
as siding, 6:56-57
source for, 26:74 (SH), 46:51 (EEH)
One Design, Inc.: address for, 71:106, 74:90
One- and Two-Family Dwelling Code:
source for, 5:45
O'Neil, Isabel: *Art of the Painted Finish for
Furniture, The,* cited, 60:81
O'Neill, Don: house by, 31:92
O'Neill and Perez: house by, 38:66-71
Oney, Rick: mentioned, 38:38 (CSH)
Online Access Guide Magazine: address
for, 46:60
Onslow-Ford House: construction of,
27:26-31
Onsrud Cutter: address for, 55:63
Oostdik, Dennis: light-fixture
reproduction by, 61:86

Opalight gaslight: source for, 14:31
Openings, Inc.: address for, 55:79
Operation Solar, Northeast Utilities:
address for, 53:89
Optimum Value Engineering (OVE):
books on, cited, 84:49
criticized, 85:4
details of, 84:46-49
framing, publication on, 23:48
Ore-bin house: pictured, 32:100
Oregon:
ADA tests in, 37:65
architecture of, book on, 33:88
heat-exchanger workshop of, 23:80-82
home conservation credits in, 5:65
Home Demonstration Program of, 29:68
solar tax credits in, 3:12
tempered-glass skylight code of, 18:36
(DWS)
Oregon Cutting Systems: address for,
61:82
Oregon Scientific: ultrasonic tape,
reviewed, 78:54-55
Oregon Strand Board: address for, 83:42
Oregon Water-Heater Heat Pump:
source for, 5:65
Oribin, Edwin: on box beams, 71:76-77
(MFC)
Oriented strand board: (OSB)
associations for, 67:81
buckle prevention for, 81:57, 58
cart for, reviewed, 81:92
hurricane-proofness of, 78:85, 79:4
information on, 65:53
and moisture, 67:78, 70:4
nail-holding ability of, 67:78-79
non-swelling, 37:80
and post-hurricane codes, 85:118-20
production of, 67:79
sealed-edge, source for, 75:94
for sheathing, 37:69 (FRC)
siding from, 83:43-44
as subfloor, test report on, 81:102-104
uses of, 67:77-78, 80
Oringderff, Barbara: *True Sod,* 31:54
Orion Marketing & Sales, Inc.: address
for, 72:90
Orlando, Joanne M., ed.: *Old House
Journal Catalog, The,* reviewed, 70:120
Ornament:
book on, 61:69
casting, 1:36-39, 5:10 (FWS)
designing, books on, 69:87
plaster, sources of, 1:62
Victorian, cards for, 1:66
See also Casting. Molding.
*Ornamental Carpentry of 19th-Century
American Architecture* (Karp):
mentioned, 18:53
Orr, Harold:
energy-efficient designs of, 24:82
on sealing houses, 28:82

at superinsulation conference, 22:18
(CSH)
Orr, Wilson and David: direct
Meadowcreek, 37:75
Orta, Nick: stonework by, 36:70-75
Orton, Steve: on header, 62:87 (MFC)
Orton, Vrest: *Forgotten Art of Building a
Good Fireplace, The,* cited, 3:43, 47:8,
51:18 (CBS)
Osborn, Thomas D.: floors by, 79:90-91
Osborne, Daniel: house by, 18:44-49
Osborne (C. S.) and Co.: address for,
57:94
OSHA: *See* Occupational Safety and
Health Administration.
Osharow, Neil: discusses tools, 18:17
Osheyack, Gary: mentioned, 26:68
OSHRC: *See* Occupational Safety and
Health Review Commission.
Osmose Wood Preserving: address for,
50:20
Oster, John: reviews *Photovoltaics,* 12:72
Osterberg, Arvid: on farmhouse remodel,
12:46-49
Oswalt, Tom: mentioned, 31:92
O'Toole Randal: addresses conference,
49:98
Ottomans: triangular, 12:31
Oulette, Robert A.: *Chainsaws,* cited,
78:43
Outer Banks: address for, 63:49
Outhouses: Arts-and-Crafts style, 67:87
Outwater Plastic Industries: address for,
58:40 (REM), 62:92
OVE: *See* Optimum Value Engineering.
Ovens: *See* Ranges.
Overhead Door Corp.: address for, 52:69
Oviatt, Alfred Jr.: *How to Buy Construction
Lumber,* 8:14
Owen, David: *Walls around Us, The,*
reviewed, 83:120
Owens-Corning Fiberglas Corp.:
address for, 50:49, 64:45 (EF), 66:50
compressed fiberglass 703, 35:63
Derbigum HPS, 37:26 (BK)
type-K fiber, 27:12
Warm-N-Dri insulation, 29:12
Owner Built Home, The (Kern): cited,
7:42, 28:68, 72
*Owner-Builder's Guide to Fireplaces,
The* (Kern and Magers): source for, 22:6
*Owner-Builder's Guide to Stone
Masonry, The* (Kern, Magers and
Penfield): mentioned, 3:30 (CBS)
Owner-Built Pole Frame House, The
(Kern): reviewed, 8:70
Oxalic acid: for stain removal, 29:16, 49:26
Ozone:
production of, 63:59-60
safe levels of, 63:60

Pace Industries, Inc.: address for, 46:73
Pacific Clay Products: concrete roof
  shingles of, 22:18 (CSH)
Pacific Power and Light: heat-pump
  water-heater policy of, 5:65
Pacific Rents: MED offset hinges of, 19:10
Pacific Wood Windows: windows, 44:67
  (FRC)
Pads:
  for carpets, adhesive, reviewed, 54:92-94
  for machinery,
    rubber waffle, source for, 62:18 (CSH)
    sheet-rubber, 35:60
  nonslip work-base, reviewed, 55:92-94
Paeco, Inc.: address for, 55:79
Paint:
  acrylic,
    high-quality, 62:46-48 (SH)
    vs. oil-based, 19:10-12
    primers for, 19:10-12
  alkyd resin, waterproof, 70:65 (EEH)
  anti-fungal, effectiveness of, 72:66
    (REM)
  Arts-and-Crafts style, source for, 54:100
  for bathroom vanity under glass, 84:81
  bonding agents for, 16:8
  book on, 4:62
  cans of,
    drain holes in, 14:14
    handles for, improved, 70:34
    lip plug for, 63:26-28
  caulk for, baseboard, 61:26
  cleanup,
    hand cleaner for, 42:59 (DWS)
    mineral spirits for, 42:59 (DWS)
  cold-weather handling of, 51:42
  Colonial reproduction, source for, 63:48
  colors of,
    blending, 67:58
    choosing service for, 62:104
    range in, 56:50
    samples of, 55:74
  conditioner for, 83:86
  corrosion-resistant, 29:74, 75
  decorative finishes with, 60:78-82
    publications on, 60:81
    schools for, 60:81
    supply sources for, 60:80
  deglosser for, 60:80
  as design element, 82:85
  as design without, 46:70-73

dilute, 26:77 (SH)
  as stain, 19:12, 68:38-39
dropcloths for, from shades, 49:26
end-grain bleeding of, preventing, 67:58
epoxy, 27:12
  industrial-grade, 33:32 (CBS)
  marine, 73:73
  qualities of, 70:47-48
  sources for, 69:66, 70:49
exterior, 81:47
  applying, 27:55
  bilge, source for, 61:70
  choosing, 27:54-55
  oil vs. latex, 62:37 (EF), 75:48 (REM),
    81:46, 83:4-6
  spraying of, precautions for, 62:41
    (EF)
failures in, 12:8-10, 74:98
Federal grey, source for, 54:57
fillers for, recommended, 71:72
French high-quality, reviewed, 61:90-92
high-VOC, avoiding, 73:67
historic, research aid on, 65:55
interior vs. exterior, 70:14
latex,
  applying, 67:70
  below-ground, 2:35
  coats of, 67:70
  disadvantages of, 67:69
  high-quality, 9:24
  perm rating for, 19:67
  spraying vs. rolling, 67:68
  over texture, 67:67-68, 71
  toxicity of, 10:10, 67:67
  over wallpaper, 39:10
  and water-soluble stains, 39:10, 67:71
for lead, 53:79 (REM)
lead,
  detector kit for, 71:96
  disposing of, 84:75
  safe removal of, 62:39 (EF), 76:4, 84:75
  testing for, 84:75
for log building, 14:53
marine, source for, 70:48, 73:73
masking for, 42:55 (DWS), 42:56 (DWS)
methods for, 1:33 (FWS)
mixing, by vehicle, 47:32
nontoxic, 81:106
  citrus-oil based, 73:69
  discussed, 69:8
  low-biocide, source for, 73:69
  sources for, 67:90-92
oil-based,
  additive for, 60:28
  below-ground, 2:35
  vs. latex, 19:10-12
  for moisture control, 19:12
  perm rating for, 19:67

old,
  analyzing, 53:57
  wet-sanding prep of, 44:24-26
patching for, with epoxy, 62:37, 40-41
  (EF)
for pewter effect, 60:82
for plaster, 57:42
polyurethane, sunlight-resistant, two-
  part, 85:75
power washing for, 62:38 (EF)
over preweathered wood, disadvised,
  76:106
primers for,
  back priming with, 81:56, 84:63
  oil-based stain killer, 68:45 (FC)
  recommended, 62:41 (EF)
  rust-proofing, 62:41 (EF)
  spray, 42:57 (DWS)
problems with, book on, 62:36 (EF)
recycled, 81:106
removal of, 4:18, 57:39
  by abrasives, 1:33, 16:66 (DWS, FWS)
  from brick, 8:6
  with chemicals, 16:66-69 (DWS), 78:4
  experimental gentle, 4:8-9
  by heat, 3:4, 16:66 (DWS)
  methods for, 62:37, 38-39 (EF)
  precautions for, 2:64
  with sawdust, 69:30-32
for restoration, 9:24
restoration of, book on, 24:86
retarders for, 17:32 (CSH)
roofing,
  aluminum and steel, 62:20 (CSH)
  copper-resin, 24:46
  fluorocarbon, 24:46
  heat-reducing, 70:16
  for metals, 24:46, 41:4
  polyester, 24:46
  silicone-modified, 24:46
rubber-based, below-ground, 2:35
sandblasting, 34:64 (BK)
sand-coated, 61:71
sanding, 42:58 (DWS)
scrapers for, 36:16, 62:39 (EF)
screen-printing, source for, 78:73
over sealants, 61:40-41, 42
shields for,
  aluminum-foil, 57:28
  drywall corner-knife as, 54:24
for solar collectors, 1:30
sponged, 60:79
spray, 42:54-59 (DWS)
  nozzle cleaning for, 61:26, 62:28
  oil vs. latex enamel, 42:59 (DWS)
  respirators for, 42:55 (DWS)
stack, method for, 43:20
stain killers for, 67:71, 68:45 (FC)
stilt aids for, 32:16

strainers for, making, 63:28
surface preparation for, 12:8, 42:58
  (DWS), 62:36-41 (EF)
thinning, naphtha for, 42:57 (DWS)
translucent, from tung oil, 31:27 (CSH)
trays for,
    liners for, 53:28
    makeshift, 49:26
    plastic-sheet, 25:16
for trim on stone houses, 63:20
vapor-barrier, 37:65, 73:69
    perm rating for, 19:67
    sources for, 6:55, 9:8, 19:68, 78:69
Victorian, books on, 43:102, 66:47
video-scanner selecting of, 70:112
as visual aid, 28:53 (FWS)
whitewash, simulated, 79:55
and wood moisture, 81:54, 56, 57
woods for, 50:16
See also Brushes. Coatings. Color.
    Glazing. Paint rollers. Sprayers.
    Whitewash.
Paint Problem Solver: cited, 62:36 (EF)
Paint removers:
    flammability of, 16:82
    methylene chloride, publication on,
      1:33 (FWS)
    peel-away method for, 76:4
    with sawdust, 69:30-32
    toxicity of, 10:10
    using, 16:66-69 (DWS), 84:72-75
Paint rollers:
    caddy for, 40:16
    care of, 67:70
    cleaning, with hose, 42:18-20 (CSH)
    covers for, 67:69
    narrow, using, 61:26
    poles for, 67:69
Painted Ladies (Baer *et al.*): source for,
    35:72
Painted Ladies Revisited (Pomada and
    Larsen): cited, 66:47
**Painting and Decorating Contractors of
    America:** *Paint Problem Solver,* 62:36
    (EF)
Painting Inside and Out: source for, 4:62
Pairis Enterprises:
    address for, 55:92, 83:98
    Spoiler Sky Hook, 24:10
Palanza, William: on mosaic tile, 36:64-67
    (BK)
Palermini & Associates: address for,
    76:104
Palladio, Andrea:
    book on, 45:122
    Four Books of Architecture, 42:74
    house after, 38:84-89
    Poplar Forest after, 42:74-79
    Villa Capra by, pictured, 38:86

Palladio Guide, The (Constant):
    reviewed, 32:86
Palmer, Les: on building pains, 40:98
Palmer Industries: address for, 73:69
Palms, John: stair by, 6:20
Paloma Industries, Inc.: tankless water
    heaters, 12:18, 40:57-5 (CSH)
Panasonic Co.: drill-driver, reviewed,
    62:94-96
Panek, Julian R., and John Philip Cook:
    Construction Sealants and Adhesives,
    cited, 65:45
Panel: *See* Wainscot.
Panel Clip: metal connectors, 43:49 (FRC)
Panelectric Heating Systems: address
    for, 76:8
Paneling:
    adhesives for, 58:75
    alder, 39:32
    barn boards as, 22:14
    for ceiling, 56:74-77
    ceramic tile, laminated, 39:90
    with contoured horizontal strips, 61:74-
      75
    coverage of, figuring, 31:84
    dimension guide for, 31:84
    fiberboard as, 71:72
    fiberglass-reinforced plastic, 72:62
    finish on, improving, 5:10-12
    fireproof, cement-bonded
      particleboard, 70:63 (EEH)
    fluted, with applied beads, 71:44, 45
      (REM)
    framed, reproduction, 77:87-88
    glued, 30:23
    Greene-and-Greene, 72:38
    horizontal cherry, 15:76, 77, 78 (CSH)
    with mahogany plywood, 17:29, 33-34
      (CSH)
    Masonite bas-relief, 57:47 (REM)
    1x6s, grooved, 75:49 (REM)
    patterned, 33:77
    penta-treated, sealant for, 15:21
    pine, 59:45, 46, 47
    sealers for, 39:10
    varnish for, 72:62
    veneered, 31:49 (FWS)
    V-groove for, 8:12
Panels:
    "beaded Victoria," source for, 74:75
    curved, making, 58:38, 40 (REM)
    for doors, 83:59, 60
    large, cart for, reviewed, 81:92
    raised,
      with drywall, 44:89
      for fireplace surround, 45:79 (EEH)
      no-rout method for, 82:14-16
    scribing, 77:60, 61
    See also Wainscot.
Pantries:
    as airlock, 13:68, 71
    butler's, remodeling, 79:87, 89

Pants:
    knee patches for, with glue, 51:28
    patches for, padded, 47:28-30, 70:100
Papa, Byron:
    on clear finish, 48:74-78
    on rolling latex paint, 67:67-71
    on spray painting, 42:54-59 (DWS)
Paper:
    for drafting, 26:58-60 (TB)
    honeycomb structural, 36:89, 81:106
    laminated structural,
      mentioned, 37:84
      reviewed, 36:89
    rice,
      applying, 15:71 (FWS)
      for skylights, 27:30, 31
      sources for, 27:63
    synthetic, source for, 69:43 (EEH)
    walls from, 66:102
    See also Builder's paper.
Para-bolt anchor bolts: source for, 29:34
    (FRC)
Paragon Glass, Inc.: address for, 73:74
Paral, Rob:
    on appropriate-technology books,
      64:110-12
    on homeless programs, 61:100-102
    on inlaid gutters, 61:46-49
Paralyzed Veterans of America: services
    of, 55:8-10
Parana pine (Araucaria angustifolia):
    for paint, 42:55 (DWS)
Parging:
    book on, cited, 62:20 (CSH)
    over stone masonry, 62:20-22 (CSH)
    See also Stucco.
Paridee, Dustin: quoted, 29:89
Park, Kip:
    on compact cabin, 55:42-44 (SH)
    on energy demonstration, 47:104-106
    on foundations, 48:66-69 (MFC)
    on future windows, 55:81
    reviews computer program, 51:96
    on R-2000 program, 34:86
    on superinsulated tract houses, 24:82
    on ventilation conference, 55:102-104
Parker, Don: on solar house, 51:72-75
    (EEH)
Parker, G. Robert: builds maritime
    house, 73:51-55
Parker, H. F.: *Simplified Engineering for
    Architects and Builders,* mentioned, 7:28
    (TFH)
Parker Hannifin Corp.: address for, 49:87
Parker (L. C.) House: described, 36:24-29
    (CSH)
Parlon NT4: source for, 35:77
Parrish, Trisha: remodels kitchen, 73:16-
    20
Parry, Charles H.: quoted, 19:66
Parry, William: *Parry's Graining and
    Marbling,* cited, 60:81

Parry's Graining and Marbling (Parry):
cited, 60:81
Parsec Inc.:
address for, 49:75 (EEH)
house wrap, 39:90
Parsons, Fletcher: on log building, 13:14
Particleboard:
allergen-free substitute for, 54:16
association for, 65:72, 67:81
for cabinets, 30:59 (BK)
cart for, reviewed, 81:92
cement-bonded exterior/interior, 70:63 (EEH)
chainsaw cutting of, 78:40
densities of, 67:79
discussed, 67:79
with electronically cured finish, 62:76
as floor underlayment, 67:79-80
for floors, 19:59, 39:39, 40, 43, 67:80 (FRC)
information on, 65:54
medium-density, 40:36 (FWS)
with melamine-saturated paper finish, 62:76
nail-holding ability of, 67:79
offgassing of, 67:80, 81
perm rating of, 19:67
safety of, 65:72
sawblades for, 72:47 (MFC)
screws for, 34:45 (TB)
sealing, cautions against, 54:16
toxicity of, 55:104
uses of, 67:80
Partin Limestone Products Inc.: Cal-White marble sand of, 20:52 (FWS)
Partitions:
arches as, 80:64, 67
cabinets as, 80:80
and ceiling separations, booklet on, 29:92
fireproof, 5:32
of lapped boards, 3:24, 26, 27
partial, 80:70
of plastered jute, 5:32
of plastered wire lath, 5:32
splined wood, 2:27, 29
temperature-moderating, 80:57
See also Room dividers. Walls.
Partner Industrial Products, Inc.: cut-off saw, reviewed, 62:80-84
Pascack Valley Stone Co.: reused Connecticut brownstone from, 5:39
Paslode Corp.:
address for, 68:94
nail guns, 15:49, 51 (TB)
cordless, mentioned, 82:92
discussed, 47:74-75 (FC)
framing, reviewed, 56:52, 53, 54-55

Impulse power, 32:82
Impulse propane, reviewed, 33:82 (TB)
pneumatic tools, 15:53 (TB)
Paso Robles Carbide: address for, 53:40, 55:37 (FC)
Passive Home Program (Florida): mentioned, 40:73 (EEH)
Passive Solar Design Handbook:
for AirCore systems, 30:52 (CBS)
mentioned, 3:46, 16:10, 16, 21:59 (EEH)
reviewed, 16:14
Passive Solar Energy Book, The
(Mazria): mentioned, 5:53, 19:63, 65, 21:56, 45:116 (DWS, EEH)
Passive Solar Industries Council:
address for, 71:47
Passive Solar Design Strategies,
cited, 71:47, 84:85
reviewed, 56:110, 79:120
services of, 23:51
Passive Solar Space Heating and Cooling: source for, 23:51
Pasto, Cris: manufactures flooring persuader, 84:96-98
Patagonia, Inc.: address for, 50:62
Patios:
and adobe, 48:32
in brick mosaic, 64:80-83
canopy for, 72:88
enclosed, with windowed garage doors, 80:43
flagstone, 45:58
on garage roofs, 43:16
integrated modular, 9:64
shades for, movable, 11:35
Tudor-style, 47:58
See also Decks.
Patkau, John: on Edmonton house, 32:24-28 (CSH)
Pattern Language, A (Alexander *et al.*): cited, 46:62 (TFH)
Patterned Concrete Industries:
patterning tools of, 7:6
Patterns: cardboard, hint for, 84:41
Pattison, Bob: mentioned, 27:72, 75
Patty, R. L.: rammed-earth research of, 19:10
Pau lope: source for, 73:68
Paul, Tessa: *Tiles for a Beautiful Home,* reviewed, 62:112
Pause, Michael: as joint author. *See* Clark, Roger.
Pavers: grass-crete perforated, for steep sites, 80:45
Paxton, Joseph: mentioned, 32:4
PC-SIG: address for, 56:36
PDQ Building Blocks: foam forms, 40:86
PDQ Industries, Inc.: foreign/American hybrid door hardware, 39:92
Peabody Noise Control, Inc.: address for, 58:57

Peace of Mind in Earthquake Country
(Yanev): source for, 29:38 (FRC)
Peachtree Doors and Windows, Inc.:
address for, 55:79, 76:75 (FC)
Avanti Insulated Doors, 6:60
4-ft. patio doors, 39:72
Peacock, C. M.: reviews Mitchell, 34:92
Peake, Jud:
on decking and sheathing, 37:66-69 (FRC)
on framing layout, 21:69-77 (FRC)
on portable circular-saw use, 3:33-35 (TB)
on rafter squares, 10:56-61 (TB)
on routers, 55:36-41 (FC)
on scribed ellipse, 8:50-51 (FWS)
Peake, Ron: ceramics by, 59:91
Peal-and-Seal aluminum strip: source for, 42:22 (CSH)
Pearl Abrasive Co.: address for, 64:83
Pearson, David: *Natural House Book, The,* reviewed, 61:106
Pease Industries:
address for, 53:68
Ever-Straight Door, 6:60
Peaveys:
for pulling plates to line, 39:10
using, 8:31 (TFH)
Peckham, Pama: ceramics by, 59:88-89
Pecora Corp.:
Duramem, 40:32
glazing tape from, 25:12
Pedestals: limestone carved, 54:73
Pediments:
defined, 20:60 (FWS)
limestone, cutting of, 37:56, 61
neon backlighted, 33:75
Pee Dee Brick Co.: paraffined bricks of, 23:12
PEG: *See* Princeton Energy Group.
Pegboard: carrying hook for, 7:12
Pegg, Brian F.: as joint author. *See* Stagg, William D.
Pehoski, Joseph: iron work by, 48:85
Pelican Industries: address for, 72:88
Pella Rollscreen Co.:
address for, 52:66, 64:87, 65:77, 66:66 (EEH, REM)
window production of, 60:47, 51 (FC)
Pella Windows and Doors:
address for, 55:79, 59:82, 76:75 (FC)
bow windows of, modified, 44:65, 66 (FRC)
small-light double-pane windows from, 40:86
sponsors conference, 19:22
windows, for ventilation, 17:63 (DWS)
Pelli, Cesar: on architects, 20:26
Pellicoro, Nicola: toolbox of, 74:86
Pellitteri, Phil: on wood-infesting insects, 60:64-69 (REM)
Pelton wheels: described, 15:66

Pemko Manufacturing Co.: address for, 58:57, 76:56

Pencils:
clothespin-fitted, 72:26
for drafting, 26:58, 59 (TB)
drywall-screw extender for, 67:26
for frozen wood, 72:26
fuse clip holder for, 15:18
grease, advantage of, 72:26
mechanical,
    advantage of, 72:26
    guaranteed, 77:58
old, butt joinery for, 85:30
for renovation, 12:51 (TB)

Penetrating-oil finishes: *See* Finishes.

Penetrol paint additive: source for, 17:32 (CSH)

Penfield, Lon: as joint author. *See* Kern, Ken.

Penfield, Paul: on perils of Paul, 41:106 (BK)

Pennsylvania: building code changes in, 3:10

Pennsylvania Energy Office: house by, 82:102

Pennsylvania Governor's Energy Council Home Energy Cost Estimator: cited, 33:56

Penofin finish: *See* Performance Coatings, Inc.

Pentachlorophenol:
cautions with, 15:21, 37
discussed, 63:63 (MFC)
EPA status of, 15:21
exterior use of, 15:21
interior sealants for, 15:21, 37
levels of, 63:64 (MFC)
for log buildings, 14:51, 53
pressure treatments with, 15:21
for redwood, 3:8
toxicity of, 1:6, 13:14, 14:51, 53
uses of, 13:14
vehicles for, 15:21, 37
See also Wood preservatives.

Pentair: buys Porter-Cable, 18:18

Penthouses:
building, strategic problems of, 31:63-65
scaffolds for, 31:65

Pentox: for logs, 8:8

Pentron Work Lights: reviewed, 50:94

Penwalt Corp.: Kynar 500 paint, 24:46

Penzotti Pete's: address for, 70:100

Percolation tests: method for, 3:36-37 (BK)

Perfection Corp.: address for, 82:58

Performance Coatings, Inc.:
address for, 52:66, 62:76, 68:72 (EF)
Penofin finishes, source for, 37:29, 39:54 (BK, CSH)

Pergola: defined, 29:48

Perkins, Alan: reviews miter saw, 85:104-106

Key to books:

(BK)   Building Baths and Kitchens
(CBS)   Building with Concrete, Brick and Stone
(CSH)   Craftsman-Style Houses
(DWS)   Building Doors, Windows and Skylights
(EEH)   Energy-Efficient Houses
(EF)   Exterior Finishing
(FC)   Finish Carpentry
(FRC)   Frame Carpentry
(FWS)   Building Floors, Walls and Stairs
(MFC)   More Frame Carpentry
(REM)   Remodeling
(SH)   Small Houses
(TB)   Tools for Building
(TFH)   Timber-Frame Houses

Perlite: in block work, 31:38, 41, 36:73 (CBS)

Perlite Institute: address for, 31:38 (CBS)

Perma-Chink Systems, Inc.:
address for, 47:94
backer rod for, 47:22
latex caulk, 32:75
qualities of, 28:6

Perma-Door: source for, 6:60

Permalite insulation: source for, 36:73

Permanent Wood Foundations: cited, 68:66

Permanent wood foundations: *See* Foundations: all-weather wood.

Permanent Wood Foundations, Inc.: address for, 68:62

Permeance: defined, 19:67

Perry, Brian: window seat by, 66:91

Personal Protective Equipment: source for, 34:55 (TB)

Pest control: environmentally sound, advice on, 60:67 (REM)

Pesticides: danger of, 64:6

Petersen Aluminum Corp.: roofing brochure from, 32:6

Peterson, Roger: quoted, 46:79

Petit Durathane Paint Co., Inc.: boat varnish of, 19:35 (DWS)

Petrochemicals: avoiding, 73:67

Pettit Marine Paint Co., Inc.:
address for, 73:73
bedding compound, 25:76

Pettyjohn: as joint author. *See* Lehr.

Pewter:
acid-etched, sheets of, 82:85, 86
simulating, with paint, 60:82

Pfeiffer, Bruce Brooks: *Treasures of Taliesin,*
cited, 41:31
reviewed, 34:92

Pfeiffer, Peter L.:
on energy-efficient design, 80:54-58
on seaside solar, 60:56-59 (EEH)
on sun-angle calculator, 80:26

Phase-change systems: *See* Hot-water heaters.

Phelps, Bill:
on AirCore floor, 30:50-54 (CBS)
on arched dormer, 23:66-67
on cabin, 44:38-41 (SH)
on cordless drills, 35:38-42 (TB)
on small solar house, 21:56-59 (EEH)
on Teton house, 18:40-43

Phelps, John: on gabled house, 84:64-68

Phenolic:
board, for retrofits, 39:10
foam, source for, 35:8
insulation, ozone depletion and, 49:102
See also Glue: phenol-formaldehyde.

Phenoseal adhesive caulking:
source for, 15:40 (EF)
waterproof nature of, 6:23

Philips Lighting Co.: address for, 54:51, 67:92, 76:45 (REM)

Phillips, Morgan W., and Judith E. Selwyn: *Epoxies for Wood Repairs in Historic Buildings,* 16:21, 62:41 (CSH, EF)

Phillips, Robert: metal trim by, 43:80-81

Phillips Brothers Supply: masonry fasteners, 41:57 (CBS)

Phillips Drill Co.: Redhead anchor bolts, 29:34 (FRC)

Phleps, Hermann: *Craft of Log Building, The,*
cited, 15:4, 34:50
reviewed, 17:80

Phoenix Enviro-Tech: heat pumps, 26:68

Photovoltaics. *See* Electricity.

Phragmites communis: *See* Reed.

Physical Climatology (Sellers): mentioned, 9:16

Picea spp.: *See* Spruce.

Pickens, Dan: on carving limestone, 54:72-75

Pickling: described, 60:81-82

Pickups:
anti-noise caulking of, 72:28
back support for, adding, 69:32
bed extender for, reviewed, 81:94
canopy rack for, 44:4
cargo planks for, adjustable, 71:26
dump bed for, sliding, 16:12
flag holder for, 54:28
panel-carrying system for, 78:28
roof rack for, 41:14
tie-downs for, sliding locking-pin system for, 72:90
tool storage for, 8:10, 41:58-59 (TB)
tool-retrieval aids for, 85:81
trash liner for, 68:30

Picnic shelters: roofed, simple, 75:86

Picton, Jim:
on Clover Knoll house, 55:82-87
on flashing, 11:64-65 (DWS)
on installing skylights, 11:59-61 (DWS)
reviews gas nail gun, 33:82 (TB)
reviews Sawbuck, 12:14
on worm-drive saws, 24:36-40 (TB)

Picture Book of Log Homes (Mackie):
reviewed, 27:84

Pieper, Paul J., Jr.:
on levels, 37:80
reviews clamps, 54:92
reviews Diamond Whetstone, 48:91
reviews gripper pad, 55:92-94
reviews nail spinner, 49:94
reviews screw extractor, 74:90
on rolling tool bench, 69:73-74

Pier-and-girder foundations:
constructing, 54:60-61

Pierce, Don: on scaffold incident, 67:98-100

Pierce, Doug: on solar farmhouse, 37:70-75

Pilaroscia, Jill: on color, 74:40-45

Pilasters:
bases of, repairing, 19:35, 36 (DWS)
building, 3:14, 16-17
defined, 20:60 (FWS)
Greek Revival, 1:49
limestone, corner, 37:61
stone-simulating, 9:21, 22

Pilchuck Glass School: glass technique
studies, 39:8

Pine *(Pinus* spp.):
for clapboards, 49:4
color matching, 48:78
decay resistance of, 63:63 (MFC), 69:16
Eastern white *(P. strobus),* for
clapboards, 31:37
glazing, 59:50-51 (SH)
hardness group of, 40:69 (FRC)
lodgepole *(P. contorta),* hardness group
of, 40:69 (FRC)
old heartwood, source for, 56:92
ponderosa *(P. ponderosa),* for framing,
4:54 (TFH)
red *(P. resinosa),*
hardness group of, 40:69 (FRC)
for log building, 44:10
for shingles, 12:52, 28:66
Southern long-leaf yellow *(P. palustris),*
woodwork in, 39:76
Southern yellow *(P. echinata),*
association for, 84:4
hardness group of, 40:69 (FRC)
span capability of, 33:43 (FWS)
as subfloor, test report on, 81:102-104
treated, handling, 63:64 (MFC)
sugar *(P. lambertiana),*
for framing, 4:54 (TFH)
for millwork, 49:40 (REM)
for timber framing, 13:6, 16:6, 30:6
white stain for, 75:49 (REM)
See also Parana pine.

Pinecrest: address for, 51:90

Pinsonneault, Marc: window-seat storage
by, 85:95

Pioneer Energy Products:
ductwrap of, 1:62
hot-water heater insulation of, 1:62
pipewrap of, 1:62
water-saver faucets of, 1:62

Pioneer History of Custer County, A
(Butcher): mentioned, 31:54

Pioneer Materials, Inc.: address for, 83:62

Pipe:
ABS, for plumbing, 29:52 (BK), 39:33-37
(BK)
bender for, 21:16
cutting jig for, 63:26
for floor-heat conveyance, 7:37-38
(DWS)
flue, assembly clamp for, 74:24-26
heavy-duty, 50:83
insulation for, 1:62
plastic,
broken, removing, 75:28
cut-off jig for, 74:24
polybutylene,
advantages of, 39:90
crimping, 78:75, 76, 78, 79:8
factory mutual approved, 47:6
for fire-sprinkler systems, 47:6
fittings for, 27:71, 39:90 (CBS), 78:79,
79:8
floor installation of, 21:12
installing, 78:74-78
oxidation of, 81:82
qualities of, 21:12, 26:12
in radiant-floor heating, 22:68, 70, 71,
26:12 (CBS)
for sprinkler systems, 44:43 (BK)
steadying, cat's-paw for, 78:75
tie-downs for, 27:71 (CBS)
polyethylene,
qualities of, 50:83
in radiant-floor heating, 22:68 (CBS)
polypropylene, for radiant-floor
heating, 22:68 (CBS)
polystyrene, qualities of, 50:83
polyvinyl chloride (PVC),
drainpipe, as concrete forms, 28:16
for fire-sprinkler systems, 44:43, 47:6
(BK)
for plumbing, 29:52 (BK)
trench-drain, 50:85
tubing cutter for, 39:34 (BK)
See also Drain lines. Metalbestos.
Plumbing. Radiant-floor heating.
various metals.

Pipe threaders:
ratcheted, 17:53 (BK)
using, 17:53 (BK)

PIRF: *See* Floors: perimeter-insulated
raised.

Pisé: *See* Earth construction.

Pitch: *See* Asphalt. Bitumens.

Pitch board: uses of, 10:61 (TB)

Pitch line: defined, 10:63 (FRC)

Pitch (roof): defined, 10:63 (FRC)

Pitha, Jay: concrete-block fireplace of,
15:20-21

Pitt, William B.: on perils of renovation,
7:64

Pittcon Industries, Inc.:
address for, 81:43
raised-panel drywall, 44:89
Softforms extrusions, 37:81

Pittsburgh-Corning Corp.:
address for, 59:110, 67:62
glass blocks, 37:46, 47, 49, 50 (DWS)
panel reinforcing, 37:48, 49 (DWS)

Piwarski, Frank: designs stoves, 42:68
(CBS)

Place of Houses, The (Moore, Allen and
Lyndon):
cited, 52:36 (TFH)
query list in, 45:102
reviewed, 45:116

Place to Live, A (film): reviewed, 1:66

Plain 'n Fancy Kitchens: address for,
65:73

Planers:
bevels with, jig for, 17:37 (DWS)
blade sharpener for, discontinued,
18:18
curved molding on, jig for, 76:73, 74-75
(FC)
dust collection for, 71:24
knife sharpener for, *in situ,* 65:96
new, mentioned, 82:92
portable, reviewed, 31:76
roller table for, site-built, 57:26
safety labels for, 37:81
workstation for, reviewed, 71:94
See also Molder/planers.

Planes:
block, 12:51, 76:80-82 (FC, TB)
choosing, 78:4-6
butt-mortise, 76:83-84 (FC)
reviewed, 49:95
chamfer, 76:83, 84 (FC)
compass, 11:40, 41 (DWS)
18th-century, reproduction of, 11:41
(DWS)
jack, 4:22 (TFH)
Japanese,
books on, 76:82 (FC)
tuning of, 8:16
using, 76:81, 82 (FC)
metal, restoring, 4:24-25 (TFH)
multi-, 11:37 (DWS)
power,
compared, by brand, 54:76-79
described, 54:76
11-in., 35:56 (TB)
safety with, 14:45 (TB)
sharpening, 14:45 (TB)

for timber framing, 4:22, 28:59 (CSH, TFH), 55:58
types of, 14:42 (TB)
rabbet, 4:22, 24 (TFH), 76:81 (FC)
rounding-over, 76:83, 84 (FC)
router, 4:22 (TFH)
sharpening, 76:84-85 (FC)
shoulder, 76:81, 83 (FC)
smooth, 4:22 (TFH)
soles of, truing, 76:81 (FC)
source for, 76:82-83 (FC)
tuning, 78:6
See also Sharpening.

Planetary Design Corp.:
address for, 71:106

Planet-Era Action New Shelter Institute:
address for, 72:98

Planned unit development (PUD):
Boulder (CO) requirements of, 10:42
explained, 19:46-47
See also Subdivisions.

Planning and Designing Lighting
(Effron): reviewed, 54:106

Plans:
book of, 4:62
Cracker-style energy-efficient, source for, 68:102
early collections of, 53:88
for Gypsy wagon, 50:87 (CSH)
historic,
books on, 52:10-12
source for, 47:44 (TFH), 52:8-12
for owner-builders, 5:14
for solar houses, 1:9, 5:16
stock,
discussed, 53:85-88
sources for, 53:89
storage for, 51:26
for superinsulated houses, 32:90
Victorian, 4:58, 71:71

Planters:
atop bookcases, 75:47, 49 (REM)
dormer niche for, 70:42-43
high cantilevered, 81:84
stone, large, 3:21, 25

Plants: pollution-fighting, 69:102

Plaster:
acrylic compound, 23:66
advantages of, 28:50 (FWS), 53:50 (SH)
thermal, 51:61
aging, 56:50, 51
applying, 31:59-62 (FWS)
over block, 15:74 (FWS)
over chimney, 75:45
bonding agents for, 15:74 (FWS), 23:10-12, 28:10, 43:10
books on, 31:80, 60:106, 62:20 (CSH), 77:120
brackets of, 28:52 (FWS)
castings of, 53:57
attaching, 60:16
source for, 51:85 (MFC)

ceiling in, coved, 6:19
cement, sprayed, 66:55
for chimneys,
curing, 75:45
finish-coat, 75:45
clay/dung, 30:30
cleaning, 4:18
compound for, quick-drying, 62:60
over concrete, 15:74 (FWS)
costs of, 31:62 (FWS)
coves in, matching, 15:10
cratered, reproducing, 12:8
crowns in,
carved, running, 67:12
curved, running, 67:12
curved, 63:55, 57 (REM)
cutlines on, readable, 84:28
cutting, 11:10
with reciprocating saw, 68:45 (FC)
decorative,
book on, 47:8
"compo" mix for, 47:6-8
composition molding of, 43:41-42 (FWS)
fibrous casting of, 43:41-43 (FWS)
materials for, 47:6
delamination of, discussed, 49:16-18
on domed ceiling, 34:61 (FRC)
drawbacks of, 31:62 (FWS)
drilling, vacuum for, 28:16
dust from, minimizing, 22:10
expansion joint for, sheet-metal, 34:61 (FRC)
exterior, premixed, 75:45
float for, carpeted, 20:78
for free-form walls, 66:55
glass fibers for, 23:12
glue bond for, 77:30
historic, research aid on, 65:55
holes in,
crackless, 54:26-28
cutting and trimming, 18:12
for horizontal surfaces, 26:41
insulation over, 31:8, 33:4
joint compound over, 28:10
on jute scrim, 5:32
Keene's, using, 34:64 (BK)
kinds of, proprietary, 23:12
lath for, 23:10-12
bonding agent for, liquid, 23:12-14
corner, for restoration, 23:12
Cornerite, 23:12
diamond-mesh copper-bearing, 17:12
Japanese, 4:54 (CSH)
metal, 31:58, 59 (FWS)
metal, right-side-up of, 22:67 (BK)
nails as, 32:73
rock, 20:76, 31:58 (FWS)
strip, for restoration, 23:12
vapor-barrier mesh-paper, 31:27 (CSH)

loose, dealing with, 2:6, 4:9
mixing, 20:76-78, 31:60, 61 (FWS)
moldings, 28:50-52 (FWS), 33:10
foam-core, 39:92
form for, 28:50-51 (FWS)
run-in-place, 57:40-42
thick, 19:74, 75, 77
mud, 43:33 (CSH)
mud and straw, 4:54 (TFH)
for no-paint surface, 46:73
old, problems with, 8:72
old-to-new matching of, system for, 4:19-20
ornamental,
painting, 57:42
repairing, 50:67, 68, 57:38-42
perlite, 31:58 (FWS)
perm rating of, 19:67
pigmented, 20:78
over plywood, 76:59
preserving, book on, 77:120-22
over pumice-crete, 77:56
quick-set, 34:64 (BK)
radiuses in, 31:58, 59 (FWS)
removing, 4:18, 13:39-40, 22:10
repairing, 5:6, 6:8-10, 9:10-12
booklet on, 72:108
chicken-wire skim-coat, 22:43
corner, 15:16-18
around new door, 68:46 (FC)
with scribed patch, 68:28
tips for, 72:108
restoration of, 56:85-86
book on, 24:86
risks with, 34:51 (TB)
sand, 31:58 (FWS)
using, 51:61
sculpture, exterior grotesque, 78:89
sealer for, 82:68
sealing, for paint, 12:8
skim coating of, 17:30, 32 (CSH)
Structo-Lite, 5:50
vs. stucco, 70:14
explained, 71:6, 74:6
over stucco netting, 5:50
supply sources for, 57:39, 40
Swedish putty, reproducing, 12:8
textured, smooth finish over, 28:10
three-coat, modern, 82:68
tools for, 31:4, 61
and trim, 31:62 (FWS)
two-coat, 31:58-62 (FWS)
as vapor barrier, 82:14
veneer,
base board for, 68:87
process of, 15:72-74, 28:10 (FWS)
system for, 4:19-20, 28:10
See also Adobe. Casting. Stucco.

Plaster of Paris:
  mixing, 1:37 (FWS)
  mold release for, 1:37 (FWS)
  See also Casting.
Plastering (Stagg and Pegg): reviewed, 31:80
Plastering Plain and Decorative (Millar): cited, 47:8
Plastering Skills (Branden and Hartsell): reviewed, 31:80, 77:120
Plaster-Weld: source for, 28:10, 43:10
Plastic:
  anchors, described, 41:56 (CBS)
  burning safely, 74:4
  honeycomb panels, 36:89
  supplier of, reviewed, 44:89
  See also *various kinds and forms.*
Plastic Components: address for, 50:95
Plastic solvent adhesives: *See* Glue.
Plastic laminate:
  applying, on both sides, 47:28
  backsplashes in, 75:65
  bending plywood for, 55:96
  over curves, 62:61
  designer nonglossy, 30:60 (BK)
  edgings for, hardwood, 69:51, 54, 78:66-67
  estimating for, 75:60
  filing, 75:64, 65
  filling, 78:67
  forms of, 75:60
  gluing, 30:61 (BK), 62:61, 75:64-65
    spacers for, 29:16, 61:24
    spray adhesive for, 75:62, 64
  inlaid, 49:62 (SH)
  moldings of, 77:42
  qualities of, discussed, 77:40-42
  samples of, express-mail, 69:102
  sawblades for, 30:60 (BK), 72:47 (MFC)
  seams in, 41:8, 75:61, 63-64
  sink clips with, 75:65
  striped, source for, 62:61
  substrate for, 75:61, 63
    acclimation of, 75:62-63
    attaching, 78:28, 79:8
  tools for, 75:60-61
  ungluing, 75:65, 77:8
  working with, 75:60-65
  See also Countertops.
Plastilene: molds from, 1:37 (FWS)
Plastique Exterior Tung Oil: mentioned, 17:64 (DWS)
Plate joinery: *See* Joinery: plate.
Plate rail:
  Arts-and-Crafts style, 22:59 (CSH)
  continuous pine, 67:36, 37
  sectioned, 63:48, 49
  self-scribing, two-piece, 18:12
Plates:
  caulking, 6:10
  curved, 31:70-71
    laminated, 7:17 (FRC)
  cutting, 3:34 (TB)

Key to books:

(BK)   Building Baths and Kitchens
(CBS)   Building with Concrete, Brick and Stone
(CSH)   Craftsman-Style Houses
(DWS) Building Doors, Windows and Skylights
(EEH)   Energy-Efficient Houses
(EF)   Exterior Finishing
(FC)   Finish Carpentry
(FRC)   Frame Carpentry
(FWS)   Building Floors, Walls and Stairs
(MFC)   More Frame Carpentry
(REM)   Remodeling
(SH)   Small Houses
(TB)   Tools for Building
(TFH)   Timber-Frame Houses

  defined, 3:33, 34 (TB)
  detailing, 22:33 (FRC)
  double top, 22:36 (FRC)
  exposed, anchors for, 29:74-75
  final fixing of, 23:69 (FRC)
  kinds of, defined, 21:71 (FRC)
  layout of, 21:69-77 (FRC)
  persuaders for, 39:10
    commercial, 39:10
  precuts in, 21:16
  reinforcing, for added load, 7:21-22 (BK)
  repairing, 6:38, 32:57-58 (FRC)
  roof, described, 10:63, 65 (FRC)
  structural consideration for, 27:4
  top,
    failure in, 6:36, 37 (FRC)
    lining up, 23:70-71 (FRC)
  wiring groove in, 6:10
Playhouses: Gothic, building, 61:43-45 (SH)
Pleko Products, Inc.:
  address for, 46:43
  source for, 18:8
Plexiglas:
  roof of, 38:66, 70
  source for, 10:33 (DWS)
  window of, large, 17:77 (SH)
  See also Glazing: acrylic.
Pliers:
  locking, for standing-seam roofing, 39:63
  for renovation, 12:51 (TB)
Plimoth Plantation: cruck building at, 42:43 (TFH)
Plinth: defined, 20:60 (FWS)
Plochere: address for, 55:74
Plug In Sure: cord lock, reviewed, 42:88
Plugs:
  cutting, on site, 67:28
  tapered, cutters for, 85:108

Plumb and line:
  braces for, 7:12, 8:10
  importance of, 23:68 (FRC)
  level for, extendable, 23:80
  of plates, 23:69 (FRC)
  plumb-bob hanging for, 50:30
  powder-actuated fasteners for, 23:69 (FRC)
  push stick for, 23:69 (FRC)
  scissor lever for, 8:12
  sequence for, 23:68 (FRC)
  solo, aid for, 72:88
Plumb bobs:
  chalk-box string storage for, 9:10
  door hanging with, 74:64-65 (FC)
  hanging, 50:30
  kinds of, 25:69 (TB)
  projecting points with, 25:67-69 (TB)
  reels for, 11:14, 28:6
  sheath for, 12:50 (TB)
  in spring-loaded reels, reviewed, 83:92
  steadying, 9:10, 69:32
  string for, 25:64, 69 (TB)
  tips for, making, 51:26
  wind-up, making, 24:22
Plumb Co.:
  broad hatchets, 30:49
  framing hammer, 23:32 (TB)
  rigging ax, 23:33 (TB)
Plumb cut: defined, 10:63 (FRC)
Plumbing:
  ABS vs. PVC pipe in, and disinfectant, 62:18 (CSH)
  adding, to remodel, 78:58
  air-gap inlet for, 54:46, 48
  and airtight drywall approach, 37:64
  anti-freeze for, safe, 57:4
  balloon stop-flow method for, 72:28
  in balloon-truss system, 24:69
  basement insulated box for, 7:7-8
  books on, 19:82, 54:48
  brass no-solder, 65:96
  cast-iron,
    dealing with, 17:53-54, 55 (BK)
    desirability of, 79:20
    vs. PVC, 74:60-61
  centralizing, 52:14
  chases for, 52:39 (TFH)
    ceiling, 65:51 (TFH)
    floor, 77:51, 52
    roof, 66:87
  cleanouts in, 29:54 (BK)
  closet flange for, offset, 17:53 (BK)
  codes on, sources for, 5:45, 29:51, 39:37 (BK)
  for cold climates, 10:52 (SH)
  components of, 29:51-52 (BK)
  copper for, 17:53 (BK)
  costly, 3:59 (EEH)
  designing, 81:4
  for dishwashers, 54:46-48
  and door retrofits, 68:43 (FC)

drainage system for, 44:39-40 (SH)
drain-line disguise for, 49:61, 62 (SH)
drain-line sizes for, 29:53 (BK), 49:52 (MFC)
earthquake proofing, 64:62, 64 (MFC)
faucets for, ceramic temperature-sensing, 75:92-94
faucets, plugging in, 7:10
fittings for,
  brass, 22:6-8
  Calder, 17:54, 55 (BK)
  dielectric, 17:52, 53, 21:4-6, 22:8 (BK)
  galvanized, quality of, 79:8
  glossary of, 29:55 (BK)
  plastic, 17:53, 54, 21:6 (BK)
fixtures for, European, 35:34
framing for, 49:51-53 (MFC)
freeze-proofing, 47:8
galvanized for, 17:53 (BK)
for handicapped, 53:70, 71
in kitchen soffits, 67:72, 73 (REM)
layout of, 29:52-54 (BK)
lead in, avoiding, 73:67
line sealer for, source for, 60:54
locating, with volt meter and nail, 76:30
materials for, 29:52 (BK)
noise elimination in, 36:10, 58:54, 79:20, 82:6
odors from,
  diagnosing, 62:18 (CSH)
  killing, 62:18 (CSH)
old, evaluating, 17:53 (BK)
openings for, sealing, 78:70
outlets for, oversized, 5:35
pipe isolators for, 36:10
pipe supports for, 10:40 (BK)
pipe-cutting jig for, 63:26
plastic, book on, 33:88
with plastic pipe, cut-off jig for, 74:24
plastic-drain,
  insulating, 79:20
  quieting, 82:6
polybutylene, source for, 60:54
punctured, finding, 56:26
in rammed-earth building, 34:38
repairing, with radiator hose, 30:10
in restorations, 24:86, 29:65, 67
in sand foundation base, 8:38, 39 (EEH)
sealing walls around, 66:66 (EEH)
sheathing around, 37:67 (FRC)
sizing, 78:74-75
  supply-line, 48:12-14
in slab-on-grade, 60:53-54
society for, 76:106
solder with, lead-free, using, 57:14
sources for, mail-order, 44:4
with steel framing, 32:71 (FRC)
tees in, adding new, 17:52, 53, 54 (BK)
in timber frames, 79:54
tool bags for, 42:66 (TB)
tool kit for, 39:37 (BK)
trap-arm considerations in, 29:54 (BK)

tree for, 4:33
in truss frames, 5:57 (FRC)
tubing cutter for, racheting, 53:94
valves for, pressure-balancing, 53:70
and vapor barriers, 9:59, 24:82, 29:70, 72
vent stacks for,
  flashing, 56:80
  locating holes for, 63:28
vents for, 1:34-35, 29:53-54 (BK)
  alternatives to, 5:35
  flashing of, 9:50 (SH)
  mechanical, 4:4
  placement of, 44:41 (SH)
  sealing, 61:76 (EF)
Vola components for, 1:62
waste lines in, exposed copper, 43:73, 74 (SH)
water lines of, dry-ice freezing, 76:28
water-conserving, books on, 5:12
for wetlands, 57:63-64
See also Hot tubs. Hot-water heaters. Metals: galvanic corrosion. Septic-tank systems. Showers. Sinks. Soldering. Sprinkler systems. Toilets.
Plumbing for Dummies (Fredricksson):
  mentioned, 19:82
Plumb-It:
  address for, 58:44
  level, source for, 23:80
Plumleigh, Laird: ceramics by, 59:88-89
Pluswood Indiana: address for, 81:72
Plywood:
  air/vapor barrier for, 42:60-61
  associations for, 3:9, 51:82, 58:75, 63:65, 67:81, 72:98, 83:45, 85:118 (MFC)
  avoiding, 46:70-73
    through alternatives, 73:67
  batten system for, 19:32, 33
  benderboard, for dormer framing, 65:84 (MFC)
  bending, 83:62-63
    reviewed, 55:96
  box beams from, information on, 72:98
  Bruynzeel, 9:21, 22
  buckle prevention for, 81:57, 58
  building with, book on, 4:62
  for cabinets, 30:59-60 (BK)
  carriers for, 7:12, 42:20 (CSH)
  carts for, 81:92, 83:30
  CDX, perm rating of, 19:67
    as sheathing, 19:68
  characteristics of, 32:33 (FRC)
  clips for,
    metal, 43:49 (FRC)
    ply, 37:68 (FRC)
  corrugated, 36:89
  curving, 7:19-20 (FRC)
  cutting,
    chainsaw, 78:40
    guides for, 76:63-64 (MFC)
    jig for, 1:22-23 (TB)

  no-splinter methods for, 76:63-65 (MFC), 77:10
  production, 74:76
  table for, simple, 81:67
for decking, 37:66 (FRC)
delivery of, forklift, 37:67 (FRC)
Douglas-fir vs. yellow pine, moisture absorption of, 81:57
doweled, to hardwood, 69:51, 53
edgings for, 30:60 (BK)
  wood, 19:14, 69:51, 53, 78:66-67
exterior,
  glues in, 73:68
  grades of, 71:6
for floors, 19:59-60, 80:71 (FRC)
for forms, 44:34-37 (CBS)
  release-coated, 69:96
  reusing, 66:84
  source for, 78:48
foundations of, 5:40-42 (FRC)
framing with, books on, 84:49
house of, early, 19:28-33
hurricane-proofness of, 78:85
and hurricanes, post-Andrew codes for, 85:118-20
information on, 65:53
interior vs. exterior, 70:14
jointed, twin-arrow, reviewed, 53:98
jointing, table-saw, 44:24
kerfing, for bend, 68:58
low-toxicity, source for, 56:6
manufacture of, early, 19:32
marking of, with masking-tape, 76:65 (MFC)
medium density overlay (MDO), for jigs, 28:39 (FWS)
nail pattern for, 54:61
nail removal from, tool for, 32:54 (TB)
nails for, 85:46-47
nine-ply, 58:39 (REM)
vs. OSB, in hurricanes, 79:4
overlay for, hardwood, applying, 69:52-53
pickup cargo system for, 78:28
pilferage protection for, 21:16
rabbet-dado for, 30:60 (BK)
sawblades for, 72:47 (MFC)
  jigsaw, 33:60 (TB)
sealant for, 46:73
sealer for, tilework, 51:63
for sheathing, 37:67 (FRC)
sheathing platform for, 37:68 (FRC)
siding from, 83:42-43
siding gauge for, 5:7
staples for, 37:69 (FRC)
strength of, as joist sisters, 68:16
for subfloors, 13:42, 43 (FWS)
  test report on, 81:102-104

supply of, in crises, 78:100-102
table-saw extensions for, 30:60, 61 (BK)
tongue-and-groove,
    installing, 19:59, 60, 20:14, 40:4, 47:30
        (FRC)
    persuader for, 43:20
    on roofs, 37:68 (FRC)
treated, toxicity of, 56:14
types of, 37:69 (FRC)
T-111 siding, 3:57, 58, 59, 20:10 (EEH)
    for roof, 20:10
U.S.-Canadian tariffs on, 81:106
veneer for, iron-on, 69:53
veneer-core, water-resistant, 9:21, 22
See also Foundations: all-weather
    wood.
Plywood Design Specification:
mentioned, 18:14
Pneumatic tools: See Air compressors.
Pocket Caddy: reviewed, 63:92-94
**Pocket Guide to the National Electric
Code** (Fischer): reviewed, 44:94
Pocket Size Carpenter's Helper, The
(Bailey): reviewed, 46:104
Poison Control Center: national number
for, 42:57 (DWS)
Polaroid Business System: address for,
68:96
Pole building:
backfilling for, 17:45 (SH)
books on, 8:70, 15:37, 83:77
bracing for, 67:4
and cantilevered construction, 15:27-29
ceramic "lids" for, 49:26
construction of, 8:65, 9:43-45, 15:32-36,
    17:40-45 (EEH)
with exterior poles, 15:32-36, 17:40-45
    (SH)
flashing for, movable, 39:28, 29-31
against flooding, 3:56-57 (EEH)
with interior poles, advantages of, 15:28
logs for, 9:43
off-square, dealing with, 39:28-29
plumbing, 15:35-36
pole preservatives for, 15:27, 37
pole setting for, 15:28, 34-35, 83:78
poles for, harvesting, 64:58-59
on rock, 39:27-28
sites for, 15:27, 32
Sonotube-reinforced, 39:28
staircases in, 39:29, 30, 31
three-story, 15:26-27, 28-29
twelve-level, 39:26-32
Pole Building Design: source for, 15:37
Pollack, Roslyn G.: on builder liability,
49:76-77

Pollman, Dieter: quoted, 35:59 (TB)
Pollock, Roger: bookcase by, 58:86
Poly Plastic and Design Corp.: laminated
polyethylene of, 19:22
Poly-C insulation: source for, 31:38 (CBS)
Polycel One: source for, 15:59
Polycutter pneumatic cutter: reviewed,
43:92
Polydrain: address for, 50:85
Polyester resin: molds from, 1:37 (FWS)
Polyethylene:
aluminized, cost of, 8:30 (TFH)
/asphalt, 25:72, 29:12
for AWWF wrap, 68:65
below-ground use of, 2:35
cold-weather handling of, 51:42
cross-laminated, source for, 19:22, 34:68
    (SH)
degrade of, heated, 34:69 (SH)
durability of, 22:18 (CSH)
40-mil, 22:12, 32:46-47, (BK)
for gravel-bed foundation, 68:64
mentioned, 19:22
perm rating of, 19:67
seamless, 46:71-72
sheeting,
    air/vapor barrier, 15:59, 19:22, 68,
        20:36, 21:59, 25:82, 29:68, 31:8, 34:68,
        39:90, 43:73, 61:106 (EEH, SH)
    air/vapor barrier, Swedish standards
        for, 22:18 (CSH)
for sod roofs, 51:45
source for, 29:68
3-ply, 36:12
tubing of, high-density, for floor
    heating, 22:68 (CBS)
using, 34:68 (SH)
UV-stabilized,
    avoiding, 46:70-73
    puncture-resistant, 68:64
vapor barriers of, case against, 37:62, 65
Polyisocyanurate insulation: See
Insulation: polyisocyanurate.
Polymer Extruded Products Inc.: Korad
acrylic film, 24:46, 28:6
Polyplastex International: Synskyn, 39:74
Polypropylene: for radiant-floor heating,
22:68 (CBS)
Polyseamseal: address for, 68:45 (FC)
Polyshim tape: source for, 11:63 (DWS)
Polystyrene:
in earth-sheltered roofs, 16:52
expanded,
    adhesives for, 24:59
    ant susceptibility of, 20:6
    fire ratings of, 24:59
    flammability of, 13:4
    for foundations, 26:10
    heat deformation of, 24:59

perm rating of, 18:33, 19:67, 24:55, 59
    (CBS)
over plates, 33:4
for roofs, 20:10
extruded,
    for foundations, 18:8, 33, 26:10, 43:20
    resistance of, to ants, 20:6
mastic for, waterproof, 18:34 (CBS)
mentioned, 18:33 (CBS)
for models, 42:49 (FWS)
ozone depletion and, 49:102
perm rating for, 19:67
over plaster, 33:4
See also Stress-skin panels.
Polyurethane:
avoiding, 73:67
foam,
    with acrylic, 10:33 (DWS)
    as adhesives, discussed, 65:41, 44
    over adobe, 22:43
    casting with, 1:38-39 (FWS)
    under concrete, commercial sheets
        for, 24:76
    as exterior spray, 13:6
    vs. fiberglass, for roofs, 24:6
    fire ratings of, 24:59
    fire-retardant barrier for, sprayed,
        33:75
    foil-faced boards of, using, 19:68,
        20:10
    over metal, 33:75
    perm rating for, 19:67, 24:55, 58-59
    as slab insulation, 26:10
    source for, 1:39 (FWS)
    spray, two-part system of, 20:31
    on stone masonry, 15:14
insulation, ozone depletion and, 49:102
nontoxic, sources for, 67:92
See also Membranes. Paint. Varnish.
Polyvinyl chloride (PVC):
paint for, 50:49
pipe cement, for gluing electrical tape,
    9:12
sheets, below-ground use of, 2:35
See also Membranes. Pipe.
Poly-void packing: source for, 37:49
(DWS)
Pomada, Elizabeth, and Michael Larsen:
Daughters of Painted Ladies, cited, 66:47
Painted Ladies Revisited, cited, 66:47
Pond Publishers:
address for, 53:89
Ponds:
backyard building of, 13:6
books on, 13:6
See also Pools.
Ponds and Water Gardens (Heritage):
cited, 13:6
Pony walls: defined, 19:55 (FRC)

Pools:
   artesian, 59:58, 61
   constructing, 12:48, 49, 80:66, 67
   as heat storage, 12:48
   interior/exterior, 3:21, 23, 26, 27
   of limestone block, 38:66
   waterproofing membrane for, 20:12,
      24:86
Pope, George: cabin by, 18:84
Poplar Forest: building of, 42:74-79
Popovac, Vladimir: on masonry stoves,
   71:50-54
Porcelain: refinishing, 44:10
Porches:
   adding, 65:24
   Arts-and-Crafts style, 59:52-53 (CSH)
   bench balustrade for, 66:89
   brackets of, backing for, 75:74
   brownstone, repairing, 9:21-24
   cantilevering, 72:82 (REM)
   Colonial,
      addition, 5:22-24
      arched, 63:45, 46
   columns for,
      commercial, 73:50
      replacing, 2:15-17, 23
   for cooling, 40:74, 76 (EEH)
   curved ends for, 52:53, 54
   decking of, replacing, 2:17
   decks with, 6:22-23
   detailing for, 26:72, 77
   early Southern, 29:49
   entablature for, 6:24-25
   false-front, 42:112
   fascia of, replacing, 2:16, 17
   finish for, 27:55
   flashing, 75:73
   floors,
      flashing for, 57:28
      framing for, 73:50
      screens for, 72:82 (REM), 77:30-32
   foundations for, 75:74
   fungi protection with, 72:66 (REM)
   Galveston ornate, 39:78-79
   glossary of, 29:48
   Greek Revival, adding, 6:22-25
   grills for, notched pine, 4:65
   for handicapped, 53:71
   handrails for, 2:16, 17
   history of, 29:47, 50
   jacking up, 2:14-15
   with latticed gables, 28:73, 74
   membranes for, torch-down, 66:50
   narrow east, 84:89
   new, 29:50
   ornamental work of, 14:60-61
   pickets for, 2:16, 17
   repairs for, 75:72-74
   under roof monitor, 19:47, 48, 49
   roofs for, 6:24
      extensions for, 14:24-25
      lightweight, 72:82, 83 (REM)

   rot-resistant, building, 81:44-47
   for saltboxes, 37:36, 37
   screened, 66:37 (SH), 73:86, 80:52, 53
      building, 51:50-53, 72:81-83 (REM)
      sleeping, 36:70, 71
      small, 74:55
      splined no-paint, 75:94
   sculptural studio, 2:56-59
   second-level, 26:72-75
   sequential, to core, 15:64-65
   shed-dormer, 24:47-51 (FRC)
   shoring, for repairs, 69:67-68 (REM)
   solar-pool enclosure, 12:47-49
   solar-room conversion of, 15:42-43
   Spanish-style, 38:66, 67, 69, 70
   for sun moderation, 34:10
   of sunken sunspace, 19:47, 48, 49
   timber-framed, 5:12
   as transitional spaces, 80:52
   Victorian,
      four-square, adding, 71:60-63 (REM)
      new small, 71:73
      tiny, 48:70, 73 (SH)
      two-story, building, 66:48-50
   See also Decks. Porticoes. Screens.
      Stoops. Verandahs.
POR-ROK concrete: source for, 34:64 (BK)
**Port Austin Level and Tool
   Manufacturing Co.:** address for, 58:45
**Port Orford cedar (Chamaecyparis
   lawsoniana):**
   for framing, 4:54 (TFH)
   floors of, 4:56 (TFH)
   house in, 43:28-33 (CSH)
Port Townsend (WA) Boatworks: trusses
   by, 39:69 (TFH)
Porta-Nails, Inc.: address for, 49:66
Porta-Tools: nail guns, 13:45 (FWS)
Porter, Tom: Architectural Color, cited,
   74:45 (EF)
Porter (W. H.) Inc.: address for, 67:35
**Porter-Cable Professional Power Tools,
   Inc.:**
   address for, 48:62 (FC, MFC), 63:75, 70:53
      (FC), 74:92
   circular saws, reviewed, 63:75, 77
   discussed, 18:18
   door buck, 31:30 (TB)
   drills,
      cordless, #800, 35:38, 40-42 (TB)
      VSR, reviewed, 82:36-41
   hinge butt mortising template, 31:29, 30-
      31 (TB)
   jigsaw blades, 33:60 (TB)
   jigsaws, 26:82
      model 7648, 33:58, 59, 61, 62 (TB)
   laminate stripper, 75:61
   laminate trimmer, 75:61
   lock mortiser, 81:61

   miter saw #7700, reviewed, 85:104-106
   plunge routers,
      model 693, reviewed, 57:96
      reviewed, 71:79, 82-83, 84 (FC)
   pocket cutter, reviewed, 83:92-96
   Power Block Plane #167, 14:42 (TB)
   power planes, reviewed, 54:76, 77, 78-79
   random-orbit sanders, reviewed, 64:94-
      96, 77:69, 70-71, 72, 73
   router #690, for mortising, 31:29 (TB)
   Saw Boss, reviewed, 44:88
   screw guns, 34:43, 45 (TB)
   Speedtronic 7¼-in. saw, 18:18, 24:41 (TB)
   Tiger Saw reciprocating saw, 16:45, 46,
      49 (TB)
      reviewed, 41:84
   trim saw #314, reviewed, 48:40-43
   Versa Plane #653, 14:42, 43 (TB)
   worm-drive saw, 4½-in., 24:40 (TB)
   See also Rockwell.
Portholes: stained-glass, 52:45
Porticoes:
   defined, 29:48
   dome-and-column, 50:56-57
   restoring, 61:67-70
Portland cement:
   as adhesive, 65:41, 45
   See also Concrete.
Portland Cement Association:
   address for, 47:60, 55:68, 62:20 (CSH),
      65:53, 71:16
   Cement Mason's Guide, 44:14
   on concrete mesh, 48:90
   Critique of Plywood Basements and Wood
      Foundations, A, 23:49
   on efflorescence, 25:10
   Homeowner's Guide to Building with
      Concrete, Brick and Stone, The, 62:112
   information from, 44:37 (CBS)
   pamphlet from, on control joints, 44:37
      (CBS)
   Plaster and Stucco Manual, The, 62:20
      (CSH)
   publications from, 23:50
   Recommended Practices for Laying
      Concrete Block, 46:104
   Resurfacing Concrete Floors, 15:14
   services of, 23:50
   slab-repair information from, 32:10
   water cautions of, 30:67 (CBS)
**Portland Cement Plaster (Stucco)
   Manual:** source for, 47:60
Portland General Electric: heat-pump
   water-heater policy of, 5:65
Portland (ME) Museum of Art: Federal
   fence of, 25:73-77
Positive Energy Conservation Products:
   address for, 46:45
Post, Irwin L.: on insulated doors, 10:46-
   47 (DWS)

Post, Irwin L. and Diane L.: on wood foundations, 5:40-42 (FRC)

Post, Jerry: gate post by, 48:84

Post-and-beam construction:
adding,
to existing wall, 12:47-48
second-story, 9:29, 30, 31
beams for, composite, 3:57, 58, 8:39 (EEH)
bolted, 46:62, 63 (TFH)
butt joints for, strapped, 1:54
California style, 1:52-55
cantilevered, with braces, 55:71
columns for, metal, 48:50-51, 53
connectors for,
intersect custom, 39:72
joist hangers for, 19:69, 70 (EEH)
post-to-concrete, 39:53, 72 (CSH)
for double envelopes, 11:66, 67, 68
earthquake-proofing, 64:60-61 (MFC)
flanges for, 3:57, 58 (EEH)
floors for, plank-and-beam, 33:41-43 (FWS)
Greene-and-Greene style, 22:55-57 (CSH)
gusset plates for, angled, 19:69, 70 (EEH)
insulation,
hung-wall, 8:28-30 (TFH)
retrofit for, 39:10
joinery for, 39:72
laminated,
Japanese-influenced, 16:58-64 (TFH)
site-built, 75:80-81, 82-83
light, 50:79-81 (SH)
mentioned, 46:49-53 (EEH)
modular, laminated, 2:28, 29
nailed, designing, 40:71-72 (FRC)
panels for,
cam-locking, 46:81-82 (TFH)
concrete, 48:48-53
post caps for, 39:74
rebar with, 1:54
Rex Roberts-modified, 28:69-70
shell for, insulated, 19:70-71 (EEH)
for sodded solar cube, 34:28, 29 (DWS)
for spa, 58:59, 61 (CSH)
for steep sites, 39:71
tree support in, 6:67 (FRC)
trusses in, curved, 27:26-31
wiring for, 39:74
by women, 13:18
See also Saltboxes. Stress-skin panels. Timber framing.

Post-Modernism: banality of, 38:100-102

Posts:
anchors for, metal, 57:65-66
on block walls, prescriptions for, 83:18
carved, 25:27-28, 30
connectors for, 43:45-46, 48, 49 (FRC), 79:69
copper caps for, 72:40
cut-off jig for, 40:16
exterior, end-grain sealer for, 72:41
fake, building, 65:51 (TFH)
frost jacking of, preventing, 79:66
gate, Galveston, 39:79
gunstock, carved, 28:59-60 (TFH)
holes for, digging, 79:67, 69
of laminated teak, 49:44-45
plumbing trick for, 41:14
porch, repairing, 75:74
with preservatives, and end grain, 55:20
puller for, 79:30
removing, 77:32, 81:28
round, pouring, 79:67-69
scribing to, 77:62-63
socket for, metal, commercial, 56:92
straps for, 4:65
wooden, setting, 79:68
See also Beams.

Potlatch Corp.: address for, 55:60

Pottery House:
building of, 41:26-31
original, 41:31

Pound, Albert: on shoji sash, 8:75

Poured Concrete Wall Contractors Association of America: address for, 48:69

Powder-Actuated Tool Manufacturers' Institute: Powder-Actuated Fastening Systems Basic Training Manual, 21:34 (TB)

Powder-actuated tools: See Tools.

Powell, Niles T.: on copper soldering, 10:40-41 (BK)

Power inverters: reviewed, 51:92

Power Tool Institute:
Safety Is Specific, 34:55 (TB)
safety manuals of, 22:6

Powernail Co.: address for, 49:66

Powers, Alan: as joint author. See Aslet, Clive.

Pozzi Window Co.:
address for, 55:79, 76:75 (FC), 84:86
windows of, 60:48, 51 (FC)

PPG Architectural Finishes: address for, 83:86

PPG Industries:
Duranar paint, 24:46
high-performance glass of, discussed, 41:84-86

Practical Electrical Wiring (Schwan): mentioned, 8:45

Practical Home Energy Savings (Bill): reviewed, 76:118

Practical House Carpenter, The (Benjamin): mentioned, 1:49

Practical Photovoltaics (Komp): cited, 62:71

Practical Pole Building Construction (Seddon): cited, 83:77

Practical Stonemasonry Made Easy (Kennedy): source for, 44:57

Praeger Brush Co.:
address for, 48:78
white China bristle brushes, 42:59 (DWS)

Prairie School: house after, 52:62-67

Prather, Fred: on architects, 20:26

Pratt and Lambert, Inc.:
address for, 54:57, 72:62, 81:47
Fabuloy, 44:41 (SH)
stain, 32:27 (CSH)
Water Beader, 30:49

Pratt house: restoration of, 72:36-41

PRC sealant: qualities of, 9:56

Precast Lintels for Concrete Masonry Construction: source for, 74:50

Precedents in Architecture (Clark and Pause): reviewed, 45:120

Prefabricated houses:
Arts-and-Crafts style, source for, 54:100
metal-shed, 33:73-75
Scandinavian, 23:84
at conference, 28:82
small modular, 5:14
steel, 22:26-30
Wallframe system for, customized, 62:72-77
See also Mail-order. Sears, Roebuck. Small houses.

Preiss, Richard: reviews rail-boring jigs, 63:90

Prentice, Blair: as joint author. See Kapland, Helain S.

Prentiss, Jeffrey: on San Juan Island cabin, 52:36-40 (TFH)

Prescolite, Inc.: address for, 69:49 (EF)

Preserva Products, Inc.: address for, 73:68

Preservation: See Historic preservation. Restoration.

Preservation and Conservation:
reviewed, 4:58
source for, 5:39

Preservation and Energy Conservation (slides): mentioned, 1:66

Preservation Assistance Division, Park Service: address for, 65:55

Preservation Briefs (National Park Service): reviewed, 72:108
Preservation Briefs No. 1 (Mack), mentioned, 4:4

Preservation Institute for the Building Crafts (Windsor, VT): 1985 workshop by, 27:82-83

Preservatives: See Wood preservatives.

Pressure Sensitive Tape Council: address for, 65:45

Pressure testing: as marketing tool, 22:18 (CSH)

Prestique Plus: address for, 59:55 (CSH)

Prest-On: address for, 84:48

Prestressed Concrete Institute: hollow-core plank information from, 25:71

Prevention of Cracked Ceramic Tile Thin-set over Concrete Slabs: source for, 23:50

Preway Heat Mizer fireplace:
mentioned, 1:45 (EEH)
source for, 10:44

Priat, Roland: mentioned, 33:65, 67

Price Brothers Tool Co.:
address for, 74:78, 85:60
Versa-Level, 42:86-88

Price, Don:
on cobblestone cottage, 54:83 (TFH)
on garage apartment, 69:62-63 (REM)
on Island cabin, 46:80-83 (TFH)

Primavera Systems: address for, 69:80

Prince, Bart:
on solar building, 11:54-58
on studio addition, 2:56-59

Princeton Energy Group: on acrylic glazing, 10:30, 31, 32, 33 (DWS)

Princeton Plans Press: plans from, 53:86, 89

Principles of Attic Ventilation: cited, 56:41

Principles of Low Energy Building Design in Warm, Humid Climates: reviewed, 30:80

Privy (Strombeck): cited, 53:89

Procedure for Classification of Stains Which Develop on Wood in Service (Dost): cited, 47:16

Procon: vane pump, 29:88

Proctor, Jody: mentioned, 29:30

Proctor, Robert: mentioned, 28:81

Proctor Products Co.:
address for, 56:62 (EEH)
Little Pee-Vee, 39:10
wall jacks of, 22:38 (FRC)

Product Application Guide: cited, 71:59 (MFC)

Production of Houses, The (Alexander *et al.*): reviewed, 33:88

Products Research and Chemical Corp.: address for, 70:49

Professional Dome Plans (Hill): reviewed, 65:108

Professional Handbook of Building Construction, The (Allen): *See Fundamentals of Building Construction* (Allen).

Progressive Power Tools Corp.: chainsaw/bandsaw blade, 39:90

Project Notebook (LeGwin): reviewed, 77:122

Prokosch, Andy: mentioned, 5:14

Proper Use and Care of Hand Tools, Pliers, Screwdrivers, Wrenches, Striking & Struck Tools: source for, 34:55 (TB)

Key to books:

(BK)	Building Baths and Kitchens
(CBS)	Building with Concrete, Brick and Stone
(CSH)	Craftsman-Style Houses
(DWS)	Building Doors, Windows and Skylights
(EEH)	Energy-Efficient Houses
(EF)	Exterior Finishing
(FC)	Finish Carpentry
(FRC)	Frame Carpentry
(FWS)	Building Floors, Walls and Stairs
(MFC)	More Frame Carpentry
(REM)	Remodeling
(SH)	Small Houses
(TB)	Tools for Building
(TFH)	Timber-Frame Houses

Propylene glycol: as collector fluid, 1:30

Proskiw, Gary: in R-2000 program, 34:86

ProSoCo, Inc.:
address for, 84:72
Sure Klean Efflorescence Control System, 25:10
Sure Klean 600 Detergent, 43:55 (CBS)

Prosopis: *See* Mesquite.

Protech Systems Inc.: address for, 70:79

Protractors: combination, source for, 67:90

Prowler, Donald: *Modest Mansions,* reviewed, 40:90

Prudential Metal Supply Corp.: copper nails of, 20:42 (EF)

Prusa, Dave: mentioned, 38:38 (CSH)

Prusa, Rudy: mentioned, 38:38 (CSH)

Prybars: *See* Wrecking bars.

Pseudotsuga menziesii: See Douglas fir.

PTI: glazing tape from, 25:12

Publication Index: on structural plywood, source for, 23:49

Publicover, Scott: on excavating wine cellar, 81:68-71

PUD: *See* Planned Unit Development (PUD).

Pueblo Bonito:
research center of, 18:63
stone-veneer types in, 18:63, 64

Puget Power: heat-pump water-heater policy of, 5:65

Pulleys:
source for, 13:49 (DWS)
for timbers, 8:31

Pulls:
aluminum extruded, 62:61
bit for, 46:41 (REM)
source for, 83:72
cabinet,
jig for, 43:20
rubber, 30:58-59 (BK)
chrome, source for, 75:49 (REM)

copper test-cap, 70:91
cross-shaped, 67:72, 75, 76 (REM)
drawer, 30:58-59 (BK)
finger, bits for, 83:72
hand-forged, 67:57
installation jig for, multi-purpose, 71:26
making, 42:34 (DWS)
neoprene, source for, 66:50
for pocket doors, 54:66 (FC)
porcelain, 71:72
from resin board,
chunks, 66:55
sculpted, 66:55
routed, 83:70, 72
source for, 30:59 (BK)
template for, 85:52

Puls, Ric: on worksite table, 81:67

Pulsifer, Daphne: gate by, 52:89

Pumice:
quarried, in roofs, 5:50
See also Block: pumice. Concrete: pumice.

Pumps:
bilge, source for, double-action, 67:63
DC, source for, 24:82
foot-operated galley, source for, 67:63
geared magnetic, 29:88
$\frac{1}{25}$-hp, 72:14
pitcher, source for, 10:55 (BK)
solar-powered, sources for, 60:16
submersible, grounding codes for, 67:96
sump, discussed, 50:86

Punches: self-centering screw, 12:51 (TB)

Purafil, Inc.: address for, 46:72

Purdy Inc.: address for, 48:78, 67:69

Pureheart Redwood: address for, 70:106

Purlins:
built-up, 52:59 (CSH)
defined, 10:63, 67, 68 (FRC)
hangers for, 43:45, 46-47 (FRC)
installing, 4:45-47, 10:68, 69 (FRC), 60:86-87 (MFC)
log, 53:6
exposed, 44:38-41 (SH)
method for, 10:63, 67, 68-69 (FRC)
for octagonal roof, 34:60-61 (FRC)
sizing, 4:46 (FRC)

Purpleheart (*Peltogyne* spp.):
with fir, 35:34
framing with, 57:68-70 (TFH)

Purpose-made Joinery (Foad): reviewed, 69:108-10

Purser, Michael W.: on floor finish, 67:52-55, 85:61-63

Push brooms: strengthening, 24:24

Put-Line portable drafting board: reviewed, 56:94

Putnam, R. E., and G. E. Carlson: *Architectural and Building Trades,* reviewed, 47:112

Putnam Rolling Ladder Co., Inc.: address for, 52:98, 55:86, 84:55

Putting Food By (Hertzberg, Vaughan and Greene): cited, 72:14

Putty:
application of, 47:52 (EF)
colored, source for, 69:4
exterior, applying, 62:41 (EF)
knives for,
cleaning, 24:24
for renovation, 12:51 (TB)
loosening, 5:7
nontoxic, sources for, 67:90-92
for paint preparation, 62:41 (EF)
softener for, 60:26-28
source for, 62:41 (EF)
See also Fillers.

PVC: *See* Gaskets. Polyvinyl chloride.

Pye, David: *Nature and Art of Workmanship, The,* cited, 23:6, 52:58 (CSH)

Pyramid house: advantages of, 23:72

Pyrok, Inc.: address for, 70:63 (EEH)

Q-Bond Corp. of America: surface-bonding mix, 12:37 (CBS)

Q-Dot Corp.: heat-pipe heat-recovery ventilator, 34:33, 34 (DWS)

Quad-pane windows: source for, 34:68 (SH)

Quality Building Conference & Exhibition: discussed, 72:100

Quality Hardware Manufacturing Co., Inc.: address for, 54:65 (FC)

Qualls, George: mentioned, 33:26

Qually, Paul: house by, 27:64-65

Quantum Chemical: address for, 50:60

Quarton, Barr: hand-forged tools from, reviewed, 49:95

Quarve-Peterson, Julee: *Accessibility Book, The,* reviewed, 63:106

Quercus: See Oak.

Quick Wall surface-bonding mix: source for, 12:37 (CBS)

Quic-kut outlet cutter: source for, 23:61 (FWS)

Quiet Indoor Revolution, The (Konzo and MacDonald): reviewed, 81:114, 83:6

Quik Bolt: source for, 29:34 (FRC)

Quik Drive Fastening Systems, Ltd.: address for, 62:94

Quik Drive U.S.A., Inc.: screw gun, reviewed, 85:70-71

Quikcrete surface-bonding mix: source for, 12:37 (CBS)

Quinlan, Mike: mentioned, 30:66 (CBS)

Quinn, Peter: house by, 43:72-74 (SH)

Quinn, William: on water-tower house, 24:92

Quivik, Fred: at superinsulation conference, 22:18 (CSH)

Quoins:
block for, stuccoed, 54:87 (TFH)
stone, cutting, 37:58

Quonset huts:
contemporary rendering of, 33:24-30
history of, 33:73
made-over, 67:20

R. B. Industries: molder/planers, reviewed, 55:50-55

Rabbets: with router, 18:74-76 (DWS)

Rabbitt, Patrick: on framing turret, 68:56-59

Racal Health & Safety: address for, 58:90

Rack-R: address for, 72:88

Radial-arm saws:
benchtop, 36:88
cold-weather precautions for, 50:60
with compound-miter capacity, reviewed, 57:59, 60-61
fences for, sliding-stop, 74:76
kerfing with, 82:61
miter jigs for, 17:16
newel-post shaping with, 6:21 (CSH)
portable, 36:88
radial-table, reviewed, 46:90
Rockwell, safety retrofits for, 43:96
safety with, 34:53, 55, 37:14 (TB)
labels for, 37:81
stands for,
from steel desks, 58:24
wheeled storage, 69:71-72
steel-cutting wheel for, 32:68 (FRC)
for tenons, double-bladed, 36:49 (TFH)
for timber framing, 36:48, 49, 50 (TFH)
See also Table saws: Norwegian turntable.

Radiant barriers:
association for, 58:98
described, 49:75 (EEH), 52:68
and heat buildup, 40:12
method for, 58:96-98
publications on, 58:98
for roofs, 70:18

Radiant Technology: address for, 59:102

Radiantec Co.: address for, 85:87

Radiant-floor heating:
Alaskan, 19:69-70 (EEH)
automated, 53:76
with brick floors, 37:10
cast-iron, 12:28, 32
commercial, 73:45 (EEH)

concrete for, 27:69 (CBS)
in concrete, 80:49, 82:68
ceiling, 30:37, 39
slab-on-grade, 60:55
controls for, 18:6, 22:69-70, 71, 27:70-71, 29:4-6 (CBS)
copper,
life span of, 27:69 (CBS)
and sand, 38:34
design for, 22:69, 71, 24:10, 26:4, 27:69-70, 58:61, 60:55 (CBS, CSH)
durability of, 18:6
electric, 30:23, 75:69-72
and electromagnetic fields, danger from, 82:20 (CSH)
failure of, 81:80, 82
with fireplace duct, 66:39 (SH)
heat sources for, 22:70, 27:71 (CBS)
heat-transfer plates for, 85:87
history of, 22:68 (CBS)
installing, 22:70, 26:4, 12, 27:71 (CBS), 62:74
with metal pans, 60:58-59 (EEH)
polybutylene, 21:12, 26:4, 27:70-71 (CBS)
oxidation in, 81:82
publications on, source for, 65:102
in slab,
floor coverings over, 24:10
insulation for, 22:69 (CBS)
suspended, 58:59-61 (CSH)
wood over, 18:6, 24:10
solar, 14:10, 16:4, 30:38, 37:10, 68:53
collectors for, 30:38
under subfloors, plywood, 85:86-87
supply source for, 62:74
system for, 51:74-75 (EEH), 58:60-61 (CSH), 73:81
with tile floors, 85:87
tubing for, 22:68 (CBS), 77:54
Swedish, 58:61 (CSH)
underperformance of, 22:68 (CBS)
under wood, 6:66, 18:6, 24:10, 38:75-77 (TFH)
with wood stoves, 26:12
in Wright house, 3:23
See also Masonry stoves: k'ang.

Radiators:
old, using, 67:72, 76 (REM)
Swedish low-profile, source for, 38:28 (EEH)
thin-profile, reviewed, 59:102
wood covers for, 6:66

Radios:
and cooler combined, reviewed, 81:92
protective box for, 33:16, 34:4

Radio Shack: ultrasonic tape, reviewed, 78:54-55

Radon:
and air infiltration, 77:65
books on, 51:16, 53:110, 55:108, 70:8
Contractor Proficiency Program, 67:51
contractors dealing with, finding, 67:51

dangers from, 1:12, 5:4, 15, 22:16
  lack of, 65:102
detector for, 51:16
entry routes of, 67:47, 48, 70:4-6
fans against, 66:68 (EEH), 67:49-50, 70:4-8
information on, 65:55
levels of,
  dangerous, 67:47-48
  reducing, 66:68 (EEH)
liability with, 61:98
sealing against, 51:14-16, 61:41-42, 63:82
  (EEH), 67:48-49
seminars in, 70:112
system controlling, 73:68
testing for, 67:51, 70:4
venting against, 67:48, 49, 50-51, 75:48
  (REM), 78:68-71
waterborne, 67:51
Radon Environmental Monitoring, Inc.:
  address for, 67:51
Radon Industry Directory, The
  (Siegelman): reviewed, 53:110
Radon Reduction Methods (USGPO):
  cited, 51:16
Radva Corp.: address for, 62:73
Rafco Products: patterning tools of, 7:6
Rafters:
  adding, for addition, 24:49, 50 (FRC)
  anchors for, 43:48 (FRC)
    hurricane, 57:54
  backing bevels for, finding, 76:49 (MFC)
  barge, 10:69 (FRC), 59:53, 55 (CSH), 60:87
    (MFC)
    Carpenter Gothic, 61:43, 44, 45 (SH)
    decorative projections for, 81:50-51
    defined, 10:65, 69 (FRC)
    double matching cuts for, 19:14
    furring out, for shingles, 28:64
    gallery of, 76:86-87
    pendented, 48:70, 72 (SH)
    thatching on, 22:73
    Victorian, making, 76:46, 50 (MFC)
  beams for,
    box, 55:43-44 (SH)
    built-up I-, 32:36
    steel I-, 16:51, 52, 53
    wood I-, 56:58, 60 (EEH)
  bearing for, 60:84 (MFC)
  bench for, 10:67 (FRC)
  blocking for, 60:86 (MFC)
  books on, 10:60, 66, 28:31-32, 44:67 (FRC,
    TB)
  calculator for, 10:61, 36:62-63 (FRC), 76:48
    (MFC, TB)
  cheek cuts for, 28:33, 34, 35, 37 (FRC),
    68:78 (MFC)
  for circular roofs, brackets for, 8:26
    (CBS)

collar ties for, 60:86 (MFC), 66:71, 72
  adding, 77:18-20
  alternating, 77:18-20
  cross, 51:72-73, 74 (EEH)
  exposed fir, 76:50 (MFC)
  let-in, 29:58 (CSH)
  metal, 73:87
  nails for, 85:47
  placement of, 10:63, 68-69 (FRC)
  steel, 70:62, 65 (EEH)
  strengthening, 56:84
  wooden-pinned, 39:4
common, 10:56-58, 63, 66, 67, 68, 28:33-35
  (FRC, TB)
common difference for, 10:66 (erratum,
  15:6, FRC)
composite, 8:38-40 (EEH)
compression-ring, brackets for, 30:40
for conical roofs, 25:54, 28:4 (FRC)
connectors in, internalized, machinery
  for, 35:56-57 (TB)
copper caps for, 12:12
cripple-jack, 10:63 (FRC)
for cross gables, framing, 76:46-50
  (MFC)
curved, 21:38
cutting, 28:33 (FRC)
  chainsaw, 28:37 (FRC), 78:41
  ends of, 60:87 (MFC)
  gang, 10:66-67 (FRC), 60:83-84 (MFC)
decay problems with, 68:6-8
for dome ceiling, 34:59-61 (FRC)
double-beveled, cutting, 5:7
dummy tails for, 27:43 (FRC)
epoxy repair of, 72:41
for eyebrow dormer, 65:81-83 (MFC)
for eyebrow roof, 44:66-67 (FRC)
for "falling" eaves, 74:82-85 (MFC)
fireblocking for, 25:12
fly, 10:63, 69 (FRC)
gable-end, figuring, 60:87 (MFC)
gusseting, 9:6
hanger kerf in, 27:16
hangers for, 43:47 (FRC)
hip, 10:58-59, 63, 66, 67, 68, 28:33, 34, 35
  (FRC, TB)
  figuring, 57:78-83 (CSH, MFC)
  by square, 28:6
  trusses for, 59:55 (CSH)
hip-jack, 10:63, 65, 28:33 (FRC)
horses for, 60:83, 84 (MFC)
illustrations of, 10:63, 28:33 (FRC)
installing, 10:62, 67-68 (FRC)
  two-man method for, 60:85-86, 87
    (MFC)
insulation baffles for, 29:70
jack, 79:60-61
  common difference for, 10:66 (FRC)
  common distance for, 68:77-78 (MFC)
  compound cuts for, 16:8
  described, 10:62, 63, 66, 67 (erratum,
    15:6), 15:8, 68 (FRC)

no-math method for, 68:77-78 (MFC)
  for octagonal roof, 32:36
and king post, plan of, 11:45 (SH)
king-common, 10:63, 65, 68, 28:33 (FRC)
laminated-veneer, 50:44 (MFC), 66:79-80
  (SH)
layout for,
  string aids for, 25:67 (TB)
  tool for, 21:20
lengths of, determining, 10:61, 62, 66
  (TB), 28:33, 34, 35 (FRC), 60:86 (MFC)
mathematics of, 57:83 (MFC)
mock-up of, on mudsills, 11:45 (SH)
models for, 28:32 (FRC)
nails for, 85:47
new, over old, 32:4
number of, figuring, 60:86 (MFC)
for octagons, 30:42-45
  bay, 26:12 (erratum, 27:6)
opposing, gusset-joined, 66:45
pattern, defined, 10:63
plans for, 28:32-33 (FRC)
and plate connection, strengthening,
  74:36-39 (MFC)
post connections to, 9:43
  fancy, 5:9
premarking, 82:44
on ring beam, 54:62, 58:51-52
round, 46:62, 64 (TFH)
run of, 28:33, 37 (FRC)
screwed and bolted, 68:72, 73 (EF)
sizing, 13:8
for soffits, 63:69 (MFC)
span of, sheathing for, 37:69 (FRC)
span tables for, 77:110
  source of, 23:50
stacking, 82:44-45
steel, 2:24 (CSH)
strengthening, 13:8
superinsulated gusseted, 17:10, 20:12
tail cuts for, 69:42 (EEH)
  no-math method for, 68:75, 77 (MFC)
tails of, carved, 59:52, 53, 54, 55 (CSH)
tee for, 60:84 (MFC)
template for, 79:61
tie-rods for, steel, 79:86
timber, raising, 1:21 (TFH)
timber-framed,
  repair of, 1:51
  squaring, 57:69-70 (TFH)
tools for, 10:60-61 (TB)
trimmer, 10:63 (FRC)
truss makeover of, 55:69 (REM)
trussed, 20:12, 56:64-65 (FC), 71:74, 76-77
  (MFC)
valley,
  "California" technique for, 79:58-61
  closed in, 11:4
  compound cuts for, 16:8
  described, 10:58-59, 62, 61, 63 (TB),
    28:33, 35-36 (FRC)

framing of, simplified, 79:58-61
   no-math method for, 68:74-78 (MFC)
vents for, commercial, 56:63 (EEH)
from warped stock, 48:71-72 (SH)
wedged, 1:54
See also Purlins. Ridge beams. Roofs.
Ragan, Bob:
   address for, 56:6
   limestone carving by, 54:72-75
Raible, John: staircase by, 60:74-77
Railings:
   angled rounded, 32:27 (CSH)
   Australian simple, 53:62, 64-65
   baluster paint aid for, 85:32
   benches as, 69:46-47, 49 (EF), 80:45,
      82:52-53
   beveled, grooved, 26:72, 77
   boring jigs for, reviewed, 63:90
   bracket for, handcarved wooden, 67:57
   cables for, plastic-coated, 45:69
   Chinese Chippendale modified, 80:74
   from closet poles, 80:45
   copper-pipe, 1:58, 53:46 (SH), 70:91
   cypress, 45:8
   deck, installation gauge for, 49:28
   designing, 29:46 (FRC), 66:20, 22 (CSH)
   dovetailed, 48:1, 35
      cherry, 2:51 (SH)
   dowels for, spring-loaded, 11:14
   over drywall partition, 11:45 (SH)
   around elevated hall, 52:85, 86
   exterior, 31:71, 45:41
      weatherproof construction for, 70:68-
         69 (EF)
   fastening, importance of, 77:8
   for fences, 25:75
   freeform, wooden, 47:78 (MFC)
   for French balcony, 75:49 (REM)
   Greene-and-Greene restoration, 72:39-41
   hand,
      codes on, 30:4
      codes on, height for, 39:54 (CSH)
      copper-pipe, 56:69, 71 (CSH)
      detail of, 37:31 (FWS)
      Douglas fir, 28:41 (FWS)
      iron, curved safe, 57:4
      kinds of, 36:57 (FWS)
      laminated, curved, 39:54 (CSH)
      laminated, exterior, 54:82 (EF)
      laminated, making, 37:33 (FWS)
      laminated, walnut, 55:62, 63
      production of, 35:58-59 (TB)
      safe, 55:6
      veneered, 36:61 (FWS)
   for handicapped, 53:71
   inlay for, 45:80 (EEH)
   joining, 70:88, 91
   and ladder support, integral, 65:86
   laminated, cherry, 1:54
      making, 62:30
      spiral, 48:38-39
      walnut, 25:47-48 (BK)

Key to books:

(BK)   **Building Baths and Kitchens**
(CBS)   **Building with Concrete, Brick and Stone**
(CSH)   **Craftsman-Style Houses**
(DWS) **Building Doors, Windows and Skylights**
(EEH)   **Energy-Efficient Houses**
(EF)   **Exterior Finishing**
(FC)   **Finish Carpentry**
(FRC)   **Frame Carpentry**
(FWS) **Building Floors, Walls and Stairs**
(MFC) **More Frame Carpentry**
(REM) **Remodeling**
(SH)   **Small Houses**
(TB)   **Tools for Building**
(TFH)   **Timber-Frame Houses**

lapped uptilted, 45:75 (CSH)
library formal, 31:50 (FWS)
for maple staircase, building, 60:74-77
nails for, 85:47
ogee, shaping, 70:88, 90
pierced, 3:67
plain, 45:57
plank-with-cap, 66:50
for porches,
   rot-resistant, 81:47
   screened, 72:82, 83 (REM)
removable, 48:24
returns for, 70:88
   code on, 67:4
sanding, contoured blocks for, 61:26
simplified, 39:30, 31
with snakes, 73:64, 65
staircase, simple, 62:45
steel, 49:58 (SH), 51:85 (MFC)
   aircraft-enameled, 66:86, 87
   custom, 62:88-89
   miminal, 85:73
   painted formed, 61:50, 52, 54 (SH)
   pipe, 45:60, 62, 63 (SH), 47:83 (SH)
   source for, 41:46
   stainless, 42:37
   tubing, 70:65 (EEH), 79:80, 83-84
   temporary, urgent need for, 47:82 (SH)
   for upstairs gallery, 68:37
   urns for, 48:70, 73 (SH)
   wooden shaped, clamps for, 74:26
   Z-joint for, 60:26
Rainer, Ivan: staircase by, 49:78-82
Rainey, Will: on bulkheads, 33:31-35 (CBS)
Raising:
   for addition, 59:74-77 (REM)
   of arches, A-frame, 20:66, 67
   in balloon-truss system, 24:67-68
   of bents,
      steel, 23:76
      timber-framed, 11:18
   with block and tackle, 11:17

by children, 34:98
derricks for, 34:10
gin poles for, 34:10
jacks for, 22:38, 29:16 (FRC)
   walking, 2:5
Japanese, 24:63-64 (TFH)
for new footings, 28:12
pivot braces for, 11:14
   nailed plates as, 8:12
   strapped plates as, 8:12
of roofs, 67:64-66 (REM), 72:54-56 (REM),
   78:57-58
safety nail stops for, 11:14
with stakes, 1:4
for timber framing, 6:44 (TFH)
tractor-and-block, 1:19-21 (TFH)
tree protection in, 2:4
of walls,
   disaster with, 33:94
   framed, 3:6, 22:37-38 (FRC), 82:47
   jacks for, 22:38 (FRC)
   second-story, 11:14
   settled, process of, 85:20-22
Rake: defined, 10:63 (FRC)
Rake boards: *See* Rafters: barge.
Rake molding: *See* Molding.
Rake walls: *See* Walls: gable.
Ralph Wilson Plastics Co.:
   address for, 65:86
   800-number for, 69:102
Rammed earth: *See* Earth construction.
Rammed Earth Co.: houses by, 34:37,
   38-39
***Rammed Earth Designs for the Desert
   Southwest*** (Schmidt): source for, 34:39
Rammed Earth Experience, The
   (Easton): source for, 34:39
Rammed Earth Solar Homes: houses by,
   34:37, 38
Rammed Earth Works: address for, 71:104
Ramos, Don: house by, 31:92
Ramps: for handicapped, 53:67-68, 69, 71,
   55:87
Ramset Fastening Systems:
   address for, 41:57 (CBS)
   described, 21:30 (TB)
   powder-actuated tools from, 21:30, 34
   (TB)
Ramsey, Dan: *Complete Foundation and
   Floor Framing Book, The,* reviewed,
   46:104
Ramsey and Associates: address for,
   52:100, 53:89
Rand, Charles: house by, 52:74-77 (SH)
Rand, Ellen, and Florence Perchuk:
   Complete Book of Kitchen Designs, cited,
   77:45
Randolph, Octavia Porter:
   reviews *Ceramic Houses,* 40:90
   reviews Fathy, 47:110
   reviews Jencks, 35:94

Random Lengths: lumber prices in, 8:14

Ranges:
  commercial, 71:43 (REM)
  cooktop, 7:67 (BK)
  exhaust fan for, #1912J, 67:72, 76 (REM)
  German, 40:67 (BK)
  hoods for, 40:67 (BK), 67:73, 74 (REM)
    cantilevered, 61:54 (SH)
    grain-hopper, 28:52, 53 (FWS)
    stainless-steel, 40:65, 67 (BK)
    wood-faced, 45:51 (CSH)
  insulation for, 2:54 (BK)
  microwave, solar-powered, 8:47
  selecting, 2:54, 55 (BK)
  small gas, source for, 60:45 (SH), 75:67
  wood,
    building, 21:62-65 (CBS)
    fire-resistant wall behind, 67:73
      (REM)
    masonry, cast-iron parts for, 21:62
      (CBS)
    old, sources for, 21:63 (CBS)
  See also Masonry stoves.

Rantis, Daryl: on solar farmhouse, 37:70-75

Raschko, Bettyann B.: *Housing Interiors for the Disabled and Elderly,* 35:45 (BK)

Rasmussen, Steen E.: *Experiencing Architecture,* reviewed, 45:116

Rasps: for jigsaws, 33:60 (TB)

Rastra Building Systems, Inc.:
  address for, 76:39
  cement/polystyrene blocks of, 83:108
  insulation of, using, 76:41

Ratch-Cut RC 1125: reviewed, 53:94-96

Raven Industries, Inc.: address for, 55:68, 66:49, 68 (EEH), 68:64

Ravens Metal Products, Inc.: aluminum sheets, 33:32 (CBS)

Rawlplug Co., Inc.:
  address for, 41:57 (CBS), 73:73
  stud anchor bolts, 29:34 (FRC)

Ray, Colin: renovation by, 28:26-30

Ray, W. Redmore: mentioned, 16:6

Raymond E. Enkeboll Designs, Inc.:
  address for, 66:106

Raynes Enterprises: Groove-V-Guide, 37:81

Readybuilt Products Co.: address for, 63:49

Real Goods: address for, 80:104

Realist Co.: level-transits, 37:45 (TB)

Reardon, J. Thomas: on shingle-style house, 52:52-56

Rebar:
  bender for, 26:64-65 (CBS), 55:28
  cutting, 44:34 (CBS)
  fiberglass, source for, 70:49
  guards for, 49:26
  mentioned, 44:34 (CBS)
  placement of, 47:4, 6
  retrofitting, with epoxy, 70:47, 49
  sizing system for, 63:106
  supports for, 69:61
  threaded, 33:34 (CBS)
  tie-rod, 33:34-35 (CBS)
  ties for, 26:65 (CBS), 47:4
  using, 44:34, 35, 36, 37 (CBS)

Reciprocating saws:
  blades for,
    bimetal, 16:47 (TB)
    broken, reshaping, 7:10
    choosing, 16:46-48 (TB)
    installing, 16:48 (TB)
    locks for, 60:26
    offset, adaptor for, 2:5
    plaster-cutting, 8:8, 11:14
  buying, 16:45-46 (TB)
  composition-roof cutting with, 11:14
  discussed, 7:60, 18:18
  fast-cut, 35:90
  gas-powered, 36:88
    reviewed, 41:84
  larger, reviewed, 65:92
  maintenance of, 16:49 (TB)
  resawing with, 23:14
  siding removal with, 2:5
  using, 16:45, 49 (TB)
  See also brand names.

Recommended Practices for Laying Concrete Block (Portland Cement Association): reviewed, 46:104

Recommended Specifications for Adobe and Construction Details: source for, 30:39

Record: smooth plane #04½, 4:22 (TFH)

ReCraft 90 house: manual on, 85:126

Recreation Products: address for, 65:92

RectorSeal Corp.: address for, 77:67

Recycling:
  books on, cited, 76:104, 83:110
  building materials from, 81:104-106
  center for, 81:104-106, 85:124
  house from, 85:124
  products from, catalog of, 85:124
  strategies for, 83:108-10
  wood look-alike from, 85:122

Red Cedar Shake and Shingle Bureau:
  on copper and shingles, 49:40 (REM)
  Design and Application Manual for Exterior and Interior Walls, cited, 54:42-44 (EF)
  exposure recommendations of, 8:60
  services of, 23:50

Red Devil:
  One-Time Spackling, 30:57 (DWS)
  scrapers, 12:51 (TB)

Red Head:
  anchor bolts, source for, 29:34 (FRC)
  powder-actuated tools from, 21:34 (TB)

Red Top:
  Regular Gypsum plaster, source for, 23:12
  Wood Fiber plaster, source for, 23:12

Reddi-Form, Inc.:
  address for, 76:39
  insulation of, using, 76:41

Reducing Home Building Costs with OVE Design and Construction (NAHB): cited, 21:6, 23:48, 84:49

Redwood Restoration (Syracuse, NY): bell-tower work by, 30:42-45

Redwood (*Sequoia sempervirens*):
  acids of, and zinc, 24:44
  association for, 3:9, 33:90, 83:45
  bark, siding from, 3:66
  for bending, 17:64 (DWS)
  decay resistance of, 61:12-14, 63:63 (MFC), 69:16-18
  as decking, booklets on, 33:90
  exterior finishes for, 52:66-67
  fire rating of, 33:90
  grades of, 18:7, 33:90
  hardness group of, 40:69 (FRC)
  house of, 1:52-55
  limits of, 4:33
  nailing, booklet on, 33:90
  for pole building, 15:32
  preservatives for, 3:8-9
  recycled, source for, 70:106
  sapwood vulnerability of, 18:7
  for shingles, 12:52
  as siding, 33:90
    finger-jointed, 83:41-42, 43
  for solar collectors, 1:30
  stability of, 33:90
  termite resistance of, 33:90
  for timber framing, 30:6
  vulnerability of, 75:4, 77:4
  wax for, 52:80-81
  working quality of, 9:23

Reed, Bill and W. G.: newel post by, 71:88

Reed, Mortimer P.: *Residential Carpentry,* reviewed, 35:69-70 (TB)

Reed Manufacturing Co.: tubing cutters, 39:34 (BK)

Reed (*Phragmites communis trin*): for thatching, 22:74, 76-77

Reef Industries: address for, 55:68

Reef Tank Owner's Manual, The (Tullock): cited, 72:63

Reel, Kip: cabin restorations by, 14:46-51

Reemay, Inc.: address for, 68:83

Reese, Ilse: restoration plan by, 49:39-43 (REM)

Reeves, Mike: mentioned, 30:45

Reflective Insulation Manufacturers Association: address for, 58:98

Refracrete: source for, 36:32 (CBS)

Refrasil fire-resistant material: source for, 24:82

Refrigeration

Refrigeration: information on, 46:48
Refrigerators:
custom, 38:59
dangerous gas, rebate for, 71:106
DC homemade, 8:47
efficient, 2:64
flush-faced, 43:79
  source for, 43:79
small, source for, 75:67
source for, 14:54-56 (BK)
under-counter,
  custom, 38:59
  self-defrosting, 44:52 (SH)
  source for, 60:45 (SH)
Reggio Register Co.:
address for, 10:49 (SH)
registers of, reviewed, 60:96
***Regional Analysis of Ground and
Above-Ground Climate*** (Labs): chart
from, 21:60-61
Registers:
cast-iron, 10:49, 60:96 (SH)
between sill and floor, 37:27 (BK)
Rehab Right (Kapland and Prentice):
reviewed, 2:62
Rehabilitation: *See* Renovation.
Restoration.
REI Co-op: headlamp, 4:6
Reich, Jonathan: on building instruction,
45:106-10
Reif, Daniel K.:
Solar Retrofit, 5:52
on solar site evaluation, 5:52-53 (DWS)
Reinke Shakes: copper shingles, 39:90
Reischauer, Edwin O.: *Japanese, The,*
praised, 34:92
Reitz, Michael: publishes *New England
Builder,* 20:80-81
Rejuvenation House Parts: work of, 16:44
Rekdahl, Eric K.:
on drafting, 26:58-62 (TB)
on kitchen expansion, 7:21-23 (BK)
on pole house, 39:26-32
on ridge vents, 21:53 (DWS)
on second-story addition, 9:28-31
on timber-frame remodel, 52:46-51
  (TFH)
Relative humidity:
and construction, 68:8
controlling, 19:68
defined, 19:67
high, symptoms of, 19:68
levels of, 19:68, 68:8
See also Moisture.
Relay Primer, A (Thomsen): cited, 68:108
Reliance Manufacturing Corp.: address
for, 70:104
Remington Fastening Systems: hammer-
detonated tools, 21:32, 34 (TB)

Remodeler's Handbook (ed. Williams):
reviewed, 3:61
Remodeling:
anecdote of, 62:126
Arts-and-Crafts style, 44:50-53 (SH)
  kitchen, 67:72-76 (REM)
attic kneewalls in, 74:14
of attic to studio, 64:84-87 (REM)
of bathrooms, 22:65-67 (BK), 76:66-69
  (REM)
of bedroom, into two, 74:60-61
books on, 74:98, 78:8
of Cape, 78:56-59
for ceiling, coffered, 84:69-71
computer programs for, 35:66 (TB),
  83:122
concrete slab for, topped, 19:47
contract for, model, source for, 60:100
costs of, 19:49
curtain wall for, reviewed, 76:94-96
of duplex, 26:33-37
for elderly's suite, 65:76-79 (REM)
entry change with, 30:32-35
exhibit of, 1985, 26:82
of farmhouse, 12:46-49, 49:58-62 (SH)
  Shaker, 79:85-89
floors in, dropped, 32:59
of garage into library, 77:76-79 (REM),
  84:69-71
for handicapped, 73:60-65
of kitchen,
  larger, 63:54-57 (REM)
  for two cooks, 73:16-20
  from warren, 68:22
loans for, 203(K), 76:70-71
of loft, 70:80-81 (REM)
to lot requirements, 80:74-75
measurement system for, 73:20-22
models for, 27:49
of 1920s bungalow, 64:38-42 (CSH)
organization for, 44:46-49 (TB)
philosophy of, 27:53
for porch, dining-room, 71:60-63 (REM)
of porches, 65:24
to prairie style, 70:26
of ranch, 80:72-77
recycling strategies for, 83:108-10
roof monitor for, 19:47
of store and stable, 20:44-48
sunspace for, sunken, 19:47
superinsulation in, 20:35-37, 22:35-37
  (FRC)
through-and-up, 69:24
around tract house, 27:48-53
vapor-barrier paint in, 19:68
weather-protection hints for, 41:10
See also Renovation. Restoration.
  Superinsulated houses: retrofits.
Remodeling Old Houses (Stephen): cited,
78:8

Remote controls:
for handicapped, 53:68
for outlets, transmitter, 80:98
***Removal of Stains from Concrete
Masonry Walls:*** source for, 23:50
Renewable Energy News: address for,
15:62
Renovation:
Arts-and-Crafts style, 59:83-87 (CSH)
assistance groups for, 6:14
of barn, 66:60-63 (REM)
of basements, 39:38-39
bearing-wall strategies for, 55:75-77
  (MFC)
books on, 1:63, 2:62, 3:61, 4:62, 5:60, 10:70,
  14:76, 65:106
of bungalow, small cheap, 56:68-72
  (CSH)
classes in, high-school, 29:88-89
competition for, 75:102
condensation problems and, 39:10
costs of, 1:8, 3:54, 55, 4:14, 7:50-51, 10:42,
  45
of cottage, Victorian, 28:49 (FWS)
debris chute for, 58:24
disaster in, 2:66
do-it-yourself, cost of, 82:70
doors in, pocket, 7:23 (BK)
energy-sensitive, 6:14-16, 10:44-45
exhibitions, 1981, 1:9
of finish, restraint with, 19:4
floor-plan revision for, 28:50 (FWS)
footings for, 7:22-23 (BK)
framing repair in, 6:36-38 (FRC)
headlamps for, 4:6
insulation in, adding, 4:8
for integrated systems, book on, 6:58
of kitchens, 2:53-55 (BK), 26:38-39 (BK),
  40:64-67 (BK), 58:36-41 (REM)
lead poisoning from, 2:64
leveling compromises in, 14:23
for library, 26:40-42
morality of, 80:4
perils of, 7:64
planning for, 10:42, 44
plumbing insulation in, 7:6-8
of porches, 75:72-74
precautions for, 55:75 (MFC)
process of, 59:18-20
of row house, tiny, 39:38-43, 47:79-83,
  82:69-71 (MFC, SH)
of shack, hillside, 38:46-48 (SH)
solar, tax incentives for, 6:16
and Teton retrofit, 18:40-43
tools for, 12:50-51 (TB)
of tract house, 62:46-49 (SH)
of train station, Carpenter Gothic, 81:50-
  53
underlayment for, self-leveling, 48:12
urban renewal and, 1:8-9
vapor-barrier paint in, 19:68
walls in, 7:21-23 (BK)

weather-protection hints for, 41:10
windows for, 39:41
wrap-around, 3:52-53
zoning for, 10:42
See also Attics. Reconstruction.
    Restoration. *specific projects.*
Renovation (Litchfield): reviewed, 14:76,
65:106
Renovator's Supply:
address for, 48:72 (SH)
catalog of, described, 1:63
period plumbing, 42:30 (CSH)
Rensselaer Polytechnic Institute: lighting
degree program of, 69:100
Repairing Old and Historic Windows
    (New York Landmarks Conservancy):
reviewed, 84:124
Replacement Windows (SHC-BRC):
source for, 29:92
Repointing of Historic Masonry
Buildings, The (Mack and Askins):
mentioned, 4:4
Reproductions:
Arts-and-Crafts style, source for, 54:100
Scottish, source for, 54:106
Resawing: with reciprocating saw, 23:14
Residential and Commercial Sunspaces
    (Kupferer, ed.): reviewed, 68:108
Residential Asphalt Roofing Manual:
reviewed, 37:84
source for, 23:50, 57:89 (EF)
Residential Carpentry (Reed): reviewed,
35:69-70 (TB)
Residential Concrete (NAHB): cited, 44:37
(CBS), 55:68, 68:14
Residential Controls Div.: address for,
67:51
Residential Fireplace and Chimney
Handbook: source for, 57:4
Residential Indoor Air Quality and
Energy Efficiency (DuPont and Morrill):
reviewed, 75:110
Residential Standards Demonstration
Program: heat-recovery ventilators in,
34:30 (DWS)
Resilacrete: for logs, 8:8
Resin board:
adhesive systems for, 37:81
chunks of, as pulls, 66:55
color matching, 28:6
colors of, 37:81
for countertops, 77:41, 42, 84:40-45
cutting, 84:41, 42
gridded, 64:42 (CSH)
installing, 27:44-47 (BK), 34:66 (BK),
    84:44-45
literature on, 27:47 (BK)
mentioned, 37:81
possibilities of, 84:90-91
sources for, 34:64 (BK), 84:45
templates for, 84:41

Resin Systems: source for, 16:21 (CSH)
Resnick, Candy: ceramics by, 59:91
Resource Conservation Technology,
Inc.: address for, 64:45 (EF), 77:67, 81:6,
83:16
weatherstripping, reviewed, 78:94
Resource-Efficient Housing Guide:
reviewed, 53:108-10
Resources Conservation, Inc.: address
for, 84:84
Respirators:
air-hat,
    homemade, 36:16
    reviewed, 58:90
for asbestos, 24:83
cartridge, 48:74
choosing, information number on, 72:6
against lead, 61:68
source for, 10:10
for spray painting, 42:55 (DWS)
for Swedish floor finishes, 36:43 (FWS)
See also Dust. Masks.
Restoration:
air-conditioning ducts and, 29:65
of Arts-and-Crafts style, 66:24-26
assessment for, 61:67
association for, 65:45
of barn, 44:72-75
of bell tower, 30:42-45
books on, 1:33, 63, 2:62, 4:4, 58, 62, 5:39,
    60, 24:86, 34:92 (FWS), 70:120-22,
    82:112
casework in, borrowed, 4:19
of chimneys, 29:64, 65
of "cottage," 1880s, 50:64-68
courses in, 8:14-15
of Craftsman house, 52:78-82
dating in, 27:82
demolition for, 4:17
detail removal in, 1:48
difficulties of, 17:29-30 (CSH)
electrical service and, 4:19
of entryways, 4:20
epoxy in, 16:20-21 (CSH)
of finish, restraint with, 19:4
from frame to finish, 49:38-43 (REM)
framing repair in, 6:36-38 (FRC)
glass for, 59:102-104
grants for, 5:39
of Greek Revival houses, 1:48-51, 29:62-
    67, 32:56-59
of Greene-and-Greene house, 72:36-41
headlamps for, 4:6
house for, choosing, 4:16-17
information on, 65:55
insulation for, 43:4
lead in, protection from, 61:68, 62:39
    (EF)
lighting and, 4:19
loans for, 4:14
of masonry, publications on, 5:39

moldings for,
    fitting, 2:6
    foam-core, 39:92
organization for, 72:98
paint for, 9:24
paint removal in, 1:33 (FWS)
patches for, wood, 29:65
permits for, 5:39
plans for, 4:17, 29:63-64
of plaster, 4:18, 28:10
of porch, 2:14-17
    brownstone, 9:20-24
of portico, classical-revival, 61:67-71
quality in, encouraging, 17:30 (CSH)
of Quonset-hut house, 33:24-30
salvaged elements for, 7:14
source for, reviewed, 81:114
of staircases, 4:18
of stone house, 33:63-67
of stone masonry, seminar in, 72:98
of stone shell, 40:55-59
tax incentives for, 6:16
technology of, book on, 61:68
telephones and, 29:65
and urban renewal, 1:8-9
vapor-barrier paint for, 19:68
and wiring, 29:65
wood matching in, 56:84-85
workshop (1985), on, 27:82-83
of Wright's Oak Park, 56:82-87
See also Brownstone. Church
    conversion. Historic preservation.
    Renovation.
Restoration Product News: mentioned,
1:63
Resurfacing Concrete Floors: source for,
15:14, 32:10
Retaining walls: *See* Walls.
Retro Technologies, Inc.: address for,
68:66, 76:37
Retrofits:
guide for, 32:90
See also Remodeling. Restoration.
    specific details, operations.
Reuder, Leo: on owner-building, 4:10
Reusche (L.) Co.: address for, 78:73
Rev-a-Shelf, Inc.: address for, 74:78
Revel, Gary: on timber framing, 36:46-50
(TFH)
Revel, Ryan: on timber framing, 36:46-50
(TFH)
Revere Copper Products, Inc.: *Copper*
and Common Sense, 58:14
Rex, Michael: stairway by, 25:81
Rex Roberts house: construction of,
28:69-72
Rexnord Chemical Products:
ConTech adhesive, 34:59 (FRC)
PL 400 adhesive, source for, 35:8

Reynolds, Glenn: on bowstring trusses, 33:44-47 (TFH)
Reynolds, Michael:
Earthship, reviewed, 69:110
rammed earth and tires technique of, 60:120
Reynolds Metals Co.:
address for, 58:61 (CSH)
galvanized roofing, 40:74 (EEH)
R-Forms, Inc.:
address for, 76:39
insulation of, using, 76:40-41
Rheem Manufacturing Co.:
address for, 69:94, 82:58
Solaraide hot-water tanks, 3:50, 29:86-88
water heaters, problem with, 2:64
Rhino Industries: knife sharpener of, reviewed, 84:94-96
Rhoades, Duke: house by, 39:66-69 (TFH)
Rhode Island: solar tax credits in, 3:12
Ribbon joist: *See* Joists: rim.
Richards, Donna: on the Little house, 1:56-58
Richardson, Frank: mentioned, 34:59 (FRC)
Richardson, Henry Hobson:
house by, 5:60
mentioned, 9:68
Richert, Clark: mentioned, 26:52
Richmond Screw Anchor: address for, 78:50
Richter, H. P.: *Wiring Simplified,* 4:4
Riddell, Robert: *New Elements of Hand Railing, The,* 43:38 (FWS)
Ridge beams:
carved, extended, 6:67 (FRC)
curved, 21:38
defined, 10:63, 63, 67-68 (FRC)
installing, 10:63, 67-68, 28:35, 56:64-65 (FC, FRC)
laminated-veneer lumber, 50:44 (MFC)
offset, 4:47 (FRC)
retrofitting, 81:53
Russian patterned, 26:96
tree support for, 6:67 (FRC)
See also Rafters.
Ridge caps: *See* Roofing.
Ridge Tool Co.:
address for, 46:57, 58:45 (BK)
aluminum wrench, 12:51 (TB)
backsaws, 12:51 (TB)
tubing bender, 46:57
tubing cutter, 39:34 (BK)
Ridgeboards: *See* Ridge beams.
RidgeMaster: address for, 61:80 (EF)
Ridgepoles: *See* Ridge beams.
Riechers, A. F.: *Full Length Roof Framer, The,* 10:60 (TB)
Riedel, Karl: on ultrasonic measuring tools, 78:54-55

Rifkind, Carole: *Field Guide to American Architecture, A,* reviewed, 2:62
Rigger, Ralph: on barrier-free house, 53:67-71
Riggs, J. Rosemary: *Materials and Components of Interior Design,* reviewed, 30:78
Right-to-Know Pocket Guide for Construction Workers: reviewed, 62:114
Rigi-Dor: source for, 6:60
Riley, Stephen:
on garage doors, 74:57-59 (MFC)
on Sun Valley Manhattan, 62:58-61
Rindlaub, Curtis: on rolling hatch, 48:54-57
Ring, Douglas: on brick floors, 33:68-71 (CBS)
Ring Brick Floors: floor sealer, 33:70 (CBS)
Ringel, John: pictured, 38:8
Rinnai America Corp.: water heater, 12:18 (CSH)
Ripolin paint: reviewed, 61:90-92
Ripping: sawblades for, 72:47 (MFC)
Ripping bars: *See* Wrecking bars.
Rising and Nelson Slate Co.: address for, 20:39 (EF)
Rivco: sash unit, 10:51 (SH)
Rivenberg, Steve: chimney repairs of, 9:16
Riverbend Timber Framing:
chain mortiser use of, 22:16
cited, 40:44 (TFH)
stress-skin panels, 24:59
Riveting: riveter for, 67:40 (EF)
Rix, Robert:
reviews first-aid kits, 58:90-91
reviews Holladay, 55:108-10
RJD Industries, Inc.: address for, 78:50
RMI Design: address for, 72:90
RMK Enterprises: panel supplies, 40:12
Roadside Geology (Alt and Hyndman): cited, 50:86
Robern, Inc.: address for, 75:49 (REM)
Robert A. M. Stern Architects: New American Home by, 32:82
Robert Consolidated Industries Inc.: Woodlife finish, 27:75
Robert H. Peterson Co.: address for, 77:79 (REM)
Robert Larson: address for, 84:63
Robert Owens Installing Co.: address for, 52:98
Roberts, J. Stewart: on Usonian house, 66:56-59 (SH)
Roberts, Louis O.: house by, 40:28-32
Roberts, Rex: *Your Engineered House,*
built, 28:68-72
costs of, 30:4
Roberts, Ron: reviews Branden and Hartsell, 77:120

Roberts Consolidated Industries, Inc.: address for, 48:71 (SH)
Robert's Woodworking: threaded wooden connectors from, 35:31
Robertson, Richard: on cottage, 33:48-52 (SH)
Robertson, Robert: on bathroom built-ins, 13:60-63 (BK)
Robidoux, Larry:
reviews bungalow book, 31:80-82
reviews Gowans, 37:90
reviews Lewis book, 29:90
Robinault, Isabel P.: *Functional Aids for the Handicapped,* 6:51
Robinson, David: on Central Park shelter, 21:66-68
Robinson, Sidney: *Architecture of Alden Dow, The,* mentioned, 10:24
Robinson Iron: work of, 16:44
Robtee Resin Systems: epoxy consolidants, 16:21 (CSH)
Rochester Area (MN) Vocational Technical Institute: superinsulation forum report from, 22:16-18
superinsulation conference by, 28:82
Rochlin, Davida:
porch exhibit by, 20:22
on porches, 29:47, 50
Rock beds: *See* Thermal mass.
Rockhill, Dan:
on architectural models, 41:32-35
on being a builder, 45:20-28
on concrete belvedere, 30:64-69 (CBS)
on decks, 12:58-60
on levels, 58:42-45
on prefab metal building, 33:72-75
quoted, 35:66 (TB)
reviews Brown, 37:88
on slate-roofed cottage, 47:56-60
on solar house, 26:72-77
on stemwall foundations, 44:32-37 (CBS)
Rockland Industries, Inc.: address for, 70:55 (EEH)
Rocklath plaster base: source for, 12:23 (CSH, TFH)
Rocklite concrete aggregate: source for, 20:52 (FWS)
Rockwell, Ed: molding by, 40:34-37 (FWS)
Rockwell International Power Tool Division:
belt grinders, 18:59 (TB)
circular saw #542, for timber framing, 35:55 (TB)
hinge butt mortising templates, 31:31 (TB)
miter saws,
carbide blades for, 21:4
model 34-10, 19:42-43, 44, 45 (TB)
power, brake on, 20:4
Porta-plane, 14:42, 45 (TB)
radial-arm-saw retrofits, 43:96

Sawbuck, 19:42 (TB)
  bearings in, 14:4
  blades for, 14:4, 18:17
  evaluated, 12:14-16
  modified, 31:49 (FWS)
  stainless rails for, 25:4-6
sells Porter-Cable, 18:18
Unisaw,
  extensions, 30:60 (BK)
  for moldings, 2:49 (FWS)
See also Delta International Machinery
  Corp. Porter-Cable.
Rocky Mountain Institute:
  *High-Efficiency Showerheads and
  Faucets,* cited, 84:83
  publications of, reviewed, 53:108-10
  Resource-Efficient Housing Guide,
  reviewed, 53:108-10
  *Water-Efficient Technologies for the
  Urban-Residential Sector,* reviewed,
  53:108-10
  Waterless Toilets, cited, 53:110
Rodel, Kevin:
  on Poliquin house, 47:44, 46 (TFH)
Rodman, Warren: stonework of, 14:63
Roean Industries, Inc.: address for, 70:100
Roeser (G. P.), Inc.: address for, 57:39
Roesner, William E.: on kitchen remodel,
  67:72-76 (REM)
Rogers, Benjamin T.: on solar adobe,
  58:80-85 (EEH)
Rogers, Sherry A.: *E. I. Syndrome, The,*
  mentioned, 49:6
Rohm and Haas Co.:
  address for, 19:12
  Plexiglas, 10:33 (DWS)
ROKI Associates: cathedral-ceiling
  insulated truss of, 19:22
Roland, Ron: trim by, 45:44-48 (TFH)
Roll Former Corp.: electric roof-crimping
  machine, 32:59
Roll-a-way Insulating Security Shutters:
  address for, 76:16
Roller supports:
  plan for, 23:16
  site-built, 44:26, 57:26
  stand for, 29:16
Rollers: skate wheels for, 48:56
Roll-top house: construction of, 25:38-41
  (EEH)
Roman tub: *See* Bathtubs: hexagonal
  tiled.
Romex: described, 8:44-45
Rondavels:
  building of, solar, 30:29-31
  origin of, 30:29
*Roof Cutter's Secrets to Framing the
  Custom House, A* (Holladay):
  reviewed, 55:108-10
Roof Frames for 7/4 House Designs
  (SHC-BRC): source for, 29:92

Key to books:

(BK)   Building Baths and Kitchens
(CBS) Building with Concrete, Brick and Stone
(CSH) Craftsman-Style Houses
(DWS) Building Doors, Windows and Skylights
(EEH) Energy-Efficient Houses
(EF)   Exterior Finishing
(FC)   Finish Carpentry
(FRC) Frame Carpentry
(FWS) Building Floors, Walls and Stairs
(MFC) More Frame Carpentry
(REM) Remodeling
(SH)   Small Houses
(TB)   Tools for Building
(TFH) Timber-Frame Houses

Roof Framing (Gross):
  cited, 57:78 (CSH, MFC)
  reviewed, 60:106
Roof Framing (Siegele): discussed, 28:31-
  32 (FRC)
Roofers: risk rating of, 34:51 (TB)
Roofing:
  acrylic-shingle, 23:72, 73-74, 75, 76-77
  for additions, 24:50-51 (FRC)
  adventure in, 73:118
  aluminum, 24:42, 44, 32:6
    litho plates for, 21:18
    ribbed, 11:34, 35
    shake, 58:61 (CSH)
  asphalt,
    book on, 57:89 (EF)
    compatibility of, 9:4
    corrugated, 6:55, 56-57, 20:10, 26:72,
      73, 74, 46:51 (EEH)
    in hot climates, 82:67
    hot-mopped, disadvantages of, 32:46
      (BK)
    information on, 65:53
    recycling, 69:102
    removing, 33:16
    roll, 20:10
    roll, decorative use of, 22:54, 58
      (CSH)
    roll, double-coverage, 28:72
    roll, perm rating of, 19:67
    roll, vertical, 83:78, 79
  asphalt-organic, 26:72, 73
  asphalt-shingle,
    color of, and heat buildup, 61:77 (EF)
    diamond-shaped, 63:4, 80:49
    vs. fiberglass, 57:85 (EF)
    hurricane-proofness of, 78:84-85, 87
    indictment of, 84:112
    installing, 57:84-89 (EF), 60:4-8
    manual for, 3:63
    rounded-edge, reviewed, 72:88
    self-sealing, source for, 38:38 (CSH)

  stapling, 58:68 (EF)
  stapling, disallowed, 78:84
  vent space with, 51:74 (EEH)
  weather-resistant, 64:92
  vs. wood, help on, 23:49
associations for, 43:16, 57:89 (EF),
  60:100, 84:112
bitumen/plastic/aluminum roll, 9:4
books on, 23:50, 37:84
built-up,
  for solarium, 17:65 (DWS)
  substitutes for, 9:4
channel-vented, 26:4
cheap insulated, 20:10
concrete-shingle,
  from sewage aggregate, 22:18 (CSH)
  source for, 63:84 (EEH)
copper, 23:66, 24:42
  and acid rain, 75:59
  lead-caulked, 32:65
  lead-coated against acids, 49:4
copper/asphalt seamless, 23:66, 67
copper-shingle, 43:30, 32-33 (CSH)
  movement allowance for, 46:4
earthquake-proofing, 64:60-61 (MFC)
eave shield for, 57:86 (EF)
estimating, 57:85 (EF)
felt, nails for, 53:18
felt underlayment for, 57:85-86 (EF)
fiberglass, built-up, 66:87
fiberglass-shingle, 59:55 (CSH)
  avoiding, 73:68
  multicolored, 51:69, 71
  from recycled thermoplastic, 78:104
  recycling, 69:102
  source for, 66:80 (SH)
  textured, over imperfections, 24:50
    (FRC)
over foam-core panels, 62:56, 57 (TFH)
galvanic action and, 50:6
galvanized, 3:58 (EEH), 8:65 (EEH),
  20:10, 24:42, 43, 44, 46, 40:74 (EEH),
  84:67-68, 85:72
  painting, 15:62
glass, 13:66 (SH)
glass-shingle, 80:42, 44
gravel, 72:14-16
hammers for, gauged, 57:94-96
handbook on, cited, 67:6
for hot climates, 70:16-18
hurricane-proof, 78:82-84
information on, 65:54, 55
lead, 25:59-61
lead-coated copper plates for, 32:65,
  61:48, 63:4
life of, and ventilation, 25:12
membranes for, 16:8, 20:12, 29:12, 34:28,
  47 (DWS), 43:16, 51:53, 52:56, 58:16,
  79:82, 81:81
  acrylic-latex elastomeric, 50:49
  butylated-asphalt, 15:59
  choosing, 72:16

elastomeric, 9:4
elastomer-sheet, 12:58, 59, 60, 34:28, 29 (DWS)
EPDM, 82:67-68
EPDM, sealant for, 61:37
flame-bonded, 37:26, 27 (BK), 50:49
modified bitumen, flashing posts into, 70:71 (EF)
polyethylene, 52:56
rubber single-ply, 43:16
steel-elastomeric, 11:57
metal, 8:41 (EEH)
   coatings for, 24:46
   corrosion with, 24:46
   corrugated, with epoxy and silicone, 33:29
   cutting, 26:16
   discussed, 24:42-46
   electric crimper for, 32:59
   fastening, 24:45-46, 40:74 (EEH)
   for hot climates, 70:16-18, 80:57
   length problems with, 56:62 (EEH)
   machines for, 24:44, 45
   product guides to, 32:6
   sheathing for, 65:14
   siding as, 41:40-41
   over stress-skin panels, 48:12
mineral-felt roll, 26:10
nailers in, 20:10
neoprene walk-on, 59:82
plywood-strip, rubber-painted, 65:38
for porches, 75:73
removing,
   protective slide for, 28:16
   tool for, 40:10
ridge caps for, curved copper, 4:64
roll, 5:30, 33, 9:4
   with ash overlay, 63:118
for roof decks, 80:70, 77
roofing fabric for, 57:88-89 (EF)
rubber, 32:65
   compound for, 52:39 (TFH)
   source for, 32:65
for seashore, 65:79, 74:69 (REM)
shingle, 10:8, 44:61, 62, 45:56, 58
   adding, to expanded roof, 67:66 (REM)
   aging, 56:50-51
   algae-stained, remedying, 63:10
   anti-fungal copper wire for, 49:40 (REM)
   applying, 12:54-56
   association for, 49:40 (REM), 77:16
   backpack for, 78:28
   bandsaw jig for, 48:72, 73 (SH)
   books on, 23:50
   books on, metric, 67:104
   border in, decorative, 61:53 (SH)
   for Carpenter Gothic playhouse, 61:44, 45 (SH)

cedar, 79:87, 88
cedar, fireproofing, 77:16
circular saw for, 58:68 (EF)
for cones, 25:54 (FRC), 68:58
copper flashing and, problems with, 2:4, 49:4
cost of, 12:52
over curved dormers, 20:31-33
for curves, forming, 45:83-84
over curves, jig for, 20:31
cutting, 10:8
cypress, 25:62-63
cypress, finding, 30:8
decorative, gallery of, 65:88-89
dimensions of, 12:52
fancy, 1:62, 46:75 (BK)
felt under, 32:10, 84:16
finish for, 54:45 (EF)
fire-resistance of, proved, 65:102
fire-resistant, reviewed, 79:112
fire-treated, 47:8
fish-scale, making, 48:70, 72 (SH)
5-in., source for, 25:62
flashing for, 9:48-50, 12:56, 57 (EF)
freeform, 64:50-53
freeform, undulating, 19:84
gallery of, 57:90-91
for gazebo, 55:83-84
grades of, 18:8, 28:66-67
grey, matching flashing to, 73:75
Hollywood, 1:55
homemade, 30:46-49
information on, 65:53-54
and insulation, 56:37
irregular, 31:72-73
Japanese-style, 4:53, 54, 19:40 (BK, TFH)
for low-pitched roofs, 35:71 (TB)
materials list for, 12:52
over membrane, 64:53
nails for, 30:49, 85:47
of octagon, 30:45
organic reroofer, source for, 82:6
ornamental, 18:53-55
ornamental, book on, 18:53
permeability of, 19:68
pilot holes in, 10:8
pitch for, 46:4
porous underlayment for, reviewed, 79:100
preservatives for, 30:49
over purlins, 6:47, 8:60 (TFH)
red vs. white cedar for, 18:8
removing, protective slide for, 28:16
ridge caps for, 58:70 (EF)
on ridges, 12:56-57
sassafras, 6:47 (TFH)
sawtooth, 2:60
seasoning of, 10:8
shake, felt strips with, 32:10

sheathing for, 12:53-55
sheathing for, solid vs. open, 8:8
over sheathing, uneven, 21:68
with skylights, 45:76, 77 (EEH)
sources for, 28:66-67
southern pine, 84:4
tools for, 12:52
treated, 11:8
24-in., 68:85
valley flashing for, 1:5
in valleys, 9:50, 12:57 (EF)
ventilation for, 61:76 (EF)
Victorian use of, book on, 29:90
white cedar, sources for, 30:4
woods for, 12:52
shingle-thatch, 58:67-71 (EF)
   asphalt, reroofing, 11:12-14
   fire danger of, reducing, 11:8
   installing, 23:53-56
   treated, source for, 11:8
slat,
   Cotswold, book on, 49:114
   Cotswold, installation of, 49:69-71
slate, 43:59, 60 (CBS)
   books on, 5:12, 20:39, 37:84 (EF), 47:59
   broken, replacing, 76:8
   care of, 23:6
   Chinese, source for, 80:67
   costs of, 20:39 (EF)
   cutting, 19:41, 21:8 (BK)
   deterioration of, 20:38, 39 (EF)
   eave flashing for, 22:4
   eaves for, lifting, 23:4-6
   increasing weathertightness of, 53:18
   installing, 20:40-43 (EF), 47:59-60
   jigsaw blades for, 33:60 (TB)
   nails for, 20:40, 22:4 (EF)
   production of, 71:65-68
   psi of, 32:33 (FRC)
   random salvaged, 33:76
   reconstituted, 57:96
   repair of, 50:65-66, 61:24
   restoration of, book on, 24:86
   roofing felt under, 23:4
   snips for, 23:6
   snow guards for, 20:42, 43 (EF)
   sources for, 20:39 (EF), 54:54
   temporary roof for, 53:18
   tools for, 20:40, 27:16 (EF), 71:68
   used, using, 66:77
   in Wales, 23:4
sod, 34:25, 26, 28, 35:75, 77 (DWS), 51:44-45, 52:76 (SH), 56:78-81
   membranes for, 34:28, 35:77 (DWS)
   schematic of, 71:38-39 (EEH)
and solar panels, 59:65-67 (EEH), 69:18
standing-seam,
   baked-enamel, 75:59
   book on, 7:60
   conical, 30:38, 40, 41
   copper, 10:20, 24, 55:58, 60

copper, triangular-pieced, 58:52

figuring, 39:61, 62

flashing for, 9:8, 39:65

galvanized, 45:65, 69

hurricane-proofness of, 78:84

installing, 39:62-65

machines for, 24:44

metals for, 39:61

premolded, 76:58

skylights in, 36:10

slope limits for, 39:65

soldering, 39:65

staple gun for, 57:86 (EF)

steel,

advantages of, 15:62

aluminized, 24:43

corrugated, 2:18, 19, 20, 24 (CSH)

Cor-Ten, 24:42, 43, 27:4-6, 59:42, 45, 47

costs of, 15:62, 84:68

cutting, 20:16

factory coatings for, 24:46

paint for, 62:20 (CSH)

panel, 15:62

panel, alloy-coated, 52:73

panel, installing, 15:62, 17:4, 25:53

panel, prepainted, 15:61, 62

stainless, 24:42-43

weathering, 19:6, 24:42, 43, 27:4-6

stripping, clean method for, 57:26

tar,

compatibility of, 9:4

discussed, 64:43-44 (EF)

hot, 27:29, 31, 32:28 (CSH)

paper, temporary, wire hold-down for, 85:32

resurfacing, 7:8

tarring, how-not-to, 36:102

terne, 24:44, 39:62, 41:4

advantages of, 39:61-62

disastrous coatings for, 44:10-12

installing, 24:42-46

lengths of, 39:62

paint for, 44:12

painted improperly, restoring, 44:10-12

rustproofing, 41:4

source for, 24:44, 39:62

weights of, 39:62

thatch,

of African rondavels, 30:30, 31

Dutch supplier of, 39:90

early American, 11:76

examples of, 19:23, 22:72

process of, 22:73-76

roof pitch for, 24:4

simulating, 58:67-71 (EF)

tools for, 22:74, 75

vocabulary of, 22:73

tile, 9:45, 18:47-48, 24:31, 37:84, 45:70-71, 72, 51:60 (CSH)

adhesive for, 78:84

association for, 60:41, 65:61 (EF)

barrel, 24:31 (CSH)

barrel, as gutters, 24:29, 30 (CSH)

concrete, 14:27, 28, 37:84, 60:38-39 (EF)

concrete, source for, 43:77

cooling effects of, 74:106

custom, 60:38 (EF)

dividing, 65:61 (EF)

flashing for, 60:38, 65:56, 57, 59, 60 (EF)

framing for, 24:31-32 (CSH)

for hot climates, 70:16-18

hurricane-proof installation of, 78:84-85

installing, 60:38-41, 65:56-60 (EF)

installing, tips for, 69:4-6

Japanese, 4:54 (TFH)

Japanese, installing, 45:74-75 (CSH)

source for, 24:31, 60:38, 41 (CSH, EF)

terra-cotta, 45:38-41

types of, 60:36-38 (EF)

underlayment for, 60:38, 65:56 (EF)

tool bags for, 42:66, 67 (TB)

tools for, 10:56-61, 65, 39:62-63 (TB)

translucent panels for, 65:36-37, 38, 39, 72:82, 83 (REM)

for tropics, 85:72, 75

underlayment for, 39:62

vented, installing, 9:26, 27

ventilated panels for, 61:78 (EF)

ventilation for, 61:76 (EF)

zinc, 24:42, 44

See also Flashing. Membranes. Metals: galvanic corrosion of. Roofs.

Roofing compounds:

as chinking, 28:6

precautions with, 32:48 (BK)

against termites, 6:53

Roofing Industry Educational Institute:

programs of, 60:100

Roofmaster Products Co.: address for, 84:55

Roofs:

adding, 64:38, 39 (CSH)

new-over-old, 57:43-47 (REM)

for additions, 6:24, 25, 24:48, 49-51, 30:34-35 (FRC)

Arts-and-Crafts style, framing, 69:41, 42 (EEH)

aspen-leaf, 58:49, 52

asymmetrical shingled, 31:72-73

barn, rebuilding, 44:72-75

beam pockets for, 53:6

beams for,

built-up, 52:59 (CSH)

compound curved I-, 73:44, 45 (EEH)

perimeter, 34:72, 73

ring, concrete, 25:59-61

side-loaded, retrofitting, 81:53

wood I-, 52:55

bonnet, double-pitched, 38:80 (CSH)

books on, 10:60, 66, 30:78 (TB), 55:108-10, 60:106

bow, building, 20:8, 33:45-47 (TFH)

braces for, 10:67-68 (FRC)

brackets for,

setting up, 57:85 (EF)

using, 36:38 (TB)

built-from-the-inside, 33:52 (SH)

built-up, for decks, 12:58

bullnosed, 53:63, 65

calculator equations for, 10:61 (TB)

California, framing, 58:78-79 (MFC)

cantilevered, 41:39, 65:38, 39, 66:36, 37, 38 (SH), 66:87

failure of, 81:81-82

ground-level, 38:30, 34

chimney penetrations of, fire codes on, 69:78

circular,

framing, 35:76

rafter-bracket layout for, 8:26 (CBS)

for cisterns, 10:53 (BK)

clamp lift for, 76:28

climbing gear for, 23:76

for coffered ceilings, 75:36-40 (MFC)

cold,

airspace for, 64:4

book on, 63:42

building, 63:42-44, 65:14

color for, 74:42 (EF)

compression-post supported, 21:66, 67, 68

concrete, 6:29, 35

concrete self-venting, 63:36, 37, 39-40

and condensation damage, 61:76-77 (EF), 63:18

conical, 25:54-55, 59, 60, 28:4, 30:39-41 (FRC), 68:57-58

cantilevered support for, 52:54, 55

log, ceiling shot of, 18:3

for turret, 68:57-59

connectors for, split-ring, 8:29, 30 (TFH)

continuous multi-level, 19:76-77

for cooling, 36:71, 49:75 (EEH)

cross-gable,

discussed, 51:36 (CSH)

framing, 76:46-50 (MFC)

with cupolas and transoms, framing, 83:55, 56

curved, 66:75

compound-, 29:29, 30, 31-32

framing, 38:42, 38:42-44

with curved timbers, 21:38

decking for, 2x6, 24:6

decks as, 7:8, 12:58-60, 51:52-53, 84:12

solid laminated, 20:30, 31, 32, 33

tiled, 82:81

as design core, 38:60-61, 108 (CSH)
designing, 10:28-29, 80:85, 87, 85:93
     for materials efficiency, 84:46-47
for dormers, 35:49-50 (FRC)
dormers in, adding, 15:12, 28:26-30
double, 8:28, 29-30 (TFH)
drain for, 18:28
drainage pans for, 75:83-84
earthquake-proofing, 64:62, 64 (MFC)
for earth-sheltered houses, 7:36-37
     (DWS)
eaves for, 10:63 (FRC)
     braced-beam, 85:72, 75
     sheathing, 37:67-68 (FRC)
     in wet country, 66:43-44, 70:74-75
     widening, 75:59
English, early, 60:71
for entrances, 10:26, 29
estimates for, 27:34
evaluating, 10:42, 43
evolution of, 10:26, 27
exposed,
     framing, 36:72-75
     insulation for, 32:74
extending, 3:54-55
eyebrow, 44:64-68 (FRC)
with "falling" eaves, framing, 74:82-85
     (MFC)
felt for, under shingles, 84:16
finials for, Carpenter Gothic, 61:43, 44,
     45 (SH)
fire sprinklers for, 44:45 (BK)
flammability of, study on, 62:104
flat, 32:28 (CSH), 39:71
     designing, 75:83-84
     discouraged, 74:4
     metal roofing disadvised for, 58:14-16
     problems with, 3:51
     in snow country, 37:25, 26, 45:61 (BK,
          SH)
     system for, 55:84
from flat to peaked, 1:40-42 (FRC)
foam panel over decking,
     disadvantages of, 44:40 (SH)
folding, 85:148
framing, 10:62 (FRC)
     analyzed, 1:40-42, 15:8 (FRC)
     books on, 55:108-10, 57:78 (CSH, MFC)
     calculators for, 57:70 (TFH)
     clamps for, 74:70 (FC)
     clips for, 63:42
     gusset blocks for, 82:28
     instruction sheet on, 29:92
     with laminated-veneer lumber, 50:44-
          45 (MFC)
     re-, 14:24-25
frieze blocks in, 7:42, 10:63, 68 (FRC)
gable, 51:70, 71
     as archetype, 28:73
     ridge support for, 10:67 (FRC)
     structure of, 10:63, 65, 15:8 (FRC)

Key to books:

(BK)   Building Baths and Kitchens
(CBS)   Building with Concrete, Brick and Stone
(CSH)   Craftsman-Style Houses
(DWS)   Building Doors, Windows and Skylights
(EEH)   Energy-Efficient Houses
(EF)   Exterior Finishing
(FC)   Finish Carpentry
(FRC)   Frame Carpentry
(FWS)   Building Floors, Walls and Stairs
(MFC)   More Frame Carpentry
(REM)   Remodeling
(SH)   Small Houses
(TB)   Tools for Building
(TFH)   Timber-Frame Houses

     upturn for, 22:57-58 (CSH)
     ventilation in, 7:52-53 (DWS)
     wind vulnerability of, 78:82, 83, 85-86
gable-end, 10:63, 67, 24:14 (FRC)
     detailing for, 84:66
     as solar overhang, 22:10
gardens on, 48:49
for glassed gable end, 66:43-44
glazed, integral shading ladders for,
     16:26, 28
glossary for, 10:63 (FRC)
glulam, with 3-in. decking, 77:52-54
gypsy-wagon arched, 50:88-89 (CSH)
hammer-beam, 48:44-45 (TFH)
headers in, 10:63 (FRC)
heat gain through, controlling, 40:74
     (EEH)
for heavy snow loads, framing, 37:26
     (BK)
for high winds, 54:60, 62
hip, 52:83, 86
     center-supported, 55:58-60
     Dutch, 79:50, 51
     framing, 69:44-45 (MFC)
     in French manner, 57:68-70 (TFH)
     hurricane resistance of, 57:68, 78:86
          (TFH)
     Prairie School, 52:62, 67
     over rectangle, 11:44-45 (SH)
     with ring beam, 57:64, 65, 66
     ring-support system for, 20:30
     steel connectors for, 6:50
     on two sides, 66:79 (SH)
historic, restoring, 61:67-68
for hot climates, 70:16-18
hot unvented, theory of, 63:84 (EEH)
hurricane damage to, 57:104, 128
hurricane-proof, 78:82, 87
hyperbolic/paraboloid, 11:34, 35
I-beam and truss, welded, 82:65
ice dams on, preventing, 18:42, 63:42,
     71:14, 75:16

ice-and-water barrier for, source for,
     65:79 (REM)
ice-house insulated, 9:26, 27
insulation for, 1:9, 8:40, 18:47, 54:62
     (EEH)
     adding, 78:64, 65 (REM)
     board, 18:47
     renovation, 1:9
     rigid-foam, 58:61 (CSH)
     rigid-foam vs. fiberglass, 24:6
     tapered, 75:83
Japanese, 4:52, 53 (TFH)
ladders for, source for, 84:55
ladders in, 10:63 (FRC)
layout of, 10:62, 65, 12:4 (FRC)
     tees for, 10:61-63, 65-66 (TB)
loads from, redistributing, 81:87
with log members, 7:31
low sheltering, 73:51
metal connectors for, 85:47
multi-gabled, 84:64, 66, 67-68
multiple-form, 10:26, 27
nail guns for, 15:49, 53 (TB)
nails for, 85:47
of new to old, framing, 32:4
octagonal, 46:80, 83 (TFH)
     bay, 26:12 (erratum, 27:6)
     domed, 34:56-61 (FRC)
     lantern for, 32:37
     ring-tensioned, 24:76, 32:35-36, 63-64
oriented strand board on, 67:78
outriggers on, 10:69 (FRC)
     defined, 10:65. 69 (FRC)
overhangs for, deep, 70:65, 84:66, 67, 68
     (EEH)
     forms of, 10:28, 29
     fungi-prevention, 72:66 (REM)
     glazed, 80:42, 44
     insulating, 37:63
     measurements of, 55:57
     for solar designs, 84:86
     stuccoed wire-mesh, 40:29, 31-32
     support for, 23:14
     in tropics, 85:72, 75
panels for, tapered, 68:86
for photovoltaic systems, framing,
     72:75 (EEH)
pitch of,
     for asphalt, 72:16
     early, 13:25 (TFH)
plans for, 10:65 (FRC)
plates in, 10:63 (FRC)
pop-up in, 27:52-53
prefab homemade, 35:52-53 (BK)
production framing of, 60:83-87 (MFC)
     62:4
pumice for, 34:65, 66 (BK)
pyramidal, 25:92, 26:6
     46:74-75 (BK)
radiant barriers for, 40:11, 74
     49:75 (EEH), 80:55-57

radiation losses from, 15:12
and rain, weight of, 67:100
rainwater catchments for, 85:72, 74
raising, 67:64-66 (REM), 78:57-58
    intact, 72:54-56 (REM)
rake in, 10:63 (FRC)
rebuilding, weather protection for, 41:10
removing, 44:72-73, 58:76-77 (MFC)
repair of, 50:65-66
replacing, for third-floor addition, 74:47-
    49 (REM)
ridge dormers for, 5:30
ridge height of, 10:67 (FRC)
ridge truss for, built-up, 56:60, 61-62
    (EEH)
ridges for,
    sizing, 60:85 (MFC)
    strengthening, 64:85-87 (REM)
rise of, 28:33 (FRC)
    defined, 10:63 (FRC)
    finding, 24:12
round, 7:54, 55
run of, defined, 10:63 (FRC)
Russian ornamentation for, 26:96
safety with, 10:67 (FRC)
    OSHA standards for, 61:102
Scandinavian, 40:51, 53
sealers for, temporary, 34:66 (BK)
second-story, adding on, 58:76-79 (MFC)
shed, 28:68, 69, 70-72
    adding, reinforcement for, 24:51
        (FRC)
    canopy, framing, 78:16
sheltering, 52:67
shingled, gallery of, 57:90-91
simple cabin, 55:43-44 (SH)
single-form, 10:26, 27
skylights as, 15:31
slat, Cotswold, 60:70, 71
slope of, and wind resistance, 78:85
snow guards for, cast-aluminum, 53:16-
    18
solar panels as, tax credits for, 3:4
span for, measuring, 10:65 (FRC)
spiral-raftered, 18:69, 70, 71
sprockets for, 47:58, 59
steep,
    book on, 37:84
    danger of, 37:74-75
    overhung, 46:64-65 (TFH)
straightening, 9:6, 15:43
strengthening, 66:71, 72
stress-skin panels for, 39:73
string measurement for, 10:62 (FRC)
for structural strength, 79:82, 83
for superinsulated houses, 15:61
temporary, 3:6
tile, framing for, 24:31-32 (CSH)
timber-framed, 6:44 (TFH)
    54:84, 85, 86, 87 (TFH)
    as addition, 52:46, 48, 51 (TFH)

tools on, non-slide aid for, 62:28
for tower, framing, 74:68
two-pitch, 51:72, 73 (EEH)
Tyvek with, 25:82
unit rise of, defined, 10:63 (FRC)
unit run of, defined, 10:63 (FRC)
vapor barriers for, 8:28-30 (TFH), 65:14
vaulted stuccoed brick, 23:26-29
ventilation for, 2:5, 5:7, 15:12, 21:51-53,
    57:46, 61:76-77 (DWS, EF, REM)
vents for, under sheathing,
    commercial, 56:63 (EEH)
videos on, reviewed, 60:106
warm unvented, 61:77 (EF)
Whale house shingled, 19:84
white, for cooling, 11:30, 33 (EEH)
See also Cornices. Cupolas. Eaves.
    Flashing. Gutters. Purlins. Rafters.
    Ridge beams. Roofing. Sheathing.
    Skylights. Soffits. Vents.

Room dividers:
custom, source for, 43:94
forged, 75:77, 78
Roosevelt, Theodore: birthplace of, 5:36-
    38, 39
Root Cellaring (Bubel): cited, 72:14
Root cellars:
books on, cited, 72:14
design for, basement, 72:14
stone, 39:57, 60 (CBS)
Rope:
as decorative element, 15:26, 28
trucker's hitch in, 8:33 (TFH)
See also Knots. String.
Ros, Mat: mentioned, 34:55 (TB)
Rose (W.) Inc.: address for, 43:52 (CBS)
Rosen, David: on rustic shelter, 21:66-68
Rosenbaum, Marc:
on analyzer programs, 71:46-49
on energy-efficient house, 65:62-65 (SH)
on solar hot water, 68:50-55
wins design competition, 75:102
Rosenberg, N.: *Microclimate,* 9:16
Rosenblum, Chip: on homemade
    hardware, 63:66-68
Rosette Maker: reviewed, 48:90-91
Roskind, Robert: *Building Your Own
    House,* cited, 53:47, 50 (SH)
Ross, Howard: on air quality, 5:15
Ross, Jean: on animal hazards, 32:98
Ross, Ken: on Bolton House, 17:28-34
    (CSH)
Ross, Larry: on Lindbergh box house,
    74:116
Ross, William Post: bathroom by, 26:80
    (BK)
Rossbach, Sarah: *Feng-shui,* reviewed,
    45:116

Rot:
and air infiltration, 77:65
nontoxic preventative for, 67:90-92
Roth, Ed: reviews chain mortiser, 63:90-92
Roto Stella skylights: flashing for, 11:65
    (DWS)
Round houses:
constructing, 18:69-71
See also Silos.
Rousseau: MiniSaw PortaMax, reviewed,
    64:71
Router Master pad: reviewed, 55:92-94
Routers:
balusters with, 35:79 (FWS)
bases for, 27:37-39 (TB)
    adjustable, 49:26
    self-centering, 83:61
bead cutters for, large, 62:74
bearings in, checking, 79:75
bit bearings for, homemade, 41:69
    (CSH)
bit blanks for, large, 55:63
bits for, 27:37-39 (TB)
    bearing-guided, 55:36-37 (FC)
    bearing-over, making, 13:12
    bearing-over-cutter trim, 10:38, 39
    care for, 27:39 (TB)
    custom, 70:90
    diamond, 51:63
    face-frame, 55:36, 41 (FC)
    face-inlay, 58:41 (REM)
    flush-cutting trim, 10:38, 39
    panel pilot with drill point, source
        for, 53:18
    pattern grinding of, 18:75 (DWS)
    quirk-bead, 28:61 (TFH)
    roundover, sharpening, 47:32
    slot cutter, 78:92
    slot cutter, adjustable, 64:92
    storage for, 56:26
    tongue-and-groove, sets of, 46:12
    two-flute hinge-gain, 53:40 (FC)
bushings for, 27:40 (TB)
care of, 27:42 (TB)
choosing, 27:36-37 (TB)
climb cutting with, 55:39-40 (FC)
collets of, maintaining, 79:75
column-turning jig for, 64:55-57
Corian cutting with, 27:46 (BK)
curves with, compound, 7:19 (FRC)
cutouts with, 49:28
dadoing jig for, 1:23 (TB)
depth adjustment for, 55:40 (FC)
dovetails with, indexed, 55:41 (FC)
drip edges with, 39:14
drywall-cutout, 81:41
fences for, 27:39-40 (TB)
    adjustable infeed, 55:40-41 (FC)
fluting with, 9:21-22
    jig for, 54:55-56, 64:55-56
glue joints with, 85:65
grooves with, spaced, 61:74

guide systems for, 55:36-37 (FC)

hand, 4:22 (TFH)

hand drills as, 71:26

hinge templates for, 28:4, 31:28-31, 68:45 (FC, TB)

   reviewed, 70:104-106

hinge mortising with, 16:12, 26:29-31 (DWS)

for housed stringers, template for, 74:90-92

jointing with, 1:23, 55:40-4, 83:58 (FC, TB)

for laminate trimming, 75:61

milling fixture for, German, 35:59 (TB)

miters with,

   double-angle, 15:18

   lock, 55:64

moldings with, 18:74-76 (DWS)

   jig for, 51:24

mortises with,

   jig for, 35:79 (FWS), 83:60

   latch, 79:44

   lock, 81:61

   stair-tread, 48:57

   stringer, jig for, 55:38-39 (FC)

   templates for, 10:38-39, 79:45

pattern cutting with, 55:40-41 (FC), 81:51-53

plastic-laminate trimming with, 9:41 (BK)

plunge, 27:36-37 (TB)

   discussed, 71:78-80 (FC)

   maintaining, 79:75

   removable-base, reviewed, 57:96

   reviewed, 71:78-84 (FC)

   stringer jig for, 28:38-40 (FWS)

quirks with, 43:36, 37 (FWS)

for resin board, 84:42

safety with, 27:42 (TB)

stone shaping with, 51:63

tables for, 55:39-41 (FC)

   homemade, 1:23 (TB)

   sliding, 55:41 (FC)

table-saw mounting of, 1:23, 18:74 (DWS, TB)

templates for, 27:40 (TB)

   hinge butt, 55:37-38 (FC)

   timber-framing, 10:38

tenons with, 18:74-76 (DWS)

   slip, 27:40-42 (TB)

for timber joinery, 36:50 (TFH)

trammel jig for, 27:10

   making, 56:67 (FC)

trim-joinery jig for, 41:69 (CSH)

using, 27:39 (TB)

for weatherstripping groove, 68:45 (FC)

workpiece gripper pad for, 55:92-94

workstation for, reviewed, 71:94

See also brand names. Laminate trimmers.

Row houses: renovation of, 39:38-42, 47:79-83 (MFC, SH), 82:69-71

Rowe, Ellis: toolbox of, 74:87

Rower, Ken: mentioned, 45:46 (TFH)

Rowland, Amy Zaffarano: *Handcrafted Doors and Windows,* 36:41 (DWS)

Rowland, Mitch: on timber-framing machines, 35:55, 56 (TB)

Roy, Robert L.:

   Cordwood Masonry Houses, mentioned, 2:68

   on cordwood sauna, 2:68

Roybal house: features of, 5:46-47

Roybal, Richard: house by, 48:32-36

Roycroft Associates: address for, 54:100

R-Plus Industries: address for, 56:40

RTV silicone rubber:

   molds from, 1:36-37 (FWS)

   sources for, 1:39 (FWS)

R-2000 Energy Analysis Program (Canada):

   computer program of, 34:86

   reviewed, 61:106

   workshops of, 34:86

Rubber:

   antioxidant for, 48:57

   latex liquid, casting with, 1:37 (FWS)

   restorative for, 40:16

Rubbermaid, Inc.: address for, 75:28

Rubbol finish: source for, 1:6

Ruby Chemical Co.: Rubyfluid Soldering Flux, 39:65

Rucker, Debra G.: on solar house, 84:85-89

Rucker, Terence:

   on random-orbit sanders, 77:68-73

   on worm-drive saws, 70:66-67

Ruddick, J. N. R.: log-building study by, 34:50

Rudolf Bass Inc.: address for, 70:53 (FC)

Rule Industries:

   address for, 57:69 (TFH)

   Fit-Al bimetal blades, 16:47 (TB)

   Planetor bit, 28:40 (FWS)

Rules: bricklaying, 43:53 (CBS)

Runtal North America, Inc.:

   address for, 59:102

   radiators, source for, 38:28 (EEH)

Rural electric cooperatives: heat-pump water-heater policy of, 5:65

Rural Housing Improvement (Winchedon, MA): mentioned, 6:14

Russell, Dean: reviews plastering book, 31:80

Russell Swinton Oatman Design: plans from, 53:86, 88, 89

Russian fireplaces: *See* Masonry stoves.

Rust:

   on ironwork, removing, 16:44

   preventing, vapor cube for, 49:94

   stains from, removing, 49:26

Rustoleum Corp.: address for, 53:79 (REM), 70:49

Ruthling, Ford: sculpture by, 48:33

Rutt: address for, 65:73

Ruyle, Kim: on cellular concrete, 30:76

R-value:

   calculating, 30:6

   and compression, 29:4

   on concrete, 20:10

   discussed, 33:57

   handbook for, 10:46 (DWS)

   of hardwood, 39:10

   of high-performance glass, 41:84-86

   labeling of, 1:10

   and moisture, 41:4

   See also Insulation.

Rybczynski, Witold: *Looking Around,* reviewed, 84:124

Ryder, William: mentioned, 27:72, 76

Ryerson Steel Co.: address for, 73:79

Ryobi America Corp.:

   address for, 63:76, 70:53 (FC)

   carving blade from, 64:96

   chain mortiser,

      reviewed, 63:90-92

      unavailability of, 22:16

   circular saws, reviewed, 63:75-76, 77

   compound-miter saws,

      model RA-200, reviewed, 57:59, 60-61, 62

      reviewed, 83:64, 66, 67

   cut-off saws, reviewed, 62:81-84

   detail sander, reviewed, 83:96-98

   drills, VSR, reviewed, 82:36-41

   jigsaw #JSE 60, 33:61, 62 (TB)

   planers, portable #AP-10, 31:76

   plunge routers, reviewed, 71:79, 82, 83, 84 (FC)

   portable table saws, reviewed, 64:72-74

   power planes, reviewed, 54:77, 78-79

   radial-arm saws, benchtop, 36:88

   random-orbit sanders, reviewed, 77:71, 72

   reciprocating saws,

      gas-powered, 36:88

      model EJ-100, reviewed, 41:84

   table saws, #BT 3000, reviewed, 75:92

   thickness planers, mentioned, 82:92

   trade practices of, 82:104

Saarinen, Eero: reflecting windows by, 44:78-79

Sachs, Harvey: on indoor air quality, 22:16

Sackett, Jim:

   Japanese housing report by, 28:82

   on Japanese imports, 46:96

Sacks, Alvin M.: on deep foundations, 69:58-61

Safety:
accidents, causes of, 65:102
and asbestos, 24:82-83, 50:66-67
associations for, 34:52, 55 (TB)
books on, 51:104
34:55 (TB)
source for, 64:74
in brazing, 63:67, 68
and building alone, guidelines for, 55:56
of carbon monoxide, 5:15
with chainsaws, 61:82, 78:39
and chemicals, handbook of, 73:67
of chlordane, 5:12
with circular saws, 55:56, 63:77
in coatings, sources for, 67:90-92
code requirements for, 50:59
cold-weather, 50:60-63
with composition board, 67:80, 81
and creosote, 62:18-20 (CSH)
and cumulative injuries, 64:66-69
with cut-off saws, 62:80
and electromagnetic fields, 82:20 (CSH)
ensuring, 10:10
environmental,
booklet on, 55:108
organization for, 62:104-106
factors influencing, 34:51-55 (TB)
fire-prevention association for, 64:106
of floor finishes, 67:54, 55, 72:4-6
and foam-core panels, 62:53, 56 (TFH)
and foot injuries, 79:56-57
of formaldehyde, 5:15
and gas refrigerators, 71:106
in hammering, 62:4
with hand tools, guide for, 84:6
with handsaws, 81:6
with hazardous materials, booklet on,
62:114
house for, 50:102
household, organization for, 60:102
of indoor air pollution, 5:15
insulated wiring for, color-coded, 84:98
of insulation, 2:64-65, 56:37, 42
with jacks, 51:6-8
with ladders, 57:85 (EF)
with laminated-veneer lumber, 50:44
(MFC)
of latex paints, 67:67
in lead removal, 76:4
of low air-change rates, 1:10-12, 5:4
with masonry blades, 50:18
in metal polishing, 63:68
of methylene chloride, 3:4
with molder/planers, 55:51, 54-55
with nail guns, 56:57
NIOSH number for, 72:6
OSHA inspections for, 69:100
with outlets, during painting, 67:68
in overhead work, 50:4
and ozone, 63:60
in paint removal, 62:39 (EF), 84:74-75

of paint strippers, 2:64, 10:10
of paints, 10:10
with particleboard, 65:72
with particleboard fumes, 54:16
of pentachlorophenol, 1:6, 14:51, 53,
15:21, 27
in pours, 78:4
with power planes, 54:78
pre-amputation advice for, 53:102-104
products for, 34:55 (TB), 58:90-91
source for, 61:84
of radon, 5:15, 51:14-16
with railings, 77:8
regulations and, 34:52-53 (TB)
on roofs,
OSHA standards for, 61:102
while shingling, 60:8
of sanding, 10:10
with scaffolding, 67:98-100
shoes for, 81:4
and sick-house hazards, publications
on, 55:108
sneakers for, steel-toed, 69:96
and space heaters, 51:42
of spraying, 10:10
stair design for, 65:66-68
of sulfur dioxide, 5:15
with table saws, 64:74, 83:80-81
cautionary tale for, 55:100
with table-saw sliding tables, 56:4
with tile saws, 70:60
in tiling roofs, 65:61 (EF)
in tool wiring, 82:41
with wet saws, 51:63
in wood burning, 70:79
of wood preservatives, 10:10, 56:14,
63:63, 65 (MFC)
See also Building codes. Fire:
prevention of. First-aid kits. Healthy
houses. Injuries. National Fire
Protection Association. Radon.
Respirators. Scaffolding. *specific
machine, process or product.*
Ventilation.
Safety Is Specific: source for, 34:55 (TB)
*Safety Standards for Stairways and
Ladders* (OSHA): cited, 84:53
Sage Advance Corp.: address for, 68:54
St. George, Michele: on sewage
aggregate, 22:18 (CSH)
Saint Products: address for, 67:90
Saint Sophia: dome of, 25:4
Salaman, R. A.: *Dictionary of Tools,*
reviewed, 47:112
Salt: phase-change, for heat, 50:63
Saltboxes:
balloon framing for, 4:46 (FRC)
evolution of, 4:44, 13:25-26 (FRC, TFH)
garage-apartment plan for, 34:67-69
(SH)

for greenhouse, book on, 7:60
open-plan, framing, 4:44-47 (FRC)
solar-adapted, 2:50-52 (SH)
Salvadori, Mario, and Robert Heller:
Structure in Architecture, 7:28 (TFH)
Salvage:
books on, 28:86, 67:104
house from, 66:74-77
newspaper for, 46:62 (TFH)
Salvaged Brick: source for, 23:49
Salvaging Old Barns and Houses
(Abrams): reviewed, 28:86
Samuel Cabot, Inc.:
address for, 52:67, 66:45
stains, 44:88
Samuel Yellin Metalworkers: work of,
16:44
San Francisco Institute of Architecture:
address for, 63:100
San Francisco Victoriana: address for,
51:85 (MFC)
Sandaro: address for, 79:75
Sanders:
belt, metal grinding with, hazard of,
49:28
belts for,
lacquer-thinner cleaning of, 54:26
nondirectional, 64:96
detail, reviewed, 83:96-98
orbital, for stone polishing, 51:63
pole, for drywall, 8:57, 32:69 (FRC, FWS)
power,
auto belt-tracking, 18:17
belts for, cleaning, 11:14
belts for, reversing, 11:4, 14:4
drum (floor), 14:58, 59 (FWS)
edging (floor), 14:58, 59 (FWS)
for moldings, 14:45 (TB)
for paint removal, 1:33 (FWS)
random-orbit,
cordless, 77:69-70
for floors, 64:94-96
reviewed, by brand, 77:68-73
table for, 70:34
Sanding:
contoured blocks for, 61:26
of crown molding, 74:81 (FC)
die grinder for, pneumatic, 47:67
of exterior surfaces, 62:39 (EF)
of finish, 48:77
floor, process of, 7:6, 14:58-59 (FWS)
sanders for, random-orbit, 64:94-96
with molder/planer, 55:55
on table saws, disc for, 72:28
Sanding blocks: making, 50:30
Sanding sealers:
and alkyd-resin, 8:6
discussed, 48:75
and polyurethane, 8:6
spraying, 48:75, 77

Sandpaper

Sandpaper:
for clear finish, 48:77
double-sided tape with, 27:16
lacquer-thinner cleaning of, 54:26
non-tear, source for, 74:81 (FC)
Sandrin, Michael: gate by, 52:90
Sandrisser, Barbara: house by, 45:70-75, 89 (CSH)
Sands Level and Tool: address for, 58:45
Sandvik handsaws: discussed, 20:69 (TB)
Sanfilippo, Steven: house by, 33:96
Sanford, Al: quoted, 8:16
Sanford, Jim:
acrylic glazing of, 10:31, 32-33 (DWS)
mentioned, 25:38 (EEH)
Santarsiero, Tom: on kitchen cabinets, 85:53
Santo, Sherril: on farmhouse remodel, 49:58-62 (SH)
Sanyo Fisher: address for, 75:94
Sargent, Tom: mentioned, 29:33
Sarnafil Inc.: address for, 65:79 (REM)
Sash:
cord, source for, 64:49 (FC)
eyebrow, making, 76:72-75 (FC)
kinds of, 18:72, 73 (DWS)
making, sequence for, 18:72-77 (DWS)
in restorations, 29:67
wood for, 18:72 (DWS)
Sashco Sealant: address for, 62:41 (EF)
Saskatchewan Conservation House:
discussed, 9:56
Sassafras *(Sassafras albidum)*: shingles from, 6:47 (TFH)
Saudi Arabia: traditional housing in, 49:100-102
Saum, David: on air quality, 46:96
Saunas:
cedar yurt, 13:76
cordwood, 2:68
Finnish, building, 51:42-45
heat of, using, 69:43 (EEH)
and laundry combination, 33:52 (SH)
woods for, 34:8
See also Showers: steam, generating units for.
Saussey, Hunter: mentioned, 29:74
Savage, Craig:
on computer research, 46:58-60
on jigsaws, 33:58-62 (TB)
Macintosh Construction Forum, reviewed, 68:108
on molding, 57:48-51
on pneumatic nailers, 47:72-75 (FC)
on routers, 27:36-42 (TB)
trim by, 49:91
Trim Carpentry Techniques, cited, 57:51
Savidge, Bill: staircase by, 49:78-82
Saving Our Ancient Forests
(Zuckerman): reviewed, 75:110
Saw Saver: reviewed, 55:92
Saw set: using, 20:70, 71 (TB)

Sawblades:
brick-cutting, 64:82-83
carbide-tipped,
cleaning, 72:44 (MFC), 75:4, 77:10
danger with, 34:54 (TB)
diamond whetstone for, 13:12
discussed, 72:43-47 (MFC)
noise-limited, 72:44 (MFC)
reviewed, 50:95
sharpening, 72:44 (MFC)
thin-kerf, source for, 64:70
cleaning, 8:12
combination, 24:33-34 (TB)
covers for, 51:24
crosscut, 24:33 (TB), 72:47 (MFC)
negative-rake, 58:77 (MFC)
for plywood, 76:63-65 (MFC)
sharpening, 24:34-35 (TB, TB)
for stone, 51:63
Teflon-coated, reviewed, 56:92
types of, 24:33-34 (TB)
waxing, 62:28
Sawbuck: *See* Rockwell: Sawbuck.
Sawdust: bricks from, 15:10
Sawhorses:
bench substitute for, quick, 81:28
clamping system for, 6:8
clamps for, 74:72, 73 (FC)
folding, 3:9, 6:8, 10:12, 75:26
source for, 71:94
knockdown toolbox, 9:10
making, 43:56-57 (TB), 50:30
metal legs for, 65:47 (FC)
outlet for, 53:28
radial-arm-saw jig for, 47:32
ripping on, anchors for, 53:26
as roller stands, 29:16
saw hook for, 71:26
steel-tubing, 54:24
variable-height notched, 18:12
Sawing: waste-side mark for, 68:28
Sawklip: source for, 24:10
Sawmills:
bandsaw portable, 35:90
chainsaw,
book on, 41:51 (TB)
carriage-and-track, 41:49-51 (TB)
chainsaws for, 41:51 (TB)
homemade, 10:35, 36-37 (TB)
log cabins with, 7:29-31
saws for, 10:35 (TB)
sources for, 7:31, 42:41 (TFH)
large mechanized, 47:40-42
portable, 51:70
Saws: *See* Bandsaws. Bits: hole-saw. *brand names.* Chainsaws. Circular saws. Cut-off saws. Handsaws. Miter saws, power. Radial-arm saws. Reciprocating saws. Table saws. Tile saws.
Saw-Tech Industries, Inc.: chainsaw blade, reviewed, 43:96

Sawzall:
blade lock for, 60:26
See also Reciprocating saws.
Sayko, Sam: on solar program, 33:84
Scaffolding:
care with, 67:98-100
designing, 10:67 (FRC)
discussed, 62:37-38 (EF)
electrocution danger from, NIOSH booklet on, 72:100
folding, source for, 71:94
homemade, 18:54
jacks for, 20:4
braced, 18:14
ladders for, 8:12, 57:85 (EF)
need for, 10:67 (FRC)
non-skid, 68:28
on outriggers, for turret, 68:58
plank supports for, wall-bolted, 57:28
rafter-tail attached, 35:14
roof brackets for, 12:55, 36:38, 57:85 (EF, TB), 49:40 (REM)
swing, 31:65
wall brackets for, 12:52-53
Scandinavian style:
fixtures, sources for, 35:34
prefab houses, 23:84, 28:82
Scarf joints: *See* Joinery.
Scawthorne, Dr. Charles: quoted, 34:86
Schaplow, Terry: on radon liability, 61:98
Scheck, Gerald: iron work by, 48:81, 83
Scheduling for Builders (Householder): reviewed, 46:104
Schiffer, Herbert F.: *Shaker Architecture,* cited, 79:88
Schindler, R. M.:
apartment units of, 6:6
book on, 4:30
concrete use of, 14:70
houses by, 4:26-33, 7:4
mentioned, 16:6
and Richard Neutra, 19:29
Schinkel, Karl Friedrich: influence of, 70:64 (EEH)
Schipa, Gregory:
on reproduction doorway, 11:36-41 (DWS)
on restoration, 1:48-51
Schipper, Lee:
addresses conference, 33:84
on Swedish houses, 28:82
Schlage Lock Co.:
keyless deadbolt by, 48:65 (FC, MFC)
lockset, interconnected, 48:62-63, 64 (FC, MFC)
Schlender, Shelley: on Haertling house, 58:49-53
Schlerman, Carl: on first framing, 71:126
Schmidt, Tom:
houses by, 34:35, 36-37
Rammed Earth Designs for the Desert Southwest, 34:39

Schmuecker, Tom: paint removal by, 16:66-69 (DWS)

Schnaser, Gene: on nail pulling, 32:53-55 (TB)

Schneider, Paul: on making sinks, 51:54-57

Schnittker, John M.: on power trowel, 83:52-53

Schools: *See* Instruction.

Schramm: 125-cfm compressor, 34:39

Schreier, Curtis: door by, 29:32, 33

Schroeder, Roger:
on stone-ender construction, 6:42-47 (TFH)
as joint author. *See* Sobon, Jack.

Schuttner, Scott:
on cold-weather work, 50:60-63, 51:41-42
on deck foundations, 79:64-69

Schutz, Robert: gate by, 52:88

Schwan, W. Creighton:
on electrical outlet boxes, 8:44-45
Practical Electrical Wiring, 8:45

Schwartz, Barry: on remodeling house, 28:49-53 (FWS)

Schweikher, Paul:
career of, 16:62-63 (TFH)
home by, 16:58-65 (TFH)
house site of, 16:84

Schweitzer, Robert, and Michael W. R. Davis: *America's Favorite Homes,* reviewed, 77:120

Schwob, Bill: photographs of, 5:60

Schwolsky, Rick, and James L. Williams: *Builder's Guide to Solar Construction, The,* reviewed, 18:78

Scofield (L. M.) Co.:
address for, 66:86
Lithochrome Chemical Stain of, 11:10, 28:69

Scorps: for log scribing, source for, 34:49

Scotland: book on, reviewed, 54:106

Scott, Charles: on Norwegian corner posts, 72:84-85

Scott, Kathy: on penthouse, 31:63-65

Scrapers:
cleaning, 24:24
making, for crown molding, 74:81 (FC)
for renovation, 12:51 (TB)

Screen printing: method for, 78:72-73

Screen Tight: address for, 75:94

Screens:
attaching, over frame, 21:16
coated fiberglass, source for, 57:75 (FC)
for decks, 46:66, 69 (EF)
door, 51:50, 51, 52
making, 36:39-41 (DWS), 57:72-75 (FC)
sliding, 48:72, 73 (SH), 51:51-52, 53
sliding, automatic, 65:77 (REM)
storm, making, 62:6
8-ft. wide, 59:82

Key to books:

(BK)   Building Baths and Kitchens
(CBS)   Building with Concrete, Brick and Stone
(CSH)   Craftsman-Style Houses
(DWS)   Building Doors, Windows and Skylights
(EEH)   Energy-Efficient Houses
(EF)   Exterior Finishing
(FC)   Finish Carpentry
(FRC)   Frame Carpentry
(FWS)   Building Floors, Walls and Stairs
(MFC)   More Frame Carpentry
(REM)   Remodeling
(SH)   Small Houses
(TB)   Tools for Building
(TFH)   Timber-Frame Houses

exterior, bamboo-faced, 68:72, 73 (EF)
folding *shoji,* 65:36-37, 38-39
pocket sliding, 8:74
retractable, 64:48 (FC)
rolling, source for, 60:50 (FC)
shingled, 45:85
sliding, 30:23
stretching, 58:24
various metal, supplier for, 54:4
window, making, 50:73 (FC)
wood-strip, 7:38 (DWS)

Screw eyes: brace installation of, 30:10

Screw guns:
for metal framing, 32:68 (FRC)
models of, 34:42-45 (TB)
Quik Drive attachment for, reviewed, 62:92-94
reviewed, by brand, 85:69-71
screws for, 34:44-45 (TB)
self-feed,
advantages of, 85:68-69
reviewed, 46:90
sources for, 34:45 (TB)

Screw hooks: driving, 55:26

Screwdrivers:
avoiding, 67:6
extended power,
criticized, 84:4-6
making, 83:28
for renovation, 12:51 (TB)
reshaping, as scribers, 14:14
square-tipped, making, 46:26

Screws:
adapter, for railing, 65:86
for adobe, 30:41
anchors for, reusable drywall, 62:94
bag for, reviewed, 62:94
bugle-head, 32:68 (FRC)
caps for, plastic, 58:41 (REM)
for concrete,
described, 41:55 (CBS)
source for, 65:86

damaged,
extractor for, 74:90
removing, 75:26
drywall, 10:4, 34:42-45 (TB)
brittleness of, 64:65 (MFC)
countersinking, 78:28
types of, 81:38-40
uses of, 6:8, 10:4, 12:51 (TB)
zinc-plated bugle-head, source for, 51:48 (EF)
epoxy thread repair for, 63:26
for exterior siding, 75:54 (EF)
framing, 32:68 (FRC)
hardened, 57:28
for headers, vs. nails, 64:8-10
hook-, installation aid for, 85:32
knockdown fastener, 74:77
lubricant for, silicone caulk, 61:24
old, hole-saw remover for, 81:26, 84:28
organizers for, 12:51 (TB)
for particleboard, 34:45 (TB), 67:79
plugs for,
angled, 71:24
from leather punch, 84:28
presanded, 19:14
tapered, 85:108
Quadrex, 34:45 (TB)
reinforcing, with epoxy, 70:47
for renovation, 12:51 (TB)
for screw guns, 34:44-45 (TB), 85:68-69
self-tapping, 34:45 (TB)
all-weather, 82:96
slot cleaning for, 49:26
square-drive, advantages of, 55:59
stainless,
source for, 63:92
with washers, 46:52 (EEH)
in stripped metal, solution for, 69:30
TAPCON, 41:55 (CBS), 61:74
tapered vs. machine, 69:74
tapping, 34:45 (TB)
Teks, 34:44, 45 (TB)
for treated lumber, 63:64, 65 (MFC)
trim-head, 32:68 (FRC)
of various metals, source for, 63:92
and wood shrinkage, 81:55-56
See also Screw guns.

Scribers: for log building, making, 53:83

Scribing:
ceiling boards, with spiling battens, 77:60-62
of patches, 68:28
pencil for, 77:58
scribers for,
double-bubble level, 2:39, 34:49-50
homemade, 11:12
large, 5:25 (DWS)
from screwdriver bits, 14:14
from spade bits, 79:30
V-block and pencil, 81:42
V-notched square as, 20:16
techniques of, 77:58-63

Scroll saws: *See* Jigsaws.

SCS: *See* Simple Caulk and Seal method.

Scully, Vincent: *Shingle Style and the Stick Style, The,* reviewed, 45:120

Sculpture:
exterior, gallery of, 78:88-89
freeform welded, 10:76
glass, 73:89

Sculpture Associates:
Hydrocal, 29:66
synthetic rubber casting material, 29:66

Sculpture House:
address for, 54:75
casting supplies from, 1:39, 5:10 (FWS)

Sealants:
acoustical non-drying, 46:72
air-infiltration-preventing, 77:67
applying, 61:39
associations for, 61:42, 65:45
backer rods for, 61:38
for baseboards, 61:26
bedding-compound, 61:70
bond breakers for, 61:38
books on, 61:42
and chemical incompatibility, 72:80 (FC)
for chemically sensitive, 46:73
containers for, 61:36, 37
cord, 61:37
epoxy, sources for, 70:49
foam, 47:54 (TFH), 61:37
applicator for, precise, 39:92
disadvised, as fire stop, 49:4
solvent for, 39:92
against formaldehyde, 46:73
for foundations, 63:82 (EEH)
gap for, 61:37-38, 39
guns for,
air-powered, 61:36
metal tips for, 61:39
for gutters, 67:40, 42 (EF)
liquid, 61:37
for noise control, 58:54, 57
non-ozone-damaging, 85:18
nontoxic, 81:106
for plaster, 82:68
PRC, qualities of, 2:56
removable, 61:37
silicone vs. urethane, 72:78, 80 (FC)
specialty, 61:37
supply sources for, 61:42
types of, evaluating, 61:36-37, 40-41
for vapor-retarder joints, 61:106
See also Caulk.

Sealed Insulating Glass Manufacturers Association (SIGMA):
address for, 51:78 (FC)
glazing recommendations of, 11:4

Sealers:
acrylic liquid, for concrete, 66:86
for air/vapor barriers, 9:56
for brick, 2:45, 14:35 (CBS), 82:20 (CSH)

clear, 64:49 (FC)
for concrete cold joints, 2:36
exterior, 46:71
homemade, 10:8
for flooring, 27:12
against formaldehyde, 46:73
for logs, 8:8
marine adhesive, 33:46 (TFH)
for masonry, 81:71
nontoxic, 73:68
sources for, 67:92
non-yellowing, 59:56 (CSH)
polyurethane, roll-and-daub
application for, 46:41 (REM)
for rammed earth, 11:23
for tilework, 79:20-22
waterproof, source for, 60:54
See also Paint: air/vapor barrier.

Searchlink computer service: described, 46:60

Sears, Roebuck and Co.:
compound-miter saws, reviewed, 83:65, 66-67
Craftsman tools, 7:60
reciprocating saws, discussed, 16:46 (TB)
screwdrivers, 12:51 (TB)
drills, VSR, reviewed, 82:36-41
hinge butt mortising template, 31:31 (TB)
houses by, mail-order, 28:42-45, 37:90
jigsaws, scrolling-head, 33:61-62 (TB)
kitchen cabinets, 7:60
miter saws, 19:42, 44 (TB)
compound-cut radial, 20:4-6
molder/planers, reviewed, 55:50-55
reviewed, 62:51
water heaters, defective, 2:64

Seating: design booklet for, 53:14

Second Generation Passive Solar Systems: source for, 30:52 (CBS)

Secrets of the Old Growth Forest (Kelly): reviewed, 57:114

Section modulus: defined, 7:25, 26 (TFH)

Security: closet for, 57:26-28

Seddon, Leigh:
Low-Cost Green Lumber Construction, cited, 7:42
Practical Pole Building Construction, cited, 83:77

Sedge (Cladium mariscus): for thatching, 22:73, 77

Sedgwick Lifts, Inc.: address for, 73:104

Seeley, Jeff: mentioned, 25:44, 29:74 (TFH)

Seep 'n Seal epoxy: mentioned, 16:20, 21 (CSH)

Seibold, Llewellyn: on budget craftsmanship, 52:57-61 (CSH)

Seiko Instruments USA, Inc.: ultrasonic tape, reviewed, 78:54-55

Select Home Designs: address for, 53:89

Selected Resource Guide on Accessible Environments for the Disabled: reviewed, 32:86

Selects-Finish, Commons-Boards: source for, 17:8

Selkirk Metalbestos:
address for, 46:14
chimneys, types of, 12:8

Sellers, David:
on acrylic glazing, 10:30-33 (DWS)
on Skidompha house, 17:76-79 (SH)

Sellers, P.: *Physical Climatology,* 9:16

Sellery, David: toolbox of, 74:86

Selvin, Nancy: on screen-printing tiles, 78:72-73

Selwyn, Judith E.: as joint author. *See* Phillips, Morgan.

Semler, Paul: extendable level by, 23:80

Semling-Menke Co.: Insulated Door, 6:60

Senco Products, Inc.:
address for, 58:68 (EF), 68:64
coated nails, 15:51 (TB)
nail guns, 15:51 (TB)
pneumatic, discussed, 47:74-75 (FC)
reviewed, 56:52, 53, 54-56, 57
pneumatic tools, 15:53 (TB)

Senf, Norbert: on masonry-heater emissions, 71:54

Septic-tank systems:
described, 3:37-38 (BK)
information on, 64:102
maintenance of, 3:38-39 (BK)
percolation tests for, 3:36-37 (BK)
in poorly drained ground, 14:37
tree roots in, 23:10
See also Drain lines. Plumbing.

Sequoia sempervirens: *See* Redwood.

Serdy, Jim: on solar hot water, 68:52-53

Servais, James:
house by, 53:46-50 (SH)
reviews gas nail gun, 33:82 (TB)
on two-coat plaster, 31:58-62 (FWS)

Servais Design and Construction, Inc.:
bathroom by, 80:91

Servel Corrective Action Committee:
number for, 71:106

Service core: freestanding, 46:36

Setting Ceramic Tile (Byrne): cited, 56:47, 69:57

Seventh Old House Catalog, The (Grow, comp.): reviewed, 70:122

Sewage: aggregate from, 22:18 (CSH)

Sewage disposal: *See* Septic-tank systems.

Sewall, Stephen:
on Federal fence, 25:73-77
on Federal mantel, 54:54-57
on replacing sills, 19:34-36 (DWS)
on screen doors, 57:72-75 (FC)

Sewer lines: *See* Drainage systems.

Shacks:
building, for movie, 56:48-51
modular knockdown job-site, 21:44-45 (TB)

Shades:
louvers for, exterior, 79:70-71, 72-73
porch-roof, draped burlap for, 72:83 (REM)
roll, exterior, 5:33
for sloped surfaces, 31:34 (DWS)
track-mounted, exterior, 11:35
venetian, wire-strung, 64:87 (REM)
See also Shoji.

Shading masks: making, 5:52, 53 (DWS)

Shafer, Jonathan F.: on curved casings, 67:82-85 (FC)

Shakeproof Co.: Teks screw, 34:43, 45 (TB)

Shaker Architecture (Schiffer): cited, 79:88

Shaker houses:
book on, cited, 79:88
design of, 79:87-88
remodel of, 79:85-89

Shakertown Siding:
address for, 54:44, 57:45, 82:84, 83:41 (EF, REM)
shingles, mentioned, 1:62, 25:62

Shakes: *See* Roofing: shingle.

Shaklee: addresses for, 46:72-73

Shands, Paul: constructs penthouse, 31:63-65

Shapers:
book on, 50:72 (FC)
cutters for,
cope-and-pattern, 58:38 (REM)
cope-and-stick, using, 72:52 (FC)
custom, 61:68
radius roundover, 60:74
hold-down for, 50:73 (FC)
moldings on, curved, 72:53 (FC)
sash making with, 50:72-73 (FC)
sliding jig for, 50:72-73 (FC)
staircase elbows on, jigs for, 60:74-77
stock feeders for, source for, 34:55 (TB)

Shapiro, Andrew M.: *Homeowner's Complete Handbook for Add-on Solar Greenhouses and Sun-spaces, The,* reviewed, 29:90

Sharpening:
alumina/ceramic system for, 77:94-96
buffing in, 18:61 (TB)
of chisels, 4:25 (TFH)
of drill bits, 4:25 (TFH)
honing in, 18:59-60 (TB)
of plane irons, 4:25 (TFH)
system for, 76:84-85 (FC)
process of, 18:58-61 (TB)
sandpaper for, 18:56 (TB)
value of, 18:56 (TB)

Shaving horses: for shingles, 30:48

SHC-BRC: *See* Small Homes Council-Building Research Council.

Shear: defined, 7:25, 27, 28, 32:30-31 (FRC, TFH)

Shears:
plastic-laminate, 75:61
for thatching, 22:75

Sheathing:
for A-frame houses, 20:67
asphalt-impregnated, 8:30 (TFH), 66:48
vs. plywood, 4:44 (FRC)
board, 37:69 (FRC)
as bracing, 85:56
buckled, cause of, 81:57-58
capillary breaks for, commercial, 56:42
cardboard, foil-faced, 80:57
clips for, 43:49 (FRC)
cutouts in, with router, 49:28
cutting in place, 3:34 (TB)
fastening of, with stud gun, 23:76, 77
foam, effectiveness of, 56:38
form plywood for, 66:84
glue for, disadvised, 85:47
gypsum panels for, 73:58
hurricane-proofing, 78:85
insulating, 28:12, 31:70
for moisture control, 50:100
jig for, 37:14
laminated reflective, 49:73-74 (EEH)
molsture problems with, and asphalt-impregnated paper, 56:42
nail guns for, 15:53 (TB)
nailing, in hurricane areas, 79:4
nails for, 85:46-47
oriented strand board as, gluing of, 67:78, 85:47
particleboard for, cement-bonded, 70:63 (EEH)
pine, advantages of, 74:56
plywood, 37:67-69 (FRC)
removal of, tool for, 32:54, 55 (TB)
sequence for, 82:44
as shear wall, 54:60-61
for shingles, 54:42 (EF)
solid vs. let-in, 35:8-10
support hooks for, making, 78:30
for tight radii, 65:83 (MFC)
tongue-and-groove,
installing, 55:60
laminated, custom, source for, 55:60
traditional, advantages of, 47:47 (TFH)
for turret, 68:58
twin-arrow jointed plywood, reviewed, 53:98

Sheaths: leather, making, 51:26-28

Sheehan, Sean:
on balloon framing, 62:62-63 (MFC)
on forests, 59:4

Sheetrock: *See* Drywall.

Sheldon, George: book of, reprinted, 29:90

Shell Oil Co.: polybutylene pipe, 21:12, 26:12, 27:70 (CBS)

Shellac: *See* Finishes.

Shells: over entrances, 3:14, 17-18 (DWS)

Shelter Institute:
Astrolon, 8:30 (TFH)
film by, 1:66
hung-wall system of, 8:28-30 (TFH)
mentioned, 10:48, 52 (SH)

Shelter (Kahn, ed.): reviewed, 62:114

Shelter, 1973: quoted, on straw-bale construction, 24:71, 72

Shelter-Kit houses: described, 5:14

Shelters: Central Park, building, 21:66-68

Shelters on the Plains: mentioned, 31:54

Shelton, Jay: *Wood Heat Safety,* 11:10

Shelves:
board-and-bar-stock, 52:37, 40 (TFH)
built-in, 10:25, 32:42
cantilevered, 12:31
clips for, source for, 69:53
in closets,
for kitchens, 66:67 (EEH)
plywood sheathing for, 81:28
concealed-mount, 60:44, 45 (SH)
Danish system, 31:76
display, adjustable lighted, 80:54
facings for, inlaid, 65:86, 87
fiberboard for, 71:72
glass ceiling-hung, 75:47 (REM)
granite, 51:62
heavy utility, supporting, 21:45 (TB)
ladder for, rolling, 65:86, 87
library, maple, 65:85-87
mantel-flanking, 49:43 (REM)
in modular design, 66:59 (SH)
open, building, 63:55, 57 (REM)
peg-hole jig for, 58:36 (REM)
pins for, brass, 65:86
pivoting-sliding, 74:75, 78
plate-groove lining for, 52:98
plate-joined, 70:51, 52, 53 (FC)
rests for, 9:38 (BK)
rod-hung, 4:6
roll-out, making, 69:51, 53
scribing, 77:60
semicircular, 49:61, 62 (SH)
soffit-retracting, 34:75
steel, source for, 53:44 (SH)
in stone partition, 80:57
between studs, 47:89
supports for, drilling for, 79:79
swing-up mechanisms for, 67:75 (REM)
tenon-supported, 44:52, 53 (SH)
understair, 49:26
uprights for, foam-sandwich, 65:86, 87
U-shaped, bevel joint for, 60:26

Sheridan, Patrick: on Laguna Beach remodel, 59:83-87 (CSH)

Sherman, Joe:
on house revival, 32:56-59
on IASTE conference, 49:100-102

on preservation workshop, 27:82-83
on renovation classes, 29:88-89
reviews *Roots,* 53:108
on Shelburne restoration, 50:64-68
Sherwin-Williams:
address for, 62:48 (SH)
tile stain of, 1:55
Zinc-Clad #5, 29:74, 75
Sherwood, Gerald: *How to Select and Renovate an Older House,* 28:86
Shibata, Tetsuo: bookcase by, 58:87
Shims:
box file for, 46:26
sizing, 51:24
table-saw jig for, 58:26
Shingle style:
Block Island, 19th-century, 45:83
book on, 45:120
cabin in, 46:80-83 (TFH)
contemporary, 45:82-87, 89
house in, building, 52:52-56
Shelburne house in, 50:64-68
solar, building, 12:64-67 (EEH)
Shingle Style and the Stick Style, The (Scully): reviewed, 45:120
Shingles: *See* Roofing. Siding.
Shining Examples: described, 4:62
Shirts: for job sites, 79:6-8
Shivers, Natalie: *Walls and Moldings,* reviewed, 77:120
Shoes:
fashionable safety, source for, 81:4
for job sites, 79:57, 81:4
safety, source for, 69:96
seaworthy, 43:116
sneaker, steel-toed, 69:96
Shoji:
American-style, 45:70-71 (CSH)
catalog for, 51:90
ceiling, 29:58, 59-61 (CSH)
custom, source for, 75:94
modified, 19:39, 41 (BK)
sash-adapted, 8:75
sliding door, 29:56-57 (CSH)
storage box for, 45:71 (CSH)
See also Lighting. Screens.
Shooting boards:
for circular saws, 76:64-65 (MFC)
for miters, 76:82 (FC)
Shopcarts: address for, 81:92
Shope, Allan:
on house raising, 59:74-77 (REM)
storehouse by, 67:87
Shophelper: anti-kickback feeders, 34:55 (TB)
Shoppell, Robert: *Shoppell's Modern Houses,* cited, 53:88
Shoppell's Modern Houses (Shoppell): cited, 53:88
Shorea spp.: *See* Mahogany, Philippine.

Key to books:

(BK)   Building Baths and Kitchens
(CBS)   Building with Concrete, Brick and Stone
(CSH)   Craftsman-Style Houses
(DWS)   Building Doors, Windows and Skylights
(EEH)   Energy-Efficient Houses
(EF)   Exterior Finishing
(FC)   Finish Carpentry
(FRC)   Frame Carpentry
(FWS)   Building Floors, Walls and Stairs
(MFC)   More Frame Carpentry
(REM)   Remodeling
(SH)   Small Houses
(TB)   Tools for Building
(TFH)   Timber-Frame Houses

Shoring:
crib, 69:68 (REM)
for porches, 69:67-68 (REM)
rake (wall), 69:68-69 (REM)
for wall removal, 55:76, 77 (MFC)
wedges for, 69:68 (REM)
Short Log and Timber Building Book, The (Mitchell): reviewed, 34:92
Shotcrete panels:
hurricane-proofness of, 78:100
source for, 78:100
See also Gunite.
Shoveling: stance for, correct, 85:78, 79, 80
Showerlux U.S.A.: address for, 52:112
Showers:
acrylic, mortar base for, 73:87
base for, plywood-membrane, 70:81 (REM)
/bathtubs,
integral cast, 4:31, 33
hexagonal tiled, 9:65, 67
blocking for, 22:35-36 (FRC)
circular, 49:59 (SH)
copper, 26:80 (BK)
Corian kit for, 69:63 (REM)
curtainless angled, building, 79:62-63
diagram of, 32:46 (BK)
doors for, steam-tight, 52:112
fiberglass, foam support for, 23:14
with glass panels, 80:88
glass-block, 80:77, 82:70
for handicapped, 65:77, 79 (REM), 76:55, 56
headroom for, slanted, 76:69 (REM)
houses for, gazebo, 46:74-75 (BK)
layout for, 21:72, 77 (FRC)
mortar for, 32:50-52 (BK)
in octagonal house, 24:76, 77
outdoor stone, 5:8

pan liners for,
membrane for, 20:12, 32:46-48 (BK)
no-leak, 80:98
pans for, retrofitting, 68:30, 70:14-16
pressure changes in, avoiding, 65:14-16
quarter-round, 73:73
recessed attic, 21:29
semicircular, 36:68-69 (BK)
showerheads for, water-saving, 1:62, 61:66, 84:82-84
steam, generating units for, 52:110-12
subfloor for, 32:47 (BK)
tile,
handmade, 56:43
layout for, 32:49 (BK)
repairing, 22:12
wall substrates for, 32:49-50 (BK)
and water-saving devices, 85:4-6
whole-room, 21:40-41, 42, 25:47 (BK)
See also Membranes.
Shrader Bellows: Cinva-Ram, 26:77 (SH)
Shrode, Terry: on vinyl floors, 22:44-49 (BK)
Shurcliff, William A.: *Superinsulated Houses and Double-Envelope Houses,* reviewed, 6:58
Shutters:
catalog for, 51:90
construction of, 17:35-39 (DWS)
counterbalanced, vertically drawn, 17:44 (SH)
custom insulated, 53:14
greenhouse, making, 13:48-49 (DWS)
hurricane-proof, making, 78:86
insulated, source for, 43:92-94
louvers for, making, 17:37, 27:37, 40 (DWS, TB)
parallelogram pierced, 12:31, 32
post groove for, 8:38, 39 (EEH)
R-value of, 13:48 (DWS)
sliding panel, 8:74
vandal-proof, 30:69 (CBS)
wood for, 20:12
See also Zomehouse.
SICA: polyurethane caulking, 12:4
Side cut: defined, 10:63 (FRC)
Side cutters: for renovation, 12:51 (TB)
Sidewalks: placement of, 48:67
Sidewinder Reel Products: address for, 76:94
Siding:
aluminum, 83:45
corrugated, 52:72, 73
enameled, 39:71
and foil-faced backer board, 19:68
ventilation of, 19:68
asphalt, corrugated, 6:55, 56, 57
association for, 83:45

board-and-batten, 52:39 (TFH), 59:40-41, 45, 47 (SH), 83:41, 43
    annual-ring placement in, 54:14
    battens for, 12:28, 31, 75:48 (REM)
    as camouflage for foam-core, 67:37
    in caulk bed, 43:74 (SH)
    described, 7:42
    horizontal, 43:72-74 (SH)
    installing, 75:53-56 (EF)
    nailing patterns for, 1:6, 4:9, 9:45, 54:14, 75:52, 56 (EF)
    nails for, 75:56 (EF)
    Norwegian variant on, 80:59
    painting, 75:52-53, 56 (EF)
    with plywood, 61:44 (SH)
    as post-and-beam exterior, 28:68-70, 71
    reversed, 44:76, 79, 81
    screwed, 55:58, 59-60, 75:54 (EF)
    variations for, 75:52, 57, 58 (EF)
book on, cited, 83:45
cedar,
    beveled, alternate-exposure, 59:55-56 (CSH)
    finger-jointed, 66:49
    interior, 75:84
    prestained grey, 45:33, 34, 37
    roughsawn, 45:65, 69
    vertical, care for, 66:73
cement-based plank, 83:45
    reviewed, 77:96
    warranty for, 85:8
Ceramicboard, 39:90
clapboard, 83:40-41, 43
    corners in, 6:46 (TFH), 40:10, 50:4
    defined, 31:35
    and dormers, 49:4
    gauges for, 40:16, 47:1
    grades of, 31:37
    inside/outside, 66:38, 39 (SH)
    installing, 47:48-52 (EF), 49:4
    making, by hand, 11:76
    mills for, 31:35-37, 47:48 (EF)
    nail setting with, 47:52 (EF)
    nails for, 49:4
    packing strip with, 49:4
    permeability of, 19:68
    scarf joints for, 31:37, 51:28
    and shingles, 68:82, 85
    story pole for, 47:50 (EF)
    2x12, 52:48, 51 (TFH)
    white-stained, pictured, 52:52-53, 54, 56
    wood for, 31:37
clapboard-and-shingle, 31:66, 67, 52:56
continuous course, 6:47 (TFH)
for curves, 7:19-20 (FRC)
    with greenwood, 64:52
cutting, with reciprocating saws, 68:45 (FC)

detail of, 66:46
Douglas-fir stained, 61:53 (SH)
drop, 44:75
durability of, 83:43, 44-45
estimates for, 27:34
fiber-cement, 81:106
    composite panel, 59:82
    as replacement, 82:14
finger-jointed, 83:41-42
finish for, 3:8-9, 10:8, 32:10-12, 66:38 (SH)
galvanized metal, vertical, 83:83, 85
for garage doors, 74:59 (MFC)
gauges for, 5:7, 59:56 (CSH)
grade of, and stain, 84:4
green-wood, nailing, 29:74-76
hardboard exterior, vulnerability of, 78:86, 87
hardboard, source for, 71:72
installation holder for, 71:26
installing, 85:8
over insulation, rigid, 56:38
interior/exterior, 66:43
lap, 2x12, 52:48, 51 (TFH)
low-maintenance, 76:57-58
Masonite, 52:59 (CSH)
mildewcide for, 32:12
nail guns for, 15:49 (TB)
nail lengths for, 81:56
nails for, 85:47
permeable, 19:68
plywood as, 55:73
    disadvised, 75:48 (REM)
polypropylene, 83:45
pre-painting, rack for, 60:28
priming, timing recommendation for, 60:100
rain screen for, 78:71
redwood, 59:60
    bark, 3:66
    board-and-batten, 79:70-74
    maintaining, 52:66
removing,
    with saws, 2:5
    tool for, 32:54 (TB)
rough-textured, finish for, 12:8-10
for round forms, 44:79-80
router-beaded, 59:40-41 (SH)
sawing vertically, base-strip guide for, 67:28
for seashore, 65:79 (REM)
sheet,
    cart for, 83:30
    installer for, 83:28-30
shingle,
    around arch, strategy for, 57:14
    association for, 54:44 (EF), 83:45
    book on, 54:42-44 (EF)
    circular-saw corner trimming of, 3:34 (TB)
    and clapboards, 31:66, 67, 68:82, 85
    and copper flashing, problems with, 49:4

    on corners, 8:62, 25:63, 28:66
    for Craftsman house, 51:38, 40 (CSH)
    curved, 57:52, 54, 55-56
    discussed, 83:41, 43
    of dormers, 28:66
    double-coursed, 66:59 (SH)
    exposure for, 49:40 (REM), 80:44, 45
    fancy, applying, 54:42-45 (EF)
    finish for, 51:40 (CSH), 62:76, 68:85
    flashing for, 28:63, 64
    grades of, 8:60
    guide strip for, 28:65
    installing, 8:62, 28:65, 62:76
    irregular, 31:72-73
    jig for, 32:6
    materials list for, 8:60, 28:67
    ornamental, 18:53-55
    patterned, 27:80-81
    perspective trick with, 81:124
    prefab panels of, 57:45 (REM), 82:84
    preparation for, 8:60-62, 28:63-65
    replacing, 28:67
    rosin paper with, 25:63
    Russian, 26:96
    scuffed, restoring, 67:28
    shaping, 56:69 (CSH)
    sheathing for, 8:60
    shelf for, 19:14, 28:67
    with solar design, 45:76, 77 (EEH)
    square-butt patterned, 14:25
    staplers for, 32:6, 33:52 (SH)
    supply sources for, 54:44 (EF)
    tools for, 28:63
    Victorian, 25:62-63
    white-stained, pictured, 52:52-53, 54, 56
southern pine, 84:4
splines for, metal, 29:16
stains for, 59:60
stains on, dealing with, 47:16
steel, 83:45
    corrugated, 7:68
sunbursts for, 74:46, 49 (EF, REM)
support hooks for, making, 78:30
tongue-and-groove, 83:41, 43
    1½-in., 73:81
trimming bottom of, guide for, 20:14
T-111, stained, 46:49, 51 (EEH)
underlayment for, 50:100
vinyl, 83:44-45
    with acrylic, 10:33 (DWS)
    association for, 83:45
    damage from, 82:14
    and foil-faced backer board, 19:68
    high-quality, 47:94
    recyclers of, 75:100
    sheet, cutting, 20:16
    ventilation of, 19:68
waferboard and cedar, 80:49
waterproofing, 82:14
window-sill grooves for, 8:43 (DWS)

wood,
    association for, 64:10
    back priming, 21:58 (EEH), 81:56
    drying for, 55:57
    over foam-core, 64:10-12
    installation rules for, 64:10-12
and wood shrinkage, 81:56-57
wood-composition, 83:42-44
yellow poplar, 55:59
See also Shingle style.
Siegel, Carolyn Robbins: on adobe
    addition, 82:64-68
Siegele, H. H.:
    on cheek cuts, 28:37 (FRC)
    Roof Framing, 28:31-32 (FRC)
    Steel Square, The, 28:31-32 (FRC)
Siegelman, Larry: *Radon Industry
    Directory, The,* reviewed, 53:110
Siegrist, Peter: on ranch-house buildup,
    55:69 (REM)
Sika Corp.:
    address for, 58:14, 70:49, 73:81, 77:67
    Sikaflex adhesive sealant, 33:46 (TFH)
Sikkens Corp.:
    address for, 47:22, 51:53
    mentioned, 1:6
Sikkim: architectural influence of, 45:71,
    73 (CSH)
SIL-ACT Silane concrete sealant: source
    for, 33:32 (CBS)
Silglaze 1200 caulking: for solar
    collectors, 1:32
Silicone:
    solvent for, 72:80 (FC)
    See also Sealants.
Silkman, Hawley: mentioned, 27:72, 75
Sills:
    attaching, 77:81-82
    bolt holes in, locating, 77:82
    bolt marker for, 18:4, 19:55 (FRC)
    compound-curved, 7:18, 19 (FRC)
    concrete, casting, 18:46
    concrete embedding of, 16:37, 4 (CBS)
    epoxy repair for, 50:68
    fasteners for, powder-actuated, 21:30-34
        (TB)
    foundation/post connections for, 4:45
        (FRC)
    gaskets for, expanding, 83:16
    jacks for, 21:71-72 (FRC)
    layout for, 19:55, 21:74, 75, 24:48 (FRC)
    moisture barriers for, 18:4, 46:71
    mud,
        over block work, 84:57
        nut crater for, 78:41
    repairing, 4:34-37, 38, 32:57 (FRC), 49:39
        (REM)
    rotted, replacing, 53:77-79 (REM), 77:16
    sealer for, 77:83
    steel I-beam, 11:30, 31, 33 (EEH)
Silos: as houses, 7:54-57, 44:58-62
Silva wool: in roof, 8:40 (EEH)

Silver: nobility of, 21:4
Silver, Chuck: reviews NAHB show, 82:94-
    96
Silver Metal Products Inc.: metal
    connectors, 43:49 (FRC)
Silverstein, Murray:
    on courtyard house, 80:82-87
    on peaking a flat roof, 1:40-42 (FRC)
    on roofs, 10:26-29
    on Schindler house, 4:26-33
    staircase by, 49:78-82
Simmonds, Anthony:
    on bed alcove, 76:42-45 (REM)
    on conspicuous demolition, 80:4
    on eave skylights, 70:40-44
    on site-built cabinets, 79:76-79
Simonds, John: *Landscape Architecture,*
    reviewed, 45:116
Simple Caulk and Seal method (SCS):
    described, 77:64-67
Simpler, Al: on solar-powered cabin, 8:46-
    48
Simplex Manufacturing Co.: address for,
    49:73 (EEH), 80:57
Simplex Time Recorder Co.: address for,
    50:65
***Simplified Engineering for Architects
    and Builders*** (Parker): mentioned, 7:28
**Simpson, John W., and Peter J.
    Horrobin, eds.:** *Weathering and
    Performance of Building Materials, The,*
    mentioned, 26:4
Simpson Strong-Tie Co.:
    address for, 50:42, 51:82, 56:50, 57:54, 66,
        62:59, 63:42, 67:61, 92, 74:14, 59, 79:69,
        81:87, 82:18, 85:55 (CSH, MFC)
    angle ties L-90, installing, 29:37, 38 (FRC)
    hold-downs,
        for foundations, 9:30
        model HD-2a , recommended, 44:6
    hurricane ties, using, 29:74, 75
    metal connectors, 43:49 (FRC)
    metal hangers, uses of, 21:27, 28
    steel bracket post-base, 17:14, 39:53
        (CSH)
Simpson Timber Co.: Thermal Door, 6:60
SINCO Products Inc.: safety products,
    34:55 (TB)
Singer Co.,: heat pumps, 26:68
Single-Ply Roofing Institute: address for,
    43:16, 64:45 (EF)
Singley, Jeremy: on economical design,
    52:12-24
Sinks:
    bases for, installing, 85:50
    ceramic, making, 51:54-57
    certification program for, NAHB, 76:108
    chopping block for, 21:43
    copper, 14:4, 21:41, 42, 43, 26:80 (BK)

Corian, avoiding seams with, 66:73
drain placement of, 29:52 (BK)
faucet-sprayer for, wall-mount, 27:45, 47
    (BK)
flower-shaped ceramic, 26:80 (BK)
for handicapped, 76:58
height-adjustable, 34:74
industrial, 10:51, 52 (SH)
installation of,
    conventional, defects in, 27:44 (BK)
    in solid-surface resin board, 84:44
Japanese-style, 16:64 (TFH)
lignum vitae carved, 30:22, 23
recessed, below tile, 18:6
selecting, 2:54 (BK)
steps for, retractable, 45:52 (CSH)
triangular stainless, 7:67 (BK)
ultra-modern Italian, reviewed, 68:94-96
well-designed, 66:106
with wood carvings, 80:89
See also Porcelain: refinishing.
Sinnott, Ralph:
    on apprenticeship trauma, 67:114
    on English competition, 61:98-100
Sioux Chief Manufacturing Co.: Tube
    Talons plastic clips, 27:71 (CBS)
Sioux Tools, Inc.:
    random-orbit sanders, reviewed, 77:73
    VSR drill of, reviewed, 82:36-41
Siplast: Veral roofing, 23:66
Siris, Jane: penthouse design by, 31:63-65
Site layout:
    alligator clips for, 23:14
    batter boards in, 11:26, 27, 25:67, 28:16
        (CBS, TB)
    for decks, 79:64, 68-69
    elevations in, 11:27, 28 (CBS)
    excavation lines in, 11:28 (CBS)
    for handicapped-accessible house,
        53:67, 71
    levels for, line, 25:66, 67 (TB)
    markers for,
        flour-shaker, 29:16
        iris pin, 67:26
    plumb bobs with, 25:67-69 (TB)
    pour depth in, 11:28 (CBS)
    squaring up, 11:26, 27-28 (CBS), 79:66, 68
        three-four-five rule for, 11:27, 77:80
            (CBS)
    stake driving for, 34:16
    stake replacement insurance for, 51:58
    string for, 25:67-69 (TB), 26:16
    tools for, 11:26, 27, 12:50-51 (CBS, TB)
Site layout:
    tools for, reviewed, 67:90
    transit for, laser, 18:12-14
    See also Levels. Plumb bobs. String.
        Transits.
Sites:
    choosing, 85:89-91
    house relationships to, 28:74-75
    magnetic variation of, 5:52 (DWS)

microclimates in, 9:14-16
planning of, 4:29, 23:50, 51
solar evaluation of, 5:52-53, 9:14 (DWS)
See also Landscaping. Solar design.

Sivaco Fastening Systems: address for, 56:54

Skaates, George:
on drainage systems, 29:51-55 (BK)
on toilet installation, 46:54-57 (BK)

Skidompha house:
building of, 17:76-77 (SH)
problems in, 17:79 (SH)

Skil Corp.:
address for, 63:76, 68:96, 70:53 (FC)
belt sander #1400, 18:17
circular saws, reviewed, 63:76, 77
drill, VSR, reviewed, 82:36-41
hinge butt mortising template, 31:29, 30-31 (TB)
plunge routers, reviewed, 71:79, 83 (FC)
power planes, reviewed, 54:77, 78-79
random-orbit sanders, reviewed, 77:71
saw #5525, reviewed, 79:102-104
saws for timber framing,
model 860, 4:23 (TFH)
model 5103N, 4:23 (TFH)
model 5201N, 4:23 (TFH)
Speedmatic #510, 4:23 (TFH)
trim saws, #5510, reviewed, 48:40-43
worm-drive saws,
chainsaw conversion kit for, 60:84 (MFC)
clips for, 24:10
model 559, 25:4
model 77, 24:37, 38, 40, 41 (TB)
6½-in., 24:40 (TB)

Skilsaw: *See* Circular saws.

Skilton, Dave: on sidewall shingles, 54:42-45 (EF)

Skimcoat: *See* Plaster: veneer.

Skin: sunblock for, 46:90

Skinulis, Richard: as joint author. *See* Mann, Dale.

Skydell, Robert: on octagonal greenhouse, 32:34-37

Skylids: described, 26:56, 26:57

Skylights:
acrylic, installing, 50:49
angled, 20:45, 48
for attic conversion, 13:41, 28:29, 30
barrel-vault, 76:56, 57
in bay, 74:52
in bay eaves, adding, 70:40-44
over bed alcove, 76:43 (REM)
for below-grade rooms, 56:70, 71 (CSH)
boxed, 5:51
buying, 11:59 (DWS)
caulking for, 3:48

chimney-abutting, 48:36
in cold roofs, 63:44
condensation with, 65:62 (SH)
Craftsman wood-trimmed, 29:56-57, 58 (CSH)
curbless,
building, 18:36-39 (DWS)
with corrugated roof, 23:10
installing, 13:4
thermal break for, 20:12
ventilated, 48:90
custom, 70:44
diamond-shaped, 49:62 (SH)
disadvantages of, 12:44 (REM)
domed acrylic, 50:56, 57
domed large, 47:81, 82 (MFC, SH)
drywall around, moisture-resistant, 63:52
in earth-sheltered houses, 16:52
energy-efficient, 69:42 (EEH)
flashing for, 3:48, 49, 11:60-61, 62, 64, 65 (DWS), 56:80-81, 58:71 (EF), 65:59, 60 (EF)
curb, 15:8
J-, 65:60 (EF)
water-tight, 49:83
framing for, 18:36-38 (DWS)
glass for, 11:59, 62, 21 (DWS)
codes on, 49:14-16
illuminated leaded, 20:77, 78-79
installation rules for, 16:21 (CSH)
stained, 49:6
tempered vs. laminated, 49:14-16
glass-block, reviewed, 59:110
glazing problems with, 12:48
glazing tape for, 25:12
hipped ridge, 20:29, 30
installing, 11:60 (DWS)
safely, booklet on, 61:102
insulation for, 35:8
sliding-panel, 28:46-48 (DWS)
in kitchen, 30:23
lean-to, 78:64-65 (REM)
with laminated-veneer lumber, 50:45 (MFC)
lighting in, 27:61 (BK)
making, 11:62-64 (DWS)
over pool, 12:48-49
pyramidal, source for, 73:59
reflectors for, Sunbender, 26:57
remote control for, 59:106
rice paper for, 27:30, 31
ridge-running, as heat source, 7:36, 37, 38 (DWS)
on ring beam, 58:51-52
rolling-hatch, making, 48:54-57
in roof overhangs, 80:44, 58
roofing and, 11:60 (DWS)
round, 21:28, 29, 27:51
R-value in, increasing, 17:8
sash for, hot-bed, 5:30

sealant for, 48:36
shades for, 50:49, 55:48-49 (FC), 59:65, 66 (EEH)
shallow, mullioned, 28:52, 53 (FWS)
shuttered, 2:30, 31, 32 (EEH)
site-built ridge, 55:45-49 (FC)
sliding-panel system for, 29:60-61 (CSH)
sloped-wall, 57:53, 55
with solar collectors, 1:32
solar-bronze acrylic, 15:31
source for, 73:50
storm panels for, 65:62 (SH)
structural considerations with, 11:59-60 (DWS)
tape for, 11:62 (DWS)
tempered, custom, 48:36
for thermosiphon systems, 3:48-49
venetian blinds for, wire-strung, 64:87 (REM)
ventilated,
commercial, 61:78 (EF)
vertical, 54:62
ventilating, 61:78 (EF)
source for, 62:48 (SH)
weatherproofing, 7:37 (DWS)
See also Cupolas. Glazing: sloped. Roofing: glass.

Slate:
blackboard, using, 21:8
See also Roofing.

Slate Roofs: source for, 47:59

Slave board: explained, 17:37 (DWS)

Sleep: positions for, proper, 85:81

Sleeping lofts:
basket, for bedrooms, 4:27, 31, 32-33
diagonal, 11:43 (SH)
rustic, 44:41 (SH)

Slicks:
bent, straightening, 62:22 (CSH)
design of, 64:12
hand-forged, 49:95
using, 4:22-23, 12:23, 26 (CSH, TFH, TFH)

Slide-Right: address for, 82:96

Sliding bevels: *See* Bevel gauges.

Sloan, Samuel L.: *Sloan's Victorian Buildings,* reviewed, 11:70

Sloan-Miyasato: lighting fixtures, 43:33 (CSH)

Slope (roof): defined, 10:63 (FRC)

Small, C. Jeffrey: farmhouse remodel by, 49:58-62 (SH)

Small Homes Council-Building Research Council:
address for, 56:16, 65:55
Basic Construction and Materials Takeoff, 23:48-49
described, 29:92
Kitchen Planning Standards, 23:48-49
publications from, 29:92
slide sets from, 29:92
Solar Orientation, 23:48-49
Wood Frame Floor Systems, 23:48-49

Small houses:
advantages of, 33:48, 38:12 (SH)
Arts-and-Crafts style, 59:52-56 (CSH)
balconies for, 38:36, 37, 39 (CSH)
books on, 40:90, 85:132
design for, 11:42-45, 13:64, 66, 33:49-50, 38:12-14, 36-38, 100, 42:53, 73:82, 87 (CSH, SH)
earth-bermed open, 66:36-39 (SH)
Edwardian, 59:48-51 (SH)
energy performance of, 38:100
energy-efficient, 82:102
English Cotswold, 60:70-73
Hawaiian, 61:58-61 (SH)
height in, 11:43, 44 (SH)
Honda hillside, 53:46-50 (SH)
hybrid walls for, 67:35
long-range planning for, 75:66-67
lumber buying for, direct, 67:36
multiple, savings in, 59:70 (SH)
north-slope solar heated, 21:56-59 (EEH)
plans for, 59:70-73 (SH)
pole foundation for, cantilevered, 13:64 (SH)
porches for, 38:36, 37 (CSH)
sale prices of, 38:14, 100
speculative, 67:34-37
techniques for, 74:52-56
tower, 80:68-71
trapezoidal, 45:60-64, 89 (SH)
Tudor slate-roofed, 47:56-60
Usonian, 81:78-82
utility areas for, 13:64 (SH)
very, gallery of, 67:86-87
for West, 42:50-53 (SH)
Wright-inspired, 65:36-39
See also Playhouses. Shacks.
Small Hydro-Electrics: turbine, Model 90, 15:68
Small Spaces (Brown): reviewed, 85:132
Smart House: address for, 65:55
Smart houses: information on, 65:55
Smart Kitchen, The (Goldbeck): reviewed, 58:106
SmartLevel:
line-scribing clips for, 58:6
reviewed, 53:94
SMC Pneumatics, Inc.: address for, 49:87
Smirniotopoulos, Peter: reviews drill driver, 62:96
Smith, Ashley: on sculpted house, 57:52-57
Smith, Brent: on high-water house, 17:40-45 (SH)
Smith, Edward: reviews photovoltaics, 24:80-82
Smith, Greg: on baseboard installation, 76:51-53 (FC)
Smith, Henry: reviews forklift, 61:90
Smith, Jim: wellhouse by, 67:87
Smith, Kathryn: reviews Pfeiffer, 34:92

Smith, Thomas Gordon: on Bernard Maybeck house, 2:18-25 (CSH)
Smith, Todd A.: on roofing shingles, 57:84-89 (EF)
Smith & Co.: address for, 62:41 (EF)
Smith (A. O.):
PGCS water heater, 27:71 (CBS)
water heater, defective, 2:64
Smith and Hawken Tools: address for, 30:78
Smith (L. J.), Inc.: address for, 82:61
Smith Level Co.: address for, 58:45
Smithsonian Institution:
conservation slides, 1:66
ornament cards, 1:66
Traveling Exhibition of Victorian architecture (1981), 1:9
Smoke detectors:
alarm levels of, 2:65
placing, 46:98
temperature-sensitive, 50:65
using, 46:96-98
Smolen, T. F.: on raised-panel wainscot, 19:50-53 (FWS)
Smulski, Stephen:
on construction adhesives, 58:72-75
on glulams, 71:55-59 (MFC)
on treated lumber, 63:61 (MFC)
on wood shrinkage, 81:54-59
Smyth, Bart: on lighting, 15:54-55 (BK)
Snakes: source for, 47:28
Snap cutters: using, 17:54 (BK)
Snap ties: *See* Metal connectors.
Snap'Em Circulators:
address for, 81:53
source for, 33:12
Snieckus, Mary Ann: on rondavels, 30:29-31
Snow:
guards, cast-aluminum, source for, 53:18
radiant-heat removal of, 53:76
roof provisions for, 21:57-58 (EEH)
Snow, Jane Moss: *Bathroom Design,* reviewed, 47:112
Snow and Neally: froes, 30:48
Snyder, Gary: house by, 9:42-45
Snyder, Tim:
on Alden Dow complex, 10:20-24
on chain mortisers, 22:16
on chimney repair, 9:16
on curved-truss house, 14:27-29
on house moving, 5:18-21
on log-building course, 13:14
on masonry exchange program, 32:82
on NESEA conference, 19:22
on New Orleans preservation, 7:14
on octagon houses, 9:25-27, 24:73-77
on photovoltaics, 8:47
on plank-floor span charts, 33:43 (FWS)
on prefab steel house, 22:26-30
on ranch remodel, 30:32-36

reports on Denmark, 31:76-77
on restoring Fountainhead, 12:27-33
reviews design books, 20:80
reviews tools, 31:76
on roll-top house, 25:38-41 (EEH)
on round house, 18:69-71
on Sears, Roebuck houses, 28:42-45
on sidewall shingling, 8:60-62
on slate roofing, 20:39 (EF)
on solar house, 16:26-30
on stone-faced block work, 13:36-38 (CBS)
on stress-skin panels, 24:58-59
on Tidewater house, 29:73-77
on Timber Framers' Guild, 29:86
on timber-framing course, 11:16-18
on underground building conference, 7:14
on veneer plaster, 15:72-74 (FWS)
Soap: odorless biodegradable, 46:72
Soapstone: information on, 39:42
Sobon, Jack: mentioned, 29:86
Sobon, Jack, and Roger Schroeder:
Timber Frame Construction, reviewed, 27:84
Society for the Preservation of New England Antiquities: address for, 65:55, 67:4
Society of the Plastics Industry, Inc.: address for, 74:104
Sockets: for renovation, 12:51 (TB)
Sod houses:
about, 31:54-57
pictured, 58:120
See also Earth construction.
Sod Walls (Welsch): source for, 31:54
Soderstrom, Neil: *Chainsaw Savvy,* cited, 78:43
Sodium montmorillonite: *See* Bentonite.
Sofas:
with bed, slide-out, 66:89
built-in, 9:66, 21:36, 49:60, 61, 62 (SH), 73:61, 74:52
cantilevered, 15:77, 79 (CSH)
drawers under, curved-laminated, 15:77 (CSH)
L-shaped built-in, 66:90
Mackintosh, 54:39, 40-41
storage in, 47:88
Soffits:
angled, in solar design, 51:72, 73, 75 (EEH)
with cathedral ceiling, 83:54, 56
cedar tongue-and-groove unpainted, 56:58 (EEH)
colored, 10:29
compound curved, laminating, 44:68 (FRC)
curved interior divider, 56:63 (EEH)
defined, 15:39, 40, 20:60 (EF, FWS)
dropped, in kitchens, 67:72, 73 (REM)
figuring, for ells and main, 68:75 (MFC)

framing, 63:69 (MFC)
horizontal vs. pitched, 68:75-76 (MFC)
hyperbolic, 6:55
insulating, vent protection for, 56:39
interior, 52:65
    exterior-matching, 66:58-59 (SH)
    with light fixtures, 73:73
    lighting, 9:64, 65, 66
    radiused, 26:41-42
    two-tiered, 49:61 (SH)
with laminated-veneer lumber, 50:45
    (MFC)
mahogany-trimmed, 67:72, 73 (REM)
metal-framed, 32:71 (FRC)
plants on, 62:48 (SH)
for plumbing, 79:54
production framing of, 73:58
slate, 47:60
for slate roofs, 47:60
snap-together, 52:73
steel frame for, 70:65 (EEH)
vents for, 7:52, 53 (DWS), 78:58
    continuous, 51:70-71
    continuous-strip, 9:4
    and fire blocking, 23:12, 25:12
    protecting, 29:70
wide, 73:54

Software Catalogue for Home Builders:
source for, 33:88

Software Directory for Builders (NAHB):
reviewed, 75:110

Soil cement:
block press for, 26:77 (SH)
blocks from, incised, 26:77 (SH)
tile floor from, 27:56, 59
tile-stamping tools for, 27:56, 58
See also Earth construction: cob.

Soil Mechanics in Engineering Practice
(Terzaghi and Peck): cited, 50:86

Soils: solar absorption of, 9:14

Soko Hardware: rice paper, 27:63

Sokoliuk, Wally: repairs foundations,
48:68-69

Solar: *See also* Electricity: photovoltaic.
specific elements or systems. Thermal
mass. Zomehouse.

Solar Alternative Inc.: *Glass Glazed Site-
Built Solar Collector,* reviewed, 15:22

Solar Audio Visual Electronics: source
for, 24:82

Solar Collector, The: source for, 30:80

Solar collectors:
black foil for, 10:51 (SH)
demonstration of, 30:80
fire hazards with, 1:30, 2:4
insulating, 1:30, 2:4
publications on, 30:80
for radiant-floor heating, 30:38, 41
roof, construction of, 1:28-32
site-built, 16:28
    active-passive, 16:28
water preheater, 6:56, 57

Key to books:

(BK)   Building Baths and Kitchens
(CBS)   Building with Concrete, Brick and Stone
(CSH)   Craftsman-Style Houses
(DWS)   Building Doors, Windows and Skylights
(EEH)   Energy-Efficient Houses
(EF)   Exterior Finishing
(FC)   Finish Carpentry
(FRC)   Frame Carpentry
(FWS)   Building Floors, Walls and Stairs
(MFC)   More Frame Carpentry
(REM)   Remodeling
(SH)   Small Houses
(TB)   Tools for Building
(TFH)   Timber-Frame Houses

Solar Components Corp.:
address for, 70:56 (EEH), 73:70
See also Kalwall Corp.

Solar design:
absorptance values for, 2:6
active, 25:38-39 (EEH)
air movement in, 33:40 (EEH)
in angled sections, 8:37-41 (EEH)
assistance in, 3:63, 33:90, 65:52, 53, 55
associations for, 30:80, 56:110, 71:47
attitudes toward, 5:16
back-up heating in, 33:40 (EEH)
belvederes in, 3:58, 59 (EEH)
books on, 3:46, 7:60, 16:14, 18:78, 23:49,
    51, 30:52, 35:71, 37:88, 45:116, 70:120,
    79:120, 84:85, 110 (CBS, TB)
calculators for, 80:26
centers for, 30:80, 74:106
    regional, 3:63
on Colonial theme, 2:50-52 (SH)
components for, 60:16
computer software for, 21:59 (EEH)
cooling with, 19:64, 26:77 (EEH, SH)
costs of, 12:66, 59, 33:40, 84:89 (EEH)
courses in, 69:100
in cube, 34:24-29 (DWS)
in desert, 66:82
Dryvit and concrete, 1:43-47 (EEH)
ducts for, sniffer, 26:74 (SH)
earth sheltering and, 19:63 (EEH)
efficiency of, 21:59 (EEH), 59:62-67 (EEH)
electrical system for, 51:92
for enclosed porch, 15:42-43
of envelope houses, book on, 28:86
for erratic climate, 29:28-33
examples of, 45:76-81 (EEH), 46:61-65
    (TFH), 77:50-54
fascia boards in, angled, 66:57, 59 (SH)
fiber-optic transmission of, 51:96
floors in, concrete, 12:66 (EEH)

in French-American style, 26:72-77
glass for, coated-film, 26:74 (SH)
glazing for, 33:37 (EEH)
heliodon for, 13:18
house shapes for, 84:86
insulation for, 12:66, 67 (EEH)
Kalwall with, 19:63-65 (EEH)
materials for, high-tech, 11:54-58
microclimates and, 9:14-16
noise transfer in, 8:40 (EEH)
on north slope, 21:56-59 (EEH)
for Northeast, 33:84
octagon, 9:25-27
orientation for, 19:62, 63 (EEH)
    and magnetic variation, 5:52
        (erratum, 15:4-6, DWS)
overhangs for, arched, 12:64, 66 (EEH)
panels for, heat-producing, 71:106
passive, 3:20-27, 46:49-53, 51:72-75, 58:80-
    85 (EEH)
performances of, 8:40, 11:50 (erratum,
    12:4), 15:75, 25:40, 26:37, 74-76 (CBS,
    CSH, EEH, SH)
plans for, 3:63, 53:87, 89, 62:68, 69
prediction system for, 16:14
radiation balance and, 9:14
for retrofits, 33:38-39 (EEH)
Rex Roberts types, 28:68-72
and shade, 5:52 (DWS)
shading mask for, 5:52, 53 (DWS)
sites for, 3:19, 5:52-53 (DWS), 84:85-86
skylights in, 28:46 (DWS)
sliding-door panels for, insulated, 15:42-
    43
solar contribution in, 30:52 (CBS)
solar load ratio,
    explained, 21:59 (EEH)
    source for, 16:14
Southwestern, low-cost, 5:16
standard units in, 12:66 (EEH)
with stone, 43:58-61 (CBS)
sun-angle calculator for, 80:26
sunlight control for, 12:67 (EEH)
systems for, 10:49-51, 16:28-29 (SH),
    68:50-55
tax incentives for, 1:10, 3:10-12, 6:16
for temperate climates, 84:85-89
temperatures and, 9:14-16, 12:67 (EEH)
thermal network simulation for, 30:52-
    53 (CBS)
thin-mass, 11:47-50 (CBS)
traditional, 60:56-59 (EEH)
trees and, 5:52 (DWS)
ventilation in, 33:37-40 (EEH)
Victorian-style, 31:66-71
windows in,
    heat-activated collector, 16:28
    insulation for, 33:38, 40 (EEH)
    sizing, 84:86
    south gable-end, 22:10
    wooden awning, 15:42-43

Solar Earthbuilder International: source for, 34:39

Solar Electric Home, The (Davidson and Komp): reviewed, 24:80

Solar Electric Systems: source for, 24:82

Solar Energy Group: *Passive Solar Design Handbook,* reviewed, 16:14

Solar Energy Industries Association: address for, 65:52

Solar Energy Research Institute: glazings by, 33:37 (EEH)

Solar Hardware Supply Co.: mentioned, 1:63

Solar Home Planbook: source for, 33:84

Solar hot water: *See* Hot-water heaters.

Solar Oriented: heat pumps, 26:68

Solar Rating and Certification Corp.: program of, 68:55

Solar Research: address for, 29:88

Solar Soft Inc.: Sunpas solar software, 21:59 (EEH)

Solar Technology Corp.: *Household Conservation Catalog* from, 1:63

Solar Technology Institute: address for, 69:100

Solar Water and Pool Heating Course Manual: reviewed, 30:80

Solar Water Heater Book, The: described, 4:62

Solar Works: collector of, 29:88

Solaraide hot-water tanks: source for, 29:86-88

Solar-Bond absorber plates: for site-built collectors, 1:32

Solarex Corp. Technology Center: silicon-cell production of, 72:75 (EEH)

Solarflair III Domestic hot-water heat pump: mentioned, 5:65

Solariums:
 for adobe houses, 17:63-67 (DWS)
 book on, reviewed, 68:108
 curved roof, frame for, 17:64 (DWS)
 defined, 33:37 (EEH)
 vs. greenhouses, 35:4
 as heat source, 18:42-43, 60:58-59 (EEH)
 on octagon, 34:57 (FRC)
 soffit vents for, 2:31 (EEH)
 stone-walled, 43:61 (CBS, SH)
 three-level slant-glass, 46:49, 52 (EEH)
 ventilation in, 17:63 (DWS)
 See also Greenhouses. Skylights. Solar design.

SolaRoll: source for, 6:56, 57

Solder:
 50-50 vs. 60-40, 67:4
 forms of, 10:40 (BK)
 for lead-coated copper, 61:48, 49, 63:4
 lead-free, 46:72
 using, 57:14
 nobility of, 21:4
 silver-bearing low-temperature, 29:88

types of, 10:40 (BK)

workability of, 67:4

Soldering:
 copper, 47:63 (EF)
 defined, 10:40 (BK)
 flux for, 10:40, 41 (BK)
 flux-brush storage for, 48:24
 of galvanized sheet metal, 67:41 (EF)
 of guttering, 61:48-49
 irons for, for leaded glass, 23:41 (DWS)
 of leaded glass, 23:40-41 (DWS)
 of pipes,
  clogging after, 7:10
  drainage for, 35:14
  drying for, 35:14, 36:4
 process of, 10:41 (BK)
 for solar collectors, 1:30
 tiny tip for, making, 77:32
 torches for, 10:40 (BK)
 water flow block for, 8:12
 See also Copper.

Solid-Flue Chimney Systems, Inc.: address for, 70:79

Solite gaslight: source for, 14:31

Sollman, Philip S.:
 on bathroom, 25:47-49 (BK)
 on bedroom addition, 46:38-41 (REM)
 on cherry house, 61:72-75
 on crafted house, 15:75-79 (CSH)
 on kitchen, 71:42-45 (REM)
 on wardrobe closet, 83:70-73

Solutions: source for, 49:50

Solvents:
 avoiding, 73:67
 for label removal, 58:26
 protection against, 10:10
 for silicone, 72:80 (FC)

Sommer and Maca Industries: glaziers' supplies, 20:8

Songey, Mark:
 on template mortising, 10:38-39
 on timber templates, 10:38-39

Sonin: ultrasonic tape, reviewed, 78:54-55

Sonneborn Building Products:
 address for, 77:67
 concrete wax curing-compound, 26:74 (SH)
 Hydrocide sealant, 15:48 (CBS)

Sonosheen concrete wax: source for, 26:74 (SH)

Sonotubes: *See* Forms.

Soto, Benny: stonework by, 45:40-43

Soundproofing: *See* Noise.

Source, The, computer service: described, 46:60

South Carolina:
 home conservation credits, 5:65
 solar tax credits in, 3:12

South County Post and Beam: address for, 54:44 (EF)

South Dakota:
 energy standards in, 33:84
 heat-pump water-heater policy in, 5:65
 solar tax credits in, 3:12

Southcoast Shingle Co.: address for, 54:44 (EF)

Southeast Millwork, Inc.: address for, 75:94

Southern Building Code:
 on concrete mesh, 48:90
 on skylight glass, 49:14

Southern Cypress Manufacturers Association: address for, 30:8

Southern Forest Products Association:
 address for, 63:65 (MFC), 65:53
 Exterior Wood in the South, cited, 84:4
 Guide to Southern Pine Shakes, cited, 84:4
 How to Build Storm-Resistant Structures, 23:50
 publications from, 23:50

Southern Pine Inspection Bureau:
 address for, 81:16
 grading rules from, 33:43 (FWS)

Southern Screw: particleboard screws, 34:45 (TB)

Southwall Technologies, Inc.:
 address for, 53:16, 80:71, 81:102
 coated glass, 26:74 (SH)

Southwest Solaradobe School:
 book on, 67:96
 classes of, 67:96-98

Southwestern arts: book on, 67:58

Sowden House:
 construction of, 14:66-73, 84
 textile blocks in, 16:4

Space heaters:
 for cold-weather work, 51:42
 danger from, 1:12
 water vapor from, 22:10

Space Saver packing systems: reviewed, 35:91

Space, Time and Architecture (Giedion): quoted, 46:79

Spacewall International: storage systems, 35:91

Spackle:
 as filler, 30:57 (DWS), 71:72
 source for, 30:57 (DWS)
 See also Drywall.

Spaeth, David: on Farnsworth House, 46:32-37

Span: defined, 10:63 (FRC)

Span Tables for Joists and Rafters: source for, 23:50

Spandrels: of molded foam, 39:92

Spanish houses:
 Mission, embellished, 34:76, 77
 as prototypes, 38:68
 Revival, house in, 45:38-43

Sparfil International, Inc.: address for, 31:38 (CBS), 46:71

Spark's Southwest Inc.: address for, 70:65 (EEH)

Spas:
building, 58:58-61 (CSH)
heat exchangers for, automated, 53:76
moisture control for, 79:24
source for, 58:61 (CSH)
See also Hot tubs.

Speaking of Windows (SHC-BRC): source for, 29:92

Speaking tubes:
book treating, 11:70
described, 8:8
historic use of, 6:12, 9:8-9
physical requirements of, 9:9

Spears, John: on quad pane, 20:22

Spec Guide, The: reviewed, 37:88

Spec Point sheets: source for, 31:84

Special Home Products, Inc.: address for, 67:92

Specialty Products Co.: address for, 46:55 (BK)

Specialty (T. F.) Sawmilling, Inc.: lumber from, 83:112

Specialty Tools and Fasteners Distributors Association: address for, 41:56 (CBS)

Speck, Lawrence: house by, 70:61-65 (EEH)

Spectra Physics: levels, 37:45 (TB)

Spectra-Tone: address for, 56:50

Spectrum Glass: address for, 76:66 (REM)

Speed Fastener Corp.: hammer-detonated tools, 21:32, 34 (TB)

Speed Square: evaluated, 10:60-61 (TB)

Speedemon automatic chalkline: reviewed, 43:94-96

Speiser, Jane: on ferro-cement, 13:50-53 (CBS)

Sperber Tool Works: chainsaw mills, 7:31, 42:41 (TFH)

Spexarth, Michael:
on pier and grade-beam foundations, 16:34-37 (CBS)
on stepped foundations, 26:63-65 (CBS)

Spielman, Patrick: *Gluing and Clamping,* cited, 65:45

Spiling battens: using, 77:60-62

Spiral Manufacturing, Inc.: address for, 59:106

Spires, David: reviews Alexander, 33:88

Spiro, Steven:
furniture by, 47:77 (MFC)
on staircase, 47:76-78

Spiroll International: drawing protector, 26:62 (TB)

Splinters: loupe for, 68:28

Spoiler Sky Hook: source for, 24:10

Sportronics Inc.: peanut lights, 8:47

Spotnails, Inc.:
nailers,
discussed, 47:73, 74-75 (FC)
reviewed, 56:52, 53, 54-55, 56
pneumatic tools, 15:53 (TB)

Sprachman, Robert: *trompe l'oeil* by, 81:124

Spratt, Steven: on matching brickwork, 63:70-71

Sprayers:
air-compressor, 48:76
airless, 42:57 (DWS), 48:75-76
for latex, 67:68
technique for, 48:75-76

Spring, Paul:
on Arthur Brown, 11:34-35
on bridging, 19:56 (FRC)
on circular saws, portable, 24:41 (TB)
on curved wall, 7:16-20 (FRC)
on extendable level, 23:80
on framing hammers, 23:32-35 (TB)
on framing lumber, 8:14
on layout vocabulary, 21:71-72 (FRC)
on ordering concrete, 13:33 (CBS)
on plastic laminates, 9:41 (BK)
on rammed-earth conference, 10:16-17
reviews Litchfield, 14:76
reviews *New England Builder,* 20:80-81
on ridge vents, 21:51 (DWS)
on Schweikher house, 16:58-64 (TFH)
on solar conference, 24:80
on stair terms, 17:58 (FWS)
on stud-wall framing, 22:31-39 (FRC)
on tools, 18:17-18

Springer Co.: gaslights, 14:31

Sprinkler Systems: source for, 44:42 (BK)

Sprinkler systems:
codes on, 44:42 (BK)
explained, 44:42-45 (BK)
installing, 44:43-45 (BK), 47:6
mentioned, 4:57 (TFH), 66:87
propylene glycol for, 48:4
residential heads for, 47:6
spacing requirements for, 48:4
valves in, 47:6

Spruce (*Picea* spp.):
decay resistance of, 63:63 (MFC)
Sitka (*P. sitchensis*), hardness group of, 40:69 (FRC)
for timber framing, 26:10
white (*P. glauca*), shrinkage of, 19:69 (EEH)
and wood preservatives, 44:59

Spruce-pine-fir (SPF): hardness group of, 40:69 (FRC)

Spruill Products: address for, 52:73

Spyderco, Inc.: address for, 77:94

Squangle: evaluated, 10:60 (TB)

Square-D Co.: ground-fault circuit-interrupter cover plates, 9:4

Squareness: *See* Site layout: squaring up.

Squares:
adjustable, source for, 67:90
aluminum T-, for drywall, 8:54 (FWS)
books on, 10:60 (TB)
calipers from, 40:16
circles with, 54:24
described, 10:56 (TB)
framing,
for rafters, 10:56-61, 28:6 (TB)
for stairs, 27:16
unit measurement with, 10:56 (TB)
wall heights on, 10:60 (TB)
rafter,
decimal-foot conversion scale for, 75:50 (MFC)
jack-placement tables for, 75:50-51 (MFC)
for renovations, 12:50 (TB)
sling for, rieviewed, 56:92
Speed, evaluated, 10:60-61 (TB)
tape, source for, 67:90
testing, for twist, 4:21 (TFH)
for timber-framing, 4:21, 12:24, 15:4 (CSH, TFH)
triangular, source for, 60:84 (MFC)
truing, 4:24 (TFH)

SSHC, Inc.: address for, 75:72

Stabila Levels: address for, 58:45

Stackpole, Edouard A., and Melvin B. Summerfield: *Nantucket Doorways,* cited, 77:89

Stadshaug, Gaylord: house by, 39:66-69 (TFH)

Staedtler (J. S.): drafting tools, 26:58 (TB)

Stagg, William D., and Brian F. Pegg: *Plastering,* reviewed, 31:80

Staging: *See* Scaffolding.

Stahl Industries, Inc.: Staytex thermal barrier, 33:75

Stained Glass Overlays, Inc.: address for, 47:95, 48:4

Stainer, John: mentioned, 28:60 (TFH)

Stains (finishes):
aniline, vs. oil, sunlight damage to, 82:102
applying, 47:30-32
for color adding, 83:86-87
color of,
evening, 58:16-18
matching, 83:86-87
commercial, 22:57 (CSH)
components of, 24:12
for concrete, 40:10-12
and incompatible finishes, 40:10-12
from dye, Procion, 31:48 (FWS)
exterior, 22:57, 32:27, 59:60, 73:75 (CSH)
applying, 27:54, 55
pre-treatment for, 45:41
source for, 45:41, 68:85

Stains (blemishes)

failure of, 32:10-12
for fir, 71:73
latex, 26:77 (SH), 28:72
making, 82:102
mildewcide for, 32:12
nontoxic, sources for, 67:90-92
oil, problems with, 28:72
with paint and Floetrol, 83:86
paint as, dilute, 39:10, 68:38-39
over paint, peeling, 12:10
with penetrating oil, 71:73
for pine, 75:49 (REM)
for plywood walls, interior, 85:73, 75
over preweathered wood, discussed,
   76:106-108
reapplication of, 24:12
semi-transparent, exterior, 52:52-53,
   54, 56
   source for, 83:86
for siding, 52:52-53, 54, 56, 59:60
   Douglas-fir, 61:53 (SH)
   T-111, 46:49, 51 (EEH)
source for, 28:72, 44:88
storage life of, extending, 71:26
with Swedish floor finish, 36:44 (FWS)
for tile, 1:55
water-repellent, 61:14
and wax, 25:31, 27:76
white, 75:49 (REM)
with wood preservatives, 44:88
wood-floor, tests for, 67:53
wood-graining, process with, 85:18-20
See also Finishes.

Stains (blemishes):
blue, dealing with, 1:6, 29:10-12
books on, 47:16
exterior, dealing with, 47:16
fungal, removing, 1:6, 29:10-12
gasoline for, 13:8
lye for, 13:8
from mold, 25:12
removing, 29:16, 49:26
   with Fuller's earth, 13:6-8
   oily, 13:6-8, 15:14
   with steam, 15:14
   from water, 49:26, 56:86
sealers for, 13:8
Stairbuilding (Townsend): cited, 43:37
(FWS)

Staircases:
adobe/wood, 5:51
angle of, 52:16
Arts-and-Crafts style, 6:20-21 (CSH),
   57:47 (REM), 59:84-85 (CSH), 69:43
   (EEH)
   contemporary, 49:78-82
assembly of, 17:61-62 (FWS)
for attic renovation, 28:28, 30
against AWWF wall, 68:65
balusters in,
   ceiling-height, 59:38-39 (SH)
   copper, 70:93

Key to books:

(BK)   **Building Baths and Kitchens**
(CBS)   **Building with Concrete, Brick and Stone**
(CSH)   **Craftsman-Style Houses**
(DWS)   **Building Doors, Windows and Skylights**
(EEH)   **Energy-Efficient Houses**
(EF)   **Exterior Finishing**
(FC)   **Finish Carpentry**
(FRC)   **Frame Carpentry**
(FWS)   **Building Floors, Walls and Stairs**
(MFC)   **More Frame Carpentry**
(REM)   **Remodeling**
(SH)   **Small Houses**
(TB)   **Tools for Building**
(TFH)   **Timber-Frame Houses**

   dovetailed, 43:37-38 (FWS), 55:64-65
   iron, 37:30, 31 (FWS)
   jointer shaping of, 6:21 (CSH)
   layout for, quick, 77:30
   making, 70:69 (EF)
   octagonal, 18:52 (FWS)
   paint aid for, 85:32
   production of, 18:52, 28:40-41, 35:79,
      36:58-59 (FWS)
   spacing, 70:70 (EF)
   spacing, calculating, 72:4, 72:4-6
   spacing, child-proof, 55:6
   spacing, safe, 65:68
   square-top, 36:57, 58 (FWS)
   square-tubing, 54:82 (EF)
   steel, 26:46-47
   taper-top, 36:57, 58, 59 (FWS)
   Victorian, 48:70, 73 (SH)
balustrades for,
   acrylic, 15:60, 62
   for bridges, 68:71-72 (EF)
   building, 39:44-45, 48 (FWS)
   Chinese Chippendale, 32:75, 59:61
   cutout, 52:45
   exterior, drainage for, 9:23-24
   for Federal fence, 25:75
   laminated, 53:91
   limestone, 37:60
   linked, 52:87
   over-the-post, 36:57 (FWS)
   post-to-post, 36:57 (FWS)
   stone-simulating, 9:23-24
   welded metal, 57:57
   wood with steel, 1:54
benches in, 6:66
blocking for, 82:51
of blocks, L-shaped, 48:35-36
bolts in, rail, 39:45-46 (FWS)
books on, 30:78, 41:94, 43:35, 37, 38
   (FWS)
   reviewed, 64:110, 69:108-10
boring jigs for, reviewed, 63:90

builders of,
   contemporary, 43:34-39 (FWS)
   finding, 43:39 (FWS)
   listed, 53:104
building, on site, 62:42-45
cantilevered, 35:75, 76, 78-79, 40:6
carpeted, paint shield for, 54:24
carriages for, 17:59-61, 60 (erratum, 19:6,
   FWS)
carved, 16:75-76, 21:36, 38-39 (FWS)
   timbered, 25:27, 29
central post, 9:60, 13:8, 40-41, 34:8
cherry, 1:59, 38:75 (TFH)
chipped, epoxy repair for, 70:48
circular,
   clamps for, site-built, 74:24
   commercial iron, 10:50, 51 (SH)
   exterior, 9:60-61
   plastered, 51:60-61
   plywood-veneered, 53:90-91
   on poles, 8:27 (CBS)
   sprinkler system for, 39:30
   square, 39:29, 30, 31
   stress-tested, 79:132
   tower, 56:69, 71 (CSH)
clamps for, irregular-angle, 74:73 (FC)
code on, 67:4
in Colonial style, 63:47
concrete,
   circular, wood encasement of, 55:62-
      65
   finish tips for, 44:14-16, 46:4, 6
   forms for, 49:28
   spiral, construction of, 20:50-53
      (FWS)
   textured, 66:43, 45
   and tile, 6:30, 33
curved, kit for, reviewed, 59:104-106
custom,
   metal, 62:88
   source for, 56:61 (EEH)
deck, 29:46 (FRC), 69:47 (EF)
designing, 17:57 (FWS)
dismantling, 1:16 (FWS)
with double approach, 52:46 (TFH)
double-helix, 42:45-49 (FWS)
   computer-generated, 59:63, 65 (EEH)
   custom, source for, 77:54
easings for, 39:45 (FWS)
exterior, 3:57 (EEH), 81:44-47
   angled, 66:61 (REM)
   brownstone, flashing of, 20:10-12
   of carved sandstone, 68:73 (EF)
   circular, 9:60-61
   curved, 31:67, 70-71
   redwood, 25:81
   stone, 19:74, 77
   stone, dry-laid, 76:60-62
   stone, with iron handrails, 66:76
   stone, treads for, 51:58

stone-filled, 25:81
stringer methods for, 76:16
surfacing for, 54:80, 81 (EF), 81:46
surfacing for, carborundum, 32:27 (CSH)
weatherproof construction for, 70:68-71 (EF)
winding, building, 51:46-49 (EF)
finish for, 39:48 (FWS)
urethane/tung oil, 70:91
with flagpole, 28:74, 75
folding,
    installing, 48:14
    insulated hatch box for, 56:37
    insulator kit for, 67:92
    10-ft. rise, 43:70, 71 (TB)
formal, 31:44-45, 49-50 (FWS)
framing for, 17:57 (FWS)
gauges for,
    marking, 35:14
    using, 10:61 (TB)
glass block with, 45:60-61, 62, 64 (SH)
glass/maple, building, 60:74-77
glossary for, 1:14, 15, 17:58, 36:57 (FWS)
glue for, 39:48 (FWS)
Greek Revival, 1:50
handrails of, 6:21, 16:72, 77, 17:57, 28:40-41, 35:79, 37:31, 33 (CSH, FWS)
    assembly of, 39:47-48 (FWS)
    board cap as, 80:53
    clamps for, 74:26
    half-wall, Arts-and-Crafts style, 82:85, 86
    iron, 57:4
    joining, 56:26
    safe, 55:6, 65:66, 68
    sections for, 36:57 (FWS)
    simple, 26:46-47, 39:30, 31
hatchway for, 38:44, 45, 108
headroom for, 17:57 (FWS)
inlays for, cherry, 49:82
Italianate Victorian, 84:60, 61
laminated, 43:35, 36 (FWS), 47:76-78, 55:63, 56:62 (EEH)
laminating, 16:70-77, 17:4, 37:31-32, 42:46-49 (FWS)
landings for,
    bow, 6:18, 20 (CSH)
    curved, 48:45 (TFH)
    dimensions of, 65:68
    extended, 39:30, 31
    minimal, 55:6
    suspended, 16:30, 64:85-86 (REM)
    torsion-box, 13:40, 41
    windows in, 80:53
    as wood box, 39:60 (CBS)
layout for, 17:59, 28:39-40 (FWS)
lengths for, safe, 65:68
lifts for, 53:68, 69
lighting, 2:20-22, 25 (CSH)
lock miters in, riser-stringer, 55:64
L-shaped, building, 67:44-46

making, book on, 50:69 (FC)
miraculous, pictured, 42:45 (FWS)
miters for, vertical, 52:66
moldings for, drop, 31:45 (FWS)
nails for, 1:17 (FWS), 85:47
naturally lighted, 56:61 (EEH)
newel posts for, 28:40-41, 36:57, 58, 39:47 (FWS)
    brass, 39:30, 31-32
    cherry octagonal, 68:87
    diamond-inlaid, 64:40, 41, 42 (CSH)
    exterior, 36:12-14, 84:60-63
    gallery of, 71:88-89
    installing, 82:63
    layout for, 39:45 (FWS)
    radial-arm-saw shaping of, 6:21 (CSH)
    round simple, 32:27 (CSH)
    threaded-rod reinforced, 49:81, 82
nosings for,
    bull, discussed, 64:10, 82:60-63
    butt-jointed, 52:60 (CSH)
octagonal, 18:50 (FWS)
open, 62:49 (SH)
    for air flow, 8:65, 66, 67 (EEH)
    L-shaped, 49:42, 43 (REM)
openings for, earthquake-proofing, 64:64 (MFC)
open-riser, 69:43 (EEH)
parts for, commercial, 55:63
pitchblock for, 39:45 (FWS)
plans for, 19:6
platform for, 1:17 (FWS)
posts for, octagonal, 18:51 (FWS)
prefab 2x4, source for, 74:90
problems in, treating, 1:14-18, 31:8 (FWS)
Queen Anne grand, 50:67
on radius, for deck, 83:74-76
rebuilding, with threaded-rod clamps, 74:26
red-oak windowed, 75:85
reinstalling, 20:90
renovating, 82:70, 71
for restored farmhouse, 79:89
restoring, 1:51, 4:18, 56:84, 85
rise for, 17:57 (FWS), 76:61
    between-landings, code on, 42:49 (FWS)
    determining, 67:44
risers for, 17:59, 61, 62, 37:32-33 (FWS)
    curved steambent, 49:81-82
    open, 80:74
riser/tread,
    design for, safe, 65:66-67
    template for, adjustable, 48:90
run for, finding, 17:57 (FWS)
safe,
    designs for, 65:66-68
    tips for, 65:68
of saplings, peeled, 12:76
sawblade for, 39:45 (FWS)
sculpted, 12:49

ship's heavy, making, 48:54, 55, 57
silo-contained, 38:56, 58
simple, 8:67 (EEH), 50:81 (SH), 73:48, 50
skirtboards of,
    fiberboard, 71:73
    fitting to, foam shims for, 76:30
    installing, 71:4-6
    notched, 68:60-61
    scribing, 77:60
Southern Building Code on, 74:92
in Southern long-leaf yellow pine, 39:76
spiral,
    apitong, 68:41
    balusters in, 70:90-91
    book on, 70:90
    building, 70:86-91
    hollow-post, 48:37-39
    laminating, 70:89-90
    metal, 45:61, 62, 64 (SH), 80:104
    steel, source for, 75:48, 49 (REM)
    wooden exterior, 54:80-82 (EF)
on stepped face frame, 15:70-71 (FWS)
steps for,
    bullnose, making, 82:60-63
    flagstone, 15:76, 77 (CSH)
stock, production of, 36:56-61 (FWS)
storage in, 47:89, 49:26, 59:86 (CSH), 85:95
storage under, 15:70-71 (FWS)
story pole for, 49:79
stringers for, 16:70-71, 72, 18:51-52, 28:39, 40 (FWS)
    building, 67:46
    housed, router template for, 74:90-92
    jigs for, 28:38-40 (FWS), 55:38-39 (FC)
    ornaments on, 29:66
    shrinkage in, avoiding, 84:14-16
surfaces for, safe, 65:67-68
surfacing, 39:48 (FWS)
suspended, 83:84
as thermal chimneys, 31:70
tiled, 61:52 (SH)
    simple, 64:87 (REM)
in tower,
    glass block, 37:50-51 (DWS)
    light-filled, 80:74
treads for, 16:72, 17:57, 61, 62, 18:51-52, 28:39, 40, 37:32-33 (FWS)
    ferro-cement, 13:51, 52-53 (CBS)
    inlaid, 47:78 (MFC)
    jigs for, 35:59 (TB), 78:30
    laminated, 35:78, 39:92 (FWS)
    oblique, 9:64, 67
    over old anchor holes, 78:30
    rabbets for, blind, 47:77 (MFC)
    tusk-tenoned, 32:75
of tree trunks, 30:88
turnouts for, 39:45 (FWS)
types of, 17:56-57 (FWS)
Victorian Acadian, 73:37
volutes for, 36:56, 57, 59, 39:45 (FWS)
    source for, 82:61

wainscoting for, making, 40:37 (FWS)

widening, 39:42

width of, 5:34, 57

winders for, 39:46 (FWS)

    boxed, 67:44-46

    designing, 67:44-46

and wood shrinkage, 81:58-59

See also Ladders. Railings. Ramps.

Stairways and Ladders (OSHA):

    cited, 84:53

Stakes: driving, 34:14-16

Stamped Concrete Impressions Inc.:

    patterning tools of, 7:6

Stanadyne-Moen Group: address for, 53:70

StanChem, Inc.: Incralac, 34:6

Standard Building Code:

    18th-century, 5:46-47

    history of, 5:44

    source for, 5:45

Standard Practice for Curing Concrete (ACI): cited, 55:68

Standard Structural Details for Building Construction (Newman): reviewed, 47:110

Standards for Rehabilitation:

    mentioned, 4:4

Standex Energy Systems: heat-recovery ventilators, 34:34 (DWS)

Stanley, Lars:

    metal work of, 62:88-89

    on mica, 57:96

Stanley Works:

    address for, 58:45, 69:92, 74:73 (FC), 76:92

    carpenter's vise, 35:91

    chalklines, 25:69 (TB)

    hammers,

        Compo-Cast deadblow, 39:63

        Steelmaster framing, 23:32 (TB)

    hinges, stamped brass, 39:92

    levels, 37:80

    multiplane #55, using, 11:37 (DWS)

    plumb bobs, 25:69 (TB)

    rabbet planes, 4:22 (TFH)

    router #071, 4:22 (TFH)

    saws, 12:51 (TB)

    screw punch, self-centering, 12:51 (TB)

    screwdrivers, Jobmaster, 12:51 (TB)

    smooth planes #4½, 4:22 (TFH)

    Sta-Tru Door, 6:60

    Surform, 12:51 (TB)

        for drywall, 8:54 (FWS)

    tape Power Lock II, 12:50 (TB)

    Wonder bar, 12:51, 32:55 (TB)

Stanley-Bostitch: framing nailers, reviewed, 56:52, 53, 54-55

Staplers:

    cordless siding, source for, 76:96

    electric, using, 2:52 (SH)

    ergonomic, reviewed, 85:102

    mail-order source for, 57:94

    manual adjustable, 75:72

    pneumatic,

        for cabinets, 13:61, 62 (BK)

        safety seminars for, 49:102

    for roofing felt, 57:86 (EF)

    source for, 58:68 (EF)

Staples:

    in earthquake-proofing, 64:65 (MFC)

    for flooring, 81:104

    in hurricane areas, 78:85, 79:4

    for sheathing, 40:6

    stainless-steel, 63:92, 68:64

    See also Nail guns: fasteners for.

Star Expansion Co.: address for, 41:57 (CBS)

Star Heat Exchanger Corp.:

    heat-recovery ventilators, 34:34 (DWS)

    model 100J-B, 42:62

Star Manufacturing Corp.:

    metal siding, 41:40

    translucent plastic, 41:40

Star Technology Corp.: insulated curtains, 34:29 (DWS)

Starbuck, Beth: ceramics by, 59:88

Starch: as glue, 65:41, 45

Starflake Millworks: address for, 63:40

Starr, Edward: *History of Cornwall, Connecticut, A,* cited, 49:38 (REM)

Starr, John: on White Mt. house, 56:58-63 (EEH)

Starrett (L. S.) Co.:

    address for, 53:58, 67:90

    level-transits, 37:45 (TB)

    plumb bobs, 25:69 (TB)

State Industries:

    address for, 82:58

    defective water heaters, 2:64

State-of-the-Art Report on Ferrocement: cited, 50:49

States Industries, Inc.: address for, 58:39 (REM), 74:75

Sta-Tru Door: source for, 6:60

Stave construction: discussed, 46:77-79

Staytex thermal barrier: source for, 33:75

Stead, Craig F.:

    on drywall finishing, 23:60-65 (FWS)

    on reciprocating saws, 16:45-49 (TB)

    on renovating carriage house, 10:42-45

    on renovating tools, 12:50-51 (TB)

Steam bending:

    physics of, 48:46 (TFH)

    pipe steamer for,

        on-site, 15:16

    safety in, 17:6

    of shingles, 23:55-56, 58:68 (EF)

    with steam iron, 49:81-82

    in the shower, 69:54

    of timbers, 48:46-47 (TFH)

Steamist Co., Inc.: address for, 52:112

Steam-Whirl: address for, 52:112

Stecker, Sam: discusses staircases, 36:58 (FWS)

Stedman, Myrtle: on adobe house, 5:46-47

Steel:

    anti-oxidant for, 51:40 (CSH)

    bimetal, 16:47 (TB), 62:65

    characteristics of, 32:33 (FRC)

    corrosion of, 10:4, 62:64, 65, 66

    cutting, with drill and hacksaws, 54:26

    epoxy paint for, industrial, 33:32 (CBS)

    expandability of, 79:82-83

    galvanized, discussed, 62:65-66

    load capacity of, 34:4

    nobility of, 21:4

    rebar, bender for, 26:64, 65 (CBS)

    rusting of,

        explained, 62:66

        non-, alloy of, 19:6

    rustproofing of, electrical, 33:32 (CBS)

    sacrificial anodes for, 33:32 (CBS)

    sandblasting, 33:28, 30

    sealer for, 33:30

    stainless,

        acid-resistant, 12:8

        for countertops, 77:44, 45

    tool M2, 16:47 (TB)

    wrought, defined, 19:4-6

    See also Beams: steel. Framing: steel. Ironwork.

Steel houses:

    book on, reviewed, 47:110

    See also Framing: steel. Lustron houses. Steel-plate house.

Steel Joist Institute: address for, 82:67

Steel Square, The (Siegele): discussed, 28:31-32 (FRC)

Steel, Terry:

    creations of, 17:92

    on wrought iron, 17:46-51

Steelcote: address for, 51:40 (CSH)

Steel-Framed Drywall Systems: source for, 30:6

Steelite Corp.: metal roofing from, 33:29

Steel-plate house: illustrated, 4:68

Stegmeier Corp.: Poly-void packing, 37:49 (DWS)

Stein, Jay:

    on automated home system, 53:72-76

    on furnaces, 46:44-48

    reviews radiators, 59:102

    reviews registers, 60:94-96

Stein, Robert: on Mullgardt, 52:82

Steltzer, Ulli: on igloos, 1:68

Stenciling:

    Art Nouveau, 54:37, 38-40

    described, 60:78, 80

    Mermaidic, 45:87

Stenstrom, David:

    on Federal fence, 25:73-77

    on porch restoration, 9:21-24

Stephen, George: *Remodeling Old Houses,* cited, 78:8

Stepladders: *See* Ladders: step.

Steppan, Mark: mentioned, 28:77

Steps: *See* Staircases.

Stereo systems:
cabinets for,
Spanish Revival, 45:42, 43
upright, 38:62 (CSH)
DC, source for, 24:82
prewiring for, 23:14
cautions about, 25:4

Sterl, Scott W.: on remodel, 64:38-42 (CSH)

Sterling Cark Lurton Corp.: address for, 47:52 (EF)

Sterling, Raymond, William Fanan and John Carmody: *Earth-Sheltered Residential Design Manual,* reviewed, 16:14-16

Stern, Arthur: lamp by, 38:65 (CSH)

Steve Ditch Associates: epoxy countertops, 35:91

Stevens, Mark: *MacMillan Small Business Handbook, The,* cited, 62:79

Stevenson, Matilda: on Zuñi plastering, 18:63-64

Stewart, Glen:
builds beach house, 31:22-27 (CSH)
Greene-and-Greene lamp by, 17:34 (CSH)

Stewart, Zach: house by, 18:44-49

Stick layout: *See* Story poles.

Stickley, Gustav:
books on, 36:29 (CSH)
Craftsman Homes, 36:29 (CSH)
house plans of, 53:88
houses by, 36:24-29 (CSH)
light fixtures by, 36:27-28 (CSH)
More Craftsman Homes, 36:29 (CSH)
See also Arts-and-Crafts style.

Stiebel Eltron, Inc.:
address for, 82:102
water heaters, 12:18 (CSH)

Stihl: chainsaw #090, 41:51 (TB)

Stillwater Products, Inc.: address for, 72:88

Stilp, Harley: builds tower, 37:50 (DWS)

Stilts:
as finishing aid, 32:16
for plastering, 15:72, 73 (FWS)
sources for, 23:63 (FWS)
using, 23:63 (FWS)

Stirewalt, Edward N.: as joint author. *See* Maycock, Paul.

STK Canada: address for, 75:72

STO Energy Conservation, Inc.: acrylic plaster compound, 23:66

STO Industries Inc.:
address for, 77:57
synthetic stucco, 43:77

Stocker Brothers: floor by, 79:91

Stockly, Holmes: arbor and gate by, 49:44-45

Sto-Cote Products, Inc.:
address for, 46:72, 83:48
Tu-Tuf vapor barrier, 2:32, 19:22, 29:68, 34:68 (EEH, SH)

Stoddard, Gregory: on cabinet repair, 58:118

Stodola, Rick: on dust-collection system, 60:63

Stokes, William: on porch conversion, 15:42-43

Stolle Corp.: address for, 83:45

Stolwijk, Jan A. J.: on air quality, 5:15

Stone:
cutting,
boring in, 9:42, 43
business of, 37:56-61
limestone,
carving, 54:72-75
carving, source for, 56:6
cutting of, 37:56-61
source for, 68:85

Stone, Mark Van: on ornamental lettering, 72:48-49

Stone Glamour concrete sealant: mentioned, 16:57 (CBS)

Stone, Log and Earth Houses (Berglund): source for, 34:39

Stone masonry:
Aggraglaze for, 9:45
alignment for, 27:65-66, 67 (CBS)
anchors for,
adhesive, 26:82
truss, 39:90
arches in, 33:64, 65, 39:58 (CBS), 84:58, 59
form for, 58:47, 48
Arts-and-Crafts style organic, 24:29-30 (CSH)
ashlar, with fieldstone, 45:57-59
associations for, 37:59
banker for, 49:56, 57
basalt, 8:24 (CBS)
batterboards with, 49:54, 55
beam brackets in, 8:26 (CBS)
bedding compound for, 25:76, 27:65, 66 (CBS)
over block, 84:56-59
block corners with, 5:32
block imitation of, split-faced, 52:86
and block, insulated, 43:58-61 (CBS)
bond beams for, 48:80
books on, 5:39, 58:48
broken, reinforcement rods for, 5:38
with Campito sandstone, 9:45
caps for, 8:26, 27, 27:67 (CBS)
cautions for, 8:24 (CBS)
chamfering, 51:63
Chinese houses of, 55:88-89
cleaning, 3:32, 5:39, 8:26, 35:37 (CBS), 48:12, 63:20

cobble over block, house in, 54:83-87 (TFH)
conservation association for, 71:104
corner blocks in, limestone, 33:65
cutting, 51:63
decay of, 5:37
doors for, 14:64
dressing, 6:45, 35:37, 40:49 (CBS, TFH)
drunken, with round rocks, 82:88-89
earthquake-resistant, 8:23, 26 (CBS), 63:102
"farmer," 80:48, 49
fasteners for, powder-actuated, 21:30-34 (TB)
faux, 60:82
fieldstone fitted, 21:36-37, 41
finish for, 55:87
interior, 70:65 (EEH)
supply source for, 51:63
fireplaces of, fieldstone, 26:69-71 (CBS)
floors in,
mortar for, 68:48-49
porphyry, 70:65 (EEH)
sealing, 68:49
stone for, 68:47, 48
underlayment for, 68:47-48
footings for, 27:65, 67 (CBS), 49:54
forms for, 3:30, 14:62, 63-64, 65, 39:58 (CBS)
slip, 51:68-71
foundations for, 41:68 (CSH)
foundations of,
insulating, 18:6
repairing, 69:68-69 (REM)
waterproofing, 17:8, 69:14-16
gable ends for, board-and-batten, 39:59 (CBS)
and glass, joining, 45:58, 59
with granite, 52:48-49 (TFH)
over block, 58:46-48
exterior details in, 51:62
slabs for, 51:61-63
video on, 71:106
walls of, 45:74 (CSH)
guides for, 49:56
gutters for, integral, 24:30 (CSH)
headers for, 8:26 (CBS)
heat sculpting, 51:63
houses of, 18:44
French, 33:63-67
instruction in, 74:106
faxed, 70:112
over insulated core, 70:63 (EEH)
insulating, 3:22-23, 25, 28-29, 9:6, 17:8, 19:12, 51:70, 71
with urethane foam, 13:6, 15:14
joints for, 45:58
finishing, 44:57
joy from, 30:86
with lava, 38:79-83 (CSH)
laying, 5:37, 8:24, 13:37-38, 18:47 (CBS), 44:56, 51:69-70

levels for, 58:43-44, 45
  laser, 84:94
limestone, 36:70-75
  simulating, 69:69 (REM)
  types for, 37:56
  veneer, 80:55, 57
load of, 8:23 (CBS)
marble fragments in, 33:24-25
materials for, 3:30, 31 (CBS)
Mexican, 22:84
milestones in, 12:76
moisture in, capillary, 15:14
moss removal for, 48:12
muriatic acid and, avoiding, 68:49
old, book on, 49:114
openings in, 51:70
  retrofitting, 46:12-14
painting, 62:22 (CSH)
panels of, precast, 85:82-83
parging, 62:20 (CSH)
pickling, 62:22 (CSH)
plumbing, 13:37, 18:46 (CBS)
pointing, 8:24, 27:66-67 (CBS)
polishing, 51:63
over post-and-beam, 39:56-60 (CBS)
quarrying, 35:35-37 (CBS)
with quartzites, 42:73 (CBS)
quoins for, 43:58 (CBS)
reinforcing, 3:29-30, 31 (CBS)
repair of, 5:36-39, 44:54-57
restoring,
  book on, 24:86
  seminar in, 72:98
with river rock, adhesion improvement
  for, 72:28
rock for, 27:65 (CBS)
  quality of, 49:55-57
  quarried, 8:24 (CBS)
  used, 66:75
rock rollers for, coil-spring, 53:30
rubble ashlar, 3:20, 21, 23
Scottish harling over, 54:38, 41
sealants for, 20:12, 27:12
  dangers with, 5:39
  nontoxic, source for, 67:92
sealing, 51:63
seam orientation in, 54:38, 41
17th-century, 6:46, 47 (TFH)
shaping for, 58:46-47
shower in, 5:8
for staircases, exterior dry-laid, 76:60-62
story poles for, 49:54-55
strength of, 32:33 (FRC)
  vs. concrete, 9:6
stuccoed, problems with, 54:38, 41
templates for, aluminum foil, 33:16
Texas infill, 70:61-65 (EEH)
tools for, 3:30, 8:24, 15:4, 35:36 (CBS),
  49:57, 68:47
  sources for, 55:6-8, 58:46
traditional, workshops in, 54:100-102
for trim, 49:91

and trim, joining, 45:58
uses of, 3:28 (CBS)
vapor barriers for, 17:8, 19:12, 51:70-71
varicolored, paint hues with, 63:20
as veneer, 13:36-38, 36:73-74, 41:38-39
  (CBS)
walls in,
  building, 3:31-32 (CBS)
  cavity, 48:80-82
  designing, 3:29-30 (CBS)
  dry, gravel grout for, 23:14
  stepped, 18:71
waterproofing, 3:31 (CBS)
wedge keeper for, 44:24
windows in, 14:64, 65, 24:30 (CSH)
wire ties for, 41:39
wood disguised as, 9:20-24
See also Anchors. Concrete: cast
  "stone" from. Efflorescence.
  Flagstone. Metal connectors. Mortar.
  Repointing.
Stone masons: exchange program for,
  32:82
Stone-end house: construction of, 6:42-47
  (TFH)
Stoneham, William: murals by, 45:52-53
  (CSH)
Stonitsch, Gus: sawmill of, 20:29
Stools:
  Arts-and-Crafts style, 52:78
  portable work, 30:55 (DWS)
Stoops:
  defined, 29:48
  large simple, 73:54
Storage:
  creating space for, 53:43-45 (SH)
  in house "spine," 80:81
  ideas for, 47:88-89
  on-site caddy for, 49:28
  overhead compartments for, 80:70, 71
  in stairs, 47:89, 49:26, 59:86 (CSH), 85:95
  behind truck seat, 51:26
  wall, systems for, 35:91
  See also Closets. Shelves.
Storefront for Arts and Architecture: as
  resource, 66:16
Storehouses: example of, 67:87
Storm, Per Palle: sculpture by, 46:120
Story poles:
  for block work, 15:46 (CBS)
  for cabinet construction, 58:36 (REM)
  commercial, reviewed, 83:98
  for drawer slides, 83:72
  extension measuring version of, 22:14
  Japanese, 4:52-53 (TFH)
  1940s use of, 11:29-33 (EEH)
  for sidewall shingling, 8:62
  for timber framing, 13:27 (TFH)
  trench depths with, 11:28 (CBS)
  using, 51:69
  for wall raisings, 58:62
  for windows, 50:70, 71-72 (FC)

Stovall, David: on computer-aided
  design, 49:46-50
Stoves: *See* Ranges. Wood stoves.
Straight Poop, The (Hemp): cited, 49:53
  (MFC)
Straightedges: truing, 4:24 (TFH)
Strandlund, Carl: Lustron houses by,
  22:26-30
Strang, Gary: on straw-bale studio, 24:70-
  72
Strangstad, Lynette: on heat pumps, 14:16
Straps: *See* Metal connectors.
Strasser, Peter:
  on restoration, 29:63-67
  staircase by, 30:88
Straub, Calvin: on framing, 46:78
Straus-Edwards, Lydia: ranch remodel
  by, 30:32-36
Straw-bale building: construction of,
  24:70-72
Strawderman, David:
  on double-hung windows, 64:48-49 (FC)
  on French-door retrofit, 68:42-46 (FC)
  reviews weatherstripping tool, 60:92
Stress-skin panels:
  advantages of, 24:55
  bits for, making, 56:28
  book on, 26:4
  cam-lock, 46:81-82 (TFH)
  composite, waferboard and
    plywood/aluminum, 39:71
  cores for, source of, 24:59
  custom, suppliers of, 39:73
  discussed, 27:4
  as floors, 24:58, 40:12
  and foam sealants, cautions for, 49:4
  installing, 24:55-58, 59, 25:46 (TFH)
    on roofs, 51:74 (EEH)
  manufacture of, 24:58
  metal roofing over, 48:12
  roof panels for, vented, 26:4
  sandwich of, 45:47 (TFH)
  sealant for, 47:54 (TFH)
  source for, 38:74 (TFH)
  for timber framing, 25:42-43 (TFH)
  types of, 24:58-59, 25:43 (TFH)
  wiring in, 24:59, 25:46, 29:76 (TFH), 47:53-
    55 (TFH)
  See also Walls.
String:
  knots for, 25:64-65 (TB)
  spools for,
    acrylic, 37:14
    butterfly, 16:12
  types of, 25:64 (TB)
Striplath: source for, 23:12
Stripping: *See* Paint: removal of.
Strombeck, Janet A. and Richard H.:
  Backyard Structures, cited, 53:89
  Bridges and Cupolas, cited, 53:89

Gazebos and Other Garden Structures, cited, 53:89
Privy, cited, 53:89
Structo-Lite plaster: source for, 5:50, 34:64 (BK)
Structural Antiquities Unlimited: masonry repairs by, 5:36
Structural Board Association: address for, 67:81
Structural Development, Inc.: address for, 51:82 (MFC)
Structural Insulated Panel Association: address for, 64:10
Structural Slate Co.: address for, 20:39 (EF)
Structures: or Why Things Don't Fall Down (Gordon): reviewed, 45:116
Stucco:
  over adobe, 5:49-50
  adobe, pumped and sprayed, 21:20-21
  applying, 47:60
    timing for, 73:59
  Art Nouveau, 31:92
  over block, 67:59, 63
    applying, 40:12
  for block wall, freestanding, 36:12
  blocking for, 22:35 (FRC)
  bonding primer for, 18:8
  books on, 47:60
    cited, 62:20 (CSH)
  brush-on, 68:66
  of cement mortar, 33:65
  over chicken wire, 7:36 (DWS)
  Chinese houses of, 55:88-89
  cobblestones of, cultured, 81:71
  cold-weather problems with, 30:41
  coloring, 66:54
  for concrete, 15:14
    deteriorating, 15:14
    polymer-based, 30:76
  control joints for, 47:60
  crack patchers for, source for, 66:55
  cutting, with carborundum blade, 68:44, 46 (FC)
  delaminating of, causes for, 30:6-8
  earthquake-proofing, 64:61 (MFC)
  efflorescence with, detecting, 32:4
  exterior synthetic, 63:82, 83, 84 (EEH)
  exterior-grade, 40:32
  for extreme temperatures, 80:64-66
  finish for, 50:49
    elastomeric/acrylic, 77:57
  flashing with, 47:59
  French lime, 30:76
  over hot tub, 69:66
  over insulation, foundation, 18:33-35 (CBS), 76:37
  insulation retrofit for, 56:41
  interior, 42:52, 53 (SH)
    for mass, 17:45 (SH)
    plywood backup for, 19:40 (BK)
  for Japanese bathhouse, 19:40 (BK)

Key to books:
(BK) Building Baths and Kitchens
(CBS) Building with Concrete, Brick and Stone
(CSH) Craftsman-Style Houses
(DWS) Building Doors, Windows and Skylights
(EEH) Energy-Efficient Houses
(EF) Exterior Finishing
(FC) Finish Carpentry
(FRC) Frame Carpentry
(FWS) Building Floors, Walls and Stairs
(MFC) More Frame Carpentry
(REM) Remodeling
(SH) Small Houses
(TB) Tools for Building
(TFH) Timber-Frame Houses

  lath for, 68:59
    board, information on, 71:106
    installing, 18:34-35 (CBS)
    metal, isolating from flashing, 49:4
  moisture damage to, 32:4
  paint for, 16:8, 18:8
    sand-coated, 61:71
  paint on, removing, 16:8, 18:8
  paper under, vapor-barrier mesh, 31:27 (CSH)
  permeability of, 19:68
  pigmented, 21:43
  vs. plaster, 70:14, 71:6, 74:6
  polymer-based, 30:76
  premixed,
    cement commercial, 54:86 (TFH)
    source for, 75:45
  problems with, 55:70
  process of, 18:35 (CBS)
  over pumice-crete, 77:56
  with quoins, 64:39, 40 (CSH)
    built-up, 59:48-49 (SH)
  over rammed earth, cited, 54:86 (TFH)
  repairing, 30:8
    filler for, 56:41
  Scottish harling, 54:38, 41
  over seams, 31:27 (CSH)
  spray for, silicone silicate, 54:41
  spray, hopper prop for, 79:30
  over straw, 24:71-72
  synthetic, 47:94
    cement for, 18:8
    over dome, 46:42-43
    houses in, 43:75-79, 82:82
    insulating latex, source for, 43:77
  in tropics, 85:75
  trowel for, rubber, 31:4
  over wood frame, 45:38
  See also Dryvit Systems, Inc. Earth construction: cob. Parging. Thin-mass houses.

Studies:
  in bedrooms, 75:85
  open, 37:34, 35, 37
  See also Offices.
Studies and Executed Buildings by Frank Lloyd Wright: reviewed, 45:122
Studios:
  Arts-and-Crafts style, 51:36-40 (CSH)
  attic, 64:84-87 (REM)
    light-filled, 81:86, 87
  clerestory in, 27:73, 75, 76
  design around, 4:26-33
  detached, 27:72, 73, 75
  house and, 77:50-54
  house-integral private, 33:49, 50 (SH)
  music, soundproofing, 35:60-63
  for painting, 50:78-81 (SH)
  photography, and guest house, 61:58-61 (SH)
  plan sources for, 53:89
  Victorian log, 48:70-73 (SH)
  weaving, 51:58-63
  See also Offices.
Stulb Co.: address for, 63:48
Stump house: featured, 23:92
Sturdi-bond adhesive: source for, 34:49
Styrofoam: *See* Polystyrene.
Styrofoam, blueboard: *See* Polystyrene, extruded.
Subcontractors: *See* Builders.
Subdivisions: cluster, 59:68-73 (SH)
Subfloors: *See* Floors.
Subject Bibliography: source for, 23:48
Subzero Freezer Co., Inc.: refrigerators, 43:79, 44:53 (SH)
Sucka, La: vent, publication on, 30:80
Suckno Brothers: staircases, 36:61 (FWS)
Suddarth, Stephen:
  on hinge-butt templates, 31:28-31 (TB)
  on leveling tools, 37:39-45 (TB)
  on miter saws, 29:86
  on tetrahedron house, 6:48-50
Sudjic, Deyan, ed.: *House Style Book, The,* 36:94
Sugarman, Josh: on framing lumber, 8:14
Sulfur dioxide: problems from, 5:15
Sullivan, Charles, Eileen Woodford, et al.: *Maintaining Your Old House in Cambridge,* reviewed, 68:108
Sullivan, Louis: role of, 9:68
Summerson, John: *Classical Language of Architecture, The,* reviewed, 45:120
Sun Light heliodon: source for, 13:18
Sun Ray: absorber plates, 3:49
Sun, Wind and Light (Brown): reviewed, 37:88, 45:116
Sun-angle calculators: source for, 80:26
Sunbender reflectors: pictured, 26:57
Sunblock: reviewed, 46:90

Sunbursts:
  in clapboarding, 51:14
  elliptical clapboard, 14:10
  gable, 74:46, 49 (EF, REM)
Sundance Spas: address for, 69:46 (EF)
Sundberg: as joint author. *See* Durbahn, Walter E.
Sundials: magnetic float switches, 29:88
Sundows: explained, 16:28
Sun-Earth Buffering and Superinsulation (Booth and Boyles): reviewed, 28:86
Sunflake windows: mentioned, 6:54
SunGain:
  glass, described, 26:74 (SH)
  insulating film, in quad-pane, 20:14
Sunglasses: for cold-weather work, 50:62
Sunhouse: reviewed, 37:88
Sunlight to Electricity in One Step (Maycock and Stirewalt): reviewed, 12:72
Sun-Lite Premium II glazing panels: for site-built collectors, 1:32
SunQest: address for, 68:54, 55
Sunrise Industries: address for, 58:61 (CSH)
Sunrooms: *See* Glazing: sloped. Solariums.
Sunset Books:
  Garden Pools, Fountains, and Waterfalls, 13:6
  Western Garden Book, 9:16
Sunshine, Donald:
  about, 45:130
  house by, 45:65-69, 89
Sunshine Makers, Inc.: address for, 62:38 (EF)
Sunspaces: source for, 23:50
Sunspaces: *See* Solariums.
Sun-tempering: *See* Design: sun-tempered. Landscaping.
Suntime, Inc.: phase-change systems, 10:18
Suntronics: woodstove water heater, 24:64 (TFH)
Sunworks: copper absorbers, 3:49
Super Good Cents Technical Reference Manual: source for, 37:65
Super Sampson laminated polyethylene: mentioned, 19:22
Superbar prybar: source for, 32:55 (TB)
Superhouse (Metz): reviewed, 15:22
Superinsulated House, The (McGrath): mentioned, 19:69 (EEH)
Superinsulated houses:
  air quality in, 22:16-18, 35:4
  air/vapor barriers for, 9:57 (erratum, 11:4-6), 13:4, 17:10, 19:66, 70, 34:68 (SH)
  books on, 4:8, 6:58, 15:22, 28:86, 32:90
  building, 63:81-85 (EEH), 70:54-56 (EEH)
  building paper for, 11:4-6, 13:4
  in Cape format, 56:58-63 (EEH)

  cautions for, 21:59, 33:57 (EEH)
  ceilings in, 9:59
  chases in, electrical, 17:10
  chimneys in, 9:59
  components of, 6:58
  conferences on, 19:22, 22:16-18, 28:81-82
  cooling systems for, 15:61
  costs of, 11:6, 15:62, 17:4, 22:18, 34:69, 66:67 (CSH, EEH, SH)
  crawl spaces with, disadvised, 40:12
  designs for, integrated, 66:4
  doors in, 9:57, 58
  double-wall use in, 22:18 (CSH)
  electric, 22:18 (CSH)
    design for, 66:65-66 (EEH)
    energy program for, 66:65 (EEH)
  forum report on, 22:16
  frame shrinkage in, equalizing, 11:4-6, 13:4
  framing alternatives for, 8:8
  gas heat in, 22:18 (CSH)
  gases in, 9:59
  heating systems for, 5:57 (FRC), 63:85 (EEH)
  humidity in, 9:59
  information on, 65:52
  insulating, 4:8, 21:58-59, 28:81 (EEH), 70:55 (EEH)
  Larsen-truss retrofit of, for slab house, 23:10
  moisture problems in, 46:96
  organization for, 28:82
  performance of, 15:58, 61, 62, 17:4, 38:53, 66:4, 67-68 (EEH)
  plates for, doubled, 11:4-6
  plumbing stacks in, 9:59
  pressure testing of, 22:18, 28:81 (CSH)
  rafters for,
    gusseted, 17:10, 20:12
    super, 17:10
    trussed, 20:12, 34:68 (SH)
  retrofit, 20:35-37
    costs of, 22:18 (CSH)
    Larsen-truss, 20:35-37
  roll-top, 25:38-41 (EEH)
  roofs for, 9:58-59, 15:61
  selling, 22:18 (CSH)
  shed roof post-and-beam, 17:4
  stress-skin floor for, 40:12
  tract, 24:82
  types of, 9:56
  ventilation of, 28:81-82, 34:69 (SH)
  walls for, 9:56, 66:68 (EEH)
    stand-off, 15:58, 59-61, 17:4
  windows for, 9:57, 58, 70:55-56 (EEH)
  wiring in, 34:68 (SH)
  wrap 'n strap, 34:68 (SH)
  See also Framing: with truss-frames. Heat-recovery ventilators.
Superinsulated Houses and Double-Envelope Houses (Shurcliff): reviewed, 6:58

Superinsulated Retrofit Book, The (Argue): mentioned, 22:18 (CSH)
Superinsulation Building Newsletter: source for, 23:51
Superinsulation in Housing Conference (Rochester, MN, 1985): discussed, 28:82
Superinsulation Information Service:
  conference by, 28:81
  services of, 23:51
  Superinsulation Building Newsletter, 23:51
Superintendent of Documents: address for, 65:54
Superior Autovents: Bayliss vents, 32:37
Superior Clay Corp.: address for, 74:49 (REM), 85:8
Superior Distributing Co.: address for, 69:53, 81:72
Superior Propane: gaslights, 14:31
Support Systems for Buildings (Lewis): reviewed, 34:92
Suprenant, Bruce A.: on concrete curing, 55:66-68
Sure Klean:
  Efflorescence Control System, source for, 25:10
  fireplace cleaner, source for, 37:8
  600 Detergent, source for, 43:55 (CBS)
Sure Seal: address for, 48:36
Sure Seal Glazing System: installing, 34:66 (BK)
Surell:
  address for, 84:45
  See also Countertops: resin board.
Surewall:
  source for, 12:37 (CBS)
  using, 46:62, 65 (TFH)
Surface bonding: *See* Block: surface-bonded.
Surrounds: *See* Mantels.
Surveying: *See* Site layout.
Susanka, Sarah:
  house by, 38:49-53
  on Prairie house, 52:62-67
Sussman, Art, and Richard Frazier: *Handmade Hot Water Systems,* 46:65 (TFH)
Sutherland Welles, Ltd.: address for, 73:70
Sutton, Eli:
  deck by, 39:52-55 (CSH)
  designs Craftsman remodel, 29:57-61 (CSH)
Suzuki, Makoto: *Wooden Houses,* reviewed, 12:72
Svane, Poul: mentioned, 31:76
Swamp cooler: workings of, 17:45 (SH)
Swamps: *See* Wetlands.
Swan Secure Products, Inc.: address for, 58:61, 63:92 (CSH)
Swann, Robert: on land trusts, 17:20

Swanson, Wilmot: house by, 12:76
Swanson Tool Co.: Speed Square, 10:60-61 (TB)
Sweden:
  house systems of, discussed, 28:82
  housing research tax in, 23:84
  Masonite I-beam walls of, 22:18 (CSH)
  polyethylene standards in, 22:18 (CSH)
  prefab housing in, 23:84
  triple-function air-to-water heat pump of, 22:18 (CSH)
  See also Prefabricated houses: Scandinavian.
Swedish Trade Council: address for, 40:54 (erratum, 41:4)
Swedish Wooden House: address for, 23:84
Swedlow Inc.: Acrivue A, 10:33 (DWS)
Sweet williams: using, 8:31, 32, 14:48 (TFH)
Sweet's Catalog File:
  address for, 43:39 (FWS)
  computer access to, 46:59
  described, 37:29 (BK)
Swensson, Carl: Japanese trimwork by, 45:72, 89 (CSH)
Swietenia spp.: *See* Mahogany.
Swimming pools:
  dehumidifier for, 45:80 (EEH)
  gunite, 42:31 (CSH)
  as heat mass, 20:10
  humidity from, controlling, 20:8-10
  insulating, 20:10
  lap, 45:39, 40, 77, 79-81
  publications on, 30:80
  rock-wall surrounded, 59:83-84 (CSH)
Swiss Foundry: work of, 16:44
Sybron, Inc.: Nalgene containers, 38:58
Sygar, Richard: chronicles house, 75:66-67
Sylvania Lighting Center:
  address for, 54:51
  fixtures, 15:57 (BK)
Sylvax Corp.: Inogon Level and Angle Indicator, 27:82
Symons Corp.: address for, 73:73
Symphony program: for contractors, 35:66 (TB)
Syn Skyn fiberglass: source for, 39:74
Syndesis Studios: address for, 66:102
Synergetics, Inc.: mentioned, 33:29
Synopses: source for, 40:54
System, The (Mace): discussed, 35:45 (BK)
System 150 insulated forms: reviewed, 53:96-98
System Platon membrane: source for, 40:54
System Three Resins: address for, 70:49
Syvanen, Bob:
  on baseboard, 34:40-41 (FWS)
  on brick floors, 14:32-35 (CBS)
  on building fireplaces, 20:54-58 (CBS)

Carpentry, reviewed, 3:60
  on casings, 30:55-57, 33:53-55 (DWS)
  on chimneys, 21:46-50 (CBS)
  on clapboards, 47:48-52 (EF)
  on concrete, 13:34-35 (CBS)
  on cornice construction, 15:38-41 (EF)
Drafting, 43:67 (TB)
  on drafting basics, 43:62-67 (SH, TB)
Drawing House Plans with Bob Syvanen, 43:67 (TB)
  on drywall, 8:52-57 (FWS)
  on flashing, 9:46-50 (EF)
  on insulated, parged foundations, 18:33-35 (CBS)
Interior Finish, 8:52 (FWS)
  mentioned, 7:36, 37 (DWS)
  on rafter tails, 27:43 (FRC)
  reviews Sawbuck, 12:14-16
  on roof shingling, 12:52-57
  on shed-dormer addition, 24:47-51 (FRC)
  on sidewall shingling, 28:63-67
  on skirtboards, 68:60-61
  on staircases, 17:56-62 (FWS)
  on stairway remodeling, 26:46-47

T

- -

T. C. Manufacturing: address for, 64:92
Tabb, Phillip: house by, 34:56-61 (FRC)
Tabberson, William: on Prairie house, 38:84-89
Table saws:
  accidents with, 34:53 (TB)
  blades for,
    plastic-cutting, 84:42
    truing, 61:26
  brake for, 56:4
    reviewed, 58:91
  cornstarch on, for sliding ease, 84:41, 42
  crosscut jig for, 9:33-34 (BK)
  cutting guide for, 48:60
  dado blade for, hybrid, 40:87
  dangers of, 83:80-81
  edger jig for, 53:60-61
  extension for, 30:60, 61 (BK)
  featherboard for, reviewed, 69:94-96
  fences for, 64:71
    rip, homemade, 1:22-23 (TB)
    sandpaper-gripping, 56:4
    source for, 53:58
  finger joints on, 30:62 (BK)
  fluting jig for, 61:70
  frame-and-trim, 12:14-16, 14:4
  handrail shaping on, 60:77
  homemade, 1:22-23 (TB)
  jointing jig for, 44:24
  kickback prevention with, 34:53 (TB)
  miter jig for, 1:23 (TB)

  molding on, 2:48-49 (FWS)
    brick, 16:12
    crown, 74:80-81 (FC)
  Norwegian combination, 26:82
  Norwegian turntable, reviewed, 51:90-92
  plastic laminate on, 9:41 (BK)
  plywood on, accessories for cutting, 74:76
  portable,
    by brand, 64:70-74
    care of, 64:74
    choosing, 68:4
    tables for, 64:71
  rabbets on, housed, setup for, 77:30
  raised panels with, 19:50-51 (FWS)
  risk rating of, 34:51 (TB)
  as router tables, 1:23 (TB), 55:39 (FC)
  safety with, 34:53 (TB), 64:74
    labels for, 37:81
  sanding discs for, 72:28
  scarf-joint jig for, 53:61
  shim-shingle jig for, 58:26
  sliding tables for, 54:45 (EF)
    improving, 56:4
    making, 53:58-59
    portable, reviewed, 75:92
    safety with, 56:4
  stock feeders for, source for, 34:55 (TB)
  tapers on, 54:56
    jig for, 13:12
  tenons on,
    jig for, 19:51, 52, 36:41 (DWS, FWS), 48:73 (SH), 69:52-53
    round, 55:26
  tuning, 53:58
  workstation for, reviewed, 71:94
  See also brand names. Roller supports. Sawblades. Wet saws.
Tables:
  Art-Deco pedestal, 14:68-69
  built-in, 12:31
    deck, 30:35
    tile, 31:68-69
  chopping-block, 63:55, 57 (REM)
  circular convertible, 23:74-75
  coffee, hexagonal, 9:66
  dining,
    built-in, 24:76, 77
    movable, 30:23
  flip-up bed, 46:39 (REM)
  fold-down, 53:45 (SH)
  Mackintosh, 54:37, 40
  night, built-in, 74:56
  pedestal, 62:47, 48 (SH)
  pine, laminated, 45:66
  Spanish colonial, 48:34, 35
  tiled, 63:38
  trestle, 58:40 (REM)
Taco, Inc.:
  circulating pump, 33:12
  zone valves, 27:71 (CBS)
Tagg, Russ: stonework by, 45:73, 74 (CSH)

Tail cut: defined, 10:63 (FRC)
Talbot, Antony; *Handbook of Doormaking, Windowmaking, and Staircasing,* cited, 50:69 (FC)
Taliesin: seminars at, 38:102-106
Taliesin Associated Architects: Wright house plans from, 41:31
Tallman, Hap: makes brackets, 35:72-73
Tamarack: *See* Larch.
Tambours:
 for appliance "garage, " 58:38, 40 (REM)
 architectural, source for, 66:102
 oak-veneered, commercial, 72:62
 tracks for, plastic, 58:40 (REM)
Tamms Industries Co.: address for, 70:49
Tampers: for rammed earth, 34:35, 36, 39
Tan oak (*Lithocarpus densiflorus*): for floors, 24:64 (TFH)
Tanaka, Rick: bath fixtures by, hand-thrown, 36:68, 69 (BK)
Taney Supply and Lumber Corp.: staircases, 36:61 (FWS)
Tankenaka Museum: described, 65:6
Tankless Water Heater Corp.: Thermar water heater, 12:18 (CSH)
Tanzer, Kim: on Durham house, 52:83-87
Tap Plastics:
 address for, 69:66
 Syn Skyn fiberglass, 27:63
Tape:
 aluminum, with asphalt adhesive, 42:22 (CSH)
 double-sided, 27:16
 drywall fiberglass, 26:41
 glazing, 25:12, 34:4
 plumber's, as strapping, 29:38 (FRC)
 preshim, source for, 11:62 (DWS)
Tape measures:
 high-quality, source for, 74:90
 magnetized holder for, reviewed, 74:90
 reviewed, 64:96
 scratch pads on, 67:28
 silicone spray for, 67:28
Tape, sealing: *See* Caulk.
Tapers: on table saw, 13:12, 54:56
Tapes and Tools: address for, 81:74
Taping banjo: finding and using, 23:60-63 (FWS)
Tar: *See* Asphalt. Bitumens.
Tar Heel Mica Co.: address for, 57:96
Tar paper: *See* Builder's paper.
Tarcher, Ben: Craftsman house, 6:18-21 (CSH)
Target Products, Inc.:
 address for, 64:82, 70:59
 wet saws, 36:64 (BK)
Tarkett: address for, 58:57, 59:73 (SH)
Tarule, Rob: makes clapboards, 11:76
TASSO wall covering: source for, 35:34
Tatachook: sculpture by, 6:18, 19 (CSH)
Taub, Richard: on assembled trim, 79:46-49 (EF)

Key to books:

(BK) Building Baths and Kitchens
(CBS) Building with Concrete, Brick and Stone
(CSH) Craftsman-Style Houses
(DWS) Building Doors, Windows and Skylights
(EEH) Energy-Efficient Houses
(EF) Exterior Finishing
(FC) Finish Carpentry
(FRC) Frame Carpentry
(FWS) Building Floors, Walls and Stairs
(MFC) More Frame Carpentry
(REM) Remodeling
(SH) Small Houses
(TB) Tools for Building
(TFH) Timber-Frame Houses

Taxodium distichum: See Cypress, bald.
Taylor, David: reviews saws, 46:90
Taylor, Jeffrey: roofing tale by, 46:118
Taylor, Joseph A.: on ceramics work, 59:88-89
Taylor, Lonn, and Dessa Bokides: *New Mexican Furniture,* cited, 67:58
Taylor, Peter: deck by, 45:47 (TFH)
Taylor, Steve: builds guest house, 73:71-75
Taylor Building Products: Uni-Door, 6:60
TayMac Corp.: address for, 77:96
Teahouses:
 examples of, 44:82-83
 thatched, 67:86
Teak (*Tectona grandis*):
 bleaching, 22:12
 cabinets of, 13:60-63 (BK)
 finish for, 22:10-12
 flooring of, 22:10-12
  refinishing, 7:6
 gluing, 13:63 (BK)
 hot-water cleaning of, 22:12
 working with, 49:44
Teak oil: *See* Finishes.
Teal Cedar Products: address for, 54:44 (EF)
TEC, Inc.: address for, 65:45
Techlidan, Inc.: address for, 58:44
Technical Carpenter, The (Walmsley): reviewed, 69:108
Technical Services, ProSoCo, Inc.: fireplace cleaner, 37:8
Technics and Architecture (Elliott): reviewed, 82:112
Techniques of Staircase Construction (Mannes): reviewed, 41:94
Tech-Ops Landauer, Inc.: address for, 51:16, 67:51

TECO Products Co.:
 address for, 50:42, 69:47, 72:55, 73:74-75 (EF, MFC, REM)
 metal connectors, 43:49 (FRC)
Tecton Laminates Corp.:
 address for, 50:42 (MFC)
Tectona grandis: See Teak.
Tedrick, Bryan: gates by, 63:86
Tegola Canadese: asphalt/copper shingles, 39:90
Teks screw gun: described, 34:43, 44 (TB)
Teledyne Isotopes, Inc.: address for, 67:51
Telephones:
 compartment for, 15:78, 79 (CSH)
 for handicapped, 53:68
 preplanning for, 23:14, 25:4
 in restorations, 29:65
 wall-bin book holder for, 10:75
 yellow-page computer access to, 46:59
Television: cable, preplanning for, 23:14
Telpro, Inc.: address for, 50:52
Temcor heat-pump water heater: mentioned, 5:65
Templace: address for, 79:42
Templates:
 adjustable curved, reviewed, 68:94
 of aluminum foil, 33:16
 for door hanging, 26:29-31 (DWS)
 for hinge routing, reviewed, 70:104-106
 hinge-butt mortising, 31:28-31 (TB), 55:37-38 (FC)
  accessories for, 31:31 (TB)
  capacities of, by brand, 31:29, 30, 31 (TB)
  router bits for, 31:29 (TB)
  routers for, 31:29 (TB)
  using, 31:29-31 (TB)
 for lockset mortises, 79:45
 with masking tape, 85:30
 for rafters, 79:61
 in timber framing, 4:21 (TFH)
Temple-Inland Forest Products Corp.: address for, 66:48, 82:94
Temples: Japanese, lumber for, 83:112
Templeton, Duncan: as joint author. *See* Lord, Peter.
Tempmaster Enterprises Inc.: heat pumps, 26:68
Tenax Corp.:
 address for, 48:90
 C-Flex plastic mesh, reviewed, 48:90
Tendinitis: preventing, 64:68-69
Tennessee:
 home conservation credits in, 5:65
 solar tax credits in, 3:12
Tennessee Valley Authority:
 heat-pump water-heater policy of, 5:65
 solar houses by, 1:9
Tennis elbow: preventing, 64:69
Tenoners: German massive, 35:58 (TB)

Tenons: *See* Joinery.

Tension: defined, 7:25, 32:29 (FRC, TFH)

Tension ties: *See* Metal connectors: strap.

Tepromark International: duckboarding, 37:28 (BK)

Termites: *See* Insects.

Terms of the Trade (Dean): reviewed, 47:112

Terraces: *See* Patios.

Terra-cotta: blocks, for bathroom, 21:40, 42

Terrell, John: on pole house, 83:77-79

Terry, Sam: glass by, 42:80-81 (DWS)

Terzaghi and Peck: *Soil Mechanics in Engineering Practice,* cited, 50:86

TESS fireplace: *See* Thermal Energy Storage Systems.

Testor Corp.: cement for wood models, 22:51 (FRC)

Teton house: construction of, 18:40-43

Tetrahedron house: building, 6:48-50

Tex Enterprises: address for, 52:39 (TFH)

Texas:
architecture of, vernacular, 70:61-65 (EEH)
farmhouse-style house for, 36:70-75
New American Home 1985 for, 28:73-77
pension-fund mortgages in, 4:14
solar tax credits in, 3:12

Texas Carved Stone: work at, 54:72-75

Texas Diamond Tools, Inc.: address for, 70:59

Texas Forest Products Laboratory: address for, 77:16

Texas Tempered Glass: address for, 48:36

Texim International: address for, 80:102

Texmate: meter, 8:47

Thallon, Rob:
on dry-stack block, 16:54-57 (CBS)
on framing headers, 72:57-61
Graphic Guide to Frame Construction, cited, 71:112
measurement system of, 73:20-22
on *Pattern Language, A,* 36:51-55
on skylights, 18:36-39 (DWS)

Thatch: *See* Roofing.

Thatcher's Craft, The: source for, 22:77

Thaw, Harry K.: shoots White, 37:53

Theis, Chris: solar house by, 26:72-77

Thelin Thompson Co.: woodstoves of, 23:4

Theoretical length: defined, 10:63 (FRC)

Therma Manufacturing: address for, 76:39

Thermador-Waste King:
address for, 48:36
Basic Concepts of Residential Kitchen Ventilation, 40:67 (BK)
Trade-Wind 1501 Ventilator, 40:67 (BK)

Thermafibre: source for, 31:34 (DWS)

Therma-froth Systems, Inc.: Frothane, 31:38 (CBS)

Thermal Energy Storage Systems (TESS):
precast-block fireplace of, 15:20-21
sponsors conference, 19:22

Thermal Energy Transfer Corp.: heat pumps, 26:68

Thermal mass:
effectiveness of, 21:61
rock-bed storage as, 12:65-66, 25:38 (EEH)
for solar design, 19:63-64, 65, 30:52, 33:38, 40 (CBS, EEH)
concrete, 8:38 (EEH)
water storage for, 6:54, 57, 21:56-57, 58, 37:72, 67:12-14 (EEH)

Thermal-Krete insulation:
discussed, 24:12-14
source for, 31:38 (CBS)

Thermar water heaters: source for, 12:18 (CSH)

Therma-Ray Mfg., Inc.:
address for, 53:76
electric heating panels, in ceilings, 10:52 (SH)

ThermaSol, Ltd.: address for, 52:112

Therma-Stor Products Group: address for, 78:70

Therma-Tru Entry System: source for, 6:60

Thermax: *See* Insulation: isocyanurate.

Thermo Dynamics, Ltd.: address for, 68:54

Thermography: advantages of, 58:4

Thermo-ply radiant barrier:
in shutters, 13:48, 49 (DWS)
source for, 40:74 (EEH)

Thermosiphon systems: *See* Hot-water heaters.

Thermostats:
about, 46:47, 48
easy-reading, 44:89
functioning of, 33:56
light-sensitive, reviewed, 83:92
for radiant-floor systems, 27:70 (CBS)

Therrien, Gary: mentioned, 18:50 (FWS)

Theuer, Robert: bathroom by, 80:88

Thiede, Arthur: on log palace, 41:108

Thincoat: *See* Plaster: veneer.

Thin-mass houses:
construction of, 11:46-50 (CBS)
floors of, 41:47, 48
performance of, 11:49-50 (CBS)
retrofitting as, 11:50 (CBS)

Thinners:
kerosene as, 15:18
nontoxic, sources for, 67:90-92

Thinset:
explained, 65:45
exterior, heat-resistant, 50:77
latex additive for, for heat resistance, 71:54

for tile, 22:67, 25:35, 36, 37:8 (BK)
epoxy, 17:70, 72 (BK)
heat-resistant, 71:54

30 Energy Efficient Houses (Wade): cited, 46:80 (TFH)

32mm cabinetry: *See* Cabinets.

This Old House (Vila and Davidson): discussed, 5:60

This Old House Kitchens (Thomas and Langdon): cited, 77:45

Thomas, G., and C. Doebley: *Cape May,* 14:61

Thomas, Michael R.: on barrier-island building, 54:58-62

Thomas, Peter Adrian: on waterfront house, 59:62-67 (EEH)

Thomas, Steve, and Philip Langdon: *This Old House Kitchens,* cited, 77:45

Thomas Catalog File: described, 23:51

Thomas Industries Inc.: address for, 49:87, 61:78 (EF)

Thomas Register of American Manufacturers:
on computer, 46:59
uses of, 23:48, 51

Thomas Ruggles house: pictured, 49:90-91

Thompson, Baggie: doghouse by, 67:87

Thompson, Benjamin, Count Rumford:
career of, 3:40 (CBS)
fireplaces of, 3:40-43 (CBS)

Thompson, Jon H.: on new roof, 57:43-47 (REM)

Thompson, L. Dennis: bathroom remodeling by, 22:65-67 (BK)

Thompson, Ned: reviews sander, 83:96-98

Thompson (E. A.) Co. Inc.: address for, 46:71

Thompson Wood Heaters: outdoor-air provision in, 23:4

Thompson's Water Seal: mentioned, 17:64 (DWS)

Thomsen, H. Skip:
More Power to You!, reviewed, 68:106-108
Relay Primer, A, cited, 68:108

Thomsen, Jay: coffered ceiling by, 75:40-42 (MFC)

Thomsett, Michael C.: *Computers,* reviewed, 36:94

Thoracic outlet syndrome: preventing, 64:69

Thorite: source for, 40:12

Thorn water heaters: mentioned, 12:18 (CSH)

Thorndike, John: octagon house, 34:56-61 (FRC)

Thornton, Judith: on house drama, 49:126

Thoro Systems Products:
address for, 48:12, 54:86, 63:82, 66:55, 70:54, 75:45, 81:71, 85:82 (EEH, TFH)
for dry-stack block, 16:57 (CBS)
stucco materials, 40:12, 32
Thorobond, 28:10, 43:10

Thoroseal Plaster Mix, source for, 40:12
Thoroseal waterproofing, 6:55, 25:72, 30:69, 40:12 (CBS)
Thorpe, John:
mentioned, 32:61
Threaded rod:
coil, nuts for, 14:6
continuous coil, 14:6
strength of, calculating, 9:6
3-C Co.: lamination glue, 44:75
3-M Corp.:
address for, 48:74, 70:49, 74:81 (FC), 81:76
coated glass, 26:74 (SH)
dust masks #8710, 42:55 (DWS)
800-number for, 42:55 (DWS)
mastic adhesive 4289, 24:59
Nextel solar coating, 1:30
panel adhesive, 40:12
sewage aggregate process of, 22:18 (CSH)
sponsors conference, 19:22
SunGain film of, 20:22
3-M Industrial Abrasives: address for, 64:96
Threshold Technical Products, Inc.:
address for, 67:51
Thuja spp.: *See* Cedar.
Thumbs: arthritis of, preventing, 64:67-68
Thunander Corp.: screw-gun supplies, 34:45 (TB)
Thunderware, Inc.: address for, 49:50
Thurston, Kendall: treehouse by, 37:100, 40:4
Tibbets, Joe: *Earthbuilders' Encyclopedia,* cited, 67:96
Ticksticking: procedure for, 20:49 (FWS)
TIES: *See* Initiative for Environmental Sensitivity in Construction, The.
Tigelaar, Leffert: on Lundie's cabins, 80:59-61
Tile:
absorption of, 17:74 (BK)
adhesives for, 58:75
plastic, 62:76
angles in, cutting, 17:73 (BK)
Arts-and-Crafts style, 26:81 (BK)
source for, 54:100
associations for, 59:89, 65:45, 85:16
from auto windshields, 81:104
backer board for, 37:8, 85:16
cement-bonded particleboard, 70:63 (EEH)
backer rod for, 85:16
for backsplashes, kitchen, 68:67-69
base for, 24:12, 36:65 (BK)
bathroom, with seconds, 76:68-69 (REM)
biters for, 17:70, 73 (BK)
in board form, 39:90

books on, 13:10, 17:74, 18:4, 23:49, 50 (BK), 56:47, 62:112-14
Ceramicboard laminated, 39:90
Chinese, 3:67
for roofs, 55:88-89
on circular shower, 36:68-69 (BK)
cleaning, 22:12, 79:20-22
composition, removing, 84:28
over concrete,
cracked, repairing, 68:14-16
underlayment for, 68:14
corner, 25:36 (BK)
for countertops, 77:42-43
making, 47:82-83 (SH)
V-cap installation for, 44:12-14
coverage of, calculating, 36:64 (BK)
cracks in, causes of, 24:10-12
curb with, 32:52 (BK)
curves in, 17:73, 22:67 (BK)
custom, 41:70-75, 76, 77 (FWS)
source for, 71:54
cutters for,
pneumatic, 43:92
snap, 17:70, 71-72 (BK), 70:57-58
cutting, 4:39-40, 25:36, 36:64-65 (BK, CBS), 68:69
decorative modules of, reviewed, 59:106-10
decorative use of, 34:76
Delft, source for, 54:54
design for, 69:56-57
books on, 69:57
edge trim for, wood, 19:14
encaustic, book mentioning, 11:70
exterior, 16:8
Japanese, 2:59
setting, 50:77
waterproofing membrane under, 20:12
fiber/cement, 81:106
on fireplace, 37:8
first course of, leveling, 32:52 (BK)
fitting of, to baseboard, 14:14
flatness of, ensuring, 22:67 (BK)
floor,
mortar for, 85:16
thinset for, 85:16
gallery of, 59:88-91
glazed, 17:74 (BK)
perm rating for, 19:67
granite, 75:83, 84
grid-sheet planning for, 72:26
grounds for, 13:61 (BK)
grout for, 17:75, 25:37, 32:52, 36:66 (BK)
epoxy impervious, 77:42, 43
heat-resistant, 71:54
placing, 68:69
redoing, 22:12
siliconing, 78:28
soil-matched, 61:60 (SH)
using, faxed advice on, 70:112
waterproof, 22:12

grout gun for, 5:6
handmade,
Dutch, source for, 68:67
process of, 56:43-47
high-relief, 6:34
holes in, drilling, 63:28
for hot tub, 69:66
house of, 6:30-35
information on, 65:54
inlaid, in countertop, 69:51, 54
installing, 56:47
faxed advice for, 70:112
jigsaw blades for, 33:60 (TB)
latex admix for, 17:75, 25:33-35 (BK)
lath for, 22:67 (BK)
layout for, wall, 68:68-69
making, supply sources for, 56:44
marble, 69:55-57
with matched tiles, 80:76-77
marker for, aluminum, 76:30
masking-tape aid for, 85:30
mastic for,
all-purpose, 68:68
avoiding, 73:67
heat-resistant, 13:10
type-A, 17:31 (CSH)
membranes for, isolation, 61:12
Mexican, 63:38, 41
floor, 59:60, 61
paver, 17:74 (BK), 61:54 (SH)
source for, 60:92
modular, source for, 52:108-10
molded, for masonry stoves, 71:54
mortar for, 70:14, 71:54
heat-resistant, 71:54
vertical, 37:8
mosaic, 17:74 (BK)
for curves, 49:59 (SH)
decorative, 36:67 (BK)
floor, 26:38, 39 (BK)
method for, 36:64-67 (BK)
organic, 66:53, 54
nippers for, 70:57
on non-combustible surround, 13:10
paper for, water-resistant, 22:67 (BK)
patterns for, offset, 43:79
pavers, 1:55, 17:74, 23:30 (BK)
pencil for, 72:26
planning for, 22:67 (BK)
quarry, 17:74 (BK)
over radiant-floor heating system, 77:54
roller for, 56:44
roof, adhesive for, source for, 65:58 (EF)
round,
cutting, 4:39-40 (CBS)
tiny, 62:76
rubber, 46:52, 53 (EEH)
saws for, 69:56, 70:58-60
screen-printing, 78:72-73
sealing, 79:20-22, 84:16
for service areas, 66:80-81 (SH)

setting, 13:52, 17:72-73, 32:50-52, 41:75 (BK, CBS, FWS)
over slabs, 85:16
slip-resistant, 1:62
source for, 76:68 (REM)
spacing, fudge factors for, 25:36 (BK)
subfloors for, 17:70, 18:4 (BK), 61:12, 85:16
substrate for,
    plywood, 70:14
    uniform, 85:16
terra-cotta oil-sealed, for floors, 67:76 (REM)
tests for, by mail, 69:102
thinset for, 22:67, 25:35, 36, 37:8 (BK)
    explained, 65:45
    exterior, temperature-resistant, 50:77
    heat-resistant, 37:8, 71:54
tinting, cautions for, 63:56 (REM)
tools for, 17:70 (BK)
trim, 17:73-75 (BK)
under trim, cutouts for, 65:30
types of, 17:74 (BK)
V-cap, 25:36-37 (BK)
    installing, 44:12-14
vinyl sheet for, 40-mil, 36:69 (BK)
on walls, kitchen, 26:38, 39 (BK)
walls of, on plywood, 17:31 (CSH)
wax for, turpentine-based, 67:76 (REM)
Wonderboard with, 24:10-12
around woodstove, 66:66, 67 (EEH)
See also Backer board. Membranes. Soil cement.

Tile Council of America:
address for, 65:45, 54, 85:16
Handbook for Ceramic Tile Installation, 23:50
on membranes, 61:12
services of, 23:50
tile tests of, 69:102

Tile Creations: address for, 67:76 (REM)

Tile Heritage Foundation: address for, 59:89

Tile Indoors and Out (Burch): cited, 69:57

Tile saws:
antifreeze with, cautions for, 70:60
portable vs. standard, 70:58-59
using, 36:64-65 (BK), 70:59-60
water heater for, 70:60

Tile-Redi: address for, 80:98

Tiles for a Beautiful Home (Paul): reviewed, 62:112

Tiller, Alvin R.: as joint author. *See* Diffrient, Niels.

Tillotson, Steve: house by, 38:66-71

Tilly, Stephen:
designs Victorian modern, 31:66-71
house by, 28:31-37 (FRC)

Tilting board: defined, 22:73, 75-76

Timber Building in Britain (Brunskill): source for, 42:44 (TFH), 44:4

Timber Construction Manual:
cited, 71:59 (MFC)
mentioned, 6:6, 7:28 (TFH)
source for, 55:58

Timber Frame Construction (Sobon):
mentioned, 42:44 (TFH)
reviewed, 27:84

Timber Frame Homes (Kupferer, ed.):
reviewed, 68:108

Timber Framers Guild of North America:
address for, 49:100, 65:53
conference of, 49:98-100
environmental concerns of, 56:104
1985 meeting of, 29:86
1993 project, 82:106

Timber framing:
for additions, 5:12
    log-cabin, 34:50
advantages of, 11:16
association for, 77:104
beams for,
    moving, 8:31-33, 34:14 (TFH)
    summer, 6:42-44 (TFH)
bents of,
    close-spaced, 38:74-75 (TFH)
    raising, 11:18
on block walls, prescriptions for, 83:18
bolts in, problems of, 19:8
books on, 15:4, 27:84, 47:45 (TFH), 68:108
boring machine for, 55:58
braces for, 40:43, 45 (TFH)
    exterior, 52:50 (TFH)
    gunstock, designing, 54:16
brackets with, for heavy loads, 33:10
and brick infill, 64:24
of bridges, Canadian, 77:104
for cabin, 52:37, 39-40 (TFH)
CADD program for, reviewed, 60:92-94
of ceilings, system for, 65:48-51 (TFH)
chain mortiser for, reviewed, 63:90-92
chainsaw/bandsaw blade for, 39:90
chisels for, 4:22, 12:23 (CSH, TFH)
of clerestories, 25:10
conference on, 49:98-100
crane for, shop-built, 55:59, 60
cruck, 42:40-44 (TFH)
dating of, 27:82
dismantling of, 11:51-52
dovetails in, 7:6
dragon and cross in, 47:45-46 (TFH)
drilling for, 4:23 (TFH)
drywall with,
    finish aid for, 50:95
    installing, 63:53
for earthquake country, 40:43-45 (TFH)
European, 35:54-59 (TB)

finish for, interior, 45:47 (TFH)
floors for, plank-and-beam, 33:41-43 (FWS)
formulae for,
    bending, 7:27-28 (TFH)
    deflection for, 7:24-27 (TFH)
    shear, 7:27, 28 (TFH)
frame/foundation attachment in, 7:6
framing square with, 15:4
framing, and upstairs platform, 28:58, 61-62 (TFH)
girts in, trussed, 6:36, 37 (FRC)
glue in, disadvised, 55:16
guild for, 49:98-100
for Habitat for Humanity, 56:104
history of, 13:23-25, 19:22-23, 24:54-55 (TFH)
hung wall, insulating, 8:28-30, 28:62 (TFH)
information on, 65:53
insulating, 4:8, 11:18, 64:24
    for sound control, 62:18 (CSH)
Japanese-style, 4:55, 43:29, 31-32, 33 (CSH, TFH)
joinery in, 11:17-18, 15:4, 36:46-48 (TFH)
    four-way, 20:4
kits for, custom, 79:52
layout for, 16:40-41 (TFH)
machinery for, 36:48-50 (TFH)
mallets for, 4:23-24 (TFH)
marking, 4:22, 16:39-40 (TFH)
measuring, 4:21-22 (TFH)
mechanicals in, 79:52
metal connectors for, 55:58-59, 61
    machines for, 35:56-57 (TB)
modified, for small house, 67:35
mortise and tenon in, 4:21, 7:6, 10:38-39, 11:17, 12:24-25, 39:59 (CBS, CSH, TFH)
Norwegian-style, 72:84-85, 80:60-61
ornamental, 28:58-62 (TFH)
plans for, 47:44 (TFH)
posts in,
    girt number for, 18:7-8
    queen, considerations for, 47:16
    shouldered, 6:42 (TFH)
radio-transceiver aid for, 34:50
reassembly of, 11:52-53
remodel of, enclosure-style, 79:85-89
restoration of, 49:38-43 (REM)
roofs for, 54:84, 85, 86, 87 (TFH)
    hip, 20:30, 32, 33, 38:77 (TFH)
    ventilating, 61:78 (EF)
saws for, 4:23 (TFH)
seminars in, 70:112
sequence for, 36:50 (TFH)
17th-century, 13:25 (TFH)
for shingle-style house, 79:50-55
shrinkage in, 7:6

simulated, 69:62 (REM)

slick for, straightening, 62:22 (CSH)

squaring up, 4:21, 22, 12:22-24, 24, 57:69-70 (CSH, TFH)

with steel column, central, 55:58-59, 61

stone-faced, 39:56-60 (CBS)

stress-skin panels for, 24:54-58, 25:42, 27:4, 36:46, 47, 50 (TFH)

structural engineering with, 7:24, 28 (TFH)

studs with, 2x4, 47:47 (TFH)

templates for, 4:21, 10:38-39 (TFH)

tenons in, 12:25, 14:6, 8 (CSH, TFH)

Tidewater-style, 34:100, 36:46-50 (TFH)

timbers for,
    care of, 47:16
    curved, 48:44-47 (TFH)
    handling, 55:58-59
    staining, 29:10-12
    steambent, 45:44-48 (TFH)
    tropical hardwood, 57:68-70 (TFH)

tools for, 11:17, 15:4
    power, 35:54-59 (TB)

Tudor,
    problems with, 64:24
    tithe-barn style, 52:46-51 (TFH)

utilities strategy for, 52:39 (TFH)

wood for, 5:10, 7:6, 13:6, 16:6, 26:10, 29:4, 30:6
    drying, 28:10-12, 30:6
    rough, allowances for, 11:17

workshops in, 55:100, 82:106

See also Beams. Bents. Corbels. Insulation: foam-core panels for. Metal connectors. Mortisers. Post-and-beam. Raising. Stress-skin panels.

Timber Products Inspection: address for, 81:16

Timber scribes: in timber framing, 4:22 (TFH)

Timberframe Housewrights: seminars of, 70:112

Timbering: western, 47:38-40

Timberline shingles: source for, 29:76, 38:38 (CSH)

Timberpeg: address for, 54:100, 79:52

Timbers: *See* Beams.

Time capsules: leaving, 77:10

Timeless Way of Building, The (Alexander *et al.*):
    discussed, 36:51-55
    cited, 37:71

Tin: nobility of, 21:4

Tin houses: building, 59:20-24

Tinner's hammers: for standing-seam roofing, sources for, 39:63

Tinsnips:
    aviation, for standing-seam roofing, 39:63
    for renovation, 12:51 (TB)
    sharpening, 79:30

Tiny Houses (Walker): reviewed, 44:94

Tiquktak, Tookillkee: igloo by, 1:68

Tischler und Sohn: window production of, 60:48, 51 (FC)

Tjernlund Products Inc.: address for, 49:18

TNT Workwear: address for, 70:100

Tobin, Stephen R.: bathroom by, 80:90, 91

Todaro, John: casting, 1:36-39 (FWS)

Todol Products, Inc.: address for, 77:67

Toenailing: *See* Nailing: toe.

Toilets:
    alcove for, 76:66, 67, 68 (REM)
    back-flush, 7:23 (BK)
    compost, 61:64-65
    dual-flush, 63:94
        performance of, 63:8
        reviewed, 82:94-96
    for handicapped, 69:63 (REM)
    incinerator, 61:64, 65, 66
    installing, 46:54-57 (BK)
    with in-wall tanks, reviewed, 78:94
    layout for, 29:53-54 (BK)
    leaky, repairing, 40:16
    lid sink for, 80:102-104
    low-flow, 67:63
        information on, 64:102
        performance of, 61:65-66, 63:6-8
        regulations on, 48:102
        reviewed, 61:62-66
        tests of, 76:106
    low-flush, Swedish, 80:70
    outdoor, Arts-and-Crafts style, 67:87
    placement of,
        corner, 23:16
        and framing, 49:51-52 (MFC)
    quality of, assessing, 50:20
    rear-discharge, 60:44 (SH), 63:94
    removing, for floor work, 84:30
    space requirements of, 29:52 (BK)
    stabilizers for, 46:55 (BK)
    up-flush, choosing, 78:16
    water use of, 65:102
    waterless, 5:12
    water-saving, 70:56 (EEH), 85:4-6
    See also Plumbing. Septic-tank systems.

Tokonohmah: example of, 4:57 (TFH)

Toller, Brian: superinsulated house, 15:58-62

Toll-Free Digest: using, 23:48

Tolpin, Jim:
    on closet wardrobe, 78:44-47
    on kitchen cabinets, 74:74-78
    reviews cabinet lift, 78:92
    on scribing, 77:58-63

Tols, Inc.: address for, 64:94

Tom Joyce Architectural Blacksmithing: address for, 67:58

Tome, April: on ranch-house buildup, 55:69 (REM)

Tongs: roofing, using, 39:63

Tongue and groove: *See* Joinery.

Tool bags: leather, alcohol-forming, 46:26

Tool belts:
    adjustments for, 42:22 (CSH)
    ear-protector hook for, 77:32
    kinds of, 42:64-65 (TB)
    for ladder, 42:22 (CSH)
    materials for, 42:67 (TB)
    nail liners for, 29:16
    nylon, 36:89
    power-tool clips for, 75:28
    skindiver's,
        quick release, 44:6
        weight belt for, 22:14
    sources for, 42:65 (TB)
    suspenders for, 42:64, 65 (TB)
        Army pack, 42:22 (CSH)
    3x5 cards in, 42:22 (CSH)

Toolboxes:
    American Plywood Association, 29:40 (TB)
    bucket, pipe dividers for, 82:26
    compartments for, fitted, making, 76:28
    construction of, 31:4
    contest for, winners of, 74:86-87
    dental chest for, 54:24-26
    display case, 29:40-41 (TB)
    handles for, 54:28
        offset, 26:16
    handsaw bracket for, 58:26
    job-site wheeled, making, 69:75
    materials for, 29:41 (TB)
    multi-purpose, 39:14
    need for, 29:39 (TB)
    open shoulder, 29:39-40 (TB)
    portable, making, 69:4
    runners for, 54:28, 58:24
    shoulder strap for, 54:28
    stool as, 30:55 (DWS)
    for vehicles, 8:10, 41:58-59 (TB), 44:4, 49:95, 57:71
    wheeled, reviewed, 50:94-95

Tool Crib of the North: address for, 65:8

Tool Kaddie: reviewed, 50:94-95

Tool Works: chisels of, 12:23 (CSH, TFH)

Tools:
    appropriate-technology, books on, 64:110-12
    battery-powered,
        cold-weather precautions for, 50:60
        essential, 67:62
    book on, reviewed, 51:104
    brake for, reviewed, 58:91
    buying, tips for, 83:69
    catalogs of, 12:51 (TB)
    cords for,
        cold-resistant, 50:60
        color-coded, 36:16
        extension heavy-duty, making, 76:30
        extension, storing, 76:92-94
        locks for, 42:88

proper length of, 85:120
recall of, 71:106
winding, 57:14
dropped, retriever for, 67:28
evaluating, book on, 7:60
feed tables for, 34:55 (TB)
hand,
older English, source for, 65:8
safety manual for, 84:6
heavy, sling system for, 19:14
Japanese,
dumping charge of, 82:104
museum of, 65:6
lube for, low-viscosity gear, 50:60
mail-order, 65:8
companies for, reviewed, 62:50-51
numberless measuring, discussed, 57:94-96
outlets for,
overhead-weighted, 25:16
right-angle, 83:30
powder-actuated,
publication on, 21:34 (TB)
sources for, 21:34 (TB)
types of, 21:30-32 (TB)
using, 21:33-34 (TB)
for renovation, 12:50-51 (TB)
shopping for, 12:51 (TB)
silicone spray for, 67:28
solar power for, 51:92
speed control for, source for, 77:70
stands for, from steel desks, 58:24
storage for, behind-seat, 58:26
wiring for, safety-insulated, color-coded, 84:98
work supports for, 34:55 (TB)
See also Air compressors. Extension cords. Machinery. *specific tool or machine.*
Tools on Sale: reviewed, 62:51
Top Cat: address for, 61:80 (EF)
Torches:
for brazing, 63:66-67
using, 10:41 (BK)
Torchio, Greg: pictured, 38:8
Torp, Bill R.: on learning work, 64:130
Torque:
defined, 24:41 (TB)
measurements of, variation in, 24:41 (TB)
Torrence Window Co.: address for, 52:51 (TFH)
Torsion boxes: construction of, 13:40, 41
Totten, Charles: ceramics by, 59:90
Tousain, David: on stone masonry, 58:46-48
Towards a Symbolic Architecture (Jencks): reviewed, 35:94
Towel racks:
on bent rod, 30:22
sculpted, 38:45
strengthening, 37:14

Key to books:

(BK) Building Baths and Kitchens
(CBS) Building with Concrete, Brick and Stone
(CSH) Craftsman-Style Houses
(DWS) Building Doors, Windows and Skylights
(EEH) Energy-Efficient Houses
(EF) Exterior Finishing
(FC) Finish Carpentry
(FRC) Frame Carpentry
(FWS) Building Floors, Walls and Stairs
(MFC) More Frame Carpentry
(REM) Remodeling
(SH) Small Houses
(TB) Tools for Building
(TFH) Timber-Frame Houses

Towers:
bell, restoring, 30:42-45, 33:4-6
concrete-block, 21:37, 41, 43
contemporary, 41:66, 67 (CSH)
glass-block, 37:50-51 (DWS)
ladders for, 45:87
shingled, 45:82-85
shingle-style, 46:80-83 (TFH)
Victorian, 52:77 (SH)
wood-frame, 35:76, 77
Townhouses: *See* Row houses.
Townsend, Gilbert: *Stairbuilding,* 43:37 (FWS)
Toy boxes: roll-out under-stair, 15:70, 71 (FWS)
Trace Engineering: address for, 51:92
Traco: address for, 55:79
Tract housing: *See* Housing developments.
Tradition 3 Thousand: address for, 53:57
Trailers: model of, Smithsonian-quality, 83:130, 132
Traister, John E.: *Vest Pocket Guide for Builders and Contractors,* reviewed, 43:102
Trammels: shop-built, 61:68
Trane Co.: heat pumps, 26:68
Transite insulation board: cautions with, 2:54 (BK)
Transits:
bearing for, ensuring, 58:77 (MFC)
brands of, discussed, 37:45 (TB)
for decks, 29:43 (FRC)
described, 37:39-40 (TB)
one-person shots with, 83:30
using, 37:40-44 (TB)
Transoms:
diagram of, 3:14, 16 (DWS)
Greek Revival, 1:49
Trapnell, Baylor H.: small house, 42:50-53 (SH)

Trash: truck liner for, 68:30
Travaco Laboratories: epoxy, 16:21 (CSH)
Travers, Richard: mentioned, 25:38 (EEH)
Traylor, Nancy: reviews Moyer, 85:132-34
Treadwell, Albert: toenailing, 9:51 (FRC)
Treasures of Taliesin (Pfeiffer):
cited, 41:31
reviewed, 34:92
Treatise on Stairbuilding and Handrailing, A (Mowat):
reviewed, 41:94
source for, 43:35 (FWS)
Treehouses:
building, 14:41 (SH)
moving, 40:4
plans for, 5:14-15, 14:41 (SH)
retreat in, 37:100
Trees: *See* Forests.
Trelleborg House: address for, 23:84
Trellises:
Arts-and-Crafts style, 82:83
with awnings, 34:10
cantilevered, 1:59, 57:54
for cooling, latticed, 60:56, 58 (EEH)
entryway, 45:40, 41
examples of, 75:86
flashing, 61:24-26
hinged, 31:14
integral exterior/interior, 18:27, 29-32
integral-to-building, 20:75, 76, 51:50-53
for shade, 80:62
suspended redwood, 39:55 (CSH)
Tremco Manufacturing Co.:
Acoustical Sealant, 42:61
address for, 58:14, 57
butyl tape,
Exolite compatibility of, 17:65 (DWS)
qualities of, 3:48-49, 4:7, 10:32, 25:12 (DWS)
mentioned, 14:12
Mono-sealant, 3:48, 4:7, 9:56, 32:37
Polyshim tape, 3:49, 11:63 (DWS)
polysulfide JS709 sealant, 8:16
Preshim spacer-rod tape, 11:62 (DWS)
Tremont Nail Co.:
address for, 49:64, 63:48, 77:88, 78:58
nails from, 11:53
rose-head, 43:73 (SH)
spiral, 20:67
Trenches: roots in, Sawzall for, 15:16
Trend-Lines:
address for, 55:94, 74:90
reviewed, 62:51
Trestles:
pipe, 36:35-36 (TB)
for scaffolding, 36:35 (TB)
Trichloroethylene: plants removing, 69:102
Trigger finger: preventing, 64:67
Tri-Guards Inc.: address for, 53:68

Trim:
adding, 6:8
Arts-and-Crafts style, 29:56-57, 36:26-27, 42:30 (CSH)
back-priming of, 21:58 (EEH)
battens as, 68:87
butt-jointed, 49:41, 43 (REM)
  filling, 49:28
  rabbeted, 31:27 (CSH)
caps for,
  gap-hiding, 28:49, 53 (FWS)
  horizontal, 45:53 (CSH)
carved, source for, 66:104-106
casing,
  arched, 69:82-84
  bullnose, 74:63, 64 (FC)
  making, 72:50, 52-53 (FC)
cedar, horizontal, 32:26-28 (CSH)
chalk-rail, 64:87 (REM)
cherry, 15:76, 77, 78 (CSH)
cherry and walnut, 68:87
closet resource for, 53:26
Colonial, 63:48-49
color for, 74:42 (EF)
conference on, 1982 , 13:14
corner blocks, rosette, cutter for, 48:90-91
corner-block, mitered, 79:48 (EF)
curved, laminating, 6:10
custom,
  builder of, 45:48 (TFH)
  from stock components, 79:46-49 (EF)
for doors,
  custom, 79:46-49 (EF)
  heavier, 70:32
Douglas fir, 49:91
drip edges for, router-made, 39:14
in drywall, 63:50-53
for Edwardian addition, 59:50 (SH)
exterior,
  curved-in-place, 68:58-59
  designing for weather, 36:12-14
  glue for, 36:14
  metal for, 43:80-81
  Port Orford cedar, 45:73, 74 (CSH)
  restoring, 82:14
  source for, 59:40 (SH)
  wood for, 36:14, 82:4-6
Federal, 31:46, 47 (FWS)
fiberboard, 71:72
finish for, 45:48, 53, 48:75-78, 49:91 (CSH, TFH)
  lacquer, 77:79 (REM)
  natural, 75:84
  nautical, 38:45
  oil/varnish, 68:39
  varnish, 22:58 (CSH)
  wax, 66:45
fire codes on, 69:78
fitting, 21:16-18
flashing for, in shingling, 28:64
glossed, painting, 67:70

for Gothic Revival house, 59:38, 40 (SH)
granite, 49:91
grooved, 29:61 (CSH)
half-lap scarf joint on, 38:82 (CSH)
in hardwoods, contrasting, 38:88-89
integral, 5:33-34
jatoba, 49:91
leveling, 58:43
  with transit, 83:30
with metal framing, 32:71 (FRC)
Mission, 31:46, 47 (FWS)
nails for, splitless, 77:49 (EF)
old,
  repairing, 62:40-41 (EF)
  stripping, 16:66-69, 19:4 (DWS)
ornate, 49:90
painting, 67:67
  spray, 42:54-59 (DWS)
  wet-sanding prep of, 44:24-26
  woods for, 42:55 (DWS)
peg-rail, 73:84
picture-rail, as room unifier, 83:56
plate-rail, Craftsman, 52:78-79, 80
racks for,
  drying, making, 79:32
  on-site, 67:26
radiused, 6:10, 41:68-69 (CSH)
removing, tools for, 19:34, 32:55 (DWS, TB)
rounded, coping jig for, 62:30
screws for, 66:49
simple, 26:77 (SH), 61:53, 54 (SH)
site-made, 49:41, 43 (REM)
sugar pine for, 49:40 (REM)
tapering, 13:12
taping off, 67:68
train, 49:91
Victorian, 42:120
  book on, 31:82
  neo-, 31:44-47 (FWS)
  new, 66:50, 71:72-73
as visual connector, 66:72-73
wood,
  plain, 52:66
  shrinkage of, 81:56-57, 58-59
  of three kinds, 64:39-40, 41, 42 (CSH)
See also Cornices. Wainscot.
Trim Carpentry Techniques (Savage): cited, 57:51
Trinkaus, Ted: on small house, 65:36-39
Trisodium phosphate (TSP): plaster cleaning with, 4:18
Troeil, A. E.: concrete forms of, 2:22, 23-25 (CSH)
Trojan Manufacturing:
  address for, 65:47 (FC)
  miter-saw stand of, reviewed, 49:94
Trombe walls:
  adobe, 5:51
  air leaks around, 12:67 (EEH)

block,
  glass, 10:48, 49 (SH)
  surface-bonded, 46:62 (TFH)
collectors for, sheet-metal plate, 5:4
convection loop in, 3:46
described, 6:12
below floor level, 29:28-30
foil for, selective-surface, 12:67 (EEH)
foundations for, 3:47
frame, 3:46-47
heating perimeters of, 10:50 (SH)
insulating for, 3:46-47
with Kalwall, 58:82-83 (EEH)
modification of, 26:34-36
performance of, 10:50 (SH)
in shingle style, 12:65 (EEH)
sizing, 3:46, 10:50 (SH)
venting, 3:47, 6:12
  through window-seat, 29:28, 30
See also Greenhouses: heat storage for.
Tropical Timbers of the World: source for, 37:84
Trow and Holden Co. Inc.:
  address for, 54:75, 55:8
  stone masonry tools, 35:36 (CBS)
Trowels:
  bricklaying, 43:52 (CBS)
  power, operating, 83:52-53
  for stucco, rubber, 31:4
Trucks: See Pickups.
True Sod (Oringderff): source for, 31:54
True Temper: Rocket framing hammer, 23:32 (TB)
Truitt and White Lumber Co.: computer-ordering system of, 69:102
Trumbull, William: porches by, 29:50
Trus Joist Corp.:
  address for, 52:55, 56:58 (EEH), 57:44 (REM), 79:82
  I-beams, 34:68 (SH)
  laminated components, 1:63, 39:92
  lenticular trusses, 29:31-32
  production at, 50:42-43 (MFC)
Truslock: reviewed, 37:80
Truss Plate Institute, Inc.: plans from, 30:26 (FRC)
Trusses:
  Arts-and-Crafts style, 51:36-40 (CSH)
  barrel-vault, 51:79-80 (MFC)
  beams for, wood I-, 56:58, 60 (EEH)
  bearing details of, 30:27 (FRC)
  for belvederes, 43:69-70 (TB)
  bow, inverted, 39:66-69 (TFH)
  bowstring,
    for domed form, 30:67-68 (CBS)
    in double-envelope, 11:68-69
    making, 33:44-47 (TFH)
  box-beam,
    curved, making, 20:8
    making, 71:76-77 (MFC)
  brackets for, 27:28-39
  built-up, exposed, 50:80 (SH)

camber in, 32:4
and chimneys, fire codes on, 69:78
chords of, bottom, removing, 66:45
collar-tie replacement of, 62:46 (SH)
components of, 30:25 (FRC)
composite, with wooden connectors, 35:29, 30-31
concrete anchors for, 39:90
costs of, 30:25 (FRC)
crossed-chord king-post, 6:18, 19 (CSH)
cutting, fiats against, 48:14
defined, 32:32 (FRC)
deflection in, 30:26 (FRC)
designing, 11:8
diamond, 30:20
drawings of, certified, 30:26 (FRC)
as ducts, 30:22
ends of, carved, 59:52, 53, 54, 55 (CSH)
fabricators of, choosing, 30:28 (FRC)
finials for, 62:74-76
Fink, 10:69 (FRC)
    modified, 7:36 (DWS)
firestops for, 32:4
floor, 19:55, 24:67, 68, 69, 25:16 (FRC), 43:75-76
    advantages of, 30:25, 26 (FRC)
    choosing, 30:26-27 (FRC)
    for mechanical chases, 77:51, 52
glue for, 44:75
glulam square, 47:84, 86-87
Gothic-arched, 14:27-29
on hammer posts, 48:44-45 (TFH)
handling, 65:38
hangers for, girder, 39:90
headers with, abutting, 62:85 (MFC)
Howe, site-built, 9:30, 31
hurricane-proofing, 78:85-86
installing, 30:28 (FRC)
instruction sheet on, 29:92
insulating, 20:12
    advantage of, 59:53, 55 (CSH)
king-post, 31:25, 26 (CSH)
    composite, 8:38, 40, 41 (EEH)
    exposed, 11:44-45 (SH), 45:38, 42
    extended, 84:65-67
laminated curved, 27:26-30
laminating, 39:69 (TFH)
Larsen, 20:35-37, 22:6, 23:10
lenticular,
    commercial, 29:31-32, 33
    making, 6:55, 57
    welded, 63:37, 38-40
mentioned, 24:68
metal connectors for, 43:48-49, 69-70 (FRC), 73:72, 73
    plates, 30:26 (FRC)
metal-web, 30:25 (FRC)
nailed, designing, 40:72 (FRC)
nails for, 85:47
for octagon, raised, 24:73, 76

open-web wood, 73:58, 59
parallel-chord, 42:61, 63, 85:73, 75
    site-built, 75:80-81, 83
plates for, 6:18, 19 (CSH)
plywood,
    commercial, 34:68 (SH)
    site-built, 30:38, 39-40, 41
prefabricated, 19:69, 70, 34:68, 37:80 (EEH, SH)
    English, 43:60 (CBS, SH)
principal-rafter, 44:73-75
publications on, 23:50
from rafters, built-up gable-end, 56:65 (FC)
raising, 14:28, 39:69 (TFH)
    by crane, 77:51
retrofitted, to rafters, 55:69 (REM), 77:77-78 (REM)
ridge, built-up, 56:60, 61-62 (EEH)
scissor, 38:80, 81, 82 (CSH)
    for insulated cathedral ceiling, 19:22
    modified, 21:58 (EEH)
    and open ceilings, 13:68, 70-71
    steel, 73:80
setting, quick-release hoist for, 68:28, 72:28
for snow loads, heavy, 37:26 (BK)
spacing tool for, reusable, 37:80
steel-web joist, 82:67
stick-built, 51:72, 73 (EEH)
strengthening, 30:27-28 (FRC)
struts in, shaped, 74:54
stud-and-gusset hybrid, 40:50, 52, 53
tension-ring, 34:59-60 (FRC)
tie-rod, 2:24 (CSH)
    for glazed gables, 61:51, 53 (SH)
    and wood, 71:74-77 (MFC)
timber-framed, carved, 62:74-75
tree-limb, 18:84
from 2x4 stock, 20:46, 47, 48
types of, 30:24, 25, 27 (FRC)
over wall studs, 82:102
and wood shrinkage, masking, 81:56-57, 58
See also Beams. Framing: balloon-truss. Framing: with truss frames. Roofs: beams for, wood I-.
Tschida, Fred: lighting by, 33:75
Tsongas, George: quoted, 46:96
Tsui, Eugene: house by, 85:148
Tubing:
    benders for, 20:53 (FWS), 46:57 (BK)
    copper, cutters for, 10:40 (BK)
    helix jig for, 20:53 (FWS)
Tuck, Seab: house by, 45:32-37, 88
Tuck-A-Way Chalet: plans for, 5:14-15
Tucker, Glenn:
    on greenhouse heat distribution, 4:48-51
    on site-built solar collectors, 1:28-32
    on Trombe walls, 3:46

Tudor style:
    book on, cited, 69:86
    fireplace in, 69:82-87
TuffTop countertops: source for, 35:91
Tullock, John H.: *Reef Tank Owner's Manual, The,* cited, 72:63
Tung oil: *See* Finishes.
Turman, Thomas Lee: house by, 11:42-45 (SH)
Turnbull, William: Los Angeles 1983 talk by, 20:22
Turner & Seymour Manufacturing Co.: address for, 67:73 (REM)
Turning: of urns, architectural, 25:76
Turrets:
    building, 68:56-59
    examples of, 25:54-55 (FRC)
    redwood, 3:68
Tu-Tuf: as air/vapor barrier, 2:32, 19:22, 29:68, 34:68 (EEH, SH)
Tweaker: reviewed, 50:94
Twitchell Lake Inn: building of, 40:38-39
Two Jack Metalworks: work by, 81:89
2000 Series Entrance Door: source for, 6:60
Tyler, Steven: on fixed-glass windows, 51:76-78 (FC)
Typical Construction Details:
    mentioned, 23:49
Tyvek:
    as air/water barrier, 21:59, 25:82 (EEH)
    vs. Barricade, 39:90
    discussed, 19:68, 20:36
    installing, 21:59, 25:82 (EEH), 43:73 (SH)
    mentioned, 31:8
    performance of, 25:82
    sealant for, 61:106
    with stand-off wall system, 15:59

U. C. Coatings Corp.: address for, 72:41
U. S. Anchor: address for, 41:57 (CBS)
U. S. Borax, Inc.: address for, 85:22, 75
U. S. Brass: address for, 54:46
U. S. Department of Agriculture: house plans from, 53:89
U. S. Department of Agriculture Forest Products Laboratory: (USDAFPL)
    address for, 50:20, 65:53, 77:108
    on condensation, 22:4
    construction manual, 1:64-66
    Exterior Finishing, 23:50
    Exterior Wood in the South, cited, 83:45
    exterior sealer of, 10:8
    Finishing Wood Interiors, 37:84
    glue information from, 55:65
    How to Buy Construction Lumber, (Oviatt), 8:14

on let-in bracing, 40:6
linseed-oil-based finish, 34:50
National Design Specifications for Wood Construction, 7:28 (TFH)
paint studies by, 60:100
Selection, Production, Procurement, and Use of Preservative-Treated Wood, 7:8
solar kilns of, 7:41
stain-blocking paint study of, 19:12
truss-frame house of, 5:54, 55 (FRC)
Wood Engineering Handbook, 65:45
Wood as an Engineering Material, cited, 81:59
on wood foundations, 5:40 (FRC)
Wood-Frame House Construction (Anderson), 13:8
Wood Handbook, 43:8
wood identification by, 56:84
See also Farmer's Home Administration.

U. S. Department of Energy:
and ADA design, 37:62
Appropriate Energy Technology Small Grant Program, 15:67
award program of, 71:106
construction information from, 23:49
energy advice from, 56:42
Energy Information Directory, 23:51
Introducing Supplemental Combustion Air, 46:46, 49:18
National Energy Information Center, services of, 23:49, 51
Passive Solar Design Handbooks, 16:10, 14, 16
publications from, 56:36
solar load ratio models of, 21:59 (EEH)
Technical Information Center, services of, 21:60, 23:51

U. S. Department of Housing and Urban Development (HUD):
booklets from, 4:62, 23:48
building-code changes of, 3:10
construction information from, 23:49
Federal Housing Administration of (FHA), 4:14
house plans from, 53:86, 87, 89
HUD User, address for, 65:54
insulating glass tests by, 11:4
National Register of Historic Places, 6:16
publications from, 32:86
reviewed, 55:108
services from, 36:92
See also Federal Housing Administration (FHA).

U. S. Department of the Interior:
mentioned, 16:21 (CSH)
Moving Historic Buildings, 5:19
Standards for Historic Preservation Projects, The, 1:33 (FWS)

Key to books:

(BK)	Building Baths and Kitchens
(CBS)	Building with Concrete, Brick and Stone
(CSH)	Craftsman-Style Houses
(DWS)	Building Doors, Windows and Skylights
(EEH)	Energy-Efficient Houses
(EF)	Exterior Finishing
(FC)	Finish Carpentry
(FRC)	Frame Carpentry
(FWS)	Building Floors, Walls and Stairs
(MFC)	More Frame Carpentry
(REM)	Remodeling
(SH)	Small Houses
(TB)	Tools for Building
(TFH)	Timber-Frame Houses

U. S. Federal Works Progress Administration: historic house plans by, 47:44 (TFH)
U. S. General Hardware: roofing-removal tool, 40:10
U. S. Government Manual: coverage of, 23:49
U. S. Government Printing Office:
bibliographies from, 23:51
Consumer's Resource Handbook, 23:49
exterior finish book from, 50:18
Federal Information Centers of, 23:49
Historic America, 52:10-12
NIOSH Recommended Standards for Occupational Exposure to Methylene Chloride, 1:33 (FWS)
Preservation Briefs No. 1 (Mack), 4:4
Radon Reduction Methods, 51:16
Standards for Rehabilitation, 4:4
U. S. Gypsum Industries, Inc.:
address for, 53:57, 57:40, 58:57, 64:96, 66:38, 73:58, 76:59, 96, 82:68, 85:16 (SH)
Cornerite, 23:12
drywall channel RC-241 of, 18:42
Durock, 37:8
extruded polystyrene, Foamular, 18:33 (CBS)
filler, Durabond 90, 23:61 (FWS)
Gypsolite, 23:61 (erratum, 24:6, FWS)
Gypsum Construction Handbook, 35:4
cited, 51:83 (MFC)
Keene's cement, 34:64 (BK), 45:80 (EEH)
plaster base of, Rocklath, 23:12
plasters,
Dual Purpose Hardwall, 31:58 (FWS)
Structo-Lite, 31:58, 34:64 (BK, FWS)
veneer, 28:10

Steel-Framed Drywall Systems, 30:6
Striplath of, 23:12
Thermafibre, 31:34 (DWS)
USG Steel-Framed Drywall System, 32:69 (FRC)
U. S. Intec, Inc.: address for, 64:45, 53 (EF)
U. S. National Park Service: workshop sourcebook from, 74:106
U. S. Paint: address for, 85:75
U. S. Plastics: Teflon rod, 31:14
U. S. Sky:
address for, 72:78 (FC)
Sure Seal Glazing System, 34:66 (BK)
U. S. Steel: Cor-Ten steel, 24:42, 43, 27:4-6
U. S. Waterproofing, Inc.: Waterproof Cement Membrane System, 11:10
UBIX Information Services: address for, 70:18
UC Industries, Inc.: address for, 76:39
Udall, James R.:
on Earth Press machines, 28:80
on Pueblo masonry, 18:62-65
U-Line Corp.: undercounter freezer, 44:53 (SH)
Ulmer, Al: recounts disaster, 37:98
Ulmia: finger clamps, reviewed, 54:92
Ultra-Fire: consultation services, 42:68 (CBS)
Ultralert detectors: source for, 39:92
Unadilla Silo Co.:
kits from, 7:54
silos of, 44:58-62
wooden containers, 38:56
Undercurrents Environmental Research Station: heat-loss studies of, 2:31-32 (EEH)
Underground Designs (Wells): mentioned, 7:39 (DWS)
Underground houses: *See* Earth construction.
Underground Plans Book I (Wells): mentioned, 7:39 (DWS)
Underground Space Center: address for, 65:55
Underground Waterproofing (Anderson): mentioned, 29:12
Underhill, Roy: *Woodwright's Companion, The,* cited, 56:14
Underlayment:
nails for, 85:47
See also Floors.
Understanding Wood (Hoadley): cited, 81:59
Underwriter's Laboratories: services of, 23:49
Unger, Fred:
on coffered ceiling, 84:69-71
on sloped glazing, 72:76-80 (FC)
Unico, Inc.: address for, 61:12

Uni-Door: source for, 6:60
Unifast Industries: address for, 41:57 (CBS)
Uniform Building Code:
  on chimneys, 21:46-47 (CBS)
  history of, 5:44
  source for, 5:45, 21:46 (CBS)
Uniform Plumbing Code:
  provisions of, 29:51-55 (BK)
  source for, 29:51, 39:37 (BK), 48:12-14
Unihab-Cambridge, Inc.: renovations of, 1:8
Uniset: powder-actuated tools from, 21:34 (TB)
United Brotherhood of Carpenters and Joiners of America: safety information from, 34:55 (TB)
United Coatings: Diathon paint, 19:76
United Gilsonite Laboratories: address for, 70:49
United Paint Manufacturing Co.: address for, 66:55
United Stand: address for, 69:39 (EEH)
United Steel Products Co.: address for, 46:68 (EF), 50:42 (MFC)
Unity Systems, Inc.: address for, 53:72, 73:70
Universal Clamp Corp.: address for, 69:96, 74:73 (FC)
University of California (Berkeley): design resources of, 45:106-10
University of Illinois Small Homes Building Council: Lo-Cal house of, 9:56
Unsettling of America, The (Berry): cited, 45:24
Upat: address for, 41:57 (CBS)
Upco:
  latex additives for, 17:75 (BK)
  mortar-grout admix, 25:34 (BK)
Upjohn Corp. Co.: Poly-C insulation, 31:38 (CBS)
UPP Inc.: Nordic floor finish, 36:42-45 (FWS)
Upton, Dean: mentioned, 20:51, 53 (FWS)
Upton, Dell, ed.: *America's Architectural Roots,* reviewed, 53:108
URBCO Products Inc.: address for, 71:96
Urea-formaldehyde: *See* Glue. Insulation.
Urethane:
  concrete coating, and compatibility, 40:12
  finish, waterborne, 85:61-63
  nonyellowing, 75:49 (REM)
  "plaster" moldings of, 39:92
  See also Insulation: foam-core panels.
Urns: architectural, building, 25:76, 77
Usonian houses: amending, 66:57 (SH)
Utah:
  dry-stack block in, 16:57 (CBS)
  solar tax credits in, 3:12

Utilities:
  core for, 3:25, 26
  in-slab, 55:82-83
  trenches for, 15:16, 17:10
Utility companies:
  aid from, 23:51
  energy-efficiency certification program of, 68:100-102
Utility knives:
  cleaning, 31:14
  sheath for, making, 51:26-28
Utility rooms:
  design for, 30:63
  modular, 52:26-28
U-value: finding, 46:48

Vacation houses: *See* Cabins. Shacks.
Vacuum Pressing Systems, Inc.: address for, 83:73
Vacuums:
  hose keepers for, 62:28-30
  recommended, 73:70
  shop, extensions for, 58:24
  See also Dust-collection systems.
Valances: *See* Lighting.
Valdez, Ray: builds Wright house, 41:28-31
Valley: *See* Rafters.
Valley Builder's Supply: dry-stack blocks of, 16:57 (CBS)
Valleys: *See* Flashing. Roofs.
Valli and Colombo: door handles by, for disabled, 48:65 (FC, MFC)
Valspar Corp.: polyurethane varnish, 14:35 (CBS)
van Altena, William: heliodon of, 13:18
Van Camp, John: limestone carving by, 54:72-75
Van Den Branden, F., and Thomas L. Hartsell: *Plastering Skills,* reviewed, 31:80, 77:120
Van Ness Water Gardens: catalog from, 13:6
Van Pelt, Garrett: turret stairwell by, 17:29 (CSH)
Van Vranken, Robert: on renovation, 82:69-71
Vandal, Norman L.:
  on curvilinear sash, 5:25-27 (DWS)
  on period moldings, 20:59-63 (FWS)
  reviews *Architectural Treasures,* 47:112
Vande Hey Roofing & Tile Co.: address for, 63:84 (EEH)
VanEE Air Exchangers: heat-recovery ventilators, 9:59
Vanex: address for, 75:78
Vanguard Energy Systems: heat pumps, 26:68

Vanply Masonry Wall Insulation: mentioned, 1:62-63
Vapor barriers: *See* Air/vapor barriers. Polyethylene: sheeting, air/vapor barrier.
Vapor pressure: defined, 19:67
Vaporseal:
  roofing membrane, 16:8
  uses of, 20:12, 29:12
Varathane:
  Plastic Oil, 6:20 (CSH)
  varnish for trim, 22:58 (CSH)
Vargas, Robert L.: on French farmhouse, 33:63-67
Vario Spade Bit Set: reviewed, 50:95
Varnish: *See* Finishes.
Vatican Art Casting Stone: for exterior use, 5:10
Vaughan, Robert: on post caps, 56:73
Vaughan: framing hammers, 23:32, 33 (TB)
Vaughan and Bushnell Mfg. Co.: Superbar, 32:55 (TB)
Vaults:
  acrylic, 28:74, 75
  barrel,
    with truss and gusset, 51:79-82 (MFC)
    with wood I-beams, 51:82-85 (MFC)
  brick, 20:8, 10
  concrete, 6:34, 35, 68
  drywall, 11:68-69
  forces in, 32:30 (FRC)
  groined, contemporary, 14:27-29
  mathematical history of, 25:4
  wooden, roof for, 20:8
  See also Boveda house.
Vegetation: solar absorption of, 9:14
Vehicles:
  anti-noise caulking of, 72:28
  tie-downs for, sliding locking-pin system for, 72:90
  See also Pickups. Toolboxes: for vehicles.
Velarde, Carmen: fireplace by, 43:76, 77, 78
Velonis, Elias:
  on house building, 13:14-16
  reviews Hackenberg, 4:58
  on rubble-trench foundations, 18:66-68 (CBS)
  on superinsulation conference, 28:82
Velux America Inc.:
  address for, 51:75, 61:78, 65:60, 62, 70:106, 73:50 (EEH, EF)
  skylights,
    in greenhouses, 4:48, 49, 51
    for retrofit, 28:29, 30
    screens in, 11:59 (DWS)
    with solar collectors, 1:32
Velva-Sheen floor conditioner: recommended, 33:70 (CBS)
Vemco Corp.: drafting machine, 26:62 (TB)

Veneer:
edge trimmer for, 81:74
information on, 23:50
iron-on, for cabinets, 81:72, 74-75
making, 83:73
metal dust, 39:90
pressure-sensitive, for cabinets, 81:74-75
roller for, 81:74, 75
source for, 81:72, 76
vacuum-bag application for, 83:73
wood-fiber, reconstituted, 39:90
wood/melamine, 39:90
Veneer and Plywood: source for, 23:50
Ventilation:
and air quality, 77:65
in attics, 7:52-53 (DWS)
book on, reviewed, 75:110
button, for abutting roofs, 38:24, 28
  (EEH)
Canadian standard for, 55:104
center studying, 30:80
for the chemically sensitive, 46:72-73
conference on, 55:102-104
continuous, system for, 78:68-71
of crawl spaces, 29:69
cross, design for, 33:37 (EEH)
doors for, hinged, 28:70-71
fans for, 2:31, 32, 34:29 (DWS, EEH)
  ceiling, 28:12
  deficiencies in, 55:102-104
  exhaust, #1912J, 67:72, 76 (REM)
heat recovery and, 65:64 (SH)
and indoor pollution, 46:96
information on, 65:52, 54, 55
kitchen, 40:67 (BK)
  cooktop, 7:67 (BK)
  standard for, 55:104
and moisture movement, 50:100
need for, 55:104, 65:65 (SH), 68:8
of roofs,
  flat, 38:34
  standing-seam, 39:62
shutters for, 50:56
  ceiling, 2:31, 32 (EEH)
  sliding, 73:64, 65
through skylight, 50:56
stack effect for, 33:37-40, 34:29 (DWS,
  EEH)
stove, 67:73, 74 (REM)
in superinsulated houses, 28:81-82
system for, 46:72
  integrated, 33:84
in tower construction, 67:60, 61
under-sheathing, commercial, 56:63
  (EEH)
units for, portable, reviewed, 50:94
whole-house, 31:70
windows for, minimum number, 73:55
wingwalls for, 30:30, 80
See also Cupolas. Heat-recovery
  ventilators. Wind turbines. Vents.

Vents:
adjustable, 28:82
area for, computing, 44:6
automatic, 34:4
books on, 56:41, 61:80 (EF)
button, 2:5, 5:7
commercial, 61:78-80 (EF)
cone, source for, 80:70
controlled seasonal, 46:96
for cross-gable roofs, 76:50 (MFC)
cupolas as, 66:61 (REM)
doors for, hopper spring-latched, 11:32
  (EEH)
for dryers, 77:20-22
eave slotted, 52:50 (TFH)
exhaust, directing, 64:20
fascia concealed, 45:85
flashing, 39:65, 65:60-61 (EF)
foam-baffle, 81:53
for fungi protection, 72:66 (REM)
gable, 61:78 (EF)
holes for, locating, 63:20
humidistat-operated, 28:82
in hurricanes, 78:86
against ice dams, 71:14
and insulation, 56:39, 41
mentioned, 5:15
mesh for, 61:80 (EF)
panels for, insulated, operable, 66:39
  (SH)
perimeter floor, 46:65 (TFH)
polyethylene corrugated, 26:82
power, discussed, 61:78 (EF)
ridge, 57:46 (REM)
  Boston framed 63:42-44, 84:68
  bronze sceen for, 52:50 (TFH)
  building, 61:80 (EF)
  caps for, need for, 75:48 (REM)
  commercial, 23:6, 33:12
  continuous, 61:77-78 (EF)
  for cooling, 40:74 (EEH)
  of copper guttering, 52:48, 50, 51
    (TFH)
  and fire blocks, 24:6
  in hurricanes, 78:86
  installing, 7:52, 53 (DWS)
  integral simple, 44:40 (SH)
  jig for, 24:22
  need for, 24:4-6
  nonbaffled, problems with, 23:6
  rainproofing, 42:4
  retrofit of, 24:4-6
  screening, 52:50 (TFH)
  shingle-over, 76:48, 50 (MFC)
  site-built, 21:51-53, 29:61 (CSH, DWS)
roof-mounted, 30:80
  purpose of, 44:4-6
soffit, 56:58 (EEH), 76:48, 50 (MFC), 78:58
  continuous, 61:77-78 (EF)
  protecting flow through, 29:70

soffit/ridge, 70:18
  baffles for, 65:96
for solar collectors, 1:32
source for, 21:52 (DWS)
spaces for, earthquake-proofing, 64:64
  (MFC)
See also Heat-recovery ventilators.
  Ventilation.
Ventuleth, John: restoration stonework
  by, 40:56-57
Venturi, Robert:
*Complexity and Contradiction in
  Architecture,*
  cited, 45:116
  reviewed, 45:120
design after, 45:32-37, 88
Veral copper-clad roofing:
source for, 23:66
Verandahs:
Australian, 53:62-66
defined, 29:48
Vergeboards: *See* Rafters: barge.
Veritas Tools, Inc.:
blind nailer, reviewed, 54:92
Snug-Plug tapered plug cutters,
  reviewed, 85:108
Vermont:
building codes and, 50:65
house appraisals in, 7:43
solar tax credits in, 3:12
Vermont American Tool Co.:
nail spinner from, reviewed, 49:94
rust prevention cube from, reviewed,
  49:94
Vermont Castings, Inc.: address for,
  65:62, 66:81 (SH)
Vermont Structural Slate Co., Inc.:
address for, 47:59
copper nails of, 20:39 (EF)
Slate Roofs, source for, 20:39 (EF)
Versa-Level: reviewed, 42:86-88
Versatile bricks: source for, 38:82 (CSH)
Vertex Insta-Foam Frothpak: source for,
  20:31
Verticel-Chicago, Inc.: Honeycomb
  panels, 36:89
Very Efficient Carpenter, The (Haun):
  cited, 77:85, 79:61, 82:48, 84:16, 85:56
*Vest Pocket Guide for Builders and
  Contractors* (Traister): reviewed,
  43:102
Veteran's Administration:
building for handicapped handbook
  from, 53:67
Minnesota home loans under, 4:14
Vickers, Amy:
on low-flush toilets, 61:62-66
on water-saving devices, 84:82-84
Victims of Fiberglass: address for, 56:42
Victoria Mansion (Maine): etched glass
  of, 24:52-53 (DWS)

Victorian style:
architecture, book on, reviewed, 46:104
books on, 4:58, 11:70, 35:72, 66:47
brackets, 35:72-73
cottage, renovated, 28:49-53 (FWS)
doors, 39:76, 78, 71:72
    screen, 36:39-41 (DWS)
fake facade, 42:120
houses, additions to, 14:22-26
Idaho-style, building, 66:64-68 (EEH)
modern, 31:66-71, 71:70-73
ornaments, cards for, 1:66
paint, book on, 43:102
plans for, 71:71
porches, 39:78-79
shingle, book on, 29:90
solar design in, 33:84
staircases, 39:76
trim,
    book on, 31:82
    copying, 71:63 (REM)
See also Plans. Shingle style.
Victorian Design Book, The: reviewed,
31:82
*Victorian Domestic Architectural Plans
    and Details* (Comstock): reviewed,
44:94
Victorian Exterior Decoration (Moss
    and Winkler):
    cited, 74:45 (EF)
    reviewed, 43:102
Videos: on bracing, 85:56
Vieques, Puerto Rico: work brigades on,
62:106
Viherjuuri, H. J.: *Sauna,* 39:4
Viking Electronics, Inc.: address for,
70:106
Vikingsholm: building of, 77:90
Vila, Bob: *Bob Vila's This Old House,*
reviewed, 5:60
Vila, Bob, and Jane Davidson: *This Old
House,* reviewed, 5:60
Village: miniature, 20:92
Villas: Italianate brownstone, 9:21-24
Vincent Metals: Color Clad roofing, 30:41
Vincent Whitney Co.: address for, 73:104
Vincent, Zu:
on ranch-house style, 25:50-53
on studio, 37:34-38
Vinci, John: mentioned, 32:61
Vinyl:
on floors, removing, 41:8-10, 42:4
40-mil, source for, 36:69 (BK)
Vinyl Siding Institute: address for, 75:100,
83:45
Viracon Inc.: high-performance glass of,
discussed, 41:84-86
Virginia: solar tax credits in, 3:12
Virutex: distributor for, 75:61
Visador-Coffman: staircase production
by, 36:59, 61 (FWS)

Vise grips: for renovation, 12:51 (TB)
Vises:
carpenter's, 35:91
folding, on portable workbench, 69:74
saw, 20:71 (TB)
sawhorse, clamps for, 74:72, 73 (FC)
source for, 69:73
threaded rod for, 14:6
wooden, on-site, 33:16
Visual Dictionary of Buildings
    (Kindersley): reviewed, 85:134
*Visual Handbook of Building and
    Remodeling, The* (Wing): reviewed,
74:98
Vita Climate Control Systems, Inc.:
tankless water heaters, 34:69 (SH)
Vitale, Edmund, Jr.:
on building permits, 7:44-45
Building Regulations, 3:10, 5:43
on building regulations, 5:43-45
Voelker, Paul D.: on custom kitchen
remodel, 58:36-41 (REM)
Vola plumbing components: mentioned,
1:62
**Volatile organic compounds (VOC)
compliance:** and floor finishes, 67:54,
85:62-63
Volclay: panels, using, 2:36, 37, 29:12
Volechenisky, Michael: on wainscot,
19:52-53 (FWS)
Von Fange, Thomas: hammers by,
copper, 40:87
von Ranson, Jonathan:
on cookstove/heater, 21:62-65 (CBS)
on stone cottage, 39:56-60 (CBS)
Vuocolo, Sal: concrete-block fireplace of,
15:20-21

Wachs, Rick: on Lucas house, 31:44-50
(FWS)
Wade, Alex:
*Design and Construction Handbook for
    Energy-Saving Houses, A,* reviewed,
7:60
Guide to Affordable Houses, cited, 25:46
    (TFH), 46:80 (TFH)
on John Winnie house, 40:55-59
reviews *House,* 32:86
reviews pole-building books, 8:70
on stress-skin panels, 25:42-46 (TFH)
30 Energy-Efficient Houses You Can Build,
    cited, 46:80 (TFH)
Wade, Alex, and Neal Ewenstein:
30 Energy-Efficient Houses You Can Build,
reviewed, 7:60

Wade Manufacturing Co.: pipe-clamp jaw
extenders, reviewed, 85:106-108
Waferboard: *See* Oriented strand board.
Waggoner, Nora R.: as joint author. *See*
May, Elizabeth E.
Wagner, E. Logan:
on bovedas, 50:74-77
on mudejar ceiling, 26:43-45
Wagner, Otto: influence of, on Neutra,
19:29
Wagner, William J.: on four-square
houses, 71:63 (REM)
Wagner, Willis H.: *Modern Carpentry,* 3:4,
35:70-71 (TB)
Wagner Spray Tech Corp.:
address for, 48:76
sprayers,
    model 350, 42:56 (DWS)
    Super #1000, 42:57 (DWS)
Wagoner, Walter: on architects, 20:26
Wahlberg, Donald E.: on ornamental
plaster, 43:40-43 (FWS)
Wainscot:
assembly of, 19:52, 53 (FWS)
backing for, 31:48-49 (FWS)
boards for, vertical, with glass inserts,
    54:37, 38-40
built-up, 22:58-59 (CSH)
defined, 20:60 (FWS)
draw-bolt assembly of, 31:49 (FWS)
drywall-resembling, 81:43
elements of, 19:50, 52-53 (FWS)
finish for, 19:53 (FWS)
installing, 19:52, 53 (FWS)
making, 40:35-37 (FWS), 85:66-67
panels for,
    drywall, 26:4
    particleboard, 40:34, 36 (FWS)
    plywood, 19:52 (FWS)
    raising, 19:50-52 (FWS)
with plate rail, 22:59, 63:48, 49 (CSH)
stiles for, 19:52, 53 (FWS)
Walas, Henry: storage unit by, 85:94
Waldrip, Bruce: on vigas, 58:85
Waldstein, Arne:
on concrete, 61:55-57
reviews concrete book, 63:106
Walker House (Wright): gate for, 25:80
Walker, Lester: *Tiny Houses,* reviewed,
44:94
Walker, Lester, and Jeff Milstein:
Designing Houses, reviewed, 18:78
Walks:
brick, mortar problems with, 30:6
concrete for, 40:47-48 (CBS)
concrete pad, cantilevered, 80:40, 45
covered, 80:81
through cut-out wall, 38:25-26, 27, 108
    (EEH)
design of, 40:46, 49 (CBS)

flagstone,
   aluminum foil template for, 33:16
   laying, 40:46-49 (CBS)
for handicapped, 53:67
for hills, steep, 38:60-61 (CSH)
on rock bases, and stone dust, 32:12
stone-in-concrete, 3:27
of wood cut-offs, 42:16
wood rounds in gravel, 5:51
See also Bridges. Patios.
Wall Partition and Layout Tool: source for, 21:20
Wallace, Alasdair G. B.:
   on attic renovation, 28:26-30
   on Cotswold cottage, 60:70-73
   on log building, 2:38-41, 14:52-53
   reviews barn book, 67:104
   reviews log-house books, 8:70, 27:84
   reviews National Trust Book, 32:86
   reviews Scotland book, 54:106
   on slat roofs, 49:68-71
   on thatching, 22:72-77
   on timber-framing workshop, 55:100
   on Victorian screen door, 36:39-41 (DWS)
Wallace, Don: on lumber grades, 56:104-106
Wallace, Kevin: uses computer, 35:66 (TB)
Wallach, Les:
   on desert greenhouse, 41:36-40
   on desert house, 66:82-87
   on design, 45:16-20
Wallen II (Maybeck): discussed, 2:18-25 (CSH)
Wallframe System: house in, 62:72-77
Wallpaper:
   Arts-and-Crafts style, source for, 54:100
   heavy-textured, 48:72 (SH)
   historic, research aid on, 65:55
   lifting of, on plaster, 49:16
   linen for, 46:41 (REM)
   ordinary, perm rating for, 19:67
   paste, removing, 64:30
   removing, 4:18
   Scottish, source for, 54:106
   sealer for, before paint, 39:10
   Swedish fiberglass, 35:34
   vinyl, perm rating for, 19:67
Walls:
   adobe,
      freestanding, 41:28
      repairing, 22:41-43
   air infiltration through, preventing, 77:65-67
   air space in, 54:62
   aluminized kraft-paper foam, 26:53, 54
   Arts-and-Crafts style, sectioned, 52:80
   backlit grill, 46:40 (REM)
   battered, 18:27-28
   bearing, long-span headers for, 55:75-77 (MFC)

block,
   circular, 28:74, 75
   sandblasted, 27:48, 49
   with service chases, 70:110
   split, 66:85
   stone-veneered, 77:74-75
bond beam for, 9:65, 66
book on, reviewed, 83:120
bow in, correcting, 9:6
bracing for, 85:54-57
   line, 23:70-71 (FRC)
   steel, 43:46, 47 (FRC)
brick,
   curved battered, 56:83
   shoring, 69:68-69 (REM)
cable ties for, 25:51, 52
ceramic textured, 59:88
for circular tower, profiled, 56:70 (CSH)
of clay, 4:53, 54, 57 (TFH)
concrete,
   earthquake-resistant, 63:102
   embedded nailers for, 69:30
   integral, 28:82
   with integral insulation, 58:50-51
   interior, 11:48, 50, 37:24-25, 27-28 (BK, CBS)
   lightweight, 31:77, 48:49-53
   rusticated, 12:28, 29, 30-33
   slip-formed, 25:56
   in solar design, 4:48-49, 8:4, 10:49, 51, 11:29-33 (EEH, SH)
   tilt-slab, 4:27-28
   waterproofing, 52:76 (SH)
continuation of, Plexiglas, 29:32, 33
corner, protectors for, 53:68
corner with, California, 29:69
costs of, by type, 11:50 (CBS)
curved, 19:69-71 (EEH)
   with bending plywood, 83:62-63
   earth-retaining, 73:45 (EEH)
   ferro-cement 13:53 (CBS)
   framing, 2:56-59, 7:17-18, 19, 56, 19:70-71, 38:28 (EEH, FRC)
   layout for, 7:16-17 (FRC)
   plates for, 7:17 (FRC)
   with pumice-crete, 77:56
   redwood/plaster, 64:53
   siding, 7:19-20 (FRC)
cut-off, for plant display and skylight, 49:60, 61 (SH)
design for, nontoxic, 73:68
display clamps for, making, 65:32
double,
   energy-efficient, 42:61
   profile of, 56:62 (EEH)
drywall, fabric-covered, 38:58, 59
earthquake-proofing, 64:62-64 (MFC)
elliptical, framing, 71:14
evaluating, 10:42, 44
on existing slab,
   building, 83:14-16
   waterproofing, 58:14

extending, 3:54-55
exterior,
   cast-in-place, 2:18, 22-25 (CSH)
   cheap, conventional, 2:29
   concrete latticework, 2:19, 23, 25 (CSH)
   curved, 31:70, 71
   floating-glass, 66:60-62 (REM)
   foldaway, reviewed, 73:100
   hardboard, vulnerability of, 78:86, 87
   hinged, 21:36, 37
   retaining, block, 47:94
   shingled, low, 38:36, 37 (CSH)
   stone, 45:38, 40
   stuccoed, 62:89
   wind-deflecting, 38:25-27 (EEH)
filled, 19th-century, 6:38 (FRC)
fire-rated, upgrading, 30:6
and floor ratio, for materials efficiency, 84:46, 47-48
foamed and painted, 40:58
forces with, discussed, 32:32 (FRC)
gable,
   brackets in, sunburst for, 14:10
   chainsaw cutting of, 7:31
   Craftsman stone, 24:29-30 (CSH)
   deck layout for, 21:72-74, 77 (FRC)
   examples of, 29:78-79
   framing of, 10:63, 69, 21:71, 22:35 (FRC)
   Greek Revival, 1:48
   height of, finding, 24:12
   off-center, 14:65
   stiffening, 66:71, 72
   vents in, 7:52, 53 (DWS)
garage, moving, 64:32
garden, pumice-crete, 77:57
gunite, 53:49-50 (SH)
half, with columns, 64:41 (CSH)
height of, standard, 21:70, 71 (FRC)
hurricane-proof, 78:82
hybrid, for small house, 67:35
insulating, 47:16-18
   convection loops in, 19:68
   as icebox, 48:58-59
   retrofitting, 20:35-37
   three-season, 73:75
   trusses for, 19:69, 70 (EEH)
interior,
   angled, 67:36, 37
   stained plywood, 85:73, 75
intersections of, studs for, 22:14
jacks for, problems with, 56:62 (EEH)
joists for, rim, 65:49-51 (TFH)
levels for, 58:43
levers for, scissor, 23:71 (FRC)
linseed oil for, 48:73 (SH)
lintels for, concrete preformed, 83:14
load-bearing, determining, 6:37 (FRC)
   removing, 7:21-22 (BK)
low-cost, 73:59

masonry,
  insulation product for, 1:62-63
  molding application for, 47:28
paint for, 67:70
panels for,
  instruction sheet for, 29:92
  with preset "glass" block, 85:108
  from recycled paper, 66:102
  reversed, 55:85
  sliding, 17:41, 42, 43 (SH)
  sliding insulated, 34:24-25 (DWS)
papered, and matching doors, 6:8
partition,
  and ADA, 37:63-65
  block, 70:110
  partial, 73:56, 57
  and vapor barriers, 29:70, 72
pine-sided, 79:53, 54
plaster,
  over plywood, 76:59
  redoing, 79:87, 88
  unpainted sand, 24:30-31 (CSH)
plumb and line of, 23:69-71 (FRC)
plywood,
  parged, 56:69 (CSH)
  single-skin, 55:72
pony, 19:55 (FRC)
  defined, 19:55 (FRC)
prefabricated,
  homemade, 35:52-53 (BK)
  load-bearing, 62:72-77
  raised, system for, 58:62-66
  Scandinavian, 40:51, 53, 54
preserving, book on, 77:120-22
presheathed, 37:67 (FRC)
privacy,
  block, 36:12
  low, 73:45 (EEH)
radiant barriers for, 40:75 (EEH), 49:73-75 (EEH), 80:57
rain screens for, 50:100
rake,
  calculator framing for, 72:67-68 (MFC)
  grid no-math framing for, 72:67-68 (MFC)
rebuilding, 44:73-75
reinforcing, temporary supports for, 70:84 (REM)
repairing, 10:44
retaining,
  analyzed, 32:32-33 (FRC)
  drainage for, 40:62, 63 (CBS)
  gunite, 40:60-63 (CBS)
  structural complexity of, 34:4
  surface-bonded block, 69:41 (EEH)
  surface-drainage matting for, 69:41 (EEH)
Rex Roberts-type, 28:69-70, 71, 72
round, detail of, 44:60
serpentine, bending plywood for, 55:96
settled, correcting, 85:20-22

Key to books:

(BK)   Building Baths and Kitchens
(CBS) Building with Concrete, Brick and Stone
(CSH) Craftsman-Style Houses
(DWS) Building Doors, Windows and Skylights
(EEH) Energy-Efficient Houses
(EF)   Exterior Finishing
(FC)   Finish Carpentry
(FRC) Frame Carpentry
(FWS) Building Floors, Walls and Stairs
(MFC) More Frame Carpentry
(REM) Remodeling
(SH)   Small Houses
(TB)   Tools for Building
(TFH) Timber-Frame Houses

shear, 81:87
  interior, 79:82
  methods for, 7:23, 29:36-38 (BK, FRC), 85:57
sheathing, 37:67 (FRC)
sheet metal, 27:52
shoji, 45:71 (CSH)
sound-proof, 31:48, 35:60-61 (FWS)
splined, 24:76, 77
stenciled, 78:80
stone,
  Chinese, 55:89
  vs. concrete, 9:6
stone-block, 36:72-73
stone-in-concrete, precast, 85:82-83
stone-veneered, 41:66-68 (CSH)
of strips, vertical, 27:50-51
stuccoed, for mass, 17:45 (SH)
stud,
  below first level, 6:4
  defined, 21:71 (FRC)
superinsulated,
  double, 66:65-66, 68 (EEH)
  profiles for, 66:68 (EEH)
texturing, 67:67-68
tiled, 6:30, 32, 33, 34
timber-framed, 4:44, 45 (FRC)
truss clips for, 43:48-49 (FRC)
2x4, double, 29:70
2x6, and insulation, 29:69-70
ventilating, 19:68, 52:68, 71
vent skin for, 49:73-74 (EEH)
water, heat storage in, 16:10
window, 3:23-26, 27
windowless, compensating for, 12:42, 43, 44 (REM)
wing, 55:43, 44 (SH)
  reinforced, 83:30
wood,
  penetrating oil on, 73:72, 73, 75
  V-grooved, 54:61, 62

See also Blocking. Partitions. Plumb and line. Raising. Trombe walls. Wainscot.
Walls and Moldings (Shivers): reviewed, 77:120
Walls around Us, The (Owen): reviewed, 83:120
Walmsley, Brian:
  Construction Geometry, reviewed, 30:78
  Technical Carpenter, The, reviewed, 69:108
Walnut, black (Juglans nigra):
  chips, for non-skid surfacing, source for, 81:47
  radial splits in, 13:8
Walsh, Valerie:
  acrylic glazing of, 10:30, 31, 32, 33 (DWS)
  on gourmet kitchen, 34:62-66 (BK)
  pot rack by, 81:89
  on thermoformed acrylic, 17:63-67 (DWS)
Walton, Michael: house by, 45:38-43, 88
Ward, Mac: wooden latch by, 10:75
Wardell, Charles:
  on composition board, 67:77-85
  on drywall, 81:38-43, 82:72-77
  on library, 65:85-87
  on photovoltaic test house, 72:70-75 (EEH)
  reviews Carmody, Christian and Labs, 74:98
  reviews energy programs, 64:104-106, 68:100-102
  reviews Heilman, 62:112
  reviews Lstiburek, 74:98
  on small houses, 74:52-56
  on tile cutting, 70:57-60
  on windows, 64:100-102
Wardrobes: for closet, making, 78:44-47
Ware, William, ed.: *Georgian Period,* mentioned, 47:112
Warm Door: source for, 6:60
Warm Windows: cost of, 8:30 (TFH)
Warmco, Inc.: address for, 59:102
Warm-N-Dri insulation: mentioned, 29:12
Warren, David: on hydro-power, 15:66-69
Warren Tool Group: address for, 74:73 (FC)
Wasco Cedar, Inc.: treated shingles, 11:8, 28:66
Wasem, Joann: on chateau, 65:120
Washers: stainless-steel, source for, 54:81 (EF)
Washing machines:
  front- vs. top-loading, 75:92
  mentioned, 2:54 (BK)
Washington:
  home conservation credits in, 5:65
  Model Conservation Standards of, house to, 42:60-63

Seattle houseboat codes in, 12:69
solar tax credits in, 3:12
Washington State Energy Office: address for, 71:49
Wasserman, Ann: renovates cottage, 28:49 (FWS)
Watching for the Wind (Edinger): mentioned, 9:16
Watco-Dennis:
  Danish oil, for cabinets, 9:38 (BK)
  exterior oil finish of, 17:64, 22:57 (CSH, DWS)
  Floor Finish, 4:20
  penetrating-oil finishes, 4:9
Watco-Minwax: address for, 77:88
Water:
  catchments for, roof, 85:72, 74
  Clearinghouse for, 64:102
  conservation act for, 84:82
  damage from, repairing, 42:12
  freezing, force of, 18:66 (CBS)
  power for, solar, 60:16
  purified, "center" for, 80:98-102
  saving,
    library on, 64:102
    strategies for, 85:4-6
  solar absorption of, 9:12-14
  toilets saving, 70:56 (EEH)
  underground activity of, 20:4
  See also Domestic hot-water systems. Drainage systems. Plumbing. Water lines.
Water and Pipes: reviewed, 33:88
Water Beader preservative: for shingles, 30:49
Water Inc.: address for, 53:45 (SH)
Water lines:
  earthquake-proofing, 64:62 (MFC)
  locating, dowser for, 75:26-28
  trench for, 17:10
Water reed *(Phragmites communis trin):* American growth of, 24:4
Water table: defined, 15:41 (EF)
Water vapor: defined, 19:67
Water-Efficient Technologies for the Urban-Residential Sector: reviewed, 53:108-10
Waterless Toilets: cited, 53:110
Waterlox Chemical and Coatings Corp.:
  address for, 46:41 (REM), 71:45 (REM), 83:73
  Waterlox tung oil, 31:27 (CSH)
Waterproofing:
  nontoxic, sources for, 67:90-92
  See also Membranes.
Waterproofing & Restoration Institute: address for, 61:42
Waterstop-Plus: mentioned, 2:36
Water-tower house: pictures of, 24:92

Watkins, M. Scott:
  on cut-off saws, 62:80-84
  reviews Craftsman conference, 54:100
  on spa room, 58:58-61 (CSH)
  on stone veneer, 84:56-59
Watson, Donald A.:
  Construction Materials and Processes, reviewed, 3:61
  heliodon of, 13:18
  as joint author. *See* Labs, Kenneth.
Watson, Jay: uses computer, 35:64 (TB)
Watson, Richard D.: on radiant heat, 75:69
Watson Malone Inc.: address for, 55:58
Wattle and daub:
  example of, 19:23
  in U.S., 13:25 (TFH)
Watts, Simon:
  on doors, 40:78
  on Marcus models, 29:100
  on sliding shutters, 8:74
  on Victorian brackets, 35:72-73
Waupaca Elevator Co., Inc.: address for, 73:104
Wax:
  acrylic water-based, 75:78
  for countertops, 1:6
  emulsion of, for end-grain sealing, 72:41
  nontoxic, sources for, 67:90-92
  nonyellowing, 33:70 (CBS)
  pigmented, as filler, 20:78
  tinted, 42:30 (CSH)
WCD-3 Design of Wood Formwork for Concrete Structures: cited, 78:53
WCSH Mesquite Production Co.: address for, 59:106
WD-40: as gummed-sticker remover, 54:28
WE Care, Inc.: address for, 48:91
Weald and Downland (England) Open Air Museum: reviewed, 19:22-23
Weather Shield Window Corp.:
  address for, 55:79
  low-e glass, 38:26 (EEH)
  quad-pane glazed units from, 20:22, 34:68 (SH)
  sponsors conference, 19:22
  Tri-pane, 34:68 (SH)
Weatherbead Insulation Systems, Inc.:
  address for, 68:45 (FC)
  channel-router tool, reviewed, 60:92
Weatherboard: *See* Siding: clapboard.
Weathering and Performance of Building Materials, The (Simpson and Horrobin, eds.): mentioned, 26:4
WeatherKing Inc.: heat pumps, 26:68
Weather-Master, Inc.: address for, 62:94
Weatherstripping:
  for Arctic, 68:100
  channel-router tool for, reviewed, 60:92
  commercial, 60:48-49 (FC)
  for commercial windows, 60:48-49 (FC)

door-bottom spring-loaded, 76:56-57
for doors, 8:35, 36 (DWS)
  in-swinging, 81:4-6
  seacoast, 74:56
  spring-loaded, 76:56-57
  thresholds of, 8:36, 9:10 (DWS)
gaskets for, 61:37
interlocking metal, 74:56
leaf-type stainless, 50:73 (FC)
router-groover for, 68:45 (FC)
silicone rubber bulb, reviewed, 78:92-94
spring-type, installing, 8:35, 36 (DWS)
V-Seal, 13:49 (DWS)
for windows, 50:73 (FC)
  heavy-duty, 73:81
  in-swinging, 81:4-6
  spring-brass, 20:8
See also Caulk. Sealants.
Weathervanes:
  gilding, 3:8
  stainless-steel and bronze, 9:75
Weaver, Gerald L.: on Trombe walls, 3:46-47
Weaver, Lawrence: *Houses and Gardens by E. L. Lutyens,* reviewed, 45:122
Weavers (J. P.): address for, 47:6
Webb, Bruce: Los Angeles exhibit by, 20:22
Webb, Philip: washes deck, 84:134
Webb & Associates: address for, 65:96
Webco Sealants: address for, 46:71
Weber, John: runs millworks, 39:75-77
Weber Bros.: address for, 67:36
Webster, William: about, 45:130
Webster, William and Tom: house by, 45:44-48, 88 (TFH)
Wedge Innovations: address for, 53:94, 58:44, 71:96
Wedges: for separating lumber, 32:53, 55 (TB)
Wedgewood Entrance System: source for, 6:60
Wedlick, Dennis: on development architecture, 80:16-20
Weeden, William B.: *Economic and Social History of New England 1620-1789,* 47:48 (EF)
Weibel, Stuart: roofs house, 73:118
Weil-McLain: gas-fired boilers, 31:69
Weinstein, Robert A.:
  on Capitol Hill townhouse, 39:38-42
  on remodel, 31:32-34 (DWS)
  as joint author. *See* Capen, Judith M.
Weiser Lock: address for, 48:64 (FC, MFC)
Weiss, Johnny: solar design course of, 69:100
Wej-It Anchoring Systems: address for, 41:57 (CBS)
Weldwood: resorcinol glue, 3:16, 42:10 (DWS)

Wellborn Paint Co.:
address for, 48:73 (SH), 50:49
adobe sealer, application of, 30:41
Wellhouses: example of, 67:87
Wells, Alfred: on treehouses, 14:41 (SH)
Wells, Malcolm:
Architect's Sketchbook of Underground Buildings, An, reviewed, 65:106-108
on earth-sheltered house, 7:34-39 (DWS)
Gentle Architecture, reviewed, 3:60
reviews Hornbostel, 67:104
stairway by, 26:46-47
on underground architecture, 73:4
Underground Designs, 7:39 (DWS)
Underground Plans Book I, 7:39 (DWS)
Welsch, Roger L.: *Sod Walls,* 31:54
Wen Products, Inc.: random-orbit sanders, reviewed, 77:72, 73
Wenco: address for, 76:75 (FC)
Wendorf, Peter: mentioned, 26:34, 36
Wentworth, Bruce: remodel by, 65:24
Werner (R. D.) Co., Inc.: address for, 84:55
West Coast Door: 2000 Series Entrance Door, source for, 6:60
West Coast Victorians (Naversen): reviewed, 46:104
West System: *See* Epoxy. Gougeon Brothers, Inc.
Westeel Rosco Ltd.: Ultraclad 88 prepainted steel roofing panels, 15:62
Western Forms, Inc.: forms by, 34:39
Western Lumber Product Use Manual: reviewed, 31:84
Western Regional Agricultural Engineering Service: *Energy Efficient Home Sites,* 23:51
Western Saw Inc.: address for, 53:38 (FC)
Western States Roofing Contractors Association: address for, 84:112
Western Wood Moulding and Millwork Producers Association: casings booklet from, 30:55 (DWS)
Western Wood Products Association:
address for, 65:53, 71:104, 77:110, 82:104, 83:45
described, 47:43
Exposed Cedar, 47:16
field aid from, 31:84
lumber-grade brochures, 17:8
1993-94 Buyer's Manual, 85:124
plank-flooring guide, 33:43 (FWS)
Product Use Manual, 23:50
publications from, 23:49, 50, 31:84, 47:40, 43
seminars of, 31:84
span computer, 13:8
and timbering, 47:38
Western Wood Species Book, source for, 23:50
wood-use campaign by, 83:112

Westex Supply Ltd.:
asphalt membrane, 35:77
Westinghouse Electrical Corp.:
address for, 9:41 (BK)
fixtures, 15:57 (BK)
Westlake, Cy: on mobile workshop, 8:58-59 (TB)
Wet saws: *See* Tile saws.
Wetlands: house for, 57:63-67
Wetzler Clamp Co., Inc.: address for, 74:73 (FC)
Wetzler, John: on septic tanks, 3:36-39 (BK)
Wexler, Paul: Japanese units by, 45:70, 72, 74, 89 (CSH)
Weyerhauser: Silva wool, 8:40 (EEH)
Wheat *(Triticum aestivum):* for thatching, 22:73, 74
Whedon Products: address for, 84:83
Wheelbarrows:
tires of, resealing, 71:24, 76:28
wooden slat-wheel, 3:7
Wheelchairs:
measurements of, 53:70, 71
See also Design: for handicapped.
Wheeler, Dan: builds simple houses, 73:82-87
Wheeler, William R.: on attic venting, 7:52-53 (DWS)
Wheeling Corrugating Co.: address for, 80:57, 84:67
Whetstones: *See* Benchstones.
Whiffen, Marcus:
American Architecture since 1788, reviewed, 2:62
Eighteenth-Century Houses of Williamsburg, The, reviewed, 43:102
Whipple, Rodger:
about, 45:130
house by, 22:54-60 (CSH)
mentioned, 31:26 (CSH)
on Spanish Revival house, 45:38-43
White, Kirby: on simple house, 14:62-65
White, Mark:
on arbor and gate, 49:44-45
balcony rail by, 3:67
reviews shingles, 64:92
on steel framing, 76:92
on truss-frames, 5:54-57 (FRC)
White, Stanford: career of, 37:53
White, Stephen: teahouse by, 67:86
White, Steven M.: on spiral stair, 70:86-91
White face: *See* Farmline Thermoply.
White Pine Institute: monographs of, 33:6
White Pine Series of Architectural Monographs, The: plans after, 53:86, 88, 89
White-Hansen, Sue Ellen: on Hawaiian house, 61:58-61 (SH)
Whiteman, Robin, and Rob Talbot: *Cotswolds, The,* reviewed, 49:114

White-Rodgers: defective thermostats, 2:64
Whitewash:
early English, 60:71
simulated, 79:55
Whitney, William: on electricity, 2:42-44
Whitney Museum (New York City): Shaker exhibit, 1986, 38:100-102
Whole Earth Access: reviewed, 62:51
Whole Earth Review: reviewed, 30:78
Whole Energy & Hardware: address for, 77:67
Widow's walks:
as height-restriction solution, 52:55, 56
metal, 43:81
Wilbern, Jack: on ranch remodel, 80:72
Wilbur, C. Keith: *Home Building and Woodworking in Colonial America,* reviewed, 79:120
Wilcox Cool Heat Solar Inc.: heat pumps, 26:68
Wild Heerbrugg Instruments Inc.: levels, 37:45 (TB)
Wiley, Drew:
on framing nailers, 56:52-57
on portable air compressors, 49:84-89
Wilk, Sanford H.:
on architecture, 63:100
on circular saws, 63:72-77
reviews Ryobi table saw, 75:92
on sawblades, 72:42-47 (MFC)
Wilkerson Corp.: address for, 49:87
Wilkes, Joseph, ed.: *Encyclopedia of Architecture,* reviewed, 50:108
Wilkes, Perry: solar design by, 5:16
Wilkins, A. D. Paul: catalogue from, 24:82
Wilkinson, Joe: on timber-frame remodel, 52:46-51 (TFH)
Willamette Industries, Inc.: address for, 62:76
Willcox, Peter:
on office, 45:28, 94
on Texas house, 36:70-75
William Marine Service: address for, 73:73
William Zinsser and Co., Inc.:
address for, 67:71
B-I-N primer-sealer, 39:10
Williamette-Greystone Inc.: dry-stack block of, 16:55 (CBS)
Williams, Benjamin, ed.: *Remodeler's Handbook,* reviewed, 3:61
Williams, Bob: on dumbwaiters, 55:86
Williams, Chuck: on barrier-free house, 76:54-59
Williams, Erin: on solar designs, 33:84
Williams, James I.: as joint author. *See* Schwolsky, Rick.
Williams, Ken: on dismantling tower, 51:118
Williams, Les: on gutters, 67:38-43 (EF)

Williams, Thomas H.:
on carving cabinets, 47:64-67
doors by, 46:84-85
Williams and Hussey Machine Co.:
knives from, custom, 40:34 (FWS)
molder/planers, 19:52 (FWS)
model W7S, 40:34 (FWS)
reviewed, 55:50-55
Williams Form Engineering Corp.:
address for, 78:50
Williams Furnace Co.: swamp coolers of,
17:45 (SH)
Williamsburg (Virginia): book on,
reviewed, 43:102
Williamson, Hugh: on landscaping, 3:19
Willis A. Roon and Sons, Inc.: house by,
39:70-74
Willis-Moody house: pictured, 39:79
Willmar Window Industries Ltd.:
address for, 55:81, 81:102
Will-Seal: address for, 58:14
Wilson, Alex: *1991 Consumer Guide to
Home Energy Saving,* reviewed, 67:104
Wilson, David Stark:
on hillside house, 51:58-63
trim by, 49:91
Wilson, Gary: mentioned, 19:38, 41 (BK)
Wilson, Jim: on concrete log cabin, 5:68
Wilson, Roy L.: *Build Your Own Energy-
Saver Home,* reviewed, 1:66
Wilson, Steve: reviews gas nail gun, 33:82
(TB)
Wilsonart Laminates:
address for, 9:41 (BK)
nonglossy laminates, 30:60 (BK)
Wilton Corp.: address for, 74:73 (FC)
Wiltshire, Ian: window seat by, 66:90
Winchester, Stephen:
on bullnose steps, 82:60-63
on hutch, 85:64-67
WINCO: generator 5888-1, 15:68-69
Wind:
allowing for, 1:42 (FRC)
building for, 54:60-61
design around, 29:28-33
joist ties against, 29:74, 75
and microclimate, 9:16
See also Energy.
Wind Energy: mentioned, 1:66
Wind turbines: access door for, 43:20
***Windlight Workshop Catalogue and
Handbook:*** reviewed, 24:80
Window Quilt:
cost of, 8:30 (TFH)
pictured, 33:39 (EEH)
for skylights, 35:8
source for, 39:51
Window seats:
under arch, 66:89
Arts-and-Crafts style, 52:78, 57:47
(REM), 66:90
for bedroom, 74:61
cantilevered, 66:84
in log house, 66:76
between closets, 66:91
column-flanked, 64:42 (CSH)
concrete, 66:91
corner, 74:69, 80:54
engawa nook as, 43:28, 29 (CSH)
oak inset, 66:50
plastered, with radiant heat, 66:91
rustic granite, 83:89
stairwell built-in, 44:81
with storage below, 66:89, 85:95
with wood storage, 66:90
Windows:
accordion, making, 41:41, 42-43 (DWS)
in adobe,
repairing, 22:41-43
vent, 5:51
aerogel, 55:81
aging, 56:50, 51
air/vapor barriers with, 9:58
aluminum,
black anodized, 37:26 (BK)
-clad casement, source for, 47:59
commercial, source for, 73:81
cost of, 83:87
-glazed, 8:42 (DWS)
headers for, 21:72 (FRC)
painted, 53:49, 40 (SH)
side tracks for, 20:8
angled vs. plumb, 8:42 (DWS)
apron for, 33:55 (DWS)
arched, 26:37, 48:53, 66:89, 76:56, 80:64,
65, 66
Colonial, 63:49
high, 78:81
inset, 25:29
installing, 56:64-67 (FC)
molding for, 63:10-12
opening for, cutting, 36:16
source for, 65:80 (MFC)
architraves for, classical hardwood,
38:88-89
area of, Jefferson's formula for, 42:78
Arts-and-Crafts style, 51:37, 38, 40 (CSH)
handmade, 69:43 (EEH)
association for, 40:86, 64:102, 81:102
awning, 50:81 (SH)
band of, 34:26, 28 (DWS)
for cooling, 52:73
source for, 43:74 (SH)
for ventilation, 44:80, 81
band of,
high, 19:31, 32, 45:43, 57, 80:55
for privacy, 80:76
bay,
as added space, 22:65, 67 (BK)
built-in, seating for, 12:41
framing, 57:78-83 (CSH, MFC)
gallery of, 60:88-89
with sofas, 74:52
to the side, adding, 70:40-44
triangular, 38:26, 27 (EEH)
two-story, 59:36, 37-39 (SH)
Victorian, 28:49, 53 (FWS)
See also Window seats.
books on, 1:66
bow,
under eyebrow roof, 44:64-68 (FRC)
framing for, 44:65 (FRC)
box,
building, 7:10
geometric, 15:26, 28
for bridging boulders, 19:77
casement, 45:40, 41, 44-45, 48, 49:62 (SH),
59:82
advantages of, 5:33
cost of, 51:77 (FC)
cremorne bolts for, 5:33
divided-light, custom, 38:72, 73, 75, 77
(TFH)
handles for, 76:94
leaded, 83:88
making, 50:69-73 (FC)
modular, 27:73, 75
in non-bearing wall, 77:52
operators for, 9:8, 50:69, 73 (FC)
pivoting, 65:77 (REM)
shades for, 5:33
in solar design, 84:86
stained glass, 6:18, 21 (CSH)
in turret, 68:58, 59
wall of, 66:79, 80 (SH)
casings for, 33:54-55 (DWS), 84:78-79
curved, building, 67:82-85 (FC)
Greene-and-Greene, 56:70, 72 (CSH)
inaccuracies in, dealing with, 19:44
(TB)
limestone, 37:60
with power miter saw, 19:44 (TB)
radiused, 20:14-16
circular, 73:48, 49, 50
concrete, 25:56, 57, 58

Key to books:

(BK)   Building Baths and Kitchens
(CBS)   Building with Concrete, Brick and Stone
(CSH)   Craftsman-Style Houses
(DWS)   Building Doors, Windows and Skylights
(EEH)   Energy-Efficient Houses
(EF)   Exterior Finishing
(FC)   Finish Carpentry
(FRC)   Frame Carpentry
(FWS)   Building Floors, Walls and Stairs
(MFC)   More Frame Carpentry
(REM)   Remodeling
(SH)   Small Houses
(TB)   Tools for Building
(TFH)   Timber-Frame Houses

in circular structures, 44:61-62

clerestory, 64:77, 67:36, 37, 76:56, 57, 82:66

east, 80:78, 80

headerless, 75:80, 79:82, 83, 84, 80:76

long, 66:37, 39 (SH)

openers for, 46:26

code requirements for, 50:59

collector, heat-activated, 16:28

color for, 74:42 (EF)

commercial,

association for, 60:50 (FC)

computer libraries of, 60:49 (FC)

divided-light, 54:87, 60:49 (FC, TFH)

divided-light, source for, 71:71

reviewed, by brand, 60:46-51 (FC)

concrete, precast, 48:80

condensation on, and placement of, 60:51 (FC)

convection with, checking, 1:5

corner placement of, 73:84, 86

counterbalanced,

chain for, 67:73 (REM)

vertically drawn shutters for, 17:44 (SH)

curlicue, 85:148

curtains for, Mylar insulating, 58:83 (EEH)

curtains for, track-held, 38:58

curved,

in Greek Revival, 1:48-49

making, 5:25-27 (DWS)

mullioned, 45:44, 47-48 (TFH)

source for, 55:92

in curved walls, 7:18, 12:66, 31:70-71 (EEH, FRC)

custom, 36:74, 44:66, 67 (FRC)

sources for, 63:40, 76:67 (REM)

Danish, 31:76

decay problems with, 68:6-8

design for, 34:8-10

functional, 16:30

for solar gain, 84:86

double-hung,

diagrammed, 33:53 (DWS)

divided-light, commercial, 59:61

installing, 33:53-55 (DWS)

insulated, 18:42

renovating, 64:48-49 (FC)

sources for, 64:49 (FC)

storm sash over, 18:42

traditional, 32:73

dowel joints for, 16:10

drywall around, moisture-resistant, 63:52

early English, 60:72, 73

energy labels for, 78:104

energy ratings of, new, 64:100-102

energy-efficient, 65:62 (SH), 81:83-87

energy-gaining, 66:4

enlarging visually, 45:33, 37

estimates for, 27:34

etched and stained, 73:88, 91

exterior, wood for, 50:16

eyebrow, 41:66, 67 (CSH)

building, 76:72-75 (FC)

sources for, 76:75 (FC)

fanlight, book review on, 64:110

films for,

low-e polyester, 69:43 (EEH)

metallic-oxide, sizing, 26:74 (SH)

reflective, 49:73 (EEH)

exterior, 54:14

fixed,

building, 51:76-78 (FC), 55:4, 56:6

detail of, 4:29, 31, 33, 12:31

heavy, 73:49

installing, 4:7, 8:42-43, 10:6 (DWS)

Rex Roberts, 28:70-71

flashing, 8:60-61, 9:47 (EF)

in shingling, 28:63

foam rope for, 4:7

frames for,

building, 66:86, 84:76-79

removing, 18:72, 77 (DWS)

framing for, 82:43, 44

failures with, 6:38 (FRC)

hurricane-proofing, 78:86-87

as frieze blocks, 85:73, 75

gable, 66:43-44

quick playhouse, 61:44 (SH)

gable-end retrofit, 21:26-27, 28, 29

glare from, Mylar for, 34:66 (BK)

glass-block, 66:50, 67:62-63

preset plastic, source for, 85:108

glaziers' supplies for, 20:8

glazing tape for, 7:37 (DWS)

glue for, 16:10

good-luck, 32:57, 59

grills for, 25:27, 29

custom metal, 62:88

stock, 39:41

grouping of, traditional, 73:47

for handicapped, 53:68

headerless, 75:80, 83, 84

headers for,

steel curved, 57:56

wood, 21:72 (FRC)

heat loss from, 66:68 (EEH)

heat-deflecting, 65:77 (REM)

high-performance, custom, 41:84-86

hinges for, brass integral pin, 50:73 (FC)

hoods for, 46:82 (TFH)

in hung walls, 8:30 (TFH)

importance of, 80:52-53

information on, 65:55

insulating,

covers for, source for, 70:55-56 (EEH)

flashing, 10:6

lighting, 16:30

making, 14:12

prolonged fog resistance in, 10:4

site-built, 24:76

site-built venting, 14:65

vinyl, 59:72 (SH)

insulation for,

movable, 35:8, 39:51

movable automatic, 34:24 (DWS)

publications on, 32:90

jacks for, split, 15:43

jalousie, 11:30, 32, 32, 33 (EEH)

interior, 68:39

Kalwall in, 16:30

lap joints for, 76:73 (FC)

large,

coverings for, 53:14

wind-bracing, 82:68

leaded-glass, 64:53

casement, 20:74, 75

making, 15:16, 23:37-41, 42:33 (DWS)

light shaft as, 81:84-85

light-directing, holographic, 76:104

lintels for, marine-grade, 67:61

in log buildings, 7:30, 31

low-e glass for, 38:26 (EEH)

making, books on, 50:69 (FC)

for masonry houses, 54:87 (TFH)

and mass ratio, 16:14

measuring for, metric vs. imperial, 60:102

in modular design, 66:59 (SH)

moldings for,

drip, raked, 61:43, 44 (SH)

wood glazing, 16:10

mullions of,

color for, 55:74

many, offset, 52:37, 39, 40 (TFH)

profiles for, 20:61, 62, 63 (FWS)

multiple-joined, custom, 70:82 (REM)

as night mirrors, 19:32

north, restricting, 45:37

old, matching, 67:14, 69:14

openings for, laying out, 21:72 (FRC)

Palladian, 16-ft., 51:80-81 (MFC)

panels for, exterior, 69:14

panes of, replaceable inner, 66:66 (EEH)

parts for, 18:77 (DWS), 44:89

Plexiglas, 17:77 (SH)

projecting, 83:56

putty in, removing, 5:7

quad-pane system for, 20:22

quarter-round, 38:45

rabbeted, for siding, 28:64

radiation-resistant sandwich, 17:64 (DWS)

rain shed for, 3:66

reflective three-dimensional, 44:78-79

reinforcing for, 34:28, 29 (DWS)

for remodel, choosing, 65:77-78 (REM)

repairing,

book on, 84:124

epoxy for, 70:48

replacing,
  booklets on, 29:92
  flange-seal trick for, 42:20-22 (CSH)
  "simple," 44:110
  system for, 1:62
restoration of, book on, 24:86
for restoration, source for, 67:14
restringing, 71:4
returns for, angled, 80:70, 71
reveal jig for, 23:14
roof, 56:59 (EEH)
  rain sensor for, 53:68
  in solar design, 51:75 (EEH)
rose-and-grey, 41:46
round, 1:55, 38:41, 43
  concrete, 48:79, 82, 83
  leaded, 83:88, 89
  molded, in cob wall, 83:89
  roof, 80:67
Russian, 36:76 (DWS)
R-values for,
  R-11.9 glass, reviewed, 81:102
  standards for, 57:6
safety, requirements for, 15:43
sash for,
  barn, 26:38, 39 (BK)
  extra-strong, 16:10 (erratum, 17:6)
  factory, 11:29, 31, 33 (EEH)
sash weights for, making, 68:30
for seacoast, 74:69
semicircular hinged, 25:58
setting blocks for, neoprene, 4:7
shades for, recessed in concrete, 48:80, 82
sheathed-over, chainsaw cutting, 78:40
shutters for,
  integral, commercial, 6:54
  interior, 79:54, 55
  rolling exterior, 76:16, 77:10
sills for, 21:71, 72 (FRC)
  angle for, 10:6
  drip kerf for, 8:43 (DWS)
  grooved for siding, 8:43 (DWS)
  self-draining, 66:86, 87
  slate, 34:50
  stone, 24:30 (CSH)
sliding, making, 41:43 (DWS)
sliding-door panels as, 15:42-43, 25:40, 41 (EEH)
solo installing, aid for, 85:32
soundproofing, 35:63
springs for, 20:8
steel industrial, 2:18, 19, 20-23 (CSH)
steel narrow-muntined, source for, 52:51 (TFH)
stepped, in tower, 80:74, 76
stone-framed, 54:38-39
stool caps for, 33:54 (DWS)
stools for, scribing, 77:60, 62
stops for, 33:55 (DWS)

storm/screen, commercial, 77:88
story poles for, 50:70, 71-72 (FC)
in stress-skin panels, 24:55, 57, 58
sunbursts for, 51:14
for superinsulated house, 70:55 (EEH)
suppliers of, choosing, 52:66
swing-up, making, 41:42 (DWS)
for Swiss chalets, 70:75
tape balances for, 20:8
tape for, butyl, 4:7
teak, 35:34
Tedlar in, 16:30
top-of-the-line, 80:58
transit-set, 15:43
triangular, tiny, 12:31
trim for, brickmold, 4:7
trimmers for, 21:71, 72 (FRC)
  split, 22:34, 35, 24:6 (FRC)
for tropics, 61:60 (SH)
ultraviolet blocking for, 55:8
unprimed, commercial, 10:51 (SH)
vacuum-gel, 56:42
and vapor barriers, 29:70, 72
as ventilators, 5:15, 16:30, 55:81
  operable low, 80:70, 71, 79, 81
vents for, temperature-sensitive, 32:37
viewing, modular, 16:30
weathertight sealing of, 55:43, 44 (SH)
wells for, inverted, 64:85 (REM)
west-facing, design of, 34:8-10
See also Glazing. Hardware. Sash.
  Screens. Shades. Shutters.
  Weatherstripping.
Windows for Energy-Efficient Buildings:
  mentioned, 1:66
Windscreens: planning, 3:19
Wine cellars:
  building, 13:8-10, 48:58-60
  excavating for, under house, 81:68-71
Wing, Charles:
  addresses conference, 33:82 (TB)
  From the Walls In, quoted, 5:4
  mentioned, 20:81
  thermal shutters by, 2:52 (SH)
  Visual Handbook of Building and Remodeling, The, reviewed, 74:98
Wing, Charles, and John Cole: *From the Ground Up,* 7:42
Wing, Daniel:
  on cumulative injuries, 64:66-69
  on gypsy wagon, 50:87-89 (CSH)
Wing, George: learns framing, 82:122
Wing Enterprises, Inc.: address for, 84:55
Wing Industries, Inc.: address for, 54:65 (FC)
Winkler, Gail Caskey: as joint author.
  See Moss, Roger.
Winner International: address for, 85:102
Winona Manufacturing, Inc.: address for, 72:62
Winooski Block: moldings of, 2:48-49 (FWS)

Winslow, Barbara:
  on design for handicapped, 6:51
  on roofs, 10:26-29
  as joint author. *See* Lifchez, Raymond.
Winter, Amos:
  insulation information from, 4:8
  stress-skin panels by, 24:58
Winter, Robert: Los Angeles exhibit by, 20:22
Winter Panel Corp.:
  organizes trip, 35:55 (TB)
  stress-skin panels, 38:74 (TFH)
Wire: binders for, Velcro, 81:28
Wire strippers: for renovation, 12:51 (TB)
Wiremold Co.:
  address for, 47:55 (TFH), 51:52
  strip outlets, 40:67 (BK)
Wiring:
  adaptors for, 12:51 (TB)
  in adobe, 30:39
  and airtight-drywall approach, 37:64
  from attic, 32:58-59
  in balloon-truss system, 24:69
  books on, 4:4, 8:45
  boxes for,
    airtight, 46:72
    filing, 30:10
    foam "gluing," 81:28
    locator jig for, 53:30
    outlet, cherry cover plates for, 15:76, 77 (CSH)
    outlet, flush casings for, 29:64, 65, 31:4
    outlet, gaskets for, 12:12
    outlet, for handicapped, 76:58
    outlet, installing, 8:45, 18:12
    outlet, insulating, 18:6
    outlet, jig for, 57:28
    outlet, location for, 25:16
    outlet, transmitter-controlled, 80:98
    outlet, trim around, 15:76, 77 (CSH)
    outlet, watertight outdoor, 77:96
    plastic vs. metal, 8:44-45
    tight-place installation of, 68:28
  cable ,
    BX, armored, 8:45
    BX, cutter for, reviewed, 55:94-96
    NM, non-metallic sheathed, 8:44
    Romex, 8:44
  for cable television, planning for, 23:14, 25:4
  chases for, 50:81 (SH), 52:39 (TFH)
    ceiling, 65:51 (TFH)
    drywall-formed, 63:53
    floor, 47:57, 55:59, 77:51, 52
    through foamboard, 55:60
    roof, 66:87
    routed ceiling, 28:62 (TFH)
    in slab-on-grade, 60:53-54
    surface, 47:55 (TFH)
  circuit-breaker numbering system for, 15:16

in cold weather, 51:42

in concrete, 48:53

    precast cellular, 30:76

conductors for, aluminum, 2:44

conduit bender for, 21:16

with conduit (EMT), thinwall, 8:45, 55:60

cord organizer for, 46:26

cover plates for,

    energy-saving childproof, 48:91

    vinyl paint for, 37:25 (BK)

and door retrofits, 68:43 (FC)

double-insulated, 34:54 (TB)

drywall cutting for, 81:41

in earthen structures, expert on, 67:96-98

evaluating, 2:43

exposed, 46:51, 52 (EEH)

    conduit, 12:45 (REM)

    conduit, support for, 48:4

extensions for, 12:51 (TB)

furring space for, 18:41-42

generator system for, 78:85

grommets for, in metal studs, 32:71 (FRC)

ground-fault protection, 6:39-41

    code requirements for, 6:39

    cover plates for, duplex, 9:4

    extension cord for, 8:4

    need for, 6:39, 34:54 (TB)

    testers for, 9:4

grounding, 2:43, 44

for handicapped, 53:70

heavy-duty extension cords for, making, 76:30

in inaccessible places, snare for, 44:26

Insulation Contact (IC) fixtures for, 20:12

joists for, prebored, 55:59

in log building, 32:75

marking, with masking tape, 85:30

in masonry, 33:66

memory jog for, 25:16

meter base for, 2:42-43

for minimum heat loss, 18:7

and noise control, 58:54, 57

no-nail zone for, 21:18

through old walls, tricks for, 11:12, 17:41, 26:16, 63:26 (SH)

openings for, sealing, 78:70

organizer vest for, 46:26

plaster canopies around, 57:40

through plates, V-grooved, 6:10

prefabricated Scandinavian, 40:53

in rammed-earth buildings, 34:38, 39

recyled, 81:106

and renovation, 55:75-76 (MFC)

in restorations, 29:64, 65

retrofitting, 50:67

rippers for, 12:51 (TB)

routes for, energy-efficient, 66:66 (EEH)

safety with, 34:54 (TB)

in sand foundation base, 8:38, 39 (EEH)

service panel for, 2:42, 43-44

source for, mail-order, 44:4

stereo planning with, 23:14, 25:4

storage reels for, 69:32

strand-twisting, trick for, 72:26

with stress-skin panels, 24:59, 25:46, 29:76 (TFH), 47:53-55 (TFH)

through stud notches, 82:102

through stud spaces, trick for, 77:32

with studs, metal, 30:6, 32:71 (FRC)

switches for,

    computer, 53:74

    float, magnetic, 29:88

    insulated placement of, 18:7

    large toggle, 46:39 (REM)

    refrigerator-door, 21:43

    three-way, 81:48-49, 82:6

    transmitter-controlled, 80:98

tape for, 12:51 (TB)

taping of, gluing ends in, 9:12

telephone planning with, 23:14, 25:4

terms for, 2:43

testers for, 12:51 (TB)

in timber frames, 79:54

tool bags for, 42:66 (TB)

of tools, for safety, 82:41

tripod wire-holder for, 60:26

in truss frames, 5:57 (FRC)

Underwriter's Laboratories for, 23:49

upgrading of, temporary, 17:14-16

and vapor barrier, 12:12, 19:68, 29:70, 72

See also Building codes. Electricity. Extension cords. Remote controls.

Wiring Simplified: (Richter), 4:4

Wirsbo Co.: address for, 58:61 (CSH), 62:74, 73:45 (EEH)

Wirth, Harry J.: on tower house, 80:68-71

Wisconsin:

    conservation tax incentives in, 6:16

    dry-stack block in, 16:57 (CBS)

    heat pumps in, 14:16

    solar tax credits in, 3:12

    water-return laws of, 14:16

Wisconsin EPS, Inc.: address for, 68:86

Wisconsin Knife Works: negative-tooth sawblade of, 18:17

Witt, Susan: on land trusts, 17:20

Wittausch, William Howard: house by, 45:38-43, 88

Wofford, John: on foundation dressing, 81:122

Wojcik, William: toolbox of, 74:87

Wolfcraft, Inc.: random-orbit sanding heads, 77:70

Wolfe, Delores: as joint author. *See* Yanda, Susan.

Wolfe, Tom: *From Bauhaus to Our House,* reviewed, 9:68

Wolfer, Jim: on cantilevered countertop, 76:58-59

Wolff, John:

    on architracting, 19:46

    garage remodel by, 19:46-49

Wolf-Gordon Inc.: address for, 46:41 (REM)

Wolfskill, Lyle A., Wayne A. Dunlap and Bob M. Gallaway: *Handbook for Building Homes of Earth,* 34:39

Wolverine Technologies, Inc.: address for, 47:94, 83:44

Womack, John Calvin:

    about, 45:130

    house by, 45:54-59, 88

Women: building instruction for, 13:16-18

Wonder Arch: source for, 33:72

Wonderbar prybar: source for, 32:55 (TB)

Wonderboard:

    edge plane for, 42:20 (CSH)

    source for, 15:8

Wood:

    air- vs. kiln-dried, 4:53 (TFH)

    association for, 65:45

    attitudes toward, 83:112

    books on, 7:28 (TFH), 64:112, 69:54

    cement for, synthetic, 18:8

    characteristics of, 32:32-33 (FRC)

    choosing, 50:16

        books for, 81:16

    compression set in, 81:59

    consultants in, 81:59

    decay of, 68:4-6

        epoxy repair of, 16:20-21, 70:48-49 (CSH)

        epoxy repair of, book on, 70:49

        stopping, 68:4-6

        temperatures for, 9:4

        treating, 68:6

    decay resistance of, predicting, 69:16-18

    defects in, 7:41

    drying, 7:41, 28:10-12

        in kiln, disadvantages of, 31:37

        in kiln, explained, 18:6

        process of, 81:16

        stickers for, 26:12

    grading of, 7:40-41, 23:59 (FWS)

    green,

        availability of, 8:14

        building with, 5:10

        building with, book on, 4:58

        buying, 7:40, 41

        costs of, 7:40, 8:49

        finish for, 1:6

        moisture content of, 7:40

        nails for, 7:41

        problems with, 7:41-42, 49

    hard, R-value of, 39:10

    by hardness groups, 40:69 (FRC)

    and humidity, 69:54, 81:56

    identification of, laboratory for, 56:84

information on, 65:53

for log buildings, 13:14

moisture in,
    books on, 81:59
    capacity of, 19:67
    and nail withdrawal resistance, 85:43

movement of, and moisture content, 43:8

oily, and epoxy bonding, 70:46-47

perfuming, 11:10

perm rating of, 19:67

pressure-treated, sawblades for, 72:47 (MFC)

prices of, 1981, 1:10

rot-resistant plantation grown, 73:68

roughsawn, calculation problems with, 4:46 (FRC)

shrinkage of,
    design for, 81:54-59
    ratios of, 61:12-14

solar absorption of, 9:14

splits in, preventing, 13:8

stinking, cleaning, 11:8-10

stress in, calculating, 4:46 (FRC)

structural,
    capacity of, 34:4
    engineering with, books on, 58:16
    glossary of, 7:25 (TFH)

used, metal detector for, 20:28-29

western, association for, 83:45

See also Stains (blemishes). *various species.*

Wood, Chris: on skunks, 60:118

Wood, Joseph: on eyebrow roof, 44:64-68 (FRC)

Wood as an Engineering Material (U. S. Department of Agriculture): cited, 81:59

Wood Book, The: cited, 46:66 (EF)

Wood Building Research Center: stain-removal booklet from, 47:16

Wood Frame Design: source for, 47:43

Wood Frame Floor Systems: source for, 23:49

Wood-frame House Construction (Anderson): mentioned, 13:8

Wood Framing Details: mentioned, 21:6

Wood Handbook (USDAFPL):
    cited, 37:84
    mentioned, 10:46 (DWS)
    source for, 43:8

Wood Heat Safety (Shelton): mentioned, 11:10

Wood Heater Program: address for, 49:98

Wood Heating Alliance: safety information from, 46:14

Wood in American Life (Youngquist and Fleischer): reviewed, 54:106

Wood Insulated Door: source for, 6:60

Wood preservatives:
    advice on, source for, 15:37
    applying, 27:55

associations for, 3:9, 63:63, 65 (MFC), 77:108

avoiding, 73:67

for beam ends, 79:24

borate, 62:57 (TFH), 63:65 (MFC), 85:75
    effectiveness of, 85:22

choosing, 27:54, 55

comparing, book on, 7:8

copper arsenate, 13:14, 15:27, 37
    ammoniacal (ACA), 15:37
    chromated (CCA), 15:37
    chromated (CCA), and spruce, 44:59
    for logs, 14:53
    toxicity of, 28:10, 56:14
    types of, 28:10

copper compounds as, 63:63-64 (MFC)

copper, toxicity of, 56:14

creosote as, 63:63 (MFC)

dangers of, 79:4-6

for decks, 61:14
    applying, 69:48, 49 (EF)

design without, 46:70-73

and finishes, 55:18-20, 77:104-108

and fungi prevention, 72:66 (REM)

and grass, 29:43 (FRC)

liquid, application for, 17:16

and metal roofing, 24:46

and nail choice, 85:45

and nail corrosion, 85:120-22

nontoxic, 14:51, 73:68

oil-borne, 63:63 (MFC)

oils as, 17:64 (DWS)

and paint, 29:43 (FRC)

pentachlorophenol, 15:37
    toxicity of, 14:53

pressure-applied, 63:62-63 (MFC)

for shingles, 30:49

for siding, 3:8-9

for sills, 48:71 (SH)

source for, 53:79 (REM)

and spruce, 44:59

stains for use with, 44:88

toxicity of, 1:6, 10:10

weathering of, 29:43 (FRC)

Wood Science and Technology Centre:
    address for, 75:100

Wood stoves:
    books on, 11:10, 30:78
    cast-iron, vs. masonry stoves, 40:4
    catalytic elements for, 40:4
        deficiencies of, 39:4
    central corner, 73:52
    chimneys of,
        heat-retaining, 66:66, 67 (EEH)
        metal two-story, 66:81 (SH)
    clearances for, 11:10
    connector pipes for, 50:4-6
    consultation services on, 42:68 (CBS)

cook, fire-resistant wall behind, 67:73 (REM)
    masonry, building, 21:62-65 (CBS)
    masonry, cast-iron parts for, 21:62 (CBS)
    old, sources for, 21:63 (CBS)

and dampers, 46:14

EPA standards for, 49:98

fisherman's, 46:83 (TFH)

hearth for, 80:50
    concrete, 73:76

heat shields for,
    copper, 44:41 (SH)
    stone, 55:84, 86
    tile, 13:10

hot-water heating systems for, 33:12, 65:62-65 (SH)

multi-fuel trash-burning, reviewed, 65:94-96

outside air for, 23:4
    need of, 28:82

pipes for, as design unit, 19:48-49

radiant-floor heating with, 26:12

safety information on, 46:14

source for, 66:81 (SH)

stovepipes for, 46:14
    visible stainless, 45:62 (SH)

surrounds for, noncombustible, 13:10 (erratum, 15:8)

through-the-wall, 51:43, 44, 45

tiny, source for, 55:44 (SH)

wood lift for, reviewed, 64:92

See also Firewood storage. Flues. Furnaces. Masonry stoves. Ranges.

Wood Structural Design Data (USDAFPL): cited, 7:28 (TFH)

Wood Ventures: registers of, reviewed, 60:96

Woodbridge, Sally B.:
    Bernard Maybeck, reviewed, 83:120-22
    Los Angeles exhibit by, 20:22

Woodcock, Johanne: library by, 61:120

Woodcraft Supply Corp.:
    address for, 55:94, 65:42, 74:73 (FC), 81:74
    bubble-level scribers, 2:39
    carpenter's vise, 35:91
    chisels, 12:23 (CSH, TFH)
    froes, 30:48
    Japanese tools, 8:15
    Mark II sharpener, 18:59, 61 (TB)
    reviewed, 62:51

WoodHeat: reviewed, 30:78

Wood-Hu Kitchens, Inc.: cabinets of, discussed, 65:71, 72

Woodlife preservative:
    exterior finish, life of, 27:75, 76
    mentioned, 6:23
    for redwood, 3:8

Woodline-The Japan Woodworker:
    chisels of, 12:23 (CSH, TFH)

Woodman, Donald: at conference, 28:81

Woodmaster Tools: molder/planers, reviewed, 55:50-55

Woodmeister Corp.: pocket-door frames of, 54:64-66 (FC)

Wood-Mizer Products, Inc.: address for, 51:70

Woodpecker Products Inc.: address for, 68:96

Woods, Donna: recalls Sowden House, 14:70, 73

Woodstone Co.: address for, 83:56

Woodward, Eric: on renovation, 42:26-31 (CSH)

Woodward, Richard:
on cabin restorations, 14:46-51
on chinking, 26:50-51

Woodward Thomsen Co.:
builds fence, 25:73, 77
restoration work of, 9:21

Woodwork Joints (Hayward): cited, 42:42 (TFH)

Woodworkers Alliance for Rainforest Protection: discussed, 65:102

Woodworkers' Store, The:
address for, 52:98, 65:74, 73:100, 79:32
reviewed, 62:51

Woodworker's Supply of New Mexico:
address for, 46:41 (REM), 75:65, 83:72
62:51

Woodwright's Companion, The (Underhill): cited, 56:14

Worden, Jon: on New American home, 28:73-77

Work belts: *See* Tool belts.

Work Right Products, Inc.: address for, 52:112

Work tree: making, 51:24

Workbenches:
for doors, 53:40, 41 (FC), 82:6
folding, trussed, 17:16
heights for, 85:81
hold-downs for, 65:30
job-site,
folding, for chopsaw, 76:30
simple, 81:28, 64-67
versatile, 11:14
wheeled, making, 69:73-74
from joint-compound buckets, 58:26, 69:32
outlets for, overhead weighted, 25:16
for panel cutting, 81:67
portable, 81:64, 66
reviewed, 71:94
for renovations, 12:50 (TB)
sawhorse-clamp improvised, 6:8
stance at, correct, 85:77
workpiece gripper pad for, 55:92-94

Worker's compensation: discussed, 18:16, 17

Working Knowledge (Harper): reviewed, 55:108

Key to books:

(BK)   Building Baths and Kitchens
(CBS)   Building with Concrete, Brick and Stone
(CSH)   Craftsman-Style Houses
(DWS)   Building Doors, Windows and Skylights
(EEH)   Energy-Efficient Houses
(EF)   Exterior Finishing
(FC)   Finish Carpentry
(FRC)   Frame Carpentry
(FWS)   Building Floors, Walls and Stairs
(MFC)   More Frame Carpentry
(REM)   Remodeling
(SH)   Small Houses
(TB)   Tools for Building
(TFH)   Timber-Frame Houses

Workmate folding tables:
mentioned, 12:50 (TB)
as miter-saw stands, 20:4-6

Works, Gloice: on owner-building, 5:14

Workshops:
air dome, over building site, 51:120
belvedered Victorian, 43:68-71 (TB)
cylindrical shingled, 8:75
dust collection for, 60:60-62
on exterior-grid plan, 43:74 (SH)
filter fans for, 48:24
/house combination, 73:76-81
job-site, 1:22-23, 29:57 (CSH, TB)
shack for, 21:44-45 (TB)
warehouse, 44:46-47 (TB)
mobile,
building, 8:58-59 (TB)
in custom trailer, 70:132
nonskid surfaces for, epoxied, 70:48, 49
portable, 27:96
space for, creating, 53:43-45 (SH)
storage for, dental-chest, 54:24-26
timber-framed, 1:19-21 (TFH)
book on, 27:84
two-story snow-proof, 44:63
Velcro ties for, 81:28
work tree for, 51:24

Worman, John: on Japanese museum, 62:128

Wray, William O.: color studies of, 2:6

Wrecking bars:
double-headed, 32:53, 54, 55 (TB)
mattock as, 2:10
for nail pulling, 32:53, 55, 32:53 (TB)
pipe, making, 2:10
source for, 32:55 (TB)
for trim removal, 19:36 (DWS)

Wrenches:
aluminum, 12:51 (TB)
socket extension for, quick, 60:28

Wright, David: mentioned, 8:38 (EEH)

Wright, Frank Lloyd:
on architects, 38:104
books on, 3:27, 34:92, 45:122, 50:108, 69:57
concrete-block use of, 14:70, 16:4-6
Dow adaptations of, 10:20
exhibit on, 47:102-10
Fallingwater by, analyzed, 32:29-30 (FRC)
finish mixture by, 20:78
fireplace of, 3:21, 25
Foundation of, Taliesin tours by, 82:106
foundations by, 3:22
foundations of, rubble-trench, 18:66 (CBS)
Fountainhead by, 12:27-33, 14:4
furniture by, 12:28
gate by, 25:80
heating systems of, 3:23
Hollyhock house by, 16:4
house after, 45:54-59, 73:42-45 (EEH)
Jacobs I house by, restoring, 81:78-82
Jacobs II house by, 3:20-27 (erratum, 4:4), 5:4
and John Lautner, 18:26
John Storer house by, 16:4
La Miniatura by, 16:4-6
light fixture by, 61:86
Little house by, reassembly of, 20:73-79
mentioned, 9:68
and Mike Wallace, 38:106
Muirhead house by, 3:22
Natural House, The, 16:4, 18:66 (CBS)
Newsletter, 3:27
Oak Park by,
book on, 56:82
restoration of, 56:82-87
Olive Hill buildings of, 4:30
and organic architecture, 38:104
Pfeiffer house by, 38:104
Pottery House by, 41:26-31
and Richard Neutra, 19:29
and Rudolph Schindler, 4:26, 30
seminars on, 38:102-106
on style, 12:4
unbuilt houses of, book on, 41:31
Unitarian church by, 3:22
and Usonian community, 66:26-28
Usonian concept of, 3:20-21
Usonian house by, public, 65:100
Usonian, houses after, 66:56-59 (SH), 80:46-49
See also Oak Park Studio (Wright).

Wright, Lloyd:
block use of, 16:4-6
furniture by, 14:68-69
Sowden House by, 14:1, 66-73, 84

Wright (P. M.) Ltd.: heat-recovery ventilators, 34:34 (DWS)

Wrought iron: *See* Ironwork.

Wunsch, Steve: teaches housing classes, 29:88-89

Wynn, Scott:
    cabinet by, 3:67
    on hand planes, 76:80-85 (FC)
    hangs doors, 74:64-65 (FC)
    on inglenook, 69:82-87
Wyoming: heat-pump water-heater policy
    in, 5:65

X-acto Co.: razor knife blades of, 22:51
    (FRC)
Xetex, Inc.: heat-recovery ventilators,
    34:34 (DWS)

Yagi, Koji: *Japanese Touch for Your House,*
    A, reviewed, 19:26
Yale, Linus: pin-tumbler cylinders of,
    48:63 (FC, MFC)
Yanda, Bill and Susan: on solar
    greenhouses, 10:17-18
Yanda, Susan, and Delores Wolfe:
    Growing Food in Solar Greenhouses,
    10:17
Yanev, Peter: *Peace of Mind in Earthquake*
    Country, 29:38 (FRC)
Yankee, Mark: toolbox of, 74:87
Yankee windows: casement windows,
    custom, 38:75 (TFH)
Yates, Richard:
    house by, 34:37, 38-39
    mentioned, 28:81
Yellow poplar *(Liriodendron*
    tulipifera):
    exterior use of, 82:4-6
    for framing, 25:10-12
    hardness group of, 40:69 (FRC)
    qualities of, 5:10, 25:10
    range of, 28:4
    for siding, 55:59
    for timber framing, 7:6
Yemen: traditional housing in, 49:100, 102
Yeskoo, Richard C.: on wine cellar, 48:58-
    60
Ying Mfg. Corp.: phase-change systems,
    10:18
York Spiral Stair: address for, 77:54
You Can Build It: source for, 23:48
Young, Bill:
    on job-site shack, 21:44-45 (TB)
    on plunge-router stairs, 28:38-41 (FWS)
Young, Blaine: house by, 48:32-36

Young, Juliana: sconces by, 30:70-71
Young, Larry S.:
    on chainsaws, 61:81-85
    on chinkless log building, 53:80-84
Young, Regan: mentioned, 45:130
Youngquist, W. G., and H. O. Fleischer:
    Wood in American Life, reviewed, 54:106
Your Engineered House (Roberts):
    cost of building, as discussed in, 30:4
    mentioned, 28:68, 69, 72
    See also Rex Roberts house.
Your Home and Your Health: mentioned,
    49:6
Youth Work, Inc.: discussed, 79:112
Yunker Industries: address for, 68:64

Zaleski Snow Guards and Roofing:
    address for, 53:18
Zander, Peter: on church conversion,
    13:67-71
Zar, Angela Marie: on renovation, 7:50-51
Zatz, David: on design, 8:25 (CBS)
Zdepski, M. Stephen: on solar cube,
    34:24-29 (DWS)
Zee Medical, Inc.: address for, 58:90, 72:90
Zeluck (J.) Inc.:
    address for, 76:75 (FC)
    small-pane insulated glass, 40:86
Zelver, Michael:
    renovates cottage, 28:49-53 (FWS)
    shop of, 43:68-71 (TB)
Zepp, Donald E.: on squares, 75:50-51
    (MFC)
Zero Weatherstripping Co., Inc.: address
    for, 58:57
Zetex fire-resistant material: source for,
    24:82
Zimmerman, Paul: compound-curve sills
    by, 7:18, 19 (FRC)
Zinc:
    alloy, as roofing, 24:42, 44
    corrosion with, 24:44, 46, 62:65, 66, 67
    nobility of, 21:4
    as roofing, 24:44
    source for, 24:44
Zinc-Clad 5 paint: source for, 29:74
Zink, Bill:
    house by, 30:4
    How to Build a House Simply, source for,
    28:68
Zip Penn: chainsaw equipment from, 7:31
Zircon International, Inc.: Anglesensor
    levels, 44:89
Zircon Water Levels: address for, 85:60
Zomehouse: described, 26:52-57

Zomeworks Corp.:
    address for, 58:84 (EEH), 68:54
    described, 26:56
Zoning ordinances:
    defined, 5:43
    for subdivision, 5:43-44
    working around, 38:55-56
    See also Building codes.
Zonolite insulation: with block, 31:38, 41
    (CBS)
Zook, Wayne H.: on cost estimating, 4:10,
    42-43
Zuckerman, Seth: *Saving Our Ancient*
    Forests, reviewed, 75:110
Zuker, Gary: house by, 83:88-89
Zummwalt, Robert: cabinets by, 7:23 (BK)
Zurawski, Edwin:
    on central vacuum systems, 60:60-62
    on framing math, 36:62-63 (FRC)
    reviews carpet padding, 54:92-94
Zwieg, Peter: Los Angeles exhibit by,
    20:22

 February/March 1981

Staircase Renovation Joseph Kitchel
Solo Timber Raising Ross Kirk
On-Site Shop Sam Clark
Four Elements of Designing William S. Cope
Site-Built Solar Collectors Glenn Tucker
Gentle Stripping Lowell Northrop
Venting the Plumbing System Michael Litchfield
Molding and Casting Materials John Todaro
Peaking Over a Flat Roof Max Jacobson and Murray Silverstein
Massive Passive
A Greek Revival Restoration Gregory Schipa
Redwood Classic Roger Barnes
Building by the Book Donna Richards

2 April/May 1981

Restoring a Porch Roy F. Cole, Jr.
Bernard Maybeck's Wallen II House Thomas Gordon Smith
A Large House on a Limited Budget Donald McNeice
Passive Cooling Chuck Mitchell and Tom Barr
Waterproofing Earth-Sheltered Houses Charles A. Lane
Round-Log Construction Alasdair G. B. Wallace
Upgrading Your Electrical Service William Whitney
The Point of Repointing Richard T. Kreh
Table-Saw Molding Bruce Andrews
Hands-On Down East Mark Alvarez
Custom Kitchen Planning Matthew Kaplan
Sculptural Studio Addition Bart Prince

3 June/July 1981

Formal Entryway Sam Bush
Landscaping for Energy Efficiency Hugh Williamson
Frank Lloyd Wright's Jacobs II House Thomas A. Heinz
Form-Based Stone Masonry Richard MacMath
On-Site Carpentry with a Circular Saw Jud Peake
The Septic Tank Revealed John Wetzler
Rumfordizing Brick by Brick Kent Burdett
A Matrix of Design Variables William S. Cope
Hybrid Trombe Wall Additions Gerald L. Weaver
Passive Solar Thermosiphon Stephen Lasar
Rebuilding a Modern House Kenneth Lelen
Florida Cracker House Mark Alvarez

4 August/September 1981

Rebuilding a Fire-Damaged House Louis S. DiGaetano and Kathleen Haugh
Tools for Timber Framing Edward M. Levin
R.M. Schindler's Kings Road House Murray Silverstein
Capping a Foundation Roger Allen
Renovating a Chimney Joseph Kitchel
Estimating Construction Costs Wayne H. Zook
Framing an Open-Plan Saltbox Pat and Patsy Hennin
Distributing Greenhouse Heat Glenn Tucker
A Modular Home Chuck Miller

 October/November 1981

Moving a House Tim Snyder
Rebuilding an Addition Nelson Denny
Making Curvilinear Sash Norman Vandal
Bow-Cot and the Honeymoon Cottage Daniel A. Levy
Restoring Brownstone Facades Sarah Latham
Wood Foundations Irwin L. and Diane L. Post
Understanding Building Regulations Edmund Vitale, Jr.
Ageless Adobe Myrtle Stedman
Solar Site Evaluation Daniel K. Reif
Truss Frame Construction Mark White

6 December 1981/January 1982

Cooperative Craftsmanship Ben Tarcher
Classical Style in a Porch Addition Ted Ewen
Contracting Your Home Charley Huddleston
Fonthill Roger Barnes
Trouble Spots in 19th-Century Framing Dan Desmond
Ground-Fault Protection Joseph H. Foley
Rhode Island Stone-Ender Roger Schroeder
House of Steel and Salvage Stephen Suddarth
Home Access for the Handicapped Barbara Winslow
Keeping Termites Out of Your Home
N62FL-Airplane House Steve Badanes

7 February/March 1982

Building a Curved Wall Paul Spring, Rick Harper and Malcolm McDaniel
Shaping Compound-Curved Sills Phil Zimmerman
Expanding a Kitchen, Step by Step Eric K. Rekdahl
Sizing Roughsawn Joists and Beams Ed Levin
An Island Retreat David K. Ford
Batten Doors Bruce Gordon
Earth Shelter on Cape Cod Malcolm Wells
Working with Green Wood Paul Hanke
Buying Green Lumber Paul Fuge
Tax Shelters Tim Matson
Getting a Building Permit Edmond Vitale, Jr.
A Russian Fireplace Paul Lang
A New Facade Angela Marie Zar
Attic Venting William R. Wheeler
A Silo House Karla Kavanaugh

8 April/May 1982

Sticks and Stones Sebastian Eggert
Hung Walls Pat Hennin
Raising Heavy Timber Trey Loy
Hanging an Exterior Door Jared Emery
Three Sides to the Sun Wink Davis
Installing Fixed Glass Windows Dale McCormick
Electrical Outlet Boxes W. Creighton Schwan
A Solar-Powered Cabin Al Simpler
Green-Wood Woes Richard Cobos
The Scribed Ellipse Jud Peake
Drywall Bob Syvanen
A Mobile Workshop Cy Westlake
Sidewall Shingling Tim Snyder
A Modern Mississippi House Robert M. Ford

9 June/July 1982

Restoring a Grand Victorian Porch David Stenstrom
Octagon House Tim Snyder
Adding Up Eric K. Rekdahl
The Kitchen Cabinet Will Hasson
Counter Intelligence Jesus Granado
Permanent Campsite Jeff Gold and Bruce Boyd
Flashing Bob Syvanen
Toenailing Albert Treadwell
Laying Brick Arches Elizabeth Holland
The Superinsulated House John R. Hughes
Outside Circular Stairway Tom Law
Unifying Site and Structure Charles F. Johnson

10 August/September 1982

Alden Dow's Studio and Residence Tim Snyder
Choosing the Right Roof Max Jacobson, Murray Silverstein and
    Barbara Winslow
Acrylic Glazing Elizabeth Holland
Cabin Cellar Tim Matson
A Mill for the Chainsaw Will Malloff
Timbers and Templates Mark Songey
Soldering Copper Pipe Niles T. Powell
Renovating a Carriage Barn Craig F. Stead
Making an Insulated Door Irwin L. Post
A Small House to Work In Rosalyn Gerstein
Underground Cistern Roy McCollum
The Rafter Square Jud Peake
Roof Framing Simplified Tom Law
Putting the Lid On Don Dunkley

11 October/November 1982

Rammed Earth Magnus Berglund
Site Layout Tom Law
In the Solar Vanguard Helen J. Kessler
The Architecture of Arthur Brown Paul Spring
Connecticut River Valley Entrance Gregory Schipa
A Little Place in the City Chuck Miller
The Thin-Mass House Max Jacobson
Barn House Alan Moyler
High-Country Studio and Residence Bart Prince
Installing a Factory-Built Skylight Jim Picton
Site-Built, Fixed-Glass Skylights Stephen Lasar
Flashing a Curb Jim Picton
Double-Envelope Addition Charlie Boldrick

12 December 1982/January 1983

An Introduction to Timber Framing Tedd Benson
Restoring Fountainhead Tim Snyder
Surface-bonded Block Paul Hanke
Refining Your Designs Herb Greene
Rock-Bottom Remodel Ira Kurlander
Transforming an Iowa Farmhouse Arvid Osterberg
The Renovator's Tool Kit Craig F. Stead
Roof Shingling Bob Syvanen
The Deck Upstairs Dan Rockhill
Curved Doors Thomas Duffy
Shingle Solar Jeffrey Ellis
Houseboat Jake Ehlers

13 February/March 1983

The Fairbanks House Ed Levin
Concrete Trey Loy
Figuring and Ordering Ready-Mix Paul Spring
Facing a Block Wall With Stone Tim Snyder
Opening Up the Attic Ira Kushner
Hardwood Strip Flooring Don Bollinger
Greenhouse Shutters Stan Griskivich
Building with Ferro-Cement Jane Speiser
Appalachian Axman's Art Drew Langsner
Bathroom Built-Ins Rob Hunt and Robert Robertson
Small House in Virginia Bruce Gordon
Church Revival Peter Zander

14 April/May 1983

Victorian Addition Steve Larson
Curved-Truss House Tim Snyder
Gaslight Tim Matson
Putting Down a Brick Floor Bob Syvanen
Shelter from the Storm Brian Berkey
Treehouse Alfred Wells
Portable Power Planes Geoff Alexander
Log-Cabin Legacy Richard Woodward
Log-Building to Last Alasdair G. B. Wallace
Designing a Functional Kitchen Sam Clark
Floor Sanding Don Bollinger
Porch Ornamentation Betsy Levine
Keeping It Simple Kirby White
Lloyd Wright's Sowden House John Beach

15 June/ July 1983

Steep-Site Solution Charles Miller
Pole House in the Treetops Thomas B. Moore
Pressure-Treated Poles Kenneth E. Jurgens
Cornice Construction Bob Syvanen
Cottage Sunspace William Stokes
Building a Block Foundation Dick Kreh
Nail Guns Angelo Margolis
Toward the Right Light Bart Smyth
Keeping Out the Cold Brian Toller
The Architect as Builder Lasse Jaakola
Smokehouse Edward Nichols
Hydro-Power on a Small Scale David Warren
Storage Stair Tom Bender
Veneer Plaster Tim Snyder
Handcrafted in Stone and Wood Philip S. Sollman

16 August/ September 1983

A Slice off the Cube Tim Snyder
Foundations on Hillside Sites Ronald J. Barr
A Pier and Grade-Beam Foundation Michael Spexarth
Timber-Frame Layout Tedd Benson
Decorative Ironwork Rachel Carley
Reciprocating Saws Craig Stead
Underground Retreat Elizabeth Holland
Dry-Stack Block Rob Thallon
At the Top of the Mountain Paul Spring
Stripping Trim Mark Alvarez
Building a Helical Stair Rick Barlow
Sculpted Stairway Jody Norskog

17 October/November 1983

Resurrecting the Bolton House Ken Ross
Building Louvered Shutters Rob Hunt
Above the Flood Brent Smith
Making Counterbalanced Shutters Brent Smith
Wrought Iron Terry Steel
Remodel Plumbing Steve Larson
Designing and Building Stairs Bob Syvanen
A Glossary of Stair Terms Paul Spring
Southwest Sunspace Valerie Walsh
Random-Fitted Panels Fletcher Cox
Laying a Tile Floor Michael Byrne
Ceramic Tiles Charles Miller
Skidompha House David Sellers

18 December 1983/January 1984

John Lautner's Mauer House Alan Hess
Insulating and Parging Foundations Bob Syvanen
Curbless Skylights Rob Thallon
Teton Remodel Bill Phelps
A House of Stone and Clay Magnus Berglund
Octagonal Spiral Stairs Tom Dahlke
Patterning Shingling Jake Ehlers
On the Edge John Lively
The Stonemasons of Pueblo Bonito James Udall
Rubble-Trench Foundations Elias Velonis
Round House Tim Snyder
Making Window Sash John Leeke

19 February/March 1984

Neutra's All-Plywood House Thomas S. Hines
Replacing an Oak Sill Stephen Sewall
Japanese-Style Bath House Kip Mesirow
Power Miter Saws Geoff Alexander
Garage Remodel Mark Alvarez
Raised-Panel Wainscot T. F. Smolen
Modified Wainscot Design Michael Volechenisky
Floor Framing Don Dunkley
Bridging Midspans Paul Spring
Designing for a Temperate Climate William Bechhoefer
The Vapor Barrier Dan Desmond
Superinsulating the Non-Box Ed McGrath
House in the Boulders Betsy Levine

20 April/May 1984

Briarcombe Jeff Morse
Retrofit Superinsulation John R. Hughes
Roofing with Slate David Heim
Converting a Store and Stable Robert Hare
Ticksticking Sam Clark
Concrete Spiral Staircase Dennis Allen
Building a Fireplace Bob Syvanen
Period Moldings Norman L. Vandal
Arched A-Frame Frank Cawley
Handsaws Tom Law
Frank Lloyd Wright Comes to the Met Thomas Harboe and Vincent Lepre

21 June/July 1984

Attic Remodel Glen Jarvis
Powder-Actuated Tools Steve Larson
Wharton Esherick's House and Studio Charles Miller
Job-Site Shack Bill Young
The Fireplace Chimney Bob Syvanen
Ridge-Vent Options Doug Amsbury, Eric Rekdahl
Architectural Stained Glass Jim Furman
A Little House with a Big View Bill Phelps
Climate and Energy-Efficient Design Charles Lane
A Stone Cookstove and Heater Jonathan von Ranson
Rustic Shelter D. Robinson, D. Rosen and A. Jaroslow
Laying Out for Framing Jud Peake

22 August/September 1984

Lustron Tim Snyder
Stud-Wall Framing Paul Spring
Rescuing an Old Adobe Paul G. McHenry, Jr.
Installing a Sheet-Vinyl Floor Terry Shrode
Making a Structural Model Mark Feirer
Greene and Greene Revival John Lively
About the Business of Building Sam Clark
A Remodeled Bath Dennis Allen
Radiant-Floor Heating Dennis Adelman
Thatching Alasdair G. B. Wallace

23 October/November 1984

O'Neil Ford's Boveda House Gene and Mary Carolyn George
Lynn Ford, Craftsman Mary Lance
Framing Hammers Paul Spring
Leaded Glass Doug Hechter
The Double Envelope Joseph Burinsky
Information Sources for Builders Mark Feirer
Shingle Thatch Gary Cooke, Mike Lienemann and Barry Huber
Custom Wood Flooring Paul Fuge
Drywall Finishing Craig Stead
Building an Arched Dormer Bill Phelps
Plumb and Line Don Dunkley
The Plastic Castle Charles Miller

24 December 1984/January 1985

The James House Charles Miller
Site-Sharpening Saw Blades Tom Law
The Worm-Drive Saw Jim Picton
Power Saws: Rating the Ratings Paul Spring
Metal Roofing J. Azevedo
A Shed-Dormer Addition Bob Syvanen
Etched Glass Chris Denison
Enclosing the Timber Frame Jeff Arvin
How Stress-Skin Pannels are Made Tim Snyder
In the Japanese Tradition Dennis Tucker
The Balloon-Truss System John Amos
Straw-Bale Studio Gary Strang
Raised Octagon Tim Snyder

25 February/March 1985

The Nicolai Fechin House John Lively
Tiling a Mortar-Bed Counter Michael Byrne
Roll-Top House Tim Snyder
Building with Stress-Skin Alex Wade
A Dutchman's Bath Philip S. Sollman
Starting Simple Zu Vincent
Framing a Conical Roof Geoff Alexander
Humboldt House John Mahony
Shingle Sleuthing Tom Law
Plumb Bobs, String and Chalkboxes Trey Loy
Concrete-Plank Roof Clifford Hackett
Rebuilding a Federal-Period Fence Stephen Sewall and David Stenstrom

26 April/May 1985

Hanging Interior Doors Tom Law
Rehabilitating a Duplex Rich Lopez
Kitchen Conversion Howard Katz
A Personal Library David Gerstel
Rebuilding a Mudéjar Ceiling Logan Wagner
New Balustrade, New Stairway Bob Syvanen
Chinking Log Walls Charles McRaven
Chinking Formulas Richard Woodward
Zomehouse Jeffrey Cook
Drafting Tools Eric Rekdahl
Stepped Foundations Michael Spexarth
Home Heating with a Heat Pump Jack Horst
Maine Stonework Jeff Gammelin
A Compact Passive-Solar House Dan Rockhill

27 June/July1985

Charles Warren Callister's Onslow-Ford House Alan Hess
The Art and Science of Estimating Sal Alfano
Routers Craig Savage
Dummy Rafter Tails Bob Syvanen
Corian Kitchen Countertops Michael O'Hare
New Life for a Tract House Nancy Clark
Designing for Remodels Will Bruder
The Outdoor Finish William Feist
Soil-Cement Tile Floor Magnus Berglund
Making Wooden Light Fixtures John Birchard
The Structural Stone Wall Stephen Kennedy
Warm Floors Michael Luttrell
Country House and Studio Victor Lazzaro

28 August/September 1985

Moving into the Attic Alasdair G. B. Wallace
Roofing Framing Revisited Scott McBride
Plunge-Router Stairs Bill Young
The Sears Pre-Cut Tim Snyder
Movable Insulation for Skylights Larry Medinger
A Revamped Victorian Barry Schwartz
Drawing Up a Contract Sal Alfano
A Carved Timber Frame William R. Cadley
Sidewall Shingling Bob Syvanen
Building a Rex Roberts House Magnus Berglund
The New American Home Jon Worden

29 October/November 1985

Jersey Devil's Hill House Steve Badanes
Seismic Retrofits David Benaroya Helfant
The Carpenter's Toolbox Tom Law
Deck Design Scott Grove
The American Porch Davida Rochlin
Drainage Systems George Skaates
Craftsman Remodel Peter Malakoff
Greek Revival Townhouse Peter Strasser, Vincent Lepre
  and Jim Boorstein
Energy Detailing Daniel Hill
A Tidewater House Tim Snyder

30 December 1985/January 1986

Jack Hillmer's Ludekens House Alan Hess
Parallel-Chord Floor Trusses E. Kurt Albaugh
The Rondavel Mary Ann Snieckus
Ranch Redress Tim Snyder
Rounded Solar Adobe Neal Bloomfield
Rebuilding a Victorian Bell Tower Al DeDominicis
Busting Shingles Drew Langsner
An AirCore Floor Bill Phelps
Casing a Door Bob Syvanen
The Flush-Fit Cabinet Paul Levine
Design for Living Lena Lawrence
A Concrete Belvedere Dan Rockhill

31 February/March 1986

Craftsman-Style Beach House Tim Andersen
Hinge Butt Mortising Templates Stephen Suddarth
A Slice and Stretch Addition Judith M. Capen and Robert A. Weinstein
Radially Sawn Clapboards Tod Cheney
Insulated Masonry Walls Bion D. Howard
Musings of a Maine Architect Jacqueline M. Michaud
Trimming Out the Main House Rick Wachs
Working with a Lumberyard Doug Ferrell
Sod Houses Andrew Gulliford
Two-Coat Plaster James Servais
Manhattan Penthouse Elizabeth Holland
Victorian Modern Mark Feirer

32 April/May 1986

Northern Prairie House John Patkau
Building Basics Thomas Koontz
Octagonal Orchid House Robert Skydell
Infill House with a View Charles Miller
Mudrooms Tim Matson
A Mortar-Bed Shower Michael Byrne
On Pulling Nails Gene Schnaser
Lessons Learned at the Clapp House Joe Sherman
Frank Lloyd Wright's Oak Park Studio Don Kalec and Amy Abernathy
Light-Gauge Steel Framing Steve Mead
Reconstructing a Log House Jeff Haegler

33 June/July 1986

James Fitzgibbon's Daniel House Peter Calandruccio
Building a Concrete Bulkhead Will Rainey
Sunspaces Richard MacMath
Laying a Plank Floor Paul Hanke
Building Timber Bowstring Trusses Glenn Reynolds
The Covered Bridge Cottage Richard Robertson
Casing a Double-Hung Window Bob Syvanen
Home Energy Myths Dan Desmond
Jigsaws Craig Savage
Grand Chaquard Robert L. Vargas
Brick Floors Douglas Ring
Tom's Wonder Building Dan Rockhill

34 August/September 1986

Solar Cube M. Stephen Zdepski
Heat-Recovery Ventilators John R. Hughs
Rammed-Earth Portfolio Magnus Berglund
Installing Baseboard Bob Syvanen
On Screw Guns and Screws M. F. Marti
Scribe-Fitting a Log House Robert W. Chambers
Job-Site Safety Mark Feirer
A Domed Octagon John Thorndike
Gourmet Kitchen Remodel Valerie Walsh
A Superinsulated Saltbox Howard Faulkner
Monsanto House of the Future Alan Hess

35 October/ November 1986

Eurostyle Rustic Graeme Means
From Boulders to Building Blocks Charles Miller
Cordless Drills Bill Phelps
Accessible Kitchen Remodel Sam Clark
Shed-Dormer Retrofit Scott McBride
Building a Sauna Ric Hanisch
Power Tools and the Timber-Frame Revival John Lively
Soundproofing a Music Studio Gene De Smidt
Microcomputers for Builders William Oberschulte
Carpentry Texts Tom Law
Victorian Brackets Simon Watts
The Bench Spiral Boh Helliwell
Building a Cantilevered-Tread Spiral Staircase John Grunwald

36 December 1986/January 1987

Craftsman Houses John Lively
K'ang Jeffrey J. Smith
Scaffolding Scott McBride
A Breath of Fresh Air Alasdair G.B. Wallace
Swedish Floor Finish Don Bollinger
The Tidewater Timber Frame Gary Revel, Ryan Revel and Brent Clark
Another Framer Turns to Power Tools Stan Lesser
Working with *A Pattern Language* Rob Thallon and David Edrington
Traditional Stairways Off the Shelf Kevin Ireton
Framing with Trigonometry Edwin Zurawski
Mosaic Tile William Palanza
Half-Moon Bath Marg Shand and Harold Sandstrom
Hill-Country Hideout Peter Willcox

37 February/March 1987

High-Style Asceticism Craig Savage
Newport Stairway Reproduction Dale Nelson
A Room of My Own Zu Vincent
Levels and Transits Stephen Suddarth
Installing Glass Block Michael Byrne
Building a Glass-Block Stair Tower Ronald W. Haase
The Montauk Association Houses Tim Snyder
Stanford White: Architect, Impresario, Voluptuary
The Best Little Stone Business Near Houston Mark Feirer
A Limestone Primer Bill McDonald
The Oregon Field Test Jim Maloney
Decking and Sheathing Jud Peake
Homework in the Ozarks S. Downen, S. Koehn, D. Pierce and D. Rantis

38 Spring 1987

On the Mountainside A. J. Davis
An Angular Solution John and Sandra Larson
Good and Small Sallie Hood and Ron Sakal
By the Sea Gunnar Hansen
A New View Sudi Scull
Putting *A Pattern Language* to Work Dale Mulfinger
Amtrak House Earl P. Carlin
Facade Roof Dean Jones
Medina River Ranch Eugene George
Woodstock House Peter S. Brock
Hawaiian Retreat Charles Miller
Prairie Formality William Tabberson

39 April/May 1987

Homestead House Eric Rekdahl
A Family Affair Ruth Glick
Roughing in the Drain Lines George Skaates
A Capitol Hill Townhouse Judith M. Capen and Robert A. Weinstein
Particleboard as a Flooring Material Howard Frank Itzkowitz
Installing Manufactured Stair Parts Sebastian Eggert
Earth and Sky Brian Lockhart
A Rambling Deck Christopher Grover
Stoneoak Jonathan von Ranson
The Classic "Tin" Lid Matt Holmstrom
Curved-Roof Bungalow Bonnie Cullen
Norman Carver's Folkhouse Mark Feirer
The Promise of Modern Architecture Norman F. Carver, Jr.
Island City Woodworks John Lively

40 June/July 1987

Light from Within Tim Snyder
Molding Character Douglas Honychurch
Earl Covey, Adirondack Builder John E. Barrows
Earthquake-Country Timber Frame Jeff Arvin
Earthquakes and the Richter Scale Paul Beatty
Laying Flagstone Walks Joe Kenlan
Swedish Prefab Houses Craig Savage
John Winnie Restored Alex Wade
Gunite Retaining Wall Ken Hughes
Kitchen Overhaul Gillian Servais
The Engineered Nail Edward Allen
Southern Comfort Ted Hutton

41 August/September 1987

Pottery House Charles Miller
Architectural Models Dan Rockhill
Desert Greenhouse Les Wallach
Screen-Porch Windows Douglass Ferrell
Tradition and Innovation Max Jacobson
Chainsaw Mill Harold Sandstrom and Marg Shand
Concrete and Masonry Fasteners Kevin Ireton
Pickup-Truck Tool Storage Ray Lincoln
Framing Doghouse Dormers Scott McBride
An Estate in Bonny Doon Eric Hoffman
Architectural Ceramics Peter King

42 October/November 1987

A Craftsman-Style Renovation Eric Woodward
Art-Glass Door and Window Bob Berg
A Sound Deck Elizabeth Martin
Cruck House Jack Sobon
Double-Helix Stair Robin Ferguson
Raven Hill Baylor H. Trapnell
Spray-Painting Trim Byron Papa
Mandating Energy Efficiency Gerry Copeland
Tool Pouches Douglass Ferrell
Masonry Heater Hybrid G. Karl Marcus
Thomas Jefferson's Poplar Forest E. Kurt Albaugh

43 December 1987/January 1988

Adapting the Japanese House Len Brackett
Three Custom Stairbuilders Kevin Ireton
Ornamental Plaster in England Donald E. Wahlberg
Metal Connectors for Wood Framing Bruce R. Berg
Bricklaying Basics Dick Kreh
Sawhorse Tom Law
Converting the Forge Grahame Collyer
Drafting Basics Bob Syvanen
Backyard Shop Charles Miller
House in the Woods Howard Katz
South of Denver Lee Moller

44 February/March 1988

Stemwall Foundations Dan Rockhill
Vacation Cabin Bill Phelps
Residential Fire Sprinklers Steve Mead
Organizing the Project David Gerstel
Better Home and Garden Ann Christoph
Repairing Old Stonework Stephen Kennedy
Cape Breton Roundhouse John Kerr
Up in the Sierra Bruce Greenlaw
Tying a Bow to an Eyebrow Joseph Wood and Robert Caine
European Cabinet Hardware Paul Levine
From Eyesore to Asset George Nash
Geometry in the Green Mountains Eliot Warren Goldstein

45 Spring 1988

A Sense of Scale Kem Gardner Hinton
Sketches of Spain Rodger Whipple
A Timber Frame in the Hudson Valley William Webster
A View Of the Redwoods Charles Miller
Along the Edge John Calvin Womack
Small House in Ski Country Graeme Means
A House for Joanna Donald Sunshine
Eastern Details, Western Framing Douglas Hamilton
Pool House Stephen Lasar
Mermaid Hill Herman Hassinger

46 April/May 1988

The Farnsworth House Revisited David Spaeth
Found Horizon Philip S. Sollman
Deca Dome Eric Lipson
Blowing Hot Air Jay Stein
Pennsylvania Snowbelt House Scott McArthur
Installing a Toilet George Skaates
Telecommunication for Builders Craig Savage
Mountain Passive Robert McGahey
A Deck Built to Last R. W. Missell
Allergy Free in Ottawa John R. Hughes
A Gazebo Showerhouse Charles Ballinger
A Tale of Two Systems Kevin Ireton
Island Victorian Don Price

47 June/July 1988

From Forest to Grade Stamp Charles Miller
A Hip-Roofed Timber Frame Christopher Hyde
Siding with Clapboards Bob Syvanen
Wiring in Stress-Skin Panels Jeff Arvin
Tudor Hardtop Dan Rockhill
Chimney Cricket Scott McBride
Carving Cabinets Thomas H. Williams
Running the Company David Gerstel
Finish Nailers Craig Savage
Arboreal Stairway Steven Spiro
Capital Gains Edward S. Fleming, Jr.
The Caretaker House Paul Hanke

48 August/September 1988

Casa Paloma Charles Miller
A Hollow-Post Spiral Stair Peter Lucchesi III
Circular Trim Saws Bruce Greenlaw
Curved Timber Ed Levin
Blue Heron House Ted P. Lehn
Hatch on Wheels Curtis Rindlaub
Building a Wine Cellar Richard C. Yeskoo
Door Hardware Kevin Ireton
Cracked Foundations Kip Park
Victorian Log Studio Peter Lauritzen
Clear Finishes Byron Papa
House in the Catskills Marlys Hann

49 October/November 1988

Saving the Old Daggett Place Kevin Ireton
Teak Arbor and Gate Mark White
Low-Cost Computer-Aided Design David Stovall
Framing with the Plumber in Mind Peter Hemp
Guidelines for Laying Stone Walls Joseph Kenlan
Farmhouse Remodel Sherril Santo
Installing a Plank Floor Don Bollinger
The Cotswold Slat Roof Alasdair G. B. Wallace
Raised in Florida Herb Beatty
A Builder's Liability Roslyn G. Pollack
A Staircase Comes out of the Closet Miles Karpilow
Caulk-Free Corners David Marshall
Portable Air Compressors Drew Wiley

50 December 1988/January 1989

Laminated-Veneer Lumber Mark Feirer
Ferrocement Home Office Berry Langford
Shop-Built Drywall Lift Tim Hanson
House in the Caribbean Michael S. Kollman
Notes from a Building Inspector Steven R. Fredrickson
Out in the Cold Scott Schuttner
Restoring the Shelburne House Joe Sherman
Cranking Out Casements Scott McBride
Laying Up Brick Bovedas E. Logan Wagner
A Modest Studio on the Maine Coast Jane Lamb
Foundation Drainage David Benaroya Helfant
Gypsy Wagon Daniel Wing

51 February/March 1989

A Craftsman Studio Charles Miller
Materials in Cold Weather Scott Schuttner
A Traditional Finnish Sauna Stanley Joseph
Building a Winding Outdoor Stair Thor Matteson
Two-Story Summer Addition Daryl E. Hansen
Hand-Formed Ceramic Sinks Paul Schneider
Timber, Plaster and Granite David Stark Wilson
Installing Crown Molding Tom Law
Building a Slip-Form Wall Doug Miller
Linear Solar House Don Parker
Building Fixed-Glass Windows Jay Chesavage and Steven Tyler
Building Barrel Vaults Gerry Copeland and Lamar Henderson

52 Spring 1989

San Juan Island Cabin Jeffrey Prentiss
Steamboat House Joanne Kellar Bouknight
Tudor Timber Frame Eric Rekdahl and Joe Wilkinson
Down-East Shingle J. Thomas Reardon
The Art of Workmanship Llewellyn Seibold
A Companionable Prairie Home Sarah Susanka
Space-Age Cracker Style Steve Badanes
The House under the Garden Charles Miller
Mullgardt Rescue William Dutcher
Natural Selections Kim Tanzer

53 April/May 1989

Production-Line Jamb Setting and Door Hanging Larry Haun
Building a Multi-Purpose Room Louaine Collier Elke
The Honda House James Servais
A History of Brick Manufacturing Kevin Anderson
Singular Details Scott McBride
Table-Saw Tools M. Felix Marti
Two Hundred Years of the Australian Verandah Brooks Heard
A Barrier-Free House Ralph Rigger
An Automated Home System Jay Stein
Replacing Rotted Sills George Nash
Chinkless Log-Building Larry S. Young
Stock House Plans Joanne Kellar Bouknight

54 June/July 1989

The Hill House Charles Miller
Decorative Sidewall Shingles Dave Skilton
Installing a Dishwasher Peter Hemp
A Guide to Fluorescent Lighting Clay Belcher
Building a Federal-Style Mantel Stephen Sewall
Building on a Barrier Island Michael R. Thomas
Pocket Doors Kevin Ireton
About Old Pocket Doors James Boorstein
A Greek Revival Addition Joseph Beals
Carving Limestone Dan Pickens
Portable Power Planes Hugh Foster
Backyard Spiral Richard Norgard
Cobblestone Cottage Don Price

55 August/September 1989

Router Control Jud Peake
Canadian Retreat Kip Park
A Site-Built Ridge Skylight David K. Gately
Molder-Planers Bruce Greenlaw
A Well-Engineered House William E. Burdick
Circular-Stair Retrofit John Alexander
Curing Concrete Bruce A. Suprenant
Ranch-House Add-Up April Tome and Peter Siegrist
Two Houses by Harwell Hamilton Harris Joanne Kellar Bouknight
Installing a Long-Span Header Matt Holmstrom
High-Performance Glazing Paul Fisette
Windows Into the Future Kip Park
The House on Clover Knoll Jim Picton
The Dumbwaiter Bob Williams

56 October/November 1988

Thermal Insulation Charles Miller
Making Tiles by Hand Peter King
Building for the Silver Screen Tommy Lusk
Framing Nailers Drew Wiley
White Mountain Cape John Starr
Installing Arch-Top Windows Douglas Goodale
Bungalow Transformation Paul E. Ohannesian
A Decorative Post Cap Robert Vaughan
A Cherry-Paneled Ceiling Glenn Guerra
Roofing with Sod David Easton
Restoring Wright's Oak Park Home Ann Abernathy and Len Fieroh

57 December 1989/January 1990

Ornamental Plaster Restoration David Flaharty
Razing the Roof Jon H. Thompson
Estimating and Buying Molding Craig Savage
Livable Sculpture Ashley Smith
Getting an Angle on Compound Miters David DeCristoforo
Cracker House in a Hammock Robert H. Gore
Framing with Purpleheart Dennis Darrah
Camper-Shell Toolbox Neal Bahrman
Building Wooden Screen Doors Stephen Sewall
Arbitration Andrew H. Diem
Framing a Bay Window with Irregular Hips Don Dunkley
Roofing with Asphalt Shingles Todd A. Smith

58 February/March 1990

Custom Kitchen Remodel Paul D. Voelker
Spirit Levels Dan Rockhill
Laying a Granite-Faced Wall David Tousain
Haertling's Aspen Leaf House Shelley Schlender
Quiet Please Russell DuPree
Adding a Craftsman Spa Room M. Scott Watkins
Raising Finished Walls Jean Dunbar
Built-Up Cedar Roofing Steve Dunleavy
Construction Adhesives Stephen Smulski
Framing a Second-Story Addition Alexander Brennen
Solar Adobe Benjamin T. Rogers
Vigas Bryan Waldrip

59 Spring 1990

A Modest House in Bucks Country Jeremiah Eck
A Big Barn at Big River John Birchard
Backyard Edwardian Richard Fearn
Budget Bungalow Gerry Copeland
Louisiana Country House Errol Barron
The Buzzards Bay House Peter Adrian Thomas
A Cluster of Cottages Daniel Milton Hill
Raising a House Addition Allan Shope
Resisting the Weather on the Outer Banks Frank Harmon
Laguna Beach Remodel Patrick Sheridan

60 April/May 1990

Tile Roofing J. Azevedo
An Attic Studio Apartment Robert Malone
Selecting Wood Windows Joanne Kellar Bouknight
A Slab-On-Grade Foundation for Cold Climates George Nash
Seaside Solar Peter L. Pfeiffer
Central Vacuum Systems Ed Zurawski
Sucking Up the Small Stuff Rick Stoda
Wood-Infesting Insects Phil Pellitteri
Cottage in the Cotswolds Alasdair G. B. Wallace
A Staircase of Glass and Maple Scott McBride
Decorative Painted Finishes Victor DeMasi
Marbleizing a Mantle Robert D'Angelo
Framing a Gable Roof Larry Haun

61 June/July 1990

Caulks and Sealants Bruce Greenlaw
Building a Gothic Playhouse Stephen Elkins
Replacing an Inlaid Gutter Rob Paral
A House in Friday Harbor Gordon Lagerquist
Forming Concrete Walls Arne Waldstein
Hawaiian Ohana House Sue Ellen White-Hanson
Low-Flow Toilets Amy Vickers
Restoring the East Portico of Montgomery Place Geoffrey Carter
A Study in Cherry Philip S. Sollman
Venting the Roof Kevin Ireton
Chainsaws Come out of the Woods Larry S. Young

62 August/September 1990

Painting Exteriors Robert Dufort
A Site-Built Stair Alexander Brennen
Tract-House Transformation Stan Malek
Mail-Order Tools Ron Greenman
Foam-Core Panels Steve Andrews
Manhattan Comes to Sun Valley Steve Kearns and Stephen Riley
Balloon-Framing a Rake Wall Sean Sheehan
Metal Corrosion Ana Diaz
Off-Line Electrical Systems Ezra Auerbach
Panelized Frame, Customized Finish Richard Irland
Structuring Your Business Sidney Hymes
Portable Electric Cut-Off Saws M. Scott Watkins
Header Tricks for Remodelers Roger Gwinnup

63 October/November 1990

Camino Con Corazon Steve Badanes
Framing a Cold Roof Steve Kearns
A Colonial Sampler Bruce Greenlaw
Drywall Detailing Dennis Darrah
The Heart of the House Bill Mastin
Electronic Air Cleaners David F. Menicucci
Preservative-Treated Wood Stephen Smulski
Homemade Hardware Chip Rosenblum
West Coast Overhang Don Dunkley
Matching Existing Brickwork Steven Spratt
A Survey of Sidewinders Sanford H. Wilk
Decorative Floor Inlays Don Bollinger
Airtight in Massachusetts Paul Fisette

64 December 1990/January 1991

A General Remodel and a Major Addition Scott W. Sterl
Single-Ply Roofing Harwood Loomis
Double-Hungs Restrung David Strawderman
The Sea Ranch Chapel Timothy Carpenter
Making Classical Columns Joseph Beals
Poles for Building Warren Johnson
Riding Out the Big One Ralph Gareth Gray
Working without Pain Daniel Wing
Portable Table Saws Bruce Greenlaw
Fitting in Seattle Richard Beckman
Brick-Mosaic Patios Scott Ernst
Attic Art Studio Kevin Ireton

65 February/March 1991

A Smaller House to Serve a Richer Life Ted Trinkaus
Builders' Adhesives Ross Herbertson
A Chop-Saw Workstation Scott King
Building a Timbered Ceiling George Nash
Information Resources Vincent Laurence
Putting on a Concrete-Tile Roof J. Azevedo
When Architecture Meets Energy Efficiency Marc Rosenbaum
Design Guidelines for Safe Stairs Gregory Harrison
Manufactured Kitchen Cabinets Kevin Ireton
Wooden Miter Boxes Tom Law
A Family at Home Stuart Baker
Raising an Eyebrow James Docker
A Home Library Charles Wardell

66 Spring 1991

Wisconsin Wizardry Kelly Davis
A House in Burnaby Fred Thornton Hollingsworth
A Newcomer on Grand Avenue W. Scott Neeley
Rainbow Hill James T. Hubbell
Adapting Usonian J. Stewart Roberts
New Life for the Adelman Barn Louis Mackall
Superinsulated in Idaho Jonathan Marvel
Simplicity with Style Duo Dickinson
Salvaged in Ohio Clyde R. Kennedy
Escape from Manhattan Jeffrey Dale Bianco
Desert House Les Wallach

67 April/May 1991

The Dot Houses Robert Foulkes
Replacing Rain Gutters Les Williams
Building an L-Shaped Stair Larry Haun
Radon Mitigation in Existing Homes Christopher Meehan
Performance Testing of Floor Finishes Michael W. Purser
Pueblo Modern Craig W. Murray
Coral Cabana George Brewer
Growing Up in Minnesota Steven Jantzen
Rolling Interior Latex Wall Paint Byron Papa
Recipe for a Kitchen Remodel William E. Roesner
Composition Panels Charles Wardell
Making Curved Casing Jonathan F. Shafer

68 June/July 1991

Sam Maloof's House Charles Miller
French-Door Retrofit David Strawderman
Installing a Hammer-Cut Stone Floor Paul Hollaway
Solar Hot Water For the '90s Marc Rosenbaum
Framing a Turret Addition Patrick Rabbitt
Installing Stair Skirtboards Bob Syvanen
Permanent Wood Foundations Bill Eich
Tiling a Backsplash Tom Meehan
Tassajara Makeover Gene DeSmidt
Valley Framing for Unequally Pitched Roofs George Nash
Cutting Crown Molding Stephen Nuding
Suburban Refuge Joseph G. Metzler

69 August/September 1991

An A.O.B. House Timothy Clark
Ceiling Joists for a Hip Roof Larry Haun
A Quality Deck John Baldwin
Building a Butternut Kitchen Rex Alexander
Boneyard Marble Jay Latta
Deep Foundations Alvin M. Sacks
Make Room for Trudy Don Price
An Energy-Efficient Hot Tub Ron Milner
Taking a Load Off W. Whitie Gray
Tools on Wheels William Lego, J. Azevedo, Paul Pieper and
　　　Linden Frederick
Fireplace and Chimney Codes John Lloyd
Job Closeout Stephen Mead
Baronial Inglenook Scott Wynn

70 October/November 1991

Skylights in the Eaves Anthony Simmonds
Construction Epoxies Ross Herbertson
Plate Joinery on the Job Site Kevin Ireton
Superinsulated Saltbox on the Coast of Maine Elsa Martz
Tools and Techniques for Cutting Tile Charles Wardell
Cool Details W. Scott Neeley
Maintaining a Worm-Drive Saw Terence Rucker
Railing Against the Elements Scott McBride
Swiss Chalets Drew Langsner
Relining a Chimney Brian Carter
Facelift for a Loft Richard Ayotte
A Cantilevered Kitchen Addition Robert Gleason
A Freestanding Spiral Stair Steven M. White

71 December 1991/January 1992

Expressing a Site Alfred DeVido
New Kitchen for an Old House Philip S. Sollman
Modeling Home Energy Use Marc Rosenbaum
Building a Tiled Masonry Heater Vladimir Popovac
Glue-Laminated Timbers Stephen Smulski
Sizing Up a Structural Beam Christopher DeBlois
Frugal Four-Square Fixup Linda Mason Hunter
Slate Quarrying and Shingle Manufacture Jeffrey Levine
Change Orders David Gerstel
Affordable Victorians Charles Miller
All Trussed Up Eliot Goldstein, Edwin Oribin
Plunge Routers Gregg Carlsen
Installing Two-Piece Crown Dale F. Mosher

72 February/March 1992

A Greene and Greene Restoration Charles Miller
Examining Carbide-Tipped Sawblades Sanford Wilk
Ornamental Lettering Mark Van Stone
Building Interior Doors Joseph Beals
Pop-Top Remodel Brian McMahon
Framing Headers and Corners Rob Thallon
An Aquarium Room Divider Louise Haberfeld
Wood-Destroying Fungi Terry Amburgey
Building Rake Walls Larry Haun
A Photovoltaic Test House Charles Wardell
Designing and Building Leak-Free Sloped Glazing Fred Unger
A Screened-Porch Addition Jerry Germer

73 Spring 1992

An Acadian Cottage Leslie Barry Davidson
An Arc in the Woods Charles Miller
A Small Maine House Ted Marks
In the Arts and Crafts Tradition G. Robert Parker
Elegance on a Shoestring John Brooks
Some Things Bold, Some Things Blue William Dutcher
An Environmental Showcase Kevin Ireton
House on the River Steve Taylor
Shop at Home Charles Miller
Three Simple Houses Dan Wheeler

74 April/May 1992

Strengthening Plate-to-Rafter Connections Stanley H. Niu
Understanding Color Jill Pilaroscia
Going Up Michael J. Crosbie
Site-Casting Concrete Lintels Joe Fetchko
Building Small Charles Wardell
Framing for Garage Doors Steve Riley
Sweet Teen Suite Peter James
Ordering and Installing Prehung Doors Steve Kearns
The Lookout House John S. MacDonald
Clamps on Site Felix Marti
Hybrid Cabinet Construction Jim Tolpin
Making Curved Crown Molding John La Torre, Jr.
Falling Eaves Scott McBride

75 June/July 1992

Building Coffered Ceilings Don Dunkley, Greg Lawrence and
    Jay Thomsen
Chimney with a Twist Carl Hagstrom
Big Ideas for Small Spaces Howard Katz
Updating the Rafter Square Donald E. Zepp
Installing Board-and-Batten Siding John Birchard
Pondside Gazebo Alan Guazzoni
Making Plastic-Laminate Countertops Herrick Kimball
Small, But Sited Right Richard Sygar
Electric-Radiant Floors Bruce C. Kaercher, Jr.
Renovating Old Porches George Nash
Architectural Ironwork Tom Joyce
Room to Mingle Michael Corlis

76 August/September 1992

Foundation Forms that Insulate Mark Feirer
Bed Alcove Tony Simmonds
Framing a Cross-Gable Roof Scott McBride
Running Baseboard Efficiently Greg Smith
A House Without Barriers Chuck Williams
Building a Cantilevered Counter Jim Wolfer
A Dry-Laid Stone Stairway Dick Belair
Cutting Against the Grain Larry Haun
Jewelbox Bathroom Jeff Morse
Funds for Fixer-Uppers Dave Ames
Simple Joinery for Custom Windows David Frane
Where to Buy Eyebrow Windows Mark Feirer
Small House, Big Heater Albie Barden
Hand Planes for Trim Carpentry Scott Wynn

77 October/November 1992

Choosing Kitchen Countertops Kevin Ireton
Rethinking the Cornice Return Scott McBride
Framed with Concrete and Glulams Rich Griendling
Building with Pumice-Crete Vishu Magee
Basic Scribing Techniques Jim Tolpin
Controlling Air Leakage Jim Maloney
Random-Orbit Sanders Terence Rucker
A Stone and Glass Addition Christopher Hall
Converting a Garage into Living Space Neil Hartzler
Framing a Crawl-Space Foundation Larry Haun
A New 19th-Century House Aileen J. Barth

78 December 1992/January 1993

Using Chainsaws on the Job Site Scott McBride
Simple Closet Wardrobe Jim Tolpin
Forms for Tall Concrete Walls William Doran
Ultrasonic Measuring Tools Karl Riedel
Salvaging a Small Cape Rick Moisan
Using a Handsaw Tom Law
Wide-Open Kitchen Remodel Matthew Adams Longo
Hardwood Edgings for Plastic Laminate Paul Levine
Beating Indoor Air Pollution Mike Nuess
Decorating Tile at Home Nancy Selvin
Plumbing with Flexible Pipe Rex Cauldwell
Frederick Church's House Jean Dunbar
Hurricane Warnings Charles Miller

79 February/March 1993

Installing Locksets Gary M. Katz
Trimming the Front Door Richard Taub
Timber Frame, Shingle-Style Wrapper Lynn Hopkins
Job-Site Foot Injuries John England
Simplified Valley Framing Larry Haun
Small Bathroom, Walk-In Shower Rich Griendling
Deck Foundations that Last Scott Schuttner
Designing for a Hot Climate Thomas Leach
Maintaining a Plunge Router Gregg Carlsen
Site-Built Kitchen Tony Simmonds
Cantilevered Hillside House Eliot Goldstein
Renovating a Shaker Farmhouse Stephen Lasar

80 Spring 1993

Live Large, Look Small David Hall
Beneath Green Gable Roofs John Eifler
Building for Unknown Clients David Carse
Beating the Heat Peter L. Pfeiffer
Minnesota Lake Cabins Dale Mulfinger and Leffert Tigelaar
The House that Healed the Land Jeff Gold
High Living in a Small Space Harry J. Wirth
Transforming a Suburban Ranch Jack Wilbern
Home in the Hills Cathi and Steven House
Courtyard Connections Murray Silverstein

81 April/May 1993

Installing Drywall Charles Wardell
Porches that Won't Rot Kevin M. Mahoney
Wiring Three-Way Switches Thomas Johnson
Train-Station Renovation Mark Goldman
Detailing for Wood Shrinkage Stephen Smulski
Installing Mortise Locksets Gary M. Katz
Simple Workbenches Tom Law
Digging a Basement the Hard Way Scott Publicover
Refacing Kitchen Cabinets Rex Alexander
Pressure-Sensitive Veneer Herrick Kimball
Restoring the Jacobs House John Eifler
A House of Light Richard M. Beckman

82 June/July 1993

Survey of ⅜-in. VRS Drills Herrick Kimball
Framing Walls Scott McBride
Don't Forget the Blocks Larry Haun
A Comfortable Outdoor Bench David Bright
Electric Water Heaters Rex Cauldwell
Making a Bullnose Starting Step Stephen Winchester
A Southwest Addition Carolyn Robbins Siegel
Row-House Renovation Robert Van Vranken
Taping and Finishing Drywall Charles Wardell
A Small House on a Rocky Hillside Kathleen Kenny
Adapting the Craftsman Style André Fontaine

83 August/September 1993

Choosing Siding Scott Gibson
Pouring Concrete Slabs Carl Hagstrom
Operating a Power Trowel John M. Schnittker
A Well-Lit Addition Robert L. Marx
An Elegant Site-Built Door John Birchard
Simple Curved Corners Scott M. Carpenter
A Survey of Compound-Miter Saws Jim Chestnut
Custom Closet Wardrobe Philip S. Sollman
Fantail Deck Stairs José L. Floresca
Building a Pole House John Terrell
Losing a Fingertip Kevin Ireton
A Contemporary Farmhouse Charles Miller

84 October/November 1993

Making a Solid-Surface Countertop Sven Hanson
Economical Framing E. Lee Fisher
Ladders Bruce Greenlaw
Stone Veneer on Concrete Block M. Scott Watkins
Building an Exterior Newel Post Peter Carlson
A Cascade of Roofs John Phelps
A Simple Coffered Ceiling Fred Unger
Removing Exterior Paint Stephen Mead
Shop-Built Window Frames Joseph Beals III
Vanity under Glass Charles Metcalf
Water-Saving Showerheads and Faucets Amy Vickers
Practical Solar Design Debra G. Rucker

85 December 1993/January 1994

All About Nails John McLeod III and Joseph R. Loferski
Installing Kitchen Cabinets Tom Law
Wall Bracing Larry Haun
Making and Using Water Levels Herrick Kimball
Using Waterborne Floor Finishes Michael Purser
A Built-In Hardwood Hutch Stephen Winchester
A Survey of Self-Feed Screw Guns Felix Marti
Mango House Peter Mullen
Avoiding Back Pain Chris dunn
A Concrete Fire Wall John Liczwinko
Mixing Forced-Air and Boiler Heat Richard D. Groff
A House that Fits its Site Dale Mulfinger

(BK)
Builder's Library
Building Baths and Kitchens

Designing a Functional Kitchen
The Kitchen Cabinet
Counter Intelligence
The Flush-Fit Cabinet
European Cabinet Hardware
Corian Kitchen Countertops
Random-Fitted Panels
Installing a Sheet-Vinyl Floor
Custom Kitchen Planning
Expanding a Kitchen, Step by Step
Kitchen Overhaul
Gourmet Kitchen Remodel
Accessible Kitchen Remodel
Kitchen Conversion
High-Style Asceticism
Toward the Right Light
Making Wooden Light Fixtures
Mosaic Tile
Tiling a Mortar-Bed Counter
Laying a Tile Floor
A Mortar-Bed Shower
Drainage Systems
Venting the Plumbing System
Underground Cistern
Roughing In the Drain Lines
The Septic Tank Revealed
Installing a Toilet
Soldering Copper Pipe
Remodel Plumbing
Residential Fire Sprinklers
Bathroom Built-Ins
Finishing Touches
Half-Moon Bath
Details
A Remodeled Bath
A Gazebo Showerhouse
Building a Sauna
A Dutchman's Bath
Great Moments in Building History
Japanese-Style Bath House

(CBS)
Builder's Library
Building with Concrete, Brick and Stone

Concrete
Small-Job Concrete
Gunite Retaining Wall
Building with Ferro-Cement
Stemwall Foundations
Rubble-Trench Foundations
Building a Concrete Bulkhead
Concrete and Masonry Fasteners
Building a Block Foundation
Insulating and Parging Foundations
Insulated Masonry Walls
Dry-Stack Block
Surface-Bonded Block
Site Layout
Stepped Foundations
Facing a Block Wall with Stone
Foundations on Hillside Sites
A Pier and Grade-Beam Foundation
A Concrete Belvedere
Radiant-Floor Heating
Warm Floors
An AirCore Floor
The Thin-Mass House
Bricklaying Basics
Putting Down a Brick Floor
Brick Floors
Building a Fireplace
Laying Brick Arches
Renovating a Chimney
Rumfordizing Brick by Brick
A Russian Fireplace
The Fireplace Chimney
Maine Stonework
Masonry Heater Hybrid
A Stone Cookstove and Heater K'ang
Form-Based Stone Masonry
The Structural Stone Wall
Stoneoak
From Boulders to Building Blocks
Sticks and Stones
Converting the Forge
Laying Flagstone Walks

(CSH)
Great Houses
Craftsman-Style Houses

Craftsman Houses
Eastern Details, Western Framing
Greene and Greene Revival
Good and Small
An Estate in Bonny Doon
A Craftsman-Style Renovation
Northern Prairie House
The Art of Workmanship
The James House
A View of the Redwoods
Facade Roof
A Rambling Deck
Bernard Maybeck's Wallen II House
Mullgardt Rescue
Resurrecting the Bolton House
Bungalow Transformation
Laguna Beach Remodel
Adapting the Japanese House
Cooperative Craftsmanship
Hawaiian Retreat
Adding A Craftsman Spa Room
Budget Bungalow
Handcrafted in Stone and Wood
A Craftsman Studio
A General Remodel and a Major Addition
Craftsman-Style Beach House
Craftsman Remodel
Gypsy Wagon

(DWS)
Builder's Library
Building Doors, Windows and Skylights

Connecticut River Valley Entrance
Formal Entryway
Hanging an Exterior Door
Hanging Interior Doors
A Breath of Fresh Air
Finishing Touches
Batten Doors
Making an Insulated Door
Mudrooms
Replacing an Oak Sill
Casing a Door
Spray-Painting Trim
Stripping Trim
Finishing Touches
Curved Doors
Making Curvilinear Sash
Making Window Sash
Screen-Porch Windows
Casing a Double-Hung Window
Installing Fixed-Glass Windows
Architectural Stained Glass
Finishing Touches
Etched Glass
Leaded Glass
Art-Glass Door and Window
Solar Cube
Installing Glass Block
Building a Glass-Block Stair Tower
Greenhouse Shutters
Details
Building Louvered Shutters
Site-Built, Fixed-Glass Skylights
Flashing a Curb
Movable Insulation for Skylights
Southwest Sunspace
Solar Site Evaluation
Curbless Skylights
Acrylic Glazing
Heat-Recovery Ventilators
Installing a Factory-Built Skylight
Earth Shelter on Cape Cod
A Slice and Stretch Addition
Ridge-Vent Options
Attic Venting

(EEH)
Great Houses
Energy-Efficient Houses

Superinsulated Saltbox on the
  Coast of Maine
Massive Passive
On the Mountainside
Airtight in Massachusetts
Roll-Top House
White Mountain Cape
Pool House
A Photovoltaic Test House
The Buzzards Bay House
Expressing a Site
The Double Envelope
Seaside Solar
Pennsylvania Snowbelt House
Designing for a Temperate Climate
An Arc in the Woods
Shingle Solar
Linear Solar House
A Little House with a Big View
Superinsulated in Idaho
Three Sides to the Sun
Sunspaces
Superinsulating the Non-Box
An A.O.B. House
Solar Adobe
In the Solar Vanguard
Cool Details
Southern Comfort
Florida Cracker House
Raised in Style
Passive Cooling
A Modern Mississippi House

(EF)
Builder's Library
Exterior Finishing

Trimming the Front Door
Painting Exteriors
Understanding Color
Decorative Sidewall Shingles
Installing Board-and-Batten Siding
Siding with Clapboards
A Quality Deck
A Deck Built to Last
Tassajara Makeover
Railing Against the Elements
Building a Winding Outdoor Stair
Backyard Spiral
Single-Ply Roofing
Venting the Roof
Built-Up Cedar Roofing
Roofing with Slate
Putting on a Concrete-Tile Roof
Tile Roofing
Roof Shingling
Roofing with Asphalt Shingles
Flashing
Chimney Cricket
Rethinking the Cornice Return
Cornice Construction
Replacing Rain Gutters

(FC)
Builder's Library
Finish Carpentry

Installing Crown Molding
Installing Two-Piece Crown
Making Curved Crown Molding
Making Curved Casing
Cutting Crown Molding
Hand Planes for Trim Carpentry
A Chop-Saw Workstation
Plunge Routers
Cranking Out Casements
Building Fixed-Glass Windows
A Site-Built Ridge Skylight
Installing Arch-Top Windows
Selecting Wood Windows
Simple Joinery for Custom Windows
Double-Hungs Restrung
Designing and Building Leak-Free
  Sloped Glazing
Wooden Miter Boxes
Plate Joinery on the Job Site
Router Control
Clamps on Site
Finish Nailers
Running Baseboard Efficiently
Door Hardware
Building Interior Doors
Production-Line Jamb Setting and
  Door Hanging
Pocket Doors
Building Wooden Screen Doors
Ordering and Installing Prehung Doors
French-Door Retrofit

(FRC)
Builder's Library
Frame Carpentry

Building Basics
Wood Foundations
Capping a Foundation
Floor Framing
Parallel-Chord Floor Trusses
Laying Out for Framing
Plumb and Line
Stud-Wall Framing
Building a Curved Wall
Light-Gauge Steel Framing
Truss-Frame Construction
Making a Structural Model
The Engineered Nail
Toenailing
Metal Connectors for Wood Framing
Framing with Trigonometry
Putting the Lid On
Roof Framing Simplified
Dummy Rafter Tails
Roof Framing Revisited
Framing a Conical Roof
A Domed Octagon
Framing an Open-Plan Saltbox
Seismic Retrofits
A Shed-Dormer Addition
Finishing Touches
Shed-Dormer Retrofit
Peaking over a Flat Roof
Framing Doghouse Dormers
Tying a Bow to an Eyebrow
Trouble Spots in 19th-Century Framing
Decking and Sheathing
Deck Design
Details

(FWS)
Builder's Library
Building Floors, Walls and Stairs

Designing and Building Stairs
Double-Helix Stair
Traditional Stairways off the Shelf
Installing Manufactured Stair Parts
Octagonal Spiral Stairs
Three Custom Stairbuilders
Plunge-Router Stairs
Building a Helical Stair
Sculpted Stairway
Concrete Spiral Staircase
Building a Cantilevered-Tread
  Spiral Stair
Outside Circular Stairway
Newport Stairway Reproduction
Storage Stair
Staircase Renovation
A Revamped Victorian
Ornamental Plaster in England
Molding and Casting Materials
Drywall Finishing
Drywall
Two-Coat Plaster
Veneer Plaster
The Scribed Ellipse
Hardwood Strip Flooring
Floor Sanding
An Uncommon Application
  for Particleboard
Laying a Plank Floor
Ticksticking
Custom Wood Flooring
Swedish Floor Finish
Installing Baseboard
Trimming Out the Main House
Molding Character
Raised-Panel Wainscot
Modified Wainscot
Gentle Stripping
Period Moldings
Table-Saw Molding
Architectural Ceramics

(MFC)
Builder's Library
More Frame Carpentry

Framing a Second-Story Addition
Permanent Wood Foundations
Framing a Gable Roof
Ceiling Joists for a Hip Roof
Valley Framing for Unequally
 Pitched Roofs
Framing a Cross-Gable Roof
Updating the Rafter Square
All Trussed Up
Examining Carbide-Tipped Sawblades
Cutting Across the Grain
Building Rake Walls
Balloon-Framing a Rake Wall
Strengthening Plate-to-Plate Rafter
 Connections
Riding Out the Big One
Building Coffered Ceilings
Building Barrel Vaults
Header Tricks for Remodelers
Installing a Long-Span Header
Framing a Bay Window with
 Irregular Hips
Raising an Eyebrow
Framing for Garage Doors
Composition Panels
Glue-Laminated Timbers
Laminated-Veneer Lumber
Preservative-Treated Wood
West Coast Overhang
Falling Eaves
Framing with the Plumber in Mind

(REM)
Builder's Library
Remodeling

Going Up
Growing Up in Minnesota
Razing the Roof
Pop-Top Remodel
Ranch-House Add-Up
Raising a House Addition
Rock-Bottom Remodel
Converting a Garage into Living Space
Make Room for Trudy
A Family at Home
A Greek-Revival Addition
Attic Art Studio
Bed Alcove
Facelift for a Loft
Found Horizon
Jewelbox Bathroom
Wide-Open Kitchen Remodel
Custom Kitchen Remodel
The Heart of the House
New Kitchen for an Old House
A Cantilevered Kitchen Addition
Recipe for a Kitchen Remodel
A Screened-Porch Addition
Frugal Four-Square Fixup
Big Ideas for Small Spaces
Taking a Load Off
Replacing Rotted Sills
Saving the Old Daggett Place
New Life for the Adelman Barn
Wood-Infesting Insects
Wood-Destroying Fungi

(SH)
Great Houses
Small Houses

The Covered Bridge Cottage
A Superinsulated Saltbox
Tract-House Transformation
Escape from Manhattan
A Little Place in the City
Backyard Edwardian
Victorian Log Studio
Canadian Retreat
House in the Woods
A Modest Studio on the Maine Coast
When Architecture Meets
 Energy Efficiency
The House under the Garden
An Attic Studio Apartment
A Cluster of Cottages
Adapting Usonian
A Modest House in Bucks County
Raven Hill
Vacation Cabin
Better Home and Garden
The Honda House
A Compact Passive-Solar House
Above the Flood
Wisconsin Wizardry
A House in Friday Harbor
Capital Gains
Hawaiian Ohana House
A Small House to Work in
Building a Multi-Purpose Room
Mandating Energy Efficiency
Skidompha House
Farmhouse Remodel
Building a Gothic Playhouse
Small House in Virginia
Treehouse
Small House in Ski Country
Hands-On Down East
A New View

(TB)
Builder's Library
Tools for Building

(TFH)
Great Houses
Timber-Frame Houses

Drafting Basics
Drafting Tools
Job-Site Safety
Plumb Bobs, Strings and Chalkboxes
The Rafter Square
Scaffolding
On-Site Carpentry with a Circular Saw
Sawhorse
Handsaws
Site-Sharpening Sawblades
The Worm-Drive Saw
Power Saws: Rating the Ratings
Power Miter Saws
Jigsaws
Reciprocating Saws
Chainsaw Mill
A Mill for the Chainsaw
Power Tools and the
  Timber-Frame Revival
Framing Hammers
Powder-Actuated Tools
Nail Guns
Power Nailing without Hoses
Levels and Transits
Portable Power Planes
On Screw Guns and Screws
Routers
Cordless Drills
Hinge Butt Mortising Templates
On Pulling Nails
The Carpenter's Toolbox
The Renovator's Tool Kit
On the Edge
Tool Pouches
Pickup-Truck Tool Storage
On-Site Shop
Job-Site Shack
A Mobile Workshop
Organizing the Project
Backyard Shop
Carpentry Texts
Microcomputers for Builders

An Introduction to Timber Framing
Earthquake-Country Timber Frame
A Tudor Timber Frame
Timber-Frame Layout
Sizing Roughsawn Joists and Beams
Solo Timber-Raising
A Timber Frame in the Hudson Valley
Tools for Timber Framing
The Fairbanks House
Rhode Island Stone-Ender
A Carved Timber Frame
Mountain Passive
Cruck House
Raising Heavy Timber
At the Top of the Mountain
A Modular Home
In the Japanese Tradition
Cobblestone Cottage
Building with Stress-Skin
Wiring in Stress-Skin Panels
Foam-Core Panels
Island Victorian
Framing with Purpleheart
Hung Walls
Building Timber Bowstring Trusses
Curved Timber
Curved-Roof Bungalow
A Timbered Ceiling
A Hip-Roofed Timber Frame
Woodstock House
San Juan Island Cabin
The Tidewater Timber Frame
A Day at the Raisings

All in one place...the best of

Fine Homebuilding Great Houses Books

Here are the best design articles on a broad array of topics taken from the past 12 years of *Fine Homebuilding*. These articles can't be found in any other collection.

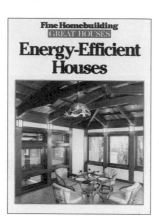

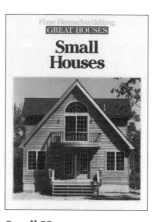

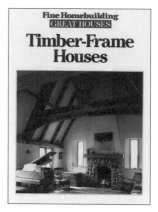

Craftsman-Style Houses
HARDCOVER, COLOR, 160 PAGES,
116 PHOTOS, 74 DRAWINGS,
ITEM 070164, $24.95

Energy-Efficient Houses
HARDCOVER, COLOR, 160 PAGES,
195 PHOTOS, 63 DRAWINGS,
ITEM 070191, $24.95

Small Houses
HARDCOVER, COLOR, 160 PAGES,
102 PHOTOS, 68 DRAWINGS,
ITEM 070176, $24.95

Timber-Frame Houses
HARDCOVER, COLOR, 160 PAGES,
207 PHOTOS, 101 DRAWINGS,
2 CHARTS, ITEM 070177, $24.95

Direct from *Fine Homebuilding*'s most popular columns...

In the past two decades, thousands of *Fine Homebuilding* readers who've solved building problems or found techniques that make the process easier have sent their discoveries to us.

We publish the best of them in our two most popular features—"Tips & Techniques" and "Q & A." The best of these columns is collected in four paperback books.

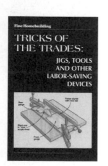

Tricks of the Trades: Jigs, Tools and Other Labor-Saving Devices
SOFTCOVER, 224 PAGES,
146 DRAWINGS, ITEM 070204, $10.95

Tips & Techniques for Builders
SOFTCOVER, 256 PAGES,
ITEM 070080, $10.95

Questions and Answers about Building
SOFTCOVER, 256 PAGES,
ITEM 070084, $10.95

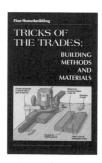

Tricks of the Trades: Building Methods and Materials
SOFTCOVER, 224 PAGES,
170 DRAWINGS, ITEM 070205, $10.95

Fine Homebuilding magazine.

Fine Homebuilding Builder's Library

It's like having America's best builders on the job with you, ready to share their experience and wisdom. Virtually every subject of importance to residential builders is covered.

All the articles in the library volumes have appeared in *Fine Homebuilding* over the past 12 years. Each is written by an expert and is based on firsthand experience. These books are beautifully cloth-bound in a durable hardcover format.

See the information below to find out how to subscribe to this informative series.
Ask for Item **07A096.**

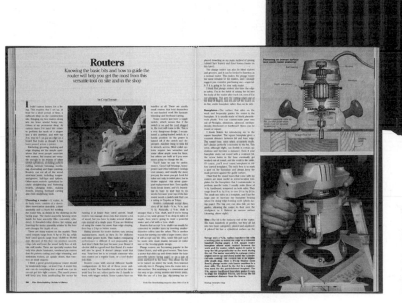

The titles in the series:

- *Frame Carpentry*
- *Building Floors, Walls and Stairs*
- *Tools for Building*
- *Building Doors, Windows and Skylights*
- *Building Baths and Kitchens*
- *Building with Concrete, Brick and Stone*
- *More Frame Carpentry*
- *Finish Carpentry*
- *Remodeling*
- *Exterior Finishing: Siding, Roofs, Decks, Porches*

To inquire about the *Builder's Library* series or any of the books on these pages, please call 1-800-888-8286 or write to The Taunton Press, 63 S. Main St., P.O. Box 5506, Newtown, CT 06470-5506.

Publisher: Jon Miller
Designer: Henry Roth
Copy/Production Editors: Peter Chapman, Ruth Dobsevage, Pam Purrone

Typeface: Cheltenham
Paper: Marcy Matte, 70 lb., neutral pH
Printer: Arcata Graphics/Hawkins, New Canton, Tenn.